INTRODUCTION TO CLASSICAL AND MODERN TEST THEORY

INTRODUCTION TO CLASSICAL AND MODERN TEST THEORY

Linda Crocker
James Algina

University of Florida

Harcourt Brace Jovanovich College Publishers

Fort Worth Philadelphia San Diego New York Orlando Austin San Antonio
Toronto Montreal London Sydney Tokyo

Library of Congress Cataloging-in-Publication Data

Crocker, Linda M.
  Introduction to classical and modern test theory.

  Bibliography: p. 482
  Includes index.
  1. Psychometrics.   2. Educational tests and
measurements.   I. Algina, James.   II. Title.
BF39.C695   1986   150′.28′7   85–17647

ISBN 0-03-061634-4

Requests for permission to make copies of any part of the work should be mailed to: Permissions, Harcourt Brace Jovanovich, Inc. Orlando, Florida 32887.

Printed in the United States of America.

    4   038   9

PREFACE

In 1904, E. L. Thorndike published *An Introduction to the Theory of Mental and Social Measurements,* which is generally hailed as the first textbook on test theory. The work was greeted with much enthusiasm by his professional colleagues, and within a short time the study of test theory was a standard part of the curriculum for graduate students in psychology and education. Over the next six decades a succession of scholars expanded, refined, and added to the body of theory that Thorndike originally described. This collective body of knowledge, known as classical test theory, provided the theoretical foundation for development of most aptitude, achievement, personality, and interest measures used in this century. Within the last twenty years, however, test theory made rapid advances which have not been recorded in traditional texts. This expansion of knowledge is attributable in part to improved computer technology, which made possible the practical applications of more sophisticated mathematical and statistical models for test score data. Increases in the number of professionals working in psychometrics and the demand for objective measurements of students' or clients' benefits from publicly funded service and educational programs also contributed to the growth of this field. Consequently, an inspection of the current contents of leading measurement journals in education and psychology will reveal that many dominant topics are relatively recent in origin. Examples of such topics include methods for developing criterion-referenced tests, item response theory, generalizability theory, and psychometric methods for investigation of bias in test items. In view of this development, a sound knowledge of classical test theory is no longer sufficient to prepare today's graduate student or the practicing measurement professional to read current literature in the field or to apply the information it contains.

Students of modern test theory must acquire a base of knowledge about classical psychometrics, but they must also be able to integrate new ideas into that framework of knowledge. This text was written to help the reader attain these ends. The reader who hopes to find only a series of ''cookbook'' steps on how to carry out any specific process, uncluttered by technical discussion or statistical symbols, will be disappointed. We recognize that ''best'' or ''most recommended'' procedures for any aspect of test development may change as new ideas and empirical findings are published. Thus it seems desirable for the students of test theory to acquire some practice in reading material that contains technical terms and symbols similar to those which will be encountered as they graduate from a textbook and begin to read the professional literature independently. At the same time, we were aware that many readers may not have had more than an introductory course in statistics. Consequently quantitative expressions are usually accompanied by verbal explanations, which we hope will not seem redundant to readers with strong quantitative backgrounds. There were times, however, when accurate or adequate treatment of an important topic required inclusion of content beyond introductory statistical methods (i.e., the material on generalizability theory and item response theory). In these cases, it seemed more important to be "true" to the material rather than to dilute it until it would appear deceptively simple and thus mislead readers about the level of expertise required to use these methods or interpret their results.

The material in this text is organized into five units: Introduction to Measurement Theory; Reliability; Validity; Item Analysis in Test Development; and Test Scoring and Interpretation. The first unit provides background information for readers with little formal training in measurement or statistics. Each of the following units presents classical theoretical approaches in the initial chapters. More recent developments are presented in subsequent chapters, accompanied by discussion of how these procedures relate to the traditional concepts. In general, the new developments in most areas of test theory require more complex statistical treatment. For this reason, the chapters within each unit tend to be ordered progressively from the simplest to the most complex material on that topic. Instructors making reading assignments should be aware that chapters in the latter part of most units can be omitted or assigned for optional reading without loss of continuity with material presented in subsequent units. If only an introduction to traditional classical test theory is desired, it can be obtained from Chapters 1 through 7, 10, 14, 17, and 19. An introduction to recent topics in psychometrics, for those with a background in classical test theory, can be found in Chapters 8, 9, 15, 16, 18, and 20.

The computational exercises and questions at the end of each chapter are an integral part of the text. They were developed specifically to illustrate applications of the theoretical concepts presented in the chapter, and they offer the reader an opportunity for active involvement in application of test theory to current measurement problems. The answers to many of the computational exercises appear in Appendix B.

Writing a textbook is an arduous, frustrating, and humbling, but richly rewarding, experience. The sources of frustration and humility in this case were the insufficiencies of our own knowledge and our seemingly limitless capacity for logical, computational, and grammatical errors as we sought to organize, simplify, and accurately translate the ideas of others into a pedagogical work. The rewards in this effort derived from having the opportunity to study the original works of many professional colleagues and from the generous support and assistance we received from so many quarters. We are indebted to students of test theory at the University of Florida who encouraged this undertaking and offered constructive suggestions for the manuscript as it was developed. Foremost among those were Diane Buhr, Sherry Kragler, and Darla McCrea who assisted in making revisions and preparing end-of-chapter exercises. In addition, we received helpful reviews and comments from a number of professional colleagues. We are particularly indebted to Jeri Benson, James Impara, and William Mehrens who read and reacted to the manuscript in its entirety. Also Robert Brennan, Dale Harris, Maria Llabre, Richard Lomax, Stephen Olejnik, and Hariharan Swaminathan offered valuable suggestions for selected chapters. The difficult task of typing the manuscript was shared by Edna Richardson, Alesia Sheffield, Dorothy Padgett, Elsie Voss, and Madonna Trautvetter. The editorial staff at Holt, Rinehart, and Winston Inc. were extremely helpful. This work has been greatly enhanced by all of their contributions. Portions of the manuscript were written while the first author was on sabbatical leave from the University of Florida and receipt of that award is gratefully acknowledged. Most of all, we appreciate the enduring support and encouragement we received from Tim, Beth, and John and from Elizabeth, David, and Leah.

L.C.
J.A.

CONTENTS

ix

UNIT V   Test Scoring and Interpretation

INTRODUCTION TO CLASSICAL AND MODERN TEST THEORY

UNIT ONE

Introduction to Measurement Theory

Chapter 1

WHAT IS TEST THEORY?

Whatever exists at all exists in some amount. To know it thoroughly
involves knowing its quantity as well as its quality.

E. L. Thorndike, 1918

The beginning student who embarks on the study of test theory often poses such
questions as

What is test theory and why is it needed?
How does it differ from learning to administer and use specific tests?
Did test theory originate with psychology, or is it a "new" field of study?
How is test theory related to research design and statistics?

This chapter should provide at least partial answers to such questions. In the following sections we will define basic terms, describe special problems encountered in
the measurement of psychological constructs, explain the broad purpose of test
theory in relation to these problems, and review the historic origins of this discipline. Finally, we will draw the distinctions between test theory and other aspects of
social science research and evaluation.

To understand the need for test theory, it is first necessary to understand something about the fundamental nature of *measurement, constructs,* and *psychological
tests.* Weitzenhoffer (1951) described measurement as "an operation performed on
the physical world by an observer." To Stevens (1946) measurement was "the
assignment of numerals to objects or events according to rules." Lord and Novick
(1968) and Torgerson (1958) enhanced the precision of Stevens' definition by noting that measurement applies to the properties of objects rather than to the objects
themselves. When a physical chemist measures the molecular mass of a compound
or a biologist determines the bacterial count in a drop of pond water, these are
measurements of specific attributes of the object under investigation. In a similar

3

vein, a school psychologist does not measure a child but a specific physical attribute of the child such as height or weight or a psychological attribute such as vocabulary development, social maturity, or knowledge of basic addition. Psychology is traditionally defined as the study of behavior and attributes which characterize an individual's behavior in home, work, school, or social settings are commonly called *psychological attributes* (or by some authors, *psychological traits*). Unlike physical attributes, the psychological attributes of an individual cannot be measured directly as can height or weight. Psychological attributes are *constructs*. They are hypothetical concepts—products of the informed scientific imagination of social scientists who attempt to develop theories for explaining human behavior. The existence of such constructs can never be absolutely confirmed. Thus the degree to which any psychological construct characterizes an individual can only be inferred from observations of his or her behavior.

Let us consider, through an example, the process of construct formation and how it leads to the measurement of attributes. Suppose a developmental psychologist, working in a preschool, notices that in a variety of play activities some children repeatedly try to direct the activities of others. After observing this kind of behavior consistently over time and in different contexts for the same individuals, the psychologist may begin to label such behaviors as "socially dominating." This psychologist has invented a theoretical construct that encompasses a number of similar behaviors. But inventing a construct is not the same thing as measuring that construct. Before any measurement of the construct can be made, it is necessary to establish some rule of correspondence between the theoretical construct and observable behaviors that are legitimate indicants of that construct. This process is called *establishing an operational definition*. In the example, to measure social dominance the psychologist must specify what types of behavior in the preschool play setting are considered "dominating." Then the psychologist must devise a plan for obtaining samples of such behaviors in a standard situation and recording observations for each child in a standard format. This requires the development of an instrument, or "test," for the construct of social dominance. Broadly speaking, a *test* may be defined as a standard procedure for obtaining a sample of behavior from a specified domain. As used in this text, the term *test* refers to procedures for obtaining a sample of an individual's *optimal performance* (as typified by an aptitude or achievement test on which examinees are instructed to do their best) or a sample of an individual's *typical performance* (as on questionnaires or inventories where respondents report their typical feelings, attitudes, interests, or reactions to situations). Another approach to sampling typical performance is a standard schedule and list of behaviors which may be used by an observer who records behavior displayed by subjects in naturalistic settings. When a psychologist prepares a list of behaviors to be checked or rated by an observer using a predetermined schedule, when a chemistry instructor writes a set of multiple-choice items on the activity level of elements in the periodic chart, or when a counselor has clients rate how anxious they would feel in a list of social situations, each has devised a test, in the broadest sense of the word. We shall use the term in that sense.

Measurement of the psychological attribute occurs when a quantitative value is assigned to the behavioral sample collected by using a test. In other words a measurement has been taken when the psychologist tallies the number of "socially dominating" acts on the checklist that a child displayed during a five-minute observation period, or when the chemistry instructor counts the number of items a student answered correctly and records the total score. From such measurements of observable behavior, the test developer draws an inference about the amount of the theoretical construct that characterizes an individual.

Why do psychologists and educators attempt to measure constructs that cannot be directly observed? In education and psychology, a construct provides an efficient and convenient method for labeling a number of similar behaviors. Without such constructs for classifying and describing individual atomistic behaviors, most attempts to observe complex behavioral phenomena would dissolve into chaos and confusion. Consider the wide array of words, actions, and interactions that can occur in a single day in a single classroom. Cronbach (1969) probably understated the case when he asserted that studying the activities of a classroom is at least as difficult as studying a hurricane. An observer who attempted to record and describe each individual act in this setting would soon be overwhelmed by the task. Furthermore, any attempt to predict, control, or determine the cause of each isolated behavior would be virtually hopeless. Through the use of constructs, however, the observer can begin to classify and group instances of similar behavior and communicate in compact terms what has been witnessed. Such constructs are the basic building blocks of theories about human behavior. At the simplest level, a psychological theory is a statement of the possible relationship between two psychological constructs or between a construct and an observable phenomenon of practical consequence. Ultimately through empirical investigation and substantiation of such theories, it may be possible to predict or control certain patterns of behavior. To achieve this goal, however, it is usually necessary to quantify the observations of behavior representing the constructs posited by the theorist.

PROBLEMS IN MEASUREMENT OF PSYCHOLOGICAL CONSTRUCTS

Because psychological constructs are abstractions which can only be assessed indirectly, the design of instruments to measure such variables presents several challenging problems. Consider three illustrative situations in which the measurement of a psychological construct is desired:

1. A personnel psychologist wants to develop a test of mechanical aptitude for job applicants for an industrial firm.
2. A school psychologist wants to develop a scale to assess teachers' attitudes toward physically handicapped students.
3. A fifth-grade teacher wants to develop a unit test of students' skills in long division.

Although the constructs mechanical aptitude, attitude toward handicapped children, and skill in long division are quite diverse, in each case the test developer must cope with at least five measurement problems common to all psychological assessments.

1. No single approach to the measurement of any construct is universally accepted. Because measurements of a psychological construct are always indirect, based on behaviors that are perceived as relevant to the construct under study, there is always the possibility that two theorists who talk about the same construct may select very different types of behavior to define that construct operationally. Let us take the case in which the test developer wants to assess the students' skill in long division. Since no one can look directly into the students' heads and see how much long division they know, the test developer must designate some behaviors the students can display to permit inference about the extent of their knowledge in this subject. One reasonable approach is to require the students to solve a series of division problems; another approach is to ask them to describe sequentially the steps involved in performing long division; still another is to ask them to detect errors in a solution to a problem in long division. Obviously different measurement procedures would result from these different operational definitions and might well lead to different conclusions about the students' levels of knowledge.

2. Psychological measurements are usually based on limited samples of behavior. In the example, it would be impossible to confront the students with all possible problems in long division that they might be expected to solve. Thus any attempt to measure their skills in this area must involve only a sample of all such problems. Determining the number of items and the variety of content necessary to provide an adequate sample of the behavioral domain is a major problem in developing a sound measurement procedure.

3. The measurement obtained is always subject to error. Most psychological measurements are based on a limited sample of observations and usually are taken at only one point in time. Let us consider again the students taking the examination in long division. If they take the same examination twice in succession, it is unlikely that their scores will be identical because of the effects of fatigue, boredom, forgetfulness, guessing, careless marking, or misscoring. If they take a different form of the examination, their scores may change because of variation in content as well as the factors just mentioned. Such inconsistencies in individuals' scores due to sampling of tasks or occasions must be regarded as errors. Thus a persistent problem in psychological measurement is how to estimate the degree of error present in a given set of observations.

4. The lack of well-defined units on the measurement scales poses still another problem. Does the fact that examinees can answer none of the items on a long-division test indicate that they have "zero" mastery of this skill? If Sue answers 5 items correctly, Joe answers 10, and Steve answers 15 items correctly, can we assume that the difference in competence between Sue and Joe is the same as that between Joe and Steve? Are these three students equally spaced on the ability continuum which this examination was designed to measure? Defining the properties of the measurement scale, labeling the units, and interpreting the values derived are complex issues which also must be considered whenever a psychological instrument is developed and a scoring system devised.

   5. Psychological constructs cannot be defined only in terms of operational definitions but must also have demonstrated relationships to other constructs or observable phenomena.   A psychological measurement, even though it is based on observable responses, would have little meaning or usefulness unless it could be interpreted in light of the underlying theoretical construct. For this reason, Lord and Novick (1968) stressed that it is important for the constructs underlying psychological measurements to be defined on two levels. First, as we have already noted, the construct must be defined in terms of observable behavior. This type of definition specifies how the measurement will be taken. Second, the construct must be defined in terms of its logical or mathematical relationship to other constructs within the theoretical system. This second type of definition provides a basis for interpreting the measurements obtained. If such relationships cannot be empirically demonstrated, the measurements obtained are of no value. Obtaining evidence of how a set of psychological measurements relates to measures of other constructs or events in the real world is the ultimate challenge in test development.

TEST THEORY AS A DISCIPLINE

The study of the pervasive measurement problems just described and methods for their resolution has evolved into the specialized discipline in education and psychology known as *test theory*. The content of a course in test theory deals primarily with methods for (1) estimating the extent to which these problems influence the measurements taken in a given situation and (2) devising methods to overcome or minimize these problems.

   The purpose of a course in test theory is to help the student become aware of the logic and mathematical models that underlie standard practices in test use and construction. Awareness of these models, their assumptions and their limitations, should lead to improved practice in test construction and more intelligent use of test information in decision making. It is important to distinguish test theory from the more applied subject of educational and psychological assessment, which is usually focused on administration and interpretation of specific tests. Test theory, on the other hand, provides a general framework for viewing the process of instrument development. The mathematical models and methods traditionally studied in such a course do not rest on any particular psychological or educational theory and may be equally useful for measurement of many different psychological attributes.

Many methods of experimental design and statistical analyses used in educational and psychological research had their origin in agricultural research, where it was necessary to evaluate effects of experimental treatments under field conditions rather than in a laboratory. The principles of test theory, however, have been uniquely derived to meet the specific measurement needs of researchers in education and the social sciences.

Historic Origins

The historical development of test theory has been interwoven with the development of psychology as a scientific discipline. Test theory evolved from the efforts of psychologists in Europe and the United States as they studied a variety of psychological and educational problems. In this section, we will briefly describe the contributions of a few such individuals as illustrative of the men and women whose work has advanced test theory and its application.

GERMANY.   Beginning in the mid-1800s in the perceptual laboratories of Leipzig, Germany, Wilhelm Wundt, Ernst Weber, Gustav Fechner, and their colleagues were among the first to recognize the importance of obtaining psychological measurements under carefully controlled conditions. Previously, the study of psychology was primarily a matter of philosophical introspection and informal observation. In describing the revolutionary nature of their procedures, Wundt (1873) later wrote, "At that time the investigator who sought to employ accuracy of method in any question of psychology was challenged at every point, by philosophy as by natural science to prove that his endeavors were legitimate." Although measurement of mental abilities has expanded beyond reaction time, auditory discrimination, estimation of the relative weights of objects, or other sensory variables studied in the German perceptual laboratories, the legacy of collecting behavioral observations under carefully prescribed conditions is yet apparent in the precise instructions which accompany modern standardized tests. These instructions specify standard conditions for collecting and scoring data and allow the scores to meet the general definition of measurement.

GREAT BRITAIN.   During this same period scientists in Great Britain were engaged in work that would also have a profound effect on the measurement of human mental traits. In contrast to the Germans, the British were more interested in the study of individual differences. Foremost among these was Sir Francis Galton, whose ideas were strongly influenced by his noted contemporary and cousin, Charles Darwin.

Galton's interests were varied, and some of his methods seem unorthodox by today's standards. For example, in one article he described such informal practices as counting the objects that he could recall after a stroll in Pall Mall or noting the species of animals he could startle with a high-pitched whistle concealed in the handle of his walking stick (Galton, 1883). He also recorded detailed quantitative measurements of the physiological characteristics of subjects in his anthropomorphic laboratory. His chief contributions to the field of test theory involve original application of statistical techniques to psychological test data. In 1869, by using scores from a mathematics examination for all students at Cambridge University and an admissions examination to the Royal Military College, he demonstrated that mental abilities might be distributed in an approximation of the normal curve. Almost twenty years later, still fascinated by the nature of individual differences, Galton published an essay suggesting the correlation procedure for examining covariation in two or more traits (Dennis, 1948). British statistician Karl Pearson later developed the statistical formula for the correlation coefficient based on this suggestion. Other British scientists followed in this tradition. The most noted was probably Charles Spearman, whose well-known theory of intelligence was based on a more advanced correlational procedure that he called *factor analysis*. Today correlational methods and factor analysis remain among the most common statistical techniques used in test validation.

FRANCE. Despite the importance of previous contributions by German and British psychologists, it was the achievement of two Frenchmen, Alfred Binet and Theophile Simon (1905–1908), which moved the study of mental testing from an academic exercise to an enterprise that could have immediate application in the classroom, clinic, and workplace. These two clinical psychologists undertook the pragmatic task of devising a method that would be useful for identifying mentally deficient children in the public school population. The result was a successful procedure for measuring that trait which is generally labeled "intelligence." Although Binet is most renowned for the test that still bears his name, he also made a significant impact on test theory by demonstrating a working method for constructing and validating a test. Until Binet's breakthrough, the commonly accepted approach to test construction was to compose a set of items based on purely armchair logic and put it to use. In 1905 Binet scornfully rejected this approach, calling it "an amusing occupation, comparable to a person's making a colonizing expedition into Algeria, advancing only on the map, without taking off his dressing gown." Binet's laborious procedure required the identification of a series of tasks which discriminated among children at different age levels in sequential progression. Hundreds of items were tried with large numbers of children, and only those which successfully discriminated were retained. Binet and Simon then assembled at each age level a cluster of diverse tasks which a majority of children at that age could perform successfully, for example,

Age 3—point to the eyes, nose, mouth.
Age 7—indicate omissions in a drawing; repeat five figures.
Age 11—criticize sentences containing absurdities.

From performance on these items, Binet derived an estimate of the examinee's "mental age," which was compared to chronological age[1] to determine appropriate placement in instructional or institutional settings. Thus Binet, in addition to originating the practice of empirical item analysis, must also be credited with advancing the concept of norms as useful aids for score interpretation. It is a tribute to Binet's effort and ingenuity that the present form of the Stanford Binet Intelligence Scale still bears remarkable resemblance to the original test, which was first administered to the schoolchildren of Paris (Thorndike, 1975). It is also important to note that many modern test developers still engage in the practices of item analysis and establishment of norms, which despite considerable refinements, are still in principle much like the procedures used by Binet at the turn of the century.

THE UNITED STATES.   Although American scholars were active in the consideration of psychological problems throughout the latter 1800s, they did not begin to offer unique measurement methods until the turn of the twentieth century. For example, James McKeen Cattell is generally credited with coining the term *mental testing* in an essay written in 1890. In his writings of this period he recognized the importance of testing large samples to obtain accurate "normative" estimates, and he insisted that psychology must study the nature of errors of observation (Boynton, 1933). Yet the tests described by Cattell were primarily psychomotor or perceptual, quite similar to those used by the German experimentalists. In 1904, E. L. Thorndike published the first text on test theory, *An Introduction to the Theory of Mental and Social Measurements*. Thorndike was uncertain about how such a text would be received by his humanistic colleagues and with some trepidation offered a copy to his former mentor, William James, with the following note (Joncich, 1968, p. 290):

> I am sending you a dreadful book which I have written, which is no end scientific but devoid of any spark of human interest. You must make all your research men read it, but never look within its covers yourself. The figures, curves, and formulae would drive you mad.

Nevertheless, Thorndike's attempt to set forth a systematic consideration of measurement problems in psychology was widely acclaimed, and the study of test theory became a requirement in training many young psychologists.

From the lecture halls of Columbia, Harvard, and Stanford, researchers like Cattell and Thorndike captured the imaginations of younger colleagues and students from whose ranks originated the next generation of applied and theoretical psychometricians. These test developers adapted the work of Binet with the penchant for mass production, so prevalent in American society during this period of industrial revolution, and produced the first group intelligence tests. In 1917, as the country entered World War I, a committee of psychologists (Bingham, Gooddard, Hines, Terman, Well, Whipple, and Yerkes), who were granted a basic stipend of

---

[1] Dubois (1970) notes that the concept of the intelligence quotient (the ratio between mental age and chronological age) was not developed by Binet but by Wilhelm Stern.

$700 from the War Department, worked for three months to produce five forms of a group examination which were to be administered to all military personnel. Later a group of nonverbal tests was also devised for examinees who could not read English. These examinations were used for selection and placement of new recruits, identification of likely candidates for officers' training, discharge of personnel who were mentally incompetent, and even as evidence in court-martials (Yerkes, 1921). Inspired by their success in testing military personnel, psychologists pressed to expand the use of such intelligence tests with civilians for vocational and educational placement. It should be noted that their efforts sparked a controversy between advocates and critics of standardized testing which has continued for more than fifty years (Cronbach, 1975).

Thurstone and Chave (1929) added techniques for the scaling of attitudes to the growing literature on test development. Thurstone and others such as Kelly and Holtzinger were developing new factor analytic procedures as well. By the 1930s theoretical developments were advancing so rapidly in support of a growing testing industry that scholars in this area founded the Psychometric Society, which facilitated communication among researchers in a journal called *Psychometrika*. The publication of a more applied journal, *Educational and Psychological Measurement,* followed in 1943. With the publication of such professional journals and several authoritative texts on the subject, test theory certainly seemed to have become a full-fledged discipline spanning education and psychology.

Role of Test Theory in Research and Evaluation

To clarify the role of test theory within the broader framework of research and evaluation methodology, it is helpful to consider research in education and the social sciences as a process of inquiry consisting of well-defined stages. These may be characterized as

1. Formulating a research question or hypothesis
2. Specifying operational definitions for each variable in the hypothesis by determining how it should be controlled or measured during the study
3. Developing or selecting the instruments and procedures needed to obtain and quantify the observations on each variable
4. Testing the accuracy and sensitivity of the instruments and procedures to be used
5. Collecting the experimental data within the framework of an experimental design that will permit the original question to be answered
6. Summarizing the data mathematically, and when appropriate, conducting statistical tests to determine the likelihood that the observed results were due to chance

The tenets of test theory have greatest relevance to steps 2 to 4 in this process. It is imperative to note that step 4 usually requires collection of data and statistical summarization of the results on a preexperimental sample to insure that the instruments function effectively before any experiment or full-scale study is undertaken (steps 5 and 6). Failure to adhere to sound practices in developing and pretesting research instruments may in part account for the conflicting or ambiguous results that so often characterize educational and social science research. In the physical and biological sciences, measurement procedures are thoroughly tested before being used in any experiment. A biochemist would never attempt to analyze an unknown compound in the laboratory without spending considerable time calibrating the spectrometer to insure that it was yielding accurate wave-length readings for standard samples. In contrast, however, social scientists too often attempt to assess how an experimental program has affected a complex variable, such as the anxiety level of mental patients or the language development of preschoolers, by using virtually untried tests. The researcher who jumps directly from formulating the research question and defining the variables to collection of the experimental data is likely to come up empty-handed. Should researchers observe no differences between the treatments, they cannot know whether the treatments were ineffective or the measurements were so imprecise that the true effects of treatment went undetected. Closer adherence to the principles for sound test construction and empirical field testing of each instrument before the ultimate experiment is undertaken would do much to improve the overall quality of research in education and psychology.

ORGANIZATION OF THIS TEXT

Knowledge of test theory is crucial for any researcher or evaluator whose investigations will require development of a psychological test to measure a variable of interest. For those who use tests in classroom, clinical, or personnel settings, some knowledge of test theory is also essential. Informed selection of well-developed instruments and competent interpretation of scores are the responsibilities of all test users. Understanding the theoretical models that underlie test construction enables the practitioner to fulfill these important professional responsibilities. The purpose of this text is to promote appropriate practices in test use and development.

The material in this text has been organized into five distinct, but related, units. The first focuses on introductory concepts of measurement and scaling with which all test users and developers should be familiar. Units II and III deal with important properties of test scores (reliability and validity), which are essential if test scores are to be used in group or individual decision making. The psychometric theory underlying reliability and validity and procedures for investigating the reliability and validity of scores are presented in some depth. Obviously such knowledge is important to test developers, but it is also vital for test users to be well informed on these topics so that they can critically evaluate whether published instruments have been developed and validated in accordance with acceptable professional standards. The fourth unit is devoted to specific procedures for empirical investigations of item quality that are useful in developing new tests or in revising and improving existing ones. The fifth, and final, unit focuses on questions and issues that often arise in relation to the use and interpretation of test scores. A set of self-help exercises is provided at the end of each chapter to assist readers in testing their knowledge of material presented in that chapter.

Each unit of this text is organized to present first the traditional or classical approach to a particular test development problem. After the reader has become familiar with these methods and their applications in standard situations, some problems may be described that may not be easily resolved with traditional methods. In view of these problems, additional measurement techniques (often recent in origin) will be presented, usually accompanied by discussion of how these newer methods relate to more traditional ideas and concepts. It is not surprising that newer developments in test theory are often based on more complex statistical and mathematical models than those of their predecessors. For this reason the chapters within each unit tend to be ordered progressively from the simplest to the most complex material on that topic. The order in which topics are presented was chosen for pedagogical reasons and does not necessarily imply an endorsement or relative preference for any procedures described. Rather, we hope the reader will see that there are usually multiple approaches to solving test development problems but that these approaches may have different underlying assumptions and limitations. Informed selection of the "best" method in a given situation requires this understanding.

SUMMARY

In this chapter, basic terms such as *test, measurement,* and *construct* were defined. The usefulness of constructs was established for labeling or categorizing similar observed behaviors, and their role in theory development was explained.

The distinction between formulating a construct and developing a measurement for that construct was presented. Five problems were identified which are commonly encountered in developing measurements of psychological constructs:

1. No single way of defining a psychological construct is universally accepted.
2. Psychological measurements are based on samples of behavior.
3. Sampling of behavior results in errors of measurement.
4. The units of measurement are not well-defined.
5. The measurements must have demonstrated relationships to other variables to have meaning.

Test theory is the discipline devoted to the study of how these problems may influence psychological measurements and how to devise methods to overcome or minimize these problems. Historically, the development of test theory has been interwoven with the development of psychology itself. Modern test theory has been influenced by early contributions of German, British, French, and American social scientists. Test theory plays an important role in the overall process of research methodology by offering general methods for operationalizing or measuring variables of interest and methods for testing the sensitivity and accuracy of the measurement procedures developed.

Exercises

1. Consider the following activities and indicate whether testing, measurement, both testing and measurement, or neither is involved:
   A. An instructor assigns students to complete five problems at the end of a chapter and collects their papers.
   B. A student in experimental psychology records the time required for a rat to learn to press a bar at the sound of a buzzer.
   C. A social psychologist observes interactions between same-sex and opposite-sex persons with no prior acquaintance sitting in a double seat on a public bus.
   D. A first-grade teacher has each child copy the letters of the alphabet and places children into groups based on the number of letters correctly formed.
   E. A telephone interviewer asks each interviewee to respond to a series of yes-or-no questions concerning several commercial products.
   F. The interviewer tabulates the number of yes responses for each product given by all respondents.
2. Consider the following descriptions and decide whether the items would probably be considered to be from an optimal performance measure, a typical performance measure, or an observational performance measure:
   A. Items require students to solve word problems by using functional equations learned in physics class.
   B. Items are marked by an instructor as students in a physics laboratory perform an experiment under the instructor's supervision.
   C. Items require students to check each activity they enjoyed on a list of activities in their physics class.
   D. Items on a test of "Scientific Creativity" require reading a description of a natural phenomenon and generating as many plausible explanations as possible.
3. A new method has been devised to help adults acquire fluency in a second language. A researcher wants to determine whether this new method is more effective than a traditional method of instruction used in the past. To measure performance in fluency in a second language, the researcher decides to present subjects with a series of written passages in the second language and have them answer questions about the content; following this, subjects will listen to recorded spoken messages in the second language and answer questions about the contents. What measurement problems will be intrinsic to this procedure?
4. Consider the following testing practices and indicate which nineteenth-century psychological researcher probably should be credited with the origin.
   A. Items for a math-anxiety questionnaire are chosen by selecting items endorsed by math majors but not endorsed by students in a remedial math class.
   B. A teacher about to give a test reads aloud from the test manual: "Please read the instructions at the top of the page silently while I read them aloud. . . ."

C. A personnel-selection test is used because it has been demonstrated that scores on this test place employees in approximately the same rank order as do their supervisors' ratings after three months on the job.

5. Read the following description of a hypothetical study: "An educational evaluator wants to compare the effects of two eighth-grade science curricula. Method A requires teachers to use a specific textbook and a student workbook. Method B requires teachers to develop their own lesson plans around a series of laboratory experiments. At the beginning of the year, twelve classrooms are selected from the school district so that they are matched on teachers' years of experience. Six classrooms are randomly assigned to method A, and six are randomly assigned to method B. At the end of the year, the researcher devises 50 items on general scientific principles, applied to daily life, and administers them to all students. Each four-choice item is scored with one point for each correct answer. The researcher computes a correlation between student I.Q. scores and scores on the science test. The researcher also computes the mean number of items on the science test answered correctly for each group and contrasts these with a test of statistical significance."

Consider the following steps in the research process (problem formulation, research design, sampling, instrument development, inferential statistical analysis) and match each to one of these activities:

A. Six classrooms are randomly assigned to Method A.

B. The researcher devises 50 items on scientific principles.

C. Mean numbers of correct responses for the two groups are compared.

D. Twelve classrooms from the district are chosen.

6. For which of the activities described as 5A, B, C, or D in the preceding exercise would knowledge of test theory be most useful?

Chapter 2

STATISTICAL CONCEPTS FOR TEST THEORY

In education and the social sciences, statistics are used for two primary purposes—description and inference. Descriptive statistics summarize or describe the distribution of values for a set of observations. Inferential statistics test hypotheses about whether or not a given sample of observations has been obtained from a population with certain distributional characteristics. The study of inferential statistics is a discipline in its own right and is not the major focus of this chapter. The purpose of this chapter is to provide a review of basic descriptive statistics useful in interpretation of test scores and evaluation of test quality. Readers with a sound background in applied statistics may wish to omit this chapter.

TEST SCORES AS DISCRETE VARIABLES FOR FINITE POPULATIONS

Consider the teacher who has a classroom of 30 students or the clinical psychologist who works with 150 learning-disabled children referred to a clinic over a one-year period. Although both these professionals are interested in the characteristics of each individual, they may also wish to summarize certain characteristics of the groups for administrative reports or for program planning and evaluation. One convenient and efficient way to summarize and report information on group characteristics is through descriptive statistics.

In the study of a given population, descriptive characteristics of individuals may be either constant or variable. A _constant is a characteristic that is the same for everyone in the population_. In summarizing data on students in a typical classroom, the teacher usually does not bother to record data that are constant (e.g., each

16

student has only one head; therefore, the number of heads is a constant with the value 1). A *variable* is a characteristic that can differ for individuals in the population. Variables may be qualitative or quantitative. Eye color is a qualitative variable; weight is a quantitative variable; a test score is a quantitative variable. Suppose that a professor administers a 10-item biology quiz to 50 students, and examinees earn 1 point for each item answered correctly; no partial credit is given. Scores on this test may vary from 0 to 10. If we consider only the observed scores, the test score is a *discrete* variable because the possible values are limited to certain values or points on the real number line. In this case there is no possibility of earning a score of 2.5 or 3.75. In addition, we know that the classroom of students for whom these test scores are obtained contains a definite, countable number of students. Assuming that we have one score for each individual, we have a *finite population* of observations. The explanation of descriptive statistics that follows applies to situations in which we have a finite number of observations for a discrete variable. By convention, values computed for an entire population of observations are usually denoted by Greek letters and are called *parameters*. We will adhere to this convention in μ ρ defining basic concepts useful in describing score distributions in test theory. Unless otherwise noted, throughout Unit I concepts will be defined for a population of observations.

Frequency Tables and Graphs

Recall the biology professor who administered the 10-item test to 50 students. If the teacher wants to summarize how the group as a whole performed on this test, one sensible approach would be to determine the frequency distribution for this variable. A frequency distribution is used to specify the values that occurred for the variable and how often each value was observed. Frequency distributions are usually reported in the form of tables or graphs. Let X denote the variable, biology test score. Table 2.1 presents a frequency table representing 50 examinees' scores on a 10-item test. Possible scores on the test (values of X) range from 0 to 10 and are listed from

TABLE 2.1.   Frequency Table for Scores on a 10-Item Test for 50 Examinees

X	$f(X)$	$cf(X)$	$p(X)$	$cp(X)$
10	1	50	.02	1.00
9	2	49	.04	.98
8	3	47	.06	.94
7	5	44	.10	.88
6	6	39	.12	.78
5	12	33	.24	.66
4	11	21	.22	.42
3	5	10	.10	.20
2	3	5	.06	.10
1	2	2	.04	.04
0	0	0	.00	.00

high to low in the far left column of the table. The number of examinees earning each score, or the frequency of each value of X, is listed in the column noted $f(X)$. The third column indicates the cumulative frequency of each score value; the cumulative frequency is the total number of examinees who scored at or below a given value of X. Thus, for $X = 3$, the value of $cf(X) = 5 + 3 + 2 + 0 = 10$, the total of the frequencies for the scores 3, 2, 1, and 0. The fourth column indicates the percentage of the group who earned a given value of X; it is labeled $p(X)$ and is usually called the *relative frequency*. This is equivalent to the probability of drawing a person with that score if we select one person at random from the group. Thus, the probability of drawing one person at random with a score of 10 from the 50 examinees is $p(X) = 1/50$, or .02. The column at the far right indicates the cumulative probability for each value of X. The cumulative probability $cp(X)$ is the total of all the percentages of the group who scored at or below a given value of X.

Figure 2.1 displays a histogram of the data in Table 2.1, with possible values of X plotted on the horizontal axis. The relative frequency of any particular X value is represented by the height of the graph at that value. Thus we can see from the graph that scores of 4, 5, and 6 occurred with greater frequencies than scores of 0, 2, 9, or 10 simply by noting the heights of the graph at those points.

The description of how a set of test scores (or observations on a variable) is distributed is not limited to frequency tables and graphs. Certain descriptive statistics may also be used to convey some of the same information. At least two types of descriptive statistics must be employed to describe a score distribution—measures of central tendency and measures of variability.

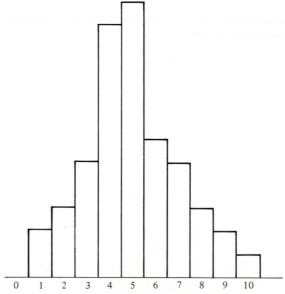

FIGURE 2.1   Frequency Histogram for Scores of 50 Examinees on a 10-Item Test

Measures of Central Tendency

Measures of central tendency represent the score of a typical individual in the group. Three such measures commonly used in reporting test scores are the mean, the median, and the mode.

THE MODE.   The mode is defined as the most frequently occurring value in a set of observations. For the data presented in Table 2.1 the mode of this distribution is 5, the score earned by more examinees than any other. It is possible for a frequency distribution to have more than one mode.

THE MEDIAN.   The median is the midpoint in the distribution of a set of observations. Theoretically it is the exact point above and below which 50% of the scores fall. It corresponds to the fiftieth percentile rank in a score distribution. For the data presented in Table 2.1, the value of the median would be somewhere between 4 and 5 points. (A computational formula for determining the exact value of the median will be presented in Chapter 19.)

THE MEAN.   The mean of a set of observations is the average value of all those observations. It is denoted as μ and is computed by using the formula

$$\mu = \frac{\sum_{i=1}^{N} X_i}{N} \tag{2.1}$$

where X_i is the score of person i and there are N people in the group. The summation sign $\sum_{i=1}^{N}$ is a common algebraic notation that means to compute the sum of all values of X beginning with the first observation and ending with the Nth observation. In computing the mean and other statistics described in this book, the reader may assume that the summation sign applies to all N observations when the lower and upper limits of i are not specified. Thus, for the set of five scores—160, 155, 145, 140, and 150—

$$\Sigma X = 160 + 155 + 145 + 140 + 150$$

and

$$\mu = \frac{\Sigma X}{N} = \frac{750}{5} = 150$$

The mean of the X distribution may also be called the expected value of X and denoted $\epsilon(X)$.

When a set of observations or test scores has already been organized into a frequency table, such as Table 2.1, the mean may be computed by using the formula

$$\mu = \frac{\Sigma f_i X_i}{N} \tag{2.2}$$

where X_i denotes a possible value of X and f_i denotes the frequency of occurrence of that value. Thus for the data in Table 2.1, the mean would be

$$\mu = \frac{1(10) + 2(9) + 3(8) + 5(7) + 6(6) + 12(5) + 11(4) + 5(3) + 3(2) + 2(1) + 0(0)}{50}$$

or

$$\mu = \frac{250}{50} = 5$$

Among the three measures used to describe central tendency, the mean is preferred for most commonly encountered test score distributions. For many of the distributions encountered in mental testing, the mean is more stable from sample to sample than the median or mode. Also the mean of a sample is an unbiased estimate of the population mean. That is, means computed from random samples of observations do not systematically underestimate or overestimate the value of the mean of the population from which the samples were drawn.

Measures of Variability

Measures of central tendency alone are seldom adequate for describing the performance of a group on a test. This is apparent if we picture a student who has just been informed that he scored 5 points on the 10-item biology test. In order to interpret how he has performed in relation to the rest of the class, the student's first question to the teacher is likely to be, ''What was the mean?'' Informed that the class mean was 7 points, the student's next question is likely to be, ''How much spread was there in the scores?'' In other words, how variable were the scores? If the student learns that most scores were concentrated between 6 and 8, he is likely to register some concern about his relatively ''low'' score. If he learns that most scores were concentrated between 2 and 9, he probably will take some comfort from the fact that there are several other scores lower than his. Although the student's raw score and the class mean are the same in these two situations, the interpretations of the score are affected substantially by the variability in the set of scores. Thus, in addition to measures of central tendency, measures of variability are also necessary to describe adequately a score distribution. The three most commonly reported measures of variability are the range, variance, and standard deviation.

The *range* of a distribution of scores is usually reported by indicating the lowest and highest scores earned. This measure of variability, however, has several undesirable properties. First, it is determined by two extreme scores (which are often affected by chance and errors of measurement), and thus the values of the range may be highly unstable from sample to sample. Second, the range offers no indication of how scores are distributed between the lowest and highest values. It is quite possible that although a given set of scores may range from 0 to 10, perhaps all scores but one are between 6 and 10. Thus the range can be misleading about the degree of variability in the scores for the entire group.

The variance and standard deviation are measures of variability that overcome the limitations of the range. These statistics are based on the simple concept of the *deviation score*. For each person with a raw score X, a *deviation score* x may be defined as

$$x = X - \mu \tag{2.3}$$

Thus a deviation score is the distance between each individual's score and the group mean. If a raw score is less than the mean, the deviation score will have a negative sign; if the raw score is greater than the mean, the deviation score will be positive. The *variance* for a group of scores is obtained by finding the average squared deviation score. This definition is denoted by the formula

$$\sigma_X^2 = \frac{\Sigma(X - \mu)^2}{N} = \frac{\Sigma x^2}{N} \tag{2.4}$$

The *standard deviation* is simply the square root of the variance:

$$\sigma_X = \sqrt{\frac{\Sigma(X - \mu)^2}{N}} = \sqrt{\frac{\Sigma x^2}{N}} \tag{2.5}$$

To illustrate the computation of the variance and standard deviation, let us return to our earlier example of five scores: 160, 155, 145, 140, and 150. Recall that the mean for these scores is 150. Therefore the deviation scores corresponding to the five raw scores are 10, 5, -5, -10, and 0, respectively. Applying Equation 2.4 to these deviation scores will give us the variance

$$\sigma_X^2 = \frac{\Sigma x^2}{N} = \frac{(10)^2 + (5)^2 + (-5)^2 + (-10)^2 + (0)^2}{5} = 50$$

Taking the square root of the variance will provide the standard deviation for this score distribution:

$$\sigma_X = \sqrt{\frac{\Sigma x^2}{N}} = 7.07$$

When test scores have already been organized into a frequency table, the variance can be computed from the formula

$$\sigma_X^2 = \frac{\sum\limits_{i=1}^{K} f_i x_i^2}{N} \tag{2.6}$$

where x_i is the deviation score for the ith possible value of X, f_i is the frequency of occurrence of this value, and K is the number of possible values of X. For the data presented in Table 2.1, the variance would be computed as follows:

$$\sigma_X^2 = \frac{1(5)^2 + 2(4)^2 + 3(3)^2 + 5(2)^2 + 6(1)^2 + 12(0)^2 + 11(-1)^2 + 5(-2)^2 + 3(-3)^2 + 2(-4)^2 + 0(-5)^2}{50}$$

$$\sigma_X^2 = \frac{1(25) + 2(16) + 3(9) + 5(4) + 6(1) + 12(0) + 11(1) + 5(4) + 3(9) + 2(16) + 0(25)}{50}$$

$$\sigma_X^2 = \frac{200}{50} = 4$$

Although the computation of the standard deviation is relatively simple, students of measurement are often unsure of its meaning. How should this statistic be interpreted in practical situations? First, remember that the standard deviation and variance are based on deviation scores. The larger the absolute values of the deviation scores, the larger will be the standard deviation and variance. Suppose that two groups of high school students respond to an attitude scale on drug abuse. When the scores are tabulated, group A has a mean score of 45 with a standard deviation of 10 points, and group B has a mean of 45 with a standard deviation of 17 points. From the larger size of the standard deviation for group B, we can conclude that students in group B are more diverse, or heterogeneous, in their attitudes about drug abuse than students in group A.

DESCRIBING INDIVIDUAL PERFORMANCE WITH Z-SCORES

Although the mean and standard deviation are most often used to describe the characteristics of group performance, these two statistics can also be used to create score transformations that will render individual scores more interpretable. The most common transformation is the z-score, computed by using the formula

$$z = \frac{X - \mu}{\sigma} \tag{2.7}$$

where X is the individual's raw score, μ is the group mean, and σ is the standard deviation. The z-score indicates how many standard deviations above or below the mean the individual score falls. Whereas the magnitude of the z-score value indicates the distance between the score of interest and the group mean in standard deviation units, the sign of the z-score indicates whether the score is above or below the mean. This use is illustrated in the test profile presented in Table 2.2. After

TABLE 2.2.   Profile of Raw Scores and Corresponding z-Scores for a Single Examinee

Profile for John Smith		
Subtest[a]	Raw Score	z-Score
Mathematics	102	−.31
Language Arts	80	1.25
Phys. Science	115	.10
Humanities	95	.83

[a]The following information is available on each subtest:

Math test, 150 items; $\mu = 110$; $\sigma = 26$
Lang. test, 110 items; $\mu = 70$; $\sigma = 8$
Phys. Sc. test, 125 items; $\mu = 112$; $\sigma = 30$
Humanities test, 140 items; $\mu = 90$; $\sigma = 6$

All means and standard deviations were calculated on the same population of examinees.

examining only the raw scores for this student, the admissions counselor might be tempted to guide this student toward enrollment in a math, science, or technical curriculum. If, however, the counselor examines the z-scores, which take into account the different means and variability of these tests, it is clear that this student might find a liberal arts curriculum more consonant with his aptitudes. In interpreting z-scores it is helpful to keep in mind that the mean of this distribution is .00 and the standard deviation is 1.00.

INFINITE POPULATIONS AND CONTINUOUS VARIABLES

There are times in test theory when we may wish to consider the distribution of a variable for an infinite population. In these situations, Equations 2.1 (for the mean) and 2.5 (for the standard deviation) are unusable. An equivalent formula to Equation 2.1, equally applicable to finite and infinite populations of observations, is

$$\mu = \Sigma p_k X_k \tag{2.8}$$

where X_k is the kth possible value of X, and p_k is the probability of occurrence of that value of X. Note that if we applied this formula to a finite population of scores (such as those in Table 2.1), it would equal the value obtained from Equation 2.1.

In a similar way, the standard deviation for an infinite population of observations is defined by the formula

$$\sigma_X = \sqrt{\Sigma p_k (X_k - \mu)^2} \tag{2.9}$$

Again, if we applied this formula to a finite set of scores, we would obtain results identical to those obtained from Equation 2.5.

It may be of interest to note that statisticians sometimes refer to the properties of a frequency distribution as *moments*. The mean, as defined in Equation 2.8, is called the *first moment about the origin of the distribution;* the standard deviation, as defined in Equation 2.9, is called the *second moment about the mean of the distribution*.

Although the scores on tests such as classroom tests, intelligence tests, or attitude scales assume a set of discrete values, the trait underlying the test performance is often regarded as a continuous variable. Consider the single item in which the examinee is asked to spell *armament*. Suppose that examinees A, B, and C all spell the word incorrectly and thus earn the same score of 0 on this item. Yet their underlying abilities to spell this word may be different. Examinee A may not even know how to begin to spell this word; examinee B may begin with *a-r-m* . . . but be unable to complete the word correctly; examinee C may spell the word as "*a-r-m-i--m-e-n-t*," thus missing the item by a single letter. Clearly there are finer divisions of spelling ability than the observed test scores reflect. Furthermore, no matter how many items are included on a test or how the scoring rules are developed, it will always be possible to conceive of an examinee who has slightly less or slightly more ability than is reflected in the observed test score. If observed scores were 40, 41, 42, and so on, it would be possible to imagine an examinee with a score of 40.5 on the underlying ability continuum; if the observed scoring scale is extended to 40.1, 40.2, 40.3, and so on, it would still be possible to imagine an examinee with a score of 40.15 on the underlying ability continuum; and so on. A continuous variable has possible values which can always be defined with smaller and smaller intervals. Between its upper and lower limits a continuous variable may assume any value on the real number line. Whenever we confront observations for a continuous variable, the formulas presented here for the mean, variance, and standard deviation are inappropriate. For continuous data, the standard operation of summation is impossible. Proper formulas for determining the moments (mean and standard deviation) for a variable with a continuous distribution require the operations of integral calculus. These will not be presented here. Nevertheless, the student should recognize that some concepts in test theory are based on the notion of a continuous variable and are consequently defined by using functions and operations from calculus.

THE NORMAL DISTRIBUTION

One central concept in test theory is the normal distribution, a theoretical distribution for a continuous variable measured for an infinite population. Beginning in the nineteenth century, mathematicians such as Quetelet and Galton were fascinated by finding that the frequency distributions for large numbers of observations on a variety of human traits often approximated the bell-shaped form that we call the *normal curve*. This was true even though the traits were measured on a discrete scale for a finite sample. Although some data distributions may resemble the shape of the normal curve, a frequency distribution of real data, based on a finite number of discrete values, can never be more than an approximation of this theoretical curve.

The theoretical normal curve (Figure 2.2(a)) is the graphical representation of a mathematical function derived by a German mathematician named Carl Gauss. The shape of the normal curve is defined by the equation

$$Y = \frac{1}{\sqrt{2\pi}\sigma} e^{-1/2(X-\mu)^2/\sigma^2} \tag{2.10}$$

In this equation, Y represents the height of the curve above a given X, σ denotes the standard deviation of the distribution of the X-scores and μ denotes the mean. The two constant values in this equation are $\pi \approx 3.1416$ and $e \approx 2.718$, which is the base of the natural logarithm system. Because the values of the mean and standard deviation differ for each sample of observations, Equation 2.10 does not define a single curve but rather a family of curves, which all share common properties.

Although Equation 2.10 may appear rather forbidding, a numeric example can be useful in dissolving some of the mystique that seems to accompany complex equations. First, let us note that $(X - \mu)^2/\sigma^2$ is simply z^2 for any value of X. Now also note that the quantity of $1/(\sqrt{2\pi}\sigma)$ will be the same for all values of X in the distribution. Assume that we wish to plot the normal distribution, which has a mean of 50 and a standard deviation of 10 points. In this case $1/(\sqrt{2\pi}\sigma)$ will be .04 for all values of X in the distribution. Let us suppose, simply for purposes of illustration, that we are interested in determining the value of Y for the score $X = 50$. In this case, the deviation score, $x = X - \mu$ will be 0, and thus $z = 0$. Therefore,

$$Y = .04e^{-1/2(0)^2}$$

Recall that any number raised to the zero power will be 1, and therefore

$$Y = .04(1) = .04$$

Now assume that we want to determine the value of Y for $X = 30$. In this case $z = -2$, $z^2 = 4$, and so

$$Y = .04e^{-2}$$

Since any number with a negative exponent may be written as a fraction with a positive exponent,

$$Y = .04(1/e^2) = .04(1/2.718^2) = .005$$

The values of .04 and .005 obtained from these solutions would give the heights of the curve above the values $X = 50$ and $X = 30$, respectively.

It should be noted that the heights of the normal curve at different values of X are *not* probabilities. Because X is a continuous variable, it is impossible to define the probability of occurrence of a particular score, such as $X = 50$. It is, however, possible to determine the probability of obtaining a value from a given score interval (e.g., 49.6 to 50.5). In calculus there is an operation called *integration,* which permits determination of the area under a curve between any two points of interest. This area gives us the probability of obtaining a score from that interval. When integration is applied to the normal curve function, it is denoted as

$$p(l \le X \le u) = \int_{l}^{u} \frac{1}{\sqrt{2\pi}\sigma} e^{-1/2(X-\mu)^2/\sigma^2} \, dx \tag{2.11}$$

where p denotes the probability, l and u denote the lower and upper bounds of the interval, and the symbols $\int$ and dx denote the process of integration for the mathematical expression that is written between them.

Test scores are frequently interpreted by discussing the proportion of cases that are likely to fall below (or above) a particular score value, assuming a normal distribution. To find the proportion of cases likely to fall below a given score value, we would simply set the lower bound of the integral Equation 2.11 to $-\infty$, set the upper bound to the score value of interest, and perform the integration. The information obtained from this procedure would be the probability of obtaining a score less than or equal to X; however, no test user of sound mind wants to solve Equation 2.11 for each possible score on the test. Fortunately there is another way for test users to obtain these probabilities without ever seeing the normal curve equation. When scores in a normal distribution are transformed to z-scores, the distribution of z-scores is called a *standard normal distribution* and has a mean of .00 and a variance of 1.00. Appendix A presents the area under the curve to the left of selected z-scores in a standard normal distribution. Each value represents the probability of obtaining a value less than or equal to z, and was computed from the integration process just described. How can Appendix A be used to obtain the proportion of examinees who would score below a particular value in a distribution that approximates a normal distribution? Simply convert the score to a z-score and then use Appendix A to look up the corresponding probability. For example, suppose the mean for a population is 100 and the standard deviation is 10. We want to know what proportion of the population should score below 110. The corresponding z-score is $z = (110 - 100)/10 = 1.00$. In Appendix A we find that the proportional area under the curve to the left of $z = 1.00$ is .84. Thus approximately 84% of the examinees in the population score at or below 110. This procedure works because the z-score is a linear transformation of the original raw score, and therefore the shape of the z-score distribution will be the same as the shape of the raw-score distribution. If the original raw-score distribution is approximately normal, the z-scores will also be distributed in this way. Thus the same proportion falls below an observed score and its corresponding z-score.

It is important to note that there are different probabilities associated with a positive or negative z-score with the same absolute value. Suppose, for example, we are interested in the probabilities of obtaining z-scores at or below the values -1.50 and 1.50. Figures 2.2(b) and (c) show the locations of these two scores, respectively. The shaded areas under the curve indicate the probability of obtaining a z-score at or below the point of interest. From this figure we can see that a much smaller area lies to the left of $z = -1.50$ than to the left of $z = 1.50$. If we now turn to Appendix A, and locate the z-score value 1.50 in column 1, we can obtain the corresponding probability of obtaining a score less than or equal to -1.50 from column 2. We see that this probability is .067. For a group of examinees with a normal distribution, we would expect only about 7% to score at or below -1.50. From column 3, we see that the probability of obtaining a score less than or equal to 1.50 is .933. Thus we would expect approximately 93% of the examinees in this group to score below this point.

All normal distributions share several characteristics that are useful in score interpretation. One of these properties is that the mean, mode, and median are always the same value—that point directly in the middle of the distribution. In addition, every normal distribution is symmetric; that is, the right and left halves of the curve are exact mirror images. Thus if we pick two points at equal distances above and below the mean, exactly the same percentage of cases will lie above and below the mean within that score interval. Finally, in every normal distribution, as shown in Figure 2.3, approximately 34% of the scores lie in the interval between μ and $\mu + 1\sigma_X$. Since the curve is symmetric, another 34% of the scores will lie in the interval between μ and $\mu - 1\sigma_X$. Thus approximately 68% of the scores in this distribution are contained between the values that lie 1 standard deviation below and above the mean. As shown in Figure 2.3, approximately 14% of the scores will lie

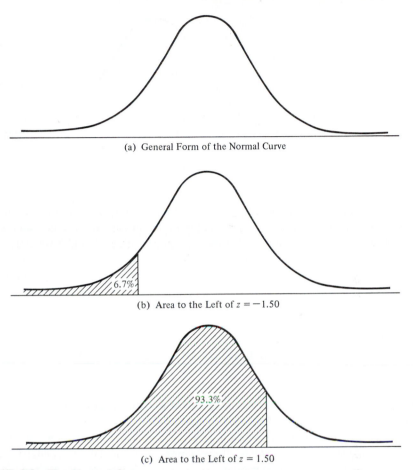

(a) General Form of the Normal Curve

6.7%

(b) Area to the Left of $z = -1.50$

93.3%

(c) Area to the Left of $z = 1.50$

FIGURE 2.2 The Normal Curve

in the interval between $\mu + 1\sigma_X$ and $\mu + 2\sigma_X$.[1] Finally we see that approximately 2% of the scores lie between $\mu + 2\sigma_X$ and $\mu + 3\sigma_X$.

Let us consider how this information is applied in describing the score distribution on a typical standardized intelligence test, where the mean is 100 points and the standard deviation is 15 points. If a large sample of students from a normal population were tested, about 68% of the sample would score between 85 and 115 because these values correspond to the points $\mu - 1\sigma_X$ and $\mu + 1\sigma_X$. Furthermore about 95% of the group would score between 70 and 130 on the test since these values correspond to the points $\mu - 2\sigma_X$ and $\mu + 2\sigma_X$. We would also expect any score below 85 to fall in the lower 16% of the score distribution; a score above 130 would

[1] To simplify this discussion, numeric values have been rounded here to the nearest whole number. To be strictly correct, we should say that 13.59% of the scores lie between the points $\mu + 1\sigma_x$ and $\mu + 1.96\sigma_x$, but this degree of precision is seldom employed in test score interpretation.

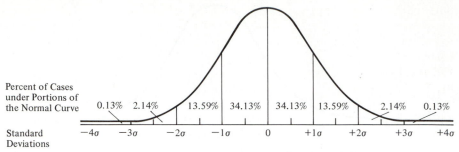

Percent of Cases under Portions of the Normal Curve   0.13%   2.14%   13.59%   34.13%   34.13%   13.59%   2.14%   0.13%

Standard Deviations   −4σ   −3σ   −2σ   −1σ   0   +1σ   +2σ   +3σ   +4σ

FIGURE 2.3   Percentage of Cases in Each Section of a Normal Curve

fall in the upper 2.5% of the distribution. Of course, it is possible to determine the percentage of cases that will lie above or below any given score in a normal distribution; but it is those percentages that are associated with 1, 2, and 3 standard deviations from the mean that are cited conventionally in presenting guidelines for score interpretation or in establishing cutoff scores for entry into programs designed to serve limited numbers of students or clients (e.g., exceptional student education programs).

DESCRIBING THE RELATIONSHIP BETWEEN TWO VARIABLES

Up to this point we have focused on the use of statistics to describe a score distribution for a single measure. There are many occasions, however, when the test constructor and test user are interested in how the scores on two different measures are related for the same individuals. For example, the clinical psychologist may be interested in how psychiatric patients' scores on the Minnesota Multiphasic Personality Inventory (MMPI) L scale (the lie scale) correspond to the number of false statements made by the same patients during their intake interviews. Similarly, the college admissions officer must be concerned about how scores for entering freshmen on the Scholastic Admissions Test (SAT) relate to their grade-point averages (GPA) at the end of the first semester; even the classroom teacher may be interested in knowing the extent to which children's scores on a reading comprehension test are related to their scores on a measure of academic self-concept. In each of these situations the test user is asking this question: What is the degree of relationship between scores (or observations) on the first measure and scores on the second measure?

When we are interested in the relationship between two variables, we probably want to know if low scores on the first variable are associated with low scores on the second variable, and if high scores on the first are generally associated with high scores on the second. Notice that we are concerned with relative values when we talk about ''high'' or ''low'' scores. Furthermore, we are interested in whether the differences among individuals' scores on the first variable are associated with pro-portionally similar differences among their scores on the second variable. Thus, we might ask how the deviation scores on X (the first variable) are related to the deviation scores on Y (the second variable). In many cases, however, the X and Y variables have been measured on very different scales. For example, if SAT score is the X variable, raw scores, and consequently deviation scores, will be expressed in hundreds of points on the X scale; whereas if GPA is the Y variable, raw scores and deviation scores may be expressed in fractions of a single point. As a convenience, those who work with such data may wish to convert the X and Y scores to z-scores so that scores for both the X and Y variables are on a common scale with a mean of .00 and a standard deviation of 1.00.

Scatterplots

One way to understand the relationship between two variables is to construct a scatterplot, in which the pair of z_X and z_Y scores for each individual is represented by a single point, as shown in Figure 2.4. Possible scores for z_X have been marked on the horizontal axis, known as the *abscissa;* possible scores for z_Y have been marked on the vertical axis, known as the *ordinate*. The coordinates for each point on the graph are determined by a pair of z_X and z_Y scores. For example, Ralph's z_X score is 2.0 and his z_Y score is 1.0. These scores are represented by the point with coordi-nates 2,1. Ruth's scores, $z_X = -.5$ and $z_Y = -.75$, are represented by another point. The scatterplot is the collection of points for all individuals in the sample. A scatterplot (and the relationship it depicts) is often characterized in terms of its direction and shape.

The direction of a relationship may be either positive or negative. With a positive

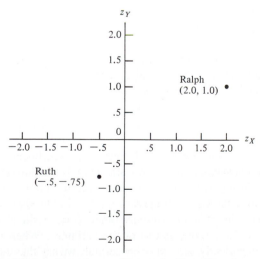

FIGURE 2.4   Plot of Points Based on z-Scores for Two Examinees

relationship, those who score high on the first variable tend to score high on the second, and those who score low on the first variable tend to score low on the second. The scatterplot in Figure 2.5(a) depicts a positive relationship between z_X and z_Y scores. We might expect to find positive relationships between variables such as job aptitude test scores and job performance, between I.Q. test scores and reading comprehension test scores, or between infants' birth weights and levels of perceptual motor development. With a negative relationship, those who score high on the first variable tend to earn low scores on the second, and vice versa. Figure 2.5(b) illustrates a scatterplot with a negative relationship. Such relationships might be found between variables such as students' absenteeism and grade-point average or scores on scales of anxiety and self-esteem.

We would like to characterize the shape of a scatterplot as resembling some geometric figure. The simplest figure that can be used to represent the relationship between two variables is a straight line. Thus, in describing the shape of a scatterplot we are often interested in how accurately this plot of points could be represented by a straight line. Figure 2.5(c) illustrates a scatterplot in which nearly all the points lie in a straight line. Such a scatterplot indicates a strong *linear* relationship between z_X and z_Y scores, because a straight line could be constructed that lies very near almost every point in the plot. Such a relationship might be observed if z_X and z_Y represented scores on two parallel forms of a math computation test, equal in length and difficulty, matched in content, and administered on the same day. The elliptical scatterplot in Figure 2.5(a) illustrates a set of data which can be represented only moderately well by a straight line. Such a relationship might be observed between such variables as motivation for achievement and grade-point average. Although there is a tendency for those who are highly motivated to have high grades in school, the rank orders of individuals on these two variables do not have perfect correspondence.

Figures 2.5(d), (e), and (f) illustrate cases in which we would say that there is little or no linear relationship between the z_X and z_Y scores. In nonlinear relationships (Figure 2.5(d) the scatterplot has a form that can be better represented by a geometric figure other than a straight line. The relationship between length of time in therapy (z_X) and level of psychological adjustment (z_Y) might be characterized by a nonlinear relationship. The circular scatterplot in Figure 2.5(e) shows little or no relationship of any kind between z_X and z_Y. There is no predictable pattern in the combinations of z_X and z_Y scores, and an individual with any given z_X score appears equally likely to have a low, medium, or high value of z_Y. The final example (Figure 2.5(f)) illustrates a case in which there is a clear linear pattern to the data but no relationship between z_X and z_Y. A statistical relationship describes the extent to which values on X may vary corresponding to variation in values on Y. If there is little or no variation in the values of the X or the Y variable, there can be little or no relationship between that variable and any other. Such a situation might occur if everyone earned the same score on one of the variables. Whenever the slant of a scatterplot becomes perfectly vertical or horizontal, we say that there is no relationship between the variables.

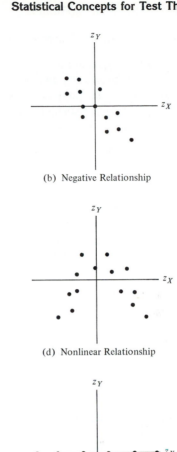

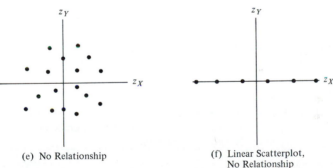

FIGURE 2.5 Scatterplots Based on z-Scores Depicting Various Relationships between X and Y Variables

Although scatterplots such as those in Figure 2.5 greatly enhance understanding of the relationships between two variables, such graphs do not permit very precise or concise descriptions of the *degree* of relationship. Two viewers might look at the same scatterplot and form different impressions about the degree of relationship represented. Furthermore, two plots may appear to be generally similar in shape and yet have some differences in locations of points which are difficult to detect or interpret from visual inspection alone. For this reason, it is useful to have a numeric index that describes the degree of linear relationship between two sets of observations for the same individuals.

The Pearson Product Moment Correlation Coefficient

One measure of the degree of linear relationship between two sets of observations is a statistic known as the *correlation coefficient*. Although there are several types, the most commonly used is the product moment correlation coefficient first conceptualized by Galton and later mathematically derived by Pearson. When the X and Y observations are expressed as z-scores, the formula for the product moment correlation is

$$\rho_{XY} = \frac{\Sigma z_X z_Y}{N} \tag{2.12}$$

where N is the number of persons. It is important to note that in computing the total cross product of the z-scores, $z_X z_Y$, must be computed for each individual prior to summing. Table 2.3 presents z-scores on aptitude test score and grade-point average for 10 individuals and illustrates the computation of the correlation coefficient.

Values of the correlation coefficient range from -1.00 to 1.00. The magnitude of this number is commonly used as a measure of the strength of the linear relationship between two variables; the sign of the number indicates the positive or negative direction of the relationship. When the value of ρ_{XY} approaches $.00$, it indicates little or no linear relationship between the variables. As the value of ρ_{XY} approaches 1.00, a strong positive linear relationship between the variables is indicated. For example, correlations reported between group and individually administered intelligence tests are frequently in the range of $.80$ to $.90$, indicating great similarity between individuals' relative performances on these two tests. By contrast, correlations between test anxiety and performance on achievement tests typically range between $-.20$ and $-.40$, indicating a relatively weak and negative linear relationship.

TABLE 2.3.   Illustrative Computation for the Pearson Product Moment Correlation Coefficient, Based on z-Scores

z_X	z_Y	$z_X z_Y$
.00	−.33	.00
−.83	−1.00	.83
1.88	1.17	2.20
.52	.50	.26
1.04	1.83	1.90
−.52	−.50	.26
.31	.00	.00
−1.98	−1.83	3.62
−.42	.33	−.14
.00	−.17	.00

$$\Sigma z_X z_Y = \rho_{XY} = \Sigma \frac{z_X z_Y}{N} = \frac{8.93}{10} = .89 \qquad\qquad 8.93$$

The product moment correlation coefficient can also be computed from raw-score data or from deviation scores. Recall that

$$z_X = \frac{X - \mu_X}{\sigma_X}$$

and

$$z_Y = \frac{Y - \mu_Y}{\sigma_Y}$$

If we substitute these quantities for z_X and z_Y in Equation 2.12, we arrive at the following raw-score formula for the correlation coefficient:

$$\rho_{XY} = \frac{\Sigma(X - \mu_X)(Y - \mu_Y)}{N\sigma_X\sigma_Y} \tag{2.13}$$

Note that the quantities $(X - \mu_X)$ and $(Y - \mu_Y)$ could also be written as deviation scores. Thus, a third expression for the correlation coefficient is

$$\rho_{XY} = \frac{\Sigma xy}{N\sigma_X\sigma_Y} \tag{2.14}$$

Again, it is important to note that the product of the deviation scores for each individual must be computed and then summed for all individuals in the group. Although three different correlation formulas have been presented, all three will yield the same numeric value. We will find the z score and deviation score formulas especially useful in many of the derivations to be presented in subsequent chapters. The computation of the correlation coefficient from raw-score data, using Equation 2.14, is illustrated in Table 2.4. (Note that the raw scores correspond to the z-scores on the aptitude test and grade-point average for the same scores reported in Table 2.2.)

Interpreting Correlation Coefficients

No discussion of the concept of the correlation would be complete without mentioning considerations in interpreting it. One issue is whether the magnitude of the coefficient is large enough to indicate an important or meaningful relationship between two variables. There are at least two criteria commonly used to judge the importance of a correlational statistic:

1. Is the correlation significantly different from .00?
2. What percentage of variance in the X observations is shared with variance in the Y observations?

To apply the first criterion, a researcher must consider the possibility that the sample under study was drawn from a population in which $\rho_{XY} = .00$. To investigate this possibility the researcher generates a range of values which will contain 95% of the correlation coefficients that would result if 100 samples of size N were drawn from a population with $\rho_{XY} = .00$. This range will be symmetric around .00. If the correla-

TABLE 2.4.   Illustrative Computation of the Pearson Product Moment Correlation Coefficient, Based on Raw Scores

X	Y	x or $(X - \bar{X})$	y or $(Y - \bar{Y})$	xy
100	2.1	0	−.2	0.0
92	1.7	−8	−.6	4.8
118	3.0	18	.7	12.6
105	2.6	5	.3	1.5
110	3.4	10	1.1	11.0
95	2.0	−5	−.3	1.5
103	2.3	3	0	0.0
81	1.2	−19	−1.1	20.9
96	2.5	−4	.2	−.8
100	2.2	0	−.1	0.0

$\mu_X = 100$ $\mu_Y = 2.3$ $\Sigma xy = 51.5$
$\sigma_X = 9.6$ $\sigma_Y = .6$

$$\rho_{XY} = \frac{\Sigma xy}{N\sigma_X\sigma_Y} = \frac{51.5}{(10)(9.6)(.6)} = .89$$

tion computed for the actual sample lies outside this range, the researcher should conclude that the observed correlation is significantly different from .00. (Remember that the researcher can be only 95% confident of this conclusion.) If the correlation computed for the actual sample falls within the designated range, the researcher is not justified in concluding that the observed correlation is significantly different from .00. To generate the necessary interval around $\rho_{XY} = .00$, the researcher must assume that the values for the 100 hypothetical samples will be normally distributed around $\rho_{XY} = .00$. Recall that in a normal distribution, 95% of the cases will fall within approximately 2 standard deviations below and above the mean. Magnusson (1967) provided the following formula for approximating the standard deviation of correlation coefficients around $\rho_{XY} = .00$:

$$\sigma_\rho = \frac{1}{\sqrt{N-1}} \tag{2.15}$$

where N is the sample size. Applying this formula when $N = 50$ would yield

$$\sigma_\rho = \frac{1}{\sqrt{49}} = .14$$

and thus 95% of the samples of size 50, drawn from a population where $\rho_{XY} = .00$, would lie within the range $.00 - 2\sigma_\rho$ and $.00 + 2\sigma_\rho$, or $-.28$ to $.28$, respectively. It should be noted that Equation 2.15 is an approximation of the standard error of the correlation coefficient, which is only accurate for reasonably large values of N. McNemar (1962) and Hays (1981) have suggested that this standard error estimation formula should be applied only when N is 50 or larger. For smaller samples a more precise method for calculating the standard error of the correlation should be used. (See Hays for details of this procedure.)

The second criterion for meaningfulness of a correlation coefficient is the value of ρ_{XY}^2. This value is interpreted as the proportion of variance in the Y-scores that is associated with variance in the X-scores. Thus, a correlation of $\rho_{XY} = .70$ means that 49% of the variance in Y was related to variance in X, but the remaining 51% of the variance in Y-scores was unrelated to individual differences on the X variable. Another way of explaining this is to consider the following example. Suppose a developmental psychologist computes the correlation between mothers' ages and children's I.Q. at age 3. This correlation is .30, and the standard deviation of the I.Q. test scores is 15; variance of these I.Q. scores is 225. In this example 9% of the variance in children's I.Q. scores is associated with their mothers' ages. Suppose now that the researcher identifies a subgroup of those children whose mothers are 25 years old. We would now expect the variation in I.Q. scores for this subgroup of children to be 9% smaller than the variance for the original population, since there is no longer any variation associated with mothers' ages. In this case the variance in I.Q. scores will be 204.75 points and the standard deviation of these scores will be 14.31. This relatively small reduction in the standard deviation of children's I.Q. scores (when variation associated with mothers' ages is removed) indicates that the relationship indicated by this correlation coefficient may be of little practical importance. Thus, we can see that correlations of moderate size must be interpreted cautiously since they indicate a relatively small percentage of shared variation in the variables under study.

Two other cautions should be noted in the interpretation of correlation coefficients. The discovery of a strong relationship between X and Y does not imply a cause-and-effect relationship between these variables. For example, an examination of the records of teachers' salaries and rates of violent crime for metropolitan areas across the United States would probably indicate a positive correlation between these variables. Yet this does not imply that raising teachers' salaries will lead to escalation of community crime rates. A more likely explanation is that both variables are a reflection of such factors as population density. Similarly, a high correlation between job satisfaction scale scores and workers' salaries cannot be interpreted to mean that the level of job satisfaction is responsible for a worker's salary. Other intervening factors (e.g., managerial concern with workers' morale) may affect both variables. Another point to remember in interpreting a correlation coefficient is that restriction of variance in the scores on the X or Y variable reduces the maximum correlation value that can be obtained. For example, suppose that for all freshmen at a large university, scores on the math subtest of the college entrance examination are correlated .75 with grades in their first college math course. Now suppose that we identify a subgroup consisting of only those students who intend to be math majors. It is quite likely that the scores for this group on the math entrance exam will be more homogeneous (less variable) than scores for all freshmen at the university. The deviation scores on the math subtest will be smaller for this select group. If we compute the correlation coefficient with these smaller deviation scores, although both the numerator and denominator of the correlation will be reduced, the effects of restricted variance are greater on the numerator. Consequently, the size of the correlation coefficient will be reduced, and the observed correlation coefficient for this homogeneous subpopulation will be less than .75. Restriction of variance in scores can also occur if the examiner unknowingly designs a test that is too hard or too easy, so that all examinees earn similar scores. Thus, whenever a low correlation coefficient is obtained, the researcher is advised to determine whether a restriction in variance has occurred, because of sample selection or some aspect of the measurement process, which may be obscuring a possible relationship between the variables of interest. Examination of the scatterplot may be helpful in this regard.

PREDICTING INDIVIDUAL PERFORMANCE

Once the test user has ascertained that there is a strong linear relationship between scores on a given test and some other variable, it may be desirable to use an examinee's test score to predict performance on that second variable. Such predictions are based on a *regression line,* which is the unique straight line that best represents a given scatterplot. Regression lines may be developed from scatterplots based on z-scores or raw scores.

The Regression Line

You may recall from basic algebra that a straight line is defined by the general formula

$$Y' = bX + c \tag{2.16}$$

where b is a constant known as the *slope of the line,* and c is a constant known as the *intercept.* The slope of a straight line may be defined as the number of scale points on the vertical axis that the line rises (or falls) for every increase of 1 scale point on the horizontal axis. The intercept is the point where the regression line touches the Y axis; it is also the value of the Y' at the point where $X = 0$. When X and Y variables are expressed in z-scores, the general formula for the regression line may be written as

$$z'_Y = m(z_X) + 0$$

where m is a constant with a different value from b'. Thus

$$z'_Y = m(z_X) \tag{2.17}$$

Thus, Equation 2.17 is simply a special case of the general formula for a straight line in which the intercept has been set equal to 0. Inspection of the z-score scatterplots in Figure 2.5 that depict linear relationships will reveal that each of them is centered around the point 0,0. This occurs because the mean of every z-score distribution is 0. Thus, the regression line for any scatterplot of z-score points must pass through the origin, and consequently, the value of the Y intercept in such a regression equation will always be 0. Figure 2.6 illustrates a regression line drawn through a scatterplot of points based on z-scores.

The reader should note that there is an important distinction between the terms z_Y and z'_Y. Each point on the scatterplot has a pair of coordinates, denoted as z_X and z_Y, which are the *actual* values of the scores observed for an individual. The regression line consists of a continuous set of points. Above any value of any individual's score z_X, there will be a point on the regression line with coordinates z_X and z'_Y. The value of z'_Y is the z-score on the Y variable that is *predicted* for an individual who earns the given z_X score. Note that for any value of z_X, it is possible to obtain a predicted z'_Y value from the regression line. This is true even for values of z_X that did not occur in the sample. Further note that for any value of z_X there is only one value of z'_Y although in the scatterplot for the actual data several values of z_Y may have occurred for a given z_X score.

Whenever a regression line is fit to a scatterplot, there are usually discrepancies between some individuals' predicted values on the Y variable and their actual values. This discrepancy, the quantity $z_Y - z'_Y$, is called an *error of prediction*. Thus, from Figure 2.7 we see that Carl's predicted z'_Y is .93, but his actual z_Y score is 1.83. If we used the regression line to predict Carl's score we would make an error of prediction of .90 z-score points. If we use the regression line to predict Cathy's z-score on the Y variable, we will make an error of prediction $-.27$ z-score points. Since it is obvious that some errors of prediction will result from using the regression line, why would we be interested in developing one for a given set of data? Suppose that z_X represents the score on a college admissions test and z_Y represents the grade-point average. If we have both sets of observations for one sample of students (e.g., the class of 1984) from this scatterplot of points, a regression line can be identified that will permit us to make predictions about the grade-point

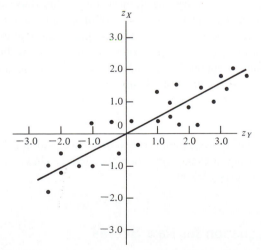

FIGURE 2.6 Regression Line for a Scatterplot Based on z-Scores

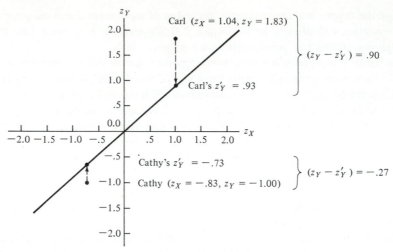

FIGURE 2.7 Discrepancies Between Actual z_Y and Predicted z_Y' Values for Two Examinees

averages of future applicants, based on their scores on the admissions test. To summarize, a scatterplot is based on use of data from a current sample for whom both sets of observations are available; but the regression line may be used to predict the performance of examinees in future samples for whom data on only one of the variables is known.

In any attempt to represent a scatterplot by a regression line, some errors of prediction are inevitable. To obtain the line of best fit, a value must be chosen for m (the slope of the line) that will minimize these errors. The quantity chosen to represent all these errors is $\Sigma(z_Y - z_Y')^2$. This quantity is referred to as the *least squares criterion*. Although we might try to find the value for the slope of the line that will minimize this quantity by trial and error, we could never be certain that we had tried all possibilities. Fortunately there is a calculus procedure (called *taking a derivative*) that is useful in identifying the minimum value for a mathematical function. When this procedure is applied to the quantity $\Sigma(z_Y - z_Y')^2$, it shows that the quantity will be minimized for the line where

$$m = \frac{\Sigma z_X z_Y}{N}$$

The right-hand side of this equation is the same as in equation 2.12, which gives the formula for the product moment correlation coefficient. Thus, we can rewrite Equation 2.17 substituting ρ_{XY} for m so

$$z_Y' = \rho_{XY} z_X \qquad (2.18)$$

Regression Equation for Raw Scores

Just as there is a raw-score formula for the correlation coefficient, there is also a formula for predicting a raw-score value, Y', from a known value of X. To demonstrate the relationship between the z-score and raw score prediction equations, let us represent z_Y' as

$$z_Y' = \frac{Y' - \mu_Y}{\sigma_Y}$$

From Equation 2.18 we know that $z_Y' = \rho_{XY} z_X$. Thus, by substitution we can say that

$$\frac{(Y' - \mu_Y)}{\sigma_Y} = \rho_{XY} \frac{(X - \mu_X)}{\sigma_X}$$

Solving for the value of Y', we have

$$Y' - \mu_Y = \rho_{XY}(X - \mu_X)\sigma_Y/\sigma_X$$

and

$$Y' = \rho_{XY}(X - \mu_X)\sigma_Y/\sigma_X + \mu_Y$$

Although this equation appears to be rather complex, we can make two simplifications. First, let us define

$$b_{Y \cdot X} = \rho_{XY}\sigma_Y/\sigma_X \qquad (2.19)$$

The constant, $b_{Y \cdot X}$, is commonly called the *regression coefficient*. Therefore, we can rewrite the raw-score equation as

$$Y' = b_{Y \cdot X}(X - \mu_X) + \mu_Y$$

By multiplication we have

$$Y' = b_{Y \cdot X}(X) - b_{Y \cdot X}(\mu_X) + \mu_Y \qquad (2.20)$$

Now let us define

$$c = -b_{Y \cdot X}(\mu_X) + \mu_Y$$

and we obtain

$$Y' = b_{Y \cdot X}(X) + c \qquad (2.21)$$

which fits the general form of the equation for a straight line.

Let us now illustrate the computation of the regression coefficient and the intercept for the regression line for predicting grade averages from aptitude test scores by using the values from Table 2.4. We can determine

$$b_{Y \cdot X} = (.89)(.6/9.6) = .06$$

The Y intercept is

$$c = -.06(100) + 2.3 = -3.7$$

Thus the regression equation is

$$Y' = .06X - 3.7$$

From this regression equation, it is simple to compute the predicted Y'-score for any individual, given the X-score. Thus, for the examinee with $X = 103$,

$$Y' = (.06)(103) + (-3.7) = 2.5$$

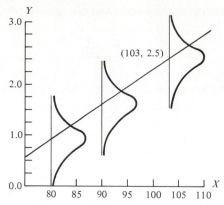

FIGURE 2.8   Distribution of Observed Y Values around Given Values of Z and Y'

Figure 2.8 shows the regression line for the raw-score values of X and Y based on data in Table 2.4. Note that when raw scores are used, the value of the Y intercept may not be 0. Thus, the regression line may not pass through the origin. Furthermore, the slope of the regression line for raw scores ($\rho_{XY}\sigma_Y/\sigma_X$) may be greater than 1.00. Finally, for convenience when plotting regression lines for raw-score data, we can start the X and Y values on the axis at some point other than 0,0.

Standard Error of the Estimate

When a regression equation is used for predicting scores for individuals, it is appropriate to wonder about the amount of error likely in such predictions. Figure 2.8 illustrates the distributions of actual Y values around the Y' value for several different values on the X variable. Such a distribution is called a *conditional distribution* because it portrays the distribution of Y values for a specific value (condition) of X. Each of these distributions has a standard deviation. Assuming that these conditional standard deviations are equal, each is known as the *standard error of the estimate*. The standard error of estimate when predicting Y' from a given value of X is denoted as $\sigma_{Y \cdot X}$ and is computed as

$$\sigma_{Y \cdot X} = \sigma_Y \sqrt{1 - \rho_{XY}^2} \tag{2.22}$$

For the data in Table 2.4 the value of $\sigma_{Y \cdot X}$ would be computed as

$$\sigma_{Y \cdot X} = (.6)\sqrt{1 - .89^2} = .27$$

To use the standard error of estimate in test score interpretation, we assume that

1. Errors of prediction are normally distributed around each Y'.
2. The distributions of these errors of prediction are homoscedastic (identical for all values of X).

Thus, we can assume that if $\sigma_{Y \cdot X} = .27$, approximately 68% of those with a predicted value of $Y' = 2.5$ will score within $2.5 \pm 1\sigma_{Y \cdot X}$ (2.23 to 2.77); approximately 95% of those for whom $Y' = 2.5$ will score within $2.5 \pm 2\sigma_{Y \cdot X}$ (1.96 to 3.04). Such estimates help us see the uncertainty of predictions made about individual scores on the basis of a regression equation.

SUMMARY

In this chapter, the use of frequency tables and graphs was reviewed as one method of summarizing a score distribution. In addition, descriptive statistics may be used to summarize the essential features of a score distribution. At least two types of statistics must be employed: measures of central tendency and measures of variability. Three commonly used measures of central tendency are the mean, median, and mode. Variability in a set of observations usually is described by range, variance, and standard deviation. Formulas for computing the mean and standard deviation for finite and infinite populations were presented and their uses illustrated.

When an individual's standing in a given distribution is of interest, the z-score is often used. A z-score indicates how many standard deviations above or below the mean the individual's score falls. The formula for the normal curve function was presented, and the standard normal distribution was defined. The values of the standard normal distribution are z-scores, and the probability of the occurrence of any score less than or equal to each particular z-value may be obtained from a standard normal z-table. This feature is a great convenience in test score interpretation because for any frequency distribution that approximates the normal curve, the percentage of examinees likely to fall above or below a certain score value can be obtained from the standard normal z-table.

When the relationship between two variables is of interest, the correlation coefficient is the appropriate descriptive statistic. Values of the correlation range between -1.00 and 1.00. The magnitude of this number indicates the extent to which the relationship between values of the first and second variable can be effectively portrayed by a straight line. The sign of the correlation indicates the direction of the relationship. The correlation coefficient may be computed by using raw score or z-score data. In interpreting a correlation, test developers and users may find it useful to square the correlation as an indicant of the amount of variance shared between the two variables. It may also be appropriate to test the statistical significance of the correlation determined for a sample.

Once the degree of the relationship between variables has been determined, it may be desirable to use an examinee's score on the first variable to predict subsequent performance on the second. Such predictions are based on use of a regression line. The regression line for a given set of data is the unique line that best fits a scatterplot of points based on the paired observations on the two variables. If the scatterplot is based on pairs of z-scores, the slope of the regression line will be the correlation coefficient alone. If the scatterplot is based on raw scores, the regression coefficient for predicting Y from X is denoted as $b_{Y \cdot X}$. It is the product of the correlation coefficient and σ_Y/σ_X. The intercept value for a regression line for z-scores is 0; for a regression line for raw scores, the intercept value is $-b_{Y \cdot X}\mu_X + \mu_Y$. In using the formula for a straight line to determine predicted values of Y for an examinee with a known value of X, some errors of prediction inevitably occur. The standard error of the estimate $(\sigma_{Y \cdot X})$ is an index of the variability likely to occur in the observed values of Y around the predicted value of Y' for examinees who have the same score on X.

Exercises

1. Suppose that a performance test of manual dexterity has been administered to three groups of subjects in different occupations. The frequency distributions are reported as follow. Answer the following questions *without* performing any calculations:
   A. In general, which group seems to have performed best on the test?
   B. Which group appears to be the most homogeneous in terms of manual dexterity? Which the most heterogeneous?
   C. Which group's frequency distribution appears to be most similar to the normal distribution?
   D. For which group would the mean and the median be most likely to differ? Why?

Score	$f(X)$ Group 1	$f(X)$ Group 2	$f(X)$ Group 3
28	1	3	1
27	2	7	4
26	3	5	3
25	7	1	4
24	5	1	3
23	1	2	4
22	1	1	1

2. Compute the mean, variance, and standard deviation for each of the three score distributions.
3. Complete the table of values for each examinee from Group 1:

	Raw Score	Deviation Score	z-Score
Joan	22	—	—
Peter	—	3	—
Edward	—	—	1.45
Cathy	24	—	—

4. For the three preceding score distributions, what raw-score values would correspond to z-scores of .00? What raw-score values would correspond to z-scores of −1.00?
5. Considering your answers to question 4, is it reasonable to say that for a given z-score, the equivalent raw score for group 3 will always be lower than the raw score for group 1? (Explain your reasoning.)

6. Assume that the following four examinees were tested as part of a large group that had an approximately normal score distribution.

Rebecca: $z = -2.15$

Sharon: $z = 2.15$

Ronald: $z = 1.50$

Sheldon: $z = .70$

   A. Approximately what percentage of examinees in the group would score lower than Rebecca?

   B. Approximately what percentage of examinees would score higher than Sharon?

   C. Approximately what percentage of examinees would have a score between Ronald's and Sharon's?

   D. Which of the four examinee's scores probably occurred more frequently in the entire group's distribution?

7. Two graduate students were assigned to convert each raw score for group 3 in Exercise 1 to its corresponding z-score. One student used the formula

$$z = \frac{X - \mu}{\sigma}$$

The second student computed the cumulative frequency for each score, divided by N, and looked up the value of z associated with this proportion in a standard normal z-table. Will these students obtain the same results? Why?

8. **A.** Suppose a variable X is normally distributed with a mean of 50 and a standard deviation of 10. What is the value of

$$\int_{45}^{55} f(X) \, dx$$

   where $f(X)$ is the normal curve equation?

   B. Rephrase question 8A as it might apply to a distribution of test scores. (Hint: see Exercise 6C.)

9. Consider the following table containing four separate test scores for seven individuals. All scores have been converted to z-scores.

	Aptitude	Reading Comprehension	Social Awareness	Self-Esteem
Examinee 1	.00	−.42	−.58	−1.44
Examinee 2	.49	.42	1.36	−.39
Examinee 3	−.41	.00	.39	−.79
Examinee 4	1.06	1.13	.19	1.05
Examinee 5	−.81	−.99	1.17	−.52
Examinee 6	1.38	1.41	−1.17	1.58
Examinee 7	−1.71	−1.55	−1.36	.52

Graph the scatterplots, illustrating the relationship between aptitude and reading comprehension, aptitude and social awareness, aptitude and self-esteem. Based on the appearance of these plots, which pair of variables has the strongest linear relationship? Is it positive or negative?

10. What are the correlations for the three pairs of variables in Exercise 9? What proportion of variance in reading comprehension is shared with variance in aptitude? What proportion of variance in self-esteem is shared with variance in aptitude?

11. Given the correlation between aptitude and self-esteem determined in Exercise 10, a teacher suggested that improving children's social awareness should also raise their aptitude test scores. Would you agree? Why? Suppose the teacher suggested that improving reading comprehension should increase aptitude scores. Now would you agree?

12. What is the predicted z-score on reading comprehension for an examinee whose aptitude score is $z = -.75$? What is the predicted z-score for this examinee on self-esteem? If the raw-score mean on self-esteem were 20 and the standard deviation 7.62, what would be the predicted raw score?

13. Two different researchers have conducted studies of the relationship between achievement motivation and internal locus of control. One researcher reports that the obtained correlation of .35 is significantly greater than .00 (at the 95% confidence level). The second researcher reports an obtained correlation of .35 and says it is not significantly greater than .00 (at the 95% confidence level). How can this discrepancy be explained? Did both researchers find the same degree of linear relationship among these variables?

14. A program evaluator has administered a pretest and a posttest to all clients in a program. The following data are obtained:

	Pretest	Posttest	$\rho_{pre,post} = .63$
mean	20	36	
std. dev.	5	3	

If Janet scored 15 points on the pretest, what is her predicted posttest score? If Tom also scored 15 points on the pretest, would he have the same predicted posttest score as Janet? Would these two examinees have the same actual posttest score? Can you give a range of points between which you might expect their actual posttest scores to fall?

15. If two examinees scored 1 point apart on the pretest, how far apart would their predicted posttest scores be? If two examinees scored 5 points apart on the pretest, how far apart would their predicted posttest scores be?

16. If you wanted to graph the raw-score regression line for the data in Exercise 14, what values would you use to represent the slope and the intercept of this line? If you wanted to graph the z-score regression line, what values would you use to represent the slope and intercept?

17. Suppose an instructor gave a 15-item quiz and weighted each item 1 point. The mean score on the test was 10 points and the standard deviation was 3 points. On this quiz the scores' correlation with scores on a preceding quiz was .56. Suppose the instructor later decided that each item should have received a weight of 5 points and so multiplied every examinee's score by 5:
   A. What effect will this have on the mean?
   B. What effect will this have on an examinee's deviation score?
   C. What effect will it have on the variance?
   D. How will it affect the correlation with scores on the preceding quiz?

18. Suppose each score in a distribution is multiplied by a constant K so that

$$X' = KX$$

and

$$\mu_X' = K\mu_X$$

Show that

$$\sigma_X'^2 = K^2\sigma_X$$

Chapter 3

INTRODUCTION TO
SCALING

If we review our definition of measurement we will note that the assignment of numbers to the properties of objects must be made according to specified rules. The development of systematic rules and meaningful units of measurement for quantifying empirical observations is known as *scaling*. Measurement scales for physical attributes were conceived in even the earliest societies. In trading, agriculture, and construction efforts it was necessary to develop arbitrary, accepted units of measure to quantify observable properties of objects. For example, early Egyptians measured length by using a unit called the *cubit,* which was defined as the length of the forearm from the elbow to the tip of the middle finger. The number of such units associated with a given object could then be counted. Thus a measurement scale is established when we define the set of possible values that can be assigned during the measurement process and state an explicit assignment rule. This assignment rule must include (or at least imply) the unit of the measurement scale. In some areas of educational and psychological measurement, a dual usage of the term *scale* has arisen. Quite often the term is also applied to a particular instrument (e.g., the Wechsler Adult Intelligence Scale or the Math Anxiety Scale). Such instruments for systematic collection of a sample of behavior are, in fact, *tests,* as defined in Chapter 1, and should not be confused with the usage of the term *scale* as it occurs in this chapter.

REAL NUMBERS AND MEASUREMENT SCALES

Recall that the real-number system is comprised of zero and all possible signed integer and decimal values between negative and positive infinity. The real-number system can be graphically represented by the real-number line, a single continuum which can be infinitely divided into smaller and smaller segments. Every value in the real-number system has a unique location on this continuum.

The real-number line has several important properties, which we will review. First, there is a fixed origin for values. Zero is the number assigned to this location. Whenever a set of numbers has a fixed zero point, we say that the set has the property of *fixed origin*. It is important-to note that the number 0 behaves somewhat differently from any other value in the real-number system. When 0 is added to any other number, the result is that other number. Thus the original value is unchanged by the addition of 0, although it would be changed by the addition of any other number. Second, the basic unit of the real-number system is the number 1 (the identity element). Moving away from the origin, each successive whole number on the real-number line is located one unit from the previous whole number. The size of this unit is a constant (it can be envisioned as the distance between 0 and 1). Thus the distances between adjacent whole numbers at any point on the number line are equal. Third, when two values from the real-number line are being compared, the absolute value of the number that lies farthest from zero is considered "greater" because it represents a greater accumulation of units than the number that lies closer to zero. Furthermore, the relationship among values in the real-number system is transitive, so that given any three values a, b, and c, if we determine that $a > b$ and $b > c$, we must conclude that $a > c$. When this relationship is true for a set of numbers, we say that the set has the property of *order*. When a number system has all these properties, it is possible to define formally the arithmetic operations of addition, subtraction, multiplication, and division, and the commutative, associative, and distributive laws for these operations can be derived.

A scaling rule establishes a link or rule of correspondence between the elements in a data system and the elements in the real-number system. A system can be defined as a collection of elements or objects that share a common property (Weitzenhoffer, 1951). We shall use the term *data system* to refer to a collection of all possible observations of a given property for a set of objects. Suppose we have a set of objects that differ observably in length. We can conceive of a variety of scaling rules which might be used to relate the observable lengths in the data system with the values from the real-number line. For example, objects might be arranged in order from shortest to longest and a number assigned to each object based on its position; the shortest object would be assigned 1, the next shortest would be assigned 2, and so on. The objects could also be compared to a standard unit such as a foot ruler and assigned numbers based on their lengths in feet. Once a scaling rule is specified and a number has been assigned to each element of the data system, these numbers are called *scale values*. The original properties (or relationships) that these scale values possessed as members of the real-number system may or may not still be viable.

LEVELS OF MEASUREMENT SCALES

Stevens (1946) identified four levels of measurement scales that differ in the extent to which their scale values retain the properties of the real-number line: these are nominal, ordinal, interval, and ratio. *Nominal* scales are those in which numbers are used purely as labels for the elements in the data system and do not have the properties of meaningful order, equal distances between units, or a fixed origin. The numbers on jerseys of football players or numbers on sweepstakes tickets are oft-cited examples. Social scientists sometimes use nominal scales in coding responses to demographic questionnaire items. For example, an item on the respondent's gender may be assigned a code of 0 for male and 1 for female, even though no quantitative distinction between the two genders is implied. The numbers merely indicate qualitative differences between categories represented by the possible responses and serve as "shorthand" labels for them. With a nominal scale any set of numbers may be used, but each unique object or response in the data system must be assigned a different number. Any other set of numbers could be substituted for the original set of numbers as long as the one-to-one correspondence between members of the sets is maintained. This is called *isomorphic transformation*. Suppose, for example, responses to an item on religious affiliation have been coded 1 for Protestant, 2 for Catholic, 3 for Jewish, and 4 for other. An acceptable isomorphic transformation would be to recode the item responses as 8 for Protestant, 6 for Catholic, 9 for Jewish, and 1 for other. It would not be permissible, however, to assign both Protestant and Catholic responses to the code of 2 during the transformation since they had unique codes in the original scaling rule. Although nominal scales allow great freedom in transforming one set of scale values for another without any loss of information about relationships among the original data, this is possible only because the original scale values assigned to the data (lacking order, distance, and origin) conveyed little quantitative information to begin with.

If the elements in the data system can be ordered on the amount of the property being measured, and the scaling rule requires that values from the real-number system must be assigned in this same order, an *ordinal* scale results. One example of a well-known ordinal scale in the physical sciences is the Mohs Hardness Scale, used by mineralogists to describe the hardness of mineral samples. This scale, in use since 1822, assigns values of 1 to talc (as the softest mineral), 2 to gypsum, 3 to calcite, and so on up to 10 for diamond. Each mineral has been assigned its numeric value based on its ability to scratch the surface of any mineral with a lower number on the hardness scale. A mineral sample that can scratch gypsum but not calcite might, for example, be assigned a value of 2.5. As noted in one geology field guide, this scale "is not an exact mathematical relationship: 10 on the scale is merely a lot harder than 9, just as 9 is somewhat harder than 8, and so on" (Pough, 1960, p. 31). As a second example, when judges in a beauty pageant rank 10 contestants from 1 to 10, using their own personal standards, these values also constitute an ordinal scale. Note that although the judges may have had great difficulty in differentiating between contestants who received ratings of 1 and 2 and relatively little difficulty in awarding ratings of 5 and 6, this information is not conveyed by the scale values. Thus ordinal scale values have the same property of order as values in the real-number system, but they lack the properties of equal distances between units and a fixed origin. Values on an ordinal scale may be converted to other values by using any rule that preserves the original information about the rank order among the data elements. Such a transformation is called a *monotonic transformation*. If five elements that comprise a data system were originally ranked 1, 2, 3, 4, and 5, these values could be replaced by the numbers 3, 10, 35, 47, and 201. On the other hand, the transformation to 10, 16, 12, 18, and 20, respectively, for the same five elements would not be acceptable since it alters the rank order of the second and third observations from their original standings.

Numbers on an *interval* scale also indicate rank order, but in addition, distances between the numbers have meaning with respect to the property being measured. If two scores at the low end of the continuum are one unit apart and two scores at the high end are also one unit apart, the difference between the low scores represents the same amount of the property as the difference between the high scores. Note how this relationship was not true for the beauty contestants rated on an ordinal scale. Although interval-level scales have the properties of order and equal distance between units, the point of origin on such a scale is still arbitrarily chosen and does not represent total absence of the property being measured. To illustrate, imagine four prisoners in a cell with only a table and a deck of playing cards. A question about their heights arises, but they have no ruler. To determine who is taller, each man must measure the other; the unit of measure chosen is the length of a single playing card. Because they do not have enough cards to measure height from the floor, they choose the table height as an arbitrary starting point, and each man's height is measured by the number of card lengths higher than the table top. Their measured heights are expressed as 12 card lengths, 11 card lengths, 10½ card lengths, and 13 card lengths. Note that any object might have been chosen as the starting point. Thus, although they now have a description of their heights on an interval scale, these measurements are relative to an arbitrary origin (i.e., they still do not know their absolute heights).

The Fahrenheit temperature scale is an oft-cited example of an interval-level scale. The reader may wonder how this can be since the Fahrenheit scale has a zero point. The zero point on this temperature scale, however, does not have the same qualities as zero in the real-number system; that is, if we added the amount of heat energy represented by 0°F to some other amount of heat energy, the total amount of available heat would be increased. In other words, zero degrees on the Fahrenheit temperature scale does not represent a total absence of heat and thus does not behave like the zero in the real-number system. Because the relative sizes of the distances between values assigned to observations contain meaningful information, transformations permissible to interval scale values are restricted. If x is a variable representing values on the original scale, and y represents the values on the transformed scale, the only transformation that will retain the information contained in the original set of values is of the form in which a and b are constants: $y = ax + b$. Thus a set of values 5, 4, 2, and 3 could be transformed to 11, 9, 5, and 7 by the transformation $y = 2x + 1$ with no loss of information about the construct under study. If, however, we tried to use a nonlinear transformation such as $y = x^2$, the values 25, 16, 4, and 9 would not have the same relationships to each other as the numbers 5, 4, 2, and 3 on the original scale.

The fourth level of measurement is the *ratio* scale, which has the properties of order, equal distance between units, and a fixed origin or absolute zero point. Many measures of physical objects are made on ratio scales (e.g., length in centimeters; weight in pounds; or age in days, months, or years). The ratio scale is so named because once the location of absolute zero is known, nonzero measurements on this scale may be expressed as ratios of one another. One prominent example is the Kelvin thermometer scale. The zero point defined on this scale corresponds to a total absence of heat. The only transformations that can be performed on ratio-level measurements, without altering the information, are of the form $y = cx$, where c is a constant. It should be noted that any set of values regarded as meeting the requirements for a ratio scale may be regarded as also meeting the requirements for an interval scale (if we are willing to accept the subsequent loss of information about the location of absolute zero). Similarly, data collected on an interval or ratio scale may also be regarded as providing ordinal-level information, and data collected on an ordinal, interval, or ratio scale certainly meet all requirements for nominal-level measurement.

It is important to remember that Stevens' four levels of measurement scales constitute a useful taxonomy, but this is not the only way to categorize or describe such levels. Torgerson (1958, p. 19), for example, talks about two levels of ordinal scales, and Coombs (1950b) posits a type of scale between ordinal and interval. An important, ongoing debate in education and psychology is whether measurements taken with psychological tests should be considered as ordinal or interval level. We will examine this issue in some detail later in this chapter. First, however, it is necessary to understand more about the scaling processes that are often applied to psychological data.

SCALING APPROACHES IN TEST DEVELOPMENT

In developing an instrument for educational or psychological assessment, the test developer is actually engaged in testing a series of hypotheses about the "scalability" of the data obtained from measurements of the proposed construct. First, a hypothesis has been implicitly formulated that the construct is a property occurring in varying amounts so that it can be quantified using the proposed scaling rule on a theoretical unidimensional continuum. Usually this is called the *psychological continuum*. Second is the question of what real-number properties (order, distance, and origin) the scale values on this continuum possess. Torgerson (1958) characterized three broad approaches the researcher may use to investigate these issues: subject-centered methods, stimulus-centered methods, and response-centered methods.

Subject-Centered Methods

With the subject-centered approach, the test developer's primary interest is in locating *individuals* at different points on the continuum. This is the purpose of most measures of aptitude or achievement and is also the major goal in the construction of many instruments in the affective domain. For example, suppose a clinical psychologist is developing a scale to measure depression; the researcher might write a set of 20 statements and classify the responses to these statements as indicative or not indicative of feelings of depression. Respondents are then awarded 1 point for each "indicative" response selected and 0 for each "nonindicative" response. Each subject's score is computed from the total of the item scores. Subjects with the higher scores are located closer to the positive end of the continuum than those with lower scores. The item scoring weights are assigned by an arbitrary decision of the scale developer, and typically all items are weighted equally. Little or no attention is given to possible differences in the items to which the subject is required to respond because the sole purpose is to "scale" the subjects. Even if the subject is permitted to respond to each item with some gradations on the response scale (e.g., a Likert response format, in which each examinee responds from "Strongly Agree" to "Strongly Disagree"), this still would exemplify the subject-centered method. As Torgerson (1958) noted, although this approach has many useful applications, it has not led to the development of scaling models that permit the researcher to *test* the scale properties of the scores derived. The total score is computed by simply *assuming* that point values assigned to each possible response form a numeric scale with the properties of order or with order and equal units.

It may seem that choosing the subject-centered, psychometric approach allows the researcher to "get off easily." At this point, no stringent tests for the numeric properties of the data must be made. In fact, however, the researcher has simply deferred addressing this question. Scores obtained from psychometric instruments must sooner or later be investigated for their qualities of reliability and validity. (Chapter 4 presents an overview of the process of developing, and investigating the reliability and validity of, subject-centered measurements. Units II and III also deal with these procedures.) If the scores obtained from this scaling approach do not have meaningful order and some approximation of equal units, they are unlikely to meet acceptable standards for reliability or validity. At that point, however, the test developer will not know whether the failure of the instrument to produce useful information is due to shortcomings in the numeric properties of the scale or inadequate validity or reliability in the measurements for the purpose under investigation.

Stimulus-Centered Methods

With the stimulus-centered approach the researcher is interested primarily in locating the positions of the stimuli (or items) on the psychological continuum. Early applications of stimulus-centered scaling in psychology were undertaken in the experimental laboratories of German perceptual psychologists in the 1800s. These researchers were called *psychophysicists* because of their interests in developing quantifiable relationships between responses to physical stimuli and the stimuli themselves. Among the psychophysicists were Ernst Weber and Gustav Fechner, who were concerned with identifying the smallest differences in physical stimuli (lights, tones, weights, etc.) that could be reliably detected by human senses. For example, to measure perception of brightness, it was common to present two lights and ask each subject to select the brighter one. Although the experimenter could determine by physical measurement which stimulus was stronger, the problem was to develop a method for scaling the subjects' responses; that is, how could the psychological continuum of ''brightness'' be scaled? Although a variety of procedures were evolved, one of the best known was to have the comparison of the two lights made repeatedly either by the same subject or by a group of subjects. Two stimuli were regarded as equal on the sensory scale when each stimulus was chosen with equal frequency (50% of the time). When a particular stimulus was chosen over the other 75% of the time, the difference between these two stimuli on the psychological scale was called a *just noticeable difference* (JND). The criterion of 75% was chosen because it was halfway between chance and perfect accuracy. The JND was used by early psychologists as the unit of measurement on the psychological continuum. Using this general scaling method, with various refinements, Weber (1846) formulated and attempted to prove empirically ''Weber's law,'' which is simply that equal increments in the strength of a stimulus would produce proportional increments of equal magnitude in the subject's sensory response. Later Fechner (1860) suggested a modification, proposing a logarithmic relationship between an increase in sensation and an increase in the physical stimulus. Although the psychophysicists devoted much effort to studying different experimental techniques for determining JNDs, they seldom considered the question of whether JNDs could be considered equal units on the psychological continuum; Torgerson (1958) noted that JNDs were simply declared to be psychologically equivalent units by definition.

Attempts at psychological scaling remained primarily the bailiwick of the perceptual psychologists until the pioneer efforts of L. L. Thurstone demonstrated that their scaling methods could be adapted to the measurement of attitudes. Thurstone showed it was possible to scale properties of stimuli that were unrelated to any physical measurement. For example, he demonstrated that the perceived seriousness of crimes could be scaled by asking judges to examine all possible pairs of crimes from a list (e.g., arson and smuggling, arson and murder, etc.) and identify the most serious crime from each pairwise comparison (Thurstone, 1927). Another of his studies involved presenting subjects with a series of statements on organized religion and asking them to place each statement on a continuum divided into equally spaced intervals, based on the strength of the sentiment toward the church expressed in the statement (Thurstone and Chave, 1929). These applications of scaling to verbal stimuli attracted the interest of sociologists, educators, and psychologists. Thurstone also proposed accompanying quantitative techniques for testing whether the scale values derived by his procedures conformed to an interval-scale model. One procedure that incorporates such a test is called the *law of comparative judgment;* another is the *law of categorical judgment.* Thurstone's ''laws'' were actually systems of equations used to estimate scale values for each stimulus. Torgerson (1958) devoted several chapters to each of these stimulus-centered scaling methods, including various methods of data collection, equations for estimating scale values, and statistical tests of goodness-of-fit between observed and estimated scale values. Such detailed treatment of the topic is beyond the scope of this chapter; however, we will briefly describe how the law of comparative judgment is applied when data are collected from judges using all possible pairwise comparisons of items.

First, it is important to understand something about the theory underlying the process. Imagine a hypothetical continuum on which we are interested in estimating the distance between two attitude statements about the use of nuclear weapons. Statement i might be something like this:

Nuclear weapons should be used only as a last resort during armed conflict.

Thurstone posited that different individuals would vary in their opinions about the strength of this statement and that these perceptions would fall in a normal distribution centered around a point on the attitudinal continuum denoted as μ_i. (This distribution is not directly observable, however.) Now, in addition, consider statement j:

Nuclear weapons should not be used under any circumstances.

Again it is assumed that individual perceptions of the strength of this statement would vary in a normal distribution around a point μ_j. The locations of μ_i and μ_j, respectively, are considered to represent the "true" locations of these two statements on the attitudinal continuum. Finally, note that for each individual, the distance between the perceived locations of statements i and j can be denoted as $(i - j)$. These distances also would vary in a normal distribution. This distribution is called the *distribution of discriminal differences,* and its mean is

$$\mu_d = (\mu_i - \mu_j)$$

The standard deviation of this distribution is $\sigma_{(i-j)}$. It is this standard deviation which serves as the unit of measurement in defining the distance between i and j on the attitudinal continuum through the expression

$$z_{ij} = \frac{(\mu_i - \mu_j)}{\sigma_{(i-j)}}$$

This expression is actually a z-score expressing the standardized difference between μ_i and μ_j, and hence is the standardized distance between stimuli i and j on the psychological continuum.

In scaling attitude statements, the researcher is usually interested in more than a single pair of statements. Thus the standardized distances are estimated for all pairs of items. For example, with three stimuli, we would obtain

$$z_{12} = \frac{\mu_1 - \mu_2}{\sigma_{(1-2)}}$$

$$z_{13} = \frac{\mu_1 - \mu_3}{\sigma_{(1-3)}}$$

and

$$z_{23} = \frac{\mu_2 - \mu_3}{\sigma_{(2-3)}}$$

Earlier we pointed out that an interval scale has an arbitrary origin. To calculate the scale values for the present example on a common scale, it is necessary to designate an arbitrary origin. Let us set $\mu_1 = 0$. Thus the scale value of item 1 is arbitrarily set to zero (and thus this scale cannot be considered to be of ratio-strength.) Now we can say that

$$z_{12} = \frac{0 - \mu_2}{\sigma_{(1-2)}}$$

$$z_{13} = \frac{0 - \mu_3}{\sigma_{(1-3)}}$$

and

$$z_{23} = \frac{\mu_2 - \mu_3}{\sigma_{(2-3)}}$$

Rearranging these equations we obtain

$$\mu_2 = -z_{12}\sigma_{(1-2)}$$

$$\mu_3 = -z_{13}\sigma_{(1-3)}$$

and

$$\mu_2 - \mu_3 = z_{23}\sigma_{(2-3)}$$

If we knew z_{12}, z_{13}, $\sigma_{(1-2)}$, and $\sigma_{(1-3)}$, it would be possible to solve the first two equations to obtain scale values for items 2 and 3. As we shall see presently, it is possible to estimate z_{12}, z_{13} and z_{23}, but not $\sigma_{(1-2)}$ and $\sigma_{(1-3)}$. In one form of the law of comparative judgment this latter difficulty is solved by assuming that the two standard deviations are equal. Denote this common standard deviation by K. Our equations are then

$$\mu_1/K = 0$$

$$\mu_2/K = -z_{12}$$

and

$$\mu_3/K = -z_{13}$$

It is important to recognize that because we arbitrarily set $\mu_1 = 0$, we can have at most an interval scale. We also know that if the scale is interval, it is permissible to transform each scale value by $a(\mu_i) + b$. Setting $b = 0$ and $a = 1/K$, we can define a new set of scale values, μ_i^*, which are related to the original μ_i values by $\mu_i^* = 1/K(\mu_i) + 0$, and so our equations for the scale values become

$$\mu_1^* = 0$$

$$\mu_2^* = -z_{12}$$

and

$$\mu_3^* = -z_{13}$$

The transformed μ_i^* value for each item i, is an indicant of its location on the continuum in relation to the item that was designated as the arbitrary origin. In the current example, the remaining problem is to estimate z_{12} and z_{13} to obtain values of μ_2^* and μ_3^* respectively.

The reader may have noticed that so far all that we know about the nature of the scale on which the μ_i^* is expressed is that it is not a ratio scale and *might* be an interval scale. Thurstone's comparative judgment procedure provides a basis for obtaining estimates of z_{ij} values from empirical observations and for testing whether these estimates are of interval strength. When two stimuli, i and j, are located at the same point on the continuum, and a group of judges are asked to indicate which stimulus is greater, we would expect that their pattern of responses would indicate some confusion in making this judgment. Specifically, we would expect that .50 of the judges would choose the response $i > j$ and .50 would choose $i < j$. As the distance between $(\mu_i - \mu_j)$ increased, this confusion should be lessened, so that perhaps .75 of the judges would choose $i > j$ and only .25 would choose $i < j$. As the distance $(\mu_i - \mu_j)$ widened still more, we might find that the judgment response distribution would be $p_{ij} = .95$ and $p_{ji} = .05$, where p_{ij} represents the proportion of judges choosing $i > j$ and p_{ji}, the proportion choosing $i < j$. Thus there is a relationship between p_{ij}, the probability of a randomly selected judge choosing $i > j$ and the distance $(\mu_i - \mu_j)$. In applying Thurstone's law of comparative judgment, it is assumed that the distribution of judges' responses in this dichotomous-choice situation is governed by the underlying normal distribution of the discriminal differences. This means that p_{ij} values can be related to z-scores by using a standard normal probability table. Thus, for example, in theory

When $p_{ij} = .50$, $z_{ij} = .00$.

When $p_{ij} = .75$, $z_{ij} = .68$.

Or when $p_{ij} = .95$, $z_{ij} = 1.64$, and so forth.

If we had only two items, the process could go no further. In scale construction, however, there are usually more than two items. The judges are asked to compare all possible pairs of items and each judgment is made independently. Thus we have an initial set of z_{ij} estimates for each item pair. Let us now consider how the data obtained from this process may be used to estimate a μ_i^* value for each item and to test whether these μ_i^* values comprise an interval scale.

1. Suppose that Figure 3.1 shows the true locations of four items on a psychological continuum. Assume that this continuum is an interval scale. Under the assumption that all the $\sigma_{(i-j)}$ values are equal, the z_{ij} values equal the distances between any two given stimuli i and j. Therefore it must be true that

$$z_{14} = z_{12} + z_{23} + z_{34}$$

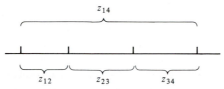

FIGURE 3.1 Additive Relationship of z_{ij} Values Where All ij Pairs Are Scaled on an Interval Continuum

In reality, even if the μ_i^* values are on an interval scale, judgments of individual pairs of stimuli are made independently, and the initial set of $\hat{z}_{ij}$ estimates obtained from judges' comparisons of possible pairs of stimuli seldom meet this condition exactly because of random errors in the judgment process.

2. The law of comparative judgment provides a set of equations, which use the initial $\hat{z}_{ij}$ values to calculate a set of $\hat{z}'_{ij}$ values that do meet the condition of additivity with minimum departure from the original set of $\hat{z}_{ij}$ values (in the least-squares sense). The assumption is that these refined $\hat{z}'_{ij}$ estimates more nearly represent the "true" picture of the relative locations of the items which would emerge if random errors of the judgment process were eliminated. (There are several different versions of this law depending on the assumptions made about the distributions of judgments.)

3. The discrepancies between the values of $\hat{z}_{ij}$ obtained empirically from the judges and the estimated values of $\hat{z}'_{ij}$ are examined by using statistical tests for goodness-of-fit. If these discrepancies are small, the psychological continuum used for rating the stimuli corresponds closely to the interval scale, which was assumed in generating the $\hat{z}'_{ij}$ values. If the discrepancies are judged to be too large (by statistical goodness-of-fit criteria), one must question the assumption of a single interval-strength continuum, which was invoked in generating the $\hat{z}'_{ij}$ values. As Torgerson (1958, p. 32) noted, the purpose of the statistical test is not to determine whether we have created a perfect scale but whether the approximation is close enough to treat this data scale as an interval numeric continuum without being "too far off."

The final set of scaled items can now be used for measurement purposes. Typically, a set of such items might be administered to a group of respondents in an agree-disagree format, and each respondent's score would be computed as the average scaled value of the items endorsed. It should be noted that the law of comparative judgment was selected for presentation here because it provides a simple illustration of how the fit of empirical data to a stimulus-centered scaling model can be tested. In the history of attitude-scale development, however, this method was soon supplanted by the law of categorical judgment because the latter did not require subjects to engage in the time-consuming task of judging all possible pairs of items, but simply required them to rank-order, sort, or place the item stimuli into categories.

Response-Centered Approaches

The most complex approaches to scaling are the response-centered. Response data are used to scale subjects on a psychological continuum, based on the strength of the items endorsed (or answered correctly); at the same time, items are scaled in terms of the strength or amount of the trait possessed by the subjects who endorse them. Two illustrations of this class of scaling procedures will be given. Guttman (1941b and 1950) described a response-scaling method known as *scalogram analysis*. Usually a fairly small number of items is used; items are worded to increase in strength so that once respondents agree with one statement, they should also agree with all statements that express weaker, but positive sentiment toward the construct and disagree with statements that express negative sentiment. An illustration of such a set of statements is

A. Clerical personnel in public employment should have the right to strike.
B. Public-school teachers should have the right to strike.
C. Nurses in state and city hospitals should have the right to strike.
D. City firefighters should have the right to strike.

Consistently logical response patterns are called *allowable response patterns*. Allowable patterns for the preceding items are shown in Table 3.1. Logically inconsistent response patterns are called *errors*. The greater the number of subjects whose responses conform to allowable patterns, the more certain we can be that these items form an ordered scale. The degree to which they do so can be assessed with the coefficient of reproducibility:

$$C = 1 - \frac{\text{total number of errors}}{\text{total number of responses}}$$

A coefficient of .90 has often been used as the criterion for demonstrating that the items form an ordered scale (Torgerson, 1958, p. 323). Procedures for assessing the distances between the items on this continuum are more complicated and will not be discussed in this chapter; however, logistic models for scaling such item responses will be discussed in Chapter 15. Practice in applying basic concepts of Guttman's scalogram analysis is provided in exercises at the end of this chapter.

Another approach to scaling both persons and items, suggested by Coombs (1950b), is known as the *unfolding technique*. Each respondent is asked to rank-order his or her preference for a set of stimuli or to rank-order a set of statements in terms of their proximity to his or her own personal belief. To understand the theory

TABLE 3.1. Allowable Response Patterns to a Guttman Scale of Four Attitude Items on Strikes by Public Employees

Allowable Patterns	Statements			
	A	B	C	D
1	+	+	+	+
2	+	+	+	−
3	+	+	−	−
4	+	−	−	−
5	−	−	−	−

behind this procedure, let us assume that we have a set of four scalable stimuli whose true location on the psychological continuum is known to us (perhaps by divine revelation). The scale for these stimuli is usually called the *joint* or *J scale* since we can consider the location of both stimuli and persons. The positions of the four stimuli on the J scale are denoted by the letters A through D in Figure 3.2(a). The midpoints between pairs of stimuli are shown in Figure 3.2(b). In this figure the point marked $\overline{AB}$ denotes the midpoint between stimuli A and B; the point marked $\overline{AC}$ identifies the midpoint of the distance between the stimuli A and C; and so on. There are six pairs of stimuli altogether, and consequently there are six midpoints marked on the scale. These six points divide the J scale into seven regions. Theoretically, if a subject's location is in region 1, when asked to rank-order the four

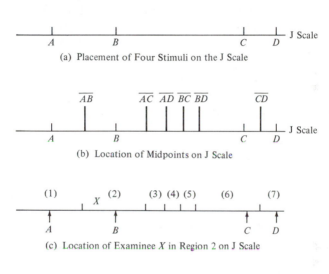

(a) Placement of Four Stimuli on the J Scale

(b) Location of Midpoints on J Scale

(c) Location of Examinee X in Region 2 on J Scale

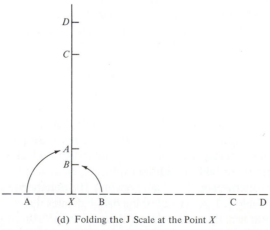

(d) Folding the J Scale at the Point X

FIGURE 3.2   Illustrations of Stimuli Placement for Coombs' Unfolding Procedure

stimuli in relation to his or her own position, the subject would give the response ABCD. If the subject's location is in region 2, he or she would respond BACD. This may be more obvious if we envision examinee X located in region 2 (see Figure 3.2(c)). If we could "fold up" the continuum at the point of X's location, it would appear as it does in Figure 3.2(d). Thus examinee X's preference orders (or ranking) for the four stimuli can be read directly from the vertical, "folded" continuum shown in Figure 3.2(d). This rank ordering of the stimuli on the vertical continuum is called an I (individual) scale. If we had a perfectly scalable set of stimuli and perfectly scalable subjects, there would be seven permissible subject-response patterns (or I scales)—one for each region on the J scale. In the example the seven possible I scales are

Subject (J Scale) Locations	Response Patterns (I Scales)
Region 1	ABCD
Region 2	BACD
Region 3	BCAD
Region 4	BCDA
Region 5	CBDA
Region 6	CDBA
Region 7	DCBA

In psychological scale development, however, we do not have the luxury of knowing the locations of the stimuli on the J scale. Instead we would begin with a set of four stimuli, not knowing if they can be ordered or what the order should be. We must try to make these inferences from observable subject-response patterns. To illustrate, let us return to the four attitude statements on strikes by public employees. We will assume that each statement is written on a different card and coded as follows:

Clerks   Clerical personnel in public employment should have the right to strike.
Teachers   Public-school teachers should have the right to strike.
Nurses   Nurses in city and state hospitals should have the right to strike.
Firefighters   City firefighters should have the right to strike.

Suppose now we administer these four statements to a sample of 200 college students, asking them to rank order the cards, placing first the statement that most closely expresses their sentiments on this issue, next the statement that comes closest after that, and so on. If this is a scalable set of statements, from our ideal model we know that we may obtain up to seven prevalent response patterns (I scales). Obtaining more than seven response patterns would indicate a lack of "scalability" for the stimuli, subjects, or both. (With real subjects, however, a small number of aberrations or error patterns would probably occur.) The obtained response frequencies are reported in Table 3.2. A perusal of the data indicates that seven of the many possible I scales were heavily used. Among them are two (and only two) that are exact mirror images: Clerks—Teachers—Nurses—Firefighters, and Firefighters—

TABLE 3.2. Illustrative Frequencies for Various Response Patterns Obtained from Coombs' Scaling of Four Attitude Statements on Striking by Public Employees

Response Pattern	Frequency	Relabeled Response Patterns after Order Determined
Clerks—Teachers—Nurses—Firefighters	41	ABCD
Teachers—Nurses—Clerks—Firefighters	32	BCAD
Nurses—Teachers—Firefighters—Clerks	30	CBDA
Nurses—Firefighters—Teachers—Clerks	29	CDBA
Teachers—Clerks—Nurses—Firefighters	24	BACD
Firefighters—Nurses—Teachers—Clerks	20	DCBA
Teachers—Nurses—Firefighters—Clerks	18	BCDA
Teachers—Firefighters—Clerks—Nurses	3	BDAC
Nurses—Firefighters—Clerks—Teachers	2	CDAB
Teachers—Clerks—Firefighters—Nurses	1	BADC

A: Clerks
B: Teachers
C: Nurses
D: Firefighters

Nurses—Teachers—Clerks. This result allows us to infer the order of the four stimuli on the J continuum, and we can now label the statements with letters ABCD to indicate their respective order placement on the J scale. (The decision of which end point to assign the letter A is arbitrary, and in this case we will substitute ABCD for Clerks—Teachers—Nurses—Firefighters, so that A represents the least favorable attitude toward strikes by public employees and D the most favorable.) As a further check on the scalability of our stimuli, note that the first two preferences in each of the seven prevalent response patterns must be adjacent scale points.

Once we have determined the order of the four stimuli, we will want to draw some inferences about the relative distances between them. Specifically, with four stimuli we are able to answer the question, Which two pair of stimuli are closer on the psychological continuum, A and B or C and D? (Rephrasing this in terms of our example, Which are perceived as closer—clerks and teachers or nurses and firefighters—in terms of their right to strike?) First recall that there are seven possible subject regions on the continuum. We must recognize that their locations are determined by the distances between the stimuli pairs. When there are only four stimuli, the location of region 4 (the middle region) depends on whether the distance between A and B is greater than the distance between C and D or vice versa. To see this, compare Figures 3.3(a) and 3.3(b). The differences between these two conditions will be reflected in the rankings given by subjects in this category. Consequently, when our empirical findings yield a prevalent response pattern (I scale) such as BCDA, we infer that the "psychological" distance between A and B exceeds the distance between C and D. (This is the case for the data shown in Table 3.2 and depicted in Figure 3.3(a).) In contrast, if the psychological distance be-

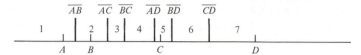

(a) When $\overline{AB} > \overline{CD}$, and Preference Order of Respondents in Region 4 Is $BCDA$.

(b) When $\overline{AB} < \overline{CD}$, and Preference Order of Respondents in Region 4 Is $CBAD$.

FIGURE 3.3 Locations of the Middle Region on the J Scale When Distances Between *AB* and *CD* Are Reversed in Size

tween C and D were greater than between A and B, Figure 3.3(b) would depict this situation and we would observe a prevalent response pattern of CBAD. With only four stimuli on the J scale, this is the only deduction we can make about the distances between the stimuli. However, when we have five stimulus points on the J scale, there will be 12 possible sets of 11 response patterns each. Using the same logical procedure followed with the four stimuli, we would now have sufficient information to determine the relative distances among all the stimuli. Coombs (1950b) pointed out that this type of scale probably lies somewhere between ordinal and interval levels because the distances between the units are not precisely determined, but rather, the relative size of these distances is known. In this limited example, we have simply used visual inspection and logic to test the fit of the data to the model; however, there are more sophisticated analytic procedures for determining the degree to which the responses fit the ideal model (see Torgerson, 1958, Ch. 14).

Readers interested in more specific application of scaling techniques to attitude inventory construction may wish to consult a source such as Dawes (1972) or Udinsky, Osterlind, and Lynch (1981), and those interested in original publications that have exercised historic influence on the field of attitude scaling should see Fishbein (1967). More detailed coverage of scaling models has been presented by Torgerson (1958) and van der Ven (1980).

SCALE LEVELS FOR SUBJECT-CENTERED MEASUREMENTS

As we have just seen, when scales are constructed and tested for the purpose of scaling the stimuli or for scaling stimuli and subjects simultaneously, various methods are available to test the degree to which scale values can be considered as ordinal- or interval-level measurements. When the subject-centered approach is used, however, there are no convenient scaling models to test whether the measurements obtained can be treated as ordinal- or interval-level information.

One argument sometimes advanced to support the notion that psychological-test data are of interval strength is the relationship between the scale values and the normal distribution. This argument usually takes one of two forms. The first is that when physical traits are measured on interval, or even ratio, scales, the distribution of values obtained for a large population frequently conforms to a normal curve. Therefore if a set of psychological measurements also conforms to a normal curve, these measurements, too, must be obtained from interval scales. There is an obvious logical fallacy in arguments of this nature. It is a bit like arguing that most nursing students are found to be females; since this new student is female, she must be majoring in nursing. A somewhat more coherent form of this argument rests on the properties of the normal curve itself. This argument takes note of the fact that under a normal distribution, the scores $1z$, $2z$, $3z$, and so on are equidistant. Thus z-scores under a normal distribution form an interval scale. When the raw scores on the test can be obtained from a linear transformation of the normalized z-scores (which is the only kind of transformation allowed for interval-strength data), the original test scores themselves are also of interval strength.

Magnusson (1967, p. 13) seems to accept this argument, stating that "equal distances on the continuum on which the normal distribution is placed are also equal units. If we construct an instrument which gives a normal distribution of obtained scores, we can thus express the positions of the individuals on this psychological continuum on an interval scale." One shortcoming of this position seems to be that by writing enough items and inspecting item responses, one can always select a subset of items so that the distribution of scores approximates the normal distribution. Yet if other items that fit the trait conceptually must be excluded to obtain this distribution, it is questionable whether there is truly a logical or mathematical relationship between positions on the underlying psychological continuum and the observed score continuum. A second problem with this argument is that although the distances between $1z$, $2z$, and $3z$ may be numerically equivalent, they may still not be equivalent in a psychological sense. Consider a classroom of children with an approximately normal distribution of scores on a reading comprehension test. From a psychological perspective, the distance between the abilities of a child who scores at the mean and one who scores 1 standard deviation below the mean $(-1z)$ is meaningful and important; but the distance between abilities of a child who scores 3 standard deviations below the mean $(-3z)$ and one who scores 4 standard deviations below the mean $(-4z)$ may be barely noticeable.

A related issue in the interval-ordinal debate over psychological test scores involves the choice of statistical operations that can be applied to these data. This Pandora's box was opened for the psychological community by Stevens (1946) when he held that "most of the scales widely and effectively used by psychologists are ordinal scales. In the strictest propriety the ordinary statistics involving means and standard deviations ought not to be used with these scales for these statistics imply a knowledge of something more than the relative rank order of the data.'' Two crystallized positions on this issue have been characterized by Burke (1963) as the ''measurement-directed'' and the ''measurement-independent'' positions. The measurement-directed group would maintain that the nature of the measurement scale dictates the types of arithmetic and statistical operations that may be performed on the data. They contend that because social scientists can rarely prove that their measurements are of interval strength, they would be wiser to use statistical operations and significance tests appropriate for rank-order data. In inferential statistics, this class of statistical tests is often grouped under the name of *nonparametric statistics*. These procedures have been described in several texts such as the one by Marasciulo and McSweeney (1977).

The measurement-independent group generally assumes the posture that once the measurements have been taken, they are numbers like any others (regardless of the original scale) and as such may be subjected to computations and statistical analyses as long as the data meet the assumptions required by the particular statistical method used. This group points out that most parametric statistical tests do not require the data to be measured on an interval scale; rather, such tests require assumptions about the distributions of the data. As long as the data meet these distributional assumptions, the group sees no need to sacrifice the statistical power and computational convenience that can be achieved through parametric statistical tests. Thorough reviews of the arguments in favor of the measurement-independent position can be found in Gardner (1975) and Ware and Benson (1975). Currently most quantitatively oriented social scientists seem to accept this position.

Ultimately, however, the issue of interval- or ordinal-level measurement is a pragmatic one. Basically the test user must ask, ''Can I use the information from scores on this test as if they were interval data?'' Consider the following set of scores for six examinees on an instructional placement test:

Student	Score
1	37
2	35
3	39
4	22
5	18
6	42

If the test user wants to divide the examinees into two groups for instruction on the basis of test scores, it is fairly easy to see that students 1, 3, and 6 would be placed in one group and students 4 and 5 in another. The problem is where to place student 2. If the test user assigns this student to group 1 on the grounds that his or her score is ''closer'' to the scores of the other group members, the test user is essentially treating these scores as if they were derived from an interval scale. If the test user places this child in group 2 on the grounds that the three top-ranking students should be in one group and the three low-ranking students in another, the test user is employing the data as if they were derived from an ordinal scale. Which course of action seems more justifiable? The answer to this question requires empirical solution. We concur with Lord and Novick (1968, p. 22) that if it can be demonstrated that the scores provide more useful information for placement or prediction when they are treated as interval data, they should be used as such. On the other hand, if treating the scores as interval-level measurements actually does not improve, or even lessens, their usefulness, only the rank-order information obtained from this scale should be used. This seems to be the one position on which nearly everyone agrees. It is often overlooked that even Stevens, who popularized the ordinal-interval debate, after criticizing the use of statistics with psychological test data, added, "On the other hand for this illegal statisticizing there can be invoked a kind of pragmatic sanction: in numerous instances it leads to fruitful results."

SUMMARY

The development of systematic rules and meaningful units of measurement for quantifying empirical observations is known as scaling. A scaling rule establishes a link or rule of correspondence between the elements in a data system and the elements in the real number system. The real-number system has the properties of order, equal distances between units, and a fixed origin. Once the numbers have been assigned to elements in a data system, they may no longer possess these properties. Stevens (1946) identified four levels of measurement scales (nominal, ordinal, interval, and ratio) which are distinguishable in terms of the real number properties that apply to them. Numbers on a nominal scale do not have meaningful order, equal units, or a fixed origin; numbers on an ordinal scale have only the property of order; interval-level scales have order and equal distances between units but no fixed origin; ratio-level scales have all real number properties. Allowable transformations for each of these levels of scales were discussed.

In developing a psychological assessment procedure the researcher must select a scaling method that will permit assessment of the extent to which the numbers used to identify positions on the psychological continuum have the properties of order and equal units. Torgerson (1958) identified three basic approaches to scale development: subject centered, stimulus centered, and response centered. Subject-centered scaling focuses on location of individuals on the psychological continuum. It is the approach commonly used in many psychological test-development efforts. Only the stimulus-centered and response-centered approaches have actually resulted in scaling models which permit the researcher to test the goodness-of-fit between empirical observations and predicted values that would result from a scale with order and equal unit properties.

Stimulus-centered scaling was illustrated by Thurstone's law of comparative judgments. The steps characterizing this procedure are: (1) creation of a p_{ij} matrix based on examination of all possible item pairs by a group of judges; (2) conversion of each p_{ij} value to a $\hat{z}_{ij}$ value using a normal curve table; (3) deriving a set of predicted $\hat{z}'_{ij}$ values; (4) testing the goodness-of-fit between $\hat{z}_{ij}$ and $\hat{z}'_{ij}$ values; and (5) designating an arbitrary origin and deriving the locations of all other items relative to it on the continuum using $\hat{z}'_{ij}$ values.

Response centered approaches permit simultaneous scaling of both stimuli and subjects. Guttman's scalogram analysis and Coombs' unfolding technique were described to illustrate this approach. The coefficient of reproducibility is used with scalogram analysis as one method for determining goodness-of-fit of the data to the model. With Coombs scaling, subjects indicate their rank-order preferences for a limited number of stimuli. Any given number of stimuli has a maximum number of allowable patterns for these preferences. A method for inferring the order of stimuli on the continuum and the relative distances between pairs of stimuli was illustrated. More complex statistical procedures for testing goodness-of-fit of response-centered scaling models were not discussed.

The issue of whether subject-centered measurement yields data of interval or ordinal strength was explored from three perspectives. Arguments that a normal distribution of scores implies an interval scale were not found to be totally convincing. The use of parametric statistics, however, seems justified as long as the assumptions required by the procedures are met, even though the researcher cannot be certain that the data are of interval strength. Finally, a sensible position seems to be that psychological test data should be treated as interval scale data when it can be demonstrated empirically that usefulness of the scores for prediction or description is enhanced by this treatment.

Exercises

1. Identify the type of transformation that follows and the type(s) of data to which such transformations may be legitimately applied:
   - **A.** 37 _____ 75
     - 26 _____ 53
     - 54 _____ 109
     - 28 _____ 57
     - 32 _____ 65
   - **B.** 12 _____ 5
     - 15 _____ 4
     - 18 _____ 3
     - 21 _____ 0
     - 24 _____ 2
     - 15 _____ 4
   - **C.** 22 _____ 87
     - 25 _____ 102
     - 19 _____ 19
     - 6 _____ 5

2. Consider the following responses of 10 subjects to the four items on strikes by public employees (see allowable response patterns shown in Table 3.1).

	Items			
Subject	A	B	C	D
1	+	+	+	+
2	+	−	+	+
3	+	+	−	−
4	+	−	−	−
5	+	+	−	−
6	−	−	−	−
7	+	−	+	−
8	−	+	+	−
9	+	−	−	−
10	−	+	−	−

    A. Rank-order the items based on the number of positive responses given to the item.

    B. Identify those subjects who did not make allowable response patterns.

    C. For those subjects who made allowable response patterns, rank-order them, from those who hold most to those who hold least favorable attitudes on strikes by public employees.

    D. Which item responses would need to be changed to make the response patterns of unscalable subjects conform to allowable patterns? How would this information be helpful to the test developer for future item revision?

    E. What is the coefficient of reproducibility for this set of items? How should it be interpreted?

    F. Suppose a test developer proposes writing 40 items for a scalogram analysis. What difficulties might be encountered?

3. Consider the topics of corporal punishment of school children, the use of nuclear weapons in warfare, or capital punishment of convicted murderers. Try to develop a three-to-five item scalogram on one of these topics. Indicate what you would consider the allowable response patterns.

4. After examining the data in Table 3.2, indicate the "region" on the continuum (numbers from 1 to 7) in which a subject must be located to give each of the response patterns indicated.

5. For each of the following measurement situations, indicate the approach to scale development that seems most appropriate. (Choose among the subject-centered, stimulus-centered, and response-centered approaches.)

    A. A marketing researcher wants to assess the appeal of 10 different magazine ads for a single commercial product.

    B. A college professor wants to develop a test for assigning final grades in a chemistry course.

    C. An educational psychologist wants to develop a set of math problems on basic skills, using problems of increasing difficulty, which can be used for diagnostic placement of students. His goal is to identify the student's instructional level by assuming that once the student misses at least three items in succession, that student will answer no more items correctly.

Chapter 4

PROCESS OF TEST CONSTRUCTION

In Chapter 3 we noted that the goal of most measurement in education and the social sciences is the location of individuals on a quantitative continuum with respect to a particular psychological construct. This was called "subject-centered measurement." The purpose of this chapter is to describe a process that can be followed in test construction for subject-centered measurement. The focus of this chapter is on a systematic approach to test construction that has wide applicability to various types of tests. The steps in this process can be listed as follows:

1. Identify the primary purpose(s) for which the test scores will be used
2. Identify behaviors that represent the construct or define the domain
3. Prepare a set of test specifications, delineating the proportion of items that should focus on each type of behavior identified in step 2
4. Construct an initial pool of items
5. Have items reviewed (and revise as necessary)
6. Hold preliminary item tryouts (and revise as necessary)
7. Field-test the items on a large sample representative of the examinee population for whom the test is intended
8. Determine statistical properties of item scores and, when appropriate, eliminate items that do not meet preestablished criteria
9. Design and conduct reliability and validity studies for the final form of the test
10. Develop guidelines for administration, scoring, and interpretation of the test scores (e.g., prepare norm tables, suggest recommended cutting scores or standards for performance, etc.)

The preceding list of steps probably represents the minimum effort required to ensure that test scores will have the essential technical qualities to serve as useful

66

measurements. Many professional test developers include additional steps in the sequence or repeat some steps several times. The sequence presented here is intended primarily as a guide to novice test developers who may undertake construction of a test for a local research or evaluation study. The main focus of this chapter is on the first six steps in the process, which are intrinsic to the initial production of a test. Procedures for executing the remaining steps (7 through 10) are the major topics of subsequent units of this text.

IDENTIFYING PURPOSES OF TEST SCORE USE

A systematic process for test development should be grounded in consideration of the basic purposes for which the test scores will be used. For example, suppose a reading expert has been commissioned to develop a test of reading comprehension for entry-level college students. Ultimately information from scores on such a test might be used for making admissions, placement, or diagnostic decisions. Yet it is doubtful if a single test could be developed to meet all these needs optimally. As we will see in Chapter 5, a test to discriminate among examinees over a broad range of ability (or temperament) should be composed of items of medium difficulty (so that variance of examinees' scores will be maximized). On the other hand, a diagnostic test, used to identify areas of specific weaknesses for low-ability students, must contain a substantial number of items which are relatively easy for the population of examinees as a whole. Similarly the content of a test designed to assess minimum competency would probably differ from that of a test designed to select applicants for a competitive educational program. Clarifying the major purposes for which test scores will be used and establishing priorities among these probable uses greatly increases the likelihood that the final form of the test will be useful for the most important purpose it is to serve.

IDENTIFYING BEHAVIORS TO REPRESENT THE CONSTRUCT

As a general rule, the process by which psychological constructs have been translated into a specific set of test items has remained private, informal, and largely undocumented. Cronbach (1970), Roid and Haladyna (1980), and Shoemaker (1975) have discussed this subject with particular emphasis on the development of achievement tests. Typically the test developer will conceptualize one or more types of behavior which are believed to manifest the construct and then simply try to "think up" items that require these behaviors to be demonstrated. Unfortunately this approach can result in omission of important areas of behavior or inclusion of areas that are relevant to the construct only in the mind of this particular test developer. Such an approach results in a highly subjective and idiosyncratic definition of the construct. To broaden, refine, or verify the view of the construct to be measured, the test developer should engage in one or more of the following activities:

1. *Content analysis.* With this method, open-ended questions are posed to subjects about the construct of interest, and their responses are sorted into topical categories. Those topics that occur predominantly are taken as major components of the construct. For example, Jersild (1952) published results of a content analysis of compositions by children describing themselves, and the resulting categories served as the basis for generating items for two widely used inventories designed to measure children's self-concepts (Gordon, 1967; Piers and Harris, 1964).
2. *Review of research.* Those behaviors that have been most frequently studied by others are used to define the construct of interest. The test developer may use an eclectic approach or select the work of one particular theorist in specifying behavioral categories to be represented by test items.
3. *Critical incidents.* A list of behaviors is identified that characterizes extremes of the performance continuum for the construct of interest. This method is usually attributed to Flanagan (1954), who asked job supervisors to describe situations in which an employee had functioned with outstanding effectiveness or ineffectiveness and thereby generated a list of "critical behaviors" to use for rating job performance.
4. *Direct observations.* The test developer identifies the behaviors by direct observation. For example, a vocational counselor, developing an inventory to assess job-related stress in high-risk occupations, might find that actual observations of such workers on the job would help identify situations that are potential sources of emotional stress.
5. *Expert judgment.* The test developer obtains input from one or more individuals who have first-hand experience with the construct. Written questionnaires or personal interviews are used to collect information. As an illustration, a personnel psychologist who wants to develop a checklist for rating performance of staff nurses in a large hospital can survey a group of nursing supervisors to identify the types of performance that should be included.
6. *Instruction objectives.* Experts in a subject are asked to review instructional materials and develop a set of instructional objectives when an achievement test is being developed. An instructional objective specifies an observable behavior that students should be able to exhibit after completion of a course of instruction. Such objectives communicate to the item writer both the specific content on which items should focus and the nature of the tasks the examinees should be able to perform. A thorough description of the process of developing objectives is provided in most introductory texts in measurement (e.g., Brown, 1983; Mehrens and Lehmann, 1984; Popham, 1981).

DOMAIN SAMPLING

Many psychological constructs, such as intelligence, creativity, or moral development, are of interest primarily because of the degree to which individuals differ in the amount of that attribute. Development of a test to be used for differentiation typically involves conceptualization of major behavior components of the construct (using procedures such as those just described), production of items in these areas, and ultimately, selection of items on which the expected degree of variation in performance occurs. Items on which there is little variation are eliminated because they fail to represent the construct appropriately. Because the meaningfulness of scores on tests constructed in this fashion is derived by comparing the individual examinee's performance with the performance of others, measurements from such tests are often called *norm-referenced*.

However, in some situations there is a need to measure examinees' performance in terms of more absolute levels of proficiency. For example, such information is often needed for achievement tests when the user wants to certify whether examinees have attained a level of minimal competency in an academic subject or to evaluate the effectiveness of an instructional program. In such situations Ebel (1962) suggested a need for a "content standard score," which would have interpretive meaning for an examinee regardless of how others had performed on the test; and Glaser (1963) suggested that the term *criterion referenced measurement* should be applied to test scores that derive their meaning from the examinees' absolute levels of performance on a series of test items in which each set of items corresponds to a known level of proficiency on a criterion of importance. In developing tests for such purposes, the preceding methods of operationalizing the construct of interest are usually regarded as insufficient. Typically, in the development of a criterion-referenced achievement test, the test developer begins with a set of instructional objectives and then proceeds to define a domain of performance to which inferences from test scores will be made. This performance domain is called the *item domain*. An item domain is a well-defined population of items from which one or more test forms may be constructed by selection of a sample of items from this population. (This is sometimes called the *domain-sampling* approach to test construction.)

Obviously creating all possible items so that only a few could be used on a test would be economically and practically unfeasible in many cases. An alternative is to produce a set of item-domain specifications which are so structured that items written according to these specifications would be "interchangeable." Extensive reviews of methods proposed for defining item domains have been written by Millman (1974), Roid and Haladyna (1980), and Shoemaker (1975). One widely used approach is known as the *item specification,* or amplified objective. As defined by Popham (1974), an item specification includes sources of item content, descriptions of the problem situations or stimuli, characteristics of the correct response, and in the case of multiple-choice items, characteristics of the incorrect responses. An illustrative example is presented in Figure 4.1.

The use of item specifications is particularly advantageous when a large item pool must be created and different item writers will draft the items. If each writer adheres to the item specification, a large number of "parallel" items can be generated for an objective within a relatively short time. Furthermore, if different item writers must

Subskill   Demonstrates an ability to multiply decimals.

Item Descriptor   Decimal multiplication: computation.

Stimulus Attributes	*Response Attributes*
1. The problem should require the multiplication of two decimal numbers, fractions and/or mixed.	1. Format: All numerical choices should be aligned according to the decimal point and arranged in either ascending or descending order.
2. The problem should be written in either sentence or horizontal form. If the horizontal form is used, instructions may read "Find the product" or "Multiply."	2. Four alternative responses: a. The correct answer.
3. One of the factors should consist of 3 non-zero digits; the other should have three digits-exactly 2 of these should be non-zero digits greater than 5.	b. One foil should reflect an error in regrouping during multiplication. c. One foil should reflect an alignment error during multiplication.
4. Each of the two factors should have at least one decimal place.	d. One foil should reflect either (1) the omission of the decimal point or (2) an error in positioning the decimal point.
5. There should be no more than four decimal places in the product.	
6. At least two regrouping steps should be necessary.	3. Another possible response: "None of the above" may replace either a, b or c. This choice should appear in the fourth position.
7. In choosing the factors, no digit should be used more than twice.	

FIGURE 4.1   An Item Specification for Items on a Basic Math Skills Subtest.

From the Florida Teacher Examination Bulletin II. Used with permission of the Florida Department of Education.

be employed over time, item specifications help to ensure that items on future test forms will be reasonably equivalent to those used on previous forms.

A method providing even greater structure to the domain specification is the use of item algorithms or item forms. The term *algorithm* is more commonly applied when the items deal with quantitative content, and the term *item form* is generally applied when the item content is primarily verbal. To illustrate an item algorithm, let us consider this objective:

The student will be able to compute the difference between any two positive integers in the form $a - b = $ _____ , where $a > b$.

In this case, the algorithm is the general form of the computation to be performed: "$a - b = $ _____ , where $a > b$." Obviously a large pool of items could be generated from this algorithm by substitution of different values for the quantities denoted as a and b. An item domain can be defined by a single algorithm or by a set of several algorithms.

For verbal material, a general form of an item is written that has a fixed syntactical structure but the item stem contains one or more variable components. This form defines an entire class of items, depending on which element of the replacement set is substituted for the variable component of the item stem. An example of such an item might be

When a citrus tree displays _____(A)_____, this is probably symptomatic of
_____ .

1. nutritional deficiency
2. herbicide injury
3. cold weather injury
4. viral infection
5. bacterial infection

Replacement set (A) for this item would consist of a list of common leaf and bark pathological symptoms for this type of plant (e.g., yellowing leaves, splitting bark, rusty spots on leaves, black soot on leaves, scaling bark, mosaic pattern in leaves, bark cankers). The correct answer to this item would vary, depending on the element from replacement set (A) that is inserted in the item stem.

Even more-structured approaches to domain specification, which are similar to the use of item forms, involve "mapping sentences," have preidentified parts of speech, phrases, or clauses which may be systematically varied and located in designated positions of a sentence with a fixed syntactic structure. Guttman (1969) proposed the use of mapping sentences as part of his facet theory for identifying characteristics of items for cognitive tests or attitudinal inventories that may affect response patterns. Berk (1978) and Millman (1974) discussed the application of mapping sentences to domain definition. In the assessment of reading comprehension, Bormuth (1970) suggested a transformational grammar approach for generating test items based on a written passage, which is also similar to the item-forms method.

In considering the appropriate level of specificity required for domain definition in a given situation, several points should be considered. First, the meaningfulness of scores in a criterion-referenced test depends on (1) identifying a domain of behavior of practical importance and (2) constructing items in a way that allows test users to infer that performance on these items represents the performance that would be displayed on the entire item domain. Obviously there is a trade-off here. The more explicitly the domain is defined and the more individual subjectivity of different item writers is eliminated in selecting item form and content, the more confident test users can be that the items on a given test form represent the domain (in the sense that if a second test were constructed, it would closely resemble the first). Yet as the domain is restricted, the extent to which it is likely to be considered "practically important" may be reduced. Being able to generalize with confidence to a domain that encompasses a very limited sphere of behavior may be appropriate for some measurements but questionable in others.

Second, a related issue is whether depending upon item specifications to reduce the degree of subjectivity involved in selection of item form and content simply displaces subjective decision making from the point of item-writing to the point at which item specifications are written. The consequences of this shift require careful consideration.

Finally, if a particular item specification results in consistent production of items that are technically flawed or susceptible to response set, a test could consist of a much greater proportion of faulty items than might occur if item writers had not been constrained to follow specifications. It is important, therefore, to have the item specifications carefully reviewed prior to their use and to develop several items according to each item specification on a pilot basis so that potential flaws in the specification can be detected.

PREPARING TEST SPECIFICATIONS

Once a set of objectives, item specifications, or other categories of behavior have been chosen, the test developer needs to formulate a plan for deciding the relative emphasis that each of these components should receive on the test. Specifically there should be a balance of items so that different components of the construct are represented in proportion to the test developer's perception of their importance. If an item domain has been defined through a set of item specifications, the issue becomes, How many items on the test should represent proportionally each item specification? Without such a plan, subsequent forms of a test produced from the same set of item specifications might differ substantially if the writers emphasized some item specifications more heavily than others and the areas of emphasis changed from form to form. In the more common case, where no item specifications have been prepared, the development of test specifications usually requires the test developer to attend to two orthogonal properties of items—the substantive content and the cognitive process or operation which the examinee apparently must employ to carry out the item task. This requirement is especially critical in the development of achievement tests, as shown in the example that follows.

Consider the following objectives from the same instructional unit in a plane geometry course:

A.   Define basic terms related to circles (e.g., radius, diameter, central angle).
B.   Compute areas, distances, circumferences, and angle measures by using properties of circles.

Obviously the first objective requires primarily recall of memorized material, whereas the second requires both knowledge of these concepts and application of principles defining relationships of two or more concepts. Thus to simply specify the content to be covered by the items of a test without also indicating the levels or types of cognitive operations that should be represented does not provide adequate guidance for test development.

Several authors have suggested hierarchical systems for categorizing cognitive operations; these are useful in developing test specifications. Probably the best known of these is the taxonomy by Bloom (1956) consisting of the following major categories:

1. *Knowledge*—recall of factual material in similar form to that in which it was presented during instruction; an objective at this level might entail naming the capital cities of given states.
2. *Comprehension*—translation, interpretation, or extrapolation of a concept into somewhat different form than originally practiced or presented; an objective at this level might require recognizing nouns in sentences that have not been used in class examples or giving an example of a prime number other than those given in the text or class examples.
3. *Application*—solving new problems through the use of familiar principles or generalizations, for example, calculating the resistance of an electrical conductor by using Ohm's law when no reference to the law is made in the problem statement.
4. *Analysis*—breaking down a communication or problem into its component elements by using a process that requires recognition of multiple elements, relationships among these elements, and/or organizational principles, for example, making an identification of the genus of a new specimen plant based upon its leaf and flower characteristics.
5. *Synthesis*—combining elements into a whole by using an original structure or solving a problem that requires combination of several principles sequentially in a novel situation, for example, writing a computer program to perform a calculation on a set of data records using input, output, loop, and logical transfer statements in an efficient sequence of execution.
6. *Evaluation*—employment of internal (self-generated) or external criteria for making critical judgments in terms of accuracy, consistency of logic, or artistic or philosophical point of view, for example, writing a critical review of a journal article describing empirical research in social or personality psychology.

Bloom, Hastings, and Madaus (1971) provided additional explanation and examples of these categories. Additional systems for categorizing processes required on optimal performance tests were described by Ebel (1972), who suggested the processes of knowledge and use of terminology; recall of factual material; use of generalizations, explanation, calculation, and prediction of outcomes; and recommendations for action. Thorndike and Hagen (1977) detailed the categories of recognizing terms and vocabulary; identifying facts; identifying principles, concepts, and generalizations; evaluating information; and applying principles to novel situations. It is not uncommon for test developers to select only a few processes from any of these taxonomies or perhaps to combine categories from one or more taxonomies to suit their specific needs.

Because of the great variation in the level of cognitive processes that may occur in items covering even a single topic, test specifications should provide some guidance to item writers in terms of the levels of operation that should be represented. Test specifications should also indicate the balance that should be maintained in trying to tap these different processes for the test as a whole. One useful structure for test specifications that takes into account both content and process is known as a *table of specifications*. The table is basically a two-way grid with major content areas listed on one margin and cognitive processes on the other. An illustrative table of specifications for a subtest of a teacher certification examination is shown in Figure 4.2. (This example illustrates that process levels may be selected from more than one taxonomy.) The number in each cell is an arbitrary value weight indicating the relative emphasis in the examination that the test developer wishes to place on the content and process associated with that cell. In an achievement test, these cell weights usually reflect the amount of time devoted to mastery of material at that level during the course of instruction. The total of these cell weights should equal 100. Each weight indicates the percentage of items or points on the test that should be devoted to coverage of this content and process. Such weights determine how many items must be written to represent the cells adequately in relation to the domain of interest. In Figure 4.2, 1% of the test items should measure recall of

Content Base Category	Level			
	Knowledge	Application	Problem Solving	Totals
1. Classroom Management (Competencies 6, 12, 13, 15, 16, 17, 20, 22)	1	10	9	20
2. Development of Students (Competencies 6, 10, 11, 12, 16, 17, 20, 21, 22, 23)	1	11	11	23
3. Evaluating, Recording and Reporting Student Progress (Competencies 6, 7, 10, 12, 14, 18)	2	16	1	19
4. Instructional Materials (Competencies 10, 12, 13, 15, 21)	1	6	2	9
5. Instructional Objectives (Competencies 9, 10, 11, 12 14)		7	3	10
6. Learning and Teaching (Competencies 6, 9, 10, 11, 12, 13, 15, 17, 21, 22, 23)	2	12	5	19
TOTALS	7	62	31	100

FIGURE 4.2   Table of Specifications for the Florida Teacher Certification Examination

From the Florida Teacher Examination Bulletin I. Used with permission of the Florida Department of Education.

classroom management principles, and 10% should measure application of class-room management principles. The table of specifications also provides a convenient way to describe the test to potential users. By summing the percentages in each column, we can see that 7% of the test items measure knowledge-level skills, 62% measure application-level skills, and 31% measure problem-solving skills. Summing the percentages in each row yields the total percentage of items covering each category respectively. When the test developer has decided on the total number of items, the number of items that must be written for any cell to meet the specifications equals the cell weight times K, where K equals the total number of items on the test.

In the construction of attitude inventories or observational performance measures, the test developer may wish to use a table of specifications that involves behaviors from the affective domain. Krathwohl, Bloom, and Masia (1964) have presented a taxonomy which may be useful for this purpose. Detailed description of the five categories they proposed and examples of their use in test development may by found in Bloom, Hastings, and Madaus (1971).

ITEM CONSTRUCTION

Lindquist (1936) characterized the test developer's task as requiring two major types of decisions—what to measure and how to measure it. During item construction the latter type of decision must be addressed. Developing a pool of items to measure a construct entails the following activities:

1. Selecting an appropriate item format
2. Verifying that the proposed format is feasible for the intended examinees
3. Selecting and training the item writers
4. Writing the items
5. Monitoring the progress of the item writers and the quality of the items

If item writers will work from item forms or item specifications, the structure and format of the items may already be determined. If item specifications are not being used, it is still important for decisions about item format to be made at the outset of the item-construction phase rather than to be left to the idiosyncratic tastes of individual writers. In deciding on a common format, the test developer may wish to review similar instruments in the field and study reports of their development. The opinions of experts may also be helpful in deciding such matters as whether the examinees are sufficiently literate to take group-administered pencil-and-paper tests, whether company employees would take the time to write out responses to open-ended questions, or whether third-graders can distinguish among five points on an agree-disagree continuum. At times it may be necessary to collect data in a small-scale study, using a few prototype items to answer such questions, before producing a large number of items in a particular format.

Once an appropriate item format has been chosen, the test developer should review standard sources on item writing to glean suggestions on writing items of this type. A list of guidelines should be prepared and distributed to the item writers, particularly if nonprofessional writers are to be employed.

Item Formats for Optimal Performance Tests

For optimal performance tests (typified by aptitude or achievement tests), a wide variety of item formats may be considered. Popham (1981) has divided these formats into two major categories—those that require the examinee to generate the response (e.g., essay or short-answer questions) and those that provide two or more possible responses and require the examinee to make a selection. Because the latter can be scored with little subjectivity, they are often called objective test items. The three most widely used objective formats are

1. *Alternate choice*—a statement (or question) and two possible responses (true-false or yes-no).
    Example: The most probable cause of "sooty," black
    coating on the leaves of a citrus tree, is insect
    infestation.   **True**   **False**
2. *Multiple choice*—a stem in which the question or problem is posed; a correct response or keyed response; and two or more incorrect responses, which are called *foils*.
    Example: A citrus tree has a number of leaves coated with a black, "sooty" substance. This is probably caused by
    a. Herbicide damage
    b. Bacterial infection
    c. Insect infestation
    d. Nutritional deficiency
3. *Matching*—a statement of the principle to be used in relating the objects from two separate lists, a list of premises or stimuli, and a list of responses.
    Example: For each symptom listed in the left column, record the letter from the right column which identifies the most probable cause.

Symptom	Probable Cause
_____1. Yellow leaves	A. Cold weather injury
_____2. Splitting bark	B. Nitrogen deficiency
_____3. Rusty spots on leaves	C. Fungal infection
_____4. Mottled leaves	D. Herbicide damage
	E. Viral infection

Most introductory texts in testing and measurement devote several chapters to suggestions for writing each of these formats. For example, the reader might wish to consult Brown (1983), Mehrens and Lehmann (1984), Popham (1981), or Sax (1980). An important point that is common to all objective formats, however, is that all responses should appear logically reasonable to an examinee who does not have the knowledge or skill that the item was designed to test. For example, in a multiple-choice item, a well-written item stem accompanied by the correct response and three absurd foils is unlikely to measure examinees' knowledge in the domain intended; most examinees would be able to eliminate all but the correct choice by using only common sense, and as a result, the usefulness of the item would be reduced. To avoid this problem, foils for multiple-choice items are often constructed from common misconceptions, misinterpretations, or answers that could result from errors of computation. The point here is that in selecting item writers, the test developer should remember that construction of a good item requires not only knowledge of the material but also familiarity with the examinee population to ensure that incorrect choices will appear plausible.

As a general rule, test developers are advised to give careful thought to selecting an item format appropriate to the needs of the examinees and to avoid novel or untried formats without having a sound rationale for their use. Recently, however, some authors have called for moving beyond the use of the highly popular multiple-choice format, although the direction to take has generated strongly contrasting points of view. On the one hand, Ebel (1982) advocated broader use of more highly structured alternate-choice items—for example, "The density of ice is *(1) greater (2) less* than that of water." His point was that in many cases the domain of knowledge that is to be sampled could actually be expressed as a series of precisely stated functional relationships or principles and that each of these can form the basis of a highly structured item. Although it would appear that each item can test only a limited "piece" of information, Ebel argued that (1) a large number of such items can be asked in a relatively short amount of time, thus permitting more thorough sampling of the content domain; (2) performance on such items is less subject to the influence of extraneous factors, such as the higher level of reading ability that may be required by more complex formats; and (3) such items have greater conceptual clarity for examinees about the nature of what is being asked (or the underlying principle being tested). On the other hand, Frederiksen (1981, p. 19) suggested that in the pursuit of greater scoring efficiency, test developers may rely too heavily on highly structured formats and that this interest in what can be easily measured may overshadow consideration about what should be measured. This may leave "many important abilities untested and untaught." As one alternative, Frederiksen suggested the development of unstructured multiple-choice problem-solving tasks. Recent developmental work on such a test has been described by Ward, Carson, and Woisetschlager (1983). At this time, the issue of whether items covering the same material but using such contrasting formats actually measure the same trait has not been conclusively resolved, but the issue seems likely to spawn additional theoretical and empirical investigation.

Item Formats for Inventories

Three popular item formats for attitude and personality inventories are the dichotomous Agree-Disagree format, the Likert format, and the bipolar adjective checklist. Each of these will be briefly described.

The dichotomous Agree-Disagree format typically consists of a simple declarative statement followed by two response options. This format is illustrated by the three items:

1. Children should obey their parents without question.   **Agree**   **Disagree**
2. Children today need stronger discipline at home.   **Agree**   **Disagree**
3. Most children with behavior problems are rebelling
    against too much parental control.   **Agree**   **Disagree**

The simplest procedure for scoring such items is to decide first which end of the attitudinal continuum should be associated with high scores on the inventory. For example, for the items above, the underlying attitude could be described as a continuum between authoritarian and permissive views of parental discipline. The test developer has the option of specifying whether respondents who hold more authoritarian views should receive higher scores on the instrument or whether respondents who hold more permissive views should receive higher scores. Let us assume that the test developer wishes high scores to reflect more permissive attitudes. Next, each item is identified as being positively worded or negatively worded with respect to the construct. In our example, because the continuum is characterized in terms of "permissiveness," items 1 and 2 would be considered negatively worded and item 3 would be considered positively worded. Items are scored by awarding 1 point to the respondent for each "Agree" response given to a positively worded item and 1 point for each "Disagree" response given to a negatively worded item. The respondent's total score is the total of the item scores. For the present example, a respondent who marked "Disagree," "Disagree," and "Agree" to items 1, 2, and 3, respectively, would receive item scores of 1, 1, and 1, for a total of 3 points. Another respondent, who marked "Disagree," "Agree," and "Disagree," would have a score pattern of 1, 0, and 0, for a total score of 1.

An alternative scoring approach for the agree-disagree format involves item weighting. Each item is assigned a weighted value associated with the perceived strength of sentiment expressed toward the construct of interest. Although a variety of scaling procedures may be used to arrive at the item weights, the most well known is probably the equal-appearing intervals procedure described by Thurstone (1928). Typically, the item writer produces a large number of statements (Thurstone suggested as many as 100), which range from extremely positive to extremely negative with respect to the construct. Some statements should be nearly neutral in affect. Each statement may be written on a separate card, and the collection of statements is presented to a sample of judges for rating. With the equal-appearing intervals method, each judge is instructed to read each statement and place it along a continuum divided into 7, 9, or 11 intervals equal in width. The positive and negative end of the continuum are identified in advance for the judge; those statements that are most negatively worded are placed in categories 1 and 2, and those most positively worded are placed in categories 10 and 11. On an 11-interval continuum, the most neutral statements are placed in category 6.

The data resulting from this judgment task are used for two purposes—selection of items for the final version of the scale and assignment of weights for scoring the scale. The median of the judges' ratings is the item weight. Furthermore, the items to appear on the scale are chosen from the initial large set of items on the basis of a statistic such as Q, the semi-interquartile range:

$$Q = \frac{X_{75} - X_{25}}{2}$$

where X_{75} is the numeric value corresponding to the 75th percentile rank, and X_{25} is the numeric value corresponding to the 25th percentile rank in the distribution of ratings. Smaller values of Q indicate that judges were in fairly close agreement about the strength of sentiment expressed by the item. Items with smaller Q values are, therefore, favored in item selection although the test developer still tries to include some items from each category. When the scale is later administered to a group of respondents, each time a respondent endorses a statement, the weight value for this item is added to the respondent's total score. This total score is then divided by the number of items endorsed to obtain the average weight of the statements endorsed. The average weight is used for comparing or describing respondents' attitudes.

The second widely used item format for inventories was suggested by Likert (1932). This method requires writing a collection of statements, each of which is clearly positive or clearly negative with respect to the construct of interest. Statements neutral in affect are not included. The respondent reads each statement and selects a response from a five-point continuum ranging from "Strongly Agree" to "Strongly Disagree," as shown in the following example:

Children should obey their parents without question.
Strongly Disagree   Disagree   Neutral   Agree   Strongly Agree

The statements are not weighted or scaled prior to their administration to respondents, but respondents use the response continuum to indicate the degree of strength of their endorsement. To score items with a graded response continuum, 1 point is assigned to the response showing the lowest level of positive sentiment toward the construct; 2 points are assigned to the response showing the next highest level; 3 points to the response indicating the next highest level; and so forth. If we again assume that the test developer wants respondents with more permissive attitudes to receive higher scores, the three items from the preceding example would have scoring weights as follows:

	SA	A	N	D	SD
1. Children should obey their parents without question.	1	2	3	4	5
2. Children today need stronger discipline at home.	1	2	3	4	5
3. Most children with behavior problems are rebelling against too much parental control.	5	4	3	2	1

A respondent's total score is the sum of the points associated with the response given to each of the items.

The following are some general guidelines that may be helpful in writing and reviewing inventory items for either Likert or agree-disagree formats:

1. Put statements or questions in the present tense.
2. Do not use statements that are factual or capable of being interpreted as factual.
3. Avoid statements that can have more than one interpretation.
4. Avoid statements that are likely to be endorsed by almost everyone or almost no one.
5. Try to have an almost equal number of statements expressing positive and negative feelings.
6. Statements should be short, rarely exceeding 20 words.
7. Each statement should be a proper grammatical sentence.
8. Statements containing universals such as *all, always, none,* and *never* often introduce ambiguity and should be avoided.
9. Avoid use of indefinite qualifiers such as *only, just, merely, many, few,* or *seldom.*
10. Whenever possible, statements should be in simple sentences rather than complex or compound sentences. Avoid statements that contain "if" or "because" clauses.
11. Use vocabulary that can be understood easily by the respondents.
12. Avoid use of negatives (e.g., *not, none, never*).

Recent references on the production of attitude statements include those by Anderson (1981); Dawes (1972); and Udinsky, Osterlind, and Lynch (1981).

Another popular format sometimes used in inventory construction is the bipolar adjective pair. The origin of this format is usually attributed to Osgood, Suci, and Tannenbaum (1957), who proposed its use in the study of the semantic meaning of psychological constructs. The construct of interest is listed at the top, followed by a pair of adjectives which should represent opposite poles of a single continuum. Typically a five- or seven-point continuum is presented between the adjectives, and respondents are instructed to mark the spot on the continuum which most closely reflects their feeling. For example, in attempting to assess teachers' attitudes toward working with mentally retarded children, the following format might be used:

Mentally Retarded Child

Pretty						Ugly
Happy						Sad
Dirty						Clean

Osgood and his colleagues, after investigating a large number of diverse adjective pairs, determined that most of them could be grouped into one of three dimensions (evaluation, potency, or activity) underlying the semantic meaning of verbal constructs. They suggested a method for analyzing and interpreting responses to these items and called their instrument a semantic differential. The test developer who generates a unique set of bipolar adjectives for a specific assessment, without using these pretested pairs, must assume responsibility for determining how the responses should be scored and interpreted. In this situation, the item format should probably be described as a bipolar adjective checklist rather than a semantic differential measure.

In the development of inventory items, it is important to be aware of response sets that may affect individual examinees' behavior. *Response set* may be defined as the tendency of an examinee to respond in a certain way to a particular item format regardless of content. Guilford (1954) provided a classic identification of several common types of response sets and offered suggestions for reducing or controlling their effects. Two response sets that often affect inventory scores are acquiescence (the tendency to agree with a statement regardless of its content) and differential individual interpretations of indefinite qualifiers (e.g., *some* and *often*). Adherence to the previous writing suggestions can reduce the likelihood that items will be susceptible to response sets. Other issues related to construction of inventory items include the effects of using different types of anchor points on the response continuum (see Frisbie and Brandenburg, 1979; Lam and Klockars, 1982) or different numbers of response alternatives (see Masters, 1974; Velicer and Stevenson, 1978). Such studies again illustrate that decisions about how to measure behavior may have an impact ultimately on what has been measured.

ITEM REVIEW

As test items are drafted, it is advisable for the test developer to ask qualified colleagues to review them informally for accuracy, wording, grammar, ambiguity, and other technical flaws. "Problem" items can then be revised as necessary. In addition, once the items have been written, they should be subjected to more formal review on an item-by-item basis. Important aspects of item construction which should be considered include

1. Accuracy
2. Appropriateness or relevance to test specifications
3. Technical item-construction flaws
4. Grammar
5. Offensiveness or appearance of "bias"
6. Level of readability

Different types of expertise are required on the item review panel. For example, experts in the subject matter are best qualified to certify that the items are clearly stated and correctly keyed. They are also qualified to judge whether items are appropriate for the test specifications or item specifications. (More detailed explanation of this process is given in Chapter 10 on content validation.) Some general expertise in measurement and test construction is important for the reviewer(s) who must certify that items are free from construction flaws. For example, if items are in multiple-choice format, the technical expert should look for common flaws affiliated with this particular format (e.g., making the correct alternative longer than the others). The texts mentioned in the section on item construction can be used to identify common flaws or problems most likely to occur with a particular format. In addition, the measurement expert should identify the types of response sets most likely to affect scores on the instrument being developed and consider the susceptibility of each item to these types of response sets. Naturally, every item on a test should be free of grammatical errors, including spelling errors. Particularly, flaws in punctuation or unwieldy sentence construction may result in misinterpretation. All item reviewers should be instructed to look for grammatical errors.

Also, one or more members of the review panel should have expert familiarity with the population for whom the test is intended. These reviewers should consider whether content might be construed as offensive or seemingly "biased" toward any particular subgroup, perhaps by use of undesirable cultural stereotypes or content that is unfamiliar to certain subgroups (when this content is unrelated to the construct or knowledge domain being tested). For example, a math word problem requiring calculation of simple interest on the sales price of an object should involve an object that is appropriate for purchase by most examinees (or their families) rather than an exclusive luxury item that would more likely be purchased by upper-middle-class or wealthy families only.

For items to be used with children or adolescents, the readability level of the items should be considered when the test is being developed to measure something other than reading skills. Many standard methods for assessing readability of written passages are not appropriate for test items because of their length and structure, but one promising procedure has been described by Ironson and her associates (1984).

Item review can be carried out either before or after preliminary item tryouts. The choice of sequence is made on the basis of convenience and economy. If expert reviewers are readily available and their time is not costly, item review can be conducted before tryouts so that time in tryouts will not be wasted on faulty or biased items. On the other hand, after item tryouts many items will inevitably be revised or reworded. This creates the necessity for additional item review by the expert panel. Thus if substantial costs or effort are involved in assembling the review panel, many test developers choose to defer this activity until after preliminary item tryouts and subsequent revisions. If results of the item review are to be reported as evidence of content validity, it is especially important for the review panel to examine items in their final form.

PRELIMINARY ITEM TRYOUTS

Before the test developer has printed items in final form for a field test, it is a good idea to try out the items on a small sample of examinees. If only a limited number of subjects are available (as when participants in an experimental program are the examinees of interest), most of these subjects must be reserved for later field trials of the items. In such cases, it might be necessary to use as few as 15 to 30 subjects for the preliminary item tryouts. Items developed for commercial use may be tested on samples as large as 100 to 200. If a large number of items have been developed and testing time is limited, it is possible to administer subsets of items to different groups of examinees. Preliminary item tryouts are fairly informal, and the test developer should use this opportunity to observe examinees' reactions during testing, noting such behaviors as long pauses, scribbling, or answer-changing, which may indicate confusion about particular items. After the testing session, a "debriefing" should take place in which examinees are invited to comment on each item and offer suggestions for possible improvements.

Examination of descriptive statistics for the response distribution to each item is also recommended. This will enable the test developer to obtain a rough idea of whether the items seem to be at the appropriate level of difficulty for the group as a whole and whether there is sufficient variation in the responses to justify proceeding into a larger-scale field test. It is important to recognize that although the final decisions about which items to retain and which to eliminate are made on the basis of the large-scale field test, items are often revised extensively after reviewing the results of preliminary tryouts.

THE NEXT STEPS

After items have been through preliminary tryouts (and possibly subsequent revisions), they are ready for a full-fledged field test. The field test typically involves the administration of the items in their final draft form to a large sample of examinees representative of those for whom the test is designed. Statistical properties of the item scores are examined through a variety of procedures, known as *item analysis*. Designing item field-test studies and conducting appropriate analyses of item response data is the theme of Unit IV of this text. Typically, when norm-referenced interpretations are to be made, the test developer will use results of item analysis to "cull" those items that do not appear to function as intended. As we shall learn in Chapter 14, however, there is lack of agreement about using item analysis results to eliminate items from criterion-referenced tests.

Once a final form of the test is assembled, it is incumbent on the test developer to undertake studies of the test scores' reliability and validity. Theories and practices relevant to conducting studies of test score reliability are the topics of Chapters 6 through 9 (Unit II); validation procedures are the focus of Chapters 10 through 12 (Unit III). Suggestions for development of scoring procedures, setting standards, and providing normative data to aid in test score interpretation are presented in Unit V.

SUMMARY

In this chapter ten steps in a systematic process of test development were identified. First, the purpose(s) for which test scores are most likely to be used must be clearly specified. The most appropriate approach to test development must be chosen in light of these purposes. Second, two possible approaches to test development were described: development of a test for differentiation among individuals on a given construct, and development of a test designed to provide scores that describe more-absolute levels of proficiency in a given content area. Useful aids in identifying behaviors which may typify a construct include content analysis, review of research, critical incidents, direct observations, and instructional objectives. In the development of achievement tests for which criterion-referenced measurements are desired, the goal of test developers is to establish a well-defined item domain so that test users may infer from test scores on a sample of items proficiency with respect to the entire item domain. Consequently the item domain may be established through instructional objectives, item specifications, and item forms or item algorithms.

The third step in test construction is development of a table of specifications, which delineates the proportion of items on the test that should focus on various content and process categories relevant to the construct of interest (or item domain). Several taxonomies for categorizing behavior in the cognitive domain were presented. The most well known is the one proposed by Bloom (1956). In addition, a taxonomy proposed for behavior in the affective domain has been described by Krathwohl, Bloom, and Masia (1964).

Fourth, item construction entails selection of an appropriate item format—verifying that the format is feasible for use with the intended population—selection and training of item writers, item writing, and monitoring the progress of the item writers. Three popular objective formats for optimal performance tests are the alternate choice, matching, and multiple choice. For inventories, three widely used formats are the agree-disagree format often used with Thurstone scaling, the Likert format, and the bipolar adjective checklist. Each of these item formats was briefly described.

Fifth, items should also be subjected to review by a panel of experts who should consider such aspects as accuracy, relevance to test specifications, technical quality, grammar, potential for offensiveness or appearance of cultural or gender bias, and readability. In addition, items should be administered to small groups of examinees for informal preliminary tryouts to ascertain that examinees can follow the instructions associated with the format, to obtain estimates of the time required to take the test, and to identify items that are poorly written or ambiguous. Revisions indicated from the item review or preliminary item tryouts should be made before proceeding with formal field-testing of the items on a large sample. The final steps in test development include field-testing and item analysis, reliability and validity studies, and establishing guides for test score interpretation. These procedures are covered in subsequent units of this text.

Exercises

1. Review objectives A through L, based on the contents of Chapter 2, and classify them into cells of the table of specifications that follows.

A. Explain how a score distribution for a group of examinees may be characterized with measures of central tendency and measures of variability.

B. Compute and interpret common measures of central tendency and measures of variability.

C. Recognize the meanings of terms such as *discrete variable, continuous variable, frequency, cumulative frequency, cumulative probability, measures of central tendency, measures of variability, expected value, normal curve, standard normal curve, raw score, deviation score, z-score, correlation coefficient, scatterplot, regression coefficient, prediction equation, standard error of the estimate,* and *homoscedasticity.*

D. Convert raw scores to deviation scores and z-scores.

E. Relate z-scores based on a normal distribution to areas under the normal curve by using a standard, normal z-table.

F. Recognize situations where z-scores may be more useful than raw scores.

G. Use scatterplots to make interpretations about the nature of the relationships among the variables.

H. Compute and interpret correlation coefficients.

I. Explain the relationship between a scatterplot and its regression line.

J. Compute the values of slope and intercept of a regression line for a data set, and use these in construction of the line.

K. Use the regression equation to estimate an individual's predicted values on a criterion variable, given the score on a predictor variable.

L. Use the standard error of estimate to generate a confidence band around a predicted criterion score value.

	Distribution Parameters	Normal Distribution	Correlation/Regression	
Knowledge				10%
Comprehension				30%
Application				60%
	35%	15%	50%	

2. Assume that you wanted to construct a test covering the statistics unit by using the preceding table of specifications. You have time to administer a 30-item test.

 A. Approximately what percentage of items should be written at the levels of knowledge, comprehension, and application, respectively?

 B. Approximately what percentage of items should cover the topics of basic distribution descriptors and correlation, respectively?

 C. Approximately what percentage of items should cover correlation and regression at the application level?

3. Review the item specification presented in Figure 4.1. Develop a similar specification for the subskill "Demonstrates an ability to subtract decimals."

4. **A.** Consider the following problem from the exam of a high school physics class: "A quantity of gas was collected over water at 16°C. The pressure of the mixture of gases was 982.9 torr. The water vapor was removed and the remaining gas had a partial pressure of 969.3 torr. What is the vapor pressure of water at 16°C." If the teacher

wanted to convert this problem into an item form, identify two likely sections of the item that could be designated as the position for replacement sets.

B. Suppose that the instructor had originally designated this item as measuring the process of application. The examination is to be administered to several classes of students, who take the test in successive periods throughout the school day. Because the instructor fears that answers will be "leaked," a different form of the examination is given to each class, through the item-forms approach and substitution of different values into the problem. Later, however, the instructor observes that the classes who took the test later in the day still performed better on this item than those who took the test earlier in the day. What could account for this result?

C. Compare the major advantages and disadvantages of using an item-forms approach to test construction for the preceding situation.

5. Review each attitude inventory statement and identify technical flaws which should be corrected.

A. Working mothers should remain at home because they take jobs that may be needed by male heads of families.

B. If a mother wants to work, she should work during hours when her children are in school.

C. In the U.S., currently more than half of all mothers of school-age children are employed outside the home.

D. It is not possible for a woman to combine career and parenting responsibilities successfully.

E. A woman can sometimes combine her desire to have an intrinsically rewarding career and still fulfill her quintessential maternal obligations without experiencing undue stress.

6. A graduate student in developmental psychology is interested in constructing an inventory to assess children's self-concepts. Suggest at least three procedures that might be helpful in domain definition of this construct.

7. Suppose that a rehabilitation psychologist were interested in developing an inventory to assess attitudes of employers in the community toward hiring physically handicapped workers.

A. Identify three different procedures that could be used to define this construct, and compare the advantages and disadvantages of using each method.

B. Identify three different item formats that could be used in this situation, and write one sample item exemplifying each.

8. For a class discussion, read the article by Irvin, Halpern, and Landman (1980). Answer the questions and discuss your responses.

A. Do the authors state (or clearly imply) the basic purpose for which the test scores on the Social and Prevocational Information Battery (SPIB) are intended?

B. Which basic approach to test development seems to underlie the construction procedures described—individual differentiation or domain sampling?

C. How did the test developers determine what content should be covered in the test being developed?

D. Compare the authors' description of this study to the ten steps for systematic test development described in this chapter. Which, if any, steps were omitted? Identify those activities in the authors' description which correspond to particular steps of test development described in this chapter.

E. To what extent did the obtained correlations support the hypothesis that alternate-choice items, true-false items, and multiple-choice items measure different constructs?

Chapter 5

TEST SCORES AS COMPOSITES

A test battery is a collection of two or more separate tests designed to be administered to the same examinees. A separate score is computed for each test on the battery. A well-known example of a test battery is the Graduate Record Examination, from which separate verbal, quantitative, and analytic subtest scores are obtained. A *composite test score* is a total test score created by summing two or more subtest scores. To interpret correctly the scores of such a composite, it is important to understand how the statistical properties of subtest scores influence those of the composite score. Even more important, however, test developers must recognize that every test score is a composite. An *item score* can be defined as the number of points assigned to an individual's response to a given item. In scoring a test, the total test score is usually determined by summing the item scores. Thus each item could be considered a very short subtest, and item scores can be considered as "mini-test" scores. In this sense whenever a test score is created by summing the points awarded to an examinee on each item, that total test score is a composite.

In this chapter we will consider the statistical operations that can be performed on item scores and the relationship of the statistical properties of item scores to those of the total test score. An understanding of the relationship is crucial for effective test development because items are the building blocks of which tests are made. A test can have no property that is not a function of the items that comprise it. The test developer who seeks to create a test of sound quality must have information about the score distribution of each item and its relationship to other items in the test. In Chapter 2 we considered how the concepts of mean, variance, standard deviation, and correlation could be applied to describing the distribution of test scores. Now we will consider how these statistics can be applied to item scores and how the item statistics affect distributional properties of total test scores.

ITEM SCORING SCHEMES

Scoring schemes for most test items can be classified as either dichotomous or nondichotomous. An item is a dichotomous variable if the only possible values of the item score are 0 or 1. Examples of dichotomously scored items are

1. The space between nerve cell endings is called the
   a. Dendrite
   b. Axon
   c. Synapse
   d. Neutron
   (In this item, responses *a*, *b*, and *d* are scored 0; response *c* is scored 1.)
2. Teachers in public school systems should have the right to strike.
   a. Agree
   b. Disagree
   (In this item, a response of Agree is scored 1; Disagree is scored 0.)

As seen from these examples, items with dichotomous scoring schemes can be found on measures of either the affective or cognitive domain. They may have multiple responses, as in the first example, as long as the scoring scheme is restricted to 0 or 1 for any response given. Nondichotomous scoring schemes are those in which the range of possible points awarded to a response is not restricted to 0 or 1. Examples of items with nondichotomous scoring are

1. Write a grammatically correct German sentence using the first person singular form of the verb *verstehen*. (A maximum of 3 points may be awarded and partial credit may be given.)
2. A mentally retarded person is a nonproductive member of society.
   a. Strongly agree
   b. Agree
   c. No opinion
   d. Disagree
   e. Strongly disagree
   (Scores can range from 1 to 5 points, with high scores indicating a positive attitude toward mentally retarded citizens.)

As demonstrated in the example, most essay or short-answer items are scored with nondichotomous scoring schemes. Also, items from many attitude or performance rating scales are scored in this way.

DESCRIPTIVE STATISTICS FOR NONDICHOTOMOUS VARIABLES

Assume that Table 5.1 contains the responses of 10 persons to 5 attitude items which were scored with the strongly-agree-to-strongly-disagree continuum. Possi-

TABLE 5.1.   Responses of 10 Persons to 5 Attitude Items Scored on a 1-to-5 Scale

Person	Items					Total
	1	2	3	4	5	
1	5	5	4	3	2	19
2	2	2	3	1	2	10
3	4	4	3	3	2	16
4	2	2	2	1	2	9
5	5	5	3	5	4	22
6	1	1	2	2	3	9
7	1	2	3	1	1	8
8	4	1	3	4	5	17
9	5	3	4	4	3	19
10	2	2	3	3	4	14
Item Mean	3.1	2.7	3.0	2.7	2.8	
Item Variance	2.5	2.0	0.4	1.8	1.4	

ble score values for each item range from 1 to 5. Such a configuration is called a person-item score matrix. Each row of the matrix contains the responses of a particular examinee to all items on the test. Each column contains the responses of all examinees to a given item. In matrix notation, the location of each element in the matrix is denoted by two subscripts, for example, X_{rc}, in which the first subscript (r) denotes the row, and the second subscript (c) denotes the column. Thus X_{11} would indicate the value in the first row, first column, or the response of person 1 to item 1; in Table 5.1, $X_{11} = 5$. The symbol X_{23} denotes the value in the second row, third column, or the response of person 2 to item 3. In Table 5.1, $X_{23} = 3$. If the test constructor were interested in determining the strength of sentiment conveyed by an individual item, it would be appropriate to examine the mean score for that item. We will denote the mean score for item j as μ_j. The mean score for item 1 would be computed by using Equation 2.1:

$$\mu_1 = \frac{\Sigma X_{i1}}{N} = \frac{5 + 2 + 4 + 2 + 5 + 1 + 1 + 4 + 5 + 2}{10} = 3.1$$

Similarly the mean score for each of the remaining four items could be determined.

If the test constructor were interested in determining the variability of responses displayed by the group for an item, the variance of that set of item responses could be determined by applying Equation 2.4. For item 1, the variance of the responses can be computed as follows:

$$\sigma_1^2 = \frac{\Sigma(X_{i1} - \mu_1)^2}{N} = \frac{(5 - 3.1)^2 + (2 - 3.1)^2 + \cdots + (2 - 3.1)^2}{10}$$

$$\sigma_1^2 = 2.5$$

The test constructor may also be interested in knowing whether there is a relationship between examinees' responses to items 1 and 2. This can be determined by

TABLE 5.2. Item Intercorrelation Matrix for Item Scores Reported in Table 5.1

	1	2	3	4	5
Item 1	1.00	.73	.70	.81	.34
Item 2		1.00	.56	.48	−.16
Item 3			1.00	.47	.00
Item 4				1.00	.73
Item 5					1.00

computing the product moment correlation between the scores for items 1 and 2 for this sample, using Equation 2.13. Table 5.2 presents the matrix of values for the correlations for each pair of items on the scale. From examination of these values it is apparent that items 1, 2, 3, and 4 seem to evoke similar patterns of responses; item 5 is related to item 4, but performance on this item appears to have little relationship to performance on items 2 and 3. In subsequent sections we will discuss how such information might be useful in test construction and revision.

DESCRIPTIVE STATISTICS FOR DICHOTOMOUS VARIABLES

Mean and Variance

When items are scored dichotomously it is possible to use simplified formulas for computing the item mean, variance, and standard deviation. To derive these formulas we employ a concept known as *item difficulty*. Item difficulty (p) is defined as the proportion of examinees who answer an item correctly. The reader should note that this is a technical term, which sometimes seems contradictory to a layperson's use of the term *difficulty*. According to our definition, an item answered correctly by 85% of the examinees would have an item difficulty, or p-value, of .85, whereas an item answered correctly by 50% of the examinees would have a lower item difficulty, or p-value, of .50. Thus, the easier item actually has the higher item difficulty value. Table 5.3 displays a person-item score matrix in which each entry represents the score of examinee i on item j. Below the person-item score matrix p-values are presented for each item. This should not be surprising since

$$p_j = \frac{\text{Number of persons with a score of 1 on item } j}{N}$$

where N is the number of examinees in the group. Consider the formula for the mean of item j:

$$\mu_j = \frac{\Sigma X_{ij}}{N}$$

When all values of X are restricted to 0 or 1, ΣX_{ij} will be equivalent to the number of persons with a score of 1 on item j. Thus,

$$p_j = \mu_j \tag{5.1}$$

TABLE 5.3. Responses of 10 Examinees to 5 Items, Dichotomously Scored

Examinee	Items					Total[a]
	1	2	3	4	5	
1	0	0	1	1	0	2
2	0	0	0	1	0	1
3	1	1	0	0	0	2
4	1	0	0	1	0	2
5	0	1	1	1	1	4
6	0	1	0	0	0	1
7	1	1	1	1	1	5
8	1	1	0	1	0	3
9	1	1	1	1	0	4
10	0	0	0	1	1	2
p_j (Item Mean)	.50	.60	.40	.80	.30	
p_jq_j (Item Variance)	.25	.24	.24	.16	.21	

[a] Total score mean, $\mu_X = 2.60$.
Total score variance, $\sigma_X^2 = 1.64$.

The value for each item variance in Table 5.3 could have been computed by the traditional variance formula:

$$\sigma_j^2 = \frac{\Sigma(X_{ij} - \mu_j)^2}{N} \tag{5.2}$$

However, when items are dichotomously scored, a simpler formula for computing item variance is

$$\sigma_j^2 = p_jq_j \tag{5.3}$$

where $q_j = (1 - p_j)$. A simple algebraic proof demonstrates that Equation 5.3 is derived directly from Equation 5.2. We can expand the right-hand term of Equation 5.2 so that

$$\sigma_j^2 = \frac{\Sigma X_{ij}^2}{N} - \frac{2\Sigma X_{ij}\mu_j}{N} + \frac{\Sigma \mu_j^2}{N} \tag{5.4}$$

Because X_{ij} must equal 0 or 1, X_{ij} always equals X_{ij}^2. Therefore,

$$\frac{\Sigma X_{ij}^2}{N} = \frac{\Sigma X_{ij}}{N}$$

and this in turn equals p_j. Furthermore, because μ_j is a constant for all values of X_{ij}, the second term in Equation 5.4 can be expressed as

$$\frac{-2\Sigma X_{ij}\mu_j}{N} = -2\mu_j^2 = -2p_j^2$$

The last term in Equation 5.4, $\frac{\Sigma \mu_j^2}{N}$, is also a constant, μ_j^2, summed N times divided by N. Thus, this term equals μ_j^2 or p_j^2. We can now rewrite the item variance equation as

$$\sigma_j^2 = p_j - 2p_j^2 + p_j^2 \tag{5.5}$$

By combining like terms, we have

$$\sigma_j^2 = p_j - p_j^2$$

and by factoring,

$$\sigma_j^2 = p_j(1 - p_j) = p_j q_j$$

Thus, whenever an item is dichotomously scored, its variance may be computed by Equation 5.3. If we use this formula to compute the variance of item 1 in Table 5.3, we see that

$$\sigma_1^2 = (.50)(.50) = .25$$

This is obviously a more convenient formula for computing the variance of dichotomously scored test items than the traditional variance formula. The standard deviation of an item is given by the expression

$$\sigma_j = \sqrt{p_j q_j}$$

Correlation Coefficient

In cases where the test constructor is interested in the relationship between responses to two items, for example, item j and item k, there is also a simple computational formula for the correlation coefficient which uses p and q. This formula is called the *phi coefficient* and is denoted

$$\rho_{phi} = \frac{p_{jk} - p_j p_k}{\sqrt{p_j q_j p_k q_k}} \tag{5.6}$$

where p_{jk} is the joint proportion of students answering both items j and k correctly. Equation 5.6 is derived directly from the formula for the Pearson product moment correlation coefficient. (The derivation is fairly straightforward, and the reader who enjoys algebraic derivations may wish to try this one.) To illustrate the use of Equation 5.6, the proportion of students with each response pattern to items 1 and 2 are presented in Table 5.4. The "+" sign indicates a correct response to the item;

TABLE 5.4.   Joint Proportion Response Distribution to Items 1 and 2 from Table 5.3

		Item 1 +	Item 1 −	
Item 2	−	.10	.30	.40
	+	.40	.20	.60
		.50	.50	

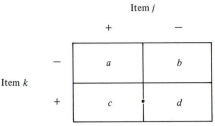

FIGURE 5.1 General Form of a Fourfold Table for Displaying Joint Item Response Frequency Distributions

the ''−'' sign indicates an incorrect response. In this case the value in the upper left-hand cell represents the proportion of the group who answered item 1 correctly but missed item 2; the value in the upper right-hand cell represents the proportion who missed both item 1 and 2; and so on. If we compute the *phi* coefficient between items 1 and 2, using Equation 5.6, we will obtain

$$\rho_{phi} = \frac{.40 - (.50)(.60)}{\sqrt{(.50)(.50)(.60)(.40)}} = .41$$

It is also possible to compute the value of the *phi* coefficient by using simple response frequencies. Figure 5.1 is a fourfold table for displaying joint response frequency data for a pair of items. The letter in each cell represents the number of persons who answered items *j* and *k* with the response pattern indicated by the cell labels. For example, the number in cell *c* would indicate the number of examinees who answered both items *j* and *k* correctly. Table 5.5 is a fourfold table for the data presented in Table 5.3 for items 1 and 2. Using these data, the *phi* coefficient between items 1 and 2 would be computed as follows:

$$\rho_{phi} = \frac{bc - ad}{\sqrt{(a + b)(a + c)(c + d)(b + d)}} \tag{5.7}$$

$$\rho_{phi} = \frac{(3)(4) - (1)(2)}{\sqrt{(1 + 3)(1 + 4)(4 + 2)(2 + 3)}} = .41$$

Thus the degree of relationship between two dichotomously scored test items may be computed by using Equation 5.6 with item difficulty data or by using simple

TABLE 5.5. Joint Response Frequency Distribution for Items 1 and 2 from Table 5.3

		Item 1	
		+	−
Item 2	−	1	3
	+	4	2

response frequencies in Equation 5.7. In using the frequency formula, the reader should be careful to label the item response table as presented here; if the response categories are rearranged, incorrect results may be obtained.

VARIANCE OF A COMPOSITE

Because most tests are scored by computing the sum of the item scores, it follows that there should be some relationship between individual item variances and the variance of the total test scores. In Table 5.3 a person-item score matrix was presented containing responses of 10 examinees to a five-item quiz. Summary statistics are presented for the item scores and the total test score beneath the matrix. If we compute the sum of the item variances for all five items, it would equal 1.10. You may be surprised to note that this sum is considerably less than the variance of the total test scores ($\sigma_X^2 = 1.64$). How can this discrepancy be explained? Obviously the total test variance is not determined solely by the individual item variances.

To understand why total test variance exceeds the sum of the item variances, it is necessary to understand the general formula for the variance of a composite. Assume that we have two item scores, denoted as X_1 and X_2, for the same examinees. It is possible to compute a total of these two item scores for each examinee, which we will denote as C:

$$C = X_1 + X_2 \tag{5.8}$$

The mean of the composite of these two scores is

$$\mu_C = \mu_1 + \mu_2 \tag{5.9}$$

The variance of a two-element composite can be determined as follows. In terms of deviation scores,

$$c = x_1 + x_2 \tag{5.10}$$

and

$$\sigma_C^2 = \frac{\Sigma c^2}{N} = \frac{\Sigma(x_1 + x_2)^2}{N} \tag{5.11}$$

By expanding the final term,

$$\frac{\Sigma(x_1 + x_2)^2}{N} = \frac{\Sigma x_1^2}{N} + \frac{\Sigma x_2^2}{N} + \frac{\Sigma 2x_1 x_2}{N} \tag{5.12}$$

By definition the first two terms of Equation 5.12 are item variances, that is,

$$\frac{\Sigma x_1^2}{N} = \sigma_1^2$$

and

$$\frac{\Sigma x_2^2}{N} = \sigma_2^2$$

The third term in Equation 5.12 can be rewritten as follows:

$$\frac{\Sigma 2 x_1 x_2}{N} = \frac{2\Sigma x_1 x_2}{N} \cdot \frac{\sigma_1 \sigma_2}{\sigma_1 \sigma_2}$$

By rearranging the terms, we can also write

$$\frac{\Sigma 2 x_1 x_2}{N} = \frac{2\Sigma x_1 x_2}{N\sigma_1 \sigma_2}(\sigma_1 \sigma_2)$$

and since the term $(\Sigma x_1 x_2)/(N\sigma_1 \sigma_2)$ is the correlation ρ_{12}, we can write

$$\frac{\Sigma 2 x_1 x_2}{N} = 2\rho_{12}\sigma_1 \sigma_2 \qquad (5.13)$$

The term $\rho_{12}\sigma_1 \sigma_2$ is called the *covariance* of X_1 and X_2. For any pair of variables, taken on the same sample, the covariance is simply the correlation of those two variables multiplied by their standard deviations.

Suppose now that we add a third item to the composite, so that

$$C = X_1 + X_2 + X_3$$

The mean of this three-element composite is then

$$\mu_Y = \mu_1 + \mu_2 + \mu_3$$

The formula for the variance of the three-element composite is

$$\sigma_Y^2 = \sigma_1^2 + \sigma_2^2 + \sigma_3^2 + 2\rho_{12}\sigma_1 \sigma_2 + 2\rho_{13}\sigma_1 \sigma_3 + 2\rho_{23}\sigma_2 \sigma_3$$

By inductive reasoning, the reader may be able to see that there will always be one variance term for each item (σ_i^2) and a pair of covariance terms for each pair of items ($2\rho_{ij}\sigma_i \sigma_j$). Thus the general form for the variance of a composite of n elements would be

$$\sigma_Y^2 = \sigma_1^2 + \sigma_2^2 + \cdots + \sigma_n^2 + 2\rho_{12}\sigma_1 \sigma_2 + \cdots + 2\rho_{n,n-1}\sigma_n \sigma_{n-1} \qquad (5.14)$$

Equation 5.14 can be more concisely stated as

$$\sigma_Y^2 = \sum \sigma_i^2 + 2\sum_{i<j} \rho_{ij}\sigma_i \sigma_j \qquad (5.15)$$

where the second summation covers all possible pairs of items i and j for which $i < j$. Thus the total variance of a composite is determined jointly by the variance of individual test items and by the covariance of all pairs of those items.

A convenient way of visualizing variance and covariance elements which contribute to composite variance is through the variance-covariance matrix. For a test that consists of n items, this matrix will be an nxn square matrix, with item variances displayed in the diagonal and the covariances displayed in the off-diagonal locations, so that the value of row i, column j, represents the covariance between items i and j (see Figure 5.2). The symbol σ_{ij} is a short form of the more complex expression for covariance, $\rho_{ij}\sigma_i \sigma_j$. It should be noted that this matrix is symmetric, which means that the element in row i, column j, is identical to the element in row j,

$$\begin{array}{ccccc}
\sigma_1^2 & \sigma_{12} & \sigma_{13} & \sigma_{14} \cdots & \sigma_{1n} \\
 & \sigma_2^2 & \sigma_{23} & \sigma_{24} \cdots & \sigma_{2n} \\
 & & \sigma_3^2 & \sigma_{34} \cdots & \sigma_{3n} \\
 & & & & \vdots \\
 & & & & \sigma_n^2
\end{array}$$

FIGURE 5.2 General Form of a Variance-Covariance Matrix.

column i; or $\sigma_{ij} = \sigma_{ji}$. For this reason it is common to see only the upper or lower diagonal of the variance-covariance matrix presented. Thus, the expression $2\rho_{ij}\sigma_i\sigma_j$ represents $\rho_{ij}\sigma_i\sigma_j + \rho_{ji}\sigma_i\sigma_j$. We can see from Figure 5.2 that a composite variance for a test with n items will have n variance terms and $n(n - 1)$ covariance terms. (There are, however, only $n(n - 1)/2$ *unique* covariance terms.) Thus the composite variance for a five-item test would consist of the sum of 5 item variance terms and twice the sum of the (5)(4)/2 unique covariance terms.

Let us now examine Table 5.6, which contains the item variance-covariance matrix for the five-item test displayed earlier (in Table 5.3). Examination of these values and their sums, as shown beneath Table 5.6, indicates how total score variance (1.60) of this test is determined by a combination of the item variances and covariances.

Finally, from inspection of the general form of the variance-covariance matrix, we can see that as a test is lengthened, the number of covariance terms increases more rapidly than the number of item variance terms. For example, if we add five items to our original five-item test, the total number of item variance terms will increase from 5 to 10, but the total number of item covariance terms will increase from 10 to 45. For test construction this has significant implications, which will be explained in the following section.

TABLE 5.6. Item Variance-Covariance Matrix for Dichotomous Item Scores in Table 5.3

	1	2	3	4	5
Item 1	.25	.10	.00	.00	−.05
Item 2		.24	.06	−.08	.02
Item 3			.24	.08	.08
Item 4				.16	.06
Item 5					.21

$$\sum \sigma_i^2 = 1.10$$

$$2\sum_{i<j} \rho_{ij}\sigma_i\sigma_j = 2(.27) = .54$$

PRACTICAL IMPLICATIONS FOR TEST CONSTRUCTION

Assume that a researcher has written an experimental form of a scale to measure test anxiety. Respondents will answer each item in an agree-disagree format so that items can be dichotomously scored. The researcher hypothesizes that test anxiety is a construct on which there are important individual differences and thus wants an anxiety scale that yields substantial score variance. After initial tryout of a short form of the scale (e.g., 20 items), the researcher finds that the variance of scores is not as large as expected and wonders how the scale could be modified to increase the variance. Considering the factors that determine total test score variance, how should the following questions be answered?

1. *Is test variance likely to increase if the number of items is increased?*   In most cases, adding items to the test should increase total test variance. For each item added, the total test variance will be increased by the sum of that item's variance and its covariances with all other items on the test. The proportional increase in total test variance will be more marked when items are added to a short test than when they are added to a longer one. This can be seen in the following situations. Suppose that the researcher adds 5 items to a 20-item scale. Assume that the average item variance on this test is .20 and the average item covariance is .10. The variance of the original 20-item test would be 42. If the researcher adds 5 items (with the same average item variance and covariances as those already on the test), the variance of the new test would be

$$\sigma_X^2 = 25(.20) + 25(24)(.10) = 65$$

This increase from 42 to 65 is a proportional increase in total test variance of 55%. Now consider a 70-item test with an average item variance of .20 and an average item covariance of .10. The total test variance of this 70-item test would be 497. If the researcher now adds 5 additional items to this test, with the same average item variance and covariance values as on the original test, total test variance would be

$$\sigma_X^2 = 75(.20) + (75)(74)(.10) = 570$$

This increase of variance from 497 to 570 represents only a 15% increase in total test variance. Obviously, considering costs of test development and administration time, there will be a point when the additional increments in test variance will not justify the additional expenditures of time and effort required. It should also be noted that if for some reason item scores are negatively correlated with one another, the addition of such items would reduce, rather than increase, total test variance.

2. *What is the optimal mix of item difficulties for maximizing test variance?* This question actually has two elements. First, is it better to write items that are nearly equal in difficulty or items that have a mixture of high, low, and medium difficulties? Consider for a moment the fact that item covariances will be larger when items are highly correlated. Logically we should recognize that high correlations between items can occur only when the same persons who respond correctly to

item i also respond correctly to item j and those who respond incorrectly to i also respond incorrectly to j. Then the items would have equal difficulties. A more precise description of the mathematical relationship between item correlations and the similarity of their difficulties was given by Gulliksen (1945), who provided a graph shown in Figure 5.3. This figure demonstrates that as the discrepancy between difficulties for items h and k increases, the maximum possible Pearson or *phi* correlation between those items declines sharply. A maximum correlation of 1.00 can be achieved only when items h and k have equal p values.

Second, to maximize test variance, as Gulliksen (1945) further noted, not only should items be approximately equal in difficulty but also they should be of medium difficulty. This is easily seen if we compute the variance for items with the following p values: .20, .40, .50, .70, and .90. Obviously as item difficulty increases from the lowest value of .20 to the medium value of .50, item variance (pq) increases from .16 to .25; after that, as item difficulties increase from .50 to .90, item variance begins to decrease from .25 to .09. Thus the values of item variances and standard deviations (which contribute to the covariance terms) will be greatest for items of medium difficulty. (It should be noted that for tests comprised of multiple-choice or true-false items, where guessing is likely to occur, it is desirable to construct items with p values somewhat higher than .50. Determining the ideal p value for such items is discussed in more detail in Chapter 14.)

3. *Should items added to the test be similar in content to those already included, or should these items attempt to cover new content areas?* Sound test development

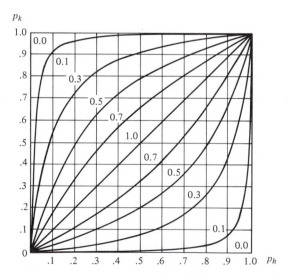

FIGURE 5.3 Combinations of p_h and p_k for which the Maximum Correlation Is 1.0, 0.7, 0.5, 0.3, 0.1, and 0.0

From H. Gulliksen (1945), The relationship of item difficulty and inter-item correlation to test variance and reliability, *Psychometrika*, 10, 79–91. Reprinted by permission.

requires the initial set of items to cover a well-defined set of domain specifications or objectives. By now, the reader probably recognizes that in adding items to a test, it is advisable to add items that will be highly correlated with items already on the test, as this allows covariances to be maximized. Nevertheless, translating this principle into item writing can sometimes be difficult. In trying to develop content for new items, the test developer may be tempted to expand the domain of material covered by the test in the hope of increasing total variance rather than trying to develop additional items based on content already covered. The former practice, however, is somewhat undesirable—first, because such additional items may detract from the usefulness of the test by altering the content domain covered, and second, because the test developer runs the risk of producing items that are not highly correlated with those already on the existing test (thus contributing little to total score variance). Thus, in situations where the test developer has already developed a test from an existing set of specifications or objectives, it is usually advisable to try to develop additional items based on that same content if items are being added primarily to increase total score variance.

4. *Is test score variance in and of itself an index of test quality?* Even on a test where the measurement of individual differences is of prime importance, maximizing total score variance is not the only consideration in test construction. Potential test users, comparing two tests designed to serve the same purpose, should opt for the test that yields scores with greater reliability and validity (which are the focus of the next two units). As we shall see, however, these two critical properties of test scores are, to some extent, dependent on the variance of the scores. Thus, for norm-referenced tests, variance is a necessary, but not sufficient, condition to insure test usefulness. By contrast, however, when description of examinees' proficiencies in the given domain is the goal of measurement (as with criterion-referenced tests), the construction or selection of items to maximize total score and item score variance may be regarded as an irrelevant consideration (see, for example, Popham, 1974; Popham and Husek, 1969).

SUMMARY

A composite test score is a total test score created by summing two or more subtest scores. An item score is the number of points assigned to an examinee's response to a given item. A total test score computed as a sum of the item scores may thus be regarded as a composite score.

Item scoring schemes may be classified as dichotomous (restricted to values of 0 or 1) or nondichotomous. For items with nondichotomous scoring schemes, traditional formulas of mean, variance, and product moment correlation are applied to describe distributions of the item scores. When items are dichotomously scored, special formulas for computing the mean and variance may be applied. These formulas use the concept of item difficulty (p), defined as the proportion of examinees who answered the item correctly. The product moment correlation for dichotomous variables can be computed with the phi coefficient.

When a test score is considered the composite of the item scores, the composite variance equals the sum of the item variances plus the sum of all item covariances. Each pair of items j and k contributes covariance equal to $2\rho_{jk}\sigma_j\sigma_k$. For a test of n items, there will be n item variances and $n(n-1)/2$ unique item covariances. Thus when the goal is to maximize total score variance, some practical test construction suggestions are:

1. Increasing the number of items increases total score variance.
2. As nearly as possible items should be as equal in difficulty, and difficulty levels should be in the medium range to maximize item covariances.
3. Items with similar content are more likely to have higher correlations (and hence higher covariances).
4. Item score and total score variances alone are not indices of test quality.

Exercises

1. Five students were given the following scores on three essay questions:

Ann:	9	8	7
Bill:	5	3	4
Carol:	8	8	7
David:	7	6	8
Erin:	6	5	7

A. Calculate μ_i and σ_i for each item.
B. What is Bill's mean score?
C. What is the mean score for the third question?
D. Determine the variability of responses displayed by the group for the first item.
E. What is the correlation between items 1 and 2? What does this tell you about the relationship between these items?

2. On a five-item math quiz, the scores for a group of 10 students are

	Item				
Student	1	2	3	4	5
1	1	1	0	0	0
2	1	1	1	0	0
3	1	0	0	0	0
4	1	1	1	1	1
5	1	0	1	1	1
6	0	1	0	0	0
7	1	1	1	1	0
8	1	0	0	1	0
9	1	1	0	0	0
10	1	1	1	0	1

    A. Which item has the highest difficulty value? What does this tell you about the item?

    B. Which item has the greatest variance?

    C. What is the standard deviation for item 3?

    D. What is the correlation between items 4 and 5?

    E. Construct a table for displaying the joint response-frequency data for items 2 and 3. Using this table, calculate the correlation between these 2 items.

    F. What is the covariance of items 2 and 3?

3. For a battery of three subtests the following variances were obtained.

For Test 1, $\sigma_1^2 = 9$.
For Test 2, $\sigma_2^2 = 25$.
For Test 3, $\sigma_3^2 = 16$.

Furthermore, the correlation between tests 1 and 2 is .81; between tests 1 and 3, .64; and between tests 2 and 3, .90.

    A. Construct a variance-covariance matrix.

    B. Determine the variance of the composite test.

4. Researchers want to develop a 10-item test to measure achievement motivation. Answers are scored by using a dichotomous scoring scheme. The researchers have heard that maximum test variance is obtained by using items of medium difficulty which are highly correlated. They therefore decide to identify a single item on which there is substantial response variance and ask that same item 10 times because these responses should be almost perfectly correlated. Is this a reasonable approach to test construction? What will be the consequence?

5. Demonstrate, by algebraic proof, that ρ_{ik} (the Pearson product moment correlation) between variables i and k is the *phi* coefficient when values of both i and k are limited to 0 or 1.

UNIT II

Reliability

Chapter 6

RELIABILITY AND THE CLASSICAL TRUE SCORE MODEL

Whenever a test is administered, the test user would like some assurance that the results could be replicated if the same individuals were tested again under similar circumstances. This desired consistency (or reproducibility) of test scores is called *reliability*. In practical terms reliability is the degree to which individuals' deviation scores, or z-scores, remain relatively consistent over repeated administration of the same test or alternate test forms. (A more technical definition will be presented shortly.) To a certain extent all psychological measurements are unreliable. For example, if an aptitude test is administered to a group of adults and they are retested two weeks later, it is unlikely that each person would earn the same score on the two testing occasions or maintain the same rank order within the group. Similarly if alternate forms of a geometry examination are given to a class of students on the same day, these students probably would not score in the same order on the two test forms. The extent of this unreliability in a set of observations is a concern for every responsible test user and test developer.

What makes test scores unreliable? Whenever an examinee responds to a set of test items his or her score represents only a limited sample of behavior—responses to a subset of many possible items from a given domain obtained on one of many possible occasions. Consequently scores obtained under these conditions are fallible and subject to errors of measurement. Error of measurement can be broadly categorized as random or systematic. Systematic measurement errors are those which consistently affect an individual's score because of some particular characteristic of the person or the test that has nothing to do with the construct being measured. For example, on some reading tests for children, the examiner says a word and the

105

examinee is required to circle the letter that indicates the beginning sound. A hearing-impaired child may hear *bet* when the examiner says *pet* and mark an incorrect response. If the test were repeated, the child would make similar errors, and this child's scores would be consistently depressed across testing occasions. Systematic errors of measurement are illustrated also by the respondent who always marks ''Disagree' when he finds an attitude scale item ambiguous. Because such tendencies persist across repeated testings with the same instrument and affect the examinee's score in a constant fashion, they are systematic errors of measurement.

By contrast, random errors of measurement affect an individual's score because of purely chance happenings. They may affect an examinee's score in either a positive or negative direction. Sources of random errors include guessing, distractions in the testing situation, administration errors, content sampling, scoring errors, and fluctuations in the individual examinee's state. Fluctuations in an individual's behavior may be general enough to affect overall test performance (as when a headache affects an examinee's performance on all items), or they may be very brief and specific (misreading a question, miscopying a math problem, or forgetting momentarily an answer). Stanley (1971) presents a detailed categorization of these individual sources of random variation. If the examinee were to repeat the same examination, the random errors that affect his or her score on the first occasion probably would not be repeated, although other random errors would undoubtedly occur.

Both random and systematic errors are a source of concern in score interpretation. Systematic measurement errors do not result in inconsistent measurement, but still they may cause test scores to be inaccurate and thus reduce their practical utility. Random errors reduce both the consistency and the usefulness of the test scores. It would be illogical to expect measurements to be useful if we did not have some confidence that they were consistent. Thus test developers have a responsibility to demonstrate the reliability of scores obtained from their tests. Such demonstrations require empirical studies, which are usually based on a theoretical model for describing the extent to which random errors influence the scores. In this chapter we will describe such a theoretical model, which has widespread application to the study of test reliability. In the next chapter we will focus on practical methods for studying reliability based on this theoretical model.

THE CLASSICAL TRUE SCORE MODEL

The classical true score model is one of the most significant issues from British psychologist Charles Spearman's fascination with the concept of correlation. From 1904 to 1913 he published logical and mathematical arguments that test scores are fallible measures of human traits, and thus the observed correlation between fallible test scores is lower than the correlation between their ''true objective values'' (Spearman, 1904). In repeated attempts to explain the terms *fallible measures* and *true objective values,* Spearman (1907, 1913) laid the foundation for the classical true score model. Many authors, most notably Guilford (1936), Gulliksen (1950), Magnusson (1967), and Lord and Novick (1968), have restated and elaborated this model into the form described here.

The essence of Spearman's model was that any observed test score could be envisioned as the composite of two hypothetical components—a true score and a random error component—expressed in the form

$$X = T + E \qquad (6.1)$$

where X represents the observed test score; T, the individual's true score; and E, a random error component. For example, on a 10-item test, John may actually know the answers to 7 items but by chance mismark 2 answers incorrectly, so that his observed score becomes

$$X = 7 - 2 = 5$$

Sarah, however, knows the answers to only 4 items but makes 3 lucky guesses, so her score is

$$X = 4 + 3 = 7$$

Finally, Ralph knows the answers to 8 items, misses an item by misreading the question, but guesses correctly on an item that he does not know. His positive and negative errors cancel each other so that his score is

$$X = 8 + 0 = 8$$

These numeric examples illustrate the additive effects of positive and negative measurement errors, but it is incorrect to infer that the examinee's "true score" as defined in the classical true score model, is some precise number of items that the examinee can answer.

Test Scores as Random Variables

A variable is a quantity that may assume any one of a set of values. A *random variable* can be loosely defined as *a variable that assumes its values according to a set of probabilities*. For example, suppose that you are about to throw a six-sided die. The number of spots that will appear on the top face of the die may be considered a random variable. This variable may take values of 1 to 6 according to a set of probabilities. On a single throw of the die, only one value occurs. This value is called a *realization of the random variable*. Although this random variable may assume only six possible values, the number of realizations of the random variable is unlimited because you can conceive of throwing the die again and again without affecting it. This leads to a second way of conceptualizing a random variable: The random variable in the example can be viewed as *a hypothetical distribution of outcomes* of throws of the die. A single throw may be considered a random sample of one outcome from this distribution of possible outcomes. It is important to note that the exact probability of occurrence of each of the values 1 to 6 is unknown and *unknowable*. We cannot simply assert that the probability of each value is one-sixth. Even if the die were manufactured to be fair, there can be no assurance that it is exactly fair. If you try to determine the probabilities empirically by tossing the die a large number of times, you get, at best, an estimate of the probabilities. With each new throw of the die, these estimates will change slightly.

Whenever an examinee takes a test, the score on that test can also be considered a realization of a random variable. Why can a test score be conceptualized in this way? First note that a test consists of a specified number of items. If the test has 50 items an examinee's score may fall anywhere between 0 and 50 (just as outcomes of the throw of the die range between 1 and 6). Before an examinee takes a test, we cannot know whether he or she will have a few or many instances of inattention, lucky or unlucky guesses, misreading of items, and so forth. Thus (prior to the administration of the examination) we can view this individual's test score as possibly assuming one of several values according to some unknown set of probabilities. This distribution of potential scores for an individual examinee can be considered a random variable, and the score actually obtained when the examinee takes the test is a realization of that random variable. To envision how to obtain an estimate of this hypothetical distribution of scores for an examinee, imagine administering this test repeatedly to the examinee, hypnotizing the examinee and instructing the examinee to forget the previous testing, then repeating this process many times. Obviously the observed scores obtained from repeated testings of this individual would fluctuate because of the errors of measurement discussed earlier. The frequency distribution of obtained scores could provide an estimate of the probabilities that would govern the examinee's score on any particular testing occasion. In this sense, an observed test score, like a throw of the die, can be considered a realization of a random variable.

It is important to realize that the score of each examinee in a testing situation represents a different random variable. That is, the probability of obtaining a given test score is independently determined from a different distribution for each examinee. Table 6.1 illustrates this fact for two examinees who take a five-item test.

TABLE 6.1.   Probabilities of Test Scores for Two Examinees on a Single Testing

Test Score (X)	Probability for Susan	Probability for Elaine
0	.00	.15
1	.02	.20
2	.18	.40
3	.50	.23
4	.25	.02
5	.05	.00

$\Sigma(X)p_{\text{Susan}} = (0)(.00) + (1)(.02) + (2)(.18) + (3)(.50) + (4)(.25) + (5)(.05) = 3.13$
$\Sigma(X)p_{\text{Elaine}} = (0)(.15) + (1)(.20) + (2)(.40) + (3)(.23) + (4)(.02) + (5)(.00) = 1.77$

(Note that this is a hypothetical illustration since these probabilities are never directly observable.) According to these two probability distributions, we would consider Susan as the more "able" examinee because the probabilities suggest that she is likely to get a higher score than Elaine when we sample just one value at random from each distribution.

Definition of the True Score

Now that we see how a random variable represents a probability distribution, it is possible to talk about the mean of such a distribution. The *expected value* of a random variable is another name for the mean of a random variable. When a random variable, denoted by X, assumes a finite number of discrete values, the expected value of X is defined as

$$\mu = \sum_{k=1}^{K} X_k p_k \qquad (6.2)$$

where X_k is the kth value the random variable can assume, and p_k is the probability of that value. For the die example, if the die were exactly fair, the expected value would be

$$\mu = \sum_{k=1}^{6} X_k p_k$$

$$= 1(1/6) + 2(1/6) + 3(1/6) + 4(1/6) + 5(1/6) + 6(1/6)$$

$$= 3.5$$

If a random variable can assume an infinite number of values, Equation 6.2 cannot be used to define the expected value. (The algebraic symbols and process used in Equation 6.2 would be replaced by a calculus procedure known as integration.) In either case, the expected value of the random variable X is denoted by $\epsilon(X)$.

When we consider the observed test score as a random variable, X_j, the *true score* for examinee j is defined as

$$T_j = \epsilon X_j = \mu_{X_j} \qquad (6.3)$$

For the two examinees in Table 6.1, the expected values of their test scores (using Equation 6.2) are 3.13 for Susan and 1.77 for Elaine. For each examinee this expected value may be considered the average of all the test scores that examinee *might* achieve on taking the test. Loosely speaking, then, the examinee's true score can be interpreted as the average of the observed scores obtained over an infinite number of repeated testings with the same test.

Given this definition it is important to note the distinction between the true score on a psychological variable and an absolute true score on a biological or physical variable. Suppose, for example, a physician suspects that a patient has a chronic liver disease. On this variable the patient has an absolute true score. He either has the disease or he does not. Even with an absolute true score, it is still possible for errors of measurement to occur. The laboratory test used to detect this disease (isoenzyme analysis) may yield different results when repeated for the same patient. Nevertheless, the patient's absolute true score exists independently of the results of these tests. We would never say that the state of the patient's liver is defined by the average value of the test results. Furthermore, no matter how many different types of tests are run, the patient will still have only one absolute true score on this variable. In contrast, the patient's true score on a psychological test is totally dependent on the measurement process used. Any systematic errors or biasing aspects of a particular test for an individual contribute to that person's psychological true score on that test. Thus if an individual's observed scores on the Wechsler Intelligence Scale are depressed consistently because of a hearing disorder or a language disability, the true score (as the average of those observed scores) will be lowered. Furthermore, if we measure intelligence with the nonverbal Raven's Progressive Matrices and the Wechsler scale, which has a verbal component, this individual will have different true scores for each test. Thus in contrast to an absolute true score, a psychological true score is a statistical concept, based on the expected value obtained from a given measurement process.

Definition of Error

According to the classical true score model, an *error* of measurement is the *discrepancy between an examinee's observed test score and his or her true score*. The error in the score for examinee j, (E_j), is thus defined as

$$E_j = X_j - T_j \tag{6.4}$$

The error, E_j, is a random variable since it is the difference between X_j, a random variable, and T_j, a constant for examinee j. The mean of the error distribution for examinee j is the expected value

$$\mu_{E_j} = \epsilon E_j = \epsilon(X_j - T_j) \tag{6.5}$$

To simplify the expression further we must employ two basic rules for operations with expected values. First, the expected value of a difference between two variables is the difference of their expected values. Therefore, Equation 6.5 can be written as

$$\epsilon E_j = \epsilon X_j - \epsilon T_j \tag{6.6}$$

Second, the expected value of a constant is just that constant; thus for examinee j,

$$\epsilon E_j = \epsilon X_j - T_j \tag{6.7}$$

Now, since $\epsilon X_j = T_j$ (from Equation 6.3),

$$\epsilon E_j = T_j - T_j = 0 \tag{6.8}$$

A loose interpretation is that the average of the error scores for an examinee over many repeated testings should be zero.

$$\mu_E = 0$$

Properties of True and Error Scores

From the preceding definitions it is possible to derive several basic principles of the classical true score model which have often been called assumptions of the model. These principles are   *Over long run errors will cancel each other out .*

1. The mean of the error scores for a population of examinees is zero ($\mu_E = 0$).
2. The correlation between true and error scores for a population of examinees is zero ($\rho_{TE} = .00$).
3. When examinees take two separate tests and each examinee's scores on the two tests (or two testing occasions with the same form) are assumed to be <u>randomly</u> chosen from two independent distributions of possible observed scores, the correlation between error scores from the two testings is zero ($\rho_{E_1E_2} = .00$).

#2. eg. error is not related to score.

These three principles describe basic properties of true scores and error scores which enable us to apply the classical true score model to the study of test score reliability. An informal description of the logical basis for each principle is presented here. Readers interested in the formal derivations should see Lord and Novick (1968, pp. 37–38).

Mean True and Error Scores

Suppose that a group of examinees has taken a test. As we have already learned, each examinee j has one true score value (T_j), which is the average observed score the examinee would earn over many repeated testings on this instrument or parallel instruments. Consequently, in theory, examinee j has a set of possible observed scores on this test such that

$$T_j = \epsilon X_j$$

The mean true score for *all* examinees in the group is denoted as

$$\mu_T = \underset{j}{\epsilon} T_j$$

where the j subscript on ϵ indicates that the expected value is taken over all persons in the group. Thus we can define μ_T, the group's mean true score, as

$$\mu_T = \underset{j}{\epsilon} \epsilon X_j \tag{6.9}$$

This double expectation notation is equivalent to saying that the average true score for the examinee population is equal to the average of all observed scores that might be earned by all examinees over many repeated testings, or that

$$\mu_T = \mu_X \tag{6.10}$$

To find the mean error score for the group μ_E, we follow the same procedure:

$$\mu_E = \underset{j}{\epsilon} \epsilon E_j \tag{6.11}$$

However, we already know that $\epsilon E_j = 0$, and thus

$$\mu_E = \underset{j}{\epsilon}(0) \text{ \large* }$$

average error for group is 0.

E = expected value.

Since the expected value of a constant is that constant it follows that

$$\mu_E = 0 \qquad\qquad (6.12)$$

It is important to remember that this principle does not guarantee that whenever a test is given, the average of the examinees' errors on that test will be zero. Collectively E_j for all the examinees constitute a population of errors, with expected value (or population mean) of zero. Administering a single test to this group of 200 examinees is equivalent to selecting a sample of these E_j values by drawing one value at random from the error scores of each examinee. The mean of this *sample* of error scores may or may not be zero.

The Correlation Between True and Error Scores

Imagine a situation in which we know the true score and all the error scores for each examinee in a population. We use these scores to construct a scatterplot with the error score scale on the vertical axis and the true score scale on the horizontal axis. Note that since each examinee has many error scores, but only one true score, there will be a fairly large number of points for each true score value earned. Suppose we find the lowest true score for any examinee in the group. There will be one or more examinees with this true score. For each examinee in the population, and consequently for each examinee with this true score, $\mu_{E_j} = 0$. Thus the mean error score for all examinees at this true score will be zero. If we locate all the error scores for this true score, they will be plotted around a mean of zero. Then suppose that we find the next lowest true score and repeat this process. Again the error scores will be plotted around a mean of zero, and so on for each true score value. Figure 6.1(a) shows such a plot for the five lowest values of T. The plot for all possible T-values will appear as in Figure 6.1(b). From this plot we can see that the correlation between true and error scores must be zero for the population of all possible observations for all examinees. This means that there is no relationship between an examinee's "ability" and the errors of measurement that affect the examinee's observed score on any testing occasion. Thus the covariance between true scores and error scores is zero, so that total observed score variance is simply the sum of true score and error variances. Knowledge of this relationship will be useful later in this chapter.

The Correlation Between Error Scores

Imagine that two tests were given to every examinee in a population and that we know the error scores for each examinee from both testings. Suppose that an examinee has a high positive error score on the first test. If you were asked to guess the value of this examinee's error score on the second test, would you guess that it would also be high and positive? Would you guess that it would be negative in value (reasoning that errors of measurement must balance out, even for a limited number of testings)? The answer is "no" in each case. Recall that each individual's error

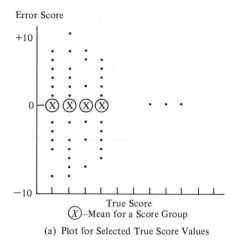

(a) Plot for Selected True Score Values

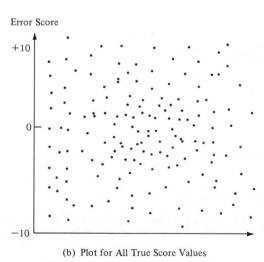

(b) Plot for All True Score Values

FIGURE 6.1 Examples of Scatterplots of True and Error Scores for a Large Group of Examinees Responding to a 10-Item Test

score on a given test is a random sample of one from an entire distribution of error scores with a mean of zero. As a result of the random sampling, there can be no relationship between the values of these two error scores, chosen from two independent distributions. Because this is true for every examinee, a scatterplot showing a point for every possible combination of error scores from the first and second tests would be similar to that constructed in Figure 6.1(b). Thus we see that the correlation between errors from distinct testings is zero. The random measurement error that affects an examinee's score on one occasion is unrelated to the measurement error for this same examinee on another testing.

$$\rho_{XT} = \frac{\sigma_T}{\sigma_X}$$

RELIABILITY INDEX AND RELIABILITY COEFFICIENT

Given the definitions of true and error scores, it seems clear that when teachers, researchers, or clinicians give a test, they know only the observed scores even though they would really be more interested in the true scores. Thus an important question is, how closely related are the examinees' true and observed scores? One index of this relationship is the correlation between these two variables. The correlation coefficient that expresses the degree of relationship between true and observed scores on a test is known as the *reliability index*. Recall that an examinee's observed score can be expressed as

$$X = T + E$$

and in deviation scores as

$$x = t + e$$

When using deviation scores we can write an expression for the reliability index as[1]

$$\rho_{XT} = \frac{\Sigma xt}{N\sigma_X\sigma_T} \tag{6.13}$$

By substituting for x, this expression becomes

$$\rho_{XT} = \frac{\Sigma(t + e)t}{N\sigma_X\sigma_T}$$

or

$$\rho_{XT} = \frac{\Sigma t^2}{N\sigma_X\sigma_T} + \frac{\Sigma te}{N\sigma_X\sigma_T} \tag{6.14}$$

Because the correlation between true and error scores is assumed to be zero, the last term in Equation 6.14 can be omitted,[2] and since $\sigma_T^2 = \dfrac{\Sigma t^2}{N}$,

$$\rho_{XT} = \frac{\sigma_T^2}{\sigma_X\sigma_T}$$

---

[1] Strictly speaking, it is incorrect to use the summation (Σ) notation here. The summation notation is only appropriate for finite populations and there is no reason to limit the presentation to a finite population. While expectation notation is more general, its use here would require an explanation of double expectation, which can be confusing for beginning students. Lord and Novick (1968, Chaps. 2 and 3) discuss the classical true score model with the double expectation approach.

[2] Since

$$\frac{\Sigma te}{N\sigma_X\sigma_T} = \frac{\Sigma te}{N\sigma_X\sigma_T} \left(\frac{\sigma_T\sigma_E}{\sigma_T\sigma_E} \right)$$

with recombination of terms, we can write

$$\left(\frac{\Sigma te}{N\sigma_T\sigma_E} \right) \left(\frac{\sigma_T\sigma_E}{\sigma_X\sigma_T} \right)$$

The first quantity in the expression now represents ρ_{TE}, which equals zero.

which simplifies to

$$\rho_{XT} = \frac{\sigma_T}{\sigma_X} \quad \text{✳}$$ (6.15)

Thus we see that the reliability index can be expressed as the ratio of the standard deviation of true scores to the standard deviation of the observed scores. Note that this is the correlation between true scores and all possible observed scores from many repeated testings. This expression would appear to have little practical value because true scores are not directly observable and we cannot get all possible observed scores for each examinee. Nevertheless, it is plausible to imagine testing a group of examinees on two occasions with the same test or with two forms of a test. When the two tests meet the requirements for parallel tests, it is possible to establish a mathematical link between ρ_{XT}, the correlation between true and observed scores, and $\rho_{XX'}$, the correlation between observed scores on two parallel tests. According to classical true score theory, two tests are defined as parallel when

1. Each examinee has the same true score on both forms of the test, and
2. The error variances for the two forms are equal.

Such tests will, as a consequence, have equal means and equal variances. It is also quite sensible (although not statistically necessary) to assume that parallel tests will be matched in content.

The _reliability coefficient_ can be defined as the correlation between scores on parallel test forms. When the reliability coefficient is defined in this way, the relationship between the reliability index and the reliability coefficient can be described mathematically.

$\rho_{XX'}$
or
$\rho_{X_1 X_2}$

Let an examinee's deviation scores on two parallel tests be denoted as x_1 and x_2. According to the model, these observed scores can be expressed as

$$x_1 = t_1 + e_1$$

and

$$x_2 = t_2 + e_2$$

The deviation score formula for the correlation between observed test scores X_1 and X_2 is

$$\rho_{X_1 X_2} = \frac{\Sigma x_1 x_2}{N \sigma_{X_1} \sigma_{X_2}}$$

By substitution this equation becomes

$$\rho_{X_1 X_2} = \frac{\Sigma (t_1 + e_1)(t_2 + e_2)}{N \sigma_{X_1} \sigma_{X_2}}$$

Through algebraic expansion, the expression becomes

$$\rho_{X_1 X_2} = \frac{\Sigma t_1 t_2}{N \sigma_{X_1} \sigma_{X_2}} + \frac{\Sigma t_1 e_2}{N \sigma_{X_1} \sigma_{X_2}} + \frac{\Sigma t_2 e_1}{N \sigma_{X_1} \sigma_{X_2}} + \frac{\Sigma e_1 e_2}{N \sigma_{X_1} \sigma_{X_2}}$$

Under the assumptions of the classical true score model, each of the last three terms in the expression can be shown to equal zero.[3] Since true score values for any individual are assumed to be equal over testing occasions, $t_1 = t_2$, and $\sigma_{X_1} = \sigma_{X_2}$ by the definition of parallel tests. Thus

$$\rho_{X_1X_2} = \frac{\Sigma t_1^2}{N\sigma_{X_1}^2}$$

or

$$\rho_{X_1X_2} = \frac{\sigma_T^2}{\sigma_X^2} \quad \text{✳} \qquad (6.16)$$

test: retest.

alternate forms.

and we see that the *reliability coefficient* can be mathematically defined as the ratio of true score variance to observed score variance (or the square of the reliability index).

In interpreting reliability information, it is important to note the distinction among:

1. $\rho_{X_1X_2}$—the proportion of observed score variance that may be attributed to variation in examinees' true scores
2. $(\rho_{X_1X_2})^2$—the proportion of observed score variance on one parallel test that could be predicted from observed score variance on the second parallel test *(regression)*
3. ρ_{XT}—the correlation between true scores and observed scores
   └ reliability index

Suppose that a test manual reports a reliability coefficient of $\rho_{X_1X_2} = .81$. The following interpretations would be appropriate. First, we may say that 81% of the observed score variance is attributable to true score variance for this examinee group. Thus $\sigma_T^2 = .81\sigma_X^2$. If the standard deviation of the observed score is 4 points, we would predict that the standard deviation of the unobservable true score distribution would be $\sigma_T = \sqrt{(.81)(16)}$, or 3.6 points. Second, we may say that $(.81)^2$, or 65%, of the observed score variance on the second test could be predicted by the variance of the observed scores on the first test. Finally, we may say that the correlation between observed scores and true scores is $\sqrt{.81}$, or .90, for these examinees.

At this point it is important to note that the reliability coefficient for a set of test scores is a purely *theoretical* concept. It is the quantity that would be obtained if we could be certain of having truly parallel tests. In Chapter 7, we will address the problem of using actual test scores to estimate this theoretical quantity. For the moment, however, we will simply point out that when real test scores must be substituted for strictly parallel measurements, it is possible to design the data collection in different ways. First, we may attempt to approximate obtaining parallel measurements by administering the same form of a test on two separate occasions to the same group of examinees. The correlation between test scores in this case is

---

[3]By using the same algebraic process as in footnote 1, the second and third terms can each be shown to equal ρ_{TE}; the last term equals $\rho_{E_1E_2}$.

often called the *coefficient of stability*. Also we could attempt to approximate parallel measurements by administering two different forms of a test, based on the same content, on one occasion to the same examinees. In this case, the correlation coefficient is known as the *coefficient of equivalence*. We could even administer two alternate test forms on separate testing occasions, yielding a *coefficient of stability and equivalence*. Each of these coefficients, however, will probably be an underestimate of the theoretical reliability coefficient which would be obtained from truly parallel measurements. Coombs (1950a) characterized this theoretical quantity as the *coefficient of precision*, defined as the correlation between test scores when examinees respond to the same test items repeatedly and there are no changes in examinees over time, or as Cronbach (1951) preferred to describe it, when the elapsed time between testings becomes infinitesimal.

alternate or parallel forms.

When the test developer's primary goal is to estimate the coefficient of precision from a set of real test scores, a *coefficient of internal consistency* is sometimes computed for scores obtained from a single administration. A number of different practical methods for obtaining internal consistency coefficients are described in Chapter 7, but understanding the origin of most of these methods requires some knowledge of the reliability of a composite of test scores.

Cronbach's alpha & related.

RELIABILITY OF A COMPOSITE

In Chapter 5 a composite was defined as a total score based on two or more subtest scores. Let us now imagine that a test developer has created two parallel forms of a test denoted as form A and form B. If these forms are strictly parallel, the reliability coefficient of either form is given by ρ_{AB}. (A common notation used to denote this reliability is $\rho_{AA'}$ or $\rho_{BB'}$.) Suppose, however, a test user desires to administer both forms and compute a total score for each examinee based on the composite score:

$$C = A + B$$

How can the reliability of these composite scores ($\rho_{CC'}$) be determined? Note that at this point it becomes rather circular to suggest that the test developer should create two additional forms of the test to provide a parallel form to the first composite score. Even if it could be done, this question could still arise: What is the reliability of the composite of all four subtests? Thus it would be useful to have a method for defining the reliability of a composite in terms of the statistical properties of its internal components. In this section, we will consider two ways in which reliability of a composite can be expressed in terms of statistical properties of its components. The first method, which uses a procedure called the *Spearman Brown prophecy*, allows us to estimate the reliability of a composite of parallel tests when the reliability of one of those tests is known. The second method, which uses a procedure known as *Cronbach's alpha*, allows us to estimate the reliability of a composite when we know the composite score variance and the covariances among all its components. For simplicity in this discussion, we will assume that we begin with a

eg: look at only 1 test.

AKA coefficient alpha

Think about reliability of a test is terms of its items –

set of parallel component tests. Later, we will consider how our results would be affected if the component tests were not strictly parallel.

The Spearman Brown Prophecy *Expresses the reliability of a composite in terms of component of the test*

To begin this derivation, let us review some simple relationships that we have learned (or that can be logically derived from what we have learned):

1. The reliability of a composite can be defined as $\rho_{CC'} = \sigma_{T_C}^2/\sigma_C^2$.
2. All parallel measurements can be shown to have equal means, equal standard deviations, and equal variances. Furthermore, when there are k parallel measurements, the correlation between any pair of these parallel measurements will be equal to the correlation between any other pair.
3. If there are k components in a composite, the variance of this composite will be the sum of k variance terms and $k(k-1)$ covariance terms.

Now we are ready to derive a formula for the reliability of a composite. Let us first define a composite of k parallel tests such that

$$C = A + B + \cdots + K \tag{6.17}$$

The observed score variance of this composite is then

$$\sigma_C^2 = \sigma_A^2 + \sigma_B^2 + \cdots + \sigma_K^2 + \sum_{i \neq j} \rho_{ij}\sigma_i\sigma_j \tag{6.18}$$

where $\sum_{i \neq j} \rho_{ij}\sigma_i\sigma_j$ is the sum of $k(k-1)$ covariance terms, and i and j denote any pair of tests from A to K. Because all the tests are parallel, all ρ_{ij} are equal, and

$$\sigma_A = \sigma_B = \cdots = \sigma_i = \sigma_j$$

Therefore we can rewrite Equation 6.18:

$$\sigma_C^2 = k\sigma_i^2 + k(k-1)\rho_{ij}\sigma_i^2$$

By factoring out $k\sigma_i^2$ from each term, we have

$$\sigma_C^2 = k\sigma_i^2[1 + (k-1)\rho_{ij}] \tag{6.19}$$

Finally we note that because i and j are parallel measures, ρ_{ij} can actually be considered the reliability coefficient of test i; and so Equation 6.19 can be written

$$\sigma_C^2 = k\sigma_i^2[1 + (k-1)\rho_{ii'}] \tag{6.20}$$

We will use this expression shortly as the denominator of the composite reliability.

Now let us turn to the true score variance for the composite C, which is

$$\sigma_{T_C}^2 = \sigma_{T_A}^2 + \sigma_{T_B}^2 + \cdots + \sigma_{T_K}^2 + \sum_{i \neq j} \rho_{T_i T_j}\sigma_{T_i}\sigma_{T_j} \tag{6.21}$$

Because true scores for each examinee must be equal on parallel measures i and j, $\rho_{T_iT_j} = 1.00$ for all tests. Furthermore, because we have parallel tests,

$$\sigma_{T_A} = \sigma_{T_B} = \sigma_{T_i} = \sigma_{T_j}$$

Therefore with k variance and $k(k-1)$ covariance terms in this true score composite, we have

$$\sigma_{T_C}^2 = k\sigma_{T_i}^2 + k(k-1)\sigma_{T_i}^2$$

This can be further simplified to

$$\sigma_{T_C}^2 = k^2\sigma_{T_i}^2 \qquad (6.22)$$

Using the expressions for $\sigma_{T_C}^2$ (from Equation 6.22) and σ_C^2 (from Equation 6.20), we can now write an equation for $\rho_{CC'}$ as

$$\rho_{CC'} = \frac{k^2\sigma_{T_i}^2}{k\sigma_i^2[1 + (k-1)\rho_{ii'}]}$$

Because $\sigma_{T_i}^2/\sigma_i^2 = \rho_{ii'}$, this fraction can be simplified to

$\rho_{CC'} = $ Rho of component

$K = $ reliability

$$\rho_{CC'} = \frac{k\rho_{ii'}}{1 + (k-1)\rho_{ii'}} \qquad (6.23)$$

ρ_{ii}

Equation 6.23 is the general form of the Spearman Brown prophecy formula, showing that reliability of a composite can be expressed as a function of the reliability of a single component (assuming that all component tests are parallel). Important uses of this formula in reliability estimation and test development practices will be discussed in Chapter 7. *Used for split-half*

Composite Reliability with Coefficient Alpha

The overall purpose of this section is to demonstrate that the reliability of a composite can be expressed as a function of the variance of the composite scores and the covariances of the tests that make up that composite. The formula to be derived here is commonly known as *coefficient alpha* (Cronbach, 1951). The following points will be helpful to the reader in understanding this derivation:

1. For any pair of tests i and j, the covariance for these tests is denoted as σ_{ij}, or

    $$\sigma_{ij} = \rho_{ij}\sigma_i\sigma_j$$

2. When tests i and j are strictly parallel, the true score variance of test i equals its covariance with true scores on test j, or

    $$\sigma_{T_i}^2 = \sigma_{T_iT_j}$$

3. For any pair of tests i and j, true score covariance equals observed score covariance, or

    $$\sigma_{T_iT_j} = \sigma_{ij}$$

Armed with this information, let us again define a composite C as the sum of k parallel subtest scores, $C = A + B + \cdots + K$; the true score composite likewise is $T_C = T_A + T_B + \cdots + T_K$. Recall that the variance of this true score composite is

$$\sigma_{T_C}^2 = \sigma_{T_A}^2 + \sigma_{T_B}^2 + \cdots + \sigma_{T_K}^2 + \sum_{i \neq j} \sigma_{T_i T_j}$$

where i and j are any pair of subtests and $\sum_{i \neq j} \sigma_{T_i T_j}$ is the sum of $k(k-1)$ terms.

Because all k parallel measures have equal variances and equal covariances with one another,

$$\sigma_{T_C}^2 = k\sigma_{T_i}^2 + k(k-1)\sigma_{T_i T_j} \tag{6.24}$$

Furthermore, from point 2 (at the beginning of this section) we know that $\sigma_{T_i}^2 = \sigma_{T_i T_j}$. Thus by making this substitution in Equation 6.24,

$$\sigma_{T_C}^2 = k\sigma_{T_i T_j} + k(k-1)\sigma_{T_i T_j}$$

which can be simplified to

$$\sigma_{T_C}^2 = k^2 \sigma_{T_i T_j} \tag{6.25}$$

From point 3 (at the beginning of this section), $\sigma_{T_i T_j} = \sigma_{ij}$, and thus by substitution,

$$\sigma_{T_C}^2 = k^2 \sigma_{ij} \tag{6.26}$$

If we use this latter expression as the true score variance of a composite, we can write an expression for the reliability of a composite as

$$\rho_{CC'} = \frac{k^2 \sigma_{ij}}{\sigma_C^2} \tag{6.27}$$

when all tests are parallel measures.

In real testing situations, however, we can never be certain that all tests in a composite are strictly parallel. In this case, it is possible to use the sum of test covariances and the composite variance to estimate the lower bound of the reliability of the composite. A lower bound to reliability is a coefficient that must be smaller than the reliability coefficient. To demonstrate this, we must establish three inequalities:

1. When k subtests of a composite may not be strictly parallel, there will be at least one subtest (subtest g) for which true score variance is greater than or equal to its covariance with any other subtest, or

$$\sigma_{T_g}^2 \geq \sigma_{ig}$$

2. For any two tests which may not be strictly parallel, the sum of their true score variances is greater than or equal to twice their covariance, or

$$\sigma_{T_i}^2 + \sigma_{T_j}^2 \geq 2\sigma_{ij}$$

3. The sum of k true score variances for nonparallel tests will be greater than or equal to the sum of all their $k(k-1)$ covariances divided by $(k-1)$, or

$$\Sigma\sigma_{T_i}^2 \geq \frac{\displaystyle\sum_{i \neq j} \sigma_{ij}}{k-1}$$

The latter inequality is the result of extending the logic of point 2 over k tests. Detailed algebraic steps are given in Lord and Novick (1968, p. 89) for the interested reader. Adding the sum of the covariances to each side of the inequality we have

$$\Sigma\sigma_{T_i}^2 + \sum_{i \neq j}\sigma_{ij} \geq \frac{\displaystyle\sum_{i \neq j}\sigma_{ij}}{k-1} + \sum_{i \neq j}\sigma_{ij} \tag{6.28}$$

The covariance sums on the right side of the inequality can be combined into a single fraction as follows:

$$\frac{\displaystyle\sum_{i \neq j}\sigma_{ij}}{k-1} + \frac{(k-1)\displaystyle\sum_{i \neq j}\sigma_{ij}}{k-1} = \frac{k\displaystyle\sum_{i \neq j}\sigma_{ij}}{k-1}$$

Furthermore, the left side of the inequality is an expression for $\sigma_{T_c}^2$, so

$$\sigma_{T_c}^2 \geq \frac{k}{k-1}\sum_{i \neq j}\sigma_{ij} \tag{6.29}$$

where $\Sigma\sigma_{ij}$ is the sum of $k(k-1)$ covariances of tests which may not be strictly parallel. If we divide each side of Equation 6.29 by σ_C^2, we have

$$\frac{\sigma_{T_c}^2}{\sigma_C^2} \geq \frac{k}{k-1}\left(\frac{\displaystyle\sum_{i \neq j}\sigma_{ij}}{\sigma_C^2}\right)$$

which is the same as

$$\rho_{CC'} \geq \frac{k}{k-1}\left(1 - \frac{\displaystyle\sum\sigma_i^2}{\sigma_C^2}\right) \tag{6.30}$$

[handwritten margin notes: $k = $ # of items; $\Sigma\sigma_i^2$ — sum of each of variances; σ_c — variance of composite *]*

The expression at the right side of Equation 6.30 is commonly known as *coefficient alpha*. To summarize, the theoretical reliability coefficient can be characterized as the coefficient of precision (i.e., the correlation that would be obtained between two perfectly parallel forms of the test if there were no changes in examinees between testings). When a composite test is made up of nonparallel subtests, we can estimate the lower bound of its coefficient of precision by using coefficient alpha. This computation requires that we know the number of subtests, the variance of the

[handwritten margin notes: theoretical concept not actual; ability can't be worse this. *]*

composite scores, and the sum of all the subtest covariances. The usefulness of this relationship will be more apparent if we recall that *any* test may be regarded as a composite and each item as a subtest. Thus, as we shall see in Chapter 7, coefficient alpha provides a convenient way to estimate the lower bound of the coefficient of precision for a test by using item response data obtained from a single administration of that test.

THE STANDARD ERROR OF MEASUREMENT

Reliability is a concept which permits the test user to describe the proportion of true score variance in a group's observed test scores. In many situations, however, the test user is more concerned with how measurement errors affect the interpretation of individuals' scores. Although it is never possible to determine the exact amount of error in a given score, classical test theory provides a method for describing the expected variation of each individual examinee's observed scores about the examinee's true score. Recall that the true score has been defined as the mean, or expected value, of an examinee's observed scores obtained from a large number of repeated testings. Figure 6.2 illustrates the distributions of several examinees' possible observed scores around their true scores within the larger distribution of scores for the total group on a single testing. Just as the total group has a standard deviation, theoretically each examinee's personal distribution of possible observed scores around the examinee's true score has a standard deviation. When these individual error standard deviations are averaged for the group, the result is called the *standard error of measurement* and is denoted as σ_E. An expression for the standard error of measurement can be derived by using the relationship

$$\sigma_T^2 + \sigma_E^2 = \sigma_X^2$$

Dividing both sides of this equation by σ_X^2,   *error is assumed to be random*
                                                            ∴ normal curve

$$\frac{\sigma_T^2}{\sigma_X^2} + \frac{\sigma_E^2}{\sigma_X^2} = 1$$

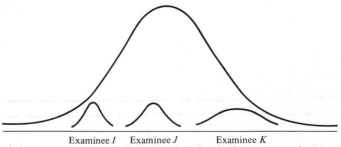

Examinee *I*   Examinee *J*   Examinee *K*

FIGURE 6.2   Hypothetical Illustration of Different Examinees' Distributions of Observed Scores Around Their True Scores

Note that the first term in the left-hand expression is the definition of $\rho_{XX'}$ so

$$\rho_{XX'} + \frac{\sigma_E^2}{\sigma_X^2} = 1$$

To solve for σ_E, note that

$$\frac{\sigma_E^2}{\sigma_X^2} = 1 - \rho_{XX'}$$

and

$$\sigma_E = \sigma_X\sqrt{1 - \rho_{XX'}} \qquad \text{\Large ✳}$$

(6.31)

[handwritten margin notes: σ_x = standard error for group]

[handwritten margin notes: $\rho_{XX'}$ = test reliability coefficient.]

Thus if the standard deviation for a set of observed test scores is known to be 10 points and the test reliability coefficient is $\rho_{XX'} = .91$, the value of the standard error of measurement could be computed as follows:

$$\sigma_E = 10\sqrt{1 - .91} = 3.0$$

Assuming that random errors of measurement are normally distributed, we would expect approximately 68% of an examinee's observed scores to lie in the interval, $T \pm 1\sigma_E$, and approximately 95% of the examinee's observed scores to lie in the interval, $T \pm 1.96\sigma_E$, or with rounding, $T \pm 2\sigma_E$.

In most testing situations, the examinee is tested once, and only one observed score is obtained. Thus even if we have an estimate of the standard error of measurement for the test, we cannot actually construct such an interval around an examinee's true score because the actual value of the true score is unknown. Instead, we use the estimated value of the standard error to create a confidence interval around the examinee's observed score of the form $X \pm 1\sigma_E$. We can be 68% confident that the true score lies within this interval. At first it may seem that some sleight of hand has been invoked to substitute the observed score for the true score in the confidence interval, but this is not really the case. Suppose that Jan's true score on a political activism attitude scale is 50 and the standard error of measurement is estimated to be 5 points. Theoretically if Jan could be tested 100 times, approximately 68 of those observed scores would lie within 5 points of the true score, between 45 and 55, but approximately 32 scores would lie outside the interval 45 to 55.

If we generated a confidence interval around each of Jan's 100 observed score values, approximately 68 of these intervals would be generated around observed scores between 45 and 55 and each of these intervals would contain Jan's true score. Testing Jan only once (as we would do in real life) is analogous to drawing a single observed score at random from this pool of 100 possible observed scores. On a single testing, there is a 68% chance that we will obtain one of the possible observed scores that lies in the range 45 to 55. When we generate a 5-point confidence interval around any of these values, that interval will include 50, the true score value. If we are unlucky enough to draw one of the 32 observed scores which lies outside the 45 to 55 interval, the 5-point interval generated around that observed score will not contain the true score value. For this reason it is important to remem-

[handwritten notes at bottom: Confidence interval — gives range of #'s from low to hi & probability that number is in there.]

[handwritten note at bottom left: ple: $\sigma_X = 15$ $\rho = .87$ $\sigma_E = 15\sqrt{1 - .87} = 5.41$]

> *if willing to be less precise can be more confident acore is in there (in CI)*

Also 95% v. useful = 2 standard deviation or 2 score of 1.96

>68% = 1 standard deviation or 2 score of 1

ber that any single observed score may be a poor estimate of the individual's true score. The standard error of measurement is useful for providing an estimate of how far the true score may lie from an observed score for an average examinee in the population, but there is no absolute guarantee that an individual's true score really falls in a confidence interval generated around the observed score. In addition, it should be noted that the value of σ_E reflects an average of many examinees' individual standard errors. It is probably not realistic to suppose that these standard errors are equal for all examinees. More specific guidelines for using the standard error of measurement in score interpretation will be presented in Chapter 7.

In 95% CI

example: observed score of 140 $140 \pm 1.96 (5.4) = 140 \pm 10.60 = 129.4 \ to \ 150.6$

(σ_E)

ALTERNATE DEFINITIONS OF TRUE SCORE AND ERROR

Until now, an examinee's true score has been interpreted as the average of a large number of observed scores earned by that examinee in repeated testings on the same test or on strictly parallel forms of the test. There are, however, alternative theories of true scores and measurement errors which use other assumptions. One well known alternative involves testing situations where we regard the test given as just one of many possible test forms that could have been comprised from a larger pool of items. In such cases, the measurement obtained is an examinee's score on a single test form, but the measurement of interest is how the examinee would have performed on the larger item pool. Lord (1955, 1957, and 1959b) redefined true scores and errors of measurement in this context, which can be described as follows. Consider a large pool of dichotomously scored items. Two or more test forms may be constructed by drawing items randomly from this pool. Such *randomly parallel test forms* need not have equal means or equal variances, nor do the items have to be closely matched in content from form to form. Examinee *a*'s true score may be regarded as the number of items in this pool which the examinee can answer correctly, but it is usually more convenient to define the true score as the *proportion* of items in the pool which the examinee can answer correctly (P_a). If we want to define the true score for examinee *a* on a test of fixed length, where *n* is the number of items, then

$$T_a = nP_a$$

Suppose we designate one randomly generated set of items as test for *g*. Then X_{ga} represents examinee *a*'s observed score on test form *g*. Obviously form *g* is only one of many possible test forms that could have been generated from the item pool. Thus there is a frequency distribution of possible test values for examinee *a*, resulting from different test forms, which are randomly distributed around T_a. The standard error of measurement for examinee *a* is defined as the standard deviation of this theoretical distribution of possible observed scores around examinee *a*'s true score.

To apply these concepts in a specific testing situation, imagine a computer item bank of 1,000 test items written to cover the content of a course in introductory psychology. Suppose that examinee Alice Doe can answer 750 items in the item bank. For Alice, $P_a = .75$. When Alice takes her final examination, a test form of 100 items will be randomly generated for her. Her true score on a test of 100 items would be

$$nP_a = 100(.75) = 75$$

On form g, however, Alice may answer 80 items correctly; on form h, she might answer 73 items correctly; and so on. Theoretically we could compute Alice's standard error of measurement by testing her repeatedly on all possible 100-item forms and computing the standard deviation of these scores. In reality we cannot do this. Instead, a practical procedure for estimating this standard error of measurement is based on the fact that the frequency distribution of Alice's scores on all possible 100-item randomly parallel tests approximates a *binomial* distribution.[4]

A binomial distribution is the type of frequency distribution that is relevant when we consider the probability of obtaining from 50 coin tosses 1 head and 49 tails, 2 heads and 48 tails, 3 heads and 47 tails, and so on. We know that there are only two possible outcomes for each toss, and there is a probability of obtaining either outcome. The general formula for the binomial distribution is

$$f(X) = \frac{n!}{X!(n-X)!} P^X Q^{n-X} \tag{6.32}$$

where, in the coin-toss example, X represents the number of times the coin comes up heads, n represents the number of tosses, P represents the probability of obtaining a head on a single toss, and Q the probability of obtaining a tail on a single toss. Three properties of the binomial distribution which will be useful in our testing situation are

1. The mean of a binomial distribution is given by the formula

$$\mu = nP$$

2. The variance of a binomial distribution is given by the formula

$$\sigma^2 = nPQ$$

3. When the variance of the distribution must be estimated from data from a sample, the formula for the sample variance is

$$\hat{\sigma}^2 = n\hat{P}\hat{Q}\left(\frac{n}{n-1}\right) \tag{6.33}$$

where $\hat{P}$ and $\hat{Q}$ are probabilities from sample data, and $\dfrac{n}{n-1}$ is a correction for obtaining unbiased estimates of population variance.

In our example, the distribution of Alice's possible test scores is similar to a binomial distribution because the selection of each item for a test form is like the

[4] Strictly speaking a binomial distribution would require an infinite item pool.

toss of a coin: As each item is chosen, it will either be an item that Alice can answer correctly or it will not. Furthermore the probability is .75 that it will be an item that Alice can answer; the probability is .25 that the item chosen will be an item she cannot answer. Alice's total score on the test is the total number of items chosen which she can answer correctly. It is directly analogous to the number of coin tosses which come up "heads." The frequency of any particular total test score could be determined from the binomial formula in Equation 6.32.

In an actual testing situation Alice would take only one form of the test. Thus we would know only her observed score on that test, X_{ga}, and her observed proportion correct, $\hat{P}_{ga}$. How can this information be used to estimate her standard error of measurement? If we regard her observed proportion correct, $\hat{P}_{ga}$, as an estimate of her population value P_a, we can use Equation 6.33 to estimate the variance of Alice's scores on all possible test forms:

$$\hat{\sigma}_a^2 = n(\hat{P}_{ga}\hat{Q}_{ga})\left(\frac{n}{n-1}\right)$$
(6.34)

By recalling that $\hat{P}_{ga} = X_{ga}/n$, and $\hat{Q}_{ga} = 1 - \hat{P}_{ga}$, we arrive at

$$\hat{\sigma}_a = \sqrt{\frac{X_{ga}(n - X_{ga})}{n-1}}$$
(6.35)

Equation 6.35 is the computational formula for the standard error of measurement of randomly parallel tests. For Alice Doe, who scored 80 points on form g, consisting of 100 items, the estimate of her standard error of measurement would be

$$\hat{\sigma}_a = \sqrt{\frac{80(100 - 80)}{99}} = 4.02$$

For another examinee, who scored 50 points on a 100-item randomly parallel test from the same item bank, the estimated standard error of measurement would be 5.02. The results of these two examples illustrate an important distinction between the binomial standard error of measurement and that from the classical true score model. With the classical true score model, typically only one standard error of measurement is estimated, but different binomial standard errors are estimated for different true scores. Binomial standard errors are larger for true scores in the middle of the possible score range and smaller for scores at the extremes. (The binomial standard error is largest when $P_a = .50$.) Because of this distinction different measurement error models may be more appropriate in some practical contexts than others.

The context for classical test theory was the measurement of individual differences using the same instrument to measure all examinees. The standard error of measurement from classical test theory is clearly useful in this context. However, if different tests are used to measure individual differences (as in a computer-generated test, which differs for different examinees) or if an absolute interpretation of the score (rather than a comparative interpretation) is of interest, other types of standard errors will be more appropriate. With dichotomously scored items, the binomial standard error is appropriate for the two situations just described. In addition, the binomial model developed by Keats and Lord (1962) and the compound binomial model developed by Lord (1965) can be used to address problems that cannot be solved with the classical true score model. For example, the binomial model can be used to estimate the degree of consistency between classifications of examinees based on observed scores and those based on true scores. This is potentially important in criterion-referenced testing. The compound binomial can be used to test whether two instruments measure the same trait. This would have potential usefulness for the investigations of test score validity. Such applications, however, are purchased at a price of stronger assumptions than are made in classical test theory. For this reason, the classical true score model will continue to be used in many situations involving a test constructed to optimize measurement of individual differences because it provides solutions to a wide range of tractible measurement problems and requires fairly minimal assumptions.

SUMMARY

Reliability refers to the consistency of examinees' relative performances over repeated administrations of the same test or parallel forms of the test. A major source of inconsistency in individual test performance is random measurement error. It is incumbent upon test developers and test users to try to determine the extent to which random measurement errors influence test performance. The classical true score model provides a theoretical framework for the development of practical reliability investigations.

The classical true score model is based on the conceptualization of an individual test score as a random variable. An examinee's score on a particular test is viewed as a random sample of one of many possible test scores that a person could have earned under repeated administrations of the same test (or a strictly parallel form of that test). Each observed test score can be regarded as the sum of the examinee's true score and a random error component. The true score is defined as the expected value of the examinee's test scores over many repeated testings with the same test. From these definitions three important properties of true and error scores may be deduced:

1. The mean of the errors for an examinee population is zero.
2. The correlation between true and error scores is zero.
3. The correlation between errors on distinct measurements is zero.

Using the classical true score model, a reliability coefficient is defined as the correlation between parallel measures. This coefficient ($\rho_{XX'}$) can be shown to equal the ratio σ_T^2/σ_X^2, the proportion of observed score variance due to true score variance. The correlation between true and observed scores on a single measure is called the reliability index and is equivalent to σ_T/σ_X.

Using test data, it is possible to estimate the reliability coefficient for an instrument in several different ways by two test administrations yielding the coefficients of stability, equivalence, or stability and equivalence. Reliability estimates from one test administration are obtained by using formulas for the reliability of a composite. When the elements of the composite may be considered to be perfectly parallel measurements, the reliability coefficient can be defined in terms of the component variances and covariances. When the components are not perfectly parallel, the lower bound of the reliability coefficient for the composite can be defined in terms of the component variances and covariances.

The standard error of measurement is defined as $\sigma_E = \sigma_X \sqrt{1 - \rho_{XX'}}$ and may be considered as the average standard deviation of examinees' individual error distributions for a large number of repeated testings. The standard error of measurement is useful for generating a confidence interval around an observed test score which has a known probability of containing the examinee's true score. The classical standard error of measurement has one value for all examinees in the population. It has been useful in many contexts when measurement of individual differences is desired. An alternate approach to the standard error of measurement has been proposed by Lord (1955) for use when a test form is generated by randomly sampling items from a well-defined domain. This binomial standard error is a function of an examinee's true score and the number of items on the test. Consequently this standard error of measurement differs for examinees with different ability levels. Such an index may be applicable in situations where different examinees take different test forms drawn from the same item pool.

Exercises

1. In each situation indicate whether the event described contributes to random or systematic measurement error in an examinee's test score.
   A. An observer rating counseling behavior during a counselor-client interview tends to rate female counselors more highly than males on items dealing with client rapport.
   B. An examinee taking a math test is distracted by noise in a nearby hallway and consequently makes an error in computing the answer.
   C. Jane often becomes so anxious during testing situations that she often leaves many items unanswered.
   D. A grader reading an essay test skips over one sentence, which renders the remainder of the student's response ambiguous.
   E. A student in a psychology class miscopies a statement from the instructor's lecture and later incorrectly answers an item based on this misinformation.
2. A three-item test is to be given to a population of four examinees. The following table shows the hypothetical proportional distribution of test scores for each examinee over many repeated testings.

Examinee	Score			
	0	1	2	3
1	.5	.5	0	0
2	.25	.25	.25	.25
3	0	0	.5	.5
4	0	.5	.5	0

A. What is the true score for examinee 3?

B. What is the true score for examinee 2?

C. What is the true score variance on this test?

D. What is the error score variance for examinee 3?

E. What is the error score variance for examinee 2?

F. What is the reliability coefficient for this test?

G. If you gave this test on two occasions, give examples of two possible sets of scores that might be obtained for these four examinees.

H. In actual testing situations, is it possible to determine test score reliability by the method used in F? Why?

3. A research psychologist administered three parallel forms of a standardized test to subjects in a study. The response sheets were scored with an optical scanner. Later the researcher was informed that the scanner had been malfunctioning, introducing occasional scoring errors at random intervals on the day the tests were scored. Because the researcher had used only the mean score for each subject averaged over the three tests, the researcher saw no need to have the tests rescored since the effects of these random errors should have been "averaged out" to zero over the three tests. Is this a correct interpretation of the assumption that the mean measurement error score should equal zero?

4. John has taken a group test of academic aptitude, earning a deviation I.Q. score of 135 points. He is then tested with an individual aptitude test, earning a deviation I.Q. of 110 points. John's teacher notes that the discrepancy between these scores is much larger than the standard error of measurement for either test. The instructor does not understand how this can happen and also wonders which test is a better measure of John's "true score." How would you explain this, using classical true score theory?

5. Show that the covariance between observed scores on two tests is equivalent to the covariance between their true scores; in other words, prove that

$$\sigma_{X_1X_2} = \sigma_{T_1T_2}$$

$$\left(\text{Remember that } \sigma_{X_1X_2} = \frac{\Sigma x_1 x_2}{N} \right)$$

6. **A.** Show that when tests i and j are strictly parallel,

$$\sigma_{T_i}^2 = \sigma_{ij}$$

B. Does knowledge of this relationship have any practical use in test development?

7. A personnel psychologist wishes to create a variable (Y) by adding together management trainees' raw scores on a measure of achievement motivation (X_1) and supervision aptitude (X_2). In a test manual the psychologist finds information on the reliabilities and variances for X_1 and X_2 and the correlation between X_1 and X_2. Derive a formula for expressing the reliability of Y in terms of these parameters.

8. Table 6.2 reports the correlations between all pairs of subtests on an achievement battery and the means, standard deviations, and alternate form reliabilities for the subtests from an administration to students at the beginning of second grade. Use the table to answer the following questions.

A. What is the correlation between Word Attack Skills and Social Studies?

B. What is the covariance between these two variables?

C. A total reading score can be formed by adding scores from Word Attack and Reading Comprehension. What is the variance of the total reading score?

D. What is the reliability of the total reading scores?

E. A cognitive psychologist forms a variable by adding together Vocabulary, Language,

TABLE 6.2.   Hypothetical Data from a Manual of an Achievement Battery for Use in Exercise 8

Subtest Name	Subtest Number	1	2	3	4	5	6	7
Vocabulary	1	1.00	.66	.63	.68	.69	.65	.69
Word Attack Skills	2		1.00	.87	.85	.61	.61	.55
Reading Comprehension	3			1.00	.83	.57	.59	.53
Language	4				1.00	.62	.62	.55
Math Concepts	5					1.00	.72	.64
Science Concepts	6						1.00	.61
Social Studies	7							1.00
Standard deviation		6.67	8.79	8.39	10.12	4.97	6.65	4.33
Mean		19.8	22.0	18.0	37.7	16.7	15.6	16.0
Alternate form reliability		.87	.95	.95	.94	.81	.90	.81

and Social Studies. What is the correlation between this new variable and the total reading score?

F. If an examinee earns a score of 22 on the Science Concepts subtest, within what interval can we be 68% sure that his or her true score lies?

G. Under the assumptions of the classical true score model, what should a scatterplot of the error scores on the math and science subtests look like?

Chapter 7

PROCEDURES FOR ESTIMATING RELIABILITY

In the preceding chapter a theoretical model was presented for characterizing the influence of random errors on test scores. According to the classical true score model, the reliability coefficient was defined as the correlation between strictly parallel tests. The reliability coefficient was shown also to be equivalent to the proportion of observed score variance that is attributable to variance in examinees' true scores. In practice, however, the test developer cannot be assured of creating perfectly parallel measurements, nor can examinees' true scores be obtained. Then how can the reliability coefficient for a set of measurements be determined? The answer is that a reliability coefficient for a set of scores can never be determined exactly; it can, however, be *estimated* for a given sample of individuals responding to a given sample of test items. Note that the term *estimate* does not refer to looking at the data and making a guess about their reliability but rather to computing a numeric value from a sample of observations, which is an estimate of the theoretical quantity under investigation. The use of a "^" above the statistical symbols for mean, variance, and correlation in this chapter signifies that these quantities are calculated for a sample rather than a population.

The purpose of this chapter is to describe the procedures commonly used to estimate test score reliability. The data to be used in estimating reliability coefficients can be collected by a variety of procedures, and there are at least two viewpoints about how one chooses the most appropriate method. One view is that the optimal procedure yields an estimate of the correlation that would be obtained if scores of strictly parallel test forms were available. Thus the reliability study is designed to minimize the effect of nonparallel measurements by using measurements that are as nearly parallel as possible. A second point of view (which forms the basis for this chapter and the following chapter on generalizability theory) is that

131

the most appropriate procedure is dictated by the intended use of the test scores. The test developer should identify the sources of measurement error that would be most detrimental to useful score interpretation and design a reliability study that permits such errors to occur so that their effects can be assessed.

PROCEDURES REQUIRING TWO TEST ADMINISTRATIONS

Alternate Form Method

Is there unreliability that comes from test content ?

Suppose that all candidates for entry into a particular health occupation must take a state board examination, which is administered under controlled conditions at a particular site on a given date. To reduce the possibility of cheating, examinees in adjacent seats take different forms of the test covering the same content. Clearly each examinee has the right to expect that his or her score would not be greatly affected by the particular form of the test taken. In this case, the errors of measurement that primarily concern test users are those due to differences in content of the test forms. Of course, administration and scoring errors, guessing, and temporary fluctuations in examinees' performance may also contribute to inconsistency of scores. To address these concerns, the test developer should estimate the test reliability coefficient by using the *alternate form* method.

develop parallel forms of test

The alternate form method requires constructing two similar forms of a test and administering both forms to the same group of examinees. The forms should be administered within a very short time period, allowing only enough time between testings so that examinees will not be fatigued. It is considered desirable to balance the order of administration of the forms so that half the examinees are randomly assigned to form 1 followed by form 2, whereas the other half take form 2 followed by form 1. The correlation coefficient between the two sets of scores is then computed, usually with the Pearson product moment formula. This correlation coefficient is called the *coefficient of equivalence*. The higher the coefficient of equivalence, the more confident test users can be that scores from the different test forms may be used interchangeably.

Any test that has multiple forms should have some evidence of their equivalence. Typically, tests of achievement and aptitude are constructed with multiple forms since some clinical, educational, or research uses require the examinee to have an opportunity to retake the examination, and the test user does not want to use the same items for the second test. Although there are no hard, fast rules for what constitutes a minimally acceptable value for alternate form reliability estimates, many standardized achievement test manuals report coefficients ranging in the .80s and .90s for this type of reliability. In addition, values of the means, standard deviations, and standard errors of measurement should be reported for each form, and these should be quite similar if the coefficient of equivalence is interpreted as a reliability estimate.

should be very similar

Test-Retest Method

Does a person's performance on test vary because of temporary issues. e.g. does performance

There are many testing situations in which one form of the test is sufficient but the test user is interested in how consistently examinees respond to this form at different times. In this situation the measurement errors of primary concern are the fluctuations of an examinee's observed scores around the true score because of temporary changes in the examinee's state. Again, however, errors due to administration, scoring, guessing, mismarking by examinees, and other temporary fluctuations in behavior may have an impact on observed scores. To estimate the impact of such errors on test score reliability, the test constructor administers the test to a group of examinees, waits, readministers the same test to the same group, and then computes the correlation coefficient between the two sets of scores. The correlation coefficient obtained from this test-retest procedure is called the *coefficient of stability*.

Evidence of the degree of stability in test scores is desirable for tests that may be used to place examinees in long-term programs. Few, if any, standards exist for judging the minimum acceptable value for a test-retest reliability estimate. Among the highest test-retest coefficients reported for commercially published tests are those of individually administered aptitude tests. For example, for subscales of the Wechsler Adult Intelligence Scale (WAIS), coefficients with values in the .70s, .80s, and even low .90s have been reported (see Wechsler, 1958). Test-retest reliabilities for personality, interest, or attitude measures are often lower than those for aptitude tests, but well-constructed instruments measuring clearly defined traits may still have test-retest coefficients in the .80s. For example, the Strong Vocational Interest Blank (1966 edition) has been reported to have short-term reliability coefficients in the .80s and long-term coefficients in the lower .60s, even after a duration of 20 years (Kaplan and Saccuzzo, 1982, p. 341). As we shall see in the ensuing discussion, critical factors in evaluating the magnitude of a stability estimate must include the elapsed time between testings and the age of the examinees as well as the nature of the theoretical trait itself.

A critical question in the design of a test-retest study is this: How much time should elapse between testings? There is no single answer. The time period should be long enough to allow effects of memory or practice to fade but not so long as to allow maturational or historical changes to occur in the examinees' true scores. The purpose for which the test scores are to be used should be taken into account in designating the waiting time. For example, consider a test to assess the level of an infant's psychomotor development. There is little danger that the baby will remember previous responses; there is, however, the strong possibility that maturation will cause changes in performance if the delay between testings is too long. Furthermore, such scores are not used for long-range prediction but are generally used for planning an immediate program of medical or psychological intervention, which will be reevaluated in a short period of time. Considering all these things, a waiting period of one day to one week might be appropriate. In contrast, consider an adult vocational interest inventory. Adults are quite likely to remember some of their responses to test items over relatively long periods, and hypothetically vocational interest should be stable over a long time span since most adults engage in the same type of job for years. Furthermore, the scores from such instruments are used to advise examinees about academic or vocational training programs which may require several weeks to several years for completion. If examinees' interests, as measured by this instrument, fluctuate greatly within the time span of a typical training period, this information should be available to potential test users. All things considered, it would not be unreasonable to allow six months to two years to elapse when conducting a test-retest study for such an instrument. Whatever the time period between testings, it is important to recognize that different test-retest coefficients may result if different time periods are chosen.

The interpretation of a stability coefficient as an estimate of reliability raises some interesting questions. When a low coefficient is obtained, does this indicate that the test provides unreliable measures of the trait, or does it imply that the trait itself is unstable? If the test user believes that the amounts of the trait that examinees possess should change over time, a basic assumption of the classical true score model has been violated and the obtained correlation coefficient is not an appropriate estimate of test score reliability. A second issue is whether an examinee's behavior is altered by the first test administration so that the second test score will reflect effects of memory, practice, learning, boredom, sensitization, or any other consequences of the first measurement. In view of these issues it is probably sensible to assume that the test-retest coefficient represents a somewhat inaccurate estimate of the theoretical reliability coefficient. Nevertheless, information on test score stability is critical to test score users in many practical testing situations.

Test-Retest with Alternate Forms *need very cooperative subjects*

Reliability coefficients may also be estimated by using a combination of the test-retest and alternate form methods. In this case, the procedure is to administer form 1 of the test, wait, and then administer form 2. If possible, it is desirable that the order of administration of the forms be reversed for half the group. The correlation coefficient between the two sets of scores is known as the *coefficient of stability and equivalence*. This coefficient is affected by errors of measurement due to content sampling in construction of the forms as well as to changes in individuals' performances over time and virtually all the other types of errors previously described. Such reliability estimates are usually lower than either a coefficient of equivalence or a coefficient of stability determined for the same test on the same group of examinees.

METHODS REQUIRING A SINGLE TEST ADMINISTRATION

There are many testing situations when a single form of a test will be administered only once to a group of examinees. The most common example is a teacher-made classroom test. The instructor usually makes up only one form and administers it to all students. Furthermore, the instructor would not necessarily expect students' performance to be consistent on this test over time since students will continue to learn (or forget) the material at different rates. Yet it is still quite appropriate to be interested in the extent to which the observed score variance for the examinees reflects their true score variance on this test at this time. As in most testing situations the examiner is not primarily concerned with how the examinees score on these items per se; usually the examiner wants to generalize from these specific items to a larger content domain of possible items that might have been asked. One way to estimate how consistently examinees' performance on this test can be generalized to the domain of items that might have been asked is to determine how consistently the examinees performed across items or subsets of items on this single test form. Procedures designed to estimate reliability in this circumstance are called *internal consistency* methods. All the internal consistency estimation procedures introduced in this chapter yield values that are functions of the correlation between separately scored parts of a test. In fact, several procedures yield values that are functions of the correlations between separately scored halves of a test. It is reasonable to think of the correlation between subsets of items as providing some information about the extent to which they were constructed according to the same specifications. If examinees' performance is consistent across subsets of items within a test, the examiner can have some confidence that this performance would generalize to other possible items in the content domain. In conducting an internal consistency study, we are primarily concerned about errors caused by content sampling, although errors of measurement because of faulty administration and scoring, guessing, and temporary fluctuations of individual performance within the testing session may also affect the internal consistency coefficient.

When examinees perform consistently across items within a test, the test is said to have *item homogeneity*. In order for a group of items to be homogeneous, they must measure the same type of performance (or represent the same content domain). The items must also be well written and free of technical flaws that may cause examinees to respond on some basis unrelated to the content. When items on a single test are drawn from diverse areas (e.g., math, history, and literature), examinees probably will not perform consistently across these items and internal consistency coefficients will be reduced. Similarly, if items come from a single area, for example, history, but some items test major concepts and others are based on minor points mentioned only in the footnotes of the text, it is again likely that internal consistency of performance will be low. Finally, even if all items are fair representatives of the content domain, but some are poorly written so that examinees may misinterpret the questions or answer based on their degrees of "test wiseness" rather than their knowledge, this will again lower internal consistency. Thus, it is always appropriate to investigate the internal consistency of a test since the internal consistency coefficient is an index of both item content homogeneity and item quality.

In the following sections two broad classes of methods for estimating the reliability coefficient for a single test administration will be presented. The first is generally denoted as "split-half" procedures. The second class of methods requires an analysis of the variance-covariance structure of the item responses. All the methods yield an index of the internal consistency of the examinees' responses to the items within a single test form.

Split-Half Methods

Using the split-half method, the test developer administers one form of the test to a group of examinees. Before scoring the test, however, the test developer divides the items into two subtests, each half the length of the original test. Thus, if a 20-item test were administered, it would be divided into two half-tests of 10 items each. The intention is to create two half-tests which are as nearly parallel as possible. Four popular methods for dividing a test into halves are to

1. Assign all odd-numbered items to form 1 and all even-numbered items to form 2
2. Rank order the items in terms of their difficulty levels (p-values) based on the responses of the examinees; then assign items with odd-numbered ranks to form 1 and those with even-numbered ranks to form 2
3. Randomly assign items to the two half-test forms
4. Assign items to half-test forms so that the forms are "matched" in content

The two half-tests are then scored separately for each examinee, and the correlation coefficient is computed between these two sets of scores. This process is illustrated in Table 7.1. Conceptually this correlation coefficient is the coefficient of equivalence for the two halves of the test. Note, however, that the coefficient obtained

TABLE 7.1. Illustrative Data for Split-Half Reliability Estimation

Examinee	Item 1	2	3	4	5	6	Subtest A (Odd)	Subtest B (Even)	Total
1	0	0	0	0	0	0	0	0	0
2	0	0	0	0	1	0	1	0	1
3	1	0	1	1	1	0	3	1	4
4	1	1	1	1	1	1	3	3	6
5	1	1	1	1	1	1	3	3	6
6	0	0	1	0	0	0	1	0	1
7	0	0	1	1	1	0	2	1	3
8	0	0	0	1	0	0	0	1	1
9	1	0	1	1	1	0	3	1	4
10	0	1	0	1	0	1	0	3	3
	Mean						1.6	1.3	2.9
	Standard deviation						1.28	1.19	2.02

$\hat{\rho}_{AB} = .34$

$$\hat{\rho}_{XX'} = \frac{2(.34)}{1 + .34} = .51$$

from this procedure is likely to be an underestimate of the reliability coefficient for the full-length test (longer tests are generally more reliable than shorter tests since errors of measurement because of content sampling are reduced). To overcome this problem, the test developer can employ the Spearman Brown prophecy formula to obtain the corrected estimate of the reliability coefficient of the full-length test. When applied to the correlation between half-tests, this formula is written as

$$\rho_{XX'_n} = \frac{2\rho_{AB}}{1 + \rho_{AB}} \tag{7.1}$$

where $\rho_{XX'}$ is the reliability projected for the full-length test and ρ_{AB} is the correlation between the half-tests. Thus, if the correlation between two half-tests of three items each is .34, the corrected reliability estimate for the full six-item test would be

$$\hat{\rho}_{XX'} = \frac{2(.34)}{1 + .34} = .51$$

Users of the Spearman Brown correction should note that this procedure is based on the assumption that the half-tests are strictly parallel. The greater the violation of this assumption, the less accurate will be the results obtained.

An alternate method for estimating the reliability from half-test scores, which does not require the use of the Spearman Brown correction, was proposed by Rulon (1939). This method involves the use of the difference score between the half-tests:

$$D = A - B \tag{7.2}$$

where A is the examinee's score on the first half-test and B is the score on the second half-test. The variance of these difference scores, σ_D^2 is used as an estimate of σ_E^2 in the definitional formula of the reliability coefficient so that

$$\hat{\rho}_{XX'} = 1 - \frac{\hat{\sigma}_D^2}{\hat{\sigma}_X^2} \tag{7.3}$$

If the difference score for each examinee in Table 7.1 is computed and the variance of these differences is determined, we obtain a reliability estimate of

$$\hat{\rho}_{XX'} = 1 - \frac{2.24}{4.08} = .45$$

Although Rulon's method is probably the simplest to use for hand computations, it is equivalent to another formula for split-half reliability estimation usually attributed to Guttman (1945) or Flanagan (Kelley, 1942).

Thus, we have seen how data obtained from administering a test only once can be divided into two parts. The scores obtained from those two parts may be treated in one of two ways:

1. The correlation between half-tests can be computed and corrected with the Spearman Brown formula.
2. The scores from the two half-tests can be used in the Rulon or Guttman methods to estimate the reliability of the full-length test.

How similar are the results obtained from the Spearman Brown and Rulon procedures? When the variances of the two half-tests are equal, the procedures yield identical estimates. Furthermore, Cronbach (1951) demonstrated that when the ratio of the standard deviations of the two half-tests lies between .90 and 1.1, the procedures yield virtually the same results. As the standard deviations grow increasingly dissimilar, correlations between half-tests corrected by the Spearman Brown technique are systematically larger than those obtained from Rulon's formula.

One drawback of using the split-half procedure with either Spearman Brown or Rulon analysis is that it does not yield a unique estimate of the test's reliability coefficient. There are many possible ways of dividing a test into halves. As Brownell (1933) noted in an early discussion of this problem, there are actually $\frac{1}{2}k!/[(\frac{1}{2}k)!]^2$ different ways of dividing the test of k items into halves, and these different divisions can result in different reliability estimates. Clearly this is cause for concern.

Methods Based on Item Covariances

The lack of a unique estimate for the internal consistency of test scores from a single sample of examinees on one occasion was a problem that received much attention in the psychometric literature of the 1930s and 1940s. Then within a relatively short time three procedures were proposed which surmounted this problem. Although they appear different in form, the three procedures described here yield identical results. The three widely used procedures are the Kuder Richardson 20, Cronbach's alpha, and Hoyt's analysis of variance. Those who wish to read test manuals, test reviews, or other test development literature must recognize the equivalence of these methods to avoid confusion. We shall use the term *coefficient alpha* to refer to this class of procedures.

COEFFICIENT ALPHA.   In 1951, Cronbach presented a comprehensive synthesis and discussion of various methods for estimating internal consistency and related them to a single general formula known as *Cronbach's alpha*. Coefficient alpha is computed by the formula

$$\hat{\alpha} = \frac{k}{k-1}\left(1 - \frac{\Sigma\hat{\sigma}_i^2}{\hat{\sigma}_X^2}\right) \tag{7.4}$$

where k is the number of items on the test, $\hat{\sigma}_i^2$ is the variance of item i, and $\hat{\sigma}_X^2$ is the total test variance. Alpha can be used to estimate the internal consistency of items which are dichotomously scored or items which have a wide range of scoring weights, such as those on some attitude inventories or essay examinations. For example, suppose that examinees have been tested on four essay items in which possible scores range from 0 to 10 points, and $\hat{\sigma}_1^2 = 9$, $\hat{\sigma}_2^2 = 4.8$, $\hat{\sigma}_3^2 = 10.2$, and $\hat{\sigma}_4^2 = 16$. If total score variance for the examination is $\hat{\sigma}_X^2 = 100$,

$$\hat{\alpha} = \frac{4}{3}\left(1 - \frac{9 + 4.8 + 10.2 + 16}{100}\right) = .80$$

To interpret this value as an estimate of a reliability coefficient, we must note that

Equation 7.4 is simply another way of expressing the formula for the reliability of a composite, which was derived in Chapter 6. In the context of a single test administration, each item constitutes one of the k subtests, and the total test score is the composite. As shown in Chapter 6, if we were willing to assume that all items were perfectly parallel subtests, coefficient alpha would represent a direct estimate of $\rho_{XX'}$ for the total test scores. In most testing situations, however, this assumption is untenable, and so we are restricted to saying that $\alpha \leq \rho_{XX'}$ (an inequality also discussed in Chapter 6). Thus, in the present example, where $\alpha = .80$, we can say that at least 80% of the total score variance is due to true score variance (or covariance that systematically affects performance across items on the test).

KUDER RICHARDSON FORMULAS. As noted earlier in this chapter, coefficient alpha can be computed by several methods other than the general formula presented in Equation 7.4. One of the best known methods is the Kuder Richardson 20. The KR 20 can be used only with dichotomously scored items. This formula was derived by Kuder and Richardson (1937) as they sought a solution to the problem that split-half methods failed to yield a unique result for a given test. Their landmark paper contained two estimation formulas, known today as the KR 20 and the KR 21. The names were taken from the numbered steps in the derivation in the journal article where the formulas were presented. The KR 20 formula is

$$KR_{20} = \frac{k}{k-1}\left(1 - \frac{\Sigma pq}{\hat{\sigma}_X^2}\right) \tag{7.5}$$

where k is the number of items in the test, $\hat{\sigma}_X^2$ is the total test variance, and pq is the variance of item i. (This formula is identical to coefficient alpha with the substitution of $p_i q_i$ for $\hat{\sigma}_i^2$.) Note that the summation indicates that the variance of *each* item must be computed and then these variances summed for all items. Table 7.2 illustrates computation of the KR 20 for the set of item responses presented in Table 7.1.

By assuming that all items were equal in difficulty, Kuder and Richardson also derived a simpler formula, which did not require computing each item variance. The KR 21 formula can be written as

$$KR_{21} = \frac{k}{k-1}\left[1 - \frac{\hat{\mu}(k - \hat{\mu})}{k\hat{\sigma}_X^2}\right] \tag{7.6}$$

where $\hat{\mu}$ is the mean total score, $\hat{\sigma}_X^2$ is the total score variance, and k is the number of items on the test. Table 7.2 also presents an example of the computations of KR 21. When all items are equal in difficulty, the KR 20 and the KR 21 methods will yield equivalent reliability estimates; however, when item difficulties vary, the reliability estimate from the KR 21 will be systematically lower than the estimate obtained from the KR 20. For this reason, it is not generally considered acceptable for a test publisher or researcher to report only the KR 21 reliability estimate for a set of test scores. Classroom teachers or other practitioners who must perform their computations with only pencil and paper or a hand calculator may find the KR 21 sufficient as a lower-bound estimate of the internal consistency coefficient of their tests.

TABLE 7.2.   Illustrative Computation of Kuder Richardson Reliability Estimates for Data in Table 7.1

Item	p	q	pq
1	.40	.60	.24
2	.30	.70	.21
3	.60	.40	.24
4	.70	.30	.21
5	.60	.40	.24
6	.30	.70	.21
			$\Sigma pq = 1.35$

$$(\hat{\mu} = 2.9, \ \hat{\sigma}_X = 2.02, \ \hat{\sigma}_X^2 = 4.08)$$

$$KR_{20} = \frac{k}{k-1}\left(1 - \frac{\Sigma pq}{\hat{\sigma}_2^2}\right) = \frac{6}{5}\left(1 - \frac{1.35}{4.08}\right) = .80$$

$$KR_{21} = \frac{k}{k-1}\left[1 - \frac{\hat{\mu}(k-\hat{\mu})}{k\hat{\sigma}_X^2}\right] = \frac{6}{5}\left[1 - \frac{2.9(6-2.9)}{6(4.08)}\right] = .76$$

HOYT'S METHOD.   Working independently of Kuder and Richardson, Hoyt (1941) developed an approach to the estimation of reliability which also yields results identical to those obtained from coefficient alpha. Hoyt's method was based on the analysis of variance, treating persons and items as sources of variation. Using standard analysis of variance notation, he defined the reliability estimate as

$$\hat{\rho}_{XX'} = \frac{MS_{persons} - MS_{residual}}{MS_{persons}} \tag{7.7}$$

where $MS_{persons}$ is the mean square term for persons taken from the analysis of variance summary table, and $MS_{residual}$ is the mean square term for the residual variance in the same table. Table 7.3 is the analysis of variance summary table for the item responses in Table 7.1 and illustrates the calculation of Hoyt's coefficient. Hoyt related his formula to the theoretical definition of the reliability coefficient by noting that $MS_{persons}$ represents the observed score variance and $MS_{residual}$ repre-

TABLE 7.3.   Summary Table for Hoyt's Analysis of Variance for Item Responses from Table 7.1

Source of Variance	Sums Squares	df	Mean Squares
Persons	6.817	9	.7574
Items	1.483	5	.2967
Residual	6.683	45	.1485

$$\hat{\rho}_{XX'} = \frac{MS_{persons} - MS_{residual}}{MS_{persons}} = \frac{.7574 - .1485}{.7574} = .8039$$

sents the error variance in the theoretical reliability expression

$$\rho_{XX'} = \frac{\sigma_X^2 - \sigma_E^2}{\sigma_X^2}$$

Because Hoyt's method requires knowledge of a slightly more complex statistical procedure than other formulas for computing coefficient alpha, the reader may wonder why it has been mentioned here. The primary reason is that analysis of variance is a general statistical procedure that is more widely available in computer software packages than are programs written specifically for computing alpha by any other method. This knowledge can save programming efforts for test users who want to use computerized data processing for estimating reliability from a single set of item responses.

As an aid to the reader in summarizing the major approaches to reliability estimation discussed in this chapter, Table 7.4 indicates the sources of error that affect type of estimate and the appropriate data-collection and analysis procedures to use for each type.

TABLE 7.4. **Summary of Approaches to Reliability Estimation**

Major Error Source	Reliability Coefficient	Data-Collection Procedure	Statistical Treatment of Data
1. Change in examinee's overtime	1. Stability coefficient	1. Test, wait, retest	1. Compute Pearson product moment coefficient, $\hat{\rho}_{12}$
2. Content sampling from form to form	2. Equivalence coefficient	2. Give form 1, give form 2	2. Compute Pearson product moment coefficient, $\hat{\rho}_{12}$
3. Content sampling, or flawed items	3. Internal consistency coefficient	3. Give one form on one occasion	3a. Divide test into halves; correlate half-test, $\hat{\rho}_{AB}$; use Spearman Brown correction: $$\hat{\rho}_{XX'} = \frac{2\hat{\rho}_{AB}}{1 + \hat{\rho}_{AB}}$$ b. Divide test into halves; use Guttman's or Rulon's formula: $$\hat{\rho}_{XX'} = 1 - \frac{\hat{\sigma}_D^2}{\hat{\sigma}_X^2}$$ c. Compute item variances; compute coefficient alpha: $$\hat{\alpha} = \frac{k}{k-1}\left(1 - \frac{\Sigma\hat{\sigma}_i^2}{\hat{\sigma}_X^2}\right)$$

Relationship of Alpha to Split-Half Estimates

With the development between 1935 and 1955 of so many procedures for estimating test reliability from a single test administration, it is no wonder that test developers in this period were somewhat confused about which method to use for estimation of internal consistency or how to interpret the estimates obtained (Coombs, 1950a). Particularly, the emergence of alpha and its counterpart procedures sparked controversy about the very nature of test reliability itself. On the one hand, theorists such as Loevinger (1947) thought that item homogeneity was an important test property but nonetheless a distinct concept from the traditional notion of test reliability, defined as the correlation between two parallel forms (or halves) of a test. Kelley (1942) questioned whether it was even reasonable to consider the reliability of one form of a test. On the other hand, Cureton (1958) and others pointed out that reliability could be properly defined as the ratio of true score variance to observed score variance; according to this definition, it seemed quite appropriate to consider the reliability of a single test form. Historically, the latter point of view prevailed, aided by Cronbach (1951), who clarified the relationship between coefficient alpha and split-half estimation procedures. His discussion contained the following points on the appropriate interpretation of coefficient alpha.

1. Coefficient alpha can be used as an index of internal consistency. It is a "characteristic of a test possessed by virtue of the positive intercorrelations of the items composing it" (Kuder and Richardson, 1937). In interpreting coefficient alpha, test users should remember that this estimate implies nothing about the stability of the test scores over time or their equivalence to scores on one particular alternate form of the test.

2. Coefficient alpha can be considered as the lower bound to a theoretical reliability coefficient, known as the *coefficient of precision.* Thus, it is not a direct estimate of the reliability coefficient but rather an estimate of the lower bound of that coefficient. If we obtain a coefficient alpha value of .75, it is impossible to know whether the coefficient of precision is actually higher than this, or how much higher it may be.

3. Alpha is the mean of all possible split-half coefficients that are calculated using the Rulon method. Put another way, if a reliability coefficient is estimated by randomly splitting the test into two halves and computing Rulon's coefficient, alpha is the expected value of that estimate.

4. One common misinterpretation of coefficient alpha is that a relatively high value for alpha indicates that the test items are unidimensional (i.e., that performance on these items can be explained in terms of a single underlying factor). Because alpha is a function of item covariances, and high covariance between items can be the result of more than one common factor, alpha should not be interpreted as a measure of the test's unidimensionality. For example, scores to items on an essay test in social studies may be determined both by examinees' writing abilities and by their knowledge of the content. Thus the test would not be considered unidimensional (measuring only one trait), but because all item scores are affected by these two abilities, the test could have a high value of coefficient alpha. Alpha can be interpreted, therefore, as the lower bound of the proportion of variance in the test scores explained by common factors underlying item performance. McDonald (1981) provides a more recent discussion of this issue, citing several examples and proofs which relate to this point.

Finally, it should be noted that coefficient alpha is generally applicable to any situation where the reliability of a composite is estimated. It could, for example, be applied to estimating the reliability of a total score based upon the sum of several subtest scores. In the most common use of alpha, each item is taken as a subtest, but we could consider the special case in which the total score is the composite of the scores on two half-tests (such as those created in a split-half reliability study). In this special case, with only two components, the coefficient is denoted as α_2 and is identical to the reliability estimate obtained by Rulon's or Guttman's method. Note that the results obtained by using α_2 depend on the composition of the two particular half-tests, and thus its value would not necessarily equal the value of coefficient alpha obtained when each item is treated as a separate component of the total test score composite.

INTERRATER RELIABILITY

For some types of instruments only one set of items is used (e.g., a list of behaviors on a performance checklist), but multiple observations are collected for each examinee by having two or more raters complete the instrument. In this situation, the consistency of the observations over raters may be of interest. To date, the most flexible and useful approach for estimating interrater reliability coefficients is through the application of generalizability, which is discussed in Chapter 8. In addition, other indices of agreement (such as the percentage of agreement among raters on codes assigned to specific items or sets of items) have been reviewed by Frick and Semmel (1978), but these indices, though informative, are conceptually different from reliability estimates and should not be considered substitutes for reliability estimates in describing an observational instrument.

FACTORS THAT AFFECT RELIABILITY COEFFICIENTS

Group Homogeneity

It is apparent that the magnitude of a reliability coefficient depends on variation among individuals on both their true scores and error scores. Thus, the homogeneity of the examinee group is an important consideration in test development and test selection. Suppose that a test has been developed to measure math anxiety. If this test were administered to a group of students in an elective honors math class, these students would probably report similar low levels of math anxiety. Consequently variance among these examinees' true scores would be low, and so would the reliability coefficient. If this same test were administered to a group of similar size composed of a cross-section of all high school students, true scores would be more likely to vary. Assuming that random error variance would be constant for these two groups of equal size, the reliability coefficient should be higher for the second group since their true score variance should account for a much larger percentage of the observed score variance. Table 7.5 presents a hypothetical example of this situation, which illustrates that a test is not "reliable" or "unreliable." Rather, reliability is a property of the scores on a test for a particular group of examinees. Thus, potential test users need to determine whether reliability estimates reported in test manuals are based on samples similar in composition and variability to the group for whom the test will be used. If the test publisher's sample is more heterogeneous on the trait being measured, a reduction in test reliability will result when the test is used on a more homogeneous sample. Parenthetically it should be noted that when a test is too hard or too easy for a group of examinees, restriction of score range and, consequently, of true score variance is likely to be the result.

Gulliksen (1950) presented a historical summary of psychometric discussion of the relationship between group heterogeneity and its effects on test reliability. Magnusson (1967, p. 75) further offered the following formula for predicting how reliability is altered when sample variance is altered:

$$\hat{\rho}_{UU'} = 1 - \frac{\hat{\sigma}_X^2(1 - \hat{\rho}_{XX'})}{\hat{\sigma}_U^2} \tag{7.8}$$

where $\hat{\sigma}_U^2$ is the variance of the new sample, $\hat{\sigma}_X^2$ is the variance of the original sample, $\hat{\rho}_{XX'}$ is the reliability estimate for the original sample, and $\hat{\rho}_{UU'}$ is the predicted reliability estimate for the new sample. It is important to note that this formula assumes that error score variances for the two groups are equal and that changes in observed score variance are due to differences in the groups' true score distributions. Since a test user can never be certain of meeting this assumption, whenever a test user's sample differs considerably from that reported by a test publisher, empirical investigation of the reliability for the new sample is appropriate.

TABLE 7.5.   Reliability Coefficients for Two Hypothetical Groups with Different True Score Variances

	Group 1	Group 2
True score variance	20	60
Error score variance	10	10
Observed score variance	30	70
Reliability coefficient	.67	.85

The dependence of classical reliability on true score variance also implies that reliability coefficients, as defined thus far, have limited usefulness in assessing the quality of information provided by a test used for screening or selection. In these cases the examiner is usually concerned only with whether the examinees score above or below a certain cutoff score. The magnitudes of the true and observed score variances (and their ratio) have less relevance for this measurement process. Reliability for tests used in this way is discussed in Chapter 9.

Time Limit

When a test has a rigid time limit such that some examinees finish but others do not, an examinee's working rate will systematically influence his or her performance on all repeated forms of the test. Thus, variance in the rates at which examinees work becomes part of the true score variance. On some tests (e.g., clerical aptitude tests or math computation tests for adults) the test constructor's goal may be to assess the ability to perform the tasks rapidly. On other kinds of tests, however, the rate of response may be irrelevant to the trait being measured. On the latter types of tests, time limits should be long enough to allow all, or nearly all, examinees to finish. Otherwise, the reliability estimate may be artificially inflated because of consistencies in performance caused by the test's time limit, when the examiner was primarily interested in the degree of consistency in test performance that might have been observed had all examinees finished the test. More detailed discussion of test speededness and the identification of a speeded test is presented in Lord and Novick (1968).

Artificial inflation of the reliability estimate will be most serious for a speeded test if the odd-even split-half procedure is used. Obviously once an examinee runs out of time, performance on all remaining uncompleted odd- and even-numbered items will be perfectly consistent, regardless of whether the items are homogeneous in content. Other internal consistency approaches will also yield inflated reliability estimates for this same reason when the test is highly speeded. Thus it is probably most appropriate to use the test-retest or equivalent form method to estimate reliability of a speeded test. A variation of the equivalent form method is to divide the items of the test into two separate half-tests and administer each half-test separately with its own time limit. The reliability of the full-length test is then estimated by using the Spearman Brown or Guttman procedure. Nevertheless, no matter what method is used, the reliability estimate of a speeded test must be interpreted with caution whenever the tasks on the test require more than the ability to perform simple tasks at a high rate of speed.

Test Length

One aspect of a test that is certain to affect both true score variance and observed score variance is test length. This is apparent if we consider a situation in which an examiner can use a test consisting of only 1 item or a test consisting of 10 items (all based on the same content). Obviously, we would place more confidence in the score from the longer test. The relationship between test length and reliability was derived in Chapter 6 in terms of the Spearman Brown prophecy formula:

$$\rho_{xx'} = \frac{k\rho_{jj'}}{1 + (k - 1)\rho_{jj'}}$$

where $\rho_{jj'}$ is reliability of a single subtest, k is the number of subtests in a composite, and $\rho_{xx'}$ is the composite reliability. Thus, if the reliability of a single subtest were .75, the reliability of a test formed from five parallel subtests would be computed as

$$\hat{\rho}_{xx'} = \frac{5(.75)}{1 + 4(.75)} = .94$$

How does this concept relate to test length? Essentially we consider the test at hand as subtest j and estimate its reliability ($\hat{\rho}_{jj'}$) by using any appropriate method. We then consider the test of new length as the composite, which contains subtest j as one element; then k is the factor by which the length of subtest j must be multiplied. For example, if test j consists of 50 items and the test of new length will consist of 150 items, the new test is viewed as a composite of three 50-item subtests, or $k = 3$. Furthermore k does not have to be an integer value; nor must k be greater than 1.00. For example, perhaps the existing test consists of 100 items, and the test developer wonders how reliability will be affected by shortening the test to 75 items. Because k is the factor by which test length must be multiplied to get new test length, $100(k) = 75$, or $k = .75$. Thus if $\hat{\rho}_{jj'} = .60$, the reliability for the shorter test would be estimated by

$$\hat{\rho}_{xx'} = \frac{.75(.60)}{1 + (.75 - 1.00).60} = .53$$

When test length is to be increased, values of k will always be greater than 1; when test length is to be decreased, values of k will be less than 1. It should be noted that increases in test reliability obtained from increasing test length follow the law of diminishing returns. That is, doubling the length of a test with reliability of .60 will increase the reliability to .75; tripling the length of such a test will increase reliability to .81; but increasing the test length to five times its original length will only result in a reliability coefficient of .88. Thus, at some point, the small increases in reliability obtained by adding more items will probably not justify the increased costs of item writing and testing time. Furthermore, the Spearman Brown projection is an accurate reflection of reliability only if the items added or removed are parallel in content and difficulty to items on the original test.

ESTIMATING TRUE SCORES

Although the value of a given examinee's true score can never be precisely determined, an estimate can be obtained from the general regression equation for predicting a value of Y from a known value of X. Recall that

$$Y' = \rho_{XY}\frac{\sigma_Y}{\sigma_X}(X - \mu_X) + \mu_Y$$

By substituting ρ_{XT} for ρ_{XY} and T' for Y', we have

$$T' = \rho_{XT}\frac{\sigma_T}{\sigma_X}(X - \mu_X) + \mu_T$$

but since $\sigma_T/\sigma_X = \rho_{XT}$, $\rho_{XT}^2 = \rho_{XX'}$, and $\mu_T = \mu_X$, we have

$$T' = \rho_{XX'}(X - \mu_X) + \mu_T \tag{7.9}$$

If we rewrite Equation 7.9 in deviation score form, where $t' = (T' - \mu_T)$ and $x = (X - \mu_X)$, we have

$$t' = \rho_{XX'}(x)$$

Since any estimate of $\rho_{XX'}$ based on real test data will almost always be less than 1.00, the value of t' will be less than x. Thus, any predicted true score for a given individual will always be closer to the group mean than the original observed score. Furthermore, the smaller the reliability coefficient, the closer the individual's predicted true score will be to the group mean. When the value of $\rho_{XX'} = 0$, for any individual $T' = \mu_{X'}$. On the other hand, as the reliability estimate approaches 1.00, the value of T' approaches the value of X.

Because estimated true scores can be easily computed, an occasional test user may advocate their use, on the grounds that estimated true scores should result in more appropriate decisions about examinees. This is not necessarily the case. As a general rule there is no advantage in estimating true scores for a single group of examinees who are to be compared on a norm-referenced basis. An instructor who computes both raw scores and estimated true scores for students will find that the means of the two distributions are the same, and furthermore, all examinees will score in the same rank order on the two distributions. Only the standard deviations of the two distributions will differ (with the standard deviation of the true scores being smaller).

In situations where examinees are allocated to different placements based on whether they fall above or below an absolute cutoff score, the use of estimated true scores can have important consequences which should be examined thoroughly before such a policy is adopted. Consider the case where examinees are to be placed into remedial or special programs based on test results. Students who score below 80 will be placed in classes for the educable mentally retarded; those who score above 130 will be placed in classes for the gifted. Suppose that Joseph scored 79 points on an intelligence scale and Karen scored 132. Using raw scores, both children would qualify as exceptional students and would be eligible for special services. Using true score estimates, however, where 100 is the group mean, and the value of $\hat{\rho}_{XX'}$ is .90, Joseph's true score estimate is

$$T'_J = .90(79 - 100) + 100 = 81.1$$

and Karen's estimated true score is

$$T'_K = .90(132 - 100) + 100 = 128.8$$

Thus, neither examinee would qualify for the special program. In contrast, consider how the results would change if, instead of the total group mean, only the subgroup mean of students in the educable mentally retarded class were used. If the mean score for this group is 65, Joseph's estimated true score would be

$$T'_J = .90(79 - 65) + 65 = 77.6$$

and on the basis of this true score estimate, Joseph would be classified as mentally retarded. This example illustrates the importance of identification of the appropriate norm group if true score estimates are to be used for decision making about individuals.

As a general rule, it is preferable to use total group means rather than subgroup means, which are based on relatively small samples and may therefore be unstable. It is definitely questionable practice to create subgroups on the basis of a test score and then use subgroup means for estimation of true scores on that test or a similar test (as illustrated in the previous example). Use of subgroup means for true score estimation is probably most justified when subgroups are formed on the basis of natural demographic or instructional variables which are unrelated to the test. For example, in estimating true scores of black, white, and Hispanic students, we might wish to use racial subgroup means rather than total group means.

Although in most situations the estimation of true scores is unnecessary, we should briefly mention that there are some types of research or evaluation where it may be advantageous. A problem that arises in some studies is the comparison of regression equations for two or more groups which have unequal mean scores on the predictors. This problem may occur in the use of analysis of covariance in non-equivalent control-group designs (Campbell and Stanley, 1963) and in item bias studies. The use of observed scores can create group differences in the regression equations that would not appear if the true scores were available. Hunter and Cohen (1974) have shown that the use of estimated true scores can overcome this problem in linear regression and reduce it in nonlinear regression analyses.

RELIABILITY OF DIFFERENCE SCORES

There are some occasions in research, evaluation, and clinical diagnosis when two tests are administered but the variable of interest is the difference between the test scores. Two common examples are these:

1. An evaluator wants to determine the gains in performance for each examinee over time, using the same test.
2. A clinician, identifying learning disabilities, is interested in the discrepancy between examinees' performance on two different tests or subtests (e.g., language processing and language production subtest scores).

In both cases, the variable of interest is a difference score, defined as

$$D = X - Y$$

where X is the score on the first measure, and Y is the score on the second. If decisions about individuals are to be based on their difference scores, it is the reliability of these difference scores that should be estimated.

The traditional formula for estimating the reliability of difference scores can be derived as follows. First we must recognize that it is possible to define the difference between true scores on X and Y as

$$T_D = T_X - T_Y$$

Since both D and T_D are linear composites of other scores, their variances can be expressed as

$$\sigma_D^2 = \sigma_X^2 + \sigma_Y^2 - 2\sigma_{XY}$$

and

$$\sigma_{T_D}^2 = \sigma_{T_X}^2 + \sigma_{T_X}^2 - 2\sigma_{XY}$$

From the basic definition of reliability, we also know that $\sigma_{T_X}^2 = \rho_{XX'}\sigma_X^2$, and $\sigma_{T_Y}^2 = \rho_{YY'}\sigma_Y^2$. We also learned in Chapter 6 that $\sigma_{T_X T_Y} = \sigma_{XY}$. Making these three substitutions, we can express $\sigma_{T_D}^2$ entirely in terms of observed score data as

$$\sigma_{T_D}^2 = \rho_{XX'}\sigma_X^2 + \rho_{YY'}\sigma_Y^2 - 2\sigma_{XY}$$

A theoretical expression for the reliability coefficient for difference scores is

$$\rho_{DD'} = \frac{\sigma_{T_D}^2}{\sigma_D^2} \tag{7.10}$$

By making appropriate substitutions for σ_D^2 and $\sigma_{T_D}^2$ and writing σ_{XY} as $\rho_{XY}\sigma_X\sigma_Y$, we have

$$\rho_{DD'} = \frac{\rho_{XX'}\sigma_X^2 + \rho_{YY'}\sigma_Y^2 - 2\rho_{XY}\sigma_X\sigma_Y}{\sigma_X^2 + \sigma_Y^2 - 2\rho_{XY}\sigma_X\sigma_Y} \tag{7.11}$$

To see how this formula operates, suppose that a researcher plans to study children who exhibit discrepancies between language-production and language-processing abilities. Hypothetical reliability data for this example are presented in Table 7.6. If the researcher finds that the correlation between language production and language

TABLE 7.6.   Hypothetical Means, Standard Deviations, and Reliability Estimates for Language-Processing and Language-Production Subtests for Children

	Language-Production Scale	Language-Processing Scale
Mean	32	40
Standard deviation	6	8
Reliability	.75	.80

processing is $\hat{\rho}_{XY} = .70$, the reliability of the difference between subtest scores would be

$$\hat{\rho}_{DD'} = \frac{(.75)(36) + (.80)(64) - 2(.70)(6)(8)}{36 + 64 - 2(.70)(6)(8)} = .34$$

If, on the other hand, the correlation between subtests were $\rho_{XY} = .30$, the reliability of the different scores would be substantially higher:

$$\hat{\rho}_{DD'} = \frac{(.75)(.36) + (.80)(.64) - 2(.30)(6)(8)}{36 + 64 - 2(.30)(6)(8)} = .69$$

Thus we see that more reliable differences will result when we choose measures that are each highly reliable but have a low correlation with each other. There are, however, some conditions which are exceptions to this general rule. For example, Zimmerman and Williams (1982) demonstrated combinations of conditions in which difference scores can be reliable when they are correlated to pretest scores.

USING ERROR ESTIMATES IN SCORE INTERPRETATION

Reliability estimates may be useful for comparing two or more tests, but in interpreting the score of an individual examinee, an index of the expected error in the test score will be more useful. Historically at least three types of errors, originally identified by Kelley (1927), have been considered relevant to the interpretation of an examinee's test score:

1. The discrepancy between the examinee's true score and observed score for a given testing
2. The discrepancy between an examinee's observed score on one test and the predicted score on a given parallel form of that test
3. The discrepancy between an examinee's true score and the estimated true score

If the test user is concerned about the first type of error, an estimate of the standard error of measurement should be employed. As noted in Chapter 6, the standard error of measurement can be viewed as the standard deviation of the discrepancies between a typical examinee's true score and the observed scores over an infinite number of repeated testings. An estimate for the standard error of measurement can be determined from the formula

$$\hat{\sigma}_E = \hat{\sigma}_X \sqrt{1 - \hat{\rho}_{XX'}}$$

where $\hat{\sigma}_X$ is the standard deviation for the observed scores for the entire examinee group and $\hat{\rho}_{XX'}$ is the reliability estimate. Table 7.7 presents an illustrative computation and interpretation of this statistic for an examinee with an observed score of 30.

Score interpretation using standard errors usually requires the establishment of a confidence interval in which we expect the score of interest to fall. In the following discussion we will use the standard error of measurement, but the points made apply

TABLE 7.7. Formulas, Computations, and Interpretations of Confidence Intervals Using Different Standard Error Estimates for the Same Examinee

$[\hat{\mu} = 26;\ \hat{\sigma}_{X_1} = \hat{\sigma}_{X_2} = 10;\ \hat{\rho}_{XX'} = .75]$

Standard Error	Formula	68% C.I.	95% C.I.	Interpretation of a 95% C.I. for Examinee with Observed Score of 30
1. Standard error of measurement	$\sigma_E = \sigma_X\sqrt{1 - \rho_{XX'}}$ $\hat{\sigma}_E = 10\sqrt{1 - .75}$ $\hat{\sigma}_E = 5$	30 ± 5	30 ± 10	We can be 95% confident that Charlotte's true score lies in the interval 20–40
2. Standard error of estimate	$\sigma_{2.1} = \sigma_X\sqrt{1 - \rho_{XX}^2}$ $\hat{\sigma}_{2.1} = 10\sqrt{1 - .75^2}$ $\hat{\sigma}_{2.1} = 6.6$	30 ± 6.6	30 ± 13.2	We can be 95% confident that if Charlotte is retested on a parallel form, her score on test 2 will lie in the interval 16.8–43.2

equally well to the other two error types. Recall from Chapter 6 that the general form of the confidence interval, using the standard error of measurement, is $X \pm 1\hat{\sigma}_E$ if we want to be 68% confident that the interval contains the examinee's true score. If we want to be 95% confident that the interval contains the examinee's true score, the interval is $X \pm 1.96\hat{\sigma}_E$, or with rounding, $X \pm 2\hat{\sigma}_E$.

Table 7.7 illustrates the use of this formula and the value obtained from its application to a given examinee's observed score on a particular test. An interpretation, using this confidence interval, is also presented for this examinee. It is important to recognize that for 95% of the examinees who took the test, the confidence intervals generated in this form would contain their true scores. Therefore, for a given examinee, such as Charlotte, there is a 95% chance that the confidence interval generated around her observed score will contain her true score. However, for any given examinee we can never say with absolute confidence that that interval will contain the true score. (Charlotte could be one of the 5% whose true scores lie outside the interval.) Furthermore, it is not necessarily true that for all examinees who earn a particular observed score (e.g., 30), 95% will have true scores within the specified interval.

There are times in test score interpretation with students, parents, or clients when discussion of the examinee's theoretical true score may not be practical. It may instead seem more advisable to discuss the score that the examinee could be expected to achieve if a particular alternate form of the test were taken. In this case the second type of error, the standard error of the estimate, should be used. The standard error of estimate for prediction of an examinee's score on form 2 from the known score on form 1 is

$$\hat{\sigma}_{X_2 \cdot X_1} = \hat{\sigma}_{X_2}\sqrt{1 - \hat{\rho}_{X_1 X_2}^2} \tag{7.12}$$

Again an example of the computation and interpretation of this statistic is presented in Table 7.7. It is interesting to note that the interval generated by using the standard error of estimate is wider than the interval based on the standard error of measurement. This is logical, however, if we remember that error of measurement on both test 1 and test 2 will affect this second confidence interval.

The third type of standard error, based on the discrepancy between actual and predicted true score values, is seldom used in practical score interpretation and thus will not be discussed here. Gulliksen (1950, p. 43) presents a formula and derivation for this standard error of measurement. We note only that confidence intervals based on this statistic are generated around the examinee's predicted true score, rather than observed score, and are smaller than confidence intervals based on the other two types of standard errors. The interested reader may wish to see Cronbach et al. (1972, p. 150) for a discussion of the utility of this standard error.

REPORTING RELIABILITY DATA

The test developer has an obligation not only to investigate the reliability of scores on the test under various conditions but also to communicate this information to potential users in an informative manner. The jointly issued *Standards for Educational and Psychological Testing* (AERA, APA, and NCME, 1985) and its immediate predecessor, *Standards for Educational and Psychological Tests* (APA, AERA, and NCME, 1974), provide useful guidelines for current professional standards to which test developers should adhere. Several points from these guidelines relevant to material in Chapters 6 and 7 are:

1. Results of different reliability studies should be reported to take into account different sources of measurement error that are most relevant to score use. Although it is appropriate to report evidence of internal consistency for an unspeeded test, such evidence is not a substitute for information on test score stability.
2. Standard errors of measurement and score bands for different confidence intervals should accompany each reliability estimate. Standard errors should also be reported in the scale units for each of the normative scores provided.
3. Reliability and standard error estimates should be reported for subtest scores as well as total test scores.
4. Procedures and samples used in reliability studies should be sufficiently described to permit users to determine similarity between conditions of the reliability study and their local situations.
5. When a test is normally used for a particular population of examinees (e.g., those within a grade level or those who have a particular handicap) reliability estimates and standard errors of measurement should be reported separately for such specialized populations.
6. When test scores are used primarily for describing or comparing group performance, reliability and standard errors of measurement for aggregated observations should be reported.
7. If standard errors of measurement are estimated by using a model such as the binomial model, this should be clearly indicated; otherwise, users will probably assume that the classical standard error of measurement is being reported.

SUMMARY

It is important for the test developer to identify the types of measurement errors which are likely to be of greatest concern to test users and to design reliability studies which will allow assessment of the effects of these measurement errors on the test scores' reliability. A variety of methods may be used to collect and analyze data in a reliability study. Among these are approaches which require two separate test administrations to the same group of examinees. These approaches are the test-retest method, the alternate form method, and the test-retest, alternate form method. Another type of reliability study involves administration of a single form of a test to a group of examinees. Analysis of data from such studies yields a coefficient of internal consistency which provides an estimate of how consistently examinees perform across items within a test during a single testing session.

One approach to assessment of internal consistency is to separately score two halves of a test for each examinee. These half-test scores may be correlated and the coefficient corrected with the Spearman Brown formula, or the difference between half-test scores may be computed and the reliability estimated by using Rulon's method. A limitation of split-half procedures is that different methods of splitting the test yield different reliability estimates. An approach that overcomes this problem is to determine the ratio of the sum of the item covariances to the total observed score variance. Three formulas, based on this principle which all yield the same results, are: Kuder-Richardson 20, Hoyt's analysis of variance, and Cronbach's alpha. Coefficient alpha is the average of all the split-half coefficients that would be obtained if the test were divided into all possible half-test combinations and the reliability estimated by using Rulon's procedure. When all items can be assumed to be equal in difficulty, the KR 21 may be used instead of the KR 20. The KR 21 can be computed from the mean, variance, and the number of items on the test.

Reliability estimates are affected by several factors in the testing situation. If a sample of examinees is highly homogeneous on the trait being measured, the reliability estimate will be lower than if the sample were more heterogeneous. Longer tests are more reliable than shorter tests composed of similar items, and the effect of changing test length can be estimated by using the Spearman Brown prophecy formula. Speededness may artificially inflate test reliability coefficients.

Given an examinee's observed score, the group mean, and the test reliability coefficient, it is possible to estimate an examinee's true score on that test. Estimated true scores are closer to the group mean than the raw scores.

Difference scores, or gain scores between two testings, are usually less reliable than the scores on either single testing occasion when errors of measurement are uncorrelated. Reliable difference scores can be obtained only by using tests which are highly reliable at each occasion and which have low correlations between them.

In interpreting test scores, at least three types of errors may be relevant: the standard error of measurement, as a measure of probable discrepancy between an individual's true and observed scores; the standard error of estimate for predicting the likely discrepancy between observed scores on two repeated testing occasions;

and the standard error of predicted true scores for the discrepancy between estimated true scores and actual true scores. Each of these standard errors can be used to generate a confidence interval around a score of interest to remind test users of the degree of fluctuation that might be expected in that score.

The AERA/APA/NCME *Standards for Educational and Psychological Testing* provides guidelines for test developers in reporting evidence on test score reliability to potential test users. Every test developer has a professional obligation to know and follow these guidelines in conducting reliability studies and reporting their results.

Exercises

1. For each situation, indicate the type of reliability estimate that would be most appropriate:
    A. A classroom teacher wishes to check on the reliability of a multiple-choice final examination in biology.
    B. A counseling psychologist wishes to develop two attitude inventories, one to be used as a pretest and one as a posttest, for a drug education program (that lasts only one day).
    C. A social psychologist develops an instrument to assess the attitude of entering college freshmen toward coeducational dorm life; each item response will be scored 2 points for "yes," 1 point for "maybe," 0 points for "no." All respondents will receive the questionnaire during orientation week.
    D. A single form of a standardized achievement test covers health science with items dichotomously scored, covering areas of nutrition, disease control, and human reproduction. The test developer wonders if a single score or content area subtest scores would be better.
    E. A nationally used college admissions examination is given in fall and spring, with a different form used on the two occasions. College admission directors want evidence that it does not matter when an applicant takes the test.
2. A dichotomously scored attitude inventory was administered to 10 respondents. The person-item score matrix is as follows:

	Items								
Persons	1	2	3	4	5	6	7	8	Total
A	1	1	1	1	1	1	0	0	6
B	1	1	1	0	0	1	0	0	4
C	1	1	0	1	0	0	0	0	3
D	0	0	0	0	1	0	1	1	3
E	1	1	1	1	1	1	1	1	8
F	1	1	1	1	1	0	0	0	5
G	0	1	1	1	1	0	0	1	5
H	1	1	1	1	1	1	1	0	7
I	1	1	0	0	0	0	0	0	2
J	1	1	1	1	1	0	1	1	7

    A. Suppose that a researcher wants to assess internal consistency of this test by using the split-half method, dividing the test into odd and even item subtests. Compute the two scores that would be obtained for each examinee by this procedure.

B. Find the correlation between these subtests.

C. What is the reliability estimate for the full-length test?

D. Based on visual inspection, would you expect a split-half procedure using the first and last halves of the test to yield a higher or lower estimate of reliability than that obtained by the odd-even split?

E. Which method of dividing the test would provide the more accurate estimate of the coefficient of precision? Justify your response.

F. What is the value of KR 20 for this test? of KR 21?

G. Explain why the values of the KR 20 and KR 21 differ.

3. The following table contains descriptive data on two hypothetical subtests of a standardized achievement battery, which has two alternate forms. Examine these data and answer the questions.

	Math Computations	Math Problem-Solving
Form A		
Mean	22	25
Stand. dev.	8	12
No. of items	35	40
KR_{20}	.83	.85
Form B		
Mean	22	24
Stand. dev.	7	12
No. of items	35	40
KR_{20}	.80	.85

A. What are the standard errors of measurement for the two forms of these tests? Is it always best to use the test form with the smallest standard error of measurement?

B. If Tom scores 20 points on the Math Computations test, Form A, generate a band which probably contains his true score (with a 68% chance of being correct). What would be the limits of the band if you wanted to be 95% certain of being correct?

C. On Form B of the Math Computations test, Jill scored 10 points and Harriet scored 29 points. What are the values of their estimated true scores?

D. The test publisher is considering shortening the Math Problem-Solving tests by five items each. Estimate how their reliabilities will be affected.

E. In the reliability study, not all students had time to finish the Math Problem-Solving test; what effect did this probably have on the KR 20 estimate?

F. Suppose that the test publisher reports a correlation of .80 between the two subtests of Form A and a correlation of .70 between the two subtests on Form B. A teacher proposes to use scores from these tests to identify students who would benefit from additional drill in basic math facts. The teacher proposes examining the discrepancy between each student's z-score on math computation and z-score on math problem solving. Students with large negative discrepancies would receive special instruction. Which of the two forms would yield the more reliable results? What are the respective reliability estimates for these discrepancy scores?

4. For the tests described in the preceding item, the test manual contains the following tables of correlational information. After the test was given, several teachers called the county testing director with concerns. Indicate which coefficients in the matrices would contain information which the director would find relevant in addressing each teacher's concern.

	Retest after 1 Day	Retest after 1 Week
Form A		
Math Comp.	.95	.86
Prob. Solv.	.87	.80
Form B		
Math Comp.	.91	.83
Prob. Solv.	.89	.78

	Form B	
Form A	Math Comp.	Prob. Solv.
Math Comp.	.85	.70
Prob. Solv.	.68	.89

A. Ms. Greenleaf suggests that her class was having an "off day" and asks if she can give the same test again on the following day.

B. Mr. Robinson says that he suspects that Form B contained too many questions based on material not covered by his text and that the other form might have been better suited for his curriculum.

C. Ms. Parker feels that the test was given too early and suggests that if given a few days later the performance of some examinees would have been substantially different.

D. Mr. Whitter would like to combine scores on the two math tests into one composite score because he believes they measure the same thing.

E. A guidance counselor wants to know whether there is a greater amount of error variance in examinees' scores because of forms or time of testing. (Students in his school were not all tested on the same form, and some were tested as much as a week earlier than others.)

5. The test manual for a personality inventory reports split-half reliabilities calculated by the formula

$$\hat{\rho}_{XX'} = \frac{4\hat{\rho}_{GH}\hat{\sigma}_G\hat{\sigma}_H}{\hat{\sigma}_x^2}$$

where G and H denote half-test scores. Prove that this is equivalent to Rulon's coefficient.

6. Beginning with the formula for KR 20 given in this chapter, derive the formula for KR 21. (State any assumptions required to complete this derivation.)

7. Compare the various split-half and item covariance methods for estimating reliability in terms of data requirements, and explain why different results may be obtained with some of these methods.

Chapter 8

INTRODUCTION TO GENERALIZABILITY THEORY

Although the procedures introduced in Chapter 7 are powerful techniques for studying reliability, they are not flexible enough to accommodate all the reliability problems that arise in mental testing. For example, suppose that 50 students write essays which are scored on a 10-point scale by each of three graders. Since the techniques in Chapters 6 and 7 are predominantly intended for use when two measurements are available for each examinee, they cannot be applied directly in this situation. As another example, suppose that a clinician, who works with exceptional children, uses alternate forms of a diagnostic test and is interested in the extent to which the two forms yield the same raw score for each child (rather than the same deviation score). Unless the alternate forms are strictly parallel (that is, parallel as defined in classical test theory), the reliability coefficient and standard error of measurement from classical test theory may give misleading results when applied in this situation. When applied to forms that are not strictly parallel, the reliability coefficient and standard error of measurement measure the consistency of z scores and deviation scores respectively. As a final example, suppose the attitudes of clients in a drug rehabilitation program are rated by four different counselors over two different counseling sessions. It might be useful to separate the extent to which variance among the counselors and variance between the sessions contribute to the error variance in these ratings. Again classical test theory, which provides for only an undifferentiated error component, cannot be easily applied to this problem.

One fruitful approach to estimation of reliability coefficients and error variance in such situations involves the use of analysis of variance. The use of analysis of variance to estimate reliability coefficients and errors of measurement has a history that dates back at least to the early 1940s. Most of the major formulas were either explicitly stated or were implicit in work by authors such as Hoyt (1951), Lindquist

(1953), and Medley and Mitzel (1963) when Cronbach, Gleser, and Rajaratnam (1963) published their first paper on generalizability theory. The major contribution of this paper and the papers by Rajaratnam, Cronbach, and Gleser (1965) and Gleser, Cronbach, and Rajaratnam (1965) was not primarily the development of new reliability formulas. Rather, it seems fair to say that the major contribution was the development of a way of thinking about reliability, which leads to procedures for choosing the reliability coefficient and/or error variance most appropriate for the situation at hand.

This chapter presents aspects of generalizability theory for what are known as single-facet and two-facet designs. A much more comprehensive treatment of generalizability theory was presented by Cronbach et al. (1972). A source that is more comprehensive than the current chapter but less comprehensive (and complex) than Cronbach et al. is Brennan (1983).

G-STUDIES AND D-STUDIES

To begin the study of generalizability theory, it is necessary to understand the distinction between a *generalizability* (G) *study* and a *decision* (D) *study*. The researcher who conducts a G-study is primarily concerned with the extent to which a sample of measurements generalizes to a universe of measurements. The universe is typically defined in terms of a set of measurement conditions that is more extensive than the conditions under which the sample measurements were obtained. Studies concerned with the stability of responses over time, the equivalence of scores on two or more forms of an instrument, or the interrelationship of subscale scores or items on a scale could all be considered G-studies. A D-study on the other hand, is one in which the data are collected for the specific purpose of making a decision. It provides data for describing examinees (for selection or placement), comparing groups in an experiment, or investigating the relationship between two or more variables.

The purpose of a G-study is to help plan a D-study that will have adequate generalizability. Thus the design of the G-study needs to anticipate the full variety of designs that may be used for the D-study. It is not possible to classify a study as a G-study or a D-study based on its design alone; the purpose of the investigator is the determining factor. Suppose that a researcher tests 2,000 children randomly selected from public schools and 2,000 children randomly selected from parochial schools in the same region, using a single standardized achievement test. If the purpose is to determine whether the test is equally reliable for students in both types of schools, this would be classified as a G-study. On the other hand, if the investigator wants to compare the mean achievement levels of the two groups and draw conclusions about possible differences in the adequacy of the two educational systems, this would be considered a D-study. In principle, an investigator should establish that the measurement procedure yields generalizable data before undertaking a D-study. In practice, however, the generalizability of the data is sometimes investigated by using the data from a D-study, but such "shortcuts" in behavioral research should be avoided when possible.

In generalizability theory a set of measurement conditions is called a *facet*. For example, suppose the performance of factory workers is rated by two supervisors under heavy, medium, and light workloads. The two sets of measurement conditions (facets) under which the measurements are taken are supervisor and workload. As a second illustration, suppose that a researcher is studying children's compositional writing. On each of four occasions, each child writes compositions on two different topics; all compositions are graded by three graders. This design involves three facets: occasion, topic, and rater.

In a D-study a facet may be treated as fixed or random. If a facet is fixed, the investigator intends to generalize to only those conditions that appear in the D-study. If a facet is random, the investigator considers the conditions in the D-study to be a sample from a larger number of conditions and intends to generalize to all these latter conditions. In either case, the population of measurements that would be obtained by measuring under all conditions is called the *universe of generalization*. A G-study is also conducted by measuring under a specific set of conditions. These conditions will typically be considered to represent a larger set of conditions. The population of observations that could be taken in all these conditions is called the *universe of admissible observations*. The results of a G-study will be useful to a researcher planning a D-study only if the universe of admissible observations includes the researcher's universe of generalization.

In classical true score theory, an examinee's true score is defined as the average of a large number of strictly parallel measurements. The true score variance is the variance of these averages, and reliability is defined as the ratio of the observed to true score variance. In generalizability theory an examinee's universe score is defined as the average of the measurements in the universe of generalization. These measurements are not assumed to be strictly parallel. One way to define a generalizability coefficient is as the ratio of universe score variance to expected observed score variance. The latter depends on the design of the D-study, and therefore, different generalizability coefficients are appropriate for different designs for D-studies. (Another definition of a generalizability coefficient is a squared correlation between universe and observed scores. We defer a discussion of this type of generalizability coefficient until later in the chapter.) Also, the universe score and, therefore, the universe score variance depend on the universe of generalization. Therefore, two researchers who intend to use the same D-study design but have different universes of generalization would require different generalizability coefficients.

In the following section we will describe how generalizability coefficients are formulated and estimated for four single-facet designs. Although many applications of generalizability theory involve multiple facets, it is easier to understand generalizability theory if we focus at first on studies involving only one facet. In the following presentation, an example involving the rating of behavior is used to illustrate the formulation and estimation of generalizability coefficients. Here the single facet consists of the raters. However the procedures described in the following sections can also be applied, for example, to situations in which the measurement facet consists of test forms, testing occasions, or test administrators.

FORMULATING GENERALIZABILITY COEFFICIENTS FOR SINGLE-FACET DESIGNS

Suppose a social psychologist is interested in correlates of shyness and intends to conduct an experiment in which two students are observed while interacting in a social setting. This experiment is a D-study. One of the students is the focus of the observation and will be referred to as the examinee. The second student is working with the psychologist, although the first student does not know this. The examinee's level of shyness will be rated on a 10-point scale. The psychologist plans to use undergraduate student assistants to do the rating. Even in this simple situation there are many possible designs for the D-study. Four such designs are the following:

1. Each examinee is rated by one rater; this rater rates all examinees.
2. Each examinee is rated by several raters; all raters rate each examinee.
3. Each examinee is rated by a different rater; there is only one rater for each examinee.
4. Each examinee is rated by several raters; there are different raters for each examinee.

In each of the four designs there is a single facet of raters. In the first two designs, every examinee is exposed to the same raters, or in more general terms, to the same measurement conditions. In this case the measurement facet is said to be *crossed* with the examinees. In the literature this crossed design is denoted as *pxi,* where *p* refers to persons or examinees and *i* refers to the measurement conditions. Data collected in a crossed design are sometimes called *matched data*. In the last two designs each examinee is exposed to different raters, or in more general terms, to different measurement conditions. In this case measurement conditions are said to be *nested* in examinees. The design is denoted as *i:p,* which is read *i* nested within *p*. In our example raters are nested within examinees. Data collected in a nested design are called *independent data*. The appropriate formula for the generalizability coefficient depends on the design the psychologist selects for the D-study he plans to conduct. Each generalizability coefficient is a ratio of universe to observed score variance. However, different generalizability coefficients are associated with each design because a different observed score variance is associated with each design. Estimation of these four coefficients depends on the design of the G-study. Initially we will consider a G-study using design 2. In this case estimation of the four coefficients involves a two-factor analysis of a variance (ANOVA) with one observation per cell. This kind of ANOVA is sometimes called a *repeated measures* ANOVA. Shavelson (1981, Chs. 16 and 17) gives a clear introduction to ANOVA. Myers (1979, Ch. 7) presents the repeated measures ANOVA.

Before turning to discussion of generalizability theory, we should note that design 1 can be considered a special case of design 2 because there is one rather than several raters. Also the generalizability coefficient for design 1 is a special case of the generalizability coefficient for design 2. In a similar fashion, design 3 and its generalizability coefficient are special cases of design 4 and its generalizability coefficient. Nevertheless, we will keep the four designs distinct in the ensuing discussion.

A Generalizability Coefficient for Design 1

Recall that our example concerns a psychologist whose research involves collecting ratings of shyness. Let us suppose the psychologist's study will be conducted next semester, and the psychologist cannot be sure which student assistant will do the rating. Nevertheless, the psychologist is interested in using data from a G-study to estimate the generalizability of the ratings that will be obtained in the future D-study. From the point of view of generalizability theory, the psychologist's situation is as follows. Because of practical considerations, only one rater will rate all the examinees in the D-study. If practicality were not a concern, the psychologist would arrange for the examinees to be rated by an indefinitely large number of trained raters. This collection of raters is the universe of generalization. Since only one rater can be used, the psychologist wants to know how well the rating made by the single rater will generalize to the average of all the ratings assigned by the raters in the universe of generalization.

Before presenting the method for estimating the generalizability of the ratings, several quantities need to be defined. Let the rating of the examinee p by the rater i be denoted by X_{pi}. As in Chapter 6 this observed score can be viewed as one of the many possible ratings that might have been assigned by rater i to examinee p. Therefore, for a particular p and i, X_{pi} is a random variable. Let T_{pi} be the mean (or expected value) of this random variable. The symbol T_{pi} represents the true score for examinee p when rated by rater i. A model for the observed rating is simply

$$X_{pi} = T_{pi} + E_{pi} \tag{8.1}$$

the same as in classical test theory. The question of how well X_{pi} generalizes to T_{pi} is the question of the reliability of X_{pi}. However, this is *not* the question which interests the psychologist at present. For student p, T_{pi} varies over raters, and over raters the mean of T_{pi} is the universe score for examinee p. This universe score is denoted by μ_p. The psychologist's generalizability question is how well the ratings in the D-study will generalize to μ_p, the universe scores. In addition to these symbols, we need to define μ_i the expected value of the true scores for examinees rated by rater i. That is, μ_i is the mean over examinees of T_{pi}. In classical test theory the expected value of the observed scores is equal to the expected value of the true scores. Similarly in generalizability theory the expected value of X_{pi}, the ratings assigned by rater i, is equal to the expected value of T_{pi}, the true scores for examinees rated by rater i. We also need to define μ, which denotes the mean over students of the universe scores. This latter mean is also equal to the mean over raters of the μ_i and is referred to as the *grand mean*. With these symbols defined, a linear model for X_{pi} is

$$X_{pi} = \mu + (\mu_p - \mu) + (\mu_i - \mu) + e_{pi} \tag{8.2}$$

Rearranging Equation 8.2 to obtain each individual examinee's deviation from the grand mean, we have

$$X_{pi} - \mu = (\mu_p - \mu) + (\mu_i - \mu) + e_{pi}$$

We see that the deviation of each examinee's score from the grand mean has three components: $\mu_p - \mu$, the examinee effect; $\mu_i - \mu$, the rater effect; and e_{pi}, a residual. The reader should note that e_{pi} is not the same as the error of measurement, E_{pi}, from classical test theory. Rather e_{pi} is equal to E_{pi} plus a component that reflects the fact that true scores assigned by different raters are not perfectly correlated. Finally we need to define several variance components:

σ_p^2, the variance of the examinees' universe scores, μ_p

σ_i^2, the variance of the rater means, μ_i

$\sigma_{e|i}^2$, the variance of e_{pi} for rater i

σ_e^2, the average over all raters of $\sigma_{e|i}^2$

$\sigma_{X|i}^2$, the variance of X_{pi} for rater i

Having defined the necessary symbols let us now turn our attention to a G-study and show how its results can be used to estimate a generalizability coefficient that is relevant to the D-study the psychologist will conduct next semester.

Suppose the psychologist conducts a G-study, using 10 examinees; the level of shyness for each examinee is rated by three raters. These data are presented in Table 8.1. Keeping in mind that the D-study will be conducted with a new rater, how can

TABLE 8.1.   Scores Assigned to 10 Essays by 3 Raters

	Rater			
Examinee	1	2	3	Average (X_{pl})
1	2	3	2	2.33
2	8	5	7	6.66
3	4	2	2	2.66
4	4	3	6	4.33
5	8	5	5	6.00
6	8	5	7	6.66
7	6	4	5	5.00
8	4	3	3	3.33
9	3	2	2	2.33
10	1	2	3	2.00
Average (X_{Pi})	4.8	3.4	4.2	4.13 (X_{pl})

these data be used to estimate the generalizability of the ratings in the D-study? Recall that in classical true score theory, the reliability of a set of scores can be defined as the ratio of true to observed score variance. It may seem reasonable, then, to define the generalizability of the D-study ratings as $\sigma_p^2/\sigma_{X|i}^2$, the ratio of universe score variance to observed score variance for the rater who will work in the D-study. A practical problem with this suggestion is that the D-study will be conducted next semester, and the psychologist is not sure who the rater in the D-study will be. Indeed the rater in the D-study may not even be one of the students who participates in the G-study. Therefore using the G-study data, we cannot estimate $\sigma_{X|i}^2$ for the rater who will work in the D-study.

However, if we consider the rater in the D-study to be representative of all the raters in the universe of generalization, our best guess about $\sigma_{X|i}^2$ is the average (or expected) observed score variance for all the raters in the universe. This average observed score variance can be shown to be $\sigma_p^2 + \sigma_e^2$. Moreover since data for three raters are available from the G-study, these data can be used to estimate $\sigma_p^2 + \sigma_e^2$. Replacing the observed score variance for rater i by the expected observed score variance for all raters in the universe of generalization, we obtain the generalizability coefficient

$$\rho_{i*}^2 = \frac{\sigma_p^2}{\sigma_p^2 + \sigma_e^2} \tag{8.3}$$

The * in ρ_{i*}^2 is used to indicate that the coefficient is appropriate for a D-study with measurement conditions crossed with examinees. Note that a critical assumption in using this coefficient, as well as the other coefficients presented in this chapter, is the claim that the raters in the G-study and the D-study are representative of the same universe of generalization. This would be assured if we could identify all the raters in the universe and sample randomly from this set. As with the current example, typically this is not possible, and so the representativeness of the raters becomes a matter of judgment.

Once the appropriate generalizability coefficient has been defined in terms of its variance components, a practical method must be devised to estimate the coefficient. The coefficient can be estimated by using the results of two-factor ANOVA of the data in Table 8.1, which can be classified in terms of two dimensions, examinees and raters. In the language of ANOVA, each dimension is called a *factor*. Each examinee constitutes one *level* of the examinee factor. Each rater constitutes a level of the rater factor. Each combination of an examinee and a rater is called a *cell*. The design in Table 8.2 is described as two-factor design, with one observation per cell because there is only one score for each examinee-rater combination.

The results of a two factor ANOVA with one observation per cell may be summarized in the form of a table such as Table 8.2. The abbreviation *SV* is for source of variance, and the entries in this column serve as labels in the table. The abbreviation *SS* stands for sums of squares, and the entries in this column are the formulas for calculating these quantities. In the usual ANOVA summary table, the numerical results of these formulas would be reported. The symbol *df* represents degrees of

TABLE 8.2.   Computational Formulas and Expected Mean Squares for a Two-Factor ANOVA

SV	SS	df	MS	EMS
Examinee (P)	$n_i \sum_p (X_{pI} - X_{PI})^2$	$n_p - 1$	$SS_p/(n_p - 1)$	$\sigma_e^2 + n_i\sigma_p^2$
Raters (I)	$n_p \sum_i (X_{Pi} - X_{PI})^2$	$n_i - 1$	$SS_i/(n_i - 1)$	$\sigma_e^2 + n_p\sigma_i^2$
Residual (R)	$\sum_i \sum_j (X_{pi} - X_{PI})^2 - SS_p - SS_i$	$(n_p - 1)(n_i - 1)$	$\dfrac{SS_r}{(n_p - 1)(n_i - 1)}$	σ_e^2

$$X_{pI} = \sum_i X_{pi}/n_i \qquad X_{Pi} = \sum_p X_{pi}/n_p \qquad X_{PI} = \sum_i \sum_p X_{pi}/n_in_p$$

freedom, and *MS* stands for mean square. The table indicates that the *MS* quantities are calculated by dividing each *SS* by its corresponding *df* value. The symbols n_p and n_i refer respectively to the number of examinees and the number of raters in the G-study. The ANOVA summary table for the data in Table 8.1 is presented in Table 8.3.

One procedure for estimating ρ_i^2* involves estimating the variance components σ_p^2 and σ_e^2, using weighted combinations of the values in the *MS* column of the ANOVA summary table. These estimates can then be substituted in Equation 8.3. To determine the formula for a variance component estimate, the investigator must examine the formulas for the expected mean squares (*EMS*) for each source of variation in the ANOVA table. These formulas identify the theoretical components of variation that are associated with the numeric mean square estimates in Table 8.3. Specifically, each *EMS* indicates the formula for the population value that is estimated by the corresponding mean square value in the summary table. Thus EMS_p, the expected mean square for the persons factor is estimated by MS_p, the mean square for persons. Now suppose that you wanted to estimate σ_p^2 from the results presented in Table 8.3. Intuitively it might seem that MS_p estimates σ_p^2 only. However, examination of the formula in the *EMS* column reveals that the MS_p value is an estimate of $\sigma_e^2 + n_i\sigma_p^2$, and so the value of MS_p cannot be used as an estimate of σ_p^2. Further inspection of other *EMS* formulas in the table reveals that MS_r is an estimate of σ_e^2. Now since

$$n_i\sigma_p^2 = (\sigma_e^2 + n_i\sigma_p^2) - \sigma_e^2$$

TABLE 8.3.   Summary of ANOVA Table

SV	SS	df	MS	EMS
Examinee (P)	92.794	9	10.310	$\sigma_e^2 + n_i\sigma_p^2$
Raters (I)	9.866	2	4.933	$\sigma_e^2 + n_p\sigma_i^2$
Residual (R)	18.780	18	1.043	σ_e^2

EMS_p can be substituted for $\sigma_e^2 + n_i\sigma_p^2$ and EMS_r for σ_e^2 to obtain

$$n_i\sigma_p^2 = (EMS_p - EMS_r)$$

and so

$$\sigma_p^2 = \frac{(EMS_p - EMS_r)}{n_i}$$

This formula illustrates that a variance component in an EMS formula can usually be isolated by creating weighted linear combinations of two or more EMS formulas in the ANOVA table. Once the proper combination has been determined, the sample estimates from the MS column are substituted into the formula for the population in order to estimate the variance components. Substituting MS terms for EMS terms we have

$$\hat{\sigma}_p^2 = \frac{(MS_p - MS_r)}{n_i} \qquad (8.4)$$

Substituting numerical results from Table 8.3 in Equation 8.4 we obtain

$$\hat{\sigma}_p^2 = \frac{(10.310 - 1.043)}{3} = 3.089$$

The formula for σ_e^2 is simply $\sigma_e^2 = EMS_r$, and so

$$\hat{\sigma}_e^2 = MS_r \qquad (8.5)$$

For our example, $\hat{\sigma}_e^2 = 1.043$. Having calculated $\hat{\sigma}_p^2$ and $\hat{\sigma}_e^2$, ρ_{i*}^2 can be estimated by using

$$\hat{\rho}_{i*}^2 = \frac{\hat{\sigma}_p^2}{\hat{\sigma}_p^2 + \hat{\sigma}_e^2} \qquad (8.6)$$

Substituting into Equation 8.6, we obtain

$$\hat{\rho}_{i*}^2 = \frac{3.089}{3.089 + 1.043} = .75$$

An alternate equation that expresses $\hat{\rho}_{i*}^2$ in terms of the various MS terms is

$$\hat{\rho}_{i*}^2 = \frac{MS_p - MS_r}{MS_p + (n_i - 1)MS_r} \qquad (8.7)$$

Substituting in Equation 8.7 we obtain

$$\hat{\rho}_{i*}^2 = \frac{10.310 - 1.043}{10.310 + (3 - 1)1.043} = .75$$

The results of applying Equations 8.6 and 8.7 should agree to within rounding error. The choice between the two equations is a matter of computational convenience. Equations, such as Equation 8.7, which express generalizability coefficient estimates as functions of mean squares will also be presented for designs 2, 3, and 4. These equations are not presented because they are preferable to equations that express generalizability coefficient estimates in terms of variance component estimates. Rather they are presented because they are common in the measurement literature.

In the preceding example the psychologist did not know which assistant would rate in the D-study. Suppose now that the psychologist knows which assistant will do the rating and wants to know how well the ratings generalize to the universe scores. Also suppose that this rater appears in the G-study. What can be done to estimate a generalizability coefficient for the ratings of this particular rater? This coefficient can be estimated if there are at least three raters in the G-study and one of the three raters is the rater who will appear in the D-study. Numbering the rater who will appear in the D-study as rater 1, the equation for estimating the coefficient when the G-study has three raters is

$$\hat{\rho}^2(X_{pi},\mu_p) = \frac{(\hat{\sigma}_1\hat{\sigma}_2\hat{\rho}_{12} + \hat{\sigma}_1\hat{\sigma}_3\hat{\rho}_{13})^2}{4\hat{\sigma}_1^2\hat{\sigma}_2\hat{\sigma}_3\hat{\rho}_{23}} \qquad (8.8)$$

Note that Equation 8.8 yields an estimate of $\rho^2(X_{pi},\mu_p)$, the squared correlation between the ratings of a particular rater and the universe scores. Lord and Novick (1968, p. 268) derived a generalization of Equation 8.8; it is applicable to more than 3 measurements. Using the data in Table 8.2 we obtain

$$\hat{\rho}^2(X_{pi},\mu_p) = \frac{[(2.573)(1.264)(.914) + (2.573)(2.043)(.790)]^2}{4(6.620)(1.264)(2.043)(.825)} = .90$$

Recall that $\hat{\rho}_{i*}^2 = .75$. Thus the two generalizability coefficients give different impressions of the generalizability of the D-study data. The reason for the discrepancy between the two coefficients is that $\hat{\rho}_{i*}^2$ refers to a randomly selected rater whereas $\hat{\rho}^2(X_{pi},\mu_p)$ refers to a specific rater. At this point the reader may wonder whether the generalizability coefficient for a randomly chosen condition will always be smaller than the generalizability coefficient for a specifically designated condition and which coefficient is preferable. First, we note that it can be shown that the coefficient for the random condition, ρ_{i*}^2 is a lower bound to the average of all the coefficients that would result if we could determine $\rho^2(X_{pi},\mu_p)$ for every rater in the universe. As a result, ρ_{i*}^2 can be larger than or smaller than $\rho^2(X_{pi},\mu_p)$. In discussing the choice between two coefficients, Cronbach, Gleser, and Rajaratnam (1963) and Lord and Novick (1968) seem to agree that in theory $\rho^2(X_{pi},\mu_p)$, the coefficient for the specific condition, is more desirable. However, Cronbach and his colleagues were concerned that accurate estimation of this coefficient might require an impractically large number of raters in the G-study. As a result of this concern, they favored estimation of the random condition coefficient. Lord and Novick, however, were more favorably disposed toward estimating $\rho^2(X_{pi},\mu_p)$. Both sources give general formulas for estimation of this coefficient.

A Generalizability Coefficient for Design 2

For the situation in which the psychologist did not know which rater would appear in the D-study, the generalizability coefficient was .75. Although this is a substantial generalizability coefficient, the psychologist in our illustration might be interested in the generalizability that would result if the ratings of two or more raters could be averaged. Let this average score be denoted by X_{pI}. Here, the capital I indicates that the score is an average over the raters in the D-study. An appropriate generalizability coefficient in this case is

$$\rho_{I*}^2 = \frac{\sigma_p^2}{\sigma_p^2 + \sigma_e^2/n_i'} \tag{8.9}$$

In Equation 8.9, n_i' denotes the number of ratings being averaged to form X_{pI}. Note that n_i is the number of raters in the G-study, whereas n_i' is the number of raters in the D-study. The major difference between the formulas for ρ_{I*}^2 and ρ_{I*}^2 is that in the latter σ_e^2 is divided by the number of raters in the D-study. This is done because averaging several ratings reduces the error variance.

The estimation of ρ_{I*}^2 is accomplished by using the results of the two-factor ANOVA. The estimation is carried out through

$$\hat{\rho}_{I*}^2 = \frac{\hat{\sigma}_p^2}{\hat{\sigma}_p^2 + \hat{\sigma}_e^2/n_i'} \tag{8.10}$$

The variance terms are again calculated through Equations 8.4 and 8.5. Previously we found that $\hat{\sigma}_p^2 = 3.089$ and $\hat{\sigma}_e^2 = 1.043$. Suppose the psychologist feels he may be able to use $n_i' = 2$ raters in the D-study. Substitution in Equation 8.10 yields

$$\hat{\rho}_{I*}^2 = \frac{3.089}{3.089 + 1.043/2} = .85$$

so increasing the number of raters to 2 increases generalizability from .75 to .85. Calculation of $\hat{\rho}_{I*}^2$ for several values of n_i' provides useful information for choosing an appropriate number of raters for the D-study. The coefficient $\hat{\rho}_{I*}^2$ can also be calculated by using the formula

$$\hat{\rho}_{I*}^2 = \frac{MS_p - MS_r}{MS_p + (n_i - n_i')MS_r/n_i'} \tag{8.11}$$

Substitution in Equation 8.11 yields

$$\hat{\rho}_{I*}^2 = \frac{10.310 - 1.043}{10.310 + (3 - 2)(1.043)/2} = .86$$

When $n_i = n_i'$, Equation 8.11 simplifies to

$$\hat{\rho}_{I*}^2 = \frac{MS_p - MS_r}{MS_p} \tag{8.12}$$

a formula that is widely reported in the literature. In passing we note that $\hat{\rho}_{I*}^2$ and $\hat{\rho}_{i*}^2$ are related by the generalized Spearman Brown prophecy formula:

$$\hat{\rho}_{I*}^2 = \frac{n_i'\hat{\rho}_{i*}^2}{1 + (n_i' - 1)\hat{\rho}_{i*}^2}$$

As with design 1 there is another coefficient that is appropriate if the raters who will participate in the D-study also take part in the G-study. This coefficient can be symbolized by $\rho^2(X_{pI},\mu_p)$ which represents the squared correlation between the observed D-study score and the universe score. Here the observed score for an examinee is the average of the scores assigned to the examinee by the raters in the D-study. As with design 1, estimation of this generalizability coefficient requires that the G-study include at least two raters in addition to the raters who will appear in the D-study. When two additional raters are included, Equation 8.8 can be used to estimate $\rho^2(X_{pI},\mu_p)$. To use Equation 8.8 in this situation, the average of G-study scores assigned to an examinee by the raters who will appear in the D-study is calculated for each examinee. The symbol $\hat\sigma_1$ then refers to the standard deviation of these scores. The symbols $\hat\rho_{12}$ and $\hat\rho_{13}$ refer to the correlation between these scores and the scores assigned by each of the two G-study raters who will not appear in the D-study.

A Generalizability Coefficient for Design 3

Suppose that it takes an extensive amount of time to observe and rate each examinee in the experiment but that a large number of assistants are available to serve as raters. In this case the psychologist might have a different assistant rate each examinee. Recall that in this case raters are nested within examinees. Let us consider the variance among the ratings of the examinees. Since each examinee is rated by a different rater, differences among examinees are influenced by differences among raters as well as by universe score differences and residual variance. As a result the observed score variance for design 3 is $\sigma_p^2 + \sigma_i^2 + \sigma_e^2$. The term σ_i^2 reflects the differences among the raters. The generalizability coefficient for design 3 is

$$\rho_i^2 = \frac{\sigma_p^2}{\sigma_p^2 + \sigma_i^2 + \sigma_e^2} \tag{8.13}$$

To signify that ρ_i^2 is used when i is nested in p, the i in ρ_i^2 is not modified by a "*".

With a design 3 G-study, estimation of ρ_i^2 involves calculating estimates of σ_p^2 and σ_e^2, using Equations 8.4 and 8.5, respectively, and in addition, requires an estimate of σ_i^2. (As we shall see with a design 4 G-study, estimation of ρ_i^2 involves calculating a single estimate of the quantity $\sigma_i^2 + \sigma_e^2$.) Using the *EMS* in Table 8.3, the following expression can be derived

$$\sigma_i^2 = \frac{(EMS_i - EMS_r)}{n_p}$$

and so σ_i^2 is estimated by

$$\hat\sigma_i^2 = \frac{(MS_i - MS_r)}{n_p} \tag{8.14}$$

Using the values of the mean squares reported in Table 8.3, we obtain

$$\hat\sigma_i^2 = \frac{(4.933 - 1.043)}{10} = .389$$

The equation for estimating the generalizability coefficient is

$$\hat{\rho}_i^2 = \frac{\hat{\sigma}_p^2}{\hat{\sigma}_p^2 + \hat{\sigma}_i^2 + \hat{\sigma}_e^2} \tag{8.15}$$

which yields, in this example,

$$\hat{\rho}_i^2 = \frac{3.089}{3.089 + .389 + 1.043} = .68$$

Comparing the generalizability coefficient for design 3, $\hat{\rho}_i^2 = .68$, to the coefficient for design 1, $\hat{\rho}_{i*}^2 = .75$, we see that there is a decrement in generalizability. However, the loss is not large. This suggests that if design 3 is practical, it is certainly a reasonable design for the psychologist's experiment. As with the other generalizability coefficients, a formula exists for calculating $\hat{\rho}_i^2$ directly from the MS:

$$\hat{\rho}_i^2 = \frac{MS_p - MS_r}{MS_p + n_i MS_i/n_p + (n_i n_p - n_i - n_p)MS_r/n_p} \tag{8.16}$$

It is important to recognize that $\hat{\rho}_i^2$, a coefficient appropriate for nested D-study designs, can be calculated by using the data from a crossed G-study design. This illustrates that a well-designed G-study permits calculation of generalizability coefficients associated with a wide variety of D-study designs. Comparison of the generalizability coefficient for several designs allows the researcher to compare and contrast D-study designs in terms of their generalizability and to pick a D-study design that is both practical and characterized by adequate generalizability.

A Generalizability Coefficient for Design 4

Suppose in the D-study it will be practical for different raters to rate each examinee but that the psychologist wants two or more ratings of each examinee. A generalizability coefficient appropriate for this design is

$$\rho_I^2 = \frac{\sigma_p^2}{\sigma_p^2 + (\sigma_i^2 + \sigma_e^2)/n_i'} \tag{8.17}$$

Again the capital I subscript on ρ_I^2 indicates that an averaged rating will be used for each examinee. Comparing Equations 8.17 and 8.13, we see that the term $\sigma_i^2 + \sigma_e^2$ is divided by n_i' in the former. Thus the use of multiple raters reduces the effects of rater variance and residual variance on the observed score variance and increases the generalizability coefficient. The formula for estimating ρ_I^2 is

$$\hat{\rho}_I^2 = \frac{\hat{\sigma}_p^2}{\hat{\sigma}_p^2 + (\hat{\sigma}_i^2 + \hat{\sigma}_e^2)/n_i'} \tag{8.18}$$

With two raters this equation yields

$$\hat{\rho}_I^2 = \frac{3.089}{3.089 + (.389 + 1.043)/2} = .81$$

TABLE 8.4.   Generalizability Coefficients for Four Single-Facet D-Study Designs

Design	Description	Number of Measurement Conditions	Observed Score Variance	Generalizability Coefficient
1	pxi	1	$\sigma_p^2 + \sigma_e^2$	$\rho_{i*}^2 = \dfrac{\sigma_p^2}{\sigma_p^2 + \sigma_e^2}$
2	pxi	n_i'	$\sigma_p^2 + \sigma_e^2/n_i'$	$\rho_{I*}^2 = \dfrac{\sigma_p^2}{\sigma_p^2 + \sigma_e^2/n_i'}$
3	$i{:}p$	1	$\sigma_p^2 + \sigma_i^2 + \sigma_e^2$	$\rho_i^2 = \dfrac{\sigma_p^2}{\sigma_p^2 + \sigma_i^2 + \sigma_e^2}$
4	$i{:}p$	n_i'	$\sigma_p^2 + (\sigma_i^2 + \sigma_e^2)/n_i'$	$\rho_I^2 = \dfrac{\sigma_p^2}{\sigma_p^2 + (\sigma_i^2 + \sigma_e^2)/n_i'}$

for this example. Once again a formula exists for estimating ρ_I^2 directly from the mean squares:

$$\hat{\rho}_I^2 = \frac{MS_p - MS_r}{MS_p + n_i MS_i/n_p n_i' + (n_p n_i - n_p n_i' - n_i)MS_e/n_p n_i'} \tag{8.19}$$

Summary of the Generalizability Coefficients for the Four Designs

So far we have formulated four generalizability coefficients, one for each of the four designs. Table 8.4 presents the observed score variance and generalizability coefficients for the four designs. We re-emphasize the fact that although a different generalizability coefficient is associated with each D-study design, all four coefficients can be estimated if the G-study data are collected using design 2. However, as we shall see in the next section, if the G-study data are collected using design 4, it is only possible to estimate ρ_i^2 and ρ_I^2, the generalizability coefficients for the designs 3 and 4.

A NESTED SINGLE-FACET G-STUDY (DESIGN 4)

It may happen that the G-study is conducted with design 4, where measurements on each examinee are obtained under different conditions. In the rating example, design 4 occurs if each examinee is rated by a different set of raters. A G-study based on design 4 can only be used to estimate generalizability coefficients for D-studies conducted with designs 3 and 4. As a result, such G-studies tend to be of less value than the G-study conducted with design 2. Moreover, for a G-study conducted with

TABLE 8.5. Computational Formulas and Expected Mean Squares for a One-Way ANOVA

SV	SS	df	MS	EMS
Examinees	$n_i \sum_p (X_{pI} - X_{PI})^2$	$n_p - 1$	$SS_p/(n_p - 1)$	$\sigma_e^2 + \sigma_i^2 + n_i\sigma_p^2$
Residual	$\sum_p \sum_i (X_{pi} - X_{pI})^2$	$n_p(n_i - 1)$	$SS_r/[n_p(n_i - 1)]$	$\sigma_e^2 + \sigma_i^2$

$$X_{pI} = \sum_i X_{pi}/n_i \qquad X_{PI} = \sum_p \sum_i X_{pi}/n_p n_i$$

design 4, new formulas are required to estimate these coefficients. When the G-study data are collected by using design 4, the formulas for estimating ρ_i^2 and ρ_I^2 are based on a one-factor ANOVA. The single factor is examinees. The ratings of an examinee are treated as replicated measurements on the examinee. Table 8.5 presents the formulas for conducting the one-factor ANOVA. A summary ANOVA table is presented in Table 8.6. These figures were obtained by applying the relevant formulas to the data in Table 8.2. Here the data are treated as if they were collected by using design 4. Formulas for estimating variance components are

$$\hat{\sigma}_p^2 = \frac{(MS_p - MS_r)}{n_i} \tag{8.20a}$$

and

$$\hat{\sigma}_i^2 + \hat{\sigma}_e^2 = MS_r \tag{8.20b}$$

In our example these formulas yield

$$\hat{\sigma}_p^2 = \frac{(10.310 - 1.432)}{3} = 2.956$$

and

$$\hat{\sigma}_i^2 + \hat{\sigma}_e^2 = 1.432$$

The coefficients ρ_i^2 and ρ_I^2 can be estimated by using Equations 8.15 and 8.18, respectively.

TABLE 8.6. Summary ANOVA Table

SV	SS	df	MS
Examinees	92.794	9	10.310
Residual	28.646	20	1.432

UNIVERSES WITH FIXED FACETS

In each of the preceding examples the investigator was interested in generalizing to a universe of generalization that included measurement conditions other than those used in the D-study. In these examples the measurement facet is a random facet. The terminology derives from the fact that the measurement conditions in the D-study are assumed to be a random sample from the more extensive set of conditions comprising the universe of generalization. In other examples the investigator wishes to generalize to a universe of generalization that includes only those conditions that appear in the D-study. In these situations the measurement facet is fixed. This section concerns generalizability theory for universes with fixed facets. D-studies conducted with designs 1 and 2 are discussed, since they are likely to be the most commonly encountered. However, similar results can be developed for designs 3 and 4.

A Generalizability Coefficient for a Design 1 D-Study with a Fixed Facet

To see the implications of treating a facet as fixed or random, recall the development of the linear model for X_{pi}. There we pointed out that X_{pi} may be viewed as one of many ratings that rater i might have assigned to examine p, and therefore for a particular p and i, X_{pi} is a random variable. The mean or expected value of X_{pi} was denoted by T_{pi} and was identified as the true score for examinee p when rated by rater i. Furthermore we pointed out that T_{pi} varies over raters, and we identified μ_p as the mean over raters of the T_{pi}.

Now suppose there are two investigators who have access to the data from a design 1 D-study. Recall that in design 1 there is only one rater, rater i, and rater i rates all examinees. The first investigator views rater i as representative of a larger universe of raters. That is, the investigator views raters as a random facet and wants to know how well X_{pi} generalizes to μ_p, the universe score of examinee p for a universe of many raters. The appropriate generalizability coefficient is

$$\rho_{i*}^2 = \frac{\sigma_p^2}{\sigma_p^2 + \sigma_e^2}$$

The second investigator is not interested in generalizing to a universe consisting of many raters. Rather, this investigator's universe of generalization consists only of rater i. As a result the investigator is interested in how well X_{pi} generalizes to T_{pi}, which is the universe score for examinee p rated by rater i. The universe score variance is the variance over examinees of T_{pi} and is denoted by $\sigma_{T|i}^2$. The observed score variance is the variance of X_{pi} and is denoted by $\sigma_{X|i}^2$. As a result, the generalizability coefficient for the second universe of generalization is $\sigma_{T|i}^2/\sigma_{X|i}^2$, the ratio of true to observed score variance for rater i and is therefore equivalent to the classical reliability coefficient for that single rater. A key point then is that even though the definitions for the universe score and the generalizability coefficient are the same for fixed and random facets, and even when the same design is to be used for a D-study, changing a facet from random to fixed changes the boundaries of the universe and consequently alters the universe score, the universe score variance, and the generalizability coefficient.

Although a generalizability coefficient appropriate for a design 1 D-study with a fixed facet can be defined, an important question is whether it can be estimated from the data collected in the G-study. The answer is that it cannot be estimated, but a lower bound can be. The estimation is carried out by using the data from a design 2 G-study in which the rater who is to appear in the D-study also appears in the G-study. With this rater in the G-study, $\sigma_{X|i}^2$ can easily be estimated by calculating $\hat{\sigma}_{X|i}^2$, the variance of the ratings assigned by the rater of interest. However, $\sigma_{T|i}^2$ usually cannot be estimated. The lower bound to $\sigma_{T|i}^2/\sigma_{X|i}^2$ is $1 - \sigma_e^2/\sigma_{X|i}^2$ (Lord and Novick, 1968). The coefficient is estimated by substituting $\hat{\sigma}_e^2$ for σ_e^2 and $\hat{\sigma}_{X|i}^2$ for $\sigma_{X|i}^2$. The quantity $\hat{\sigma}_e^2 = MS_r$, which is calculated from a two-way ANOVA of the G-study data. For rater 1 in Table 8.1 the coefficient is $1 - 1.043/6.622 = .84$.

A Generalizability Coefficient for a Design 2 D-Study with a Fixed Facet

We pointed out that when design 1 is used to conduct a D-study and the measurement facet is considered fixed, the appropriate generalizability coefficient turns out to be equivalent to the reliability coefficient from classical test theory. Similarly, when design 2 is used to conduct a D-study and the measurement facet is considered fixed, the appropriate generalizability coefficient turns out to be equivalent to the classical test theory reliability coefficient. In design 2 the observed score is the average of the scores assigned to an examinee. Thus the problem is to estimate the reliability of a composite score. As noted in Chapter 7, coefficient alpha is considered a lower bound to the reliability coefficient of such a composite. Provided that the raters who will appear in the D-study are the only raters in the G-study, coefficient alpha estimated from the G-study can be considered a lower bound to the appropriate generalizability coefficient.

USE OF GENERALIZABILITY THEORY WITH DATA OTHER THAN RATINGS

From this presentation it should be clear that generalizability theory can be profitably applied to rating data. However its applications to other types of item and test data may be less apparent. Consider as a first example a standardized achievement test with three alternate forms. Since these three forms do not constitute the only forms that could be constructed, it may be reasonable to view them as a representative sample of all possible forms that could be constructed. Now suppose a school district uses only one form in a D-study. It may be of interest to see how well scores on this one form generalize to the universe scores defined for all forms of this test that could possibly be constructed. In this case, the appropriate generalizability coefficient is $\rho^2(X_{pi},\mu_p)$. To estimate this coefficient the district must conduct a G-study using all three forms; Equation 8.8 can be used to estimate this generalizability coefficient.

As a second example, suppose a psychologist plans to study factors related to private self-consciousness. The planned study is a D-study. The psychologist develops a 20-item true-false instrument and plans to administer it to all examinees in the D-study. The items are viewed as a random sample from a universe of items that might have been used. Note that the psychologist will be able to record the item scores of the examinees in the D-study in a table like Table 8.1. The rows of the table will still refer to examinees, but the columns will refer to items. Thus the design of the D-study can be viewed as design 2, with items as the measurement facet. Since the study will be conducted with design 2, ρ^2_{I*} is an appropriate generalizability coefficient. The question that arises is what kind of G-study should the psychologist conduct in order to estimate ρ^2_{I*}. Recall that in the rating example, a design 2 study was required to estimate ρ^2_{I*}. Similarly in the current example, a design 2 G-study is required. Thus the psychologist can administer the instrument to n_p examinees, lay out the responses in a n_p by n_i table similar to Table 8.1, and use Equations 8.4, 8.5, and 8.10 to estimate ρ^2_{I*}. Here both n_i and n'_i equal 20.

It can be shown that for dichotomous data, ρ^2_{I*} is equivalent to KR 20. With a single random facet ρ^2_{I*} is a lower bound to the average of the $\rho^2(X_{pI},\mu_p)$. Thus, the psychologist can view KR 20 as a lower bound to the average squared correlation, with the universe score for tests constructed by randomly selecting 20 true-false items from a universe of items.

STANDARD ERRORS OF MEASUREMENT FOR ABSOLUTE AND RELATIVE DECISIONS

A fundamental use of the standard error of measurement is to form a confidence interval. In classical test theory the confidence interval has the form $X \pm (SEM)$, where X denotes an observed score, and SEM denotes the standard error of measurement defined in classical test theory. This interval is considered to be a confidence interval for the true score. In generalizability theory the situation is somewhat more complicated. The interval is of the form $S \pm (SEM)$. Here S denotes the score used in forming the interval. The score and standard error of measurement depend primarily on the type of decision made using the D-study data and secondarily on the design of the study or the number of measurement conditions used.

With single-facet D-studies there are four definitions of observed score variance, one for each design. For each design, the error variance associated with the design may be defined as that part of the observed score variance that is not universe score variance. The designs and associated error variances are

Design 1: σ_e^2
Design 2: σ_e^2/n_i'
Design 3: $\sigma_i^2 + \sigma_e^2$
Design 4: $(\sigma_i^2 + \sigma_e^2)/n_i'$

A standard error of measurement is defined as the square root of an error variance. Deciding which standard error to use does not necessarily depend on the design of the D-study. Rather, it depends primarily on the use to which the scores will be put in the D-study. Here it is important to distinguish between comparative and absolute decisions. A comparative decision is one made by comparing the scores of different examinees. Examples of such decisions include the use of test scores to ''grade on the curve'' and to select the top-scoring candidates for entry into an educational institution. For a comparative decision, standard error is based on the error variance for the D-study design. For example, if a design 3 D-study is conducted, the appropriate standard error is $\sqrt{\sigma_i^2 + \sigma_e^2}$.

An absolute decision is one that depends on the examinee's score alone and not on how it compares to the scores of other examinees, for example, a criterion-referenced test used to determine whether an examinee can advance to the next unit of an instructional program. The decision to advance the student is made if the examinee's score exceeds a prespecified criterion. When test scores are used to make absolute decisions and a single-facet design is used, the standard error of measurement depends on the number of conditions each examinee is measured under. If only one condition is used (designs 1 and 3), the error variance is $\sigma_i^2 + \sigma_e^2$, whereas if several conditions are used (designs 2 and 4), $(\sigma_i^2 + \sigma_e^2)/n_i'$ is the appropriate error variance. As an example of an absolute decision, suppose that a six-item test is used to decide whether a student has mastered a small unit in a mathematics curriculum. If items are treated as the measurement facet, the decisions may be viewed as being based on a design 2 D-study with $n_i' = 6$ conditions of the item facet. The error variance is then $(\sigma_i^2 + \sigma_e^2)/6$. Both σ_i^2 and σ_e^2 can be estimated by using a two-way ANOVA of the item responses.

Table 8.7 summarizes the dependency of the error variance on the type of decision. Table 8.7 also shows the score used in forming a confidence interval and the parameter estimated by the confidence interval for all combinations of single-facet designs and decision types. The rationale for and implications of the entries in Table 8.7 for absolute decision are relatively simple, and so we will present these first. With an absolute decision the score used in forming a confidence interval is simply the observed score for the design used to collect the D-study data, and the confidence interval estimates the universe score. These facts make sense, since the error incurred in making an absolute decision reflects the substitution of an observed score for the universe score. To illustrate the use of Table 8.7 with absolute decisions, suppose an instructor administered a 100-point multiple-choice final exami-

TABLE 8.7.   Scores and Error Variances to Construct Confidence Intervals Appropriate for Each Decision Type and Design Combination

Decision Type	Design	Score	Error Variance	Parameter[a]
Absolute	1	X_{pi}	$\sigma_i^2 + \sigma_e^2$	μ_p
	2	X_{pI}	$(\sigma_i^2 + \sigma_e^2)/n_i'$	μ_p
	3	X_{pi}	$\sigma_i^2 + \sigma_e^2$	μ_p
	4	X_{pI}	$(\sigma_i^2 + \sigma_e^2)/n_i'$	μ_p
Comparative	1	$X_{pi} - X_{Pi}$	σ_e^2	$\mu_p - \mu$
	2	$X_{pI} - X_{PI}$	σ_e^2/n_i'	$\mu_p - \mu$
	3	X_{pi}	$\sigma_e^2 + \sigma_i^2$	μ_p
	4	X_{pI}	$(\sigma_e^2 + \sigma_i^2)/n_i'$	μ_p

[a] Denotes the parameter estimated by the confidence interval obtained by using the score and standard error in a given row.

nation and used the results to assign grades on the following percent correct scale: .91 to 1.00, A; .81 to .90, B; .71 to .80, C; .61 to .70, D; and .00 to .60, F. Administering the examination is a D-study in which the items comprise the single-measurement facet. Because all examinees took the same items, the D-study was conducted by using design 2. The grading decisions are absolute decisions since a grade can be assigned to a student without knowing the scores of the other students in the class. According to Table 8.7, the error variance is $(\sigma_i^2 + \sigma_e^2)/n_i'$, the score used in forming the confidence interval is X_{pI}, and the confidence interval estimates the universe score μ_p. In these expressions n_i' is the number of items on the test and X_{pI} is a proportion correct score on the test. Estimation of σ_i^2 and σ_e^2 can be carried out by using a two-factor ANOVA of the D-study data.

The implications of Table 8.7 for comparative decisions are relatively straightforward. However, the rationale for the entries is somewhat complicated. We will sketch the rationale for a design 1 D-study and simply note that a similar rationale applies to the other designs. Recall that design 1 is a crossed design in which all examinees are exposed to a single-measurement condition. Suppose that we conduct a D-study using design 1 and are able to measure the whole population. This means that we know the numeric value of μ_i, the population mean score for the single-measurement condition. Under what conditions will the comparative decisions made by using the observed score X_{pi} be the same as those that would be made if we knew the universe scores for each examinee? This question is easily answered if we recognize a few facts and recall the linear model for X_{pi}. First the facts. Remember that a comparative decision involves comparing observed scores for the examinees. For design 1, comparing observed scores, X_{pi}, is equivalent to comparing deviation scores, $X_{pi} - \mu_i$, since μ_i will be the same for all examinees. In a similar fashion comparing universe scores, μ_p, is equivalent to comparing universe deviation scores, $\mu_p - \mu$. These two equivalencies are the facts we need. Now let us recall the linear model for X_{pi}:

$$X_{pi} = \mu + (\mu_p - \mu) + (\mu_i - \mu) + e_{pi} \qquad (8.21)$$

Subtracting μ_i from both sides we obtain

$$X_{pi} - \mu_i = \mu_p - \mu + e_{pi} \qquad (8.22)$$

Equation 8.22 makes it clear that a decision based on $X_{pi} - \mu_i$ will be the same as one based on $\mu_p - \mu$ if and only if these deviation scores are the same. Therefore the answer to our question is that the comparative decisions made by using the observed score will be the same as those that would be made by using the universe score, provided that $X_{pi} - \mu_i = \mu_p - \mu$. From this point of view the error incurred in making a comparative decision by using design 1 involves the substitution of $X_{pi} - \mu_i$ for $\mu_p - \mu$. As a result the appropriate confidence interval is $(X_{pi} - \mu_i) \pm (\hat{\sigma}_e^2)$, which estimates $\mu_p - \mu$. However, we usually do not know μ_i, and so we substitute the sample mean, which is denoted by X_{Pi} in Table 8.7, for μ_i. The capital P indicates that the sample mean has been taken over all persons.

To illustrate the use of Table 8.7 with comparative decisions, let us return to the example of the social psychologist. Recall that the psychologist was interested in correlates of shyness. Calculating a correlation involves comparative decisions since a correlation measures the degree to which individual differences on two variables are related. Suppose the psychologist has decided to use design 2 for the D-study. According to Table 8.7, the error variance is σ_e^2/n_i', the score used in calculating the confidence interval is $X_{pI} - X_{PI}$, and the confidence interval estimates $\mu_p - \mu$. In these expressions n_i' is the number of raters in the D-study, X_{pI} is the average rating for examinee p, and X_{PI} is the average of the X_{pI}.

It is important to remember that the observed score in generalizability theory is an average over all measurement conditions to which examinee p is exposed. It frequently happens that the corresponding total score, rather than this average score, is actually used to make the decision. In the criterion-referenced testing example, this would occur if $Y = n_i' X_{pI}$ had been used. To accommodate the use of a total score, simply multiply the error score variance by the square of the number of conditions examinee p is observed under. In the criterion-referenced testing example, the error score variance for Y would be

$$n_i'^2[(\sigma_i^2 + \sigma_e^2)/n_i'] = n_i'(\sigma_i^2 + \sigma_e^2) \qquad (8.23)$$

GENERALIZABILITY THEORY FOR TWO-FACET DESIGNS

In many situations the conditions of measurement must be classified into two or more facets. An example of a two-facet study occurs when examinees respond to several essay questions which are to be scored by several graders. The set of graders and the set of essay questions each constitutes a facet. When the conditions of measurement are classified into two facets, the theory and procedures developed for single-facet designs will not be adequate for formulating and estimating generalizability coefficients. In this section the formulation and estimation of generalizability coefficients for two-facet designs is presented. Our presentation involves the following topics:

1. Terminology for describing designs and universes of generalization
2. Universe score variance for different universes of generalization
3. Expected observed score variance for D-study designs
4. Formulation of generalizability coefficients
5. Estimation of generalizability coefficients

Terminology

Two facets are said to be *crossed* if every measurement condition of the first facet occurs in combination with every measurement condition of the second factor. For example, if each of several tests are administered on each of several occasions, the facets of tests and occasions are crossed. A facet is said to be *nested* within a second facet if different sets of measurement conditions of the first facet occur in combination with each measurement condition of the second facet. For example, suppose each of 100 students is required to respond to one essay question on physics, one on twentieth-century American novels, and one on the history of mathematics. Since the topics are quite different, one set of graders scores the physics question, another the literature question, and a third the history question. The first set of graders scores the physics essay of every examinee, and so forth. Here graders are nested within essay questions. Recall that with single-facet designs, a measurement facet can be crossed with or nested within examinees. With two-facet designs, either facet may be crossed with or nested within examinees. In the current example both graders and topics are crossed with examinees since every examinee writes an essay on each topic and is graded by each grader.

Universe Score Variance

Before describing several universes of generalization and the corresponding universe score variances, it is necessary to define the variance components used in generalizability theory for two-facet designs. These components are

1. σ_p^2, the variance due to examinee
2. σ_i^2, the variance due to the conditions of facet I
3. σ_j^2, the variance due to the conditions of facet J
4. σ_{pi}^2, the variance due to the interaction of examinees and the conditions of facet I
5. σ_{pj}^2, the variance due to the interaction of examinees and the conditions of facet J
6. σ_{ij}^2, the variance due to the interaction of conditions of I and the conditions of J
7. σ_e^2, the residual variance

The formula of the universe score variance depends on the facets, if any, that are fixed in the universe of generalization. We will present five possible universes of generalization and the universe score variance for each. However, it is important to point out that throughout our discussion of generalizability theory for two facets, we assume that a universe of generalization is defined with the measurement facets crossed. (We do not assume, however, that measurement facets are crossed with each other in the designs that can be used for G- or D-studies. It is entirely possible to use a design that has one measurement facet nested within a second measurement facet, even though the facets are crossed in the universe of generalization.) We make the assumption solely to keep the discussion from becoming more complicated than it already is. Generalizability theory can handle universes with one facet nested within another. Cronbach et al. (1972) discuss this kind of universe.

UNIVERSE 1.   In the first universe the facets are both considered random. An example of this universe is when an investigator wants to generalize over forms of a test and occasions of measurements, and both are considered to be random facets. The universe score variance is simply σ_p^2. Note that when a facet is random, the universe score variance does not depend on whether the facet is crossed with or nested within examinees.

UNIVERSES 2 AND 3.   In the second and third universes, one facet is random and one is fixed. This fixed facet is crossed with examinees. In universe 2 the I facet is fixed, and the universe score variance is $\sigma_p^2 + \sigma_{pi}^2/n_i'$. The example from universe 1 serves here, if occasions are considered random, but forms (labeled facet I) are considered fixed. In universe 3, facet J is fixed, so the universe score variance is $\sigma_p^2 + \sigma_{pj}^2/n_j'$. Universe 3 is obtained if occasions are fixed and forms are random. The symbols in n_i' and n_j' denote the number of conditions in the I and J facets in the D-study.

UNIVERSES 4 AND 5.   With universes 4 and 5 one facet is random and one is fixed. The fixed facet is nested within examinees, for example, if parents rate their child's ability to handle a series of stressful situations. Since each child has only two parents and these are different for each child, the parent facet is fixed and parents are nested within children. The situation facet is considered random. In universe 4 I is the fixed facet, there are n_i' conditions of I nested within each examinee, and the universe score variance is $\sigma_p^2 + (\sigma_i^2 + \sigma_{pi}^2)/n_i'$. In universe 5, J is the fixed facet, and the universe score variance is $\sigma_p^2 + (\sigma_j^2 + \sigma_{pj}^2)/n_j'$.

Having stated the universe score variance for each of several universes of generalization, we will present the expected observed score variance for several D-study designs. As we shall see in the subsequent section, a generalizability coefficient is expressed as a ratio of universe to observed score variance, and depends on the universe of generalization and the design of the D-study.

Expected Observed Score Variance

The definition of the expected observed score variance depends on the design of the D-study. We will present five possible D-study designs. Gleser, Cronbach, and Rajaratnam (1965) presented three additional designs.

DESIGN 1.   In design 1 the facets are crossed with each other and with examinees. Each condition of facet I occurs in combination with each condition of facet J, and each examinee is exposed to all the condition combinations. An example is when each of several tests (facet I) is administered on the same occasions and each examinee takes each test on each occasion. Cronbach et al. (1972) denoted this design by $(pxixj)$. Here p stands for persons (or examinees), i for conditions of facet I, j for conditions of facet J, and x for crossing. Thus $(pxixj)$ indicates that examinees, conditions of facet I, and conditions of facet J are all crossed. In design 1 the observed score is the average of the $n_i' n_j'$ observations, and the expected observed score variance is

$$\sigma_p^2 + \frac{1}{n_i'}\sigma_{pi}^2 + \frac{1}{n_j'}\sigma_{pj}^2 + \frac{1}{n_i' n_j'}\sigma_e^2 \tag{8.24}$$

DESIGN 2.   In design 2, n_j' conditions of J are nested in each of the n_i' conditions of I, but both facets are crossed with examinees. An example is the three essay questions (facet I), each of which is graded by three different graders (facet J). Here the graders are nested within each essay question. Each examinee takes each essay question and so is graded by each grader. Thus examinees are crossed with both essays and graders. The design is denoted by $(j:i)xp$, which is read conditions of facet J are nested in conditions of facet I and condition combinations are crossed with examinees. The observed score is the average of the $n_i' n_j'$ observations. The expected observed score variance is

$$\sigma_p^2 + \frac{1}{n_i'}\sigma_{pi}^2 + \frac{1}{n_i' n_j'}(\sigma_{pj}^2 + \sigma_e^2) \tag{8.25}$$

There is, of course, a design 2', with conditions of I nested in conditions of J. (The reader should note that when certain designs are used for G-studies it will be possible to calculate separate estimates of σ_{pj}^2 and σ_e^2, whereas with other designs it will be necessary to calculate a single estimate of $\sigma_{pj}^2 + \sigma_e^2$. The same is true for all variance components collected in parentheses in Equations 8.25 through 8.28. Each of these equations is an expression for an expected observed score variance.)

DESIGN 3.   In design 3, each condition of I occurs in combination with one condition of J, so that there are a total of $k = n_i n_j$ conditions. Each examinee is exposed to all k measurement conditions, and therefore each facet is crossed with examinees. This design is denoted by $(i,j)xp$. In the essay-grading example, this design would occur if there were one grader for the physics question, one for the literature question, and one for the mathematics question. The observed score is the average of all

k conditions, and the expected observed score variance is

$$\sigma_p^2 + \frac{1}{k}(\sigma_{pi}^2 + \sigma_{pj}^2 + \sigma_e^2) \tag{8.26}$$

DESIGN 4.   In design 4, the n_i' conditions of facet I are crossed with examinees, whereas n_j' conditions of facet J are nested within each examinee. Facets I and J are crossed. An example is when students in several courses rate their instructors with the same set of rating scales. In this example, the instructors are the examinees and students comprise the conditions of facet J. If we assume that no student is enrolled in more than one course, students are nested within examinees. Since all students used the same rating scales (facet I) and all instructors are rated with these scales, conditions of facet J are crossed with conditions of facet I and examinees. The notation for this design is $(j:p)xi$. Kane, Gillmore, and Crooks (1976) have discussed the student-rating example in detail. With design 4 the expected observed score variance is

$$\sigma_p^2 + \frac{1}{n_i'}\sigma_{pi}^2 + \frac{1}{n_j'}(\sigma_{pj}^2 + \sigma_j^2) + \frac{1}{n_i'n_j'}(\sigma_{ij}^2 + \sigma_e^2) \tag{8.27}$$

There is a design 4′, with J crossed with examinees and I nested within examinees.

DESIGN 5.   In this design, I is crossed with examinees and J is nested within examinees. In addition, J is nested in I. The design is denoted by $j:(ixp)$. As an example of this design, consider a study that attempts to measure time on task. Students are to be observed for several 15-minute periods. Each student is observed by the same n_i' observers, and so observers are crossed with examinees. Each student is observed for n_j' periods by each observer. The n_j' periods are different for each observer, and so periods (facet J) are nested in observers (facet I). Moreover no two students are observed during the same period, and so the periods are nested within examinees. The expected observed score variance for this design is

$$\sigma_p^2 + \frac{1}{n_i'}\sigma_{pi}^2 + \frac{1}{n_i'n_j'}(\sigma_{pj}^2 + \sigma_j^2 + \sigma_{ij}^2 + \sigma_e^2) \tag{8.28}$$

There is a design 5′, with J nested with examinees, I crossed with examinees, and I nested in J.

Generalizability Coefficients

Formulating the appropriate generalizability coefficient depends on the universe of generalization and the design of the D-study. Once the universe and the design of the D-study are determined, the appropriate generalizability coefficient is simply the ratio of universe to observed score variance. For example, consider the study with the physics, literature, and mathematics essays graded by several graders. Suppose the universe of generalization is defined by treating questions (facet I) as fixed and graders (facet J) as random. The universe of generalization is universe 2. If the D-study is conducted with design 2, the appropriate generalizability coefficient is

$$\rho^2 = \frac{\sigma_p^2 + \sigma_{pi}^2/n_i'}{\sigma_p^2 + \sigma_{pi}^2/n_i' + (\sigma_{pj}^2 + \sigma_e^2)/n_i'n_j'} \tag{8.29}$$

CHOOSING A G-STUDY DESIGN.   In principle, generalizability coefficients should be estimated from data collected in a G-study that is conducted prior to the D-study. This permits the researcher to judge whether the D-study data will have adequate generalizability. In designing a G-study, three issues must be confronted. First, the G-study design should be compatible with the universe of generalization the researcher has in mind. For example, a researcher wants to consider forms of a test (facet I) as a random facet and occasions of measurement (facet J) as a fixed facet in the universe of generalization. If occasions are crossed with examinees in the universe, we have universe 3. With this universe it does not make sense to use design 4 with occasions nested in examinees. The principle is that a fixed facet which is crossed with examinees in the universe of generalization should also be crossed with examinees in the G-study design. Similarly a fixed facet which is nested in examinees in the universe of generalization should be nested in examinees in the G-study design.

The second issue in choosing a design for a G-study is whether the design permits estimation of the variance components of the universe score variance. If a universe score variance includes a particular variance component, but a design does not permit estimation of this component, there is no point in considering this design as a potential G-study design. Table 8.8, which was constructed to permit the reader to address these issues, presents the designs that are useful G-study designs for each universe of generalization. Using Table 8.8 for the forms and occasions example, we see that for universe 3, designs 1, 2', 4', and 5' are useful G-study designs. The third issue in choosing a design for a G-study involves the fact that data collected with a particular design for a G-study cannot be used to estimate the observed score variance for all D-study designs. The goal is to choose a G-study design that can be used to estimate the observed score variances for the largest possible variety of D-study designs. For each D-study design, Table 8.9 indicates the G-study designs that can be used to estimate its observed score variance. For example, a G-study conducted under design 1 can be used to estimate the observed score variance for any of the eight designs used as a D-study design.

In designing a G-study, Tables 8.8 and 8.9 must be used in conjunction. Once a universe of generalization is chosen, Table 8.8 is used to identify potential G-study designs. From among these potential G-study designs the researcher should choose one that is practical and permits estimation of as many observed score variances as possible. To continue with the forms and occasions example, from Table 8.8 we found that designs 1, 2', 4', and 5' are useful designs for a G-study. Inspecting Table 8.9, we see that design 1 permits estimation of observed score variance for all the D-study designs. Therefore, if design 1 is practical, it should be used in the

TABLE 8.8. Useful G-Study Designs for Each Universe of Generalization

Universe of Generalization	Facet Description				G-Study Designs							
	Random	Fixed	Crossed with P^a	Nested in P^a	1 (pxixj)	2 (j:i)xp	2' (i:j)xp	3 (ij)xp	4 (j:p)xi	4' (i:p)xj	5 j:(ixp)	5' i:(jxp)
1	I,J	—	—	—	*	*	*	*	*	*	*	*
2	J	I	I	—	*	*	*	*	*	*	*	
3	I	J	J	—	*		*	*	*	*		*
4	J	I	—	I				*		*		
5	I	J	—	J					*			

^{a}Refers only to fixed facets. With random facets, crossing with or nesting in P do not have implications for the choice of a G-study design.

183

TABLE 8.9.   Potential G-Study Designs for Estimating Expected Observed Score Variance in D-Studies

G-Study Designs	D-Study Designs[a]							
	1	2	2'	3	4	4'	5	5'
1 (pxixj)	*	*	*	*	*	*	*	*
2 (j:i)xp		*						
2' (i:j)xp			*					*
3 (i,j)xp				*				
4 (j:p)xi					*		*	
4' (i:p)xj						*		*
5 j:(ixp)							*	
5' i:(jxp)								*

[a]The asterisk indicates that the G-study can be used to estimate the expected observed score variance in the D-study.

G-study. Note that although design 1 permits estimation of the observed score variances for all eight possible D-study designs. In choosing a D-study design for the forms and occasions example (Universe 3), we should ignore designs 2, 3, 4, and 5. Just as these were not useful G-study designs, they are not useful D-study designs for this example.

ESTIMATING GENERALIZABILITY COEFFICIENTS.   Once the G-study is conducted, an appropriate ANOVA of the data will yield estimates of the components of variance required to estimate the generalizability coefficient. Space limitations preclude a complete treatment of the ANOVA for each of the designs. However, the factors of each are given in Table 8.10, along with the expected mean squares for each factor. The expected mean squares are stated in terms of the variance components previously defined. Readers familiar with ANOVA may find some of the expected mean squares for designs 2 to 5 confusing at first. Consider, for example, the source of variance $J:I$ in design 2. Using the rules of thumb as given, for example, in Millman and Glass (1967), we would write the expected mean square as $\sigma_p^2 + \sigma_{pj}^2 + n_p\sigma_{j:i}^2$, where the last term is the variance for the conditions of j that are nested within conditions of i. However, it can be shown that $\sigma_{j:i}^2 = \sigma_j^2 + \sigma_{ij}^2$. The right-hand side of the equality is used in Table 8.10, since that notation was used in the expressions for the universe and expected observed score variance. To illustrate use of Table 8.10, consider estimating ρ^2 as defined in Equation 8.29. The necessary variance components are σ_p^2, σ_{pi}^2, and $(\sigma_{pj}^2 + \sigma_e^2)$. Based on the EMS reported in Table 8.10 for design 2, these can be estimated through

$$\hat{\sigma}_p^2 = \frac{(MS_p - MS_{pi})}{n_i n_j} \tag{8.30a}$$

$$\hat{\sigma}_{pi}^2 = \frac{(MS_{pi} - MS_r)}{n_j} \tag{8.30b}$$

TABLE 8.10. EMS for Designs 1 to 5

Design 1

SV	EMS
P	$\sigma_e^2 + n_i n_j \sigma_p^2 + n_j \sigma_{pi}^2 + n_i \sigma_{pj}^2$
I	$\sigma_e^2 + n_j n_p \sigma_i^2 + n_j \sigma_{pi}^2 + n_p \sigma_{ij}^2$
J	$\sigma_e^2 + n_i n_p \sigma_j^2 + n_i \sigma_{pj}^2 + n_p \sigma_{ij}^2$
PI	$\sigma_e^2 + n_j \sigma_{pi}^2$
PJ	$\sigma_e^2 + n_i \sigma_{pj}^2$
IJ	$\sigma_e^2 + n_p \sigma_{ij}^2$
Residual	σ_e^2

Design 2

SV	EMS
P	$\sigma_e^2 + \sigma_{pj}^2 + n_i n_j \sigma_p^2 + n_j \sigma_{pi}^2$
I	$\sigma_e^2 + \sigma_{pj}^2 + n_p n_j \sigma_i^2 + n_j \sigma_{pi}^2 + n_i(\sigma_j^2 + \sigma_{ij}^2)$
J:I	$\sigma_e^2 + \sigma_{pj}^2 + n_i(\sigma_j^2 + \sigma_{ij}^2)$
PI	$\sigma_e^2 + \sigma_{pj}^2 + n_j \sigma_{pi}^2$
Residual	$\sigma_e^2 + \sigma_{pj}^2$

Design 3

SV	EMS
P	$\sigma_e^2 + \sigma_{pj}^2 + \sigma_{pi}^2 + k\sigma_p^2$
I,J	$\sigma_e^2 + \sigma_{pj}^2 + \sigma_{pi}^2 + n_p(\sigma_i^2 + \sigma_j^2 + \sigma_{ij}^2)$
Residual	$\sigma_e^2 + \sigma_{pj}^2 + \sigma_{pi}^2$

Design 4

SV	EMS
P	$\sigma_e^2 + \sigma_{ij}^2 + n_i n_j \sigma_p^2 + n_j \sigma_{pi}^2 + n_i(\sigma_j^2 + \sigma_{pj}^2)$
I	$\sigma_e^2 + \sigma_{ij}^2 + n_p n_j \sigma_i^2 + n_j \sigma_{pi}^2$
PI	$\sigma_e^2 + \sigma_{ij}^2 + n_j \sigma_{pi}^2$
J:P	$\sigma_e^2 + \sigma_{ij}^2 + n_i(\sigma_j^2 + \sigma_{pj}^2)$
Residual	$\sigma_e^2 + \sigma_{ij}^2$

Design 5

SV	EMS
P	$\sigma_e^2 + \sigma_j^2 + \sigma_{ij}^2 + \sigma_{pj}^2 + n_i n_j \sigma_p^2 + n_j \sigma_{pi}^2$
I	$\sigma_e^2 + \sigma_j^2 + \sigma_{ij}^2 + \sigma_{pj}^2 + n_j n_p \sigma_i^2 + n_j \sigma_{pi}^2$
PI	$\sigma_e^2 + \sigma_j^2 + \sigma_{ij}^2 + \sigma_{pj}^2 + n_j \sigma_{pi}^2$
Residual	$\sigma_e^2 + \sigma_j^2 + \sigma_{ij}^2 + \sigma_{pj}^2$

and

$$\hat{\sigma}_{pj}^2 + \hat{\sigma}_e^2 = (MS_r) \qquad (8.30c)$$

The generalizability coefficient is then estimated by using

$$\hat{\rho}^2 = \frac{\hat{\sigma}_p^2 + \hat{\sigma}_{pi}^2/n_i'}{\hat{\sigma}_p^2 + \hat{\sigma}_{pi}^2/n_i' + (\hat{\sigma}_{pj}^2 + \hat{\sigma}_e^2)/n_i' n_j'} \qquad (8.31)$$

An Example

Consider an essay examination in which each examinee is to write essays on each of six topics. In studying the generalizability of the scores, the examiner wants to treat both topics and graders as random. This is universe 1, so the universe score variance is σ_p^2. Turning to Table 8.8 we find that all eight designs are useful as G-study designs. Inspecting Table 8.9 we find that using design 1 in our G-study will permit us to estimate the observed score variance for the largest variety of D-study designs. Suppose it is practical to use design 1 as a G-study and so the researcher conducts a G-study by using this design; seven examinees write essays on two topics and three graders grade each essay. Table 8.11 reports a summary of the ANOVA for the data collected in this G-study.

How can the results reported in Table 8.11 be used to choose a D-study design for collecting the examination data? Suppose the examiner feels it will be practical to have six graders in the D-study. With six graders, one possible D-study design is design 1. Labeling graders as facet J and topics as facet I, we have a D-study with $n_j' = 6$ graders and $n_i' = 6$ topics. The observed score variance for design 1 is

$$\sigma_p^2 + \sigma_{pi}^2/n_i' + \sigma_{pj}^2/n_j' + \sigma_e^2/n_i'n_j' \tag{8.32}$$

As a result the appropriate generalizability coefficient is

$$\rho^2 = \frac{\sigma_p^2}{\sigma_p^2 + \sigma_{pi}^2/n_i' + \sigma_{pj}^2/n_j' + \sigma_e^2/n_i'n_j'} \tag{8.33}$$

Another possible design is design 3. In this design each grader would grade only one topic, and so $k = n_i' = n_j' = 6$. The observed score variance for design 3 is

$$\sigma_p^2 + (\sigma_{pi}^2 + \sigma_{pj}^2 + \sigma_e^2)/k \tag{8.34}$$

and so the appropriate generalizability coefficient is

$$\rho^2 = \frac{\sigma_p^2}{\sigma_p^2 + (\sigma_{pi}^2 + \sigma_{pj}^2 + \sigma_e^2)/k} \tag{8.35}$$

The next step is to develop equations for estimating the necessary variance components for each generalizability coefficient. To estimate the observed score and

TABLE 8.11.   Summary ANOVA Table for a Two-Facet Design[a]

SV	SS	df	MS
Persons (P)	66.571	6	11.095
Topics (I)	.857	1	.857
Graders (J)	7.428	2	3.714
PI	7.809	6	1.301
PJ	54.571	12	4.547
IJ	2.285	2	1.142
Residual	152.571	12	1.087

[a]The data were collected by using design 1 ($pxixj$) of the two-facet designs.

universe score variance we must estimate σ_p^2, σ_{pi}^2, σ_{pj}^2, and σ_e^2. Using the expected mean squares for design 1 in Table 8.10, we obtain the following expressions:

$$\hat{\sigma}_p^2 = \frac{(MS_p - MS_{pi} - MS_{pj} + MS_r)}{n_i n_j} \tag{8.36a}$$

$$\hat{\sigma}_{pi}^2 = \frac{(MS_{pi} - MS_r)}{n_j} \tag{8.36b}$$

$$\hat{\sigma}_{pj}^2 = \frac{(MS_{pj} - MS_r)}{n_i} \tag{8.36c}$$

and

$$\hat{\sigma}_e^2 = MS_r \tag{8.36d}$$

Substituting the appropriate results from Table 8.11 into Equation 8.36, we obtain

$$\hat{\sigma}_p^2 = \frac{(11.095 - 1.301 - 4.547 + 1.087)}{6} = 1.055$$

$$\hat{\sigma}_{pi}^2 = \frac{(1.301 - 1.087)}{3} = .071$$

$$\hat{\sigma}_{pj}^2 = \frac{(4.547 - 1.087)}{2} = 1.730$$

and

$$\hat{\sigma}_e^2 = 1.087$$

Substituting estimates for parameters in Equation 8.33, we obtain

$$\hat{\rho}^2 = \frac{1.055}{1.055 + .071/6 + 1.730/6 + 1.037/36} = .76$$

as our estimated generalizability coefficient for design 1. Substituting estimates for parameters in Equation 8.35, we obtain

$$\hat{\rho}^2 = \frac{1.055}{1.055 + (.071 + 1.730 + 1.087)/6} = .69$$

as our generalizability coefficient for design 3. Since the two designs do not yield very different generalizability coefficients, and since design 3 demands much less time of each grader, the examiner might be well advised to choose this design.

Suppose now that the examiner feels that neither design gives adequate generalizability. The examiner notes that the largest variance component contributing to the observed score variance is the component $\hat{\sigma}_{pj}^2$, the variance due to the person by rater interaction. This effect of this component can be reduced by increasing the number of raters. For example, it may be possible to have two raters rate each essay in the D-study, with raters nested in topics and both raters and topics crossed with examinees. This is an example of design 2 with $n_i' = 6$ and $n_j' = 2$. (Note that in design 2 n_j' is not the total number of graders but the number grading each essay.)

The appropriate generalizability coefficient would then be estimated by

$$\hat{\rho}^2 = \frac{\hat{\sigma}_p^2}{\hat{\sigma}_p^2 + \hat{\sigma}_{pi}^2/n_i' + (\hat{\sigma}_{pj}^2 + \hat{\sigma}_e^2)/n_i'n_j'} \tag{8.37}$$

For our example we obtain

$$\hat{\rho}^2 = \frac{1.055}{1.055 + .071/6 + (1.730 + 1.087)/12} = .81$$

Thus, design 2 (two graders grade each topic) increases generalizability substantially over design 3 (one grader grades each essay). It also results in a modest increase over design 1 (six graders grade every essay) and requires less time per grader than design 1. However, design 2 requires 12 raters, which may be impractical. If so, then it may be best to use design 3 and increase both the number of topics and the number of graders.

SUMMARY

Generalizability theory is concerned with a set of techniques for studying the degree to which a particular set of measurements of an examinee generalizes to a more extensive set of measurements of that examinee. The first or obtained set of measurements is considered to be a representative sample from the second set. The measurements in the second set are typically hypothetical. Both sets of measurements are made under a specifiable set of measurement conditions. Here the term *conditions* refers to aspects of the measuring process such as the task presented, the time of measurement, the directions, and so forth, collectively. All the measurement conditions for the second set of measurements are called the *universe of generalization*.

The measurement conditions for each set of measurements may be classified in terms of facets. For example, if the measurement conditions are defined by the topic of an essay and the identity of a grader, there are two facets—topic and grader. A facet can be either fixed or random in the universe of generalization. If a facet refers to exactly the same conditions for the universe of generalization and the obtained set of measurements, it is a fixed facet. If the facet refers to a more extensive set of conditions for the universe of generalization, it is a random facet. Two facets can be crossed with one another or one facet can be nested in the other. Two facets are crossed if each condition of one facet can occur in combination with each condition of the second facet. One facet is nested in a second facet if each condition of the first facet can occur in combination with only one condition of the second facet. A facet can also be crossed with or nested within an examinee. Definition of the universe of generalization involves defining the facets, stating whether a facet is fixed or random, describing the crossing and nesting of facets, and stating whether each facet is crossed with or nested within examinees.

The hypothetical process of measuring an examinee under all conditions in the universe of generalization, and averaging these measurements yields the examinee's universe score. The degree to which obtained measurements generalize to the universe scores of a group of examinees can be quantified by either a generalizability coefficient or an error variance. The most common kind of generalizability coefficient is a ratio of universe to observed score variance. The universe score variance is determined by the universe of generalization, and the observed score variance is determined by the design for collecting the obtained set of measurements. The appropriate error variance depends on the use to which the test scores will be put, as well as the universe of generalization and the design for making the measurements. Two different uses are decisions which involve comparing examinees— comparative decisions—and decisions which can be made without measuring any other examinees—absolute decisions.

Generalizability theory distinguishes between generalizability and decision studies. The purpose of the former is to study the generalizability of a measurement procedure, whereas the purpose of the latter is to provide data for making decisions about examinees. A well-designed generalizability study will help the designer of a decision study to choose a design that will yield generalizable data. The designer of a decision study who has access to data from an appropriate generalizability study will use the results of an analysis of variance of the generalizability study data. These results are used to estimate generalizability coefficients and error variances for a variety of designs under consideration for the decision studies. Based on these estimates and practical considerations, the investigator can choose the most appropriate design for the decision study.

Exercises

1. Using the results reported in Table 7.1 and 7.3 carry out the following tasks:
   A. Suppose the items were a random sample from a very large pool of items. In the actual testing program a different random sample of 20 items will be drawn and administered to each examinee. Estimate a generalizability coefficient appropriate for this situation.
   B. Suppose each student will take the same 20-item test with the items drawn from the pool described in A. The test results will be used to report an estimate of the percentage of the item pool that the student knows. Calculate an appropriate confidence interval for a person who earns a score of 15 during the actual testing program.
   C. Calculate the appropriate generalizability coefficient for the situation in which each student takes the same 10 items drawn at random from the pool described in A.
2. A measurement specialist is interested in whether young children exhibit an option preference in responding to multiple-choice questions. The researcher constructs four forms of a 20-item computation test and administers all four forms to 43 third-grade students. On each form, the number of times each option is the correct answer is the same. The researcher "scores" each test by using the following scheme:

Option	Points
omit	0
a	1
b	2
c	3
d	4

The results of a two-way ANOVA of the data are presented in the following table. Calculate a generalizability coefficient that indicates whether the students tend to have consistent option preferences.

Summary ANOVA Table

SV	df	SS	MS
Examinees	42	1915.752	45.613
Forms	3	59.791	19.930
Error	126	1782.281	14.145

3. Based on each of the following descriptions of D-studies carry out the following tasks:
   A. Identify the facets in the study.
   B. State which facets, if any, are fixed in the universe of generalization.
   C. Write the symbolic formula for the universe and observed score variance.
   D. Assuming data are available from a G-study conducted with the design used for the D-study, show how you would estimate the required variance components.

   a. A 50-item multiple-choice final examination will be administered in a sociology class.
   b. A short form of the Thematic Apperception Test (TAT), consisting of 10 cards, is administered to 50 juvenile delinquents. The TAT requires the examinee to make up a short story to fit each picture. The 10 stories of the juvenile delinquents were tape-recorded, and 3 clinical psychologists rated each tape on the degree of rejection of authority. The score assigned to each juvenile delinquent is the average of the 30 ratings.
   c. In a study of factors related to writing proficiency, each participant will write eight essays: essays on two topics in each of four modes—descriptive, narrative, expository, and argumentative. Different topics are chosen for each mode, but all participants write on the same topics. The essays are scored for the number of t units, a measure of syntactic complexity. The final score for each participant is the average over all eight essays. One scorer scores all essays.
   d. A study of factors related to reading achievement is conducted. The study involves 50 third-grade classes. In the study the class is the unit of analysis. The measure of achievement used in the study is a classroom average score on the reading subtest on the Dire Achievement Test (for purposes of completing D you may assume there are an equal number of children in each classroom).

4. In a generalizability study concerned with observations of family interactions in museums, 15 randomly chosen families were observed by each of two observers in each of three exhibits. One of the variables concerned the amount of time parents attended an exhibit without interacting with a child. A summary of the ANOVA for this variable follows:

Summary ANOVA Table

SV	SS	df	MS
Families (P)	2346.955	14	167.639
Observers (I)	3.211	1	3.211
Exhibits (J)	1231.622	2	615.811
$P \times I$	18.288	14	1.306
$P \times J$	2372.377	28	84.726
$I \times J$	2.688	2	1.344
Residual	35.311	28	1.261

Using these results carry out the following tasks:

A. An investigator plans to conduct a study of the correlates of attending to exhibits without interacting with a child. Families will be observed by one rater in one exhibit. Calculate a generalizability coefficient appropriate to this design, assuming the investigator views observers and exhibits as random factors.

B. If it were practically possible for the investigator in A to increase either the number of exhibits a family is observed in or the number of observers, which would be most important to increase?

C. Suppose the investigator has access to three observers and each observer can observe families in at most two exhibits. Moreover it is practical to ask each of at least 30 families to attend up to six exhibits. Which designs are practical given these limitations? Which yields the largest generalizability coefficient?

D. Suppose the investigator plans to conduct the study by using the three exhibits in which the generalizability study was conducted. Two observers will observe in all three exhibits. The investigator views the three exhibits as fixed. Calculate a generalizability coefficient appropriate for this design.

E. Suppose the investigator plans to conduct the study in a different museum but plans to use three exhibits and two raters as in D. To which study, that in D or that in E is the generalizability coefficient, calculated in D, most relevant? Why?

Chapter 9

RELIABILITY COEFFICIENTS FOR CRITERION-REFERENCED TESTS

An achievement test usually consists of a set of items that have been chosen because they are thought to require skills and abilities representative of the goals of instruction. Glaser (1963) argued that scores on achievement tests can provide two types of information. One type is the relative position of an examinee's score in a distribution of scores. Reporting test performance as a *z*-score provides this kind of information. Here the standard used in interpreting test performance is a relative one, and the score given to the examinee is called a norm-referenced measure. The second type of information is the degree to which the student has attained the goals of instruction. A simple example is an examinee's proportion-correct score on a test covering the 100 facts of addition. If the items on the test are chosen randomly from all possible items, the proportion-correct score can be considered an estimate of the proportion of facts the student knows and can be interpreted without knowing how other examinees have performed on the test. In this example the porportion-correct score is a criterion-referenced measure.

As defined by Glaser, the principal distinction between a norm-referenced and a criterion-referenced measure is the standard to which the test performance is referenced. The term *criterion* in criterion-referenced measurement evolved from Glaser's definition of achievement measurement as ''. . . the assessment of terminal or criterion behavior.'' The term *criterion-referenced measure* is used as a substitute for the more cumbersome term *criterion-behavior-referenced measurement* and implies that the measurements are to be interpreted in terms of the criterion behaviors a student can exhibit. The term *norm* in norm-referenced measurement refers to the fact that such measurements are interpreted in terms of test norms. (See Chapter 19 for a discussion of test norms.)

In 1969, Popham and Husek emphasized that the available techniques for test construction, estimation of reliability, assessment of validity, and item analysis, were developed largely for norm-referenced measurement. From their point of view, criterion-referenced measurement required new techniques in each of these areas. Both Livingston (1972) and Hambleton and Novick (1973) formulated new indices of reliability for criterion-referenced measurement. Since the publication of these two papers, a fairly large body of literature has been devoted to formulation of reliability coefficients for use with criterion-referenced tests and to estimation of these coefficients. Aspects of this literature are reviewed in this chapter. Other reviews of this literature have been presented by Berk (1980a and b), Brennan (1980), Subkoviak (1980), and Traub and Rowley (1980).

USES OF CRITERION-REFERENCED MEASURES

If a criterion-referenced measurement is to be interpreted in terms of the criterion behaviors an examinee can exhibit, a criterion-referenced test should be designed to permit this kind of interpretation. For many writers the construction of a criterion-referenced test begins with a definition of the domain, or population, of tasks that a student should be able to perform (see Millman, 1974, for a description of procedures for domain definition). The test is constructed by sampling tasks from this domain of tasks. Two or more of these tests are called *nominally* or *randomly parallel tests*. These names derive from the fact that such tests are considered parallel in content, but unlike strictly parallel tests, need not have equal means, equal variances, or equal correlations with universe scores. Related to this method of constructing a criterion-referenced test are two purposes for the test results (Hambleton et al., 1978a). The first is estimation of the *domain score*. Loosely speaking the domain score for examinee p is the proportion of the items in the domain that examinee p can answer correctly.[1] This domain score is also the universe score from generalizability theory. Here the universe of generalization consists of all the items in the domain of items, and the universe or domain score for examinee p is the average score on all items in the universe of generalization. The second use of the test is for mastery allocation. In mastery allocation the domain score scale is divided into K mutually exclusive mastery categories defined by $(K - 1)$ cut scores, and the observed test results are used to classify examinees into the mastery categories. The most commonly cited example has one cut score and two categories, master and nonmaster. Since two different purposes for criterion-referenced test scores have been identified (domain score estimation and mastery classification), it follows that different reliability estimation procedures are required for each (Traub and Rowley, 1980).

---

[1] In this chapter we will consider only the commonly encountered measurement situation in which the domain score is considered to be a continuous variable. Readers interested in the rarer situation, where individuals are supposedly capable of performing all or none of the tasks in the domain, are referred to Traub and Rowley (1980).

RELIABILITY THEORY FOR DOMAIN SCORE ESTIMATES

Consider a situation in which a new Spanish curriculum is being evaluated, and the evaluator would like to assess the extent of each student's Spanish vocabulary. The domain is all Spanish words introduced in the curriculum. For obvious practical reasons, however, students can be tested on only a limited number of words. The evaluator intends to use each examinee's observed proportion-correct score as an estimate of the student's domain score, the proportion of the words that the student knows. But how closely do the proportion-correct scores approximate the domain scores? If we concern ourselves with tests that are constructed by random sampling from an infinite pool of items, the question can be answered through the generalizability theory presented in Chapter 8 for single-facet designs. Moreover these results can be modified to accommodate a finite pool of items (Sirotnik, 1972) and stratified sampling (Rajaratnam, Cronbach and Gleser, 1965).

From the point of view of generalizability theory, when the evaluator administers the Spanish vocabulary test, the evaluator is conducting a D-study in which examinees are crossed with items. In Chapter 8 this design was denoted as *pxi* and was labeled design 2 of the single-facet designs. The evaluator intends to use the observed proportion-correct score for examinee p as an estimate of p's domain score (or universe score). In investigating the question of how well the observed scores estimate the domain scores, two quantities are possibly of interest. One is an error variance (or its square root, which is a standard error of measurement). The second is a generalizability coefficient. For reasons discussed subsequently we prefer the error variance. Therefore let us begin by discussing an error variance that is appropriate when the observed proportion-correct score is considered to be an estimate of the domain score. Treating the observed proportion-correct score as an estimate of a domain score is an example of an absolute decision. The reader should recall from Chapter 8 that an absolute decision is made when the decision depends on the magnitude of a person's score without reference to the scores of other examinees.

As a review of concepts relevant to this discussion, the reader may wish to examine the data presented in Table 7.1, which contains a set of responses for 10 examinees to a 6-item test. In this matrix, n_p shall be the number of persons (10) and n_i the number of items (6). Table 7.2 demonstrated the computation of the Kuder-Richardson 20 reliability for these items, and Table 7.3 demonstrated how the Kuder-Richardson 20 could be estimated with Hoyt's analysis of variance procedure. Table 9.1 contains a summary of this information, which will be useful in illustrating how reliability estimates could be obtained if criterion-referenced score interpretations were to be made for scores on this test. Specifically, we see that the results of a person-by-items analysis of variance yields three quantities: mean squares for persons (MS_p), mean squares for items (MS_i), and a mean squares term for residual variance (MS_r). In Chapter 8, we learned how such mean squares estimates can be combined to obtain estimates for components of generalizability coefficients. As noted there, for a single-facet D-study such as we have here, with

TABLE 9.1.   Summary of Item Responses and Analyses of Variance Results from Tables 7.1 to 7.3 for 6 Items, 10 Persons

Examinee	Item 1	2	3	4	5	6	Total
1	0	0	0	0	0	0	0
2	0	0	0	0	1	0	1
3	1	0	1	1	1	0	4
4	1	1	1	1	1	1	6
5	1	1	1	1	1	1	6
6	0	0	1	0	0	0	1
7	0	0	1	1	1	0	3
8	0	0	0	1	0	0	1
9	1	0	1	1	1	0	4
10	0	1	0	1	0	1	3
p	.40	.30	.60	.70	.60	.30	

SV	SS	df	MS
Persons	6.817	9	.7574
Items	1.483	5	.2967
Residual	6.683	45	.1485

items treated as the facet, the variance components for persons and items can be estimated by

$$\hat{\sigma}_p^2 = \frac{(MS_p - MS_r)}{n_i}$$

$$\hat{\sigma}_i^2 = \frac{(MS_i - MS_r)}{n_p}$$

and

$$\hat{\sigma}_e^2 = MS_r$$

In the current example σ_i^2 is the variance of the item difficulties for the domain of items, and σ_e^2 reflects errors of measurement and the fact that the likelihood of an examinee answering an item correctly will vary from item to item. Using the information in Table 9.1, for this example, therefore,

$$\hat{\sigma}_p^2 = \frac{(.7574 - .1485)}{6} = .1015$$

and

$$\hat{\sigma}_i^2 = \frac{(.2967 - .1485)}{10} = .0148$$

The appropriate error variance for this design is $(\sigma_i^2 + \sigma_e^2)/n_i$. However, it is simpler to estimate the error variance by using the formula

$$\hat{\sigma}_i^2 + \hat{\sigma}_e^2 = \frac{\sum_p (X_{pI})(1 - X_{pI})}{n_p(n_i - 1)}$$

(9.1)

where n_p is the number of examinees and X_{pI} is the proportion-correct score for examinee p. This numeric value of the estimated error variance must fall in the range .00 to $.25/(n_i - 1)$. Thus for 11 items, the error variance cannot be larger than .025, and the standard error of measurement must be less than $\sqrt{.025}$, or .158. Using Equation 9.1 with the data in Table 9.1, we obtain

$(\hat{\sigma}_i^2 + \hat{\sigma}_e^2)/n_1 =$

$$\frac{.00 + .1411 + .2211 + .00 + .00 + .1411 + .25 + .1411 + .2211 + .25}{(10)(5)} = .0273$$

Since the error variance is $(\sigma_i^2 + \sigma_e^2)/n_i$, one possible generalizability coefficient for the domain score is

$$\rho_I^2 = \frac{\sigma_p^2}{\sigma_p^2 + (\sigma_i^2 + \sigma_e^2)/n_i}$$

(9.2)

Thus for our example,

$$\hat{\rho}_I^2 = \frac{.1015}{.1015 + .0273} = .79$$

This coefficient will be 1.0 if each examinee's observed proportion-correct scores *equals* the examinee's domain score. Thus high coefficients indicate accurate estimation of domain scores. However, low coefficients do not necessarily imply inaccurate estimation. To see this, consider the situation in which all examinees have the same domain score, so that $\sigma_p^2 = .00$, and consequently, $\rho_I^2 = .00$. Now if the test consisted of 11 items, the maximum error variance would be .025. Thus if the error variance estimate was only .001, the observed scores would be fairly accurate estimates of the single domain score. However, if the error variance estimate was .025, these observed scores would not be very accurate estimates of the domain score. Yet in either case $\rho_I^2 = .00$. Clearly, then, a low generalizability coefficient does not always indicate inaccurate measurement. Our point of view is that the error variance estimated by using generalizability theory is more easily interpretable than a generalizability coefficient as a measure of accuracy for domain score estimates on criterion-referenced tests.

In some cases, a norm-referenced interpretation of a domain score is of interest. In this case the question of reliability revolves around how well the observed proportion-correct score (X_{pI}) predicts the examinee's proportion-correct domain score (μ_p). If X_{pI} predicts μ_p perfectly, any norm-referenced interpretation of X_{pI} will be equivalent to the corresponding interpretation of μ_p. The generalizability coefficient

$$\rho_{I*}^2 = \frac{\sigma_p^2}{\sigma_p^2 + \sigma_e^2/n_i}$$

(9.3)

TABLE 9.2.   Effect of Variation in the Cut-Score- and Test-Length-Induced Changes in Reliability on P

Number of Items	ρ^{2b}	Cut Score (Percent-Correct Scale)[a]			
		.2	.4	.6	.8
5	.40	.81	.66	.68	.81
10	.57	.83	.71	.77	.90

[a] Mean percent-correct score is .4 for all exams.
[b] The coefficient ρ^2 is the squared correlation between observed and domain score for either form. From H. Hunyh, Computation and inference for two reliability indices in mastery testing based on the beta-binomial model, in H. Hunyh and J. C. Saunders, Solutions for some technical problems in domain-referenced mastery testing (Final Report, Project NIE-G-78-0087), National Institute of Education, Department of Health, Education, and Welfare. Adapted by permission.

Table 9.2 the mean percent correct is .4 for both forms, and the least consistent decisions result for a cut score of .4. Table 9.2 also illustrates that increasing the generalizability of the test scores by increasing the test length will have an effect of increasing the decision consistency. The increase in test length results in an increase in decision consistency for all four cut-score values. However the magnitude of the increase in decision consistency is not the same at each cut score. The trend that the larger increases in decision consistency are associated with the larger cut scores does not generalize to other situations. We can only conclude that the magnitude of the impact of test length on decision consistency is dependent on the particular situation at hand.

The results reported in Table 9.2, for each combination of test length, ρ^2, and cut score, refer to the same group of examinees. Table 9.3 presents values of P for different groups of examinees. For example the first row of the table contains values of P for five groups of examinees. Each group has a mean of 3 on each form, but domain score variability, and hence the generalizability of the test scores to the domain scores, varies across the groups. The general trends in Table 9.3 are similar to those in Table 9.2. Increasing generalizability tends to increase decision consist-

TABLE 9.3.   Effect of Group-Composition-Induced Change in Reliability and Mean Score on P

Test Mean[a]	ρ^{2b}				
	.1	.3	.5	.7	.9
3.0	.57	.63	.69	.78	.90
4.8	.96	.93	.91	.91	.94

[a] The cut score, expressed on the total score scale, is 3 for all entries in the table.
[b] The coefficient ρ^2 refers to the squared correlation between observed and domain score for either form. From H. Hunyh, Computation and inference for two reliability indices in mastery testing based on the beta-binomial model, in H. Hunyh & J. C. Saunders, Solutions for some technical problems in domain-referenced mastery testing (Final Report, Project NIE-G-78-0087), National Institute of Education Department of Health, Education, and Welfare. Adapted by permission.

ency. Thus two forms of a test will tend to yield more-consistent decisions for a group characterized by heterogeneous domain scores than for a group characterized by homogeneous domain scores. This is clearly illustrated in the first row, where decision consistency increases from left to right as variance of examinees' domain scores increases. However it is possible for decision consistency to be lower for a group characterized by greater test score generalizability. This is illustrated in the second row of Table 9.3. This table also shows that P tends to be smaller for the group with a mean score close to the cut score, as illustrated by the results reported in each column. In each column, decision consistency is lower for the group described in the first row than it is for the group described in the second row. The results were computed by assuming a cut score of 3 points on the raw-score scale. Each group in the first row has a mean score of 3.0, whereas each group in the second row has a mean of 4.8. Within a column, decision consistency is lower for the group in the first row since its mean is closer to the cut score. Table 9.3 also illustrates that substantial decision consistency can occur even when test score generalizability is low. This is illustrated in the first column of the table. For a group with a mean of 4.8, 97.7 percent of the decisions are consistent even though test score generalizability is quite low. This occurs because most of the scores are above the cut on each form, and so most of the decisions are consistent mastery decisions. It can be shown that if the scores on the two forms are exchangeable, the minimum possible value of P is .5. This value will occur if the cut score is at the median of the distribution and if the interform correlation is zero. Another factor that affects decision consistency is the similarity of the test score distributions for the two forms. Other things being equal, decision consistency tends to be smaller when the test score distributions are dissimilar.

Several suggestions have been made in the literature for transforming P to a more interpretable measure of decision-making consistency. Two of these transformations are presented in this section. Rather than trying to argue in favor of one or the other, we suggest that these two indices are simply different ways of transforming P so that the new coefficients are expressed on scales that have some interpretable scale points.

Swaminathan, Hambleton, and Algina (1974) suggest the use of Cohen's Kappa,

$$\kappa = \frac{P - P_c}{1 - P_c} \tag{9.4}$$

where P_c is the chance probability of a consistent decision. That is, the probability for the hypothetical situation in which the scores on the two forms are statistically independent. Statistical independence of the test scores implies that the decisions are statistically independent. The coefficient P_c is sometimes referred to as the *chance consistency* and is calculated by using the formula $P_c = P_1 P_{.1} + P_0 P_{.0}$. In this expression, $P_{1.}$ represents the probability of a mastery classification on one form, and $P_{.1}$ represents the probability of a mastery classification on the second form. Similarly $P_{0.}$ and $P_{.0}$ represent the probability of nonmastery classification on each of the two forms. For the data in Figure 9.1, $\hat{P}_{1.} = .5$, $\hat{P}_{.1} = .3$, $\hat{P}_{0.} = .5$, $\hat{P}_{.0} = .7$ and $\hat{P}_c = .5(.3) + .5(.7) = .5$, which means that 50 percent of the decisions would have been consistent even if the scores on the two forms had been statistically independent. Chance consistency can be viewed as a baseline for judging the actual amount of consistency observed for the two forms. The denominator of κ, $1 - P_c$, represents the maximum possible increase in decision consistency above and beyond chance consistency, and the numerator, $P - P_c$, represents the actual increase over chance consistency. Thus κ may be interpreted as the increase in decision consistency that the tests provide over chance expressed as a proportion of the maximum possible increase over chance consistency. Coefficient κ is 0 when there is no increase and 1.0 when there is maximal increase. For the data in Figure 9.1, $\kappa = (.6 - .5)/(1 - .5) = .2$. Thus 20% of the total possible increase over chance consistency was observed for the decisions based on the two forms.

It should be noted carefully that $\kappa = 0$ does not mean that the decisions are so inconsistent as to be worthless. $\kappa = 0$ may be interpreted to mean that the decisions are no more consistent than decisions based on statistically independent test scores. This consistency can be substantial. Recall that for exchangeable test forms, a minimum of 50 percent of the decisions will be consistent. Also $\kappa = 1$ may be interpreted to mean that the decisions are as consistent as those based on perfectly statistically dependent scores. The coefficient κ can assume negative values— which corresponds to the situation in which there is an inverse relationship between the scores on the two forms.

Earlier we pointed out that if two test forms are exchangeable, the minimum probability of a consistent decision will be .5. This minimum will occur if the test scores are statistically independent and the cut score is at the median of the common distribution for the two forms. Based on this minimum, an alternative to κ is

$$P* = \frac{P - .5}{1 - .5} = 2P - 1 \tag{9.5}$$

Like κ, $P* = 1$ can be interpreted to mean that decisions are as consistent as those based on perfectly statistically dependent test scores. However, $P*$ is zero when the decisions are no more consistent than those made by using statistically independent test scores that have the same distribution for each form and a cut score equal to the median of the common test score distribution. It should be noted that $P*$ can be negative when the actual test score distributions are not very similar. For the data in Figure 9.1, $P* = 2(.6) - 1 = .2$, indicating that the decision-making consistency represents a 20 percent improvement over consistency obtained from statistically independent exchangeable test scores, with a cut score equal to the median of the distribution.

Factors Affecting $P*$ and κ

Like P, the probability of a consistent decision, both κ and $P*$ are affected by the test score generalizability, the location of the cut score in the test score distribu-

TABLE 9.4.   Effect of Variation in the Cut-Score- and Test-Length-Induced Change in Reliability on P^* and κ

Index	Number of Items	ρ^{2b}	Cut Score (Percent-Correct Scale)[a]			
			.2	.4	.6	.8
P^*	5	.40	.62	.32	.36	.62
	10	.57	.66	.42	.54	.80
κ	5	.40	.20	.28	.29	.23
	10	.57	.31	.41	.39	.28

[a] Mean percent-correct score is .4 for all exams.
[b] The coefficient ρ^2 is the squared correlation between observed and domain score for either form. From H. Hunyh, Computation and inference for two reliability indices in mastery testing based on the beta-binomial model, in H. Hunyh and J. C. Saunders, Solutions for some technical problems in domain-referenced mastery testing (Final Report, Project NIE-G-78-0087), National Institute of Education, Department of Health, Education, and Welfare. Adapted by permission.

tions, and the similarity of the distributions. Tables 9.4 and 9.5 report the values of κ and P^* for the same situations used in Tables 9.2 and 9.3. Table 9.4 shows the effect on κ and P^* of test-length-induced changes on the generalizability of test scores and of changing the cut score. These results refer to the same examinees. Table 9.5 shows the effects on κ and P^* of group-composition-induced changes in test score generalizability and the location of the cut score in the test score distribution. It turns out that P^* is affected in exactly the same way as P. The index P^* tends to be smallest when the cut score is near the middle of the distribution. Also P^* usually, but not always, increases as test score generalizability increases. The index κ tends to be largest when the cut score is near the center of the distribution and always increases as test score generalizability increases. There has been some discussion in the literature about whether P^* or κ is the more appropriate index. Our point of view is that P^* and κ are alternative ways of interpreting P, and as long as the nature of the interpretation is understood, one should not be favored over the other.

TABLE 9.5.   Effect of Group-Composition-Induced Change in Reliability and Mean Score on P^* and κ[a]

Index	Test Mean	ρ^{2b}				
		.1	.3	.5	.7	.9
P^*	3.0	.14	.26	.38	.78	.80
	4.8	.92	.86	.82	.82	.88
κ	3.0	.07	.21	.36	.54	.79
	4.8	.02	.12	.27	.49	.78

[a] The cut score, expressed on the total score scale, is 3 for all entries in the table.
[b] The coefficient ρ^2 refers to the squared correlation between observed and domain score for either form. From H. Hunyh, Computation and inference for two reliability indices in mastery testing based on the beta-binomial model, in H. Hunyh and J. C. Saunders, Solutions for some technical problems in domain-referenced mastery testing (Final Report, Project NIE-G-78-0087), National Institute of Education, Department of Health, Education, and Welfare. Adapted by permission.

The final factor affecting $P*$ and κ is the similarity of the test score distributions for the two forms. Both indices will tend to decline as the distributions become more dissimilar. Indeed, neither $P*$ nor κ can reach the upper limit of 1 unless the marginal mastery and nonmastery probabilities are the same for each form.

Livingston and Brennan-Kane Indices

Thus far, we have considered only decision consistency indices which treat all inconsistent classifications as equally serious. Suppose, however, for a cut score of .70, examinee A is inconsistently classified by having proportion-correct scores of .65 on one test form and .75 on another, and Examinee B is inconsistently classified by having scores of .20 and .90. When the test developer wants to reflect the magnitude of the discrepancy of misclassification in judging the reliability of decisions, two indices may be useful. These were developed by Livingston (1972) and Brennan and Kane (1977). Kane and Brennan (1980) have presented a more formal treatment of the development of these consistency indices than we shall offer here. Recall that if the test score distributions are the same, decision consistency should depend on two factors, test score generalizability and the location of the cut score in the test score distributions. Moreover it is intuitively reasonable that a measure of decision consistency should increase as test score generalizability and/or the difference between the test score means and the cut score increases. A measure that has this property is Livingston's coefficient, which is defined by

$$K^2(X,T) = \frac{\sigma_T^2 + (\mu_T - n_iC)^2}{\sigma_X^2 + (\mu_X - n_iC)^2} \tag{9.6}$$

Here the symbols X and T are used since Livingston developed his index in the context of classical test theory. The symbol C refers to the cut score expressed on the percent score scale, and n_i is the number of items. Estimation of $K^2(X,T)$ is quite easy. If two measurements are available for each examinee, the formula

$$\hat{K}^2(X,T) = \frac{\hat{\rho}_{XX'}\hat{\sigma}_X\hat{\sigma}_{X'} + (\hat{\mu}_X - n_iC)(\hat{\mu}_{X'} - n_iC)}{\sqrt{[\hat{\sigma}_X^2 + (\hat{\mu}_X - n_iC)^2][\hat{\sigma}_{X'}^2 + (\hat{\mu}_{X'} - n_iC)^2]}} \tag{9.7}$$

can be used. Here, $\hat{\rho}_{XX'}$ is the correlation between the scores on the two forms, and $\hat{\mu}$ is the raw-score mean. If only a single form is available, the formula

$$K^2(X,T) = \frac{\sigma_X^2(KR\ 20) + (\mu_X - n_iC)^2}{\sigma_X^2 + (\mu - n_iC)^2} \tag{9.8}$$

may be used. For example, for the data in Table 9.1, if the cut score was set at .67,

$$\hat{K}^2(X,T) = \frac{4.08(.80) + [2.9 - (6).67]^2}{4.08 + [2.9 - (6).67]^2} = .85$$

A factor that affects decision-making consistency is the similarity of the test score distribution for the two test forms. When tests are constructed through sampling from a domain of items, different distributions result, in part, because items with different difficulties may end up on different forms. An index of decision consistency, which takes into account variation in item difficulty, was proposed by Brennan and Kane (1977):

$$M(C) = \frac{\sigma_p^2 + (\mu - C)^2}{\sigma_p^2 + (\mu - C)^2 + (\sigma_i^2 + \sigma_e^2)/n_i} \qquad (9.9)$$

The symbols σ_p^2, σ_i^2 and σ_e^2 were defined earlier in the chapter. The symbol μ denotes the grand mean which is estimated by $X_{PI} = \Sigma_i \Sigma_p X_{pi}/n_i n_p$. In this expression X_{pi} is the score of the pth person on the ith item. The grand mean X_{PI} can be shown to be the mean percentage-correct score for the sample. The appropriate equation for estimating $M(C)$ is

$$\hat{M}(C) = \frac{n_i(n_p - 1)\hat{\sigma}_p^2 - n_p\hat{\sigma}_i^2 - \hat{\sigma}_e^2 + (X_{PI} - C)^2}{n_i(n_p - 1)\hat{\sigma}_p^2 + (n_p - 1)\hat{\sigma}_e^2 + (X_{PI} - C)^2} \qquad (9.10)$$

Assuming a cut score of .67 and substituting in Equation 9.10, we obtain for the data in our example

$$\hat{M}(C) = \frac{6(10 - 1)(.1015) - 10(.0145) - .1485 + (.48 - .67)^2}{6(10 - 1)(.1015) + (10 - 1)(.1485) + (.48 - .67)^2} = .76$$

Because $M(C)$ includes a component for variation due to item difficulty (σ_i^2), it seems preferable to Livingston's coefficient. Yet it seems reasonable to ask: What is the relationship between $K^2(X,T)$ and $M(C)$? It can be shown that Equation 9.6 is equivalent to

$$K^2(X,T) = \frac{\sigma_p^2 + (X_{PI} - C)^2}{\sigma_p^2 + (X_{PI} - C)^2 + \sigma_e^2/n_i} \qquad (9.11)$$

Comparing Equations 9.6 and 9.11, we see that when $K^2(X,T)$ and $M(C)$ are calculated, based on a two-way ANOVA, the only difference between them is the presence of the term σ_i^2 in the denominator of $\dot{M}(C)$. As a result $K^2(X,T)$ must be larger than $M(C)$.

Comparisons of $K^2(X,T)$, $M(C)$, P, and P^*

Earlier we pointed out that P^* can be viewed as a device for interpreting P. This is not true for either $K^2(X,T)$ or $M(C)$. How, then, is a test developer to choose between P on the one hand and $K^2(X,T)$ or $M(C)$ on the other? To indicate the nature of the difference between the two, we will compare P and $K^2(X,T)$. (However, the indices P and $M(C)$ are similarly differentiated.) The coefficient P can be defined formally as follows: To any examinee who is consistently classified, assign a score or value of one. To inconsistently classified examinees assign a score of zero. Letting Y denote this new variable, P is the sum of Y values divided by the maximum possible value of this sum, which will be obtained only if all decisions are consistent. In calculating $K^2(X,T)$ the score $W = (X - n_iC)(X' - n_iC)$ is assigned to all decisions. The numerator of $K^2(X,T)$ is the average W. The denominator is the maximum possible value of this average. To illustrate the difference between

TABLE 9.6. Examples of $(X - C)(X' - C)$ for Consistent and Inconsistent Decisions

Examinee	X	X'	Classification	Y	$W = (X - C)(X' - C)$
A	10	11	Consistent	1	12
B	8	7	Consistent	1	0
C	8	6	Inconsistent	0	-1
D	10	2	Inconsistent	0	-15
E	5	8	Inconsistent	0	-2
F	4	7	Inconsistent	0	0
G	5	5	Consistent	1	4
H	3	3	Consistent	1	16

$K^2(X,T)$ and P, Table 9.6 presents hypothetical data for eight examinees on two forms of an 11-item test. The cut score for both forms was $n_iC = 7$ items. Values of Y and W are reported in Table 9.6. Since P is based on adding the Y score, it can be seen that in calculating P, all consistent decisions are given the same weight, $Y = 1$, and all inconsistent decisions are given the same weight, $Y = 0$. However since $K^2(X,T)$ is based on adding the W values, the weight given to a decision depends not only on whether it is a consistent decision for the examinee but also on how similar the scores on the two forms are for the examinee. For example both examinees C and D are inconsistently classified. However W is more negative for examinee D than it is for C since there is a more extreme difference between examinee D's scores on the two forms. Essentially this means that when an examinee has scores as disparate as 10 and 2 and is inconsistently classified, this inconsistency is more serious than when an examinee has scores of 8 and 6 and is inconsistently classified. The choice between P and indices like $K^2(X,T)$ or $M(C)$ should be based on whether the examiner agrees with the values assigned by the index to the various types of decisions.

To address the issue of how $K^2(X,T)$ and $M(C)$ are affected by changes in the cut score, let us consider one of the 11-item tests, taken by 8 examinees, used in the preceding example. Table 9.7 presents a hypothetical person-by-item response matrix to these items. Table 9.8 further reports both $\hat{K}^2(X,T)$ and $\hat{M}(C)$ for these data for a variety of cut scores. In addition Table 9.8 reports $\hat{P}$ and $\hat{P}*$ estimates determined for the two forms of this 11-item test as the cut score varies. The results indicate that in a general way all four indices are affected the same way by changes in the cut score. As was demonstrated earlier, the coefficient κ is affected in the opposite way by changes in the cut score.

Single Administration Estimates of P and κ

In the preceding discussion, estimation of P and κ required two measurements on each of the examinees. Hunyh (1976a), Subkoviak (1976), Peng and Subkoviak (1980), and Wilcox (1981b) presented single administration procedures for estimating P and κ. Both the Hunyh and the Subkoviak procedures are based on the

TABLE 9.7. Person-Item Score Matrix and Results of Person-Items Analyses of Variance for 8 Examinees on 11 Items

Examinee						Item						Total
	1	2	3	4	5	6	7	8	9	10	11	
A	1	1	1	0	1	1	1	1	1	1	1	10
B	1	1	1	0	0	1	1	0	1	1	1	8
C	0	1	1	1	0	1	1	0	1	1	1	8
D	1	0	1	1	1	1	1	1	1	1	1	10
E	0	0	0	1	0	1	1	0	1	1	0	5
F	0	0	0	0	0	0	1	0	1	1	1	4
G	1	0	0	0	0	1	1	0	1	1	0	5
H	0	0	0	0	0	1	1	0	1	0	0	3

SV	SS	df	MS
Examinees	4.715	7	.673
Items	6.704	10	.670
Residual	9.659	70	.137

TABLE 9.8.   Effect of Variation in Cut-Score on $\hat{M}(C)$, $\hat{K}^2(X,T)$, $\hat{P}$, and $\hat{P}*$

Index	Cut Score				
	.1	.3	.5	.7	.9
$\hat{M}(C)$	.94	.88	.76	.76	.88
$\hat{K}^2(X,T)$	.96	.92	.83	.83	.90
$\hat{P}$	1.00	.90	.70	.70	.90
$\hat{P}*$	1.00	.80	.40	.40	.80

binomial model developed by Keats and Lord (1962) and described in detail by Lord and Novick (1968). It should be noted that both procedures estimate P and κ for a hypothetical form that is exchangeable with the test used to gather the data. As noted earlier, if two forms are exchangeable, scores on the two forms have exactly the same distribution and the same relationship to the domain score. Exchangeability is a stronger form of equivalence than strict parallelism. One potential problem in using the Hunyh and Subkoviak procedures is that in criterion-referenced measurement, we are unlikely to be interested in an index of decision consistency between the form in use and a hypothetical form that is exchangeable with the original form. Rather we are likely to be interested in something like the average value of an index of decision consistency between all possible pairs of tests constructed by random sampling from the domain of items. What is the likely impact of this problem? Since the average value over all pairs of tests is likely to be smaller than the value for a pair of exchangeable tests, it may seem that the procedures are likely to result in a spuriously positive view of decision consistency. This would probably be true if there were not other factors to consider. However, another possible problem with these procedures is that when all examinees respond to the same items, use of the binomial model implies that all items are equally difficult—a requirement unlikely to be met in practice. Failure to meet this assumption is likely to mean that the procedures will yield values that underestimate decision consistency for an exchangeable pair of tests (Hunyh and Saunders, 1980). Thus the effects of the two problems may compensate each other to some degree.

Of Subkoviak's and Hunyh's procedures, the latter is the most well developed. It permits estimation of standard errors of P and κ. Both procedures are fairly complicated mathematically, and we will not describe the computational details here. A listing of a computer program for implementing Hunyh's procedure is available (Hunyh, 1980a). This document also includes tables that can be used to determine P and κ for tests between 5 and 10 items long. To use these tables it is only necessary to know $\hat{\mu}$, KR 21, and the cut score. KR 21 is used since, as is well known, it is the reliability of test scores that conform to the binomial model. Results reported by Subkoviak (1978) suggest that when based on as few as 30 examinees, Hunyh's procedure gives fairly accurate estimates of P and κ for strictly parallel tests with as few as 10 items.

Peng and Subkoviak (1980) showed that a simple approximation to Hunyh's procedure works fairly well. Assume that if available, the two sets of measurements

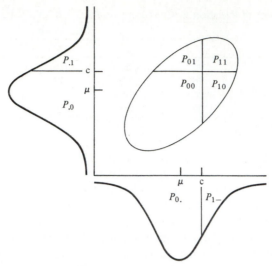

FIGURE 9.2 Bivariate Normal Distribution

would have identical normal distributions and would have a joint bivariate normal distribution. Such tests would be exchangeable. The situation is illustrated in Figure 9.2. When the test score distributions are identical, it can be shown that $P = 1 + 2(P_{00} - P_{0.})$ so $P^* = 1 + 4(P_{00} - P_{0.})$. Also it can be shown that $\kappa = (P_{00} - P_{0.}^2)/(P_{0.} - P_{0.}^2)$. Now $P_{0.} = Pr(X < n_i C)$, the probability that X is less than $n_i C$. Since the scores are assumed to be normally distributed, $P_{0.}$ can be calculated by using

$$P_{0.} = Pr\left\{z < \frac{n_i C - \mu_X}{\sigma_X}\right\} \tag{9.12}$$

where z is a standard normal random variable. The expression on the right side of the equals sign is the area to the left of $(n_i C - \mu_X)/\sigma_X$ in the standard normal distribution. To illustrate, if $\mu_X = 50$, $\sigma_X = 10$, and $n_i C = 60$, then

$$P_{0.} = Pr(X < n_i C) = Pr\left\{z < \frac{n_i C - \mu_X}{\sigma_X}\right\} = Pr\left\{z < \frac{60 - 50}{10}\right\} = .84$$

Now P_{00} is the probability that scores on both forms are less than $n_i C$, or alternatively, that each of two standard normal random variables is less than $(n_i C - \mu_X)/\sigma_X$. This probability can be found in tables of the bivariate standard normal distribution (Gupta, 1963), provided that the correlation between the two variables is known. Since in the present situation this correlation is the reliability coefficient defined in classical test theory, it can be estimated by using any of the available single administration estimates of the reliability. To approximate Hunyh's procedure, KR 21 is used. Table 9.9 presents an abbreviated table of P as a function of $z = (n_i C - \mu_X)/\sigma_X$, and ρ, the correlation between the two forms. To illustrate the calculation of P^* and κ, suppose on a seven-item test $\hat{\mu}_X = 4.5$, $\hat{\sigma}_X = 1$, KR 21 =

TABLE 9.9.   Probability That Two Standard Normal Variables with Correlation ρ Are Less Than or Equal to z

z	$\rho = .30$	.40	.50	.60	.70	.80	.90
−1.00	.0455	.0536	.0625	.0725	.0840	.0976	.1155
−0.90	.0578	.0671	.0773	.0887	.1015	.1167	.1365
−0.80	.0726	.0832	.0947	.1073	.1216	.1383	.1600
−0.70	.0902	.1020	.1147	.1286	.1442	.1625	.1860
−0.60	.1106	.1237	.1376	.1527	.1696	.1893	.2145
−0.50	.1342	.1483	.1633	.1796	.1976	.2186	.2453
−0.40	.1609	.1760	.1920	.2092	.2282	.2503	.2784
−0.30	.1908	.2067	.2235	.2415	.2614	.2843	.3135
−0.20	.2239	.2404	.2577	.2763	.2968	.3204	.3504
−0.10	.2598	.2767	.2944	.3134	.3343	.3583	.3888
0.00	.2985	.3155	.3333	.3524	.3734	.3976	.4282
0.10	.3395	.3564	.3741	.3930	.4139	.4379	.4684
0.20	.3824	.3989	.4162	.4348	.4553	.4789	.5089
0.30	.4266	.4426	.4593	.4773	.4972	.5202	.5493
0.40	.4718	.4869	.5028	.5200	.5391	.5612	.5893
0.50	.5171	.5312	.5462	.5625	.5805	.6015	.6283
0.60	.5621	.5752	.5891	.6042	.6211	.6408	.6660
0.70	.6062	.6181	.6308	.6447	.6603	.6786	.7021
0.80	.6489	.6595	.6710	.6836	.6979	.7146	.7363
0.90	.6897	.6990	.7092	.7205	.7334	.7486	.7684
1.00	.7282	.7363	.7452	.7552	.7667	.7803	.7982
1.10	.7640	.7709	.7787	.7874	.7975	.8096	.8255
1.20	.7970	.8028	.8094	.8169	.8257	.8363	.8504
1.30	.8269	.8318	.8373	.8438	.8513	.8605	.8728
1.40	.8538	.8578	.8624	.8678	.8742	.8821	.8928
1.50	.8777	.8809	.8847	.8892	.8946	.9012	.9103
1.60	.8987	.9012	.9043	.9079	.9124	.9180	.9257
1.70	.9168	.9188	.9212	.9242	.9279	.9325	.9389
1.80	.9324	.9339	.9358	.9382	.9411	.9449	.9503
1.90	.9455	.9467	.9482	.9500	.9524	.9555	.9598

Reprinted from H. Hunyh, On the reliability of decisions in domain-referenced testing, *Journal of Educational Measurement,* 13, 253–264. Copyright 1976, National Council on Measurement in Education, Washington, D.C.

.4, and $n_iC = 5$. Then using a z-score table,

$$\hat{P}_{0.} = Pr\left\{z < \frac{n_iC - \hat{\mu}_X}{\hat{\sigma}_X}\right\} = Pr\left\{z < \frac{5 - 4.5}{1}\right\} = Pr(z < .5) = .69$$

To obtain P_{00} for our example, Table 9.9 is entered by using $z = (n_iC - \hat{\mu})/\hat{\sigma}_X = (5 - 4.5)/1 = .5$ and KR $21 = .4$. Using Table 9.9, $\hat{P}_{00} = .53$. Therefore $P^* = 1 + 4(.53 - .69) = .36$, and $\kappa = (.53 - .69^2)/(.69 - .69^2) = .25$.

DECISION ACCURACY

One of the major uses for criterion-referenced tests has been for making decisions about examinees' levels of competence. In many states, high school students are granted diplomas only after surpassing a specified score on a minimum competency examination; in some professions practitioners are licensed on the basis of a minimum competency examination; in higher educational institutions, students are placed into classes for regular, remedial, or honors work, depending on their score on a criterion-referenced examination. When test scores are used in this way, one measure of the test's quality is in the *accuracy* of the decisions made on the basis of those scores (as distinct from the consistency of decisions made by repeated testings). Suppose that we could know the value of μ_p, the domain score for each examinee. We could then set a cut score, C, on the domain score scale such that all examinees with domain scores equal to or greater than C are considered to have mastered the domain of knowledge, and those with scores lower than C are considered nonmasters of this domain. Suppose also that a criterion-referenced test was administered to all examinees to classify students into two categories, which we will call *apparent masters* and *apparent nonmasters*. Examinees with test scores at or above C are apparent masters and those with test scores below C are apparent nonmasters. This decision situation can be represented as in Figure 9.3. (The difference between Figures 9.1 and 9.3 is that the former refers to the relationship between decisions made by using two different observed test scores, and the latter refers to the relationship between decisions made by using one observed test score and those that would be made if the domain scores were known.)

Inspection of Figure 9.3 shows that there are two kinds of correct decisions and two kinds of incorrect decisions possible for each examinee. The correct decisions are the true-positive and true-negative decisions. A true-positive decision occurs when an examinee who is a master in terms of the domain score is also categorized as a master in terms of the test score. The probability of a true-positive decision is labeled p_{11}. A true-negative decision occurs when an examinee who is a nonmaster in terms of the domain is categorized as a nonmaster on the basis of the test score. The probability of this decision is labeled $\hat{p}_{00}$. Inspection of Figure 9.3 also reveals

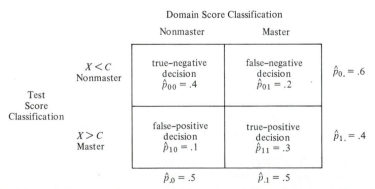

FIGURE 9.3   Probabilities of Agreement Between Domain and Test Score Mastery Classification

the two kinds of incorrect decisions that may occur. A false-positive decision occurs when a nonmaster of the domain is assigned to the mastery category by the test score, and this occurs with probability $\hat{p}_{10}$. A false-negative decision occurs when a domain master is assigned to the nonmastery category on the basis of the test score; this occurs with probability $\hat{p}_{01}$. Clearly the information provided by these probabilities will be useful in evaluating a criterion-referenced test. For example, $\hat{p} = \hat{p}_{11} + \hat{p}_{00}$, the probability of a correct decision, is a natural measure of decision accuracy and $1 - \hat{p}$, the probability of an incorrect decision, is a natural measure of decision inaccuracy. For the data in Figure 9.3, $\hat{p} = .4 + .3 = .7$, so 70 percent of the decisions are accurate.

To evaluate the degree of decision accuracy for a given test with a given cut score, the probabilities of occurrence of false-positive and false-negative outcomes must be estimated. Wilcox (1977a) presented several methods for estimating p_{10} and p_{01}, the probabilities of false-negative and false-positive errors, respectively. One of these methods uses the binomial model. Hunyh (1980d) provided tables that can be used to implement this method for tests between 5 and 10 items long. Hunyh (1980d) also developed a computer program that uses this method to calculate estimates of p_{10} and p_{01} for tests up to 60 items long. A second procedure developed by Wilcox can be carried out by hand if one has access to tables of the arcsin transformation and to tables of the bivariate normal distribution. (This procedure is described in section 4.0 of Wilcox, 1977a.) Although both methods were developed to estimate p_{10} and p_{01}, they also can be used to estimate p_{11} and p_{00}. Additional discussion of procedures for evaluating decision accuracy for a criterion-referenced test with a given performance standard is presented in Chapter 18, ''Setting Standards.''

SUMMARY

A domain of items is the population of items to which an examinee might be exposed when taking a test constructed to fit a given set of test specifications. An examinee's domain score may be thought of as the proportion of items in this domain which the examinee can answer correctly. The results of criterion-referenced tests are used either for domain score estimation or mastery allocation. As presented in this chapter, domain score estimation involves interpreting a percent-correct score on a test as an estimate of a domain score. Mastery allocation involves comparing the percent-correct score to an arbitrarily established cut score. If the percent-correct score is greater than or equal to the cut score, the examinee has apparently mastered the domain. Otherwise the examinee apparently has not mastered the domain.

Related to these two purposes for criterion-referenced tests are two reliability problems. The first concerns the degree to which an examinee's observed percent-correct score approximates his or her domain score. The second consists of two subproblems. One is the consistency of the mastery allocations made on the basis of two measurements. The second is the accuracy of the mastery allocations, that is, the degree to which the mastery decisions made from the observed test scores agree with the allocations that would be made if the domain scores were known.

When tests are constructed by random sampling of items, the generalizability coefficient ρ_I^2 and the error variance $(\sigma_i^2 + \sigma_e^2)/n_i$ can be used to quantify the accuracy of domain score estimation. Of these two, the error variance is a preferable measure since it depends only on the accuracy of estimation. The generalizability coefficient depends on the variance of the domain scores as well as the accuracy of the domain score estimates. Perhaps the simplest measure of consistency of mastery decisions is P, the proportion of examinees consistently classified as either master–master or nonmaster–nonmaster using two criterion-referenced measurements. Two possible transformations of P are $P*$ and Cohen's κ. Each of these may be viewed as a transformation of P to a new scale in which the scale points of 0 and 1 are interpretable. The sizes of P and its transformations are affected by such factors as generalizability from the observed to the domain scores, test length, location of the cut score, and similarity of the observed score distributions from the two measurement occasions. Using the binomial model, it is possible to estimate P and κ from a single test administration. Peng and Subkoviak (1980) suggested an approximation for this estimation.

The index P weights all consistent decisions equally and all inconsistent decisions equally, and therefore, does not reflect degrees of consistency and inconsistency in assignment of individuals to mastery classifications. There are, however, other indices which do reflect degrees of consistency and inconsistency. Two such indices are Livingston's $K^2(X,T)$ and Brennan and Kane's $M(C)$. $K^2(X,T)$ may be estimated from either a single test administration or from two administrations. $M(C)$ is most commonly estimated from a single test administration. $K^2(X,T)$ will be larger than $M(C)$ because the error component defined for $M(C)$ includes variation due to item difficulty.

In addition to concerns about the decision consistency that might result from criterion-referenced measurement, a second type of concern involves decision accuracy. In decision accuracy four types of decisions are defined: true positive—classifying a master as a master; true negative—classifying a nonmaster as a nonmaster; false positive—classifying a nonmaster as a master; false negative—classifying a master as a nonmaster. To evaluate the degree of decision accuracy for a given test with a given cut score, the probabilities of occurrence of false-positive and false-negative outcomes must be estimated. Wilcox (1977) and Hunyh (1980b) have described procedures which may be used in this estimation.

Exercises

1. Consider the person-item score matrix below:

Examinees				Item				
	1	2	3	4	5	6	7	8
1	0	0	1	1	0	1	1	1
2	1	1	0	1	1	1	1	0
3	1	1	1	1	1	1	1	0
4	0	0	0	1	0	0	1	0
5	1	0	1	0	1	0	0	1
6	1	0	1	1	1	0	1	0

A. What is the estimated error variance for this data set (Computed with use of Formula 9.1)?

B. What is the standard error of measurement?

C. What is the maximum possible value of the standard error of measurement for this data?

2. A researcher has run a Hoyt's analysis of variance on the item responses shown in Exercise 1 to obtain the value of coefficient alpha (KR_{20}) for these data. These results are shown below:

SV	SS	df	MS
Examinees	1.854	5	.370
Items	1.645	7	.235
Residual	7.979	35	.222

A. What is the generalizability coefficient for estimating the values of the domain scores of these examinees?

B. Does this coefficient indicate that the domain scores are accurately represented by observed proportion-correct scores on this test?

C. If this coefficient were 1.00, what would be the proportion-correct domain score for examinees 1, 2 and 3?

D. Suppose that the researcher were interested in differentiating among examinees in terms of their domain scores. What is the appropriate generalizability coefficient formula, in terms of the Mean Squares?

E. What is the value of the generalizability coefficient estimated using the formula from Exercise 2D?

F. By what other method could this value have been calculated?

3. Consider that data below indicating total scores earned in two forms of a college-level classroom examination, with 40 items per form.

Examinee	Test 1	Test 2
1	21	23
2	25	22
3	36	23
4	26	29
5	23	35
6	26	30
7	35	38
8	38	38
9	34	24
10	24	34
11	28	29
12	29	28
13	27	27
14	28	28
15	25	32
$\hat{\mu}$	28.33	29.33
$\hat{\sigma}$	4.94	5.05
$\hat{p}$	.20	

Suppose that the instructor is considering 4 possible minimum pass scores for this examination: 60% correct, 70% correct, 80% correct, and 90% correct.

    A. Determine the proportion of examinees who would be consistently classified by the two test forms, using each of the proposed scores.

    B. What is the value of coefficient kappa (κ) for these two test forms using each of the proposed cut scores?

    C. What is the value of $P*$ for the two test forms using each of the proposed cut scores?

    D. For the values of P, κ and $P*$ when 60% is the cut score, make an interpretive statement about the meaning of each of these three statistics.

    E. What is the value of Livingston's coefficient estimated from the two test forms using the cut scores of 60%?

4. A. Return to the item-examinee response matrix presented for Exercises 1 and 2. What is the value of Livingston's coefficient for this test using a cut score of .50? Using a cut score of .75?

    B. Without calculating, predict how the values of the Brennan-Kane reliability indices for these data would compare to the Livingston estimates, and explain your prediction.

    C. Compute the Brennan-Kane indices for these data using cut scores of .50 and .75, respectively.

    D. Review the Brennan-Kane formula (Equation 9.10) and indicate whether it provides an index of decision accuracy or domain score estimation accuracy. Justify your response.

    E. In what sense can the Brennan-Kane formula be considered a "norm-referenced" index?

5. A. For the purposes of this exercise assume that scores and descriptive statistics on test 1 in Exercise 3 are not available. Further, assume $\hat{\rho} = .4$. Estimate the value of κ for proportion-correct cut score of .75.

    B. What assumptions were necessary for the estimation procedure you used?

6. In describing the Fundamental Reading Competencies Test, a criterion-referenced measure with six 10-item subtests and one 5-item subtest, Ganapole (1980) reported,

    To further substantiate the reliability of the FRCT, a decision-consistency procedure was employed for both test-retest and equivalent form comparisons. Proportion of agreement indices were calculated with respect to three proficiency levels: 80%, 70% and 60%.

    Test-retest decision consistency values for subtests ranged from 72% to 88% on Form A and from 73% to 90% on Form B. . . .

    A. In the same article, the author reported that test-retest reliability estimates on Form A ranged from .50 to .71. How is it possible for these estimates to be so low?

    B. What would be the probable effect on test-retest decision consistency if all subtests were lengthened by five items?

    C. Suppose that Form A of this test were administered to a group of examinees whose domain scores were very homogeneous. How would the decision consistency indices be affected for this sample?

    D. Suppose that the test developer had instead reported decision consistency in terms of $P*$ or κ. How would these values have compared to those reported?

    E. The test developer reported that scores on this test were restricted in range, with most scores clustered at the high end of the possible score range on both occasions. In this circumstance, for which cut score would the decision consistency indices be highest?

UNIT III

Validity

Chapter 10

INTRODUCTION TO VALIDITY

Test scores are typically used to draw inferences about examinee behavior in situations beyond the testing session. Consider a quiz in eighth-grade science, a measure of egocentrism for preschool children, or a state bar examination; in each case, the examiner wants to draw an inference from the test score to some larger domain of behaviors which the examinee may exhibit now or in the future. Responsible use of test scores requires that the test user be able to justify the inferences drawn by having a cogent rationale for using the test score for the purpose at hand and for selecting this test over other available assessment procedures (Messick, 1981). Such justification has two prerequisites: reliability and validity of the test scores. A high reliability coefficient indicates that there is consistency in examinees' scores but it does not ensure that the examiner's inferences are defensible. Consider the analogy of a car's fuel gauge which systematically registers one-quarter higher than the actual level of fuel in the gas tank. If repeated readings are taken under the same conditions, the gauge will yield consistent (reliable) measurements, but the inference about the amount of fuel in the tank is faulty. Thus we see that evidence of a measurement's reliability may not be sufficient to justify the desired inference.

Cronbach (1971) described *validation* as the process by which a test developer or test user collects evidence to support the types of inferences that are to be drawn from test scores. To plan a validation study, the desired inference must be clearly identified. Then an empirical study is designed to gather evidence of the usefulness of the scores for such inferences. Three major types of validation studies are:

1. *Content* validation for situations where the test user desires to draw an inference from the examinee's test score to a larger domain of items similar to those on the test itself.

2. *Criterion-related* validation for situations where the test user desires to draw an inference from the examinee's test score to performance on some real behavioral variable of practical importance.
3. *Construct* validation for situations where "no criterion or universe of content is accepted as entirely adequate to define the quality to be measured . . ." (Cronbach and Meehl, 1955), but the test user desires to draw an inference from the test score to performances that can be grouped under the label of a particular psychological construct.

When selecting a test for a specific purpose, the test user has a clear responsibility to ascertain that the test has validation evidence appropriate to the intended use in the local situation. When no suitable validation evidence is presented by the test publisher but the test user believes that the test is potentially useful, a local validation study may be designed and conducted by the test user. Also, different types of validation studies support different types of inferences and therefore should not be considered interchangeable. Finally, to justify some inferences, more than one type of validation study may be required.

CONTENT VALIDATION

The purpose of a content validation study is to assess whether the items adequately represent a performance domain or construct of specific interest. On a vocabulary test, for example, the test user is seldom interested in whether the examinee knows only these specific word meanings but is interested in the examinee's knowledge of "words like these." In content validation, a typical procedure is to have a panel of independent experts (other than the item writers) judge whether the items adequately sample the domain of interest. Occasionally a test developer claims that writing items from a carefully specified domain insures content validity, but this does not actually constitute a content validation study. Content validation is a series of activities which take place after an initial form of the instrument has been developed. These activities may be undertaken by either the test developer or by the potential users of a test who did not participate in the test's construction. At the minimum, content validation entails the following steps:

1. Defining the performance domain of interest
2. Selecting a panel of qualified experts in the content domain
3. Providing a structured framework for the process of matching items to the performance domain
4. Collecting and summarizing the data from the matching process

Because content validation is most often employed with achievement tests,[1] the performance domain is often defined by a list of instructional objectives. Although

---

[1] In the 1970s there was considerable interest in applications of content validation to tests used for employee selection and a considerable body of literature developed on this topic. Interested readers may wish to see, for example, Gavin (1977), Lawshe (1975), and Prien (1977) for discussion of content validation in the context of personnel testing.

we recognize that other procedures may be employed for domain definition (see Chapter 4), the term *objectives* will be used in the following sections in a broad connotation to denote any list of behaviors or categories of behavior which the test developer or test user employs for domain description.

Practical Considerations in Content Validation

Planning a content validation study requires the following practical decisions:

1. Should objectives be weighted to reflect their importance?   One common procedure is to assume that all objectives stated for a given domain are equal in value. This viewpoint, however, is not universal. Katz (1958) suggested weighting or rank ordering objectives in terms of their importance before matching items to objectives and Klein and Kosecoff (1975) advocated rating the importance of each objective with a five-point scale. There is no absolute requirement that the same judges who examine the items also participate in the weighting process. In a large school district, for example, the importance weights of various instructional objectives might be obtained by surveying all teachers in the district even though only a much smaller sample would actually participate in the item-objective matching task. Another point for consideration is the nature of the instructions given to the judges who are asked to rate the importance of objectives. For example, in judging "importance" of an instructional objective, one teacher might consider the amount of classtime devoted to it; another might define importance in terms of its relationship to future learning. In content validation, the designer of the study should provide judges with a common definition of importance rather than allowing them to use idiosyncratic definitions.

2. How should the item-matching task be structured?   A sensible approach is to instruct the experts to proceed systematically through the test, matching each individual item to the list of objectives. Katz (1958) and Ebel (1956) suggested that the expert reviewer read the item and identify the correct response, just as an examinee would. Klein and Kosecoff (1975) offered three additional suggestions for facilitating the matching task: Have each item written on a separate card; compare each item to the list of instructional objectives; and record the outcome of the matching decision on a standard form. Most authors seem to have considered the matching decision as a dichotomy: Either the item matches or it does not. However, Hambleton (1980) described a procedure in which the experts rate the degree of match to a specified objective by using a five-point scale, where 1 indicates a poor fit and 5 an excellent fit. The mean or median rating for each item is then computed across judges to indicate the overall degree of match between item and objective.

3. What aspects of the item should be examined?   Judges should be supplied with clear descriptions of the item (and domain) characteristics to consider in matching items to a performance domain. Some relevant characteristics are subject matter, cognitive process or level of complexity of the performance required, stimulus (question) format or mode of presentation, and mode of required response. Consider, for example, the first-grade math objectives:

A. Add any two positive whole numbers whose sum is 18 or less.
B. Subtract any two whole numbers (each less than 20) whose difference is a positive value.

Figure 10.1 contains sample items which might be found on a test to assess performance in this domain. Item 1 matches objective A; items 2 and 3 match objective B; however, item 4 deals with subject matter not contained in either objective. Item 5 deals with appropriate subject content but seems to require a higher level of performance than implied by the objectives since it requires combination of the skills required by the two separate objectives to solve a single problem.

Even when the item content and process are appropriate for the domain of interest, the mode of presentation may cause judges to question whether an item fits the domain. For example, items 1 through 3 in Figure 10.1 could be considered inappropriate for a curriculum in which all addition and subtraction problems are taught in a vertical format rather than the linear format shown in the figure. Sometimes the mode of presentation may require examinees to display additional behaviors that lie outside the domain of interest. For example, solving item 6 in Figure 10.1 requires examinees to be able to read if the problem is to be solved correctly. Such an item clearly does not represent only the domain of basic addition and subtraction skills. Finally, the nature of the response required of the examinee may also be an appropriate consideration. An oral spelling test and a written spelling test would seem to represent somewhat different performance domains because of the nature of the required response, even though the items (stimuli) read aloud by the examiner may be identical in each situation.

When a test has been constructed with the aid of item specifications (discussed in Chapter 4), the expert panel is typically asked to judge the extent to which the item meets the specification. Although this task is fairly straightforward, it constitutes

1. $3 + 5 =$ _____.

2. $12 - 10 =$ _____.

3. $8 - 5 =$ _____.

4. $25 - 16 =$ _____.

5. $13 + 3 - 8 =$ _____.

6. Judy had 10 pennies. She lost 2. How many pennies does she have left?

    a. 2
    b. 8
    c. 10
    d. 12

FIGURE 10.1 Illustrative Problems Reviewed in Content Validation of a Primary Grade Math Test

only the first stage of a two-stage process. It is also necessary for judges to evaluate whether the item specification itself matches the objective or content area for which it was written. Again, the content, level of complexity, stimulus format, and response format may be relevant to this consideration.

4. How should results be summarized?   The question of whether a set of items adequately represents a given domain seems to be more a qualitative than a quantitative decision. Nevertheless, some quantitative indices for summarizing judges' decisions on individual items may be useful. Some indices proposed for this purpose, include

1. Percentage of items matched to objectives
2. Percentage of items matched to objectives with high "importance" ratings
3. Correlation between the importance weighting of objectives and the number of items measuring those objectives (Klein and Kosecoff, 1975)
4. Index of item-objective congruence (Rovinelli and Hambleton, 1977)
5. Percentage of objectives not assessed by any of the items on the test

Because these indices are based on very different logical rationales, there is no reason to suppose they would lead to the same conclusions about the degree of fit between a set of test items and a content domain. Several properties of these indices should be considered in choosing among them and interpreting the results. The first two indices require a reasonably large number of items (perhaps 100 or more) for meaningful interpretation. The third index is affected by variance in the number of items assessing each objective and the importance weightings. Specifically, if all objectives are weighted as equally important, or if all objectives are measured by the same number of items, the value of this correlational index would be .00.

The fourth index, described by Hambleton (1980) and Hambleton and Rovinelli (1977), can be used to assess the degree to which a given item has content validity for a set of objectives. This formula is based upon the assumption that in the ideal case an item should clearly match one and only one objective in the set. The data collection procedure reflects this assumption because raters are instructed to match the item to each objective and for each match to assign a value of $+1$ if the item measures the objective, 0 if there is uncertainty, and -1 if the item clearly does not match the objective. The index of congruence of the item i to objective k can be computed by the formula[2]

$$I_{ik} = \frac{N}{2N - 2}(\mu_k - \mu)$$ (10.1)

where N is the number of objectives, μ_k is the judges' mean rating of item i on the kth objective, and μ is the judges' mean rating of item i on all objectives. The highest possible value of item-objective congruence is 1.00, obtained only when an

---

[2]The formula presented here is a simplified version of that reported by Rovinelli and Hambleton (1977) and Hambleton (1980).

item is matched to one and only one objective by all judges. If a single item can be matched to more than one objective, its index will be less than 1.00. In the ideal pattern of I_{ik} values for a test each item should have a very high I_{ik} value for the objective it was designed to measure and low values for the other objectives.

Finally, the percentage of objectives *not* covered by a given set of items is an index of how well the entire content domain is represented by the items. Note that in the extreme case where all items on a test match only one of many important objectives, the other indices would be quite high, but this index would be low. Thus it provides a substantially different piece of information. This proportional index must be interpreted cautiously when the number of objectives in the domain is small.

Issues in Assessing Content Validity

One major problem with the approach to content validation just described is that although it is possible for all items to fit the objectives beautifully, the stated objectives may not adequately represent the domain of performance to which the test user wants to make inferences. Cronbach (1971) proposed a method for addressing this problem, called the *duplicate construction* experiment. Using this method, two independent teams of test developers would be furnished with the same definitions of relevant content, rules for sampling the domain, rules for item tryouts, and criteria for data interpretation. Each team would be asked to develop a test for some specific domain such as "knowledge of the State Motor Vehicle Code." After the two tests have been developed and administered to the same examinees, the mean of their squared difference scores on the two tests are computed. Using classical true score theory, $\Sigma(X_1 - X_2)^2/N$ equals $\sigma_{e_1}^2 + \sigma_{e_2}^2$ where X_1 and X_2 are scores on the two parallel test forms, and $\sigma_{e_1}^2$ and $\sigma_{e_2}^2$ are the error variances for the two forms. (This proof is left to the reader as an exercise following this chapter.) Error variances for the two test forms can be estimated by internal consistency procedures. Thus a ratio could be computed using sample statistics based on n examinees by

$$\frac{\hat{\sigma}_{e_1}^2 + \hat{\sigma}_{e_2}^2}{\Sigma(X_1 - X_2)^2/n}$$

As this ratio approaches 1.00, it indicates that the tests constructed by the independent teams are as similar (in terms of error variance) as the split-half tests constructed by a single team. Thus there is evidence that the objectives measured by the test are not idiosyncratic to some perception of the domain that is uniquely held by a single team of test developers. Unfortunately this procedure has seldom been used, probably because it is somewhat impractical for situations where only a single test form is needed. It would, however, not be unreasonable to use this procedure when a number of alternate forms will be needed and multiple teams of item writers might be used anyway.

A second issue in content validation is whether the question of ethnic, racial, or gender bias is relevant to content validity judgment. Strictly speaking, the judgment of content validity deals with how adequately a test item fits a specified domain. On the one hand, if the domain were defined as knowledge of English vocabulary, characteristics of the examinees (including their native spoken language or their exposure to instruction in English) would seem immaterial to this judgment of the fit between test item and domain specifications. On the other hand, if the domain were described as the ability to solve story problems in arithmetic, and the verbal stimuli of the problems were presented in English to Spanish-speaking children, accurate inferences could not be drawn from these scores about the examinees' arithmetic skills. In the latter situation the problem actually arises because of inadequate domain specification, which leads to inappropriate inferences. Clearly the domain is the ability to solve story problems, *presented in English,* using certain arithmetic skills. The test scores may still have content validity for this more strictly specified domain; the question is whether it is meaningful to attempt to describe the performance of certain examinees in that domain. This question is an issue of educational policy rather than psychometrics. So that more-informed decisions can be made regarding test use, test developers should be sensitive to basic characteristics of examinees that are prerequisite to successful test performance and include these in published descriptions of the behavioral domain sampled by the test.

Another issue is whether item and test performance data should be considered in judgments of content validity. On the one hand, Cronbach (1971, p. 457) has taken the position that "nothing in the logic of content validation requires that the universe or test be homogeneous in content. High item intercorrelations may even represent oversampling of one particular subset of behaviors in the universe." On the other hand, it does seem reasonable to expect that items matched to the same objective should display at least moderate correlations. Although such data may not be sufficient evidence of content validity (or its lack), they are almost certainly useful as evidence for the adequacy of domain definition and the content validation process. If items that were judged to fit the same objective are found to be uncorrelated in practice, the process by which objectives and items were matched, the item quality, or the adequacy of the stated objectives would seem questionable.

Finally, in passing, we note that there are several concepts encountered from time to time in measurement literature which are similar but not identical to content validity. One of these is *face validity* (Mosier, 1947) which is generally construed as the extent to which items appear to measure a construct that is meaningful to laypersons or typical examinees. In some instances, such as for certain personality inventories, it may actually be undesirable for examinees to be able to infer what is being measured by the test items; but for school achievement or employment testing, face validity may motivate examinees to perform at their best since the test appears to measure a meaningful construct. Two other concepts, fairly recent in origin are *curricular validity* and *instructional validity* (see McClung, 1978). The former refers to the extent to which items are relevant to the objectives of a specific institution's curriculum as it is formally described, and the latter refers to the extent to which teachers have provided instruction in the specific content and skills measured by the items on the test. Yalow and Popham (1983) discuss the emergence of these concepts in relation to content validity and the role they have played in recent court decisions involving states' rights to award high school diplomas based on achievement test scores.

CRITERION-RELATED VALIDATION

In many cases the test user wants to draw inferences from test scores to examinee behavior on some performance criterion that cannot be directly measured by a test. For example, a college admissions director may wish to infer from admissions test scores to academic performance in college coursework, or an examiner may wish to infer from scores on a sales aptitude test to the sales volume that applicants for a sales position might generate if hired. Before using the test scores to make decisions about admission or hiring, however, these decision makers must have evidence that there is a relationship between test score and criterion performance. This type of evidence is obtained from a criterion-related validation study.

The general design of a criterion-related validation study has the following steps:

1. Identify a suitable criterion behavior and a method for measuring it.
2. Identify an appropriate sample of examinees representative of those for whom the test will ultimately be used.
3. Administer the test and keep a record of each examinee's score.
4. When the criterion data are available, obtain a measure of performance on the criterion for each examinee.
5. Determine the strength of the relationship between test scores and criterion performance.

It is customary to distinguish between two types of criterion-related validation: predictive and concurrent. *Predictive validity* refers to the degree to which test scores predict criterion measurements that will be made at some point in the future. For example, Scholastic Aptitude Test (SAT) scores may correlate about .40 with college grade point average (CGPA), and therefore SAT scores have a degree of predictive validity with respect to CGPA. This evidence of predictive validity is the basis for justifying the use of SAT scores in making admissions decisions. College admissions directors would like to admit those students who will succeed academically in college and CGPA is a pragmatic measure of academic achievement. Because of the demonstrated relationship between SAT scores and CGPA, the use of SAT scores in admissions decisions is at least partially justified for drawing inferences about examinees' future performance. *Concurrent validity* refers to the relationship between test scores and criterion measurements made at the time the test was given. For example, if airplane navigators took a pencil-and-paper test on navigation knowledge and immediately afterward were observed and rated on their performance in an actual flight, a positive correlation would be evidence of the concurrent validity of the paper-and-pencil test. A sufficiently high correlation would justify use of the test in place of the less efficient and more costly observation system in evaluating air navigators.

Practical Problems in Criterion-Related Validation

There are several potential problems which may affect results of a criterion-related validity study. The most commonly encountered problems are identification of a suitable criterion, insufficient sample size, criterion contamination, restriction of range, and unreliability of the predictor or criterion scores. Each of these problems is discussed briefly in the following sections.

THE CRITERION PROBLEM.   Thorndike (1949) pointed out that criterion measures can be considered immediate, intermediate, or ultimate criteria. Immediate criteria tend to be readily available and relatively easy to measure (e.g., grade in a particular course, supervisor's rating of a nurse giving a hypodermic injection, time required for a secretary to type and file three standard letters). Unfortunately such criteria are often not sufficiently complete or important to be used as the sole criterion for validating a test designed to predict performance in the domain of interest. In contrast, ultimate criteria are usually recognized as being of substantial importance but may be extremely difficult to define operationally and measure. Examples of ultimate criteria might be "surgical competence," "teaching effectiveness," or "independence in activities of daily living." The reader will note that such ultimate criteria are actually *constructs,* which must be operationally defined by variables that are more directly observable.

For example, if we wanted to validate a test to predict the classroom effectiveness of future teachers, ideally the ultimate criterion would be measured with repeated observations of the teacher's performance in the classroom perhaps over a five-year period after graduation. Because this criterion is highly impractical to measure, we might be forced instead to use the intermediate criterion of rating by the student's supervising teacher during the student teaching practicum. An immediate criterion might be the grade earned by the student on a project requiring preparation of a lesson plan and delivery of a "mock" lecture to peers in an undergraduate teaching methods class. Note that as the criterion measure becomes easier to obtain, its importance or its approximation of the ultimate criterion may be reduced. This creates a dilemma in planning a criterion-related validation study. If a simple-to-measure, immediate criterion is selected, it may not be highly related to the ultimate criterion of interest. On the other hand, if an ultimate criterion is designated, the effort required to define this criterion operationally and the cost of obtaining reliable measurements of it may be prohibitive. Thus there must be a judicious tradeoff in selecting a criterion which (1) can be reliably measured within the time and cost constraints of the study and (2) will have a relationship to the ultimate criterion of interest to most test users.

SAMPLE SIZE.   When validity coefficients are estimated for small samples, sampling errors are relatively large, and the statistical power of the inferential procedures used to analyze data from the validation study may be substantially reduced. For example, Schmidt, Hunter, and Urry (1976) found that if sample sizes are between 30 and 50, a predictor that has an acceptable validity level in the population is likely to have acceptable validity levels in the samples only 25% to 35% of the time. These researchers suggest that samples of 200 or more may be needed to reflect validity levels of population data accurately at least 90% of the time. In recent years there has been increasing legal and professional expectation for test developers and test users to demonstrate validity of test scores for personnel or educational selection in each specific workplace or educational setting where tests are used. Yet within a time period reasonable for conducting a validation study, a particular organization or educational institution may have an applicant pool that is too small to permit an adequate estimation of the validity coefficient. In such cases an alternative to conducting a validation study with an inadequate sample may be to investigate the *validity generalization* of the predictor test by reviewing criterion-related validation studies reported in the literature for a particular predictor, or similar predictors, and criteria similar to the criterion in the local setting.

CRITERION CONTAMINATION.   During a validation study persons who will be able to influence examinees' criterion scores should not have access to examinees' scores on the predictor. If, for example, college professors learned how students in their classes had scored on the admissions test that was being validated, it might influence their teaching or grading practices. This is known as *criterion contamination*. On one hand, criterion contamination could artificially increase the apparent relationship between test scores and grades if instructors tended to regard students with high scores on the admissions tests as "brighter" and therefore saw their work in a more favorable light. On the other hand, criterion contamination could reduce the relationship between the predictor and criterion if instructors learned that certain students scored relatively low on the predictor and put extra effort into teaching these students. Because it is impossible to systematically predict or adjust for the effects of criterion contamination, it is important to minimize opportunities for its occurrence.

RESTRICTION OF RANGE.   Because the most common form of validity evidence is the correlation coefficient between predictor and criterion scores, it is important to recognize that restriction of the range of scores on either the predictor or criterion may result in attenuation of the observed validity coefficient. There are two ways by which selection practices may restrict the variance. First is the situation in which the test being validated is used for selection purposes before its validity has been established. (Note that this is contrary to recommended validation procedures.) All subjects who score below a certain point on the test are rejected and consequently cannot be used in the validation study because no criterion data are available for them. Thus restriction of range occurs on the predictor because of *explicit selection* on that variable. Variance on the predictor can also be curtailed if selection is made on the basis of some other variable that is correlated with the predictor test being validated. For example, when a college admissions test is being validated but during the study students are admitted on the basis of their high school grades (which are correlated to their admissions test scores), this is known as *incidental* selection.

Restriction of range may also occur if the predictor or criterion measure is so easy that all examinees earn very high scores (a ceiling effect) or so difficult that all earn very low scores (a floor effect); it may even be a function of the scaling procedure chosen (e.g., having supervisors rate workers on a four-point scale when a scale with more gradations would have allowed finer discriminations). Natural attrition is another source of restriction of range whenever subjects at the high or low end of the criterion continuum tend to leave the setting before criterion data can be collected. For example, suppose that an infant psychomotor development scale is being used to predict language development of Downs syndrome babies at age two. Many of those infants who might be expected to have the least language development because of the severity of their condition simply may not survive to the age at which the criterion data can be obtained.

Thorndike (1949, 1982), Gulliksen (1950), and Lord and Novick (1968) have discussed procedures for estimating validity coefficients for an entire group even though complete data on the predictor and criterion variables can be obtained for only a subgroup of examinees selected because of the procedures in force during the validation study. These procedures require assumptions that may not be tenable (and are seldom testable) in practical situations. One assumption is that the linear regression of Y (criterion variable) on X (predictor) is the same over all values of X, that is, for the selected and the unselected groups. Another assumption is that $\sigma^2_{Y \cdot X}$ (the variance of the criterion for examinees at any given value of X) is the same for all values of X. Lord and Novick (1968) note that errors in correcting validity coefficients may occur if these assumptions are violated, particularly if selection has not been made explicitly on the predictor scores. In summary, then, it is best to plan a validation study to avoid curtailment of variance if at all possible rather than relying on statistical correction procedures to overcome this problem.

RELIABILITY OF PREDICTOR AND CRITERION. In any attempt to assess the degree of relationship between a predictor and criterion, it would seem logical that errors of measurement should be held to a minimum. There is, in fact, a direct relationship between the correlation between X and Y and the reliabilities of the predictor (X) and the criterion (Y) and such that

$$\rho_{XY} \leq \sqrt{\rho_{XX'}}\sqrt{\rho_{YY'}} \tag{10.2}$$

Thus if we had obtained estimates of the reliabilities of predictor and criterion as $\hat{\rho}_{XX'} = .81$ and $\hat{\rho}_{YY'} = .64$, we would estimate the maximum correlation that could be obtained between these variables as .72. Later a derivation of this relationship will be presented, and its implications for interpreting results of validation studies will be discussed. For the moment it will suffice to note that it is important to collect observations for predictor and criterion under conditions that will minimize errors of measurement as much as possible and to check the reliabilities of both the predictor and criterion measures. (In some rare instances a correlation between X and Y will be observed which actually exceeds $\sqrt{\hat{\rho}_{XX'}}\sqrt{\hat{\rho}_{YY'}}$. This may occur when the reliability estimate actually underestimates the coefficient of precisions for one or both of the variables or when the assumption on uncorrelated errors of measurement between X and Y is not met.)

Although in theory, highly reliable measures of test and criterion are desirable, it is not necessarily true that the predictive power of a test is maximized by maximizing the internal consistency. Additional discussion of this problem can be found in Loevinger (1954), Lord and Novick (1968), Ebel (1968), Horn (1968), and Kane (1982). Briefly we note that as the predictor test becomes more homogeneous in content (increases in internal consistency), the correlations among items increase. Yet ideally, to account for as much variance as possible in the criterion variable, items should be highly correlated with the criterion but not with each other (Tucker, 1946). Consider the extreme example of a two-item test when the correlation between the items is 1.00. In this case the second item can account for no additional variance in the criterion that has not already been accounted for by the first item. This paradox of increasing internal consistency at the expense of reduced validity creates an issue for test developers which will be considered in Chapter 14.

Reporting and Interpreting Results of Criterion-Related Validation

The data collected in a criterion-related validation study can be analyzed in several ways. If the criterion measure is continuously distributed, the Pearson product moment correlation coefficient between test score and criterion measure can be computed. Such a statistic is called a *validity coefficient*. In some cases, however, the criterion variable may be categorical. An example might be when the criterion is the dichotomy of successful completion of a master's degree program in clinical psychology or failure to complete the program. In this case, the mean predictor test score of those who graduated could be contrasted to the mean score of those who did not graduate. A statistically significant difference between criterion group means shows evidence of a relationship between entering test score and graduation status. (As an alternative, correlational procedures appropriate for use with a dichotomous and a continuous variable are described in Chapter 14.) When the performances on predictor and criterion are both categorized (e.g., pass-fail on the predictor and success-failure on the criterion), a statistic such as the phi coefficient (or some other correlational procedure appropriate for use with categorical data) may be reported.

The validity coefficient between the test scores and criterion may not be sufficient to help potential test users judge the usefulness of the test scores for their specific needs. Additional information that may aid test users in interpreting results of a validation study includes the coefficient of determination, the standard error of the estimate, and expectancy tables.

In Chapter 2, we noted that the square of the correlation coefficient is often used in interpreting the importance of the relationship between two variables. When the two variables are a test score and criterion score, the correlation coefficient is called a *validity coefficient* and its square is called the coefficient of determination. If we find, for example, that the correlation between test score and some measure of job performance is .60, the coefficient of determination is .36, indicating 36% of the variance in job performance is related to variance in performance on the predictor test.

When test scores are to be used to predict criterion performance of individuals, it may be useful to report the *standard error of the estimate,* discussed in Chapter 2. Recall that in the formula for predicting an individual's score on Y, the criterion variable is

$$Y' = \hat{\rho}_{XY}(\hat{\sigma}_Y/\hat{\sigma}_X)(X - \hat{\mu}_X) + \hat{\mu}_Y$$

where $\hat{\rho}_{XY}$ is the validity coefficient, $\hat{\sigma}_Y$ is the standard deviation on the criterion scores, $\hat{\mu}_Y$ is the mean criterion score, and $\hat{\mu}_X$ and $\hat{\sigma}_X$ are the mean and standard deviation on the predictor test estimated for the sample in the validation study. To generate a confidence interval around an individual's predicted score, Y', we use the standard error of the estimate for the validation sample:

$$\hat{\sigma}_{Y \cdot X} = \hat{\sigma}_Y \sqrt{1 - \hat{\rho}_{XY}^2}$$

The test user who has determined an estimated Y' value for an examinee can be 68% confident that the examinee's actual Y score will fall in the approximate interval $Y' \pm 1\hat{\sigma}_{Y \cdot X}$ and 95% confident that the examinee's actual Y will fall in the approximate interval $Y' \pm 2\hat{\sigma}_{Y \cdot X}$. (An example of computation and interpretation of the standard error of the estimate has been presented in Chapter 2; see Equation 2.20.)

Finally, in explaining how accurate test scores tend to be for examinees in particular score ranges on test or criterion, it is sometimes helpful to use an expectancy table which contains the probabilities of various criterion scores for an examinee with a particular score on the predictor test. Such an expectancy table using hypothetical data is presented in Table 10.1. In this example a career skills inventory is

TABLE 10.1. Expectancy Table Showing Percentages of Trainees in Each Score Category Who Were Hired at Various Levels

Career Skills Score	Criterion Rating				Number of Trainees
	Hired above Entry Level	Hired at Entry Level	Hired on Probation	Not Hired	
101–110	0	0	0	100	3
111–120	0	0	0	100	5
121–130	0	0	33.3	66.7	6
131–140	0	0	30.0	70.0	20
141–150	0	5.6	22.2	72.2	18
151–160	3.8	11.5	34.6	50	26
161–170	8.6	28.6	28.6	34.2	35
171–180	8.5	34.0	27.7	29.8	47
181–190	22.5	47.5	23.8	6.2	80
191–200	53.6	40.2	6.2	0	97
201–210	72.3	21.4	4.5	1.8	112
211+	100	0	0	0	26

used to predict on-the-job performance of work-study students in a manpower training program. The number in each cell shows the percentage of trainees, at a given score level on the career skills inventory, who received the supervisor's recommendations (criterion), listed in columns at the top of the table. An interpretation of values in this table would be made as follows: A trainee who scores in the range 151 to 160 on the career skills inventory has a 3.8% chance of being hired above entry level, an 11.5% chance of being hired at minimal entry level, a 34.6% chance of being hired on probation and a 50% chance of not being hired.

For most clinical, educational, or personnel uses, a single test score provides insufficient data for making important decisions about individual examinees. In the event that one or more useful predictor variables have already been identified, the validation question is whether the new predictor can make a significant improvement in predicting criterion performance when added to these other predictors. Statistical procedures for addressing this question are presented in Chapter 11. Additional important considerations for interpreting validity information are discussed in Chapter 12 which deals with selection decisions.

CONSTRUCT VALIDATION

Use of psychological constructs as a basis for test development was discussed in Chapter 1. A psychological construct was defined as a product of informed scientific imagination, an idea developed to permit categorization and description of some directly observable behavior. Psychological constructs are not directly observable. Consider, for example, constructs such as "intelligence," "creativity," "field independence," or "extroversion-introversion." Lord and Novick (1968) note that to be useful a construct must be defined on two levels. First, it must be operationally defined (or semantically defined), usually by specifying the procedures used to measure the construct. Tests such as the Stanford Binet, the Remote Associates Test, the Embedded Figures Test, and the Myers Briggs Type Indicator I-E Scale illustrate operational definitions of the four constructs named. In addition, however, a psychological construct requires syntactic definition by the postulation of specific relationships between measures of the construct with (1) measures of other constructs in the theoretical system and (2) measures of specific real-world criteria. In other words, operational definition of a construct is not enough; the meaningfulness or importance of the construct must also be made explicit through a description of how it is related to other variables.

Although construct validation evidence is typically assembled through a series of studies, the process generally contains the following steps:

1. Formulate one or more hypotheses about how those who differ on the construct are expected to differ on demographic characteristics, performance criteria, or measures of other constructs whose relationship to performance criteria has already been validated. These hypotheses should be based on an explicitly stated theory that underlies the construct and provides its syntactic definition.

2. Select (or develop) a measurement instrument which consists of items representing behaviors that are specific, concrete manifestations of the construct.
3. Gather empirical data which will permit the hypothesized relationships to be tested.
4. Determine if the data are consistent with the hypotheses and consider the extent to which the observed findings could be explained by rival theories or alternative explanations (and eliminate these if possible).

From the preceding list it should be apparent that validation of the test scores on the instrument and validation of the theory about the nature of the construct of interest are inseparably linked. If the hypothesized relationships are confirmed as predicted by the theory, both the construct and the test that measures it are useful. If the hypotheses cannot be confirmed by the validation studies, the test developer cannot know whether there is a critical flaw in the theoretical construct, in the test that measures it, or both. (In this sense construct validation is somewhat like placing a bet on a daily double at the racetrack—both the theory and the test of the construct must be well constructed before there is any psychometric payoff from the gamble.)

Procedures for Construct Validation

More than any other approach to validation, construct validation requires compilation of multiple types of evidence. Four widely used approaches to construct validation will be discussed here.

CORRELATIONS BETWEEN A MEASURE OF THE CONSTRUCT AND DESIGNATED
    A classic example is the attempt to establish correlational evidence of the relationship between scores on intelligence tests and measures of school or job performance. Although it would seem illogical to argue that intelligence and school achievement are identical constructs, it can be argued that there is, or should be, a relationship between them. If this were not the case, the usefulness of intelligence as a construct would be diminished. There are no generally recognized guidelines for what constitutes adequate evidence of construct validation through correlational studies. Individual correlations may, of course, be tested for statistical significance, proportions of variance shared may be reported, and so on. Such information alone, however, is probably not sufficient without comparison with the range of values that have been reported previously by others who have developed measures of the same or similar constructs. Such information helps potential test users evaluate the strength of the evidence presented for the construct validity of the scores. In many cases the correlational approach involves application of multiple regression so that contributions of the construct of interest to variance in the criterion may be assessed relative to the contributions of other variables. (This will be discussed in Chapter 11.) Also Darlington (1970) proposed a procedure in which the test developer hypothesizes relative sizes of correlations between the construct measure and other observable variables to establish some evidence of construct validity.

DIFFERENTIATION BETWEEN GROUPS.   An example of this approach is contrasting the mean scores of males' and females' self-ratings on a sex-role perception scale to see if they differ in the hypothesized direction. Failure to find expected differences would raise doubts about either the construct of sex-role perception, the adequacy of this instrument as a measure of the construct, or both. Frequently such studies are experimental in design, with the goal of demonstrating that subjects who have received a specific treatment, designed to alter their standing on the construct, differ from subjects who have received no treatment. If expected differences are not found in such a study, the possible explanations are failure of the theory underlying the construct, inadequacy of the instrument for measuring the construct, or failure of the treatment.

FACTOR ANALYSIS.   In general, this approach involves obtaining a set of n measurements on the same examinees, computing an $n \times n$ correlation matrix between these measurements, and then using factor analytic techniques to identify some reduced number of underlying variables (called *factors*) which account for variation in the original set of n variables. A more detailed explanation of factor analysis will be presented in Chapter 13, but two general applications in construct validation will be briefly mentioned here. In the first case, a matrix of *item* intercorrelations (for n items on the same instrument) is factored to determine whether item responses "cluster" together in patterns predictable or reasonable in light of the theoretical structure of the construct of interest. Variation in responses to items that form a cluster can be attributed to variation among examinees on a common underlying factor. Such a factor, which is not itself directly observable, can be considered a construct suggested by this particular set of empirical observations. The issue is whether the constructs, empirically identified through the factor analysis, correspond to the theoretical constructs which the test developer hypothesized in developing the test. For example, in a math achievement test,[3] if items requiring execution of simple arithmetic computations clustered on one factor and items requiring solution of more complex word problems clustered on another factor, this would probably fit the test developer's expectation. If, however, several items that appear to measure the same thing (e.g., one-digit multiplication facts) clustered on different factors, this might raise questions about the validity of the construct measured by this collection of items. In the second case, a correlation matrix for a set of n different tests or measures may be factored to determine the extent to which correlations among the observed scores on these measures is attributable to variance on one or more common, underlying factors. A detailed example of this type of construct validation through factor analysis is presented in Chapter 13. Again, the critical issue is whether subtests or tests, which are supposed to measure the same construct, are empirically identified as measuring a common factor.

THE MULTITRAIT-MULTIMETHOD MATRIX.   Campbell and Fiske (1959) have described this approach as "concerned with the adequacy of tests as measures of a

---

[3] This example is offered as a simple illustration, but readers should note that factor-analysis with dichotomous item responses poses problems discussed in Chapters 13 and 14.

construct, rather than the adequacy of a construct as determined by the confirmation of theoretically predicted associations with measures of other constructs.'' With this technique, the researcher must think of two (or more) ways to measure the construct of interest. Furthermore, the researcher is asked to identify other, distinctly different constructs which can be appropriately measured by the same methods applied to the construct of interest. Using one sample of subjects, measurements are then obtained on each construct by each method; correlations between each pair of measurements are computed. Each correlation coefficient is identified as one of three types:

1. Reliability coefficients—correlations between measures of the same construct using the same measurement method. Ideally these should be high.
2. Convergent validity coefficients—correlations between measures of the same construct using different measurement methods. Ideally these should also be high, but the possible attenuation because of unreliability of the measurement methods should be considered.
3. Discriminant validity coefficients—correlations between measures of different constructs using the same method of measurement (called *heterotrait-monomethod coefficients*) or correlations between different constructs using different measurement methods (called *heterotrait-heteromethod coefficients*). Ideally these should be substantially lower than reliability or convergent validity coefficients.

To facilitate comparisons among these different types of coefficients, the correlations are arranged in a multitrait-multimethod matrix such as that shown in Table 10.2.

Data presented in Table 10.2 were reported in a study by Mosher (1968), who posited three distinct constructs labeled as ''Sex Guilt,'' ''Hostility Guilt,'' and ''Morality Conscience,'' which were measured by the multiple methods of true-false, forced-choice, and incomplete-sentence tests administered to a sample of 62 female subjects. Reliability coefficients are enclosed by parentheses and make up the diagonal of this square correlation matrix. Convergent validity coefficients are underlined. In the first three rows, there are no convergent validity coefficients because these are all correlations between measures using the same method. In rows 2A through 2C and 3A through 3C, there is one convergent validity coefficient in each row. In row 2A, the coefficient .86 represents the correlation between measures of ''Sex Guilt'' measured by true-false and forced-choice methods. In each of the lower six rows, the convergent validity coefficients are higher than the discriminant validity coefficients, offering evidence to support the proposed theory of guilt types. In addition, the relative sizes of the correlations among different traits fall in the same pattern for 7 of the 9 heterotrait triangles (Campbell and Fiske suggested that ideally the same pattern of relationship among the traits should be observed across all heterotrait triangles.) Although Campbell and Fiske recommended visual inspection for assessment of construct validity data in such a matrix, this method can be problematic because of sampling error. Recently additional analytic procedures have been suggested which may result in clearer interpretations of such data

TABLE 10.2.   Illustrative Table of Multitrait-Multimethod Matrix Data from a Study by Mosher

	Method 1			Method 2			Method 3		
	Trait A	B	C	A	B	C	A	B	C
1. True-False									
A. Sex-Guilt	(.95)								
B. Hostility-Guilt	.28	(.86)							
C. Morality-Conscience	.58	.39	(.92)						
2. Forced Choice									
A. Sex-Guilt	<u>.86</u>	.32	.57	(.95)					
B. Hostility-Guilt	.30	<u>.90</u>	.40	.39	(.76)				
C. Morality-Conscience	.52	.31	<u>.86</u>	.55	.26	(.84)			
3. Incomplete Sentences									
A. Sex-Guilt	<u>.73</u>	.10	.43	<u>.64</u>	.17	.37	(.48)		
B. Hostility-Guilt	.10	<u>.63</u>	.17	.22	<u>.67</u>	.19	.15	(.41)	
C. Morality-Conscience	.35	.16	<u>.52</u>	.31	.17	<u>.56</u>	.41	.30	(.58)

$N = 62$.

From D. L. Mosher, Measurement of guilt by self-report inventories, *Journal of Consulting and Clinical Psychology,* 32, 690–695. Copyright 1968 by the American Psychological Association. Adapted by permission of the author.

matrices for reasonably large samples. (See, for example, Lomax and Algina, 1979; Marsh and Hocevar, 1983; and Schmitt, 1978.)

Another type of evidence in construct validation is whether observations for an individual on a construct are invariant over different methods of measurement. Kane (1982) suggested investigation of this point through *analyses of variance components* obtained from application of generalizability theory (discussed in Chapter 8). It is assumed that each measurement taken for an individual represents a random sample from the universe of possible measurements that could have been obtained. This universe may vary along multiple dimensions called *facets* which may be comprised by different methods of measurement. Identification of appropriate facets in construct validation depends on the researcher's particular theory about the construct of interest and the universe to which inferences are to be made. Let us illustrate by assuming that we are interested in assessing such a construct as examinees' reading comprehension skills. It would be possible to measure this construct by using a variety of item formats (multiple choice, true-false, open-ended, matching, etc.) We might feel that the construct were more important or "generalizable" if an examinee's relative score would be the same regardless of the item format used to measure it. If we wish to see how well our findings could be generalized over item formats, we could design a G-study (defined in Chapter 8) using different item formats. Suppose we design this study so that each examinee is tested on the same *n* different item formats. (In this case we would say that the data are matched or standardized on the facet of item format.) If we wish to consider the item formats in the G-study to be a random sample of all possible item formats that might be used in future D-studies, item format is a random facet and the appropriate generalizability coefficient is

$$\rho^2 = \frac{\sigma_p^2}{\sigma_p^2 + \sigma_{pf}^2 + \sigma_e^2}$$

where σ_p^2 is variance due to persons, σ_{pf}^2 is variance due to interaction of persons and format, and σ_e^2 is due to all other unexplained sources of variation in the scores. Kane (1982) refers to this coefficient as a validity coefficient, noting that it could be interpreted as the average convergent validity coefficient obtained by randomly choosing different methods of measuring the same trait from a universe of possible methods.

The reader may note that the construction of this generalizability coefficient as an estimate of validity does not differ from the construction of generalizability coefficients presented in Chapter 8 as estimates of reliability. Does this imply that in Kane's model there is no distinction between validity and reliability? There are at least three different ways to answer this question. First, Kane specifically identifies $(\sigma_p^2 + \sigma_{pf}^2)/(\sigma_p^2 + \sigma_{pf}^2 + \sigma_e^2)$ as a coefficient for estimating reliability. Thus he restricts reliability estimates to those generalizability coefficients in which the different methods of measurement constitute a fixed facet rather than a random one. (This is an estimate of what Lord and Novick (1968) have called a "specific reliability coefficient.") Second, the distinction between generalizability coefficients as estimates of validity or reliability is conceptual, depending on the construct and the universe of generalization. For example, a test developer might consider a study of different test forms using the same method as a reliability study, but the study of different methods of measurement as a validity study.

OVERLAP AMONG APPROACHES TO VALIDATION

After digesting the material on the three different approaches to test validation, it might seem that these approaches are mutually exclusive in their applications to certain types of tests. This, however, is rarely the case. It is fairly common for the desired inferences from scores on a test to require multiple types of validity evidence. Let us consider such an example. Suppose that a researcher believes that success in college science courses is dependent upon students' abilities to read technical material with understanding. The researcher also believes that traditional tests of reading comprehension are inadequate for assessing this ability. The researcher develops a test of "ability to read technical material" consisting of reading passages selected from physical and biological science textbooks at the college level, with each passage followed by a series of multiple-choice questions on information presented in the passage. A content validation study would be appropriate to determine the degree to which the questions are relevant to the material in the passages and to ascertain how representative these passages are of texts in freshman science courses. A criterion-related validation could also be conducted to learn if performance on the test is related to grades earned in freshman science courses. Yet at this point the inference that a high score on this test means a high "technical reading ability" may not be justified. An important rival hypothesis has been overlooked. Namely, the test items may measure general scientific information that could have been acquired by students with good high school backgrounds in science. These students might have been able to answer the questions correctly without reading the passages at all; due to their better high school preparation, they may also earn higher grades in their college science courses. Thus a more complete validation would include evidence that this test measures something distinct from general scientific knowledge and from general reading comprehension or academic aptitude. Such a validation effort would include aspects of content, criterion-related, and construct validation.

Recognition of the need for multiple types of validation and the fact that constructs are often invoked in describing performance domains or defining criteria, has led some authors, such as Messick (1981), to take the position that "construct validity may not be the whole of validity, but it is surely the heart of it." The controversy over which type of validation evidence is most fundamental has been debated and discussed in the measurement literature for nearly half a century (see, for example, Guion, 1977, 1978, 1980; Loevinger, 1947; and Tenopyr, 1977). The position taken here is that the type of validation that is most important depends on the inferences to be drawn from the test scores. Debates about which type of validity evidence is most fundamental to test score interpretation may actually serve to obscure this point. Test developers and test users should think in terms of what types of evidence are most useful for supporting the inferences that will most likely be drawn from scores on the test. Validation studies should then be planned to provide such evidence. It is conceivable (and probably highly desirable) that such studies include elements of all three types of validation discussed in this chapter.

VALIDITY COEFFICIENTS FOR TRUE SCORES

In classical test theory, random errors of measurement for different variables are assumed to be uncorrelated. If this assumption is correct then the validity coefficient between observed scores on a test and some other measure of interest is lower than it would be if examinees' true scores on the two measures could have been correlated. A simple proof shows the relationship between the validity coefficient for observed scores and the corresponding validity coefficient for true scores on the same measures. Recall that in Chapter 6 it was shown that the correlation between test scores from two testing occasions could be expressed as the ratio of the covariance of the true scores to the product of their standard deviations. By the same reasoning (that errors of measurement are uncorrelated) we can now express the correlation between test score (X) and a second variable (Y) as

$$\rho_{XY} = \frac{\Sigma t_X t_Y}{N \sigma_X \sigma_Y} \qquad (10.3)$$

If we multiply this fraction by ($\sigma_{t_X}/\sigma_{t_X}$) and ($\sigma_{t_Y}/\sigma_{t_Y}$), its value will remain unchanged, so that

$$\rho_{XY} = \frac{(\Sigma t_X t_Y)(\sigma_{t_X})(\sigma_{t_Y})}{N \sigma_X \sigma_Y \sigma_{t_X} \sigma_{t_Y}} \qquad (10.4)$$

Equation 10.4 can be rewritten as the product of three separate fractions:

$$\rho_{XY} = \left(\frac{\Sigma t_X t_Y}{N \sigma_{t_X} \sigma_{t_Y}} \right) \left(\frac{\sigma_{t_X}}{\sigma_X} \right) \left(\frac{\sigma_{t_Y}}{\sigma_Y} \right)$$

and from definitions of the correlation coefficient and reliability coefficient,

$$\rho_{XY} = \rho_{t_X t_Y} \sqrt{\rho_{XX'} \, \rho_{YY'}} \qquad (10.5)$$

Because the values of $\rho_{XX'}$ and $\rho_{YY'}$ are nearly always less than 1.00, the observed score correlation coefficient (ρ_{XY}) will be less than the correlation coefficient between the true scores. An expression for the validity coefficient for the true scores can be obtained by solving Equation 10.5 for the term $\rho_{t_X t_Y}$ as follows:

$$\rho_{t_X t_Y} = \frac{\rho_{XY}}{\sqrt{\rho_{XX'}} \sqrt{\rho_{YY'}}} \qquad (10.6)$$

Equation 10.6 is sometimes called the correction for attenuation because it yields a validity coefficient that is corrected for errors of measurement in the predictor and criterion variables. It is, however, somewhat misleading to calculate and report this coefficient for a criterion-related validation study because it implies a greater degree of validity than can be achieved with the existing test and criterion measure. However, there is one situation in which examining the unattenuated validity coefficient may be justified. Consider a construct validation study in which the investigator is interested in which of two different variables is more closely related to the construct of interest. If the two criteria cannot be measured with equal reliability, the unattenuated validity coefficients may be more appropriate for comparison than the observed validity coefficients. Suppose, for example, that the observed validity estimates for a sample are $\hat{\rho}_{XY} = .40$ and $\hat{\rho}_{XZ} = .30$, but the reliability estimates are $\hat{\rho}_{XX'} = .64$, $\hat{\rho}_{YY'} = .81$, and $\hat{\rho}_{ZZ'} = .25$. Applying Equation 10.6 to this problem, we would obtain

$$\hat{\rho}_{t_X t_Y} = \frac{.40}{\sqrt{.64}\sqrt{.81}} = .56$$

and

$$\hat{\rho}_{t_X t_Z} = \frac{.30}{\sqrt{.64}\sqrt{.25}} = .75$$

Obviously use of the unattenuated coefficients may result in different conclusions about the relationships between these variables than would use of the observed score validity coefficients.

SUMMARY

Test score validity refers to the usefulness of inferences drawn from test scores for a given purpose under a prescribed set of conditions. Validation refers to the process through which empirical evidence is gathered to support the use of test scores for a stated purpose. Three major approaches to validation were presented.

Content validation is employed when it seems likely that test users will want to draw references from observed test scores to performances on a larger domain of tasks similar to items on the test. Typically, it involves asking expert judges to examine test items and judge the extent to which these items sample a specified performance domain. In designing a content validation study, decisions must be made about weighting various components of the domain, instructions to judges about the item-objective matching task, structural aspects of the item that should be reviewed, and selection of an appropriate index for summarizing the judges' ratings. Issues that may arise in the course of content validation include how well the objectives represent the domain, the meaningfulness of certain domains for examinees of different ethnic or cultural backgrounds, and whether item performance data are relevant to the judgment of content validity.

Criterion-related validation is a study of the relationship between test scores and a practical performance criterion. Practical difficulties that may occur in such studies include identification of a suitable criterion, inadequate sample size, criterion contamination, curtailment of variance, and lack of reliability in predictor or criterion measure. Results of criterion-related validation are often reported in the form of validity coefficients, but these may be supplemented with the coefficient of determination, the standard error of the estimate, or expectancy tables to help test users assess the usefulness of the test scores for particular purposes.

Construct validation is appropriate whenever the test user wants to draw inferences from test scores to a behavior domain which cannot be adequately represented by a single criterion or completely defined by a universe of content. Construct validation often requires a series of studies to test specific hypotheses about how examinees who differ on the construct of interest would differ on other related variables. Procedures for construct validation may include correlations between test scores and designated criterion variables, differentiation between groups, factor analysis, multitrait-multimethod matrix analysis, or analysis of variance components within the framework of generalizability theory. Because construct validation is almost always applicable for every type of test and for a broad variety of intended test score uses, the distinction between it and the other two approaches to validation may be somewhat artificial. The most appropriate type of validation is dictated by the type(s) of inferences to be drawn from the test scores.

Finally, it was shown that when validity coefficients are based on observed scores, these coefficients are lower than those that would be obtained if examinees' true scores on the two measures were correlated. A formula for estimating the correlation between true scores was presented and considerations on use of the unattenuated validity coefficient were discussed.

Exercises

1. Suppose a large city school district plans to institute a minimal competency testing program for hiring teachers. A study is undertaken to assess the adequacy of two commercially published tests to decide which is more appropriate for assessing performance on the skills and competencies valued in this district for beginning teachers. A panel of teachers and principals matched items on each test to a list of required skills. Each test was found to consist of 50% of items that matched one or more of the skills. What additional data might be useful in deciding which test to use?

2. Consider the sample data set containing ratings of three judges indicating the extent to which each of five items fit three different objectives, where a rating of -1 indicates a low degree of fit and a rating of $+1$, a high degree of fit.

Item	Obj. 1			Obj. 2			Obj. 3		
	J_1	J_2	J_3	J_1	J_2	J_3	J_1	J_2	J_3
1	+1	+1	0	0	0	−1	−1	−1	−1
2	+1	+1	+1	−1	−1	−1	0	−1	0
3	+1	+1	+1	−1	−1	−1	+1	+1	+1
4	−1	−1	−1	+1	+1	+1	−1	−1	−1
5	0	−1	−1	−1	0	−1	−1	−1	0

A. What is the index of item-objective congruence for each item with each objective?
B. Which items appear to measure objective 1? objective 2? objective 3?
C. Item 3 seems to fit two objectives fairly well, yet it does not have a high congruence index with these objectives. Explain. Do you consider this an advantage or disadvantage of this index?

3. Suppose two test forms (G and H) have been developed for the same content domain and both forms are administered to a single population. Using the definitions of true and error scores and the assumptions of classical true score theory, prove that

$$\Sigma(X_G - X_H)^2/N = \sigma_{e_G}^2 + \sigma_{e_H}^2$$

if test forms G and H are parallel.

4. Suppose that a test developer undertakes a contract to produce multiple forms of a professional certification examination for a state licensing board. Part of the requirement is that a duplicate construction experiment be carried out and that the ratio of total error

variances to the average squared difference score should not be less than .80. Is this experiment likely to be more successful if each item-writing team writes a very homogeneous set of items or if each team writes a heterogeneous set of items. Why?

5. Following are descriptions of several validation studies. Read each description and identify any potential problems that could affect the outcomes.

   A. A high school math teacher makes up a test for identifying mathematically gifted high school students and gives the test to 100 students in the school. On the basis of high test scores, students are permitted to enroll in a calculus course at the local junior college. At the end of the semester the test developer correlates test scores with grades in the college course. The teacher finds no significant correlation.

   B. An industrial psychologist is developing a test to screen applicants for clerical jobs in a given corporation and asks job supervisors to rate present workers on a scale with categories: "Above Average," "Average," and "Below Average." The psychologist then tests workers in the "Above Average" category and those in the "Below Average" category and compares their group means. The psychologist finds a significant difference in favor of the "Above Average" group.

   C. A developmental psychologist devises a test for social maturity in children. The test is administered to 50 students at a preschool, and parents and teachers are notified of their scores. Teachers are requested to observe the children carefully for the next three months and to keep anecdotal records on each child's behavior that would be useful in assessing level of social maturity. On the basis of these records, the psychologist ranks the children on the level of social maturity and rank orders them on the basis of their test scores. These ranks are correlated by the Spearman rank order correlation coefficient, and it is quite high.

   D. A group intelligence test was validated by correlating it with the individually administered Stanford Binet scale. Later an educational psychologist develops a shortened form of the group test consisting of vocabulary words only. Scores on the long form and the short form of the group test are correlated and found to be high and positive. The test developer now proposes using this shortened form of the group test to replace the Stanford Binet, which requires much longer to administer for each individual.

6. For each of the following situations consider the type of inference that the test user desires to make from the test score and indicate the type of validation study that would be most appropriate (content, criterion-related predictive, criterion-related concurrent, or construct).

   A. A social psychologist develops an inventory intended to identify workers in health-related occupations who manifest symptoms of "job burnout." A variety of behaviors are used to define "burnout," including high absenteeism, failure to comply with institutional policies, and strained relationships with colleagues and supervisors.

   B. A developmental psychologist specializing in adolescence develops an inventory to be administered to junior high school students for predicting who will drop out of senior high school.

   C. An observational rating scale is being developed to rate the classroom performance of first-year teachers, and experienced classroom teachers are asked to examine the items on the rating scale to see if they are relevant to effective performance.

   D. Retail sales managers' ratings of the performance of salespersons on their staffs are collected to determine if managers have an accurate perception of the sales volume produced by their employees.

E. A nonverbal academic aptitude test is developed for hearing-impaired preschool children. The test is intended as a screening measure to identify children who will have difficulty learning to read in a normal classroom.

7. The following MTMM matrix was constructed from data presented in Marx and Winne (1978). Examine this matrix of correlations and answer the questions that follow. The authors of the article report that the correlations have been corrected for attenuation. (In this study, the authors have considered subscales as traits and the different self-concept instruments as "methods" for measurement of these traits.)

	Method A				Method B			
A. Gordon's Self-Concept Inventory	1	2	3	4	1	2	3	4
1. Phys. Appear.	.70							
2. Social	.64	.64						
3. Interpersonal Adeq.	.97	.75	.73					
4. Academic Adeq.	.60	.88	.92	.66				
B. Piers-Harris Inventory								
1. Phys. Appear.	.78	.66	.63	.50	.80			
2. Popularity	.59	.59	.62	.42	.87	.79		
3. Anxiety	.53	.57	.55	.52	.72	.70	.73	
4. School Studies	.59	.81	.68	.80	.90	.86	.75	.80

(Adapted from R. W. Marx and P. H. Winne, Construct interpretations of three self-concept inventories, *American Educational Research Journal, 15,* 99–109, Table 2. Copyright 1978, American Educational Research Assn, Washington, D.C.

A. What are the reliability estimates for the four subscales on each instrument?

B. What are the convergent validity coefficients?

C. Which two of the four "traits" appear to have greatest convergent validity?

D. Which heterotrait-monomethod coefficients raise questions about the construct validity of the physical appearance trait?

E. Which heterotrait-heteromethod coefficients raise questions about the construct validity of the academic/school studies trait?

8. Suppose the researchers had chosen to report the unattenuated validity coefficients for the data matrix used in problem 7. What would these values have been for the convergent validity coefficients?

9. Given Equation 10.6 for computing the unattenuated validity coefficient, show a brief derivation of the relationship $\rho_{XY} \leq \sqrt{\rho_{XX'}}\sqrt{\rho_{YY'}}$.

10. A graduate student in clinical psychology finds in a test manual for a personality inventory that the reliability estimate of the test scores is .76, but the validity coefficient between this inventory and another inventory, which purportedly measures a similar trait, is .78. He suspects an error because he has often heard that "a test cannot be more valid than it is reliable." Is this necessarily true? Why or why not?

11. Suppose a new test of aptitude for graduate school is being developed. The test developer wants a test that correlates with first semester grade-point average with a minimum validity coefficient of .60. From a pilot study the test developer has obtained a reliability estimate for the initial set of items. Derive a formula for estimating a minimum value of K, the factor by which test length should be increased to permit the desired validity coefficient to be attained. Would lengthening the test by a factor of K insure that the minimum desired validity coefficient would be achieved? Explain the usefulness of such a formula.

Chapter 11

STATISTICAL PROCEDURES FOR PREDICTION AND CLASSIFICATION

In the preceding chapter we introduced the concepts of the test validation study and the simple validity coefficient for demonstrating the strength of the relationship between test scores and a criterion variable. Yet for most problems involving prediction of individual performance in clinical, industrial, or educational settings, the researcher has several predictor variables available. One purpose of this chapter is to describe statistical procedures which are widely used to validate the combined use of two or more variables for predicting performance on a single criterion that is continuously scored. The procedures of partial correlation and multiple regression will be described in this context. A second purpose is to describe a statistical procedure commonly used in classification of examinees when the range of values on the criterion variable is defined by two or more discrete categories. Discriminant function analysis is a technique often used in such situations. Each of the statistical procedures described here is sufficiently complex to warrant an entire book if comprehensive treatment of the topic were attempted. In this chapter the presentation will be restricted to a brief explanation of the procedure, an example of a validation study which requires its use, and presentation of typical results obtained from the analysis along with accompanying interpretation. The intent of this presentation is to provide students of test theory with the basic knowledge necessary to recognize when and how these procedures can be applied in their own test validation efforts and to understand reports of validation studies in current measurement literature which use these methods. Material in this chapter may be omitted without loss of continuity with subsequent topics covered in this text.

PARTIAL CORRELATION

There are test validation situations in which the test user has already identified one or more useful predictors but now wishes to ask, "What is the strength of the relationship between the criterion variable and some additional predictor for a sub-group of examinees who are homogeneous with respect to previously identified predictors?" As an example, let us consider a hypothetical law school admissions problem[1] in which students are admitted on the basis of undergraduate grade-point average, which is used as a predictor of first-year law school grade-point average. Suppose the correlation between this predictor and criterion is $\hat{\rho}_{YX_1} = .46$. A second possible predictor is the applicant's score on the Law School Admissions Test (LSAT), which correlates $\hat{\rho}_{YX_2} = .48$ with first-year law school grade-point average. An admissions director might be interested in knowing the strength of the relationship between LSAT and law school GPA for students who are similar in undergraduate GPA (i.e., homogeneous with respect to X_1). The statistic of interest here is the partial correlation coefficient, which is denoted as $\hat{\rho}_{YX_2 \cdot X_1}$; the subscript notation indicates that we are interested in the relationship between X_2 and Y for a subgroup of students who are homogeneous with respect to X_1. The formula for computing this partial correlation coefficient is

$$\frac{\hat{\rho}_{YX_2} - \hat{\rho}_{YX_1}\hat{\rho}_{X_1X_2}}{\sqrt{1 - \hat{\rho}_{YX_1}^2}\sqrt{1 - \hat{\rho}_{X_1X_2}^2}} \tag{11.1}$$

As this formula shows, the magnitude of the partial correlation depends not only on the correlation of X_2 with Y but also on the correlation of X_1 with Y and the correlation between the two predictors X_1 and X_2. For example, in the law school problem, if the correlation between undergraduate GPA and LSAT score were $\hat{\rho}_{X_1X_2} = .33$, the partial correlation estimate would be

$$\hat{\rho}_{YX_2 \cdot X_1} = \frac{.48 - (.46)(.33)}{\sqrt{1 - .46^2}\sqrt{1 - .33^2}} = .39$$

If, on the other hand, the correlation between the first and second predictors had been greater (e.g., $\hat{\rho}_{X_1X_2} = .60$), the partial correlation for Y and X_2 controlling for X_1 would be

$$\hat{\rho}_{YX_2 \cdot X_1} = \frac{.48 - (.46)(.60)}{\sqrt{1 - .46^2}\sqrt{1 - .60^2}} = .29$$

The latter partial correlation coefficient is lower than the former because in the latter case, there is a higher positive correlation between the two predictors. Finally, it should be noted that the partial correlation can even exceed the original correlation. If, for example, the correlation between X_1 and X_2 had been $\hat{\rho}_{X_1X_2} = -.25$, the value $\hat{\rho}_{YX_2 \cdot X_1}$ would be

$$\hat{\rho}_{YX_2 \cdot X_1} = \frac{.48 - (.46)(-.25)}{\sqrt{1 - .46^2}\sqrt{1 - .25^2}} = .69$$

[1]Values of validity coefficients for the LSAT used in this problem were reported by Powers (1982).

In each of these cases, the positive value of the partial correlation between LSAT score and law school GPA could be interpreted in a general sense to mean that for examinees who are similar in undergraduate GPA, preference should be given to those with higher LSAT scores. Furthermore the first two examples illustrate that when each of the two predictors is positively correlated with the criterion, typically the usefulness of the second predictor decreases as the correlation between the two predictors approaches 1.00.

Partial correlations can be extended to partial out any number of variables, provided, of course, that a sufficient number of examinees are available. (A common rule of thumb for sample sizes in correlational studies is to use the larger of the following: 100 subjects or 10 times as many subjects as there are variables in the study.) Although it is possible to calculate such partial correlations by hand, the description of this calculation is complicated and will be omitted here. Formulas for these calculations can be found in Pedhazur (1982). Typically these calculations are performed with the aid of a computer. It is important to note that as additional variables are partialled out, the correlation can change in sign or magnitude.

It is also important to recognize the effect of measurement error on partial correlations. The absolute value of a zero-order correlation (a correlation without any partialling) between variables perturbed by measurement error is less than the absolute value of the correlation that would have been obtained with perfectly reliable data. The partial correlation for variables perturbed by measurement error may be larger than, smaller than, or a different sign than the correlation that would have been obtained with perfectly reliable data. For a criterion and two predictor variables, the formula for correcting a partial correlation for attenuation can be written as

$$\hat{\rho}^*_{YX_2 \cdot X_1} = \frac{\hat{\rho}_{11}\hat{\rho}_{YX_2} - \hat{\rho}_{YX_1}\hat{\rho}_{X_1X_2}}{\sqrt{\hat{\rho}_{11}\hat{\rho}_{YY} - \hat{\rho}^2_{YX_1}}\sqrt{\hat{\rho}_{11}\hat{\rho}_{22} - \hat{\rho}^2_{X_1Y_2}}} \qquad (11.2)$$

where $\hat{\rho}_{11}$, $\hat{\rho}_{22}$, and $\hat{\rho}_{YY}$ denote reliability estimates. Suppose that the reliability estimates of undergraduate grade point, LSAT score, and law school GPA are .64, .87, and .67, respectively. The estimated true partial correlation between LSAT score and first-year GPA in law school (after partialling on undergraduate GPA) is

$$\hat{\rho}^*_{YX_2 \cdot X_1} = \frac{(.64)(.48) - (.46)(.33)}{\sqrt{(.64)(.67) - .46^2}\sqrt{(.64)(.87) - .33^2}} = .51$$

It is important to remember that although the estimated true partial correlation may be of interest for theoretical purposes (i.e., in construct validation), in practical situations the test user must work with predictor and criterion measurements which are less than perfectly reliable.

The preceding example concerns the use of partial correlation in the context of validating predictions. Provided that the partial correlation between first-year law school GPA and LSAT scores is significant, we can say that the LSAT has predictive validity when added to undergraduate GPA as a predictor of first-year law school GPA. Partial correlations can also be used in the context of construct validation. For example, consider the self-concept construct. Some self-concept theorists distinguish between general academic self-concept and self-concept with regard to specific academic subjects. Following this distinction, there are tests available to measure each construct. The theory suggests that achievement in a specific academic area should be positively related to both general academic self-concept and self-concept with regard to that specific academic area. Further the theory suggests that self-concept in a particular academic field should be positively related to achievement in that field even for groups that are homogeneous on general academic self-concept. The reader may recall that investigating construct validity involves determining whether test scores conform to theoretical predictions. If the test scores meet theoretical expectations, it is positive evidence for the construct validity of the tests involved.

Shavelson and Bolus (1982) collected data on achievement in science (Y), academic self-concept in science (X_1) and general academic self-concept (X_2), among other variables. The correlations among the three pairs of variables were reported as $\hat{\rho}_{YX_1} = .49$, $\hat{\rho}_{YX_2} = .41$, and $\hat{\rho}_{X_1X_2} = .73$. The correlation between science achievement and science self-concept partialling out general academic self-concept is

$$\hat{\rho}_{YX_1 \cdot X_2} = \frac{\hat{\rho}_{YX_1} - \hat{\rho}_{YX_2}\hat{\rho}_{X_1X_2}}{\sqrt{1 - \hat{\rho}_{YX_2}^2}\sqrt{1 - \hat{\rho}_{X_1X_2}^2}} = \frac{.49 - (.41)(.73)}{\sqrt{1 - .42^2}\sqrt{1 - .73^2}} = .31$$

This correlation supports the claim of construct validity for the self-concept measures since it agrees with the theoretical predictions. It should be noted that the correlations reported by Shavelson and Bolus have already been adjusted to remove the effects of measurement error. As a consequence there is no need to correct for attenuation.

MULTIPLE REGRESSION

In Chapter 2, linear regression was presented as a useful method for developing a prediction equation when scores on one predictor and one criterion are available for the same group of examinees. When two or more predictors are available, multiple regression is useful for developing a single equation to predict criterion performance from the set of predictors. Recall that the general form of the prediction equation for a single predictor variable is

$$Y' = c + b_{Y \cdot X}X \tag{11.3}$$

where X is the examinee's score on the predictor, Y' is the examinee's predicted score on the criterion, $b_{Y \cdot X} = \hat{\rho}_{YX}(\hat{\sigma}_Y/\hat{\sigma}_X)$ and $c = \hat{\mu}_Y - b_{Y \cdot X}\hat{\mu}_X$. Recall also that once a sample of scores has been used to calculate c and $b_{Y \cdot X}$, the regression equation can be used to obtain a predicted value of Y for any examinee whose score is available, provided that the examinee and the sample used to calculate the regression equation are drawn from the same population. If the absolute value of the correlation between Y and X is sufficiently high, these predicted values of Y will be fairly accurate. (A return to Equation 2.21 and the accompanying computational example may be helpful as a review of these concepts.)

An Example with Two Predictors

Although there are situations in which the test user has only one predictor, it is probably more common to find that two or more predictors are used in attempts to predict or describe examinees' performance. Indeed it is typically imprudent to use a single variable as the sole factor in decision making. To illustrate, consider a situation in which the goal is to identify a set of predictors useful for identifying children who may be lagging in cognitive development by age three; it is desirable for the predictors to be based on information available at birth. Two possible predictors in this situation are weight at birth and a scale score based on intrapartum factors determined from the case history of the pregnancy and delivery. Before these predictors are actually used, it is necessary to develop a predictive equation for combining the scores on birth weight and intrapartum factors. It is also necessary to determine how accurately the two variables predict the criterion.

The equation for predicting criterion performance from two predictors is

$$Y' = c + b_{YX_1 \cdot X_2} X_1 + b_{YX_2 \cdot X_1} X_2 \tag{11.4}$$

In our example, Y' is the predicted value of the Stanford Binet score, X_1 is birth weight, and X_2 is the score on the intrapartum variable. The terms $b_{YX_1 \cdot X_2}$ and $b_{YX_2 \cdot X_1}$ are called *regression coefficients,* and c is called the *intercept.* The numeric values for the regression coefficients and intercept are obtained by solving expressions which involve the means, standard deviations for the variables, and correlations among the pairs of variables. These statistics for the cognitive development example are presented in Table 11.1.[2]

The formulas for the regression coefficients and their numeric values for the example are

$$b_{YX_1 \cdot X_2} = \frac{\hat{\sigma}_Y(\hat{\rho}_{YX_1} - \hat{\rho}_{YX_2}\hat{\rho}_{X_1X_2})}{\hat{\sigma}_{X_1}(1 - \hat{\rho}^2_{X_1X_2})} \tag{11.5}$$

$$= \frac{19.251[.301 - (-.149)(-.111)]}{887.641[1 - (-.111)^2]},$$

$$= .006$$

and

$$b_{YX_2 \cdot X_1} = \frac{\hat{\sigma}_Y(\hat{\rho}_{YX_2} - \hat{\rho}_{YX_1}\hat{\rho}_{X_1X_2})}{\hat{\sigma}_{X_2}(1 - \hat{\rho}^2_{X_1X_2})} \tag{11.6}$$

$$= \frac{19.251[-.149 - (.301)(-.111)]}{9.121[1 - (-.111)^2]}$$

$$= -.247$$

---

[2]We thank June Holstrum for permission to use the data presented in this example and note that these data were collected as part of a study with a broader purpose than has been described here.

TABLE 11.1.   Means, Standard Deviation, and Correlations for Stanford Binet, Birth Weight, and Intrapartum Factors

	Y	X_1	X_2
Y Stanford Binet	1.000		
X_1 Birth weight[a]	.301	1.000	
X_2 Intrapartum factors	−.149	−.111	1.000
Mean	95.326	2724.900	6.445
Standard deviations	19.251	887.641	9.121

[a]Birth weight is measured in grams.

The formula and numeric value for the intercept value is

$$c = \hat{\mu}_Y - b_{YX_1 \cdot X_2}\hat{\mu}_{X_1} - b_{YX_2 \cdot X_1}\hat{\mu}_{X_2} \tag{11.7}$$
$$= 95.326 - (.006)(2724.9) - (-.247)(6.445)$$
$$= 80.568$$

Using the values of the intercept and the two regression coefficients just computed, we substitute into the general prediction equation (Equation 11.4) and obtain a specific prediction equation for this study:

$$Y' = 80.568 + .006X_1 - .247X_2$$

Thus for a child with a birth weight of 2,000 grams and an intrapartum factor of 20, the predicted I.Q. score on the Stanford Binet would be

$$Y' = 80.568 + .006(2000) - .247(20) = 87.6$$

Just as in simple linear regression, the values of the intercept (c) and the regression coefficients (b's) obtained by these procedures will minimize the discrepancies between examinees' actual Y scores on the criterion and their predicted scores (Y').

Recall that in simple linear regression the regression coefficient and the correlation coefficient have a simple relationship:

$$b_{YX} = \frac{\hat{\sigma}_Y}{\hat{\sigma}_X} \hat{\rho}_{YX} \tag{11.8}$$

In a similar fashion, regression coefficients and partial correlations have a simple relationship. The relationship between $b_{YX_2 \cdot X_1}$ and $\hat{\rho}_{YX_2 \cdot X_1}$ is

$$b_{YX_2 \cdot X_1} = \frac{\hat{\sigma}_{Y \cdot X_1}}{\hat{\sigma}_{X_2 \cdot X_1}} \hat{\rho}_{YX_2 \cdot X_1} \tag{11.9a}$$

In this expression $\hat{\sigma}_{Y \cdot X_1}$ is the standard error of estimate for predicting Y from X_1, and $\hat{\sigma}_{X_2 \cdot X_1}$ is the standard error of estimate for predicting X_2 from X_1. Although the partial correlation and regression coefficient have a simple relationship, they express different characteristics of the data. The partial correlation coefficient $\hat{\rho}_{YX_2 \cdot X_1}$ expresses the strength of the linear relationship between Y and X_2 for a group of examinees who are homogeneous on X_1. The regression coefficient $b_{YX_2 \cdot X_1}$ expresses the amount Y' changes when X_2 changes 1 point and X_1 remains constant. Thus it expresses the sensitivity of Y' to changes in X_2. The relationship between $b_{YX_1 \cdot X_2}$ and $\hat{\rho}_{YX_1 \cdot X_2}$ is

$$b_{YX_1 \cdot X_2} = \frac{\hat{\sigma}_{Y \cdot X_2}}{\hat{\sigma}_{X_1 \cdot X_2}} \hat{\rho}_{YX_1 \cdot X_2} \qquad (11.9b)$$

Relations similar to Equations 11.9a and 11.9b hold when there are more than two predictors.

These regression coefficients were calculated from raw scores for I.Q., birth weight, and intrapartum factors. Although raw scores are commonly used in regression analysis, occasionally researchers use z-scores in place of the raw scores. When z-scores are used in place of raw scores the regression equation is written as

$$z_Y' = \beta_{YX_1 \cdot X_2} z_{X_1} + \beta_{YX_2 \cdot X_1} z_{X_2} \qquad (11.10)$$

In this expression the β's indicate that the regression coefficients are calculated from standardized scores. Indeed regression coefficients calculated from standardized scores are frequently called *standardized regression coefficients*. Notice that Equation 11.10 does not include a symbol for the intercept because the intercept is always zero when z-scores are used in the regression analysis. The standardized regression coefficients have a simple relationship to the unstandardized coefficients:

$$\beta_{YX_i \cdot X_j} = \frac{\hat{\sigma}_{X_i}}{\hat{\sigma}_Y} b_{YX_i \cdot X_j} \qquad (11.11)$$

The expression says to multiply the unstandardized coefficient for a particular predictor by the ratio of the standard deviation for that predictor to standard deviation for the criterion. To illustrate, we will calculate the standardized regression coefficient for birth weight:

$$\beta_{YX_1 \cdot X_2} = \frac{\hat{\sigma}_{X_1}}{\hat{\sigma}_Y} b_{YX_1 \cdot X_2}$$

$$= \frac{887.641}{19.251} .006$$

$$= .276$$

The relationship in Equation 11.11 holds when there are more than two predictors.

The reader may wonder if standardized coefficients have any advantage over unstandardized coefficients. The advantage claimed by some is that the numeric values of two standardized coefficients can be directly compared, whereas the values of unstandardized coefficients cannot. Therefore standardized coefficients can be used to choose the more useful predictor. Why is this claim made? The reason has to do with comparability of units of measurement. The regression coefficient for X_j is the amount that the predicted value of Y changes when X_j changes 1 unit and all other X's remain constant. Thus since the unstandardized regression coefficient for birth weight is .006, two babies that are 1 gram apart in weight and have the same intrapartum factors score will differ by .006 points in their predicted I.Q. scores. Because of this interpretation of regression coefficients, any comparison of the numeric value of two coefficients involves the units of measurement of the predictors the coefficients apply to. To compare the unstandardized coefficient for birth weight (.006) to the unstandardized coefficient for intrapartum factors (.247), we must assume that one unit of measurement on the birth weight scale is equivalent to one unit on the intrapartum factors scale. Clearly this assumption is untenable. To get around this problem some researchers calculate and compare standardized regression coefficients. The assumption here is that z-scores have the same unit of measurement for all variables. For example, in predicting I.Q. from birth weight and intrapartum factors, comparison of standardized regression coefficients involves the assumption that z-scores for birth weight and intrapartum factors have the same unit of measurement. Since one unit on the z-score scale is equivalent to 1 standard deviation on the raw score scale, this assumption implies that 1 standard deviation (887.64 grams) on the birth weight scale is equivalent to 1 standard deviation (9.12 points) on the intrapartum scale. This kind of assumption needs to be weighed carefully before comparing standardized weights. In the current example this assumption seems tenuous at best. However in situations in which the predictors are measures of educational or psychological constructs, the assumption may be more tenable.

Evaluating Predictive Accuracy

Of primary importance in a validation study is the evaluation of the accuracy of the results of the prediction equation. Several statistics may be used to describe the accuracy of prediction, and conscientious reporting of validation results will usually include indices of each of the two following types:

1. A correlational measure of the accuracy of prediction
2. A measure of the probable error of prediction in estimating an individual's criterion performance score

Several statistics in each of these categories will be described in the following sections.

A CORRELATIONAL MEASURE OF PREDICTIVE ACCURACY. To develop the correlational measure of predictive accuracy it is important to distinguish between the sample prediction equation (Equation 11.4):

$$Y' = c + b_{YX_1 \cdot X_2}X_1 + b_{YX_2 \cdot X_1}X_2$$

and the population prediction equation:

$$\ddot{Y} = C + B_{YX_1 \cdot X_2}X_1 + B_{YX_2 \cdot X_1}X_2 \tag{11.12}$$

The latter equation is the one we would obtain if we had scores on the entire population of examinees. Each examinee in the population has three different values that are of interest: Y, the actual criterion score; Y', the predicted criterion score using the sample regression equation, and $\ddot{Y}$, the predicted criterion score using the population regression equation. To develop our measure of predictive accuracy, consider the following hypothetical situation. Suppose it is possible to use the sample prediction equation to calculate Y' for every member of the population. Having calculated Y', we then calculate the squared population correlation between Y' and Y. This squared correlation expresses the accuracy of Y' as a predictor of Y and is called the *squared cross-validated correlation coefficient*. It is denoted by ρ_{cv}^2 and is the correlational measure of predictive accuracy. The term cross-validated correlation implies that the accuracy of the sample prediction equation has been investigated for a group other than that on which it was derived. That is, ρ_{cv}^2 tells us about how useful the sample prediction equation will be when applied to other examinees in the population. Although ρ_{cv}^2 is of primary importance in a validation study, it is important to understand that the size of this coefficient is directly related to the sizes of two additional coefficients. One is the squared multiple-correlation coefficient (ρ^2), which is defined as the squared correlation between Y and $\dot{Y}$. The coefficient ρ^2 measures the strength of association between the criterion and the set of predictors. The second squared coefficient is $\rho_{\hat{Y}Y'}^2$, the squared correlation coefficient between the values Y' and $\dot{Y}$. Rozeboom (1981) has shown that $\rho_{cv}^2 = \rho^2 \rho_{\hat{Y}Y'}^2$, and thus the size of ρ_{cv}^2, depends on two factors. First, it depends on ρ^2, which measures how accurately Y can be predicted if we have the population equation; ρ^2 also measures how strongly the predictors are related to the criterion. Second, ρ_{cv}^2 depends on $\rho_{Y'\dot{Y}}^2$, a measure of similarity of the population and sample prediction equations. The correlation $\rho_{Y'\dot{Y}}^2$ depends primarily on the ratio of the sample size (N) to the number of predictors. If this ratio is small, $\rho_{Y'\dot{Y}}^2$ will also be small. Thus poor predictive accuracy, as measured by ρ_{cv}^2, can result from either a weak relationship between the criterion and the predictors or an insufficient amount of data for estimating the prediction equation.

To report the results of a validation study with multiple predictors, it is desirable to estimate ρ^2 and ρ_{cv}^2. With two predictors, ρ^2 can be estimated by

$$R^2 = \frac{\hat{\sigma}_{X_1} b_{YX_1 \cdot X_2} \hat{\rho}_{YX_1} + \hat{\sigma}_{X_2} b_{YX_2 \cdot X_1} \hat{\rho}_{YX_2}}{\hat{\sigma}_Y} \qquad (11.13)$$

which in our example yields

$$R^2 = \frac{887.641(.006)(.301) + 9.121(-.247)(-.111)}{19.251} = .10$$

Since this estimate of ρ^2 is quite low and since ρ_{cv}^2 must be less than ρ^2, it is not really necessary to estimate ρ_{cv}^2 in this example. We know that it will be small, and the reason is that birth weight and intrapartum factors are not strongly related to Stanford Binet scores at three years. Therefore, no matter how many examinees are in our sample, the prediction equation cannot provide very accurate predictions. Nevertheless, we shall use our example to illustrate estimate of ρ_{cv}^2.

A procedure for estimation of ρ_{cv}^2 was developed by Browne (1975) and requires calculation of two quantities (R_c^2 and R_c^4) as components of R_{cv}^2. First,

$$R_c^2 = R^2 - \frac{k(1 - R^2)}{N - k - 1} \qquad (11.14)$$

where k represents the number of predictors and equals 2 in our example. The coefficient R_c^2 is an estimate of ρ^2, which is more nearly unbiased than R^2. It is often referred to as the *adjusted* R^2. In addition, we must also calculate the value of

$$R_c^4 = (R_c^2)^2 - \frac{2k(1 - R_c^2)^2}{(N - 1)(N - k + 1)}. \tag{11.15}$$

The symbol R_c^4 was used by Browne and does *not* indicate the square of R_c^2. The squared cross-validated correlation coefficient is then estimated by

$$R_{cv}^2 = \frac{(N - k - 3)R_c^4 + R_c^2}{(N - 2k - 2)R_c^2 + k} \tag{11.16}$$

For our example, calculations of these quantities yields

$$R_c^2 = .1 - \frac{2(1 - .1)}{101 - 2 - 1} = .081$$

$$R_c^4 = .081^2 - \frac{2(2)(1 - .081)^2}{(101 - 1)(101 - 2 + 1)} = .006$$

and

$$R_{cv}^2 = \frac{(101 - 2 - 3)(.006) + .081}{(101 - (2)(2) - 2)(.081) + 2} = .067$$

As the calculations show, R_{cv}^2 is fairly small and is similar in value to R^2. Again this indicates that the lack of predictive accuracy arises because birth weight and psychomotor test score are not strong predictors of the Stanford Binet score, and not because of insufficient data to estimate the prediction equation. The reader should note that R_c^2 can be negative. If it is, zero should be substituted for R_c^2 in Equations 11.15 and 11.16. Similarly R_c^4 can be negative, and, if so, zero is substituted for it in Equation 11.16.

In contrast to the findings of the preceding example, consider another illustration of the use of R^2, R_c^2, and R_{cv}^4 based on results of a study reported by Hartley and Hartley (1976). They collected data for 57 students enrolled in a research methods course in psychology. The data consisted of 22 predictors and a measure of achievement in the course. They reported a squared multiple-correlation estimate of $R^2 = .86$ (which seems to indicate a strong relationship between the criterion and the predictors). However, if we use Equation 11.14 to calculate the corrected R^2 value, we get $R_c^2 = .77$, and so we see that the original R^2 value is somewhat misleading as a measure of the strength of relationship. Occasionally R_c^2 will be reported as an estimate of the squared cross-validated correlation (ρ_{cv}^2), but from the Hartley and Hartley example we can see that this, too, can be misleading. When we apply Equations 11.15 and 11.16 to their data, we find that $R_{cv}^2 = .64$ in this example. Clearly our impression of the predictive accuracy changes dramatically in going from R^2 to R_{cv}^2. Thus this example illustrates the importance of reporting the estimate of the squared cross-validated multiple correlation. Furthermore, since R_{cv}^2 is considerably lower than R_c^2, this suggests that collecting data for additional examinees in this study would have been useful in increasing the predictive accuracy of the sample regression equation.

There are other ways to estimate ρ_{cv}^2. One involves a cross-validation study. A typical approach here is to use half the sample of examinees to estimate the prediction equation. This equation is then applied to the second half of the data to obtain Y' values for these examinees. The simple correlation between Y' and Y values is then computed to obtain an estimate of ρ_{cv}^2. The difficulty with this approach is that half the data must be sacrificed in estimating the prediction equation.

MEASURES OF ERRORS OF PREDICTION.   Somewhat more direct measures of prediction accuracy than R_{cv}^2 can be reported in the form of the standard error of estimate and the standard error of Y'. Although the former is probably less desirable as a measure of prediction accuracy, it will be considered first because of its familiarity to the reader.

The formula for computing the standard error of the estimate for a single predictor was presented in Chapter 2 with a computational example and again in Chapter 9 with the interpretive use generally made in validation studies. The standard error of estimate for multiple predictors is calculated by

$$\hat{\sigma}_{Y \cdot \underline{X}} = \sqrt{\frac{N-1}{N-k} \; \hat{\sigma}_Y^2 (1 - R^2)} \tag{11.17}$$

where the line under the $\underline{X}$ indicates that there is more than one predictor and R^2 is the estimated squared multiple correlation. In the example of the infant data validation study, the standard error of estimate is

$$\hat{\sigma}_{Y \cdot \underline{X}} = \sqrt{\frac{100}{99}} \; (370.601)(1 - .1) = 18.355$$

Although $\sigma_{Y \cdot X}$ is widely used in reporting errors of prediction, it tends to overstate the degree of accuracy of the prediction equation because it does not reflect the fact that for any examinee, Y' (the predicted value from sample data) is only an estimate of $\dot{Y}$, the predicted value from population data.

The error of prediction $E = (Y - Y')$ can be written as

$$E = (Y - \dot{Y}) + (\dot{Y} - Y') \tag{11.18}$$

where the difference $(Y - \dot{Y})$ reflects the discrepancy between actual Y and a prediction of Y from population data, and $(\dot{Y} - Y')$ reflects the discrepancy between the value of Y predicted from population data and the value of Y predicted from sample data. A statistic that includes both these sources of error is the standard error of Y'; for two predictors the squared standard error is calculated by

$$SE_{Y'}^2 = \frac{N-1}{N-2} \; \hat{\sigma}_Y^2 (1 - R^2) \left[1 + \frac{1}{N} + \frac{1}{(N-1)(1 - \hat{\rho}_{X_1 X_2}^2)} \; (z_1^2 + z_2^2 - 2\hat{\rho}_{X_1 X_2} z_1 z_2) \right] \tag{11.19}$$

TABLE 11.2. Standard Errors of Y' for Combinations of z_1 and z_2

z_1	z_2				
	-2^a	-1^a	0	1	2
-2	19.2	18.9	18.8	18.9	19.1
-1	18.9	18.6	18.5	18.6	18.9
0	18.8	18.5	18.4	18.5	18.8
1	18.9	18.6	18.5	18.6	18.9
2	19.1	18.9	18.8	18.9	19.2

$N = 101$; $\hat{\rho}_{X_1 X_2} = -.111$
[a]Values of $z_2 = -1$ or -2 do not actually occur in the data on which this table is based.

Here $\hat{\rho}_{X_1 X_2}$ is the correlation between X_1 and X_2, $z_1 = (X_1 - \hat{\mu}_1)/\hat{\sigma}_{X_1}$, $z_2 = (X_2 - \hat{\mu}_2)/\hat{\sigma}_{X_2}$, and N is the number of examinees in the sample. Table 11.2 shows the value of this statistic for various combinations of scores on birth weight and the infant psychomotor test. Inspection of Table 11.2 shows that prediction will be more accurate for examinees with scores near the means on both predictors and least accurate for examinees with scores far away from the means on both predictors. In this example the standard error of Y' does not vary dramatically as z_1 and z_2 change. This is because $\hat{\rho}_{X_1 X_2}$ is fairly low and the sample size is relatively large. In other cases, this may not be so. Table 11.3 shows the values of the standard error of Y' that would have occurred with $\hat{\rho}_{X_1 X_2} = -.707$ and $N = 30$. Here the effect of z_{X_1} and z_{X_2} is more dramatic.

The standard error of Y' can be used to construct prediction intervals for an examinee. When the sample size is greater than 30, the examiner can construct the interval $Y' \pm S.E._{Y'}$ and be approximately 68 percent sure that the actual Y value will fall into this interval. It is interesting to note that although the standard estimate of Y' was affected substantially by the magnitude of $\hat{\rho}_{X_1 X_2}$ and N, the standard error of estimate, computed by Equation 11.17, is unaffected by these characteristics of the sample and thus can be inaccurate.

TABLE 11.3. Standard Errors of Y' for Combinations of z_1 and z_2

z_1	z_2				
	-2	-1	0	1	2
-2	20.8	19.8	19.2	18.8	18.9
-1	19.8	19.1	18.6	18.5	18.8
0	19.2	18.6	18.4	18.6	19.2
1	18.8	18.5	18.6	19.1	19.8
2	18.9	18.8	19.2	19.8	20.8

$N = 30$; $\hat{\rho}_{X_1 X_2} = -.707$.

Prediction with More than Two Predictors

When there are more than two predictors, the sample prediction equation can be written as

$$Y' = c + b_{YX_1 \cdot X_2 \ldots X_k}X_1 + \ldots + b_{YX_k \cdot X_1 \ldots X_{(k-1)}}X_k \qquad (11.20)$$

where the symbol c represents the intercept and the b's represent the regression coefficients for the k variables. The two letters to the left of the dot in the subscript of the regression coefficient identify the criterion and the predictor to which the coefficient applies. The list of letters to the right of the dot indicate the other predictors in the equation. As a concrete example of a prediction equation with more than two variables, suppose that in addition to birth weight (X_1) and scores on the intrapartum factor (X_2) in the previous example, we also had data on the mother's age at her child's birth (X_3) and the mother's socioeconomic status (X_4). Then our sample regression equation would be

$$Y' = c + b_{YX_1 \cdot X_2X_3X_4}X_1 + b_{YX_2 \cdot X_1X_3X_4}X_2 + b_{YX_3 \cdot X_1X_2X_4}X_3 + b_{YX_4 \cdot X_1X_2X_3}X_4$$

With more than two predictors, estimation of the regression coefficients is fairly complicated by hand and is usually carried out through a computer program. The same is true for R^2, $S.E._{Y'}$ and $\hat{\rho}_{Y \cdot X}$.

Selecting a Predictor Subset

When two or more predictors are available, it is important to consider whether a subset of the predictors will give predictive accuracy close to that of the full set. Indeed it is possible that a subset can yield predictive accuracy greater than that yielded by the full set (Hocking, 1976). The reason for attempting to find such a subset is to avoid collecting the data on predictors that may contribute little or nothing to predictive accuracy. For example, although two tests may correlate highly with criterion performance, if they are highly correlated with each other it is unnecessary to go to the time and expense required to administer both.

Suppose in the preceding example the researcher were interested in selecting a predictor subset that would be efficient to measure and would have reasonable predictive accuracy. There are a number of possible techniques for predictor selection, but only one method, known as *all possible subsets regression,* will be presented here. The reader interested in more detailed discussion of this and other variable selection methods can consult Hocking (1976), who has given an extensive review of methods and issues in variable selection. As the name implies, all possible subsets regression involves calculating a measure of predictive accuracy for every possible combination of predictors. These results are then used to guide the choice of an adequate set of predictors. Table 11.4 presents the results of an all possible subsets regression analysis of the variables birth weight (BW), intrapartum factor (IF), mother's age (MAGE), and mother's SES as predictors of Stanford Binet scores. The table reports R^2 for every possible combination of one predictor,

TABLE 11.4.   Results of an All Possible Subsets Regression Analysis

Number in Equation	R^2	R_c^2	Variables in Equation
1	.03		IF
1	.08		MAGE
1	.09		BW
1	.24	.23	SES
2	.09		BW, IF
2	.11		MAGE, IF
2	.15		BW, MAGE
2	.25		MAGE, SES
2	.27		IF, SES
2	.32	.32	BW, SES
3	.15		BW, MAGE
3	.27		MAGE, IF, SES
3	.32		BW, IF, SES
3	.32	.30	BW, MAGE, SES
4	.33	.30	BW, MAGE, IF, SES

two predictors, three predictors, and four predictors. These results indicate that R^2 for the four-variable model and the best three-variable models are only slightly larger than R^2 for several two-variable models. Thus a model with two of the four possible predictors seems appropriate. Since there are only small differences between the R^2 statistics for the three best two-variable models, and since SES is involved in each, this suggests that combining any of the three remaining variables with SES would provide an appropriate choice among the four available predictors. The coefficients R_c^2 are also reported in Table 11.4 to demonstrate that as the number of variables (k) increases, R_c^2 eventually reaches a maximum and then declines. The coefficient R_{cv}^2 will also be maximized at this value of k. Consequently, a plausible rule for selecting variables is to choose the number of predictors that results in the maximum R_c^2. This rule again points to choosing two predictors.

DISCRIMINANT ANALYSIS

With Two Groups

A situation that is sometimes encountered in validation research involves developing a procedure for using test data to categorize examinees into two or more groups. For example, suppose that at a particular hospital, patients have been classified into two categories, schizophrenic and depressive, based on extensive psychiatric interviews. Since the interview process takes up a large amount of the staff psychiatrists' time, it may be of interest to investigate the validity of a battery of tests for making the classifications. The battery of tests includes subtests measuring thinking disturbance, withdrawal retardation, hostile suspiciousness, and anxious depression. Kleinbaum and Kupper (1978) presented fictitious data for the situation described.

TABLE 11.5.   Illustrative Data for Discriminant Analysis

Psychiatric Group	Variable				
	Thinking Disturbance X_1	Withdrawal Retardation X_2	Hostile Suspiciousness X_3	Anxious Depression X_4	Discriminant Function Y
Depressive	5.0	6.4	6.6	10.2	−3.41
	2.9	5.3	2.5	9.2	−2.62
	2.7	5.0	2.5	10.3	−3.01
	2.5	4.7	3.5	8.6	−3.01
	1.9	4.3	4.5	11.1	−.84
Schizophrenic	7.8	6.9	3.8	6.0	−12.70
	7.6	5.6	4.2	7.3	−14.34
	7.4	5.1	5.4	4.9	−20.12
	7.2	6.0	6.0	3.6	−8.42
	3.5	5.6	3.0	11.8	−.33

From D. G. Kleinbaum and L. L. Kupper, (1978). Applied regression analysis and other multivariate methods (North Scituate, Mass.: Duxbury Press).

In Table 11.5 the psychiatric groups are the groups into which patients have been classified by the psychiatrist. The scores on X_1 to X_4 are the observed data on the four variables. The scores on Y have been calculated from the scores on X_1 to X_4. The procedure for carrying out this calculation follows.

Discriminant analysis begins with the scores of a sample of examinees for whom the correct classifications are known. These scores are used to calculate weights for combining the variables into a new variable that will eventually be used to classify examinees for whom the correct classifications are unknown. In the current example this means that the scores on X_1 to X_4 will be used to determine the *discriminant weights* a, b, c, and d for the weighted linear combination

$$Y = aX_1 + bX_2 + cX_3 + dX_4 \qquad (11.21)$$

The linear combination is known as the *discriminant function*. Once a, b, c, and d are determined, they can be used to calculate Y for patients who have not been interviewed by the psychiatrist. The reader should note the similarity between the intended use of discriminant analysis and our earlier use of multiple regression analysis. In the latter the goal was to use a sample to determine an equation that can be used to predict criterion scores for future examinees. In the former the goal is to develop an equation that can be used to classify future examinees.

Since Y is to be used to classify examinees, it makes sense that the two groups should be as different as possible on Y. A natural measure of the difference between the two groups is

$$w = \frac{\hat{\mu}_{Y_d} - \hat{\mu}_{Y_s}}{\hat{\sigma}_Y} \qquad (11.22)$$

The quantity w is the standardized mean difference between the two groups (depressive and schizophrenics). The criterion for choosing the weights is to choose a, b, c,

TABLE 11.6.   Psychiatric and Discriminant Function Classifications

		Discriminant Function Classification	
		Depressive	Schizophrenic
Psychiatric	Depressive	5	0
Interview			
Classification	Schizophrenic	1	4

and d so that w^2 is as large as possible. The mathematical procedure for choosing the weights is beyond the scope of this book but is clearly presented in Kleinbaum and Kupper (1978).

In our example the weights are $a = -3.22$, $b = 1.61$, $c = 1.15$, and $d = -.51$. Therefore, for the first depressive patient

$$Y = (-3.22)(5.0) + 1.61 (6.4) + 1.15 (6.6) + (-.51)(10.22) = -3.41$$

The scores on the discriminant function for the other patients are listed in Table 11.5. Clearly, depressive patients tend to have higher scores than the schizophrenic patients. The depressive patients' mean discriminant function score is -2.0, and the schizophrenic patients' mean is -11.2. This suggests that a reasonable rule for classifying patients involves calculating the average of the two means and classifying any patient with a discriminant function score above the average as a depressive patient. The average of the two means is

$$[-11.2 + (-2.0)]/2 = -6.6$$

Thus, any patient with a score greater than -6.6 is classified as a depressive patient; all others are classified as schizophrenic.[3]

Once the rule is developed it is important to evaluate its accuracy. A simple way to accomplish this is to use the rule to classify the patients on which the rule was developed. Since patients with scores above -6.6 are classified as depressives and others are classified as schizophrenics, the procedure results in all but the last schizophrenic patient being correctly classified. This result can be represented in a table such as Table 11.6. Based on this table, the estimated misclassification probability for depressives is .00, and that for schizophrenics is .20.

A problem with evaluating the classification rule with the data on which it is based is that the accuracy will be probably overstated. Two procedures exist for overcoming this problem. One is to apply the rule to a group of patients not used in developing the rule. One approach for doing so is to develop the rule on half the available data and evaluate it on the other half. This procedure is similar to the cross-validation procedure described for evaluating the predictive accuracy of multiple regression equations and shares the problem that half the data are ignored. The

---

[3]Use of the average mean assumes that in the population to which the rule is to be applied, depressives and schizophrenics are equally numerous. Kleinbaum and Kupper (1978) describe appropriate rules when this assumption is incorrect.

second is similar in spirit to Browne's procedure for estimating the cross-validated correlation. Kleinbaum and Kupper (1978) and Morrison (1976) describe such procedures.

In the preceding example the goal was to develop a classification procedure. With this goal, there would be little interest in making a substantive interpretation of the discriminant weights. However suppose the battery were developed to evaluate the effectiveness of psychiatric treatments, and the theory underlying the test development suggests that the battery should distinguish between depressives and schizophrenics. Further the theory suggests that these two groups will be most sharply differentiated on thinking disturbance and anxious depression, with schizophrenics exhibiting more thinking disturbance and less anxious depression than depressives. In this situation there may be some interest in interpreting Y, since Y is the variable that maximally discriminates between the two groups. The interpretation of Y is related to the construct validation of the battery.

When the goal of the analysis is the interpretation of differences between groups, several statistics may be useful. Bray and Maxwell (1982) have given a comprehensive review of these statistics. Here, only statistics that are thought to be most useful in clarifying the substantive meaning of the discriminant function will be addressed. Perhaps the most common method for using the discriminant function to interpret group differences is to inspect the size of the discriminant weights. The reasoning behind this approach may be seen by reconsidering the discriminant function for the current example. The equation for the discriminant function is

$$Y = aX_1 + bX_2 + cX_3 + dX_4 \tag{11.23}$$

Clearly, the variable with the largest discriminant weight has the most influence on Y in the sense that a change of a particular magnitude on this variable will result in the largest change in Y. To illustrate, recall that substituting for a, b, c, and d gives

$$Y = (-3.22)X_1 + 1.61X_2 + 1.15X_3 + (-.51)X_4$$

Therefore, a change of one point, for example, on X_1 results in a larger change in Y than a change of one point on X_2, X_3, or X_4. Therefore, X_1 is interpreted as having the greatest influence on Y, and X_4 has the least influence. The conclusion would be the same regardless of the magnitude considered for the change in the X's.

The problem with this approach is that it assumes that a one-point change on any one X is, in some sense, equivalent to a one-point change on any other X. In other words, it assumes that the units of measurement are the same for all variables, an assumption that is patently false in most applications. To try to get around this problem, many investigators calculate the weights that would result if each X were standardized. These weights are known as the *standardized discriminant weights* and are considered by many to be comparable from variable to variable.

In our example the standardized weights are -4.89, 1.17, 2.56, and -1.18. On the basis of these weights, thinking disturbance still contributes most to the discriminant function. However, the magnitude of its contribution, relative to withdrawal retardation and hostile suspiciousness, is judged to be larger, based on the standardized weights rather than on the original weights. On the other hand, the magnitude of its contribution, relative to anxious depression, is judged to be smaller.

As an alternative to the standardized weights, the correlations between the variables and the discriminant function can be inspected as a basis for interpreting the discriminant function. Using X_1 to illustrate the calculation of these correlations, the formula for the correlation between X_1 and Y is

$$\hat{\rho}_{Y1} = a + b\hat{\rho}_{12} + c\hat{\rho}_{13} + d\hat{\rho}_{14} \tag{11.24}$$

where the $\hat{\rho}$'s on the right side represent the correlations calculated by treating all the data as if they were contributed by one group. Thus, to calculate the correlation between the discriminant function and a variable, the correlation between this variable and each of the variables is multiplied by the discriminant weight for the other variable. These products are then summed, and the weight for the variable in question is added to the sum. In our example the correlations between Y and X_1 to X_4, respectively, are $-.89$, $-.34$, $-.35$, and $.78$, respectively. Thus, the discriminant function, on which schizophrenics tend to have low scores, exhibits a substantial negative correlation with thinking disturbance and a substantial positive correlation with anxious depression.

In choosing between inspecting the standardized discriminant weights and variable-discriminant function correlations, it is important to recognize that these two statistics answer different questions (Bray and Maxwell, 1982). The weights summarize the unique influence of a variable on the discriminant function, whereas the correlations express the shared variance between the variable and the discriminant function. Bray and Maxwell argue that the correlations are a better guide to the substantive interpretation of the discriminant function.

With More Than Two Groups

The use of discriminant analysis may be extended to the situation where several groups are involved. When there are just two groups, a single discriminant function accounts for all the differences between them. However, where we are concerned with studying differences among several groups, it is possible that group differences will be present that are not adequately represented in the first discriminant function. Some groups that are actually quite different in terms of the original variables may appear similar on the first discriminant function. In this situation more than one discriminant function will be needed to interpret group differences. In this case, the second discriminant function is the weighted combination of the original variables, which of all possible weighted combinations that are uncorrelated with the first discriminant function, maximizes the differences among the groups. The third discriminant function would be that weighted composite that is uncorrelated with either of the first two and provides for maximum separation between the groups. The maximum number of possible discriminant functions is equal to the number of variables, p, or to one less than the number of groups, $k - 1$, whichever is smaller. The procedure for computing the discriminant function when more than two groups are involved is described in Kleinbaum and Kupper (1978) and Morrison (1976).

Bray and Maxwell (1982) present an example of the use of multiple discriminant analysis to interpret differences among four groups of children classified as (1) severely disabled readers, (2) mildly disabled readers, (3) average readers, or (4) superior readers. For these children, scores on the following criterion variables were obtained: Peabody Picture Vocabulary Test (PPVT), a general verbal measure of I.Q.; Verbal Fluency Test (VF) and Similarities subtest of the Wechsler Pre-school and Primary Scale of Intelligence (SIM), two tests of verbal ability; Beery Visual Motor Integration Test (VMI) and Recognition-Discrimination Test (RD), both general nonverbal measures; and Embedded Figures Test (EF), which measures higher nonverbal abilities.

Discriminant analysis revealed two significant discriminant functions. With the standardized discriminant weights as coefficients, the two discriminant functions were

$$Y = .15(\text{PPVT}) + .10(\text{RD}) + .39(\text{EF}) + .33(\text{VF}) + .29(\text{VMI}) + .44(\text{SIM})$$

$$Y = .95(\text{PPVT}) + (-.51)(\text{RD}) + (-.58)(\text{EF}) + .37(\text{VF}) + .12(\text{VMI}) + (-.02)(\text{SIM})$$

These standardized discriminant weights indicate that the variables EF, VF, and SIM are most important for separation of groups on the first function. On the second function, PPVT has the largest standardized discriminant weight, with RD, EF, and VF contributing highly as well.

The variable discriminant function correlations are reported in Table 11.7. The first discriminant function has positive correlations with each of the variables. The strongest relationships are with EF and SIM. The relationships between the first discriminant function and the remaining variables are about equal in strength. The second discriminant function has positive correlations with PPVT and VF, negative correlations with RD and EF, and essentially no correlation with VMI and SIM. The second discriminant variable appears to contrast verbal and visual discrimination abilities.

TABLE 11.7. Variable-Discriminant Function Correlations for the Bray-Maxwell Example

Variable	Discriminant Function	
	First	Second
PPVT	.46	.52
RD	.52	−.37
EF	.73	−.36
VF	.53	.33
VMI	.50	−.10
SIM	.64	.04

From J. H. Bray and S. E. Maxwell. Analyzing and interpreting significant MANOVAs, *Review of Educational Research*, 52, 340–367. Copyright 1982 by the American Educational Research Association, Washington, D.C. Adapted by permission.

When more than one discriminant function is significant, the group means functions can be plotted geometrically as an aid in interpreting the discriminant functions and the nature of group differences. Figure 11.1 presents a plot of the group means on the discriminant functions for the four reading groups. A dot labeled with the name of a group represents the mean scores for that group on the two discriminant functions. This point on the graph is called a *group centroid*. The dot with the lines emanating from it is the centroid for the entire sample. It is apparent that the first discriminant function separates each of the groups from the others, and the second discriminant function discriminates the superior readers from the other three groups.

It is possible to plot measurements on the original variables in vectors so that an interpretation can be made of how the groups differ on these variables. Such vectors point in the direction of groups having the highest mean levels on the original variables and away from groups having the lowest mean levels. The length of each vector indicates its potency as a discriminator among the groups. (See Overall and Klett, 1972, for the procedure for plotting.) From the position of the vectors in Figure 11.1, it can be seen that PPVT mainly discriminates the superior readers from the other three groups. EF tends to discriminate among all the groups but especially separates the severely disabled from the others.

Just as in the case of one discriminant function, multiple discriminant functions can be used to classify individuals into groups on the basis of scores on the discriminant functions. The first step is to use the sample to estimate the discriminant functions and the mean for each group on each of the discriminant functions. To classify a new examinee, the examinee's discriminant function scores are calculated

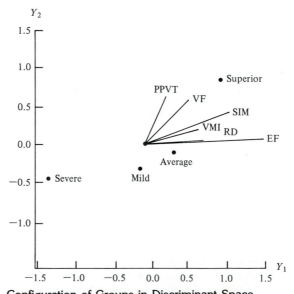

FIGURE 11.1   Configuration of Groups in Discriminant Space

From J. H. Bray and S. E. Maxwell. Analyzing and interpreting significant MANOVAs, *Review of Educational Research*, 52, 340–367. Copyright 1982 by the American Educational Research Association, Washington, D.C. Adapted by permission.

and the distance between these scores and each group's centroid is calculated. The examinee is classified as a member of the group with its centroid closest to the examinee's discriminant function scores.

SUMMARY

In this chapter statistical procedures were described for validation studies involving two or more predictors. The partial correlation coefficient may be of use when the test user is interested in the relationship between a criterion and a second predictor, assuming that examinees are homogeneous with respect to the first predictor variable. The computation of this statistic and its interpretation were illustrated for a case involving two predictors. A formula was also presented for correcting the partial correlation for the effects of measurement errors.

When a validation study is conducted to determine the effectiveness of a weighted combination of two or more predictors, the appropriate statistical procedure is multiple regression analysis. Formulas, and an example with illustrative calculations, were presented for estimating the regression coefficients and the intercept of a prediction equation involving two predictors. In addition, the general formula for a prediction equation involving more than two predictors was given, and it was noted that calculation of the regression coefficients for this case is more laborious and is usually done with a computer. In any such prediction equation, the values of the regression coefficients for the predictor variables and the intercept are chosen so that discrepancies between actual criterion scores and predicted criterion scores will be minimized for the sample used in the validation study. A method for identifying the best subset of predictors was also described and illustrated; the approach used here was called all possible subsets regression.

When the test user is concerned about the accuracy of the prediction from the regression equation, the squared multiple correlation and the squared cross-validated multiple correlation are useful statistics. The former was defined as the correlation between examinees' criterion performances (Y) and predictions of their criterion performances ($\dot{Y}$), using the population prediction equation. The latter is the correlation between examinees' criterion performances (Y) and the predictions of their criterion performances (Y'), using the sample prediction equation. An illustration was presented to demonstrate how these two correlations may differ for the same data when the ratio of sample size to the number of predictors is fairly low. Since predictions of examinees' performance must usually be made on the basis of sample data, it is the squared cross-validated multiple correlation that is of greatest interest in interpreting results of a validation study.

When the test user is concerned about the degree of accuracy in the prediction of scores for individual examinees, two statistics of interest are the standard error of the estimate and the standard error of Y'. The standard error of Y' is often preferred because it takes into account the sample size and the degree of relationship among predictors. The standard error of Y' assumes different values for different values of the predictor variables (being smallest for values near the mean).

Finally, the uses of discriminant analysis were described for situations in which the test user wishes to use the predictor variables to classify examinees into various categories of a selected criterion variable. In conducting such a validation study, the following steps are executed:

1. A discriminant functional equation is determined which is a weighted linear combination of the predictor variables.
2. A cutoff value for the discriminant function is determined to serve as the basis for the classification.
3. The accuracy of the classifications made by using the discriminant function is assessed by means of the probability of misclassification.

Exercises

1. The Minnesota Reading Assessment (MRA) is used to assess the reading skills of students in community colleges, business schools, and secondary and postsecondary vocational educational institutions, whereas the Stanford Test of Academic Skills (TASK) was designed for students in grades 8 through 13. Brown and Chang (1982) administered the MRA and the TASK reading subtest to 50 students enrolled in a vocational-technical institute. They also had access to the grade-point averages for these students. The correlation matrix for these three variables is

	MRA	TASK	GPA
MRA	1.00	.80	.60
TASK		1.00	.67
GPA			1.00

    Calculate and interpret the partial correlation between MRA and GPA controlling for TASK.

2. In the example concerning the Hartley and Hartley (1976) study, the ratio of sample size to predictors was 2.59:1, much smaller than the suggested rule of thumb of 10 to 1. The reported R^2 was .86, and R_{cv}^2 was reported to be .64. This example suggests that a small ratio of sample size to predictors will not have a drastic effect on cross validation. Calculate R_{cv}^2 corresponding to $R^2 = .50$ and $R^2 = .70$ for a situation with 57 examinees and 22 predictors (the number of examinees and predictors in the Hartley-Hartley study). What would you conclude about the kinds of situations in which examinee to predictor ratios on the order of 3 to 1 are tolerable in terms of cross validity?

3. Chissom and Hoenes (1976) reported means, standard, deviations, and correlations for two supposedly culture-free intelligence tests, the D-48 Test and the Culture Fair Intelligence Test (CFIT), and for the Science Research Associates (SRA) Achievement Test for 150 eighth-grade students. The correlation matrix and means and standard deviations follow:

	D-48	CFIT	SRA
D-48	1.00	.69	.61
CFIT		1.00	.66
SRA			1.00
μ	23.12	13.62	182.67
σ	7.88	7.66	58.41

A. Construct the regression equation for predicting SRA From D-48 and CFIT?
B. What is the predicted SRA score for a student with scores of 30 on the D-48 and 20 on the CFIT?
C. Calculate the standard error of estimate.
D. For a student with a D-48 score of 30 and a CFIT score of 20, into what range of scores can we be 68 percent sure that his or her SRA score will fall? (You can use the standard error of estimate in answering this question.)
E. With the available data is the standard error of estimate likely to overstate significantly the accuracy of prediction based on the sample regression equation? Why?

4. An alcoholic treatment facility is interested in developing a procedure for predicting which patients will return to uncontrolled drinking within six months after release from the facility. From six-month postrelease interviews, 10 patients are identified as either abstainers or controlled drinkers and 10 are identified as uncontrolled drinkers. Data are available on five variables measured during the entrance interview. These variables are the Michigan Alcoholism Screening Test (X_1), annual income in thousands of dollars (X_2), Rotter Internal-External Locus of Control Scale Score (X_3), education (X_4) and age at first drink (X_5). The data used in calculating the discriminant function equation are

	Variable				
Group	X_1	X_2	X_3	X_4	X_5
Controlled	17	24	6	16	8
Drinkers	14	21	11	11	12
and	16	23	8	14	17
Abstainers	18	26	4	12	12
	18	25	10	9	16
	17	22	12	17	14
	15	23	6	9	17
	19	25	11	10	15
	17	24	8	16	14
	18	22	5	11	16
Uncontrolled	14	25	5	11	15
Drinkers	17	28	7	13	14
	18	27	7	17	13
	12	24	4	13	11
	17	26	8	16	16
	18	29	6	15	13
	11	22	6	17	12
	14	25	9	16	15
	17	28	5	14	15
	18	26	8	16	14

A discriminant analysis yielded the discriminant function equation

$$Y = -.34X_1 + .40X_2 - .01X_3 + .14X_4 + .09X_5$$

A. Use this equation to develop a procedure for classifying future patients.
B. As a director of an alcoholic treatment facility, how would you use this rule?
C. Evaluate the accuracy of this rule by applying it to the available data.

5. The Devereux Elementary Behavior Rating Scale (DBRS) is a 47-item instrument designed to represent the full range of student behaviors occurring in regular classrooms. The scale can be scored to yield 11 subscale scores. On all subscales, except Comprehension and Creative Initiative, higher scores represent less positive behavior.

Two hundred seventeen sixth-grade students, including mainstreamed and 184 regular students, were rated by their teachers from the DBRS. The mean scores for the mainstreamed students were higher than those of the regular students for all subscales except Comprehension. Differences were minimal on Need for Closeness and Creative Initiative. The data were analyzed by using discriminant analysis. The standardized discriminant weights (SDW) and the subtest-discriminant variable correlations are reported as follows. Write a brief interpretation of the discriminant variable. What does this suggest about teachers' perceptions of the differences between mainstreamed and regular students?

Subtest	SDW	Correlation
Classroom Disturbance	.25	.76
Impatience	−.35	.67
Disrespect-Defiance	.09	.71
External Blame	.24	.77
Achievement Anxiety	.12	.54
External Reliance	−.29	.65
Comprehension	−.78	−.64
Inattentive-Withdrawn	.10	.67
Irrelevant Responsiveness	.48	.85
Creative Initiative	.40	.22
Need for Closeness	−.07	.13

Chapter 12

BIAS IN SELECTION

In the late 1960s the issues involved in using tests to select minority applicants for jobs and educational institutions began to receive increased attention in the psychometric literature. Although the possibility of bias in test scores was an issue of concern to test developers and test users, there was no clearly formulated definition of test bias which could be objectively applied to detect or remove its influence in selection situations. At first, attempts were made to develop a definition of test bias in terms of the regression lines for predicting performance from test scores of students in the minority and majority groups. (For a review of the use of regression lines, see Chapters 2 and 11.) Armed with such objective, statistical definitions of test bias, test developers hoped to construct tests that would remove bias in the selection process. However, emphasis on this line of attack soon decreased in the face of growing recognition that the issue of bias in selection is largely a question of sociopolitical values. Therefore no matter how the regression lines for minority and majority groups compare, a selection procedure or rule can be devised to fit any particular sociopolitical goal. Indeed, several selection procedures were devised that reflected very different value positions about fairness in selection.

Following this development several authors (Cronbach, 1976; Gross and Su, 1975; and Peterson and Novick, 1976) pointed out the relevance of decision theory to the problem of developing fair selection procedures, and there is now substantial agreement that decision theory provides an approach that is rationally and technically sound. As a result, several of the early selection procedures not formulated in the manner prescribed by decision theory are no longer of practical interest. Nonetheless reading and understanding the current measurement literature on bias in selection may require knowledge of some early attempts to define bias and to develop the selection models which preceded those based on decision theory. In addition to tracing the history of these definitions and selection procedures, an introduction to decision theory and its use in selection problems is provided in this chapter. However, before turning to either of these topics we must introduce some basic terms and concepts.

267

BASIC TERMS AND CONCEPTS

To begin, let us focus on the selection of examinees from a single group. Figure 12.1(a) displays a scatterplot based on the test scores (X) and criterion scores (Y) such as we might obtain from a simple validation study. Assume that a point on the Y scale, which divides the examinees into the successful and nonsuccessful groups (as depicted by the scatterplot in Figure 12.1(b), has been chosen. Suppose also that a cut-score on the X scale has been chosen so that if an examinee scores at or above the given point, the examinee will be accepted into the program, and if the score is below the point, the examinee will be rejected (Figure 12.1(c)). Now for any examinee, two outcomes are possible: success or failure on the criterion; likewise there are two possible decisions based on the predictor: accept or reject. The possible combinations of these two outcomes and two decision alternatives result in four events, depicted by the four quadrants of the scatterplot in Figure 12.1(d). The quadrant labeled A contains the true positive events (i.e., selection of an examinee who succeeds); quadrant B contains false positive events (selection of an examinee who fails); quadrant C contains true negative events (rejection of an examinee who

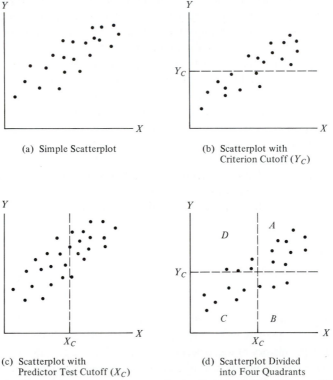

(a) Simple Scatterplot

(b) Scatterplot with
Criterion Cutoff (Y_C)

(c) Scatterplot with
Predictor Test Cutoff (X_C)

(d) Scatterplot Divided
into Four Quadrants

FIGURE 12.1 Illustrative Scatterplots with Points Based on Test Scores (X) and Criterion Scores (Y)

would fail); and quadrant D contains false negative events (rejection of an examinee who could succeed).

Three terms with a long history in the psychometric literature are based on the frequencies, or number of cases, that fall in each of the four quadrants in Figure 12.1(d).

1. The base rate—the proportion of all examinees who could succeed on the criterion, calculated using $(A + D)/(A + B + C + D)$, where the letters denote the frequency of examinees in the corresponding quadrant
2. The selection ratio—the proportion of examinees who will be selected to fill available vacancies, calculated using $(A + B)/(A + B + C + D)$
3. The success ratio—the proportion of selected examinees who succeed, calculated using $A/(A + B)$

Taylor and Russell (1939) developed an extensive set of tables which demonstrated how the validity coefficient and selection ratio interacted to affect the success ratio. The reader should note that if examinees are chosen at random from the applicant pool, the expected value of the success ratio will equal the base rate. Thus a comparison of the success ratio achieved through use of a particular predictor to the base rate indicates the degree to which use of the test improves selection decisions relative to the quality of the decisions made by selecting applicants at random.

Table 12.1 presents success ratios for various combinations of predictive validity (ρ_{XY}) and selection ratio. The success ratios were computed for the case in which 50 percent of the examinees in the applicant pool can succeed on the criterion (i.e., when the base rate is 50 percent). Inspecting the column for $\rho_{XY} = .00$, we see that the success ratio is .50. Thus when $\rho_{XY} = .00$, using the test to select applicants results in a success ratio equal to the base rate. That is, use of a test with $\rho_{XY} = .00$ is no more effective than choosing applicants at random. Inspecting the column for $\rho_{XY} = .2$, we see that when the selection ratio is .10, the success ratio is .64. Notice that with a small selection ratio (.10), using a test with a small validity coefficient $(\rho_{XY} = .2)$ can result in a success ratio substantially above the base rate that results

TABLE 12.1. Success Ratios for Different Combinations of Validity Coefficients and Selection Ratios when Base Success Ratio is .50

Selection Ratio	Validity Coefficient $(\hat{\rho}_{XY})$				
	.00	.20	.40	.60	.80
.10	.50	.64	.78	.90	.99
.30	.50	.59	.69	.79	.90
.50	.50	.56	.63	.70	.80
.70	.50	.54	.58	.62	.67
.90	.50	.52	.53	.54	.55
1.00	.50	.50	.50	.50	.50

From H. C. Taylor and J. T. Russell. The relationship of validity coefficients to the practical effectiveness of tests in selection: Discussion and tables, *Journal of Applied Psychology, 23,* 565–578.

from the strategy of selecting students at random. However if the selection ratio is .70, the success ratio is .54. Thus if we are forced to select a substantial proportion of the applicants, the success ratio may not be much greater than the base rate. This phenomenon occurs not only for tests with small validity coefficients but also for tests with substantial validity coefficients. For example, if $\rho_{xy} = .80$ and the selection rate is .90, the success ratio is only .55. In the extreme case, if we are forced to use a selection ratio of 100% (taking all applicants), the success ratio drops back to 50%; thus there is no advantage to using the test with high validity in this situation. We can summarize the relationship between these concepts as follows: *Assuming that the base rate remains constant for an examinee pool,*

1. The success ratio is high when the validity coefficient is high and the selection ratio is low.
2. If the selection ratio is increased and the validity coefficient does not change, the success ratio is reduced.
3. If the selection ratio is held constant and the validity coefficient is increased, the success ratio is increased.

It is important to note that each Taylor-Russell table was constructed for a different base rate. Thus as the base rate changed (as it might for different subpopulations), different validity coefficients and different selection ratios were required to achieve the same success ratio. If, for example, the base rate increased, a lower validity coefficient was needed to achieve the same success ratio (given a constant selection ratio). In contrast, if the base rate decreased and test validity remained unchanged, a smaller selection ratio was required to maintain the same success ratio. Although the Taylor-Russell tables are no longer widely used to predict success ratios in specific situations, it is important for test users to recognize one psychometric "fact of life" which they demonstrated. Namely, if two groups of examinees have different base rates and are selected at the same selection ratio, using a test with identical validity coefficients for each group, it will be impossible for them to have identical success ratios. Also, if two examinee groups have different base rates, and we want them to have the same success ratios, we cannot achieve this goal by using tests with identical validity coefficients and identical selection ratios. Recognition of these principles is prerequisite to understanding much of the psychometric literature on cultural bias and fair selection models.

MAJORITY AND MINORITY GROUPS

It is important to establish the meaning of the terms *minority* and *majority* groups as they are used in psychometric contexts. *Majority group* usually refers to that group of applicants who occur in the greater number in a pool of applicants for a particular educational institution or employment setting. *Minority group* usually refers to the group that has fewer candidates in the applicant pool. For example, if we are considering applicants for admission to a school of nursing, we might find that females represent the majority group and males the minority group. In considering applicants for a school of veterinary medicine, the situation might be reversed, with males constituting the majority group and females the minority group. The majority and minority group may be defined in terms of any demographic characteristic of concern to the test user (race, cultural background, age, physical disability, etc.).

The issue of fair selection can be important even when the minority and majority groups are nearly equal in size. Consider a university that admits large numbers of community college transfer students at the junior year. For a program that selectively admits junior students (e.g., schools of education or journalism), an important issue may be fairness in selection for the group who studied at the university for their first two years and the group of transfer students, even though the two groups are equally represented in the applicant pool. In this case, it does not matter how the groups are labeled.

PSYCHOMETRIC DEFINITIONS OF BIAS

Cleary (1968) argued that a test is biased for members of a subgroup of a population if consistent nonzero errors of prediction occur for its members. One situation conceived by Cleary is illustrated in Figure 12.2. Here the regression line for the total group is higher than that for the minority group and lower than that for the majority group. In this example, if the common regression line is used for prediction, performance will be underpredicted for the majority group and overpredicted for the minority group. Therefore, use of the total group regression line results in biased predictions. Darlington (1971), Hunter and Schmidt (1976), and Linn (1973) interpreted Cleary's definition to mean that a *test* is unbiased if the regression lines are the same for the majority and minority groups. If the regression lines are the same, then in a group of examinees who are homogeneous on the predictor, there are no predicted criterion score differences between the minority and majority groups. Thus Cleary's definition as interpreted by Darlington and Hunter and Schmidt requires that students of equal ability, as measured by the predictor, must have the same predicted criterion score for a test to be unbiased. In passing, at least,

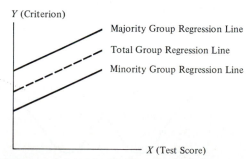

FIGURE 12.2   Regression Lines for Minority and Majority Groups Which Illustrate Cleary's Definition of Test Bias

we should note that Jensen (1980) modified the equal regression definition of test bias. He argued that a test is unbiased if (1) the regression lines of criterion scores on true predictor scores are the same for both groups, and (2) the standard errors of the predicted values (see Chapter 11) are the same for both groups. The first condition is motivated by the fact that the regression lines on observed predictor scores can be unequal, simply because of error of measurement, even when the regression lines on true predictor scores are equal. The second condition simply implies that the predictions are equally accurate for the two groups.

McNemar (1975) interpreted Cleary's definition to mean that a *selection procedure* is unbiased if separate regression lines are used for the minority and majority groups whenever the lines are not identical. The use of separate regression lines avoids the problem of consistent nonzero errors, and thus prediction is not biased. Note the shift in McNemar's position from concern with an unbiased test to concern with an unbiased (or fair) selection procedure. This shift illustrates how the question of test bias changed to the question of selection bias. The reader should also recognize that adoption of McNemar's position means that examinees with the highest predicted scores will be accepted regardless of their group memberships. Thus McNemar's definition of a fair selection procedure implicitly equates fairness with selection of examinees with the highest predicted capabilities. Clearly this is a value-laden position. It contrasts, for example, with the position that selection is

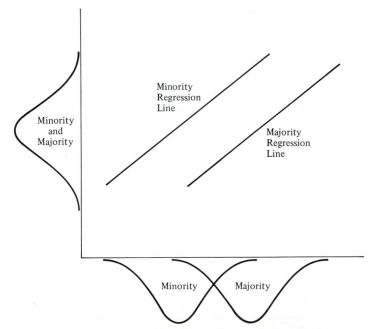

FIGURE 12.3 Minority and Majority Regression Lines with the Minority Line Above the Majority Line

fair when examinees with the highest predictor scores are chosen. Indeed McNemar's position does not necessarily lead to selecting applicants with the highest predictor scores. Consider, for example, Figure 12.3, in which minority and majority examinees have the same distribution of criterion scores, but the majority examinees do better on the predictor than minority examinees do. In this situation a minority examinee can have a lower predictor score than a majority examinee and still have a higher predicted criterion score, and thus be chosen over the majority examinee.

Thorndike (1971) offered a second definition of bias, arguing that a test is unbiased if, with any particular score considered satisfactory on the criterion (i.e., a criterion pass score), a single cut score on the predictor scale can be found so that the proportions of minority and majority members exceeding it are the same as the proportions exceeding the criterion pass score. Essentially this means that a test is fair if the minority and majority groups are as far apart on the predictor as they are on the criterion. To further characterize this definition, suppose that the standard deviations on the predictor are the same for the minority and majority groups and that this is true for the standard deviations on the criterion also. If the predictor meets Thorndike's definition, the point biserial correlation between group membership and predictor score will be equal to the point biserial correlation between group membership and criterion score.

Darlington (1971) presented two additional definitions of bias but did not argue in favor of either. One definition is that a test is unbiased if the distribution of predictor scores is the same for each group. Another definition is that a test is unbiased if the regression of the predictor on the criterion is the same in the minority and majority groups. As we noted earlier, soon after these definitions of test bias were proposed, interest in defining test bias in terms of relationships between a predictor and a criterion seemed to wane. Rather, attention was directed to the problem of defining fairness in selection and developing methods for implementing these definitions. In the next section, we will review some of these efforts.

FAIR SELECTION PROCEDURES

In exploring questions of fairness in selection, it is important to distinguish between two types of decisions—individual and institutional. Individual decision making occurs when the primary goal of the decision-making process is to maximize the benefit for a given individual. For example, when a counselor administers a vocational interest inventory and advises the examinee in terms of which career choices will be optimal, given the examinee's interests, the test score is being used for individual decision making. In contrast, institutional decision making occurs when the primary goal of the decision-making process is to achieve specific aims of an institution (e.g., to select applicants with the greatest probability of success) without regard to what is best for any particular applicant. The first point to be made about the psychometric models for fair selection considered in this section is that selection is considered to be an institutional decision. Thus the "fairness" of a selection procedure is considered in terms of the goals of the institution.

A number of models for fair selection have been proposed in the psychometric literature, and an illustrative variety of these models will be briefly described here. The six models to be described are the regression model, equal-risk employers' model, Darlington's model, equal-probability model, constant-ratio model, and conditional-probability model. The technical details for implementing each of these models will not be presented here since they may not be of general interest to all readers. These details are reported by Cole (1973), who also provided a comparison of the models in terms of predictor cut scores, percentage of minority examinees accepted, and other characteristics.

Regression Model

The regression model is based on the premise that selection is fair when the selected applicants are those predicted to score highest on the criterion regardless of their group affiliation. Thus in a situation in which 100 students are to be admitted for study in a professional school, and the criterion is overall grade-point average earned in the program, the 100 selected applicants should be those who have the highest predicted grade-point averages. To accomplish this, separate regression lines are fit for each subgroup, and the applicants chosen are those with the highest predicted grade points. Unless the regression lines for the two groups happen to coincide, examinees who have the same score on the predictor test but come from different groups will have different predicted criterion scores (see Figure 12.4). As a result, even if a member of the minority group and a member of the majority group have identical scores, they may not both be admitted. However, any selection procedure other than this one will result in a lower mean criterion score for selected

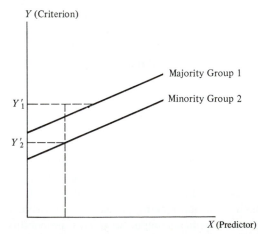

FIGURE 12.4   Using the Regression Model to Determine Predictor Test Cut Scores for Majority and Minority Groups

applicants. Thus, for an institution in which the goal is to graduate (or hire) the most highly qualified candidates in terms of criterion performance, regardless of group membership, this would be an appropriate selection model.

Equal-Risk (Employers') Model

This model requires the test user to specify a criterion pass score and also to specify the maximum tolerable probability (or risk) that an admitted candidate will fall below this score. Separate regression lines are determined for each group. Then, for each applicant a predicted criterion score is calculated (using the prediction equation described in Chapter 2), as is the risk of failure. Only examinees with a risk of failure that is smaller than the tolerable risk of failure are selected. Calculation of the probability of failure is based on the assumption of conditional normality for the criterion scores. That is, among examinees with a particular score on the predictor, it is assumed that the criterion scores are normally distributed. It is also assumed that the variances of the conditional probability distributions are the same for all predictor scores. Given these assumptions, the probability of failure is the area below

$$z = (Y_p - Y')/\sigma_{Y \cdot X} \tag{12.1}$$

in the standard normal distribution. In this expression, Y_p is the criterion pass score, Y' is the examinee's predicted score, and $\sigma_{Y \cdot X}$ is the criterion score standard deviation for all examinees at that given value of X. This standard deviation is equal to the standard error of estimate. Applicants are chosen if their probabilities of failure are less than the maximum tolerable risk. To illustrate, suppose the criterion pass score is set at 18, the maximum risk is .35, and a minority and majority member have predicted scores of 20. The standard error of estimate is 8 for the minority and 4 for the majority. For the minority group members, $z = (18 - 20)/8 = -.25$, and for the majority group member, $z = (18 - 20)/4 = -.5$. The probability of failure is .40 for the minority member and .31 for the majority member. As a result, only the majority member will be accepted. The equal-risk model is well suited to a situation where an institution wants to maintain control of the probability that an applicant will eventually fail, and wants to do so regardless of the mix of group membership that results. (It should be mentioned that if the standard errors of measurement for the two groups are identical, the equal-risk and regression models will yield identical results.) This model might seem attractive when the cost of admitting and training applicants is quite substantial.

Darlington's Model

Darlington (1971) argued that the proper approach to fair selection is to decide how much value is to be placed on selecting a minority applicant and to use this number in devising a selection procedure. He proposed to determine that value by answering the question, "How discrepant can the criterion scores for a majority and a minority member be and still have both applicants be considered equally desirable for selection?'' If we denote the size of the discrepancy by k, Darlington's selection procedure amounts to adding k to the predicted criterion score of all minority members. The selected applicants are those with the highest predicted criterion scores after adjustment by k for the applicants in the minority group. Such a model might be appropriate for an institution that has a higher priority on selecting minority candidates than on selecting the most highly qualified examinees or controlling the probability of accepting candidates who eventually fail.

Equal-Probability Model

Each of the three preceding selection models requires determining separate regression lines for the majority and minority groups and then calculating predicted criterion scores for each candidate by using the appropriate regression coefficient for the candidate's group membership. The next three procedures invoke the use of the concepts of true positive, false positive, true negative, and false negative, as depicted in Figure 12.1(d). Each of these procedures can be best understood by assuming that the test user has, through a previous validation study, obtained separate scatterplots which depict the relationship between test score and criterion performance for the minority and majority groups. We must assume also that the test user specifies a minimum acceptable criterion performance level, which is the same for both minority and majority groups. Now, in each of the following selection procedures, the test user must identify a cut score on the predictor variable for each group so that the scatterplots for the two groups are divided into four quadrants that meet conditions prescribed in the selection models.

The equal-probability model is based on the philosophy that all selected applicants should have the same chance of success regardless of their group membership. In other words, it requires the success ratio to be the same in all groups. Thus if 60% of the selected applicants in the majority group succeed on the criterion, 60% of the selected applicants in the minority group should also succeed on the criterion. To accomplish this, the cut scores on the predictor variable are located so that the quantity $A/(A + B)$ is the same for each group, where A is the number of true positives and B the number of false positives (see Figure 12.1(d)). As a result, the treatment of applicants with the same predictor score may vary, depending on their group membership, but once admitted, equal properties of each group will succeed. This model was first described by Linn (1973), although he did not advocate its use. A drawback of this model is that it may be impossible to implement if the groups differ too drastically on predictor scores (Jensen, 1980).

Constant-Ratio Model

Based on the values underlying his definition of test bias, Thorndike (1971) proposed that a selection system is fair if cut scores are set on the predictor so that the ratio of the selection ratios for the majority and minority groups is the same as the ratio of their base rates. As an example, suppose that the base rate for the majority group is 50% and the base rate for the minority group is also 50%. In Thorndike's model, if we select 20% of the applicants in the majority group, we must also accept 20% of the applicants from the minority group. As another example, suppose that the base rate for the majority group is 60% and the base rate for the minority group is 40%. The ratio of the minority to majority base rates is $40/60 = 2/3$. To meet Thorndike's requirement, the ratio of minority to majority selection rates must also be 2/3. Thus, if 20% of the majority group is selected, $13.3\% = (2/3)(20\%)$ of the minority group must be chosen.

It can be shown that the requirement of Thorndike's model is met when the quantity $(A + B)/(A + D)$ is the same for all groups. (Again the reader may wish to refer to Figure 12.1(d), where the quantities A, B, C, and D are depicted on a scatterplot.) It is for this reason that Thorndike's model is called the *constant-ratio model*. As with the other models, implementing it requires the test user to establish different cut scores on the predictor test for different groups of examinees.

Conditional-Probability Model

This model was introduced by Cole (1973) and focuses on the group of applicants who will eventually succeed. The model requires that people who can succeed should have the same probability of being selected, regardless of their group membership. For this to occur, the ratio $A/(A + D)$ must be the same for all groups of applicants (see Figure 12.1(d)). Again, to achieve this goal, different predictor cut scores are typically chosen for different groups of applicants. The quantity $A/(A + D)$ is known as the probability of selection conditional upon success, and this feature accounts for the name of the model. This model is also known as the *equal-opportunity model*.

CRITICISM OF THE MODELS

Petersen and Novick (1976) criticized the constant-ratio model, the equal-probability model, and the equal-opportunity model from two perspectives. To illustrate, consider Thorndike's model, which requires the ratio of selection to the base rate to be constant across groups. Petersen and Novick argued that if fairness requires this ratio to be constant across groups, the same logic requires the ratio of rejection to the failure rate to be constant across groups. (This is equivalent to requiring the ratio of the rejection rates for the two groups to be equal to the ratio of their failure rates.) The selection procedure based on this model is called the *converse constant-ratio model*. Petersen and Novick demonstrated that except under very special circumstances, the selection decisions under the constant-ratio and the converse constant-ratio models will not be the same. As a result they felt that both models were inappropriate. Similar arguments were presented in relation to the conditional-probability and the equal-probability models.

As Petersen and Novick pointed out, each individual must make a personal judgment about whether the failure of a selection procedure to meet both requirements of Thorndike's model and the converse constant-ratio model is really a logical contradiction. This would seem to open the way to resurrecting the constant-ratio model as well as the conditional-probability and equal-probability models. However, Petersen and Novick had a more telling criticism of these models, namely, that they were not formulated in a decision-theoretic fashion. This criticism appears to have been accepted widely in the measurement literature. In fact, Sawyer, Cole, and Cole (1976) have attempted to incorporate the values underlying the constant-ratio model and the conditional-probability model into a decision-theoretic model. Since the regression model and the equal-risk model are consistent with decision theory, Petersen and Novick were more sympathetic toward these models; however, they did point out that each model represented only one value position and that it seems unlikely that either could be universally applicable. This point should be clearer after decision theory has been introduced. With respect to Darlington's model, Petersen and Novick argued that it was not entirely consistent with decision theory but could be made so. Even so, it, too, would represent only one of many possible value systems.

DECISION-THEORETIC APPROACH TO SELECTION

Two basic methods of analysis may be used in applying decision theory to selection problems. For ease of explanation, *extensive-forms analysis* is presented first, rather than the *normal-forms analysis* used in some of the measurement literature (Gross and Su, 1975; Petersen, 1976). The basic steps in extensive-forms analysis for decision theory are these:

1. The probability of success and failure of an examinee must be determined.
2. The decision maker must assign relative value weights (called *utilities*) to each possible result—success and failure—of a selection decision.
3. The expected utility (or value) of each decision alternative—select and reject—is calculated.
4. The expected utility values for the decision alternatives are compared, and the decision with the greatest expected utility is chosen as the appropriate course of action.

The procedures and calculations involved in carrying out these four steps will be explained and illustrated in the following section.

Determining Probabilities and Utilities

Let us focus on selection in a single group. Assume that the bivariate distribution of the predictor and criterion scores for all examinees are known from past research (i.e., a validation study) and that a criterion pass score Y_c is set that divides the examinees into a successful and unsuccessful group. Since the bivariate distribution is known, the distribution of possible criterion scores is known for an applicant with

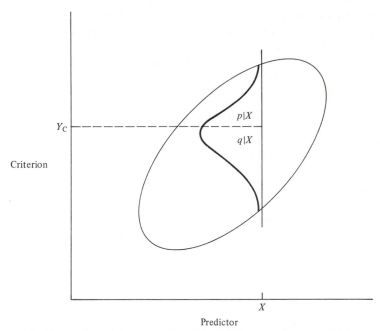

FIGURE 12.5 Illustration of the conditional Probabilities of Success ($p|X$) and Failure ($q|X$)

a particular predictor score. As a result, the probabilities of success and failure of this examinee are known. Let $p|X$ and $q|X$ represent the probabilities of success and failure for an applicant with a particular predictor score (see Figure 12.5). The quantity $p|X$ is the area above Y_c in the univariable distribution above X, and $q|X$ is the area below Y_c in the same distribution.

Recall that there are four possible events resulting from a selection decision—true positives, false positives, true negatives, and false negatives. Suppose the four possible events can be ordered in terms of their value for the decision maker. For example, true positives and true negatives are both events resulting from correct decisions and so might be seen as equally valuable. False positives and false negatives are both events resulting from incorrect decisions and are presumably less valuable than either of the correct decisions. Depending on the decision maker's viewpoint, there may be less value in one of these incorrect events than in the other. Let us assume for this illustration that the false negative event is considered the least valuable. So far, the possible events have only been ordered in value. Suppose now that the decision maker can attach numeric values to the four events indicating their relative desirability:

$$u_{tp} = 1.00$$
$$u_{tn} = 1.00$$
$$u_{fn} = .25$$
$$u_{fp} = .75$$

These numeric values are called *utilities*. The literal subscripts refer to true positive, true negative, false positive, and false negative events, respectively. (At this point we will not diverge to discuss procedures which may be used to obtain the numeric values assigned as utilities, but the interested reader may wish to consult Novick and Lindley, 1978, for references on this issue.)

Calculating the Expected Utility

According to decision theory, the rational decision about an examinee is made by calculating the average (or expected) utility for each possible decision alternative and choosing the alternative that has the largest expected utility value. For a select decision, the only possible events are a true positive and a false positive. The probability of a true positive is $p|X$, the probability of success at the examinee's X score. Similarly the probability of a false positive is $q|X$, the probability of a failure at a particular X score. The expected utility of a select decision is calculated by

$$\epsilon(u)_s = u_{tp}(p|X) + u_{fp}(q|X) \tag{12.2}$$

That is, the expected utility for a select decision is calculated by multiplying the utility of each event by its probability and adding the products over all possible events for that decision. The expected utility for a reject decision is

$$\epsilon(u)_r = u_{fn}(p|X) + u_{tn}(q|X) \tag{12.3}$$

The reader may wonder why the probabilities are the same in Equations 12.2 and 12.3. Consider $p|X$. It represents the probability of success, given a particular X score. For a select decision, a successful examinee is a true positive event. Therefore the probability of a true positive is $p|X$, and u_{tp} is multiplied by $p|X$. For a reject decision, a successful examinee is a false negative event. Therefore the probability of a false negative is $p|X$, and u_{fn} is multiplied by $p|X$ in calculating $\epsilon(u)_r$.

To illustrate, suppose, as before, that $u_{tp} = u_{tn} = 1$, $u_{fn} = .25$, and $u_{fp} = .75$. Also suppose for a particular examinee that $p|X = .4$ and $q|X = .6$. Then

$$\epsilon(u)_s = 1(.4) + .75(.6) = .85$$

and

$$\epsilon(u)_r = .25(.4) + 1(.6) = .7$$

Since the expected utility for the select decision exceeds the expected utility for the reject decision, the examinee should be selected. This is true even though the examinee has a greater chance of failure than success. The select decision is favored essentially because the utility of a false positive event is three times the utility of a false negative event.

Applying Decision Theory to Selection with Two Groups

When more than one group is involved in the selection process, the probabilities of success for examinees with the same predictor score may differ depending on their group membership. Furthermore, the decision maker may wish to assign different utility values to the various possible results of a selection for different groups of applicants. We will now illustrate how extensive-forms analysis can be applied to selection decisions involving two groups of applicants.

When there is one group there are four possible events. With two groups there are eight possible events, true positive for a majority member, true positive for a minority member, and so forth. As a result there are utilities for the eight possible events. For example, suppose the utilities for the majority group are $u_{tp1} = 1$, $u_{tn1} = 1$, $u_{fp1} = .25$, and $u_{fn1} = .5$. Further suppose that the utilities for the minority group are $u_{tp2} = 1.25$, $u_{tn2} = 1$, $u_{fp2} = .25$, and $u_{fn2} = .5$. These utilities imply that acceptance of a minority examinee who is successful is valued more highly than acceptance of a successful majority examinee. (They also imply that accepting a minority student who will be successful is more valued than rejecting a minority student who will fail.)

Suppose there are two examinees with the same predictor and that one is a minority examinee and the other is a majority examinee. Suppose that for the majority examinee, the success probability is $p_1|X = .55$ and the failure probability is $q_1|X = .45$. For the minority examinee the corresponding probabilities are $p_2|X = .52$ and $q_2|X = .48$. Thus, the majority examinee has the greater probability of success. For the majority examinee, the two expected utilities are

$$\epsilon(u)_{s1} = u_{tp1}(p_1|X) + u_{fp1}(q_1|X)$$
$$= 1(.55) + .25(.45)$$
$$= .6625$$

and

$$\epsilon(u)_{r1} = u_{fn1}(p_1|X) + u_{tn1}(q_1|X)$$
$$= .5(.55) + 1(.45)$$
$$= .725$$

Thus the majority examinee in this case would be rejected because the rejection decision has the greater expected utility.

For the minority examinee the two expected utilities are

$$\epsilon(u)_{s2} = u_{tp2}(p_2|X) + u_{fp2}(q_2|X$$
$$= 1.25(.52) + .25(.48)$$
$$= .77$$

and

$$\epsilon(u)_{r2} = u_{fn2}(p_2|X) + u_{tn2}(q_2|X)$$
$$= .5(.52) + 1(.48)$$
$$= .74$$

Thus for this case the minority candidate is accepted. This is true even though the two examinees have the same predictor score and minority examinees with that predictor score have a lower chance for success than majority examinees. The reason is that the utility for correct acceptance of minority examinees is specified to be 1.25 times the utility for correct acceptance of majority examinees.

Additional Concepts

The preceding discussion of decision theory was intended as an introduction to its use in selection problems. A more complete understanding of recent applications requires knowledge of several additional concepts, which are introduced in this section.

As we pointed out, the so-called normal-forms analysis has been more prevalent than the extensive-forms analysis in the measurement literature. With the latter, the expected utilities of the select and reject decisions are calculated for an applicant, and the decision that maximizes the expected utility is made about the applicant; separate calculations are made for each applicant. The normal-forms analysis also focuses on expected utility but is designed to determine the predictor cut score that will maximize the expected utility. Once this cut score is determined, a decision about an applicant can be made by comparing his or her predictor score to the cut score. Separate expected utility calculations for each applicant are not necessary.

To introduce the normal-forms analysis let us again focus on selection in a single group. We will again assume that the bivariate distribution of predictor and criterion score is known from past research and that a criterion pass score has been set. For presentational purposes, suppose that our knowledge about the distribution is represented by a scatterplot like the one in Figure 12.1(b). (In theoretical research such as that presented by Gross and Su, 1975, a distributional assumption such as bivariate normality is usually made. The analysis does not focus on a particular set of data but rather on the assumed distribution.) Once a predictor cut score is set, the scatterplot can be demarcated, as in Figure 12.1(d) and the probabilities of the four events— true positive, false positive, true negative, and false negative—can be determined. Note that these probabilities are calculated for the entire group of examinees. In contrast, with the extensive-forms analysis these probabilities are calculated for a particular examinee. The probabilities of the four events can be denoted by p_{tp}, p_{fp}, p_{tn}, and p_{fn}. The expected utility for the particular cut score on which the probabilities are based is

$$\epsilon(u) = u_{tp}p_{tp} + u_{fp}p_{fp} + u_{tn}p_{tn} + u_{fn}p_{fn} \qquad (12.4)$$

Note that the expected utility is a weighted sum of the utilities of the four events, and the weights are the probabilities of the four events. Note also that the difference between Equation 12.4 and Equation 12.2 or 12.3 is that the former is defined for all applicants, whereas the latter are defined for a particular applicant.

As we mentioned in introducing Equation 12.4, the expected utility is calculated for a particular cut score. The goal of the normal-forms analysis is to determine the cut score, which gives the maximum expected utility. For conceptual purposes you may think of this process as one of calculating $\epsilon(u)$ for each possible cut score and then choosing the cut score that yields the maximum value of $\epsilon(u)$. In practice, a formula for determining the cut score that maximizes $\epsilon(u)$ may be available. The normal-forms analysis can also be used to set separate cut scores for the minority and majority groups that will maximize the expected utility. Recall that there are eight events—true positives for majority members, true positive for minority members, and so forth. The normal-forms analysis maximizes the expected utility over all eight events. The expression to be maximized is

$$\epsilon(u) = \sum_{i=1}^{2} p_i(u_{tpi}p_{tpi} + u_{fpi}p_{fpi} + u_{fni}p_{fni} + u_{tni}p_{tni}) \tag{12.5}$$

where the only new term is p_i ($i = 1,2$), which represents the proportion of majority and minority students, respectively. Maximizing this expression is equivalent to adjusting two cut scores, one for the majority and one for the minority group, until the maximum expected utility is obtained. Details are given in Gross and Su (1975) for the case in which the predictor criterion distribution is assumed to be bivariate normal. Petersen (1976) showed that the procedure developed by Gross and Su can, in principle, be used with other distributions.

Another limitation in the coverage of this chapter has been that only the so-called threshold utility function has been discussed. With this utility function, the utility of any one of the events, true positive, for example, is independent of the actual criterion score eventually earned by an examinee. Or in other words, as long as two examinees are each successful, the utility of a select decision is the same regardless of any criterion score difference between the two examinees. Clearly this seems unreasonable in many situations. The utility of a salesperson whose efforts yield a profit of $2 million is certainly greater than that of a salesperson whose efforts result in a profit of $50,000. (For an interesting account of the impact of ''threshold utility reasoning'' on the GNP, see Schmidt and Hunter, 1981.) Thus utility functions other than threshold utility function should be considered in selection problems. Finally, as noted earlier, the issue of setting the numeric values of the utilities was not addressed. Both the setting of utilities and additional utility functions are discussed in Novick and Lindley (1978), who also give a large number of references to these issues.

SUMMARY

Even though a test may have empirical evidence of validity (in the form of a correlation between test scores and criterion scores), there are additional considerations in assessing the usefulness of the test scores for selection decisions. One such consideration involves constraints in the selection situation itself. Specifically, for any given base rate in an examinee population, the factors of test score validity and selection ratio interact to affect the success ratio that will be obtained. This was exemplified by use of values from the Taylor-Russell tables. It was stressed that if two different examinee groups have different base rates of success, then use of a common selection ratio and a test with identical validity coefficients for both groups will automatically result in different success ratios.

An important related issue in using a test for selection purposes is whether the selection decision is "fair" for different examinee groups. To address this issue, psychometricians developed various definitions of test bias in the 1960s. Definitions by Cleary (1968), Thorndike (1971), and Darlington (1971) were presented. An important point about these definitions is that if a test is unbiased by one definition, it is almost certain to be "biased" by the other three definitions. Furthermore criticisms of these definitions and the selection models derived from them were quick to follow their development.

Although a variety of fair selection models emanated from these definitions of test bias, those that have a basis in decision theory are generally preferred. Selection models reviewed in this chapter include the regression model, the equal-risk model, Darlington's model, the equal-probability model, the constant-ratio model, the conditional-probability model, and the decision-theoretic model. The last requires that the test user be able to assign a weighted value (utility) to each possible result of a selection decision: true positive, false positive, true negative, and false negative. Given the probability of success of a candidate with any particular score on the predictor test, the expected utility of a select decision and that of a reject decision should then be calculated. The decision alternative with the greatest positive expected utility value is the choice that should be made for a candidate with that particular predictor score. A separate set of utility weights may be established for each examinee group in recognition of the differential value to an institution or to society of the occurrence of a true positive, true negative, false positive, or false negative for different groups of examinees. These applications were illustrated through use of the extensive-forms analysis.

A final point about the various models for fair selection which have been proposed is that different models may reflect very different social values. The decision-theoretic model is recommended over others because it allows the test user to take into account all possible events that occur in the selection process, because it requires explicit public statements of the values (utilities) assigned to each of these events for each different group of examinees, and because it provides a decision rule which involves a combination of the probabilities of these events and their relative values to the decision maker. Additional topics in decision-theoretic selection models which interested readers might wish to pursue were identified.

Exercises

1. From a larger pool of eligible students, 10 male and 10 female students were chosen at random to participate in an experimental high school science program. At the beginning of the year-long program, the students were administered a science achievement test. Reported are the students' scores on the test, their grade-point averages in the program, and descriptive statistics for males and females.

	Males			Females	
Examinee	Test Score	GPA	Examinee	Test Score	GPA
1	92	3.00	11	91	3.70
2	84	2.80	12	78	1.90
3	96	3.60	13	88	3.20
4	58	2.00	14	69	1.20
5	75	2.50	15	68	2.50
6	94	3.40	16	66	3.00
7	78	2.70	17	82	3.40
8	55	1.20	18	62	1.90
9	72	1.20	19	65	2.40
10	76	1.60	20	68	2.00
mean	77	2.40		74	2.50
stand. dev.	13	.83		10	.79
correlation		.87			.78

A. The administrator of the program proposes to use a cutoff score of 70 on the science achievement test to select students into the program in future years. Success in the program is defined as a grade-point average of 2.00. Using the available data, determine whether this selection procedure is fair according to the following models.

1. Equal probability
2. Constant ratio
3. Conditional probability
4. Regression model

B. Suppose that next year the program will be able to accommodate 30 percent of the examinees. What cutoff score should be set for males and for females in order for the selection procedure to be fair according to the conditional-probability model?

C. What predictor cutoff scores should be set for males and females if the regression model is used and there is no limit on the number of applicants that can be accepted into the program?

D. According to Thorndike's definition of a fair test (not a fair selection procedure), is the science achievement test a fair test?

2. A validity study of a single predictor yields the following statistics for a majority and minority group:

	Group	
Statistic	Minority	Majority
Intercept	45.0	40.0
Slope	1.0	1.5
Standard error of estimate	5.0	4.0

If the criterion pass score is 60 and the institution is willing to accept all applicants who have at least a 75 percent chance of success, what cutoff scores should be set for the minority and majority groups?

3. Suppose the utilities for majority and minority applicants are as follows:

	Group	
Event	Majority	Minority
True Positive	1.00	1.50
True negative	1.00	1.00
False positive	.50	.75
False negative	.50	.25

The success and failure probabilities for majority and minority applicants with a particular predictor score are:

	Group	
Outcome	Majority	Minority
Success	.6	.5
Failure	.4	.5

What decisions should be made about majority and minority applicants with this particular predictor score?

Chapter 13

FACTOR ANALYSIS

When several tests are administered to the same examinees, one aspect of validation may involve determining whether there are one or more clusters of tests on which examinees display similar relative performances. The number and composition of the clusters are determined by the correlations between all pairs of tests. For example, if a battery of memory tests consists of several tests which have meaningful stimuli in the items and several which do not, it may be of interest to see whether the pattern of correlations among the tests supports the hypothesis that there are two different clusters of memory tests. Or imagine a multitrait-multimethod study in which three traits are supposedly measured. Here it may be of interest to see whether the correlations support the hypothesis of three different traits. One procedure appropriate for investigating these questions is factor analysis.

The purpose of this chapter is to provide an introductory overview of the process of factor analysis as it might be applied in an exploratory validation study with a battery of tests or some other set of measurements. First, an example with hypothetical data is presented, and basic concepts of factor analysis are explained in this context. The presentation is designed to assist the reader in answering the following questions:

1. How does the pattern of correlations among variables in a correlation matrix indicate the number of factors affecting performance?
2. What are factor loadings?
3. How are factor loadings used to identify the number of factors (or clusters of correlations) in the observed correlation matrix?
4. What are rotations?
5. How does a researcher know which set of factor loadings (resulting from different rotations) to interpret?
6. What is the difference between oblique and orthogonal solutions?
7. How are the concepts of communality and uniqueness related to reliability?

In the latter half of the chapter a complete example of a factor analysis of subtest scores on an intelligence battery is presented to illustrate interpretation of results in a realistic validation context. The chapter ends with a brief introduction to confirmatory factor analysis.

AN EXAMPLE WITH HYPOTHETICAL DATA

Suppose scores are available for a population of examinees on the subtests of the Wechsler Adult Intelligence Scale (WAIS). As is well known, the WAIS includes 11 subtests, 6 comprising a verbal scale and the other 5 a performance scale. On the basis of this gross categorization of subtests, one might hypothesize that the correlations among them will suggest two clusters of subtests. This would be confirmed by the hypothetical correlations among the subtests reported in Table 13.1. Here, each pair of verbal subtests exhibits a substantial intercorrelation, and so do each pair of performance subtests. However the correlation between any performance-verbal pair of subtests is only .15. In the language of factor analysis, the subtests measure two factors, with the verbal subtests measuring one factor and the performance subtests measuring a second factor. In contrast, if the correlations between all the tests had all been .6, for example, the correlations would indicate a single cluster of tests. That is, the tests would measure a single factor.

FACTORS AND FACTOR LOADINGS

A factor is an unobservable or latent variable, just as a true score is unobservable. Nevertheless, just as it is possible to estimate the correlation between an observed score and a true score, it is possible to calculate the correlations between tests and factors. The correlations between the WAIS subtests and the factors, indicated by the correlations in Table 13.1, are reported in Table 13.2. These correlations are

TABLE 13.1. Hypothetical Correlations among WAIS Subtests

Scale	Subtest	1	2	3	4	5	6	7	8	9	10	11
Verbal	1. Information	—										
	2. Comprehension	.65	—									
	3. Arithmetic	.65	.65	—								
	4. Similarities	.65	.65	.65	—							
	5. Digit Span	.65	.65	.65	.65	—						
	6. Vocabulary	.65	.65	.65	.65	.65	—					
Performance	7. Digit Symbol	.15	.15	.15	.15	.15	.15	—				
	8. Picture Completion	.15	.15	.15	.15	.15	.15	.50	—			
	9. Block Design	.15	.15	.15	.15	.15	.15	.50	.50	—		
	10. Picture Arrangement	.15	.15	.15	.15	.15	.15	.50	.50	.50	—	
	11. Object Assembly	.15	.15	.15	.15	.15	.15	.50	.50	.50	.50	—

TABLE 13.2. Hypothetical Factor Loadings for WAIS Subtest

Scale	Subtest	Factor	
		1	2
Verbal	1. Information	.8	.1
	2. Comprehension	.8	.1
	3. Arithmetic	.8	.1
	4. Similarities	.8	.1
	5. Digit Span	.8	.1
	6. Vocabulary	.8	.1
Performance	7. Digit Symbol	.1	.7
	8. Picture Completion	.1	.7
	9. Block Design	.1	.7
	10. Picture Arrangement	.1	.7
	11. Object Assembly	.1	.7

called *factor loadings*. Each of the verbal subtests correlates .8 with factor 1 but only .1 with factor 2. Each of the performance subtests correlates .7 with factor 2 but only .1 with factor 1. Considering the tests that correlate with each factor, factor 1 might be called a verbal factor and factor 2 a performance factor.

The correlation between a pair of tests has a very important relationship to the loadings of the two tests on the factors. When there are two factors, the relationship is

$$\rho_{ij} = a_{i1}a_{j1} + a_{i2}a_{j2} \tag{13.1}$$

In Equation 13.1, ρ_{ij} is the correlation between scores on tests i and j, a_{i1} and a_{j1} are the loadings of test i and j on factor 1, and a_{i2} and a_{j2} are the loadings of tests i and j on factor 2. To illustrate, consider the correlation between the information and digit symbol subtests. The correlation is $\rho_{17} = .15$ and the factor loadings are $a_{11} = .8$, $a_{12} = .1$, $a_{71} = .1$, and $a_{72} = .7$. Substitution in Equation 13.1 yields

$$\rho_{17} = .8(.1) + .1(.7) = .15$$

The general equation relating the test intercorrelations to factor loadings is

$$\rho_{ij} = \sum_{k=1}^{m} a_{ik}a_{jk} \tag{13.2}$$

where m is the number of factors.

ROTATION

Equation 13.1 and its generalization, Equation 13.2, are important in understanding the concept of rotation of factors. Continuing with the example of the 11 WAIS subtests, consider a new set of factor loadings reported in Table 13.3. Although this

TABLE 13.3.   Alternate Factor Loadings for the WAIS Subtests

Scale	Subtest	Factor 1'	Factor 2'
Verbal	1. Information	.6363	.4949
	2. Comprehension	.6363	.4949
	3. Arithmetic	.6363	.4949
	4. Similarities	,6363	.4949
	5. Digit Span	.6363	.4949
	6. Vocabulary	.6363	.4949
Performance	7. Digit Symbol	.5656	−.4242
	8. Picture Completion	.5656	−.4242
	9. Block Design	.5656	−.4242
	10. Picture Arrangement	.5656	−.4242
	11. Object Assembly	.5656	−.4242

set is quite different from the set reported in Table 13.2, both sets satisfy Equation 13.1. For example, denoting the factor loadings in Table 13.3 by a_{i1}^*, a_{i2}^*, a_{j1}^*, and a_{j2}^*, the correlation between the information and digit symbol subtest is

$$\rho_{17} = a_{11}^* a_{17}^* + a_{12}^* a_{72}^*$$
$$= .6363(.5656) + .4949(-.4242) = .15$$

Since the factor loadings in both Table 13.2 and Table 13.3 satisfy Equation 13.1, it is impossible to choose between the two sets on the basis of accounting for the subtest correlations. In fact there are an infinite number of sets of factor loadings all of which satisfy Equation 13.1. Any one of these sets can be obtained from a second set through a process known as *rotation*. The term *rotation* comes from a geometric interpretation of factor analysis. (We will present a geometric illustration of a rotation later in the chapter. For the hypothetical example we are currently presenting, a geometric illustration would be somewhat confusing because each of the first six subtests has the same loading on factor 1 and each has the same loading on factor 2. Similarly each of the last five subtests has the same loading on factor 1 and each has the same loading on factor 2. Thus in any geometric representation of the subtests it would be impossible to distinguish among the first six and among the last five subtests.) Different rotations are related by a mathematical transformation. For example, the factor loadings in Table 13.2 and Table 13.3 are related by

$$a_{i1}^* = .707a_{i1} + .707a_{i2} \tag{13.3a}$$

and

$$a_{i2}^* = .707a_{i1}2 - .707a_{i2} \tag{13.3b}$$

To illustrate, consider the digit symbol subtest, which has factor loadings $a_{71} = .1$ and $a_{72} = .7$. Substituting in Equations 13.3a and 13.3b we obtain

$$a_{71}^* = .707(.1) + .707(.7) = .5656$$

and

$$a_{72}^* = .707(.1) - .707(.7) = -.4242$$

The process for obtaining the numbers that transform one set of loadings to another is not really important. The key point is that when two different sets of the factor loadings are obtained by rotation, each set contains loadings on the same number of factors and accounts for the correlations equally well. Only the sizes of the factor loadings change. Also the reader should note that there is a different set of factors corresponding to each set of loadings. Thus rotating the factor loadings also changes the factors, or unobservable variables, that the test scores are being related to.

The fact that different sets of factor loadings satisfy Equation 13.2 for the same correlation matrix would not be a problem if all the sets of loadings had similar interpretations. Unfortunately, this is generally not true. For example, the two sets of factor loadings in Tables 13.2 and 13.3 suggest different interpretations of the two factors measured by the WAIS. The loadings in Table 13.2 suggest a verbal and a performance factor. Inspecting the loadings in Table 13.3, we see that all tests have a positive and fairly substantial loading on factor $1'$. This pattern suggests that factor $1'$ is a general factor measured by all the WAIS subtests. Turning to factor $2'$ we see that the verbal tests have positive loadings whereas the performance tests have negative loadings. Since the verbal and performance subtests are not negatively correlated, the pattern of loadings on factor $2'$ suggests that this factor concerns differences in the abilities measured by the verbal and performance subtests.

The two sets of factor loadings suggest different interpretations because there is a different set of factors corresponding to each set of loadings. Denote factors 1 and 2, the factors corresponding to the loadings in Table 13.2, by f_1 and f_2, and factors $1'$ and $2'$, the factors corresponding to the loadings in Table 13.3, by f_1^* and f_2^*. It can be shown that the relation between the two sets of factors is

$$f_1^* = .707f_1 + .707f_2 = .707(f_1 + f_2)$$

and

$$f_2^* = .707f_1 - .707f_2 = .707(f_1 - f_2)$$

Thus f_1^*, the factor corresponding to the first column of loadings in Table 13.3, is essentially the sum of the two factors, f_1 and f_2, corresponding to the loadings in Table 13.2. (The number .707 simply serves to make f_1^* have a variance of one.) As a result, it makes sense that the first column of loadings in Table 13.3 suggests a general factor. After all, if f_1 is a verbal factor and f_2 is a performance factor, $f_1^* = .707(f_1 + f_2)$ is a general factor measured by every WAIS subtest. Similarly, f_2^*, the factor corresponding to the second column of loadings in Table 13.3, is essentially the difference between the two factors corresponding to the loadings in Table 13.2. Again, it makes sense that the second column of loadings in Table 13.3 suggests that factor 2 concerns differences in abilities measured by the verbal and performance subtests.

If there are an infinite number of sets of factor loadings which satisfy Equation 13.2 for a given correlation matrix, how is a researcher to choose one set of factor loadings to interpret? In principle, the most appropriate set is the one that best meets the simple structure criteria developed by Thurstone (1947). Essentially these criteria imply that each test should have large loadings on as few of the factors as possible and low or zero loadings on the remaining factors. (Mulaik, 1972, gives a more complete description of simple structure.) Thus, simple structure criteria favor the loadings in Table 13.2 over those in Table 13.3.

In conducting a factor analysis, the initial set of factor loadings is obtained by using a method that permits convenient calculation of the loadings. These loadings are called *initial* or *unrotated loadings*. Typically, researchers do not attempt to interpret the unrotated loadings. The initial loadings are rotated by one of several methods. All methods essentially result in a set of transformation equations such as those in Equation 13.3. These equations are used to transform the initial factor loadings so that they approximate simple structure. The rotated loadings are then interpreted. There are two classes of rotations, *orthogonal* and *oblique*. As the names indicate, orthogonal rotations result in uncorrelated factors, whereas oblique rotations result in correlated factors, which are discussed in the next section. Detailed discussions of rotation methods are given in texts by Harmon (1967) and Mulaik (1972). Varimax (Kaiser, 1958) is the most popular method for orthogonal rotations. Direct quartimin, developed by Jennrich and Sampson (1966), is perhaps the most popular method of oblique rotation.

CORRELATED FACTORS

Factors are unobservable variables, but like any other variables they may be correlated. That is, some rotations of the factor loadings result in correlated factors; others result in uncorrelated factors. A set of factor loadings corresponding to uncorrelated factors is called an *orthogonal solution,* and a set corresponding to correlated factors is called an *oblique solution.* Table 13.4 presents an oblique solution for the WAIS subtests. The factors corresponding to these loadings have a correlation of approximately .13.

With an oblique solution the factor loadings are not correlations between tests and factors. Rather they are equivalent to regression weights. To see what this means,

TABLE 13.4. Factor Loadings for the WAIS Subtests—Oblique Solution

Scale	Subtest	Factor 1	Factor 2
Verbal	1. Information	.81	.00
	2. Comprehension	.81	.00
	3. Arithmetic	.81	.00
	4. Similarities	.81	.00
	5. Digit Span	.81	.00
	6. Vocabulary	.81	.00
Performance	7. Digit Symbol	.00	.71
	8. Picture Completion	.00	.71
	9. Block Design	.00	.71
	10. Picture Arrangement	.00	.71
	11. Object Assembly	.00	.71

consider that the Comprehension subtest has a .81 loading on factor 1 but a .00 on factor 2. The .00 loading indicates that after taking into account the statistical relationship between Comprehension and factor 1, Comprehension is not related to factor 2. Another way to say it is the correlation between Comprehension and factor 2, partialling out factor 1, is zero. The .81 loading indicates that Comprehension and factor 1 have a relationship even after factor 2 is partialled out. It should be noted, however, that a factor loading in an oblique solution is not equivalent to a partial correlation. Rather it is equivalent to a standardized regression coefficient.

For correlated factors the correlation between two tests is a function of the factor loading and the correlations between factors. For two correlated factors the relationship is given by

$$\rho_{ij} = a_{i1}a_{j1} + a_{i2}a_{j2} + a_{i1}a_{j2}\phi + a_{i2}a_{j1}\phi \qquad (13.4)$$

where ϕ is the correlation between the two factors. A similar formula holds for more than two factors.

THE NUMBER OF FACTORS

Determining the number of factors is an important step in a factor analysis. The number of factors required to explain the clustering of the measures can be anywhere between 1 and $N - 1$, where N is the number of measures. In principle, the number of factors can be determined from the relationship of the correlations between pairs of tests to the loadings of these tests on the factors. For example, if there are two factors measured by the tests, it will be possible to determine loadings of each test on two factors so that Equation 13.2 is satisfied. That is, the correlation between tests i and j and the loading of these tests on the two factors will satisfy the equation

$$\rho_{ij} = a_{i1}a_{j1} + a_{i2}a_{j2}$$

If there are m factors, the correlation between tests i and j and the loadings of these two tests on the m factors will satisfy the equation

$$\rho_{ij} = \sum_{k=1}^{m} a_{ik}a_{jk}$$

To provide a concrete example, consider the intercorrelation matrix reported in Table 13.5 for four hypothetical tests. How many factors are required to satisfy Equation 13.2 for this matrix? The answer is one, because with $a_{11} = .8$, $a_{21} = .7$, $a_{31} = .6$, and $a_{41} = .5$ as the factor loadings, any correlation in the matrix can be expressed as

$$\rho_{ij} = a_{i1}a_{j1}$$

For example, with $\rho_{12} = .56$, $a_{11} = .8$, and $a_{21} = .7$, we have

$$\rho_{12} = a_{11}a_{21} = .8(.7) = .56$$

TABLE 13.5.   Hypothetical Correlation
Matrix for Four Tests

Test	1	2	3	4
1	1.00			
2	.56	1.00		
3	.48	.42	1.00	
4	.40	.35	.30	1.00

Thus the correlations in Table 13.5 indicate that a single factor is measured by the four tests since Equation 13.2 can be satisfied with the loadings on a single factor. Suppose, however, that ρ_{14} had been .80 rather than .40, as in Table 13.5. In that case more than one factor would be required to satisfy Equation 13.2. With the four factor loadings previously listed, Equation 13.2 is satisfied for all correlations except the new ρ_{14}. For this correlation

$$\rho_{14} = .80 \neq a_{11}a_{41} = .8(.5)$$

Thus if ρ_{14} happened to be .80 rather than .40, a single factor would not account for the correlations among the four variables.

It is important to recognize that we have presented the equations relating correlations to factor loadings in terms of population parameters. Equation 13.2 will be satisfied exactly for less than $N - 1$ factors only if we know the population correlations. For correlations calculated for a sample, Equation 13.2 will typically be satisfied exactly only for $N - 1$ factors. Should this be interpreted to mean that it takes typically $N - 1$ factors to account for the correlations between tests? Most psychometricians would not take this point of view. Rather they would argue that the failure of the sample correlations to satisfy Equation 13.2 with less than $N - 1$ factors reflects sampling error in the sample correlations. With sample data, then, this problem can be thought of as the problem of determining the number of factors required for Equation 13.2 to be approximately satisfied. The degree to which it is not satisfied should be small enough to be attributed to sampling error.

THE FACTOR-ANALYSIS MODEL

Equations 13.2, 13.4, and their generalization express the correlations between tests as a function of factor loadings, and in the case of correlated factors, factor correlations. These equations can be derived from the factor-analysis model:

$$z_i = \sum_{k=1}^{m} a_{ik}f_k + u_i \tag{13.5}$$

In this equation z_i represents z-scores on test i, a_{ik} represents the loadings of test i on factor k, f_k represents scores on common factor k, and u_i represents scores on the factor unique to test i. The distinction between *common factors* and *unique factors* has not yet been introduced. Previously we referred to common factors simply as *factors*. A common factor is a factor with which two or more tests are correlated and hence contributes to the observed correlations between these tests. A unique factor is correlated with only one test. This definition, combined with the assumptions that a unique factor is uncorrelated with each common factor and that the unique factors for different tests are uncorrelated with one another, implies that the unique factors do not account for correlation between tests.

COMMUNALITY AND UNIQUENESS

An important question in a factor analysis is the portion of a test's variance that is associated with variance on the common factors. This amount is called the *communality* or the *common variance* and is calculated by

$$h_i^2 = \sum_{k=1}^{m} a_{ik}^2 \tag{13.6}$$

for uncorrelated factors. For the information subtest the communality is

$$h_1^2 = .8^2 + .1^2 = .65 \tag{13.7}$$

The communality is a number less than 1 since the test scores are expressed as z-scores in factor analysis, the variance of z-scores is always 1, and the communality is the portion of the test score variance that is associated with variance on the common factors. For two correlated common factors the formula for a test's communality is

$$h_i^2 = a_{i1}^2 + a_{i2}^2 + a_{i1}a_{i2}\phi \tag{13.8}$$

A similar formula holds for more than two factors.

The proportion of a test's variance associated with variance on its unique factor is called the *uniqueness* or the *unique variance* and is calculated by

$$u_i^2 = 1 - h_i^2 \tag{13.9}$$

For the information subtest $u_i^2 = .35$. Theoretically, the unique variance can be partitioned into two components, specific variance and error variance. The specific variance for a test is that portion of a test's true score variance unrelated to true score variance on any of the other tests. Denoting the specific variance on test i by s_i^2 and the error variance by e_i^2, an expression for the total variance (which equals 1) is

$$h_i^2 + s_i^2 + e_i^2 = 1$$

The reliable variance on the test is $h_i^2 + s_i^2$. Since $h_i^2 + s_i^2$ is a number between 0 and 1, it may be thought of as a proportion. Therefore $h_i^2 + s_i^2$ is the proportion of total variance that is reliable, or equivalently, it is the reliability of the test scores. As a result, h_i^2 can be considered a lower bound to the reliability of the scores on test i.

AN EXAMPLE WITH REAL DATA

The following example illustrates the application of factor analysis to an exploratory construct validation study involving the separate subscales of a widely used intelligence test. Guertin and Bailey (1970) reported a correlation matrix for the 11 subscales of the WAIS. The data on which the correlations are based describe the performance of 200 police officers and firefighters and were collected by Matarazzo et al. (1964). A common rule of thumb for the minimum sample size in factor analysis is to use the larger of the following: 100 examinees or 10 times the number of variables. The sample size in the example exceeds the value suggested by the rule of thumb. This correlation matrix is reported in Table 13.6.

One of the first decisions in any factor analysis is the number of factors indicated by the correlation matrix. There are a number of criteria for determining the number of factors. One is the number of eigenvalues of the correlation matrix that are greater than 1. In the next paragraph are two examples intended to explain the basis for the eigenvalues greater than one criterion. Mulaik (1972) presents the mathematical definition of eigenvalues and the mathematical rationale for the eigenvalues greater than one criterion for the number of factors.

The correlation matrix of a set of N tests has N eigenvalues. Although the process by which the eigenvalues are obtained will not be explained here, it is important to note that their relative sizes depend on the magnitudes and pattern of the correlations. Therefore, it makes sense that the pattern of eigenvalues can indicate the number of factors. For example, if all the correlations between the pairs of WAIS subtests were .7, it would make sense to say that the subtests measure one factor. For a matrix with all correlations equal to .7, one eigenvalue would be equal to 8 and the remaining eigenvalues would be equal to .3, indicating a single factor. If the correlations among the verbal subtests were .7, and the correlations between the performance subtests were .7, but the cross correlations were 0, it would make sense to say that the subtests measure two factors. With this correlation matrix, one eigenvalue would be equal to 5.2, one eigenvalue would be equal to 4.3, and nine would be equal to .7, indicating that two factors are required to account for the correlations. The eigenvalues of the correlations for the WAIS data are reported in Table 13.6. Notice that there are two eigenvalues greater than 1, which suggests that there are two factors. However, two of the other eigenvalues are close to 1, and so there may be more than two factors. Thus the results of factor analyses assuming two, three, and four factors will be reported.

Table 13.7 reports the initial or unrotated two-factor solution for the WAIS correlations. Recall that the unrotated factor loadings are calculated by a convenient method and typically must be rotated to obtain a set of factor loadings that are interpretable. In Figure 13.1 the loadings on the first initial factor are plotted against the horizontal axis, and the loadings for the second initial factor are plotted against the vertical axis. For example, to locate the Comprehension subtest on the plot, we find .63 on the horizontal axis and $-.34$ on the vertical axis. Notice that the plot suggests two clusters of variables. One cluster consists of subtests 1 through 6,

TABLE 13.6. Correlations Among the WAIS Subtests[a]

Variable	1	2	3	4	5	6	7	8	9	10	11
1. Information	1.00										
2. Comprehension	.37	1.00									
3. Arithmetic	.34	.27	1.00								
4. Similarities	.40	.25	.36	1.00							
5. Digit Span	.27	.38	.28	.22	1.00						
6. Vocabulary	.59	.46	.33	.35	.29	1.00					
7. Digit Symbol	.09	.10	.18	.08	.16	.08	1.00				
8. Picture Completion	.25	.26	.32	.31	.14	.27	.19	1.00			
9. Block Design	.27	.29	.38	.26	.18	.24	.13	.36	1.00		
10. Picture Arrangement	.22	.22	.29	.25	.15	.28	.22	.36	.30	1.00	
11. Object Assembly	.26	.24	.30	.20	.22	.26	.17	.40	.60	.25	1.00

[a]The eigenvalues of the correlation matrix are 3.79, 1.27, .98, .92, .76, .71, .64, .58, .55, .40, .35. From W. H. Guertin, and J. D. Bailey, Jr. (1970). *Introduction to modern factor analysis.* Ann Arbor, Mich.: Edward Brothers. Adapted by permission.

TABLE 13.7.   Initial Two-Factor Solution for the WAIS Data

	Factor Loadings	
Subtest	1	2
1. Information	.63	−.34
2. Comprehension	.55	−.19
3. Arithmetic	.58	.05
4. Similarities	.51	−.12
5. Digit Span	.42	−.13
6. Vocabulary	.66	−.41
7. Digit Symbol	.24	.12
8. Picture Completion	.54	.20
9. Block Design	.62	.40
10. Picture Arrangement	.47	.11
11. Object Assembly	.59	.40

which are plotted in the lower right quadrant. The second cluster consists of the remaining variables; these are located in the upper right quadrant. Notice also that the horizontal axis passes through a region that divides the subtests into two clusters. As a result subtests in both clusters have substantial loadings on Factor 1, represented by the horizontal axis.

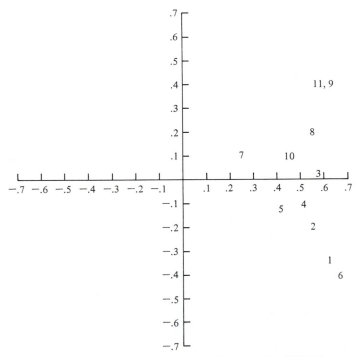

FIGURE 13.1   Plot of the Unrotated Factor Loadings for the WAIS Data

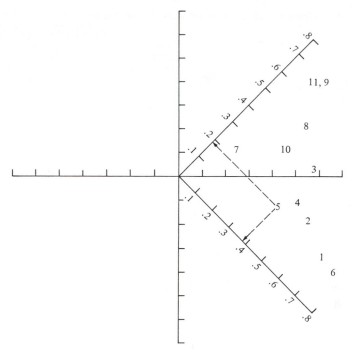

FIGURE 13.2   Plot of the Orthogonal Rotation for the WAIS Data

Rotation of the factors amounts to finding two new axes, one that passes closer to the first cluster and a second that passes closer to the second cluster. For an orthogonal solution, the new axes must be perpendicular to one another. For an oblique solution, the new axes are not perpendicular. Figure 13.2 presents an orthogonal rotation of the original axes. The process for finding a subtest's loadings on the rotated axes is illustrated for subtest 5 by the dotted lines. The rotated loadings for subtest 5 are .39 on the first rotated factor and .19 on the second rotated factor. Since an orthogonal rotation requires the axes to remain perpendicular to one another, in our example it is impossible for each axis to pass through its respective cluster of subtests. Indeed, moving one axis closer to its cluster would force the other axis to move away from its cluster. With an oblique rotation the axes are not perpendicular. Therefore with an oblique rotation each of the new axes would be located nearer to its respective cluster.

The factor loadings for a two-factor oblique solution are reported in Table 13.8. For comparison a two-factor orthogonal solution is also reported. Direct quartimin was used to obtain the oblique rotation, and varimax was used to obtain the orthogonal rotation. The correlation between the two factors for the oblique solution is .55. In reviewing the loadings in Table 13.8, the reader should keep in mind that loadings less than .30 are usually considered unimportant. The table indicates that variables 1, 2, 4, 5, and 6 load primarily on factor 1. It should be recalled that since an

TABLE 13.8. Oblique and Orthogonal Two-Factor Solutions for the WAIS Data

| | | Factor Loadings | | | |
| | | Oblique Factors | | Orthogonal Factors | |
Subtest	Communality	1	2	1	2
1. Information	.50	.75	−.06	.69	.18
2. Comprehension	.34	.54	.07	.53	.23
3. Arithmetic	.34	.29	.36	.38	.43
4. Similarities	.27	.43	.14	.45	.26
5. Digit Span	.19	.39	.07	.39	.19
6. Vocabulary	.60	.83	−.11	.76	.15
7. Digit Symbol	.07	.02	.26	.10	.25
8. Picture Completion	.33	.10	.51	.25	.52
9. Block Design	.53	−.07	.77	.17	.71
10. Picture Arrangement	.22	.16	.36	.27	.40
11. Object Assembly	.51	−.08	.77	.16	.70

oblique rotation was used, the factor loadings are analogous to regression coefficients. Thus the small loadings on factor 2 mean that once the relationships between factor 1 and variables 1, 2, 4, 5, and 6 are taken into account, there is little or no relationship between these variables and factor 2. Table 13.8 also indicates that variables 8 through 11 load primarily on factor 2, variable 3 loads about equally on both factors, and variable 7 has negligible loadings on both factors.

As noted, Table 13.8 also presents the factor loadings for an orthogonal rotation obtained from the varimax procedure. The general pattern of loadings is quite similar for the orthogonal and oblique solutions. However, the loadings for variables 2 and 4 on factor 2 are more substantial in the orthogonal solution than in the oblique. Similarly, variables 8 and 10 have more substantial loadings on factor 1 in the orthogonal solution. Thus the oblique solution simplifies a pattern that is already fairly evident in the orthogonal solution. This is fairly typical of comparisons of oblique and orthogonal factor analyses.

Table 13.9 contains the factor loadings obtained by using a direct quartimin rotation of three factors. The first factor is quite similar to the first factor of the two-factor oblique solution. The loadings on the next two factors suggest that the second factor from Table 13.8 has split into two factors. In Table 13.9 factor 2 is loaded primarily by variables 9 and 11, whereas factor 3 is loaded primarily by factors 7, 8, and 10. Inspection of the correlation matrix suggests the reason for the loadings on factors 2 and 3. The correlation between variables 9 and 11 is .60, the largest in the matrix. Also the correlation between variables 8 and 10 is .36. Variable 10 has no other correlation as high as this, whereas variable 8 has two correlations, one with variable 9 and one with variable 11, that are as high. A four-factor oblique solution is reported in Table 13.10. The loadings on the first three factors are essentially the same as those in Table 13.9. The main difference is that the loadings of variables 5 and 2 on factor 1 are reduced in going from the three- to the

TABLE 13.9. Oblique Three-Factor Solution for the WAIS Data

Subtest	Communality	Factor Loadings		
		1	2	3
1. Information	.52	.75	−.00	−.05
2. Comprehension	.34	.55	.08	−.01
3. Arithmetic	.34	.27	.18	.28
4. Similarities	.29	.39	−.04	.25
5. Digit Span	.20	.40	−.06	.03
6. Vocabulary	.60	.82	−.06	−.04
7. Digit Symbol	.11	−.04	.01	.36
8. Picture Completion	.38	.06	.19	.45
9. Block Design	.57	.03	.71	.05
10. Picture Arrangement	.35	.06	−.02	.57
11. Object Assembly	.64	−.00	.82	−.03

four-factor solution. Variable 5 has a .7 loading on the fourth factor, and variable 2 has a .28 loading. All other loadings are negligible. Inspection of the correlation matrix shows that variables 5 and 2 have a .38 correlation, which is largest for variable 5. This is probably the reason for the emergence of the fourth factor.

The interpretation of the factor analysis will focus on the four-factor solution. Factor 1 is loaded primarily by the Information, Comprehension, Similarities, and Vocabulary subtests. The Information subtest is a test of knowledge that attempts to avoid specialized academic knowledge. The Comprehension subtest is designed to measure practical judgment. Among other things it requires the examinee to say why certain practices are followed and what should be done in certain circumstances. Similarities tests the ability to determine the way two things are alike. Vocabulary, as the name suggests, requires the examinee to state the meaning of words. To some extent items on all four subtests can be answered on the basis of

TABLE 13.10. Oblique Four-Factor Solution for the WAIS Data

Subtest	Communality	Factor Loadings			
		1	2	3	4
1. Information	.57	.76	.03	−.06	.02
2. Comprehension	.36	.38	.10	.01	.28
3. Arithmetic	.34	.23	.18	.26	.08
4. Similarities	.30	.42	.01	.22	−.02
5. Digit Span	.57	.09	.02	.04	.70
6. Vocabulary	.60	.78	−.02	−.02	.06
7. Digit Symbol	.15	−.08	.01	.37	.11
8. Picture Completion	.40	.13	.23	.43	−.11
9. Block Design	.61	.03	.79	−.00	−.02
10. Picture Arrangement	.35	.14	.02	.52	−.07
11. Object Assembly	.60	−.04	.79	−.02	.03

acquired knowledge. That is, they do not necessarily require any reasoning ability. However, this may be somewhat less true of the Similarities and Comprehension subtests. For example, on the Similarities subtest an examinee may have already learned how two things, presented in an item, are alike. This item, then, can be answered on the basis of this acquired information. However, on another item the examinee may not have learned the nature of the similarity and may have to arrive at an answer by verbal reasoning. Factor 1, then, seems to reflect both verbal knowledge and verbal reasoning.

Factor 2 is loaded primarily by the Block Design and Object Assembly subtests. In the former the examinee uses cubes with red sides, white sides, and red and white sides to construct an object that matches the design of a figure presented on a card. In the latter, the examinee essentially puts together a wooden puzzle of an object. Factor 2 apparently reflects the ability to make a whole out of parts. For Block Design the examinee knows what the whole looks like and has to assemble the parts to match it. With Object Assembly the examinee must assemble parts as they go together naturally and also attempt to visualize the whole from the parts. Anastasi (1968) suggests that this factor is a combination of perceptual speed and spatial visualization, factors which have been separated in other studies.

Factor 3 is loaded primarily by Picture Completion and Picture Arrangement, and to a lesser extent by Digit Symbol. The Picture Completion subtest requires the examinee to say what part of a picture is missing. Picture Arrangement requires the examinee to put a series of pictures in an order that tells a story. Both subtests involve part-whole relationships. In Picture Arrangement the examinee must conceptualize what is happening in each picture and then recognize, or invent, the relationship that ties the pictures together. In Picture Completion, the examinee must recognize the whole picture and then generate the part that is missing. The Object Assembly and Block Designs subtests also involve part-whole relationships. It may be that although the four subtests demand similar abilities, the object tests demand some abilities not required by the picture tests and vice versa.

Factor 4 is loaded primarily by Digit Span, which requires the examinee to learn a list of digits and to repeat the list either forward or backward. This seems to be a memory factor not involved in any other subtest except perhaps Comprehension.

The choice of the four-factor solution as the one to interpret was a pedagogical decision. In practice many factor analysts would not have interpreted this solution since the fourth factor is largely defined by one variable, Digit Span, and the loading of the Comprehension subtest is hard to explain. Moreover, given the interpretation of factor 1 as verbal information and reasoning, it makes sense that Comprehension should have a single salient loading on the first factor. Since this occurs for both the two- and three-factor solutions, many factor analysts would find one or the other preferable to the four-factor solution. In choosing between the two- and three-factor solutions, the criterion of *sensibility* is likely to be important. You may recall that in going from the two- to the three-factor solution, the second, or performance, factor splits into two new factors. The new second factor is loaded primarily by Block Design and Object Assembly. The third factor is loaded primarily by

Picture Completion and Picture Arrangement. This separation seems reasonable since it suggests that the performance subtests involving manipulation require different abilities than the performance subtests involving inspection of pictures. In addition to the criterion of sensibility, the *simple structure* criteria are sometimes important in choosing the number of factors to interpret. Although it does not happen in the current example, with some data sets the simple structure criteria will be most clearly met for a particular number of factors. With fewer factors, simple structure is not met even approximately. With more factors, the factors do not make sense or are defined by too few variables. Finally, the ultimate criterion for the number of factors to interpret is *replicability*. When the same variables are investigated in different studies, the factors that are replicated in the studies are those that should be interpreted.

In addition to inspecting the factor loadings, the communality for a test should be inspected and compared to the reliability for the test. The purpose of this inspection and comparison is to determine

1. The proportion of test variance associated with common factor variance, as indicated by the communality of the test
2. The proportion of test variance that is reliable but associated with a factor specific to the test; this proportion is calculated as the difference between the reliability of the test and the communality of the test

To illustrate, consider the Comprehension subtest in the three-factor solution. It has a .55 loading on factor 1, which suggests it measures verbal knowledge and reasoning. However its communality is .34, indicating that Comprehension shares 34 percent of its variation with all three common factors. Wechsler (1958) reports a .77 Spearman-Brown corrected split-half reliability for Comprehension. (This figure was calculated for a sample of 300 examinees in the age range of 25 to 34 and is used here for illustrative purposes only.) Using this reliability figure, 33 (= 100[.77 − .34]) percent of the variation in Comprehension scores is reliable and associated with a factor specific to the Comprehension subtest. Clearly then, despite the .55 loading on factor 1, it is erroneous to consider Comprehension to be primarily a measure of the verbal knowledge and reasoning factor. In contrast, Object Assembly has a .82 loading on factor 2, a communality of .64, and a reliability of .65. Therefore, Object Assembly shares 65 percent of its variation with the three common factors. One percent of its variance is reliable and associated with a factor specific to Object Assembly. As a result Object Assembly is primarily a measure of factor 2. As a third example, Vocabulary has a .82 loading on factor 1 and a communality of .60. Consequently Vocabulary shares 60 percent of its variation with the three factors. However Vocabulary has a reliability of .95, and therefore 35 percent of its variation is reliable and due to a factor specific to Vocabulary. Thus although Vocabulary predominantly measures factor 1, it is also influenced by a factor unrelated to the other variables that measures verbal knowledge and reasoning.

An important point about factor analysis is that it simply identifies clusters of variables. Attempts to determine why these clusters exist are speculative and should be viewed as hypotheses subject to additional verification. Also with regard to the factor analysis reported in this section, the reader should recognize that the examinees were police officers and firefighters and may not be representative of adults in general. For this reason, the results of this factor analysis may differ from the results based on different types of examinees.

EXPLORATORY AND CONFIRMATORY FACTOR ANALYSIS

Research using factor analysis can be described in terms of an exploratory-confirmatory continuum. A factor analysis is purely exploratory if the investigator does not have a hypothesis, however vague, about the number or nature of the factors measured by the tests. A factor analysis is confirmatory if the investigator has such hypotheses and conducts statistical tests of them. The nature of these tests will be briefly addressed later in this section.

Very little factor-analytic research is purely exploratory. It is probably typical that the researcher has a hypothesis about the number and nature of the factors measured by the tests. For example, in the WAIS example, an investigator might have hypothesized a verbal and a performance factor. It is also true, however, that such hypotheses are not subjected to statistical tests in the typical factor analysis. Rather the factors are extracted and rotated, and a somewhat subjective judgment is made about the degree to which the results conform to the researcher's hypothesis. This failure to test the hypothesis makes a study more exploratory than confirmatory. The problem with this exploratory approach is well illustrated by the factor analysis of the WAIS data. Some researchers would interpret the two-factor solution, which gives a measure of support to the verbal-performance hypothesis. Others would interpret the three-factor solutions, which give less support to the verbal-performance hypothesis.

In a confirmatory factor analysis the researcher states a hypothesis about the numeric values of some of the parameters (factor loadings, interfactor correlations, and uniquenesses) of the factor analysis. Perhaps, most typically, the researcher states a hypothesis that certain factor loadings are zero. For example, an investigator who expected a verbal and performance factor for the WAIS data might state a hypothesis that all the performance subtests have a zero loading on one factor and all the verbal subtests have a zero loading on the second factor. This hypothesis is represented by the entries in Table 13.11. The loadings of the performance subtests on factor 1 are all zero, whereas the loadings of the verbal subtests are all zero on factor 2. A hypothesis about a numeric value has not been stated for each loading represented by an X. These loadings are to be estimated on the basis of the data, as are the other parameters—the factor intercorrelation and the uniquenesses—for which hypothesized values have not been given. The zero loadings in Table 13.11 are not estimated. They are set to zero in the estimation process.

TABLE 13.11.   Factor Loadings Under the Verbal-Performance Hypothesis

Scale	Subtest	Factors	
		1	2
Verbal	1. Information	X	0
	2. Comprehension	X	0
	3. Arithmetic	X	0
	4. Similarities	X	0
	5. Digit Span	X	0
	6. Vocabulary	X	0
Performance	7. Digit Symbol	0	X
	8. Picture Completion	0	X
	9. Block Design	0	X
	10. Picture Arrangement	0	X
	11. Object Assembly	0	X

After the factor loadings, interfactor correlations, and uniquenesses are estimated by Equation 13.2, Equation 13.3 or its generalization, whichever is appropriate, can be used to estimate the correlation between two tests. The test of the hypothesized values is essentially a comparison of these correlations with the correlations calculated from the test scores. The former correlations reflect the hypothesized values, whereas the latter do not. If the hypothesized values are wrong, the two sets of correlations should be quite different, and this difference will lead to rejection of the hypothesized values. Jöreskog (1968) presented a general approach to confirmatory factor analysis, and several examples of confirmatory factor analyses. Such analyses are usually conducted by using one of several special factor-analysis programs. Perhaps the most widely used is LISREL VI (Jöreskog and Sorbom, 1984). This program is available from Scientific Software, Inc. and as an add-on to SPSS[x].

SUMMARY

One purpose of factor analysis is to determine the number of common factors required to account for the pattern of correlations between all pairs of tests in a set of tests. A common factor is a latent or unobservable variable which is correlated with scores on two or more tests. The relationship between scores on a test and scores on a common factor is indicated by the factor loading of that particular test on that particular common factor. When the common factors are uncorrelated, a factor loading is a correlation between scores on the test and scores on the common factor. When the common factors are correlated, the factor loading is equivalent to a standardized regression coefficient based on the regression of the test on the set of common factors.

A second purpose of factor analysis is to determine the nature of the common factors that account for the test intercorrelations. This determination is rendered somewhat complicated by the fact that more than one set of common factors can account for the pattern of correlations. This is the problem of rotational indeterminancy. The problem of choosing *the* set of common factors to interpret is solved in principle by requiring the factor loadings to meet the simple structure criterion. That is, the common factors that are interpreted are the factors characterized by factor loadings that meet the simple structure criteria. In practice the problem is solved by using one of the available methods of rotation. These methods are designed to yield factor loadings that approximate simple structure.

A third purpose of factor analysis is to determine the proportion of the variance for an observed variable that is associated with common factors variance. This proportion of variance is called the *communality*. Its complement, the uniqueness, is the proportion of the variance for an observed variable unassociated with common factor variance. It can be shown that the communality of a variable is a lower bound to the reliability of that variable.

Exercises

1. The following are correlations among scores on six school subjects.[1]

	School Subject					
	1	2	3	4	5	6
1.	1.000	.439	.410	.288	.329	.248
2.	.439	1.000	.351	.354	.320	.329
3.	.410	.351	1.000	.164	.190	.181
4.	.288	.354	.164	1.000	.595	.470
5.	.329	.320	.190	.595	1.000	.464
6.	.348	.329	.181	.475	.464	1.000

A. Based on an inspection of the correlations, how many factors appear to be required to account for the pattern of intercorrelation? The varimax rotated factor loadings for a two-factor solution are

	Factor Loadings	
Subject	1	2
1. Gaelic	.229	.659
2. English	.323	.551
3. History	.086	.591
4. Arithmetic	.771	.173
5. Algebra	.720	.215
6. Geometry	.577	.213

B. Based on the factor loadings, what is the estimated correlation between scores in Gaelic and scores in Arithmetic?

[1]Reported in D. N. Lawley and A. E. Maxwell (1971). *Factor analysis as a statistical method.* New York: Elsevier Publishing Co.

C. Assuming the tests measure two factors, what accounts for the discrepancy between this estimated correlation and the correlation reported in the correlation matrix?

D. What is the communality for Geometry?

E. What is the uniqueness for Algebra?

F. What is the estimated lower bound for the reliability of History scores?

G. Assuming that the reliabilities of Gaelic, English, and History scores are approximately .75, should any of these variables be considered primarily a measure of factor 2?

H. Given the available results, how can you investigate whether additional factors are required to account for the correlations?

2. The Depression Adjective Check Lists (DACL) are used to measure brief states of depressive mood. They consist of lists of adjectives, and respondents are asked to check each adjective which describes the way they are feeling now. Roth and Lubin (1981) conducted a factor analysis of 17 adjectives from the DACL. Responses were scored dichotomously. If an indicator of depressed mood (e.g., unhappy) was checked by a respondent, it was given a score of 1. If an indicator of elevated mood (e.g., active) was *not* checked, it was given a score of 1. Other responses were scored 0. The factor loadings for a two-factor oblique solution follow. The correlation between the two factors is estimated to be .21.

	Loadings[2]	
DACL Items	Factor 1	Factor 2
Unhappy	.63	.03
Dispirited	.58	.07
Blue	.56	.01
Downcast	.56	.12
Distressed	.51	.12
Lost	.47	−.04
Forlorn	.45	.02
Lonely	.42	−.04
Broken	.39	−.02
Burdened	.39	.48
Cheerless	.34	.10
Free	−.03	.53
Good	.24	.48
Peaceful	.13	.49
Active	.08	.47
Composed	−.01	.48
Vigorous	.00	.47

A. Write an interpretation of the factor loadings.

B. How would you expect a person with a depressed mood to score on factor 1, relatively high or relatively low? Why?

C. Interpret the interfactor correlation in terms of the factors you identified in A.

[2]From A. V. Roth and B. Lubin (1981). Factors underlying the depression adjective lists. *Educational and Psychological Measurement, 41,* 382–385. Adapted with permission of the authors.

3. Answer the following questions:[3]
   A. According to Holland and Keller, Kirton believes that all individuals can be placed on a continuum ranging from adaptation to innovation. Do the results of Holland and Keller's factor analysis support this claim?
   B. Holland and Keller report a two-factor solution. Are you convinced that this is the appropriate solution to report? If not, what information would you want access to in order to decide on the number of factors to report?
   C. Considering the factor loadings reported in Table 1, do you agree with Keller and Holland's conclusion that items 28 to 31 do not measure the originality factor?
   D. Regardless of whether items 28 to 31 should be included in the first factor, do you think it is appropriate to call the first factor *originality?*

[3] Based on W. F. Holland and R. T. Keller (1978). A cross validation study of the Kirton Adaptation-Innovation Inventory in three research and development organizations, *Applied Psychological Measurement, 2,* 510–563.

UNIT IV

Item Analysis in Test Development

Chapter 14

ITEM ANALYSIS

In test construction, a general goal is to arrive at a test of minimum length that will yield scores with the necessary degree of reliability and validity for the intended uses. This is typically accomplished by field-testing a large pool of items and selecting a subset of items from that pool that make the greatest contributions to reliability or validity. In constructing a new test (or shortening an existing one), the final set of items is usually identified through a process known as *item analysis*. Item analysis is a term broadly used to define the computation and examination of any statistical property of examinees' responses to an individual test item. Item parameters commonly examined fall into three general categories:

1. Indices that describe the distribution of responses to a single item (i.e., the mean and variance of the item responses)
2. Indices that describe the degree of relationship between response to the item and some criterion of interest
3. Indices that are a function of both item variance and relationship to a criterion

In the following sections definitional formulas for some of the most popular indices of each category will be presented. Later a data example will illustrate how information from such item parameters is considered in item selection or revision decisions for norm-referenced tests. Item analysis methods for criterion-referenced tests are considered in the final sections of the chapter.

ITEM DIFFICULTY, MEAN, AND VARIANCE

When an item is dichotomously scored, the mean item score corresponds to the proportion of examinees who answer the item correctly. This proportion for item i is usually denoted as p_i and is called the *item difficulty*. This parameter was dis-

311

cussed in some detail in Chapter 5. Recall that the value of p_i may range from .00 to 1.00. As we shall see later, nearly all total test score parameters are affected by item difficulty. The total test score mean is directly related to the item difficulties because

$$\mu_X = \sum_i p_i \tag{14.1}$$

Furthermore, if we are interested in the difficulty level of an average item on the test, it can be obtained by

$$\mu_p = \frac{(\mu_X)}{k} \tag{14.2}$$

where k is the number of items on the test. When describing an examinee group's performance on several tests of different length, the average item difficulty may be preferred to the raw-score means (which vary as a function of test score length).

As shown in Chapter 5, item difficulty level controls item variance because

$$\sigma_i^2 = p_i q_i \tag{14.3}$$

There it was also established that assuming a constant degree of correlation among items, total test score variance will be maximized when $p_i = .50$. Thus it might seem surprising to learn that for most published aptitude and achievement tests designed for norm-referenced score interpretation, item difficulties typically fall in the range of .60 to .80. The reason for this lies in the item format commonly used in such tests.

To understand how item format may affect p-value, consider a format such as

$28 \times 7 = $ _____

Obviously there is little chance that an examinee who does not know the answer can supply it by guessing. Thus the observed p-value for this item and consequently its variance are primarily functions of examinees' knowledge (i.e., their true scores on this item). Now consider the same item in this format:

$28 \times 7 = $ _____
a. 186
b. 196
c. 287
d. 554

Because this item format allows some examinees to mark the correct response by guessing, the observed p-value is affected by both the examinees' true scores on the item and by guessing. Under the random guessing assumption, the observed p-value is expected to be the sum of the proportion of examinees who *know* the answer (the "true" p-value) and $1/m$ of the proportion who do not know the answer, when m is the number of choices. To maximize the total true score variance for the test it is

TABLE 14.1   Response Distributions and p_o Values for Objective Items with Different Numbers of Possible Responses

Number of Choices	Proportion Who Know Answer	Proportion Who Guess Answer	p_o	Lord's p_o
4-choice item	.50	.50/4	$.50 + (.50/4) = .62$	.74
3-choice item	.50	.50/3	$.50 + (.50/3) = .67$	.77
2-choice item	.50	.50/2	$.50 + (.50/2) = .75$	.85

necessary to maximize the item true score variances. Item true score variance will be maximized when half the examinees can answer the item based on knowledge and half cannot; however, among the half who do not know the correct answer, each examinee has a $1/m$ probability of answering the item correctly by guessing at random among the m choices. Thus the proportion of examinees who may be expected to mark the correct answer by random guessing is $.50/m$. Thus the observed difficulty of an item with maximum true score variance would be expected to be

$$p_o = .50 + .50/m$$

Table 14.1 demonstrates how p_o values are computed for items with different numbers of choices. Values calculated in this table are still probably somewhat lower than the optimal p-value for a norm-referenced test. In a simulation study Lord (1952) demonstrated that reliability is improved by choosing items with p-values even higher than those computed by adjusting for random guessing. Lord's recommended p-values are also reported in Table 14.1. From a practical standpoint, even though Lord's values are based on simulated response data, they are probably still more reasonable than those computed from the random guessing model because many examinees have some partial knowledge that enables them to eliminate one or more foils before taking a guess, thus making their probabilities of a correct response greater than $1/m$.

ITEM DISCRIMINATION

The purpose of many tests is to provide information about individual differences either on the construct purportedly measured by the test or on some external criterion which the test scores are supposed to predict. In either case the parameter of interest in selection of items must be an index of how effectively the item discriminates between examinees who are relatively high on the criterion of interest and those who are relatively low. At times there is no more adequate measure of that construct available than the total test score itself. (The classroom achievement test is a primary example of this situation.) In this circumstance, total score on all the items is used as an operational definition of the examinee's relative standing on the construct of interest. With this internal criterion, the goal is to identify items for which high-scoring examinees have a high probability of answering correctly and low-scoring examinees have a low probability of answering correctly. In achievement testing, for example, we would say that such an item discriminates, or differentiates, between examinees who know the material and those who do not. In contrast, we would be suspicious of an item on which both high and low scorers were equally successful. Such an item would not seem to measure the same construct tested by the other items. It would be even less desirable to have items that are missed by many high-scoring examinees but are answered correctly by low-scoring examinees. Such items are said to show *negative discrimination*.

Five parameters used as indicators of the item's discrimination effectiveness will be described in the following section. One of these is based on the concept of differentiating between groups of examinees defined by imposing cut scores at specific points on the criterion score distribution. The remaining four are various types of correlation coefficients. It is important to recognize that each of these parameters is equally applicable to the situation in which the item score is being related to total test performance or to the situation in which the item score is being related to performance on some external criterion variable. Although the latter practice is somewhat controversial for reasons to be discussed later, the use of an internal criterion (i.e., total test score) or an external criterion does not alter the defining formulas or computation procedures.

Index of Discrimination

One simple discrimination parameter, called the *index of discrimination,* can only be applied to dichotomously scored items. Its computation requires designating one or two points on the criterion score distribution as cut scores and separating the examinees into groups who scored below and above these cut scores. For example, if the test developer is interested in selecting items that discriminate on the internal criterion of total test score, the groups could be composed of the upper 50% and the lower 50% of the examinee group, based on total test score. If the examinee group is large, it may not be necessary to use the entire upper and lower 50%. A classic study by Kelley (1939) demonstrated that under certain conditions, a more sensitive and stable item discrimination index can be obtained by using the upper 27% and the lower 27% of the examinee group; however, when sample size is reasonably large, virtually the same results can be obtained with the upper and lower 30% or 50% (Beuchert and Mendoza, 1979; Englehart, 1965).

Once the upper and lower groups have been identified, the index of discrimination (D) is computed as

$$D = p_u - p_l \tag{14.4}$$

where p_u is the proportion in the upper group who answered the item correctly and p_l is the proportion in the lower group who answered the item correctly. Values of D may range from -1.00 to 1.00. Positive values indicate that the item discriminates in favor of the upper group; negative values indicate that the item is a reverse discriminator, favoring the lower-scoring group.

TABLE 14.2.   Illustrative Response Patterns of Ten Examinees to Three Selected Items

	Examinee									
	1 +	2 +	3−	4 +	5	6	7	8−	9	10−
Item 1	0	1	1	1	0	1	1	0	1	0
Item 2	1	1	1	1	0	0	0	1	0	1
Item 3	1	1	1	1	0	1	1	1	1	1
.										
.										
.										
Total score on 30 items	25	27	15	24	20	18	16	14	22	10

Table 14.2 displays responses of 10 examinees to selected items from a 30-item test. Normally we would require a larger sample for item analysis, and use this example only for purposes of illustration. Examinees in the upper 30% are identified with a ''+'' and those in the lower 30% with a ''−'' beside their identification numbers. Responses of these three high-scoring and three low-scoring examinees have been used to calculate D for items 1, 2, and 3 in Table 14.3. Note that although both items 1 and 2 have the same p-values (.60), their D-values differ considerably. Based on practical experience Ebel (1965) offered the following guidelines for interpretation of D-values when the groups are established with total test score as the criterion:

1. If $D \geq .40$, the item is functioning quite satisfactorily.
2. If $.30 \leq D \leq .39$, little or no revision is required.
3. If $.20 \leq D \leq .29$, the item is marginal and needs revision.
4. If $D \leq .19$, the item should be eliminated or completely revised.

One drawback of using D is that it has no well-known sampling distribution. It is not possible to answer questions such as what D-value is significantly greater than zero, or how large a difference between D-values is statistically significant? Nevertheless, because of its ease of computation and straightforward interpretation, the index of discrimination continues to be one of the most popular methods of reporting item discrimination effectiveness. It is especially appropriate for classroom test item analysis performed with hand computations.

Correlational Indices of Item Discrimination

In Chapter 2 we discussed the Pearson product moment correlation coefficient as a measure of the degree of linear relationship between two variables. If the test items undergoing development have a possible score range of 1 to 4, 1 to 5, or greater (such as items from a Likert attitude inventory), this formula is commonly used to estimate the degree of relationship between item and criterion scores. Although the

TABLE 14.3. Illustrative Computations of Item Discrimination Indices for Items from Table 14.2, where $\mu = 19.10$ and $\sigma_X = 5.17$

Item	p	μ_+	Index of Discrimination $D = (p_u - p_l)$	Point Biserial Correlation $\rho_{pbis} = \dfrac{(\mu_+ - \mu)}{\sigma_X}\sqrt{p/q}$	Biserial Correlation $r_{bis} = \dfrac{(\mu_+ - \mu)}{\sigma_X}(p/Y)$
1	.60	20.33	$(.67 - .33) = .34$	$\dfrac{(20.33 - 19.10)}{5.17}(1.22) = .29$	$\dfrac{(20.33 - 19.10)}{5.17}(.60/.3867) = .37$
2	.60	19.17	$(1.00 - 1.00) = .00$	$\dfrac{(19.17 - 19.10)}{5.17}(1.22) = .016$	$\dfrac{(19.17 - 19.10)}{5.17}(.60/.3867) = .021$
3	.90	19.00	$(1.00 - 1.00) = .00$	$\dfrac{(19.00 - 19.10)}{5.17}(3) = -.06$	$\dfrac{(19.00 - 19.10)}{5.17}(.90/.1714) = -.10$

same formula for the product moment correlation can also be used with dichotomously scored variables, special formulas have been developed that are easier to use in hand calculations when one or both variables are dichotomously scored. Four such correlational indices will be described in the following sections.

POINT BISERIAL CORRELATION.   One situation which occurs frequently in item analysis is when the test developer is interested in how closely performance on a test item scored 0 to 1 is related to performance on the total test score (or some other continuously distributed criterion). A simplified computational formula for the Pearson product moment coefficient in this situation is called the *point biserial correlation,* denoted as

$$\rho_{pbis} = \frac{(\mu_+ - \mu_X)}{\sigma_X} \sqrt{p/q} \qquad (14.5)$$

where μ_+ is the mean criterion score for those who answer the item correctly, μ_X is the mean criterion score for the entire group and σ_X is their standard deviation, p is item difficulty, and q is $(1 - p)$. Table 14.3 demonstrates the calculation of the point biserial correlations between total score and the item scores presented in Table 14.2.

The value of the point biserial correlation between an item score and total score is somewhat spurious because the item score has contributed to the total score of each examinee. If the number of items is reasonably large (perhaps 25 or more), this fact is seldom a problem. However, with a small number of items, this problem may be corrected by

$$\rho_{i(X-i)} = \frac{\rho_{Xi}\sigma_X - \sigma_i}{\sqrt{\sigma_i^2 + \sigma_X^2 - 2\rho_{Xi}\sigma_X\sigma_i}} \qquad (14.6)$$

where $\rho_{1(X-i)}$ is the correlation between an item score and the total score with that item removed, and σ_X and σ_i are the total and item standard deviations respectively.

BISERIAL CORRELATION COEFFICIENT.   If we wish to assume that the latent variable underlying item performance is normally distributed, it is possible to derive a formula for the correlation between this variable and a continuously distributed criterion such as a test score. This statistic, first derived by Pearson (1909), is called the *biserial correlation coefficient* and may be computed by the formula

$$\rho_{bis} = \frac{(\mu_+ - \mu_X)}{\sigma_X} (p/Y) \qquad (14.7)$$

where μ_+ is the criterion score mean of those who answered the item correctly; μ_X is the criterion score mean of all examinees and σ_X is their standard deviation; p is the proportion of examinees who answered the item correctly; and Y is the Y ordinate of the standard normal curve at the z-score associated with the p value for this item. For item 1 in Table 14.2, $p_1 = .60$. Because p_1 is greater than .50, turning to the standard normal curve table in Appendix A, we examine the column of probabilities (or areas to the left) of positive z scores. The area value closest to .60 is .599, and the ordinate associated with this point on the normal curve is .3867. From data in Table 14.2, we can also compute the values of μ_+, μ_X, and σ_X. Using these values in Equation 14.7, we obtain $\rho_{bis} = .36$. The calculations of biserial correlation values for items 1, 2, and 3 are demonstrated in Table 14.3. Notice that these values are somewhat different than those obtained from the point biserial correlation formula.

Mathematically, the relationship between the biserial and point biserial correlations is

$$\rho_{bis} = \frac{\sqrt{pq}}{Y}\rho_{pbis} \tag{14.8}$$

Because the value of the Y ordinate on a normal curve is always less than $\sqrt{pq}$, the value of a biserial correlation will always be at least one-fifth greater than the point biserial correlation for the same variables (Lord and Novick, 1968). This fractional difference in magnitude remains fairly moderate for items of medium difficulty; however as p-values drop below .25 or increase above .75, the difference between biserial and point biserial correlation increases sharply. Magnusson (1967) graphically demonstrated that in extreme difficulty ranges, the biserial correlation may be four times greater than the point biserial correlation between item score and total score. Notice in Table 14.3 that the ratio of the biserial to point biserial correlation is greater for item 3 (1.67) than for item 2 (1.23) or item 1 (1.28). This occurs because low item variance operates to restrict the value of the point biserial correlation. Thus test users who are comparing reports of item analyses from different studies where different correlational formulas were used should remember that biserial correlations may be systematically higher than point biserial correlations, and therefore, apparent differences in the magnitudes of the item discrimination parameters may be due to the choice of correlational formula rather than to qualitative differences in the items.

PHI COEFFICIENT. When scores from a dichotomously scored item are to be correlated with scores from a dichotomous criterion (e.g., success or failure in a rehabilitative program or a demographic characteristic such as gender), the phi coefficient described in Chapter 5 may be used. Another use of such a coefficient is to determine the degree of stability in responses to the same dichotomous item by the same examinees on different occasions. Use of phi is most appropriate when the variables involved are true dichotomies. When criterion groups are formed by imposing an artificial cutoff point on a continuous distribution, this statistic does not permit full use of the information available. In other words if all examinees whose scores fall above a cutoff score are simply classified as 1 for pass and 0 for fail, quantitative information about the differences between the scores in the passing and failing groups will be lost. Another possible limitation of phi is that its value can only be 1.00 when the p-values for the two variables are equal (because the phi coefficient, like the point biserial, is derived directly from the Pearson product moment correlation).

TETRACHORIC CORRELATION COEFFICIENT. At times the test developer may be interested in how strongly two dichotomous variables are correlated when each variable is created through dichotomizing an underlying normal distribution. In such instances the tetrachoric correlation coefficient may be appropriate. Computation of this statistic is complicated and is seldom undertaken unless the test developer strongly believes that another correlational index, such as phi, is inadequate for the purpose. One such situation is when an intercorrelation matrix of dichotomously scored items will be submitted to a factor analysis. Because values of the phi coefficient are restricted, except when both p-values are equal, such correlation coefficients are less appropriate for factor analysis than tetrachoric coefficients. The formula for the tetrachoric coefficient is not easily presented, but computer programs for estimating this coefficient are available in several standard computer packages (see, for example, Dixon et al., 1981).

Comparison of Item Discrimination Indices

Thus far five different methods for investigating item discrimination have been presented. Obviously in some situations, because of the scoring of the variables, one technique may be more appropriate than others. At other times it might be feasible to use more than one of the methods described. Thus it seems reasonable to question the similarity of results obtained from the various methods. Several empirical studies have addressed this issue. Englehart (1965) used responses from 210 examinees taking a state high school equivalency examination. Using total score as criterion, he computed a variety of item discrimination indices, including D, phi, biserial ρ, point biserial ρ, and the tetrachoric ρ. When the values obtained for each of these item indices were correlated, the correlations between pairs of discrimination statistics ranged from .85 to .99 on one form of the test and from .90 to .99 on a parallel form. Similar studies have been reported by Beuchert and Mendoza (1979), Findley (1956), and Oosterhof (1976). In most of these studies the greatest discrepancies occurred for items at extreme difficulty ranges.

In summary, the following recommendations can be offered concerning the choice of an item discrimination procedure for dichotomously scored items:

1. When items are of moderate difficulty, it makes little difference which discrimination statistic is used. If ease of computation is a major concern, D is recommended. If a test of statistical significance is desired, one of the correlational procedures should be used.

2. If the goal is to select items at one extreme of the difficulty range, biserial ρ is recommended (if it is reasonable to assume a normal distribution of the trait underlying item performance).

3. If the test developer suspects that future samples will differ in ability from the present item analysis group, biserial ρ is again recommended since the relative order of item discrimination for this statistic should remain more stable from sample to sample when samples vary in ability. Another way of saying this is that a low biserial ρ value for a sample of any ability level indicates that the item is low in discriminating power; but a low point biserial value for a sample of low ability (or

high ability) may simply be a function of the item difficulty and does not necessarily indicate that the item is a poor discriminator.

4. If the test developer is fairly confident that future samples will be similar in ability to the item analysis sample, and the goal is to select items that will have high internal consistency, it may be preferable to use the point biserial correlation (Lord and Novick, 1968). Although this has not been conclusively demonstrated, it seems logical in the view of the fact that point biserial values would be higher for items of medium difficulty, and such items would allow maximum item covariances and hence a maximum value of alpha.

5. In cases where both the item and criterion variable are scored dichotomously, the phi or tetrachoric coefficient should be used. Phi is easier to compute but will be artificially restricted when the proportions in the two dichotomies are not equal. The tetrachoric correlation is based on the assumption that the item and criterion scores arise by dichotomizing two normally distributed variables. Use of this coefficient is seldom warranted as a measure of item discrimination because of its computational complexity, but its use is strongly recommended if the correlations are to be used in a subsequent factor analysis.

ITEM RELIABILITY AND VALIDITY INDICES

The third class of item parameters often examined during an item analysis study may be typified by the *item reliability index* and the *item validity index*. Each of these is jointly a function of item score variability and item score correlation with a criterion. If the internal criterion of total test score is used, the index is defined as $\sigma_i \rho_{iX}$, where ρ_{iX} is the correlation between item and total test score. This index is called the *item reliability index*. For dichotomously scored items this formula is more commonly written as $\sqrt{p_i q_i} \rho_{iX}$, where ρ_{iX} is the point biserial correlation between item and total test score. If an external performance criterion is used, the index is defined as $\sigma_i \rho_{iY}$, where ρ_{iY} is the correlation between item score and the external criterion. When the goal of item selection is to improve test score reliability or validity by selection of items which discriminate on the criterion of interest, it has sometimes been suggested that the item reliability index (or the item validity index) should be used in lieu of the simple correlation between item and criterion because the item variance actually weights the relative contribution of a particular item to overall test score reliability or validity. If, for example, two items have equal correlations with total test score, but one item has greater variance than the other, the item with greater variance makes a greater contribution to test score reliability. Although this argument has some merit, it should be noted that as long as items with medium difficulties are chosen, there is little practical advantage in using the item reliability index instead of the item total score correlation.

There are, however, some test construction situations in which the item reliability index or the item validity index may be useful. It has been shown that total test score variance can be expressed as the sum of the item reliability indices, so that

$$\sigma_X^2 = (\Sigma \sigma_i \rho_{iX})^2 \qquad (14.9)$$

This may be useful in an item analysis where the test developer has set a desired minimal value for the total test score variance. As the process of item selection begins, the sum of item reliability indices is incremented with the selection of each additional item until the desired minimum level for total score variance is achieved. This is much simpler computationally than rescoring the test for each examinee and recomputing the variance from examinees' total raw scores with the addition of each item.

Similarly, if the test developer has set a minimum value for the internal consistency coefficient, as measured by coefficient alpha, the value of alpha can be reestimated with the addition of each new item, using only item-level data, by the formula

$$\rho_\alpha = \frac{k}{k-1}[1 - \frac{\Sigma\sigma_i^2}{(\Sigma\sigma_i\rho_{iX})^2}] \tag{14.10}$$

Where k represents the number of items selected to this point.

Finally, if the test developer wishes to specify the minimum value for a validity coefficient between a selected subset of items and some external criterion, as each new item is added, the validity coefficient can be estimated from item-level data by

$$\rho_{XY} = \frac{\Sigma\sigma_i\rho_{iY}}{\Sigma\sigma_i\rho_{iX}} \tag{14.11}$$

It should be noted that the values of variance, coefficient alpha, and validity coefficients estimated from item reliability indices are approximations when the values of ρ_{iX} are obtained from an item analysis of all items in the field-tested item pool rather than just for those items in the selected subset of items. Derivations for these formulas showing the relationships between item parameters and total test score parameters are given by Gulliksen (1950) and Lord and Novick (1968).

CONDUCTING AN ITEM ANALYSIS STUDY

Field-Testing and Item Analysis: Overview

By now it is apparent that total test scores can have no properties that are not a function of the items that comprise the test. Thus if the test developer wants test scores that have minimal measurement error or that have strong relationships to performance criteria or measures of other constructs, it is not enough to draft a set of items and "hope for the best." Once all the items have been written and revised from results of formal item review and preliminary tryouts, it is standard practice to field-test the items on an appropriate examinee sample. Results of this field test are used in the item analysis. Through item analysis the test developer identifies those items that are functioning as intended and those items that are not. In most cases the former items will be retained and the latter will be revised or eliminated from future versions of the test.

In a typical item analysis the test developer will

1. Decide what properties of the test score are of greatest importance
2. Identify the item parameters most relevant to those properties
3. Administer the items to a sample of examinees representative of those for whom the test is intended
4. Estimate for each item the parameters identified in step 2
5. Establish a plan for selection of items (or identification and revision of malfunctioning items)
6. Select the final subset of items
7. Assess whether the desired results have been achieved by conducting a cross-validation study

In the preceding sections of this chapter we identified and defined item parameters which are usually of interest because of their relationships to important total test score parameters. Formulas were presented for estimation of these item parameters. In the following sections, we focus on steps 3, 5, 6, and 7 of the previous sequel.

Sample Size

There is no absolute rule for the minimum number of examinees to use in an item analysis study. Certainly the item analysis for a test which will be widely used, such as the Graduate Record Examination or a commercially published aptitude or achievement test, should be based on a sizable, representative sample, perhaps of thousands of examinees. In contrast, a doctoral student who develops an instrument for dissertation research may have to rely on a much smaller sample. As a general rule, most item parameters described in this chapter can be estimated with relative stability for samples of 200 examinees, and so this might be considered the minimum number desired. Another longstanding rule-of-thumb (Nunnally, 1967) is to have 5 to 10 times as many subjects as items. If the test developer relies on this latter guideline, at the minimum, 20 items and 100 subjects probably should be used. Sample sizes required for parameter estimation based on item response theory (described in Chapter 15) may vary from 200 to 1,000 subjects, depending on the particular model chosen. Thus it is vital for the test developer to know what item analysis procedures will be applied when planning the item field test so that a sufficient number of examinees can be tested. Another related consideration is the need for cross validation, which will be discussed shortly. This final phase of the item analysis study requires testing subjects in addition to those whose responses were used to estimate item parameters.

Establishing a Plan for Item Selection

Historically, a controversial issue in test development has been whether it is more important to select items that correlate with total test score (resulting in test scores with higher internal consistency) or to select items on the strength of their relationship to an external criterion. On the one hand, if a polyglot of items is chosen which correlate highly with an external criterion but have little relationship with each other, the meaningfulness and interpretability of the test scores as measures of a construct will be questionable (see Travers, 1951). On the other hand, the more that items correlate with each other, the less additional variance in the criterion is likely to be accounted for by the collection of items. A key point for the test developer to remember in designating the criterion to be used for item discrimination is that the appropriateness of the criterion should be dictated by the intended purpose of the test and the likely audience it is to serve. The more it is true that the sole purpose of the test is to predict performance on a single well-defined criterion in a specific setting, the more reasonable it may be to select items which correlate with that criterion. However, such singleness of purpose in test usage is relatively rare. More commonly a test is developed to represent a domain of behavior or to predict a future performance which cannot be adequately defined by a single criterion variable. In such cases, selection of items which maximize the predictive power of the test for one particular criterion in one local setting, without requiring the items to have evidence of relationship to a broader construct of interest, will likely result in a test which will have limited usefulness in other settings, where the criteria or examinee populations differ even slightly. Thus many test developers write items to assess a trait of interest; select items from item analysis based on total score on the test; and later assess how test scores, as measures of the construct, are related to one or more external criterion variables.

In selecting field-tested items to retain for the test, the test developer usually encounters one of the following situations. In the first there are many more items than can be reasonably administered during routine test use, and to save on testing and scoring time, test users will want to administer as few items as necessary. Therefore the task is to select a subset of items which make the greatest contributions to the desired level of test score reliability or validity or with as few items as possible. The usefulness of the item reliability index (or the item validity index) for this purpose has already been discussed. In the second situation the item pool is not overly large, and the test developer wants to retain every item which makes a positive contribution to the test score parameter of major interest. In this case, a minimum level must be established for the item discrimination parameter, and all items with a discrimination parameter greater than that minimum may be retained. Ebel's (1965b) suggested criterion may be employed for assessing the index of discrimination. For correlational indices the test developer often elects to keep every item that has an item criterion correlation significantly greater than .00.

For phi and point biserial correlations, a convenient approximation for the standard error for the Pearson product moment correlation can be used to establish this level by computing

$$\hat{\sigma}_\rho = \frac{1}{\sqrt{N-1}} \tag{14.12}$$

where N is the sample size. (In using this formula we are assuming a sample size of at least 50.) Usually the minimum critical value is set at 2 standard errors above .00. Thus for a sample of 101,

$$\hat{\sigma}_p = \frac{1}{10} = .10$$

and .00 + 2(.10) = .20. Thus we would want to retain items with point biserial values of .20 or greater.

The standard error for the biserial correlation can be estimated by the formula

$$\hat{\sigma}_{bis} = \frac{\sqrt{pq/(N-1)}}{Y} \tag{14.13}$$

where p is the proportion answering the item correctly; $q = (1 - p)$; N is sample size, and Y is the ordinate of the normal curve at the value of p (Kurtz and Mayo, 1979). Again, this standard error may be used to generate the upper bound of an interval around .00, so that items with correlations greater than those expected by chance can be identified. The standard error of the biserial correlation will be smallest when $p = .50$ and will increase as p-values become extreme. Thus the stability of this statistic from sample to sample is strongly affected by item difficulty.

In developing an item selection strategy, the novice test developer may wonder how item difficulty data should influence the decision. Several points are relevant to this issue. First, item difficulty is rarely a primary criterion for item selection. For norm-referenced tests, it is generally less important than item discrimination. Second, p-values will vary from sample to sample. (The amount of sampling error in item difficulty can be estimated by using the standard error of a proportion, $\hat{\sigma}_p = \sqrt{pq/N}$, where N is the sample size.) Finally, for a test expected to discriminate reliably across a broad range of ability, items should be of uniform moderate difficulty. For years commercial test publishers constructed tests so that they consisted of a nearly even mixture of low-, medium-, and high-difficulty items. Gradually, however, this practice has been replaced by the strategy of selecting items from the medium difficulty range, with adjustments for guessing on multiple-choice items.

Two studies influential in this practice were reported by Lord (1952) and Cronbach and Warrington (1952). In general both studies showed that when items are moderately correlated with total test scores (as is usually the case), items of uniformly medium difficulty will permit more reliable discriminations among examinees of nearly all ability levels than will a collection of items with a wider spread of difficulties. More specifically, Henryssen (1971) suggested that when the average biserial correlation between item and total test score is in the range .30 to .40, the ideal item difficulty level should be between .40 and .60; but as the average biserial correlation increases above .60, a wider range of item difficulties may be acceptable. The one recognized exception to this strategy is when the test scores will be used exclusively for decision making for examinees at the upper or lower end of the distribution. For example, if a test is to be used to select applicants into a competitive professional training program and only a handful of the most qualified applicants are to be chosen, it would be appropriate to select items with relatively low p-value (difficult items), as these are more likely to result in a test that discriminates among examinees in the ability range of interest. When a test is constructed for a select segment of the population, it is important for the test developer to state this intended usage clearly since the usefulness of the test for examinees at other ability levels will be lessened.

Using Item Analysis Data in Test Revision

The following case-study in item analysis is presented to illustrate (1) detection of flawed items and (2) use of examinee response data in diagnosing potential causes of item malfunction. Data are based on responses of 50 examinees to a 35-item classroom test in an undergraduate course where a norm-referenced grading policy is used. The instructor chooses the internal criterion of total test score in computing the item discrimination indices. Data for items 21 to 35 are shown in this example.

Table 14.4 exemplifies the output information from a typical computer program that performs item analysis. Two types of item discrimination statistics, item difficulty, and the proportion of examinees selecting each response are presented. For this situation, item discrimination statistics will be useful in identifying "problem" items, but difficulty level and response distribution pattern will be useful in diagnosing item construction flaws which may have resulted in the poor discrimination.

TABLE 14.4.   Illustrative Item Analysis Results from 50 Examinees on Items 21 to 35 of a 35-Item Test

	Item Responses (%)					Diff.	Index	Point Biserial
Item	1	2	3	4	Omit	p	Disc.	Corr.
21	24	4	52	16+	4	.16	.00	−.06
22*	4	40	56+	0	0	.56	.67	.48
23*	0	76+	12	12	0	.76	.50	.45
24	4	28+	28	32	8	.28	−.17	−.12
25	16	12	0	72+	0	.72	−.17	−.29
26	0	4	52	44+	0	.44	.00	−.11
27	92+	0	8	0	0	.92	.33	.45
28*	8	68+	0	20	4	.68	.83	.61
29*	24	12	56+	8	0	.56	.50	.46
30	88+	0	0	8	4	.88	.17	.31
31	68+	12	4	16	0	.68	.17	.15
32*	20	20	8	52+	0	.52	1.00	.73
33	8	16	60+	16	0	.60	.00	.06
34*	20	20	8	52+	0	.52	.83	.59
35*	80+	0	0	4	16	.80	.50	.43

+: the keyed response
*: an effectively discriminating item
__: a poorly discriminating item

Applying Ebel's criteria for D-values, we would consider items 22, 23, 28, 29, 32, 34, and 35 to be "good" items because their D-values exceed .40. If a minimum point biserial value is set at $.00 + 2\hat{\sigma}_p$, the minimum acceptable point biserial value for this sample of 50 is .29. Thus we would select the same items chosen by the D-index plus items 27 and 30. An asterisk beside the item number in Table 14.4 indicates that the item passed on both discrimination criteria. Such items would be retained without revision. To identify items which require revision, we may use Ebel's criterion of having a D-value less than .20. These items are identified by a line under the item number in Table 14.4. On this test the six "problem items" are 21, 24, 25, 26, 31, and 33. (Note that item 30 is the only item which has an acceptable point biserial value, but an unacceptable D. In this case we are more inclined to be guided by the point biserial, which is based on all examinees' responses.)

Item 21 is a negative discriminator according to the point biserial correlation. Its difficulty level ($p = .16$) appears to be very atypical among the items on this test. In examining the distribution of responses we see that 52% of the examinees chose response 3 instead of response 4, which is keyed as the right answer. Since this is an abnormally high percentage of examinees choosing the same incorrect answer, one logical possibility is that the item has actually been miskeyed. A check of the content revealed that this was indeed the case. Item 24, also a negative discriminator, appears to be more difficult than would be ideally expected ($p = .28$). The responses are distributed almost equally across three possible choices, so it appears that examinees might have been responding at random. The relatively large number of "omits" also indicates that some examinees were confused about what was being asked. Such a pattern of responses suggests three possibilities. The wording of the item stem was so ambiguous that examinees could not understand the question, the item covered unfamiliar content for these examinees, or there is no correct response for this item. This item should probably be eliminated or rewritten completely.

Items 25 and 26 seem to have problems created by the content or construction of a particular response option. Item 25, the poorest discriminator, has a difficulty level ($p = .72$) which is only slightly greater than the ideal. From the response distribution, however, we see that option 3 has not been marked by a single examinee. The inclusion of a foil that is so obviously incorrect increases the chances that less-able examinees will select the correct answer by guessing. In revising this item, option 3 should be replaced by a more reasonable choice in the hope of attracting examinees who are uncertain of the correct response. It would also be advisable to check the answer sheets of several high-scoring examinees who missed the item to determine if they were attracted to a particular foil. Item 26, with $p = .44$, has two nonfunctional foils (options 1 and 2). A greater problem with this item, however, is that 52% of the examinees chose a single incorrect response. Obviously the content of the "correct" option should be reviewed to insure its accuracy; in addition, option 3 should be revised to make it less desirable. If option 3 is altered to make it less attractive, options 1 and 2 could also be rewritten to be more attractive. It should be noted that sometimes an ambiguity in the item stem causes large proportions of examinees to be attracted to a particular incorrect response. This possibility, too, should be checked.

For items 31 and 33, the item analysis results do not offer a particular clue to the cause of the poor discrimination. Careful examination of these items' content and perhaps a check of the incorrect responses chosen by high-scoring examinees may be necessary to identify the problem.

Finally, even though item 35 appears to have been a highly effective discriminator, this was achieved because a substantial percentage of the group did not answer the item. Because it is the last item on the test, we might suspect that the time limit should be extended slightly to allow all examinees adequate time to complete the test.

In classroom testing, most authorities recommend that item analysis data should be used as a basis for future test revision but do not advise discarding items in computing scores for the current class. When students took the test they assumed that all items would be counted, and they would probably not regard the grading policy as "fair" if the instructor elects to base their grades on only a subset of the items after the test is given. Furthermore, Cox (1965) demonstrated that a classroom test constructed only on the basis of item discrimination indices "would not validly measure the instructional objectives specified in the planning stage." In development of an experimental form of a test to be used for evaluation or research purposes, the scores of individual examinees who participated in the item analysis study are not of interest in themselves. In this case, the test developer may simply want to discard flawed items. For this reason it is advisable to produce and field-test more items than will be needed for each objective or content area, thus ensuring that an adequate number of good items will be available to construct a final test that is balanced appropriately in content. Finally, if the test constructor is responsible for ongoing maintenance of an item bank, the data may be used to identify items which are ready for immediate use. In addition, however, these data may be used to revise faulty items that can be field-tested again. Lange, Lehmann, and Mehrens (1965) demonstrated that in such cases construction of new items required almost five times longer than revision of existing items. Thus it would be inefficient to discard flawed items without attempting to revise them if future test forms over the same material will be needed.

Cross Validation

When items are selected on the basis of a statistical criterion using the responses of a given sample, the test thus constructed should be quite effective for that particular sample—more effective than it would be for any other sample of examinees. This was dramatically demonstrated by Cureton (1950), who described the development of a test in which he selected items on which students with high GPAs had fared better than students with low GPAs. Then using the same set of item responses, he recomputed total scores for each student on only the selected items and correlated these with their GPAs. The resulting correlation was .80. Only later did Cureton reveal that the "items" in this test were label tags in a cocktail shaker, and each student's responses were obtained by dumping the tags onto a table and awarding the student points for each tag that landed "face up." On each toss, there was an equal chance that a tag would land face up or face down. By random chance, some tags landed face up for a greater proportion of high-GPA students than for low-GPA students. These were the "items" retained from the item analysis. When only these items were counted and the students' total scores were computed with the same data, performance on these items appeared to be closely related to GPA. This apparently strong relationship would vanish, however, if the study were replicated and the tags were thrown again. Cross validation is analogous to putting the selected items back into the shaker and dumping them out again to see if the same items will function effectively a second time. To conduct a cross-validation study, the test developer uses only items that have been selected from the item analysis. These items are administered to a second, independent sample of examinees, and the reliability and/or validity of their scores is determined by using procedures described in Chapters 7 and 10, respectively.

Because of the effort involved in test administration, it is common in an item analysis/cross-validation study to try to collect data for both phases of the study in one testing session. This is done by administering all items in the item pool to all available examinees. Each test paper is randomly assigned to the item analysis or cross-validation condition. If, for example, 400 examinees were tested on 30 items, their answer sheets would be randomly divided into two groups of 200 each. The test developer would then use one set of 200 answer sheets to conduct an item analysis. On the basis of this analysis, suppose that 20 items were selected for the final version of the test. For the second set of 200 answer sheets, only 20 items would be used for cross validation in determining the reliability and validity estimates of interest. At times the test developer may wish to study whether similar results would be obtained regardless of which group was used for item analysis and cross validation. This can be done by using sample 1 for item analysis and sample 2 for cross validation and then replicating the study by using sample 2 for the item analysis and sample 1 for the cross validation. This is known as *double cross validation*.

Obviously the need for cross validation means that more subjects must be available than those used in the item analysis. One question which sometimes occurs in item analysis/cross validation concerns the proportions of the examinee groups assigned to the two samples. Although a 50/50 split (used in the previous example) is most common, in some cases other divisions might be more sensible. If the original item pool consisted of 50 items and only 400 examinees were available, it would be preferable to use a larger proportion of the group for item analysis and a smaller proportion for cross validation. In this case, at least 250 examinees could probably be used for the item analysis, leaving 150 examinees for the cross validation. (Note that this split was determined by following the rule of having 5 examinees per item in the item analysis study.)

ITEM ANALYSIS FOR CRITERION-REFERENCED TESTS

The usual purpose of a criterion-referenced test (CRT) is to assess performance on a set of tasks representative of a well-defined domain. For this reason CRT developers invariably employ some techniques for assuring the content validity of test items through expert judgments, which have been discussed in Chapter 10. Yet examination of empirical item response data may also be appropriate in development of a criterion-referenced test. In examining item response data the test developer is seldom looking only for flawed items. Instead the entire instructional process, the test development plan, and the item itself are under scrutiny. When an examinee group does not perform as expected on a particular item, this failure may be due to inadequacies in the instruction, the test specifications or objectives, or the construction of the item. The purpose of item analysis for CRTs is usually to investigate whether factors extraneous to the specified domain have contributed to performance on the test items. For this reason, early proponents of CRT were quick to point out that item statistics should not be a function of the item score variance for a single examinee group (see Millman and Popham, 1974; Popham and Husek, 1969). Thus the item discrimination indices described in earlier sections of this chapter seem inappropriate for CRTs.

Just as for norm-referenced tests, item analysis for CRTs should be undertaken with a clear purpose in mind. Specifically the test developer should know why information on item responses is needed and how it will be used. In certain situations, one or more of the following questions may be appropriate:

1. What is the item difficulty level?
2. Is the item sensitive to instruction (i.e., does it discriminate between those who have had the instruction and those who have not)?
3. Is there agreement among response patterns for particular items, as would be hypothesized from the test specifications?

A variety of item statistics have been suggested to answer these questions. One or more of each type will be presented here; the procedures described were chosen for their general applicability, ease of computation, and unambiguous interpretation. Readers interested in more detailed discussions of these and other analytic methods of CRT items should consult Berk (1980b); Harris, Pearlman, and Wilcox (1977); Harris, Alkin, and Popham (1974); and Lord (1980).

Item Difficulty

The difficulty level of a CRT item is generally defined as the proportion of examinees who answer the item correctly (p). Earlier discussion of this concept is relevant here except that the CRT developer should not be concerned with selecting items to maximize variance. The examination of item difficulty may, nonetheless, still be important. It is probably reasonable to determine the average or median difficulty level for each cluster of items that measures a common objective. This value can be useful for assessing the effectiveness of instruction on that objective or the adequacy of the item specification. For example, items that are extremely easy on a pretest should cause the test developer to ask whether instruction in this particular content is necessary or redundant for these examinees. Items that are extremely difficult for a group after instruction may indicate that the instruction was ineffective or that the item specification includes content or processes not covered by the instructional objective. A single item that is far easier or harder than others based on the same objective should be examined for technical flaws, unintentional clues, miskeying, or ambiguities in wording that may affect difficulty regardless of subject content. The variability among difficulties for items measuring a common objective may also provide useful information. When the difficulty levels of items tapping one objective are highly variable (and this is not because of one or two technically flawed items), review of the objective or item specification seems in order.

Instructional Sensitivity

A measure of the instructional sensitivity of an item is basically a measure of how well that item discriminates between examinees who have received instruction and those who have not. Cox and Vargas (1966) suggested a procedure whereby the same group is pretested before and posttested after instruction. The discrimination statistic is defined as

$$D = p_{post} - p_{pre} \tag{14.14}$$

where p_{post} is the proportion who answer the item correctly on the posttest and p_{pre} the proportion who answer correctly on the pretest. Values for D may range from -1.00 to 1.00, with high positive values desirable. A variation on this formula uses the responses of two separate groups, one which has received instruction and one which has not. Brennan (1972) proposed a procedure requiring use of a mastery cutoff score

$$B = (U/n_1) - (L/n_2) \tag{14.15}$$

where n_1 is the number who score above the mastery cutoff and n_2 the number below, U is the number above the cutoff who answer the item correctly, and L is the number below the cutoff who answer correctly. Because B is the difference between two proportions, it also ranges from -1.00 to 1.00, with high positive values desirable. Note that B is a measure of an item's ability to discriminate at a particular cut score.

   When the test developer wants to identify which items are relatively more or less effective in discriminating between instructed and uninstructed groups, several correlational procedures may also be used. Berk (1980b) suggested use of a correlational procedure derived by Saupe (1966) for selecting items for instruments designed to measure change. Use of this formula requires that each item be administered to the same group in a pretest, posttest design. Each examinee's item change score is computed as 1, 0, or −1, respectively, indicating a gain of 1 point from pre- to posttest, no gain, or a loss of 1 point on that item. In addition, the examinee's total scores on both pre- and posttests are computed along with the total change score defined as

$$D_{total} = Y - X \tag{14.16}$$

where Y is the total score on the posttest and X is the total pretest score. For each item the correlation between item change score and total change score can be computed by the Pearson product moment correlation between item change score and total change score. Saupe (1966) suggested a computational alternative formula for this correlation which yields results that are identical to the product moment correlation between item change score and total change score.

Two other procedures for assessing instructional sensitivity have been described by Millman (1974). For these the test developer must have item response data from separate instructed and uninstructed examinee groups. Through either partial correlation or stepwise regression, both of these methods allow the test developer to begin with a small subset of items and assess the test's improvement in instructional sensitivity with the inclusion of each additional item.

It should be noted that selection (or even revision) of items on the basis of instructional sensitivity indices may be philosophically incompatible with the purpose for which the CRT was originally developed. If the original item pool represented objectives defined by experts and constituted what examinees should know, the items sensitive to instruction may constitute only a subset of that content domain (i.e., what was taught effectively). Suppose, for example, that on one important objective, no instruction and no learning occurred. If items were selected on the basis of high values of D (Cox and Vargas, 1966) or B (Brennan, 1972), all items on this objective would be eliminated from the test. Obviously, the elimination of these items would not improve the content validity of this CRT. Further, a procedure such as Saupe's correlation of item change scores is actually designed to yield a norm-referenced measure of change; such an index results in selection of items on which there is variability in the change scores, which may not be a primary goal for the CRT developer. Thus it may not be reasonable to compute indices of instructional sensitivity routinely for every CRT. It is important to have a sound rationale for use of such information and to recognize that selection of items on the basis of such statistical criteria may not be consistent with domain mastery approaches to measurement. Instructional sensitivity indices may, however, provide useful information about the type of content that is being taught effectively or ineffectively in a particular instructional program. Use of item analysis data in this way presupposes that the test user has confidence in the item quality.

Indices of Agreement

There may be times when the test developer is interested in studying similarity of responses of one group of examinees to each possible pair of items written from the same specifications. This might be reasonable for situations in which subsequent tests will be developed by selecting items at random from the set of items now being field-tested, and the test developer wants to know if the items can be considered "interchangeable." In this case, data for each pair of item responses can be arranged in a fourfold table such as Table 14.5. Harris and Pearlman (1977) discussed a variety of statistical indices which can be applied to such data. The selection of the appropriate statistic depends on what the test developer wants to know. Some illustrative questions that a test developer might ask and a few of the indices described by Harris and Pearlman will be used to illustrate this item analytic approach. Additional probability models for the examination of item equivalence have been described by Wilcox (1977b). These models are more complex because they take into account the possibility of inappropriate responses by examinees (i.e., that an examinee may know an answer but make an incorrect response and vice versa). The procedures described here do not allow for this possibility.

As an initial example, consider the test developer who wants to know "if two items are measuring the same thing." In this case, it is appropriate to use a test of statistical independence for the responses to the two items. A simple chi square statistic can be computed with the formula

$$\chi^2 = \frac{n(ad - bc)^2}{(a + b)(c + d)(b + d)(a + c)} \tag{14.17}$$

where n is the number of persons in the sample, and a, b, c, and d are the cell frequencies in Table 14.5. This computation is illustrated in Table 14.6. This computed χ^2 statistic is compared to the value of χ^2 with 1 degree of freedom at the

TABLE 14.5. Fourfold Table for Displaying Responses to a Pair of Items

Item 1

		+	−
Item 2	+	a	b
	−	c	d

(a)

Item 1

		+	−
Item 2	+	20	5
	−	5	20

(b) Frequencies for 50 examinees.

TABLE 14.6. Illustrative Applications for Indices of Agreement and Association for Item Data from Table 14.5(b)

Illustrative Question	Formula	Computation	Illustrative Interpretation
Do these two items measure the same thing?	$\chi^2 = \dfrac{n(ad - bc)^2}{(a + b)(c + d)(b + d)(a + c)}$	$\dfrac{50(400 - 25)^2}{(30)(30)(30)(30)} = 8.68$	This computed χ^2 value exceeds the test statistic of 3.84 (for alpha = .05). Therefore the dependence in responses to these two items is significant, supporting the interpretation that the items measure the same skill or content.
What proportion of examinees passed or failed both items?	$P = (a + d)/n$	$(20 + 20)/50 = .80$	There is consistent performance on these two items for 80% of the examinees.
Did examinees perform significantly better on one item than on the other?	$\chi^2 = \dfrac{(|b - c| - 1)^2}{b + c}$	$\dfrac{(|5 - 5| - 1)^2}{5 + 5} = .10$	The computed χ^2 value does not exceed the test statistic (3.84 at alpha = .05). We fail to find a significant difference in item difficulties and thus cannot conclude that examinees have learned the content measured by one item better than the content measured by the other item.

desired alpha level. If the computed value of the test statistic is significant (as we find in our example), the responses to the two items may be regarded as dependent or associated. Failure to find a significant association between the responses to two items written from the same item specification should raise some question about the adequacy of the item specification or the technical quality of one or both of the items involved.

Finding that there is greater similarity in examinees' responses than would be expected by chance, the test developer may next wish to compute a statistic which describes the degree of that similarity. One statistic which is readily interpretable is simply the proportion of agreement, $(a + d)/n$. This is simply the proportion of examinees who responded consistently to the two items. See Table 14.6 for an illustrative computation and interpretation of this statistic. Harris and Pearlman (1977) favor this statistic because it can be averaged and meaningfully interpreted over multiple item pairs and because it is an unbiased estimator. Other statistics suitable for describing the degree of agreement in responses to a pair of items would be coefficient kappa (described in Chapter 8), Yule's Q (recommended by Harris and Pearlman), or the phi coefficient.

A slightly different question is whether the difficulties of two items are equal in the population of examinees. Put another way, the question is whether observed differences in difficulty are small enough to be attributed to sampling errors. Such a question would be appropriate if the test developer hypothesizes that because of the instructional program, the content of the two items should have been learned equally well, and the developer wishes to test this hypotheses. In this case, Harris and Pearlman suggest a χ^2 statistic of the form

$$\chi^2 = \frac{(|b - c| - 1)^2}{b + c} \tag{14.18}$$

This computed statistic is again contrasted to the value of χ^2 at 1 degree of freedom at the desired alpha level. A significant value indicates a difference in item difficulties for the sample of examinees that is too large to attribute to chance. (See Table 14.6 for this computation applied to our two-item example.)

In general, indices of item agreement may be appropriate when specific questions arise about how examinees have performed on particular pairs of items. Different questions require use of different statistical indices. It is unlikely that applying one or more of these indices to all possible pairs of items on a large test would yield meaningful information. For small item subsets (e.g., items written from the same specification or matched to the same objective in a content validation study), indices of agreement may provide empirical evidence to support rational judgments about item similarity. On some criterion-referenced tests, examinees' performance is reported separately for a number of different objectives or skill areas, often with only a small number of items measuring each objective. In such cases, investigation of the degree of agreement on item performance within objective or skill seems warranted to support the intended test score interpretations.

As a final comment, which applies to all item analyses methods for CRT, we note that Harris (1974) and Harris, Pearlman, and Wilcox (1977) took the position that if items are randomly selected from an item pool to represent a carefully structured content domain, no item should be deleted on the basis of item analysis. They contend that careful review of items during the test construction phase and a sound test development plan should be sufficient to achieve valid test scores. The role of item analysis data would be only to provide information about where the instructional system or the test development plan has failed. This view seems to imply that item writers for such a test are immune from producing flawed items, or that valid inferences about examinees' performance can still be drawn from "bad" items. This position has been criticized by Messick (1975) and has led Petersen (1979) to question whether it is reasonable to rely on samples of items in test construction when the goal is to infer to performance on some larger item domain. Thus the test user should be aware that the ways in which item analysis data are used may rest on different philosophical views about test construction and test score interpretation.

SUMMARY

Item analysis is the computation and examination of any statistical property of an item response distribution. For dichotomously scored items, the best-known descriptor is probably item difficulty (p), which denotes the proportion of examinees answering the item correctly. Item p-values are not necessarily an index of item quality; however, for norm-referenced tests, items with p values near .50 will allow total score variance, and hence reliability, to be maximized. When multiple-choice items are used, some allowance for guessing must be made so that p-values greater than .50 are ideal for maximizing total score reliability.

Indicators of item discrimination are used to assess how well performance on an item relates to performance on some other criterion. This criterion may be the total score on the test or some other variable. When total test score is used, selection of highly discriminating items leads to higher internal consistency of test scores. For items not dichotomously scored, the Pearson product moment correlation may be useful in correlating item scores with criterion scores. When the items are dichotomously scored, useful indices may be the index of discrimination (D), the biserial correlation, or the point biserial correlation. These are appropriate when there is a continuous criterion score. When the criterion is dichotomized, the phi or tetrachoric coefficient may be useful. Comparisons of these five indices indicate that their results are usually highly correlated, with greatest differences occurring for items in extreme difficulty ranges. Thus the choice among these procedures should be made on the nature of the variables, the type of information desired, and computational considerations. Formulas for calculating the standard errors of these statistics were also presented.

The item reliability index is the product of the item score standard deviation and item correlation with total test score, and the item validity index is the product of the item score standard deviation and item score correlation with an external criterion.

Total test score variance and coefficient alpha may be estimated from the time reliability indices. The total test score validity coefficient may be estimated from the item reliability and validity indices.

Typically in an item analysis study, the test developer will decide on the properties of total test scores that are of greatest interest and identify the item parameters that have greatest effect on these properties. The items are administered to a sample of examinees (usually 100 or more), and the item responses are analyzed. A plan is established for selecting the items that make the greatest contributions to the test score characteristics of interest (and possibly for identifying how malfunctioning items should be revised). After the final subset of items is selected, it is administered to a second independent sample for cross validation. (In many cases, for convenience half of the original field-test sample is held in reserve to use in the cross-validation study.)

For criterion-referenced tests, traditional item analysis indices may not be appropriate because most item discrimination statistics are designed to favor items on which there is substantial variation among examinees. This is a goal more appropriate for a norm-referenced test. Nevertheless, developers of CRTs may be interested in item difficulties, item sensitivity to instruction, and degree of agreement among specific pairs of items. Some statistical procedures proposed in the literature for investigating these types of properties were presented. Finally, it is important to note that selection of items on the basis of item analysis data may be less appropriate for CRTs than for norm-referenced tests since the representatives of the domain of interest may be reduced by such item selection on statistical criteria. Even for norm-referenced tests, the nature of the construct being measured may be altered if items are selected purely on the basis of statistical criteria without regard to the initial test specifications.

Exercises

1. Consider the following test data for 2 items and 10 persons:

Person	Item 1	Item 2	Total Score
1	0	1	12
2	0	1	15
3	1	1	16
4	0	0	10
5	1	1	7
6	1	0	5
7	1	0	6
8	0	1	10
9	1	1	15
10	1	0	13

    A. What are the indices of discrimination for the two items based on a 50/50 split? What are they based on a top/bottom 27% split?

    B. What are the biserial $\hat{\rho}$ values for these two items?

C. What are the point biserial $\hat{p}$-values?

D. How do the underlying assumptions differ in use of a biserial vs. point biserial item/total score correlation?

2. Examine the item analysis information and answer the questions that follow:

Item Number	Item Responses				Other	Item Diff.	Item Discrim.	Point Biserial Corr.
	1	2	3	4				
21	11	5	149 +	11	0	0.84	0.15	0.23
22	34	11	127 +	4	0	0.72	0.30	0.27
23	11	4	32 +	128	1	0.18	−0.13	−0.13
24	30	34	1	111 +	0	0.63	0.64	0.52
25	6	0	20	150 +	0	0.85	0.34	0.34

A. Which item appears to be most in need of revision?

B. Items 21 and 25 are nearly equal in difficulty, yet their item discrimination values differ. How can this be explained?

C. If you wanted to improve item 21, how would you try to change it?

D. Suggest at least two plausible hypotheses to account for the negative discrimination of item 23.

E. Estimate the values of the biserial correlation between item and total score for items 24 and 25.

F. What is the minimum acceptable value for the point biserial correlation if the test developer wants to be 95% certain that this statistic is significantly greater than .00?

G. Assuming a random guessing model, what is the ideal difficulty level for these items if the test developer wishes to maximize test score reliability?

3. Assume that item 21 and 22 in the preceding example were drafted according to the same item specification. The bivariate response distribution for this pair of items is

Item 21

		+	−
Item 22	+	120	7
	−	29	20

A. What statistical procedure could be used to test the hypothesis that items 21 and 22 measure the same skill or knowledge? Make the computation and state your conclusion.

B. What statistical procedure could be used to test the hypothesis that item 22 is a more difficult item than item 21? Make the computation and state your conclusion.

C. Explain how the statistic used in Exercise 3.A is related to the phi coefficient. Do these two indices provide the same information?

4. For the following situation indicate which item analysis statistic would be most appropriate. Use this key to indicate your response:

1. Phi coefficient between item scores
2. Point biserial correlation between item and total score
3. Point biserial correlation between item and external criterion score

4. Pearson product moment correlation between item and total score
5. Pearson product moment correlation between item and score on an external criterion

A. A counselor or a college counseling center wishes to select valid items on an attitude scale, to be used for predicting the behavior of college males, where each item is scored 1 to 7 and the criterion is joining a social fraternity (students are coded as "members" or "nonmembers").
B. A test constructor desires to improve the test-retest reliability of a behavior checklist where each item is scored 1 point for "yes" and 0 for "no."
C. A college professor wishes to increase the internal consistency of a 50-item unit examination which consists of 4-choice items, scored with 1 point for each item answered correctly.
D. A psychologist wishes to identify Likert-type items on which his subjects' responses are influenced by their ages.
E. A psychologist has developed an inventory to assess racial prejudice. Each item is scored on a five-point scale and was generated from a specific account of a critical incident by a large cross-section of minority group members. The psychologist is unable to identify a single behavior (which it is feasible to observe in practical time limits) that can serve as a criterion.

5. A. Derive the formula for the point biserial correlation coefficient, beginning with the Pearson product moment formula.

$$\rho_{XY} = \frac{\Sigma(X - \mu_X)(Y - \mu_Y)}{N\sigma_X\sigma_Y}$$

where X is a dichotomous variable scored 0 or 1.

B. In light of this derivation, explain why point biserial correlation values of 1.00 are seldom observed.

6. Some authors have argued that in order for scores on an instrument to have any claim to content or construct validity, there should be evidence that each item on the test correlates with total test score. Since item correlation with total score is more directly related to internal consistency, what is the logical rationale for the authors' position?

7. A graduate student has designed a dissertation study which requires measurement of attitudes of the mothers of newborn infants who have certain birth defects. The student will be obtaining subjects from all hospitals in the community with maternity wards but still anticipates having only a small sample (approximately 25 to 30) over a one-year period. Faculty on the four-person advisory committee offer four separate suggestions:

1. Use the first 15 subjects for item analysis; refine the instrument and use the last 15 subjects in the study itself.
2. Use the instrument without any item analysis and take the chance that it will provide "good" information.
3. Administer all items to all subjects; do an item analysis and eliminate bad items; then rescore the instrument for the same subjects using only the "good" items.
4. Do not conduct the study.

Discuss the advantages and disadvantages of each suggestion and decide which you favor.

8. Suppose that the test developer is considering creating a subtest consisting only of the 15 items for whom item analysis data are presented in Table 14.4. Estimate the approximate variance and reliability of scores on this subtest.

Chapter 15

INTRODUCTION TO ITEM RESPONSE THEORY

In the preceding chapter we pointed out that item selection is often based on indices of difficulty and discrimination. Although this practice works effectively in many test construction situations, it is conceivable that test development decisions could be improved by using additional information about item responses. Consider the following two items and their respective response patterns:

1. Item A is answered correctly by all examinees who earned a score of 50 points or more on the test; it is answered incorrectly by all those who scored lower than 50.
2. Item B is answered correctly by 20% of the examinees who earned 45 points, by 40% of those who earned 50 points, by 60% of those who earned 55 points, by 80% of those who earned 60 points, and by all of those who earned 65 points or more.

Clearly there is a difference in the observed pattern of item responses to these two items, which might be important for the test developer to know; yet classical item analyses statistics do not provide information about how examinees at different ability levels on the trait have performed on the item. One approach to test development which yields a more complete picture of how an item functions is known as *item response theory* or *latent trait theory*.

With item response theory the test developer assumes that the responses to the items on a test can be accounted for by latent traits that are fewer in number than the test items. Indeed, most applications of the theory assume that a single latent trait accounts for the responses to items on a test. At the "heart" of the theory is a mathematical model of how examinees at different ability levels for the trait should respond to an item. This knowledge allows one to compare the performance of examinees who have taken different tests. It also permits one to apply the results of an item analysis to groups with different ability levels than the group used for the item analysis. Naturally these features have some useful applications, which will be described later in this chapter, in Chapter 16, and in Chapter 20. Other sources of information on practical applications are Hambleton (1983), Hambleton and Swaminathan (1985), Hambleton et al. (1978b), Hulin, Drasgow, and Parsons (1983), Lord (1980), and Traub and Wolfe (1981).

The intent of this chapter is to present the basic concepts and assumptions of item response theory and to introduce four latent trait models. For one of these models, the normal ogive model, relationships between the parameters of item response theory and those of classical test theory are presented. In addition, several applications of item response theory will be outlined. Before specific latent trait models and their applications can be presented, it is necessary to lay some conceptual groundwork. Specifically, the reader must understand

1. What is meant by a latent trait
2. What constitutes an item characteristic curve
3. What the assumption of local independence means and how it is related to the dimensionality of the test

These three concepts, basic to item response theory, are described in the following sections.

BASIC CONCEPTS OF ITEM RESPONSE THEORY

Latent Traits and Item Characteristic Curves

One central concept of item response theory is the item characteristic curve (ICC). An ICC plots the probability of responding correctly to an item as a function of the latent trait (denoted by θ) underlying performance on the items on the test. (In the next section we will state more precisely what is meant when we write that a latent trait underlies performance on the items on a test.) In most applications of item response theory the ICC is assumed to have an S shape, as illustrated in Figure 15.1. The graph shows that as the score on the latent trait increases, so does the probability of answering correctly. The importance of the ICC, in contrast to item difficulty and discrimination statistics discussed in Chapter 14, is that it permits us to see how the probability of answering correctly depends on the latent trait.

It is important to correctly interpret the probability of responding correctly to an item. According to Lord (1980) there are two acceptable interpretations. For the first we must conceptualize a subpopulation of examinees at each point on the latent trait scale. The defining characteristic of each subpopulation is that its members all have the same latent trait score. (In the remainder of the chapter members of such a subpopulation will be described as homogeneous with respect to the latent trait, and a subpopulation of such examinees will be called a *homogeneous subpopulation*.) The probability of responding correctly is then interpreted as the probability that a

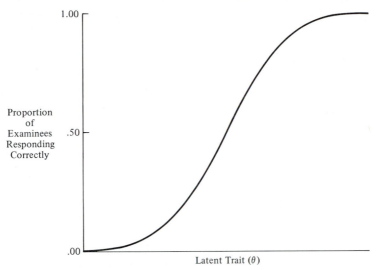

Proportion of Examinees Responding Correctly

1.00

.50

.00

Latent Trait (θ)

FIGURE 15.1   The Relationship Between Ability and Item Response

randomly chosen member of a homogeneous subpopulation will respond correctly to an item. Consider an ICC which indicates that for $\theta = 2$ the probability of responding correctly is .87. This can be interpreted to mean that the probability, that a randomly chosen examinee with $\theta = 2$ will respond correctly, is .87. An equivalent interpretation is that of the examinees with $\theta = 2$ the proportion who can answer the item correctly is .87. The second acceptable interpretation refers to a subpopulation of items all of which have the same ICC. The probability of responding correctly is then interpreted as the probability that a specific examinee will answer an item randomly chosen from the subpopulation of items. Lord (1980) specifically recommends against interpreting the probability of responding correctly as the probability that a specific examinee answers a specific item correctly. In this book we will use the first interpretation and to avoid confusion among the three interpretations will discuss the ICC as plotting the proportion of examinees who respond correctly to an item as a function of the latent trait scores.

Although the S-shaped ICC just presented is widely used in test construction, it is not the only possible type of ICC. In the ensuing discussion we will frequently discuss an ICC, such as the one in Figure 15.2. An ICC with this shape is called a *step function*. This ICC implies that there is a minimum latent trait score denoted by θ', below which examinees cannot answer the item correctly; however, any examinee with an ability level equal to or greater than θ' will respond correctly to the item. Such step functions are useful in introducing several important concepts of item response theory. However step function ICCs are less commonly used in test construction than are the S-shaped ICCs because actual test data are generally more consistent with the S-shaped curve.

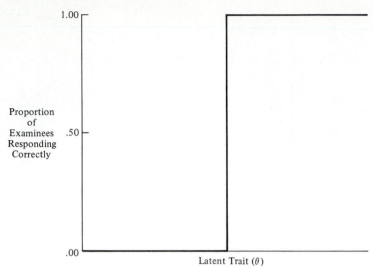

FIGURE 15.2   A Step Function ICC

Unidimensionality and Local Independence

In test theory the relationship between two variables is usually discussed in terms of whether the scores on the variables are correlated or uncorrelated. In item response theory it is common to use the more general concepts of statistical dependence and statistical independence to talk about the relationships between variables. For two dichotomously scored items these concepts can be defined in the following fashion. Let $P_i(+)$ denote the probability of answering the ith item correctly and $P_i(-)$ denote the probability of answering the ith item incorrectly. Let $P_j(+)$ and $P_j(-)$ denote the corresponding probabilities for the jth item. Further let $P(+,+)$, $P(-,-)$, $P(+,-)$ and $P(-,-)$ denote the probabilities of the response patterns defined in the parenthesis. For example $P(+,+)$ denotes the probability of answering the ith and jth item correctly. With these definitions, scores on two items are statistically independent if

$$P(+,+) = P_i(+)P_j(+), \qquad (15.1a)$$

$$P(+,-) = P_i(+)P_j(-), \qquad (15.1b)$$

$$P(-,+) = P_i(-)P_j(+), \qquad (15.1c)$$

and

$$P(-,-) = P_i(-)P_j(-), \qquad (15.1d)$$

and are statistically dependent if any of the four equalities is not met. For example if $P_i(+) = .8$, $P_i(-) = .2$, $P_j(+) = .6$ and $P_j(-) = .4$ then the scores on the two items are independent if and only if

$$P(+,+) = .48,$$

$$P(+,-) = .32,$$

$$P(-,+) = .12,$$

and

$$P(-,-) = .08.$$

Essentially the four conditions in Equation 15.1 say that items scores are independent if each probability of a response pattern to both items, that is the probability on the left side of the equation, can be calculated by knowing only the probabilities of the correct and incorrect responses to each item.

Unidimensionality is defined in terms of the statistical dependence among items. Specifically the requirement for a test to be unidimensional is that the statistical dependence among items can be accounted for by a single latent trait. This means that a test is unidimensional if its items are statistically dependent in the entire population, and a single latent trait exists such that the items are statistically independent in each subpopulation of examinees whose members are homogeneous with respect to the latent trait. Since this independence is defined for a subpopulation of examinees located at a single point on the latent trait scale, it is called *local independence*.

Two points are quite important here. The first is that local independence and unidimensionality are not equivalent concepts. For example, a test is bidimensional if two latent traits exist such that for examinees who are homogeneous with respect to both latent traits the items are independent. In general the dimensionality of a test is equal to the number of latent traits required to achieve local independence. The second point is that we can never say with certainty that a single latent trait (or any other number of latent traits for that matter) exists such that the items are locally independent. Thus local independence and the number of latent traits are always a matter of assumption. However it is possible to check the validity of these assumptions, and we will give references to the relevant literature subsequently.

Earlier we promised to state more precisely what is meant when we write that a latent trait underlies performance on the items on a test. This is simply to say that the latent trait accounts for the statistical dependence among the items. As such the latent trait is not necessarily a valid measure of the construct the test is intended to measure. Just as it is possible for a set of test scores to have high reliability but low validity, so it is possible for a latent trait to underlie performance on a set of items but be a poor measure of the construct the items were intended to measure. This, of course, implies that the items are poor measures of the construct. Thus we should not equate the notion of a latent trait with the more general notion of a construct.

To illustrate the concepts of unidimensionality and local independence, consider a hypothetical example in which a population of 200 examinees takes a test consisting of four items. Although it would be unlikely in a real testing situation, suppose that

TABLE 15.1. Response Patterns to a Hypothetical Four-Item Test

Response Pattern	Item			
	1	2	3	4
a	−	−	−	−
b	+	−	−	−
c	+	+	−	−
d	+	+	+	−
e	+	+	+	+

A "−" indicates an incorrect response and a "+" indicates a correct response.

only the five response patterns presented in Table 15.1 are observed. The responses of 40 examinees conform to each of the five patterns. These five response patterns are said to form a perfect Guttman scale. (Scales of this type were briefly discussed in Chapter 3.)

The response patterns in Table 15.1 are consistent with the idea that responses to all items depend on a single latent trait and that the ICC for each item is a step function. The step function ICCs for all four items in our example are presented in Figure 15.3. The symbols θ_1, θ_2, θ_3, and θ_4 denote the minimum latent trait scores required to respond correctly to items 1, 2, 3, and 4, respectively. An examinee with latent ability below θ_1 responds incorrectly to all four items and therefore has response pattern $-,-,-,-$. An examinee with latent ability between values θ_1 and θ_2 answers the first item correctly and the remaining items incorrectly, thus earning a response pattern $+,-,-,-$. The response patterns for examinees at other points on the latent trait scale are indicated on the horizontal axis of Figure 15.3.

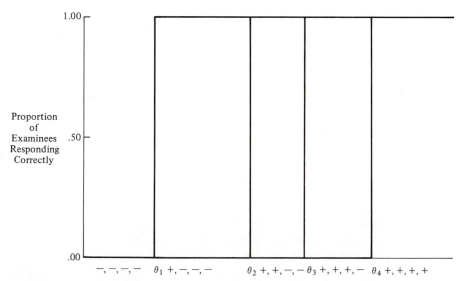

FIGURE 15.3 Step Function ICCs for a Four-Item Test

TABLE 15.2.   Joint Distribution of Responses for the Population

		Item 4 +	Item 4 −	
	+	.20	.20	.4
Item 3				
	−	.00	.60	.6
		.2	.8	

Now let us focus just on items 3 and 4. The probabilities of each possible response pattern to these items are presented in Table 15.2. These are the probabilities for the entire population of 200 examinees. By definition, the responses to these items are statistically independent if and only if Equations 15.1 hold. If we use the probabilities in Table 15.2 it is clear that Equations 15.1 do not hold for items 3 and 4. For example $P(+,+) = .20$, but $P_3(+)P_4(+) = (.2)(.4) = .08$ so $P(+,+) \neq P_3(+)P_4(+)$, and the items are statistically dependent for the entire population of 200 examinees. As a result we can view these two items as sharing a common source of variance. By using the same process with every pair of items, it can be shown that the item responses are dependent for each pair of items on the test.

The requirement for unidimensionality, however, is that a single latent trait exists such that all item pairs are locally independent. This means that the items must be statistically independent for any given subpopulation homogeneous with respect to the latent trait. We begin by examining whether items 3 and 4 are locally independent for examinees whose latent ability is equal to θ_3. (These examinees exhibit response pattern d in Table 15.1.) Table 15.3 reports the probabilities of each possible response pattern to items 3 and 4 for the subpopulation of examinees with a latent trait score θ_3. For their responses to be statistically independent the following relationships must hold:

$$P(+,+|\theta_3) = P_i(+|\theta_3)P_j(+|\theta_3) \qquad (15.2a)$$

$$P(+,-|\theta_3) = P_i(+|\theta_3)P_j(-|\theta_3) \qquad (15.2b)$$

TABLE 15.3.   Joint Distribution of Responses for the Subpopulation with $\theta = \theta_3$

		Item 4 +	Item 4 −	
	+	.00	1.00	1.00
Item 3				
	−	.00	.00	.00
		.00	1.00	

$$P(-,+|\theta_3) = P_i(-|\theta_3)P_j(+|\theta_3) \tag{15.2c}$$

$$P(-,-\theta|_3) = P_i(-\theta|_3)P_j(-|\theta_3) \tag{15.2d}$$

The notation indicates that all probabilities are defined for a subpopulation located at θ_3 on the trait. From the probabilities reported in Table 15.3 it is clear that all four relationships hold. Therefore items 3 and 4 are statistically independent for examinees with latent trait score $\theta = \theta_3$. Again, working through the same process for every pair of items and for every point on the latent continuum, we can show that the responses to all pairs of items are statistically independent once the latent trait score is held constant. Therefore the items are locally independent.

We have shown, then, that the item responses are dependent in the whole population and therefore share one or more common sources of variance. We have also shown that a latent trait exists such that for examinees who are homogeneous with respect to the latent trait, the items are locally independent. Therefore the common variance shared by the items is entirely accounted for by this single latent trait, and as a result, the test meets the requirements for unidimensionality.

Test-Free Measurement

An important point about latent trait models is that they permit examinees to be compared even when the examinees have not taken the same items. This is sometimes referred to as *test-free measurement*. To illustrate this property, suppose that an examiner knows that four items have the step function ICCs illustrated in Figure 15.3. The examiner administers the two easiest items to one examinee and the two hardest items to a second examinee. The first examinee answers the first item correctly and the second item incorrectly, and so the examiner concludes that the examinee's ability falls in the interval $\theta_1 \leq \theta < \theta_2$. The second examinee answers the third item correctly and the fourth incorrectly, and the examiner concludes that the examinee's latent ability falls in the interval $\theta_3 \leq \theta < \theta_4$. The examiner can conclude that examinee 1 has less ability than examinee 2. This example illustrates that with latent trait theory, examinees can be placed on the same scale even when they take tests containing different items, provided of course that all items measure the same latent trait. In this example, precise comparison of the two examinees' abilities was not possible because of the length of the tests. Clearly, if a larger number of items with step function ICCs could be constructed, more precise comparisons would be possible. Moreover the capability of placing examinees who have taken different tests on a common scale carries over to tests composed of items that are characterized by ICCs of other forms. Rentz and Bashaw (1977) and Marco (1977) report equating studies that use latent trait theory and depend on test-free measurement.

THE NORMAL OGIVE

As noted earlier, most applications of latent trait theory assume that the ICC has an *S* shape. One such ICC with this shape is the normal ogive, which was used in much

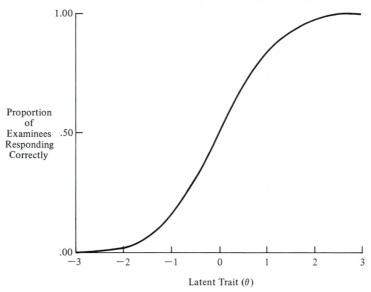

FIGURE 15.4   A Normal Ogive ICC, Mean Ability = 0 and Standard Deviation = 1

of the early work on latent trait theory (see Lawley, 1943; Lord, 1952b, 1953). Figure 15.4 illustrates several important properties of a normal ogive ICC:

1. Going from left to right, the curve rises continually. Such a curve is said to increase monotonically.
2. The lower asymptote of the normal ogive approaches, but never quite reaches, 0. The upper asymptote approaches 1.
3. The normal ogive is directly related to the normal distribution discussed in Chapter 2. There we learned that when scores are expressed as z-scores, we can use the table of the standard normal distribution to obtain the area under the normal curve to the left of any z-score. The area to the left of any z-score is a number less than 1 and can therefore be interpreted as a proportion. The standard normal ogive graphs these proportions as a function of the z-score.

When the normal ogive curve is used as an ICC, values on the horizontal axis represent the possible values of θ, the latent trait. The height of the curve above any given value of θ represents the proportion of examinees at that ability level who can answer the item correctly. The equation for the normal ogive ICC is typically written in a fashion similar to:

$$P_g(\theta) = \int_{-\infty}^{w} f(z)\, dz \qquad (15.3)$$

where the quantity $P_g(\theta)$ is the proportion of examinees with latent ability θ who answer item g correctly. The expression on the right side is the cumulative normal ogive. It means that the area between $-\infty$ and w under the normal ogive must be calculated. The quantity w is a real number and is determined by the equation

$$w = a(\theta - b) \qquad (15.4)$$

where a is a discrimination parameter for that item and b is a difficulty parameter for that item. (The parameters a and b are not, however, the discrimination and difficulty parameters from classical test theory.)

The quantity w, or its equivalent expression $a(\theta - b)$, is similar to a z-score in that $P_g(\theta)$ represents the area to the left of $a(\theta - b)$ in a standard normal distribution. Thus if an examinee has a latent ability score of $\theta = 2$, and the ICC for item g has the parameter values $a = .5$ and $b = 1.0$, for this examinee on item g,

$$w = a(\theta - b) = .5(2 - 1.0) = .5$$

Since the area to the left of .5 in the standard normal distribution is .69, use of Equation 15.3 implies that 69 percent of the examinees with $\theta = 2$ answer the item correctly. Thus if we have estimates of the a and b values for item g, and we want to know the proportion of examinees with a certain latent ability who should answer that item correctly, we simply

1. Compute the value $a(\theta - b)$, and
2. Use that value, like a z-score, to look up the $P_g(\theta)$ in a standard normal z-table.

It is important to remember that the values of the a and b parameters will vary over items on a test. Therefore in literature dealing with ICCs, these values are often denoted as a_g and b_g, where the subscript g denotes item g on a test. Thus the formal equation for the normal ogive function is usually written as

$$P_g(\theta) = \int_{-\infty}^{a_g(\theta - b_g)} f(z)\, dz \qquad (15.5)$$

where $w_g = a_g(\theta - b_g)$. To see how the difficulty parameter, b_g, operates, let us consider three items which have the same value for a_g but different values for b_g; these values are $b_1 = .5$, $b_2 = 1.0$, and $b_3 = 1.5$. The three ICCs are depicted in Figure 15.5. For each ICC the vertical dotted line indicates the latent trait score for which $P_g(\theta) = .5$. Beginning at the left, these three scores are $\theta = .5$, 1.0, and 1.5. Note that for item 1, $P_g(\theta) = .5$ when $\theta = b_1$. Similarly for item 2, $P_g(\theta) = .5$ when $\theta = b_2$; and for item 3, $P_g(\theta) = .5$ when $\theta = b_3$. Thus b_g is equal to the latent trait score at which half of the examinees answer item g correctly.

To see how the discrimination parameter, a_g, operates, consider the three ICCs in Figure 15.6. Each ICC has $b = 1.5$, but the a values for the three curves are $a_1 = .1$, $a_2 = 1$, and $a_3 = 100$. Looking at Figure 15.6 we see that the first item does not discriminate very effectively because the proportion of examinees answering an item correctly is nearly the same at every latent trait score. However, the third item, with $a_3 = 100$, discriminates very effectively between examinees with scores less than 1.45 and those with scores greater than 1.55. Indeed, for examinees with $\theta \leq 1.45$ the proportion responding correctly is less than .01, whereas for examinees with $\theta \geq 1.55$ the proportion responding correctly is greater than .99.

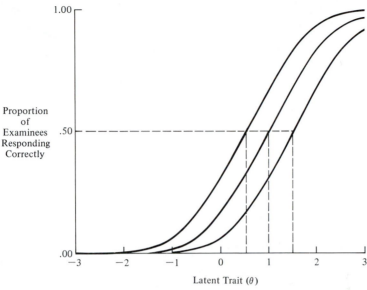

FIGURE 15.5   Three Normal Ogives with $b_1 = .5$, $b_2 = 1.0$, and $b_3 = 1.5$

Finally the second item, with $a_2 = 1$, is intermediate in terms of its discrimination. Thus a_g *is a parameter which defines the slope or steepness of the ICC.* Items that are ineffective in discriminating between different ability levels have relatively flat ICCs and low values of a_g. Items that discriminate sharply between examinees above and below a certain ability will have a steep ICC and high values of a_g. Items that discriminate moderately well across a broader range of ability levels will have a moderate rate of increase in the steepness of the ICC and thus moderate values of a_g.

The Scale of Measurement

The latent trait scale determined from Equation 15.4 has an arbitrary origin and unit of measurement. The arbitrary origin means that any one of the homogeneous subpopulations can be assigned a score of 0 since none of the subpopulations is characterized by a complete absence of the latent trait. The arbitrary unit of measurement means that after one group is assigned a score of 0, any other homogeneous subpopulation, whose members have more latent ability than members of the zero subpopulation, can be assigned a score of 1. The ability difference between these two subpopulations is then the unit of measurement. Since the unit and origin is arbitrary, it is common to choose the origin and unit so that the mean latent trait score is 0 and the standard deviation is 1 for some population of interest. As a result it is common to find ICCs drawn as in Figure 15.5, with a scale that includes both positive and negative numbers.

The values of b_g and a_g are dependent on unit and scale chosen for θ. If the unit

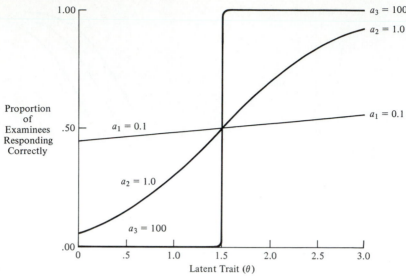

FIGURE 15.6   Three Normal Ogives with $a_1 = 0.1$, $a_2 = 1.0$, and $a_3 = 100$

and scale are changed, the values of a_g and b_g change also. Changing the unit and scale of the original latent trait scores which are denoted by θ is equivalent to transforming θ by the equation

$$\theta' = k\theta + m \tag{15.6}$$

where k and m are any real numbers. The quantity θ' is a score on the new scale. When θ is transformed to θ', b_g and a_g are transformed as follows:

$$b'_g = kb_g + m \tag{15.7a}$$

and

$$a'_g = a_g/k \tag{15.7b}$$

We can easily show that $a'_g(\theta' - b'_g) = a_g(\theta - b_g)$ and therefore $P_g(\theta)$ does not change if the unit and scale of measurement for the latent trait are changed.

RELATING ITEM RESPONSE THEORY TO CLASSICAL TEST THEORY

ICC Parameters and Classical Item Statistics

Let ρ_g be the biserial correlation between the scores on item g and the latent trait scores. Clearly this correlation is similar to item total score biserial, which is used as a discrimination index in classical test theory item analysis. If θ is normally distributed with mean 0 and standard deviation 1,

$$a_g = \frac{\rho_g}{\sqrt{1 - \rho_g^2}} \tag{15.8}$$

TABLE 15.4. Correspondence between a_g and ρ_g

ρ_g	a_g
.1	.10
.2	.20
.3	.31
.4	.44
.5	.58
.6	.75
.7	.98
.8	1.33
.9	2.06

Thus if an item has a biserial correlation of $\rho_g = .30$ with the latent trait, the value of the a parameter for the item characteristic curve is

$$a_g = \frac{.30}{\sqrt{1 - .30^2}} = .31.$$

Table 15.4 presents values of a_g corresponding to several values of ρ_g. The table shows that as ρ_g approaches 1, a_g increases, and intuitively this relationship supports the interpretation of a_g as a discrimination parameter.

The difficulty parameter of the ICC, b_g, can also be related to classical item analysis indices. Under the normality assumption it can be shown that

$$b_g = \frac{-\Phi^{-1}(p_g)}{\rho_g} \tag{15.9}$$

where p_g is the proportion-correct measure of item difficulty for item g, and $\Phi^{-1}(p_g)$ is the z-score that cuts off the area p_g to the left of z in the standard normal distribution. Thus if p_g is known, the value $\Phi^{-1}(p_g)$ can be obtained using a table such as the one in Appendix A. For example, if $p_g = .84$, $\Phi^{-1}(p_g) = 1.00$. If ρ_g for this item is .30, the value of b_g can be computed as

$$b_g = \frac{-1.00}{.30} = -3.33$$

Test Characteristic Curves and Classical Reliability

The true score on a test has a relationship to θ that can be expressed in terms of the ICCs. Explicitly,

$$T = \sum_g P_g(\theta) \tag{15.10}$$

Equation 15.10 is true regardless of the form of the ICC, and it shows that the relationship between T and θ is not statistical. The true score is a nonlinear transformation of the latent trait. Table 15.5 presents the relationship between θ and T for a hypothetical three-item test.

TABLE 15.5.   Relationship Between Latent Trait and True Scores

θ	$P_1(\theta)$	$P_2(\theta)$	$P_3(\theta)$	True Score
-2	.022	.105	.382	.51
-1	.158	.226	.460	.84
0	.500	.401	.539	1.44
1	.841	.636	.617	2.09
2	.977	.773	.691	2.44

$a_1 = 1, b_1 = 0; a_2 = .5, b_2 = .5; a_3 = .2, b_3 = -.5.$

The relationship between the observed scores (X) and latent trait scores (θ) is statistical. The regression curve for predicting X from θ scores is known as the *test characteristic curve*. This regression curve is the same as the curve relating T to θ. Therefore, an equation for X is

$$X = \sum_g P_g(\theta) + E \qquad (15.11)$$

From Equation 15.10, E is simply the error of measurement. How strong is the relationship between X and θ and how shall we interpret the strength of that relationship? Since the relationship between X and θ is nonlinear, it is appropriate to use the nonlinear correlation

$$\eta_{X \cdot \theta} = \sqrt{1 - \frac{\epsilon \sigma^2_{(X|\theta)}}{\sigma^2_X}} \qquad (15.12)$$

to measure the strength of association between X and θ. The term $\sigma^2_{(X|\theta)}$ is the variance of X for a homogeneous subpopulation. It can be shown that this variance is equal to $\sigma^2_{(E|\theta)}$ the error variance for the subpopulation. The symbol $\epsilon \sigma^2_{(X|\theta)}$, which is equal to $\epsilon \sigma^2_{(E|\theta)}$, indicates averaging the error variances over all values of θ. It can also be shown that $\epsilon \sigma^2_{(X|\theta)}$ is equal to the error variance defined in classical test theory. As a result Equation 15.12 can be rewritten as

$$\eta_{X \cdot \theta} = \sqrt{1 - \frac{\sigma^2_E}{\sigma^2_X}}$$

and is seen to be equal to the index of reliability, as defined in Chapter 6. Thus the strength of relationship between X and θ is equal to the index of reliability for scores on X.

LOGISTIC MODELS

Although the normal ogive was the predominant form for the ICC in early research on latent trait theory, it has largely been replaced today by three logistic models which require simpler computations. In the following sections, general formulas for these models will be presented, two computer programs used to estimate item parameters for these models will be discussed, and an example of the types of information obtained from one of these programs will be presented.

For each of the three logistic models the cumulative logistic distribution function is the basis for the ICC. This function has the general form

$$P_g(\theta) = \frac{e^x}{1 + e^x} \tag{15.13}$$

where e is the base of the natural logarithm system. In Equation 15.13 x is an arbitrary symbol; it does not denote an observed score. In each of the three logistic models the ICC is simply a variation of the basic formula presented as Equation 15.13. The models differ in the number of item parameters used.

Two-Parameter Model

It is convenient to begin with the two-parameter logistic model because it most closely resembles the normal ogive. For the two-parameter model,

$$x = Da_g(\theta - b_g)$$

where D is a constant which can be arbitrarily set. It is customary to set $D = 1.7$, because then $P_g(\theta)$ for the normal and logistic ogives will not differ by more than .01 for any value of θ, the latent trait score (Lord and Novick, 1968). The parameters a_g and b_g serve the same role in the logistic models as they did in the normal ogive, namely, indexing discrimination and difficulty. By making the substitution for x in the general form of the logistic model, we arrive at a formula for the two-parameter logistic model:

$$P_g(\theta) = \frac{e^{Da_g(\theta - b_g)}}{1 + e^{Da_g(\theta - b_g)}} \tag{15.14}$$

One-Parameter Model

The one-parameter logistic model may be viewed as a special case of the two-parameter model in which all items have the same discrimination parameter. Since all items have the same parameter, it will be denoted by the constant a, rather than the variable a_g. The equation for the one-parameter ICC is

$$P_g(\theta) = \frac{e^{Da(\theta - b_g)}}{1 + e^{Da(\theta - b_g)}} \tag{15.15}$$

The formula can also be written as

$$P_g(\theta^*) = \frac{e^{(\theta^* - b_g^*)}}{1 + e^{(\theta^* - b_g^*)}} \tag{15.16}$$

Where $\theta^* = Da\theta$ and $b_g^* = Dab_g$. Thus, θ^* is simply a new scaling of the ability θ, and b_g^* is expressed in terms of this new scale. Written in this way, the formula emphasizes that with the one-parameter model, the proportion of examinees responding correctly is a function of the examinees' ability and the difficulty of the item. Rasch, working with different concepts than the ICC, developed a model which is called the *Rasch model* and is equivalent to the one-parameter model. Wright (1968) gives an account of Rasch's line of development. It should be noted that there is a one-parameter normal ogive model that is analogous to the one-parameter logistic model.

Three-Parameter Model

A problem may arise in applying the normal ogive model and the one- and two-parameter logistic models to data obtained from multiple-choice or true-false items because these formats permit correct responses from guessing. The problem is that for the one- and two-parameter models, the value of $P_g(\theta)$ tends to approach zero as θ gets smaller. However, one might suspect that even for examinees with very low abilities, the proportion responding correctly will be greater than zero because these examinees can guess the correct answer. To allow for this possibility, the three-parameter logistic model can be used. The equation for the ICC in this model is

$$P_g(\theta) = c_g + \frac{(1 - c_g)e^{Da_g(\theta - b_g)}}{1 + e^{Da_g(\theta - b_g)}} \tag{15.17}$$

The parameter c_g is called the *pseudo guessing parameter*. An example of this ICC, where $c_g = .1$, is given in Figure 15.7; the ICC tends to .10 as the ability decreases. Therefore, not less than 10 percent of the examinees will answer the item correctly even for very low values of θ.

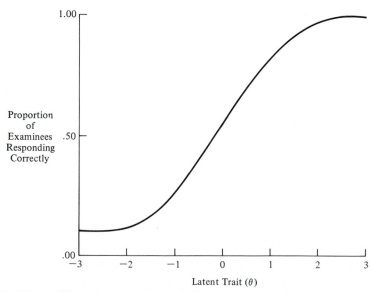

FIGURE 15.7   A Three-Parameter Logistic Ogive

ESTIMATION OF PARAMETERS

Depending on the logistic model chosen as the ICC, b_g and perhaps a_g and c_g must be estimated for each item. At least two types of estimation procedures are somewhat common. These are the *maximum likelihood* and the so-called *heuristic* or *approximate procedures*. Here, only the maximum likelihood procedures are reviewed. Swaminathan (1983) gives a more complete and technical presentation of the various maximum likelihood procedures. A well-known computer program for maximum likelihood estimation of the three-parameter model is LOGIST, developed by Wood, Wingersky, and Lord (1976). LOGIST simultaneously estimates the item parameters for all items and the latent trait scores for all examinees. This kind of procedure is referred to as a *joint maximum likelihood procedure*. When used with the three-parameter logistic, this procedure has several drawbacks. First, a substantial number of examinees may be required for accurate estimation. Hulin, Lissak, and Drasgow (1982) reported that accuracy of recovering three-parameter ICCs for 30 and 60 item tests improves significantly in moving from 200 to 500 to 1000 examinees. Accuracy does not improve as dramatically if 2000 examinees are used. Furthermore, results by Hulin et al. suggest that even larger sample sizes are needed if accurate estimation of a_g is required. Other investigations (Lord, 1968; Ree and Jensen, 1980; Swaminathan and Gifford, 1979) have similarly concluded that large sample sizes are needed to estimate item parameters. (In passing we should point out that Hulin et al. concluded that much smaller sample sizes are required if the main purpose is to estimate θ.) Second, it is not known whether the estimates of the item parameters are consistent. A procedure yields consistent estimates if it can be shown that as the sample size gets larger and larger, the estimates tend to get closer and closer to the true parameter values.

Another procedure that can be used to estimate the three-parameter model is the *marginal maximum likelihood procedure* (referred to as the *unconditional procedure* in the earlier literature). Until recently this procedure had practical limitations that precluded its use; however, Bock and Aitken (1981) developed a way of calculating these estimates that may overcome the practical problems. Bock and Aitken applied this procedure to the normal ogive model but reported that it can be applied to the three-parameter model. BILOG, a program that implements the Bock and Aitken method for the one-, two-, and three-parameter models, is distributed by Scientific Software, Inc. The principal advantage of the marginal maximum likelihood estimates is that there is reason to believe that they are consistent (Kiefer and Wolfowitz, 1956).

In North America the most widely used program for estimating the one-parameter model is BICAL, developed by Wright, Mead, and Bell (1979). This program calculates the joint maximum likelihood estimates. (Wright, Mead and Bell refer to these estimates as *unconditional estimates,* but they use this term in a different sense than Bock and Aitken use it.) These estimates are not consistent, but Wright and Douglas (1977) have developed a correction factor that makes the estimates almost consistent. In western Europe a *conditional maximum likelihood estimation pro-*

cedure is popular. Until recently this procedure was practical only with short tests, tests with fewer than 30 or 40 items (Wainer, Morgan, and Gustafsson, 1980). Recent developments (Gustafsson, 1980), however, have made this procedure practical for tests with as many as 80 to 100 items. The importance of the conditional maximum likelihood procedure is that the estimates are known to be consistent.

Interpreting Output from the BICAL Program

In this section are excerpts from the output of BICAL, the computer program developed by Wright, Mead, and Bell (1979) to implement the one-parameter (Rasch) model. This program output was chosen for presentation because it is the simplest for beginners to interpret and because it is so widely used. The interpretations are in concert with those suggested by the program's authors. It should be noted that the program provides considerable additional information to that discussed here.

In our presentation we will focus on three major types of output:

1. Item difficulty estimates
2. Examinee ability estimates
3. Item "fit" information

Our example is based on responses of 143 examinees to a 20 item, multiple-choice mathematics computation examination. (It should be mentioned that the sample size used for this illustration was slightly less than the minimum sample size of 200 commonly suggested for this program.)

Before presenting the excerpt, a brief description of the unconditional maximum likelihood procedure is in order. (The procedure is called unconditional by Wright, Mead, and Bell but is actually a joint maximum likelihood procedure.) The procedure involves a set of equations in which the item difficulty and latent trait score estimates are unknowns. Implementation of the procedure begins by calculating initial values for the difficulty and latent trait score estimates. These values are essentially guesses about the unconditional maximum likelihood estimates. The computer program uses these estimates in a procedure that produces a second set of difficulty and latent ability estimates. The second set is used to produce a third set, and so on. This iterative procedure continues until further cycles through the procedure produce only minimal change in the estimates. This final set comprises the unconditional maximum likelihood estimates.

Table 15.6 shows the first five columns of a table that provides data about the item difficulty estimates. The first column simply contains the item numbers, in this case 1 to 20. The second column reprints any arbitrary labels which the program user wishes to give to the items; in this case the item number was used, but labels suggestive of item content might also have been employed (Add, Mult., etc.). The third column, Item Difficulty, contains for each item an estimate of the ability level on the latent trait scale at which 50 percent of the examinees answered the item correctly. In other words, these are the estimated values of b_g for each item. Thus

TABLE 15.6.   Item Difficulty Data from One-Parameter Model Program, BICAL

Sequence Number	Item Name	Item Difficulty	Standard Error	Last Diff. Change
1	0001	−2.799	0.469	−2.211
2	0002	−1.375	0.291	−1.086
3	0003	0.566	0.193	0.447
4	0004	−0.218	0.217	−0.172
5	0005	−0.172	0.215	−0.136
6	0006	−1.651	0.317	−1.304
7	0007	−0.465	0.228	−0.368
8	0008	−0.037	0.210	−0.029
9	0009	−0.314	0.221	−0.248
10	0010	0.175	0.203	0.139
11	0011	−0.037	0.210	−0.029
12	0012	0.750	0.191	0.592
13	0013	0.414	0.196	0.327
14	0014	0.750	0.191	0.592
15	0015	0.092	0.205	0.073
16	0016	−0.266	0.219	−0.210
17	0017	1.682	0.192	1.328
18	0018	1.179	0.188	0.931
19	0019	0.007	0.208	0.006
20	0020	1.719	0.193	1.357

we see that item 1 was the easiest because 50 percent of the examinees with a score of −2.799 could answer this item correctly, and item 20 was the most difficult since examinees had to score 1.719 on the ability scale before they had a 50 percent chance of answering correctly. The Standard Error column contains the standard error of the difficulty estimate for each item. Thus for item 1, we can be 68% confident that the value of the difficulty parameter lies between the values −3.268 (which is −2.799 − .469) and −2.330 (which is −2.799 + .469). The column labeled Last Diff Change indicates the direction and magnitude of the adjustment made to the difficulty estimate after the program's last iteration. We see that item 19's difficulty estimate was fairly stable over the last iteration, but the estimate for item 1 changed considerably. Item difficulty data are especially useful when the test developer wants to construct a test which discriminates in a particular ability range. Such data can also be useful in construction of multiple test forms to ensure that items of similar difficulty are included on each form.

Table 15.7 presents information used to convert raw scores to ability score estimates on the latent trait scale (Log Ability). The column labeled Count presents the number of examinees earning each raw score. The Standard Errors are the standard errors for each of the ability score estimates. Note that these values are smallest for ability estimates in the middle of the score distribution and greatest for estimates at the extremes. Ability score data can be useful in establishing cut scores and equating different test forms. (These processes will be explained in more detail in subsequent chapters.)

TABLE 15.7.   Latent Ability Score Estimates from BICAL

Complete Score Equivalence Table			
Raw Score	Count	Log Ability	Standard Errors
19	18	3.48	1.12
18	14	2.60	0.81
17	11	2.05	0.68
16	15	1.64	0.61
15	9	1.30	0.56
14	16	1.00	0.53
13	12	0.73	0.51
12	12	0.48	0.50
11	2	0.24	0.49
10	6	0.0	0.49
9	3	−0.24	0.49
8	13	−0.48	0.50
7	6	−0.73	0.51
6	5	−1.00	0.53
5	1	−1.30	0.56
4	0	−1.64	0.61
3	0	−2.05	0.68
2	0	−2.60	0.81
1	0	−3.48	1.12

Table 15.8 presents information used to assess the extent to which the actual response data fit the one-parameter logistic model. It is this information which the test constructor may find useful to identify items that do not fit the one-parameter model. (However, see the discussion of goodness-of-fit tests in the section on Selection of a Model.) Look first at Table 15.8a. We see here that the examinees have been divided into six score groups. Group 1 is the group with the lowest scores; group 6 is the group with the highest scores. For each score group, the proportion of examinees who answered each item correctly is reported. For example, for item 11 we see that 20 percent of group 1 responded correctly, 61 percent of group 2 responded correctly, and so on. As the group's ability increases, we should observe an increasing percentage of the group responding correctly to the item (as is the case for item 11). These observed percentages of correct response are compared to the theoretical percentages that should have occurred if the data fit the one-parameter model. The discrepancies between the actual and theoretical percentages are reported for each score group in the Table 15.8b. The value −.15 for the first score group indicates that for item 11 the observed percentage of correct response was 15 percent too low. In other words, from the expected ICC, the proportion of correct response in this score group should have been 20% + 15% = 35%. The value .04 for the second score group on item 11 indicates that the percentage of correct response for this group was 4 percent greater than expected. Thus although 61

percent of the group was observed to answer correctly, 57 percent should have responded correctly, according to the expected ICC.

The statistical index of agreement between the observed and expected ICC is presented in Table 15.8c in the column labeled Fit Betwn. In interpreting these *t*-statistics they should be referenced to a mean of .00 and a standard deviation of 1.00. If we examine items for which this value is 2.00 or more, items 1, 4, 7, 9, and 12 might seem to have questionable fit values. (Notice that for these items, there is not a consistent increase in the proportions of examinees responding correctly for the six groups. The size of the fit statistic is affected by the magnitude of the departures from the expected ICC, but these magnitudes may be weighted differently in different regions of the curve.) A second fit statistic which may be of interest appears in the column labeled T-Tests Total; the program's authors describe this as an index of general agreement between the trait measured by the particular

TABLE 15.8a.   Item Characteristic Curve and Goodness-of-Fit Data from BICAL

Seq. Num.	Item Name	Item Characteristic Curve					
		1st Group	2nd Group	3rd Group	4th Group	5th Group	6th Group
1	0001	1.00	0.96	0.82	1.00	1.00	1.00
2	0002	0.68	0.83	0.86	0.96	1.00	1.00
3	0003	0.16	0.30	0.54	0.83	0.96	1.00
4	0004	0.44	0.35	0.75	1.00	1.00	1.00
5	0005	0.32	0.65	0.86	0.71	0.96	1.00
6	0006	0.76	0.96	0.86	0.88	1.00	1.00
7	0007	0.52	0.91	0.82	0.67	0.84	1.00
8	0008	0.32	0.61	0.64	0.83	1.00	1.00
9	0009	0.44	0.74	0.75	0.88	0.96	0.83
10	0010	0.20	0.65	0.71	0.67	0.96	1.00
11	0011	0.20	0.61	0.71	0.88	1.00	1.00
12	0012	0.16	0.35	0.64	0.83	0.76	0.78
13	0013	0.36	0.30	0.68	0.83	0.80	0.94
14	0014	0.16	0.52	0.54	0.67	0.76	0.94
15	0015	0.40	0.57	0.79	0.75	0.76	1.00
16	0016	0.36	0.52	0.86	0.83	1.00	1.00
17	0017	0.20	0.13	0.39	0.50	0.56	0.67
18	0018	0.20	0.17	0.39	0.67	0.68	1.00
19	0019	0.32	0.74	0.75	0.67	0.88	1.00
20	0020	0.04	0.13	0.21	0.58	0.68	0.83
Score Range		1–8	9–12	13–14	15–16	17–18	19–19
Mean Ability		−0.68	0.24	0.89	1.51	2.36	3.48
Mean Z-Test		0.1	0.1	−0.1	−0.1	0.1	−0.0
SD(Z-Test)		0.9	1.3	1.5	1.4	1.3	1.4
Group Count		25	23	28	24	25	18

Table 15.8b.

			Departure from Expected ICC			
Seq. Num.	1st Group	2nd Group	3rd Group	4th Group	5th Group	6th Group
1	0.11	0.00	−0.15	0.01	0.01	0.00
2	0.01	−0.00	−0.05	0.01	0.02	0.01
3	−0.07	−0.12	−0.04	0.11	0.11	0.05
4	0.05	−0.26	−0.00	0.15	0.07	0.02
5	−0.06	0.05	0.12	−0.13	0.04	0.03
6	0.04	0.09	−0.07	−0.08	0.02	0.01
7	0.07	0.25	0.03	−0.21	−0.10	0.02
8	−0.03	0.04	−0.07	0.01	0.09	0.03
9	0.03	0.11	−0.02	0.02	0.03	−0.14
10	−0.10	0.14	0.04	−0.12	0.06	0.04
11	−0.15	0.04	−0.00	0.05	0.09	0.03
12	−0.04	−0.03	0.11	0.15	−0.07	−0.16
13	0.11	−0.15	0.06	0.08	−0.07	−0.01
14	−0.04	0.14	0.00	−0.01	−0.07	0.01
15	0.08	0.03	0.10	−0.05	−0.14	0.03
16	−0.04	−0.10	0.10	−0.02	0.07	0.02
17	0.11	−0.06	0.08	0.04	−0.10	−0.19
18	0.06	−0.11	−0.03	0.08	−0.08	0.09
19	−0.02	0.18	0.04	−0.15	−0.03	0.03
20	−0.05	−0.06	−0.09	0.13	0.03	−0.02

Plus = Too many right
Minus = Too many wrong

Table 15.8c.

	Item Fit Statistics		
Seq. Num.	Fit Betwn.	T-Tests Total	Point Biser.
1	4.20	0.85	0.02
2	−1.29	0.14	0.34
3	0.77	−1.98	0.61
4	2.13	−1.12	0.55
5	0.71	−0.89	0.51
6	1.16	0.49	0.23
7	3.25	1.44	0.26
8	−0.17	−0.72	0.52
9	2.88	0.24	0.40
10	0.83	−1.02	0.55
11	0.49	−2.12	0.62
12	2.02	1.02	0.45
13	0.59	0.49	0.45
14	−0.46	0.69	0.47
15	1.25	1.31	0.36
16	0.22	−1.26	0.54
17	1.83	2.30	0.35
18	0.45	−0.52	0.53
19	1.00	0.82	0.39
20	−0.07	−1.38	0.55

item of interest and that measured by the test as a whole. Again, these values should be referenced to a mean of .00 and standard deviation of 1.00. On this fit statistic, items 11 and 17 have values in excess of 2.00. Notice that for one of these items (item 11), the point biserial correlation between item and total scores is the highest to be found among items on this test (.62). The most likely cause of misfit for this item is that its discrimination is atypical for items on this test, and thus it does not fit the one parameter model which requires the assumption of equal discrimination for all items on the test. If this is so, the misfit of this item is not due to a technical flaw in the item, but rather its relationship to the latent trait cannot be adequately represented by the one-parameter model. The authors of BICAL suggest that "Items with a between-fit t larger than 3 or 4 or a total-fit t greater than 2 or 3 should be examined for miskeying, misprinting, or other inconsistencies that might cause misfit. If the large fit statistic cannot be traced to a mechanical failure, the content of the item should be scrutinized to make sure it belongs within the realm of the variable intended." The reader is reminded that these suggestions are rules-of-thumb, and alternative criteria for judging the degree of item fit may be used.

SELECTION OF A MODEL

The question of which of the three logistic models to use in a particular situation is a rather complex one. One factor in the choice concerns how realistic the assumptions of the models are. For example, the one- and two-parameter models assume that there is no guessing. The three-parameter model can accommodate guessing, and guessing must be considered a possibility on multiple-choice and true-false items. In this regard the three-parameter model has an advantage over both of the other models. Similarly the one-parameter model assumes that the items are equally discriminating. The two- and three-parameter models can accommodate varying item discrimination. As a result, it may seem that the three-parameter model should be used with multiple-choice and true-false tests, and the two-parameter model should be used with other types of tests.

However, the ability to accommodate guessing and/or varying item discrimination is not the only criterion for choosing a model. First, it must be admitted that guessing may be negligible on some multiple-choice and true-false tests and that variation in item discrimination may be negligible on any type of test. If guessing is negligible the two-parameter model will be entirely adequate for the data, and if, in addition, variation in item discrimination is negligible, the one-parameter will be entirely adequate. This is an important consideration since use of an unnecessarily complex model will probably result in less-accurate estimates and less-adequate applications than use of the adequate, simpler model. The unnecessarily complex model will require estimation of parameters that really do not need to be estimated. Second, choice of a model depends on the extent to which an application of a simple model is robust to violations of its assumption. An application of a model is robust to violations of the assumptions of the model to the degree that the application is not affected by the violations. For example, the one-parameter logistic model assumes that there is no guessing, that all items are equally discriminating, that the items are unidimensional, and that the ICC is a cumulative logistic ogive. Although a large number of assumptions are involved, it may be that for a particular application the model yields accurate results even when one or more of its assumptions are violated. The issue of robustness to violations arises because estimation of the more complex models tends to be less practical. For example, as we noted earlier, a rule-of-thumb for the minimum sample size recommended for LOGIST is 1,000 examinees, and for the minimum sample size recommended for BICAL, 200 examinees. Thus use of BICAL is more practical. From this simple example the reader can see that an application of a simple model may be justified on practical grounds if the application is known to be robust to violations of the assumptions of the simple model.

In any application of latent trait theory, several interrelated issues must be addressed. One question is the goodness-of-fit of a model to the data. At present the most thoroughly investigated goodness-of-fit tests concern the one-parameter model. Traub and Wolfe (1981) report that the goodness-of-fit tests developed by Anderson (1973) and the measure-of-fit developed by Wright and Panchapakesan (1969) are sensitive to variations in item discrimination but not to guessing or multidimensionality. (The between t fit statistic discussed in the section on BICAL is a variation on Wright and Panchapakesan's measure of fit.) Findings such as these led Traub and Wolfe to conclude that no single statistical test is an adequate indication that a model fits the data. Rather, a series of tests to explore a variety of ways that a model may misfit data should be conducted. Traub and Wolfe and references therein and Hambleton and Murray (1983) give more details on methods for investigating goodness-of-fit. A second question that must be raised in any application is the robustness question. Unfortunately at present there is little or no guidance in the literature about the robustness of the use of latent trait models for various applications. This is an area that is in dire need of research.

APPLICATIONS OF ITEM RESPONSE THEORY

The potential usefulness of latent trait models in test construction has been demonstrated for applications such as construction of equivalent test forms, development of tests which discriminate at a particular level of ability, and the development of "tailored testing" systems. To understand how item response theory may be used for such applications, it is necessary to be familiar with three important concepts in measurement theory:

1. Invariance of item parameters
2. Information
3. Relative efficiency

These concepts are discussed in the remaining sections of this chapter, within the context of specific situations where item response theory may prove useful. It should be noted that detailed step-by-step description of how each latent trait model could be applied to the test development situations described would necessarily go far beyond the scope of this chapter. Thus the cases presented here are offered as general illustrations of areas in which interested readers might pursue further study in the references provided.

Item Calibration

Gulliksen (1950) opined that an important contribution to the theory and practice of item analysis would be the discovery of item parameters that are relatively invariant to changes in the composition of the examinee group on which the item analysis is based. The reason for this viewpoint is quite simple. If the item parameters are invariant, they can be estimated by using one group's data, and these estimates can be applied with confidence to any other group of examinees, including the whole population of examinees. We may refer to this as *invariance to selection of examinees*. Unfortunately the classical item analysis statistics—proportion correct and item-test correlation—cannot be expected to be invariant to selection of examinees. Many sources on latent trait theory, however, report that the parameters of the logistic and normal ogive ICCs are invariant to selection of examinees (see, for example, Hambleton and Cook, 1977; Lord, 1980; Lord and Novick, 1968).

The invariance of item parameters has the important practical consequence that the parameters of large numbers of items can be estimated even though each item is not answered by every examinee. This is known as *person-free item calibration*. For example, suppose we want to estimate the parameters of 75 items, but it is practical to administer only 50 items to each examinee. If the 75 items are divided into three sets, A, B, and C, two 50-item forms can be assembled. The first form consists of item sets A and B; the second, of item sets A and C. The two forms are then administered to two different groups of examinees. The responses of both groups to items in set A can be used to create a common scale on which all item parameter estimates can be expressed. This is sometimes referred to as *item calibration*. Wright and Stone (1979) have described this process in some detail for the Rasch model.

To get an idea of how item calibration can be accomplished, let us continue with the example of item sets A, B, and C and suppose all items fit the two-parameter logistic model. We have administered sets A and B to group 1 and sets A and C to group 2. Further, because of the problem of an arbitrary unit and scale of measurement for the latent trait scores, the scale has been set for group 1 so that its mean score is 0 and the standard deviation is 1. Similarly the scale in group 2 has been set so that its mean is 0 and the standard deviation is 1. Recall that b_g is defined as the point on the latent trait scale at which $P_g(\theta) = .5$. As a result the b_g's calculated for group 1 are expressed on the latent trait scale for group 1, and the b_g's calculated for group 2 are expressed on the latent trait scale for group 2. Thus the item difficulties for items in set B are expressed on the scale for group 1, and the item difficulties in set C are expressed on the scale for group 2. There are two sets of estimated item difficulties for set A, one expressed on the scale for group 1, the other on the scale for group 2. Since we can arbitrarily resolve to use the scale for group 1 to express the item difficulties for set A, the problem is that the item difficulties for set C are on a different scale than those for sets A and B. The latter problem can be overcome by using Equation 15.7a:

$$b'_g = kb_g + m$$

Where b'_g is the difficulty for item g from set C expressed on the scale for group 1; b_g is the item difficulty expressed on the scale for group 2.

  Similarly when an item discrimination is expressed on one latent trait scale, it can be transformed to a second scale by using Equation 15.7b:

$$a'_g = a_g/k$$

Thus if we knew k and m, it would be possible to transform the difficulty and discrimination parameters for each item in set C on the scale for group 2 to the scale for group 1. How can k and m be determined? Recall that for items in set A the difficulty parameters have been expressed both on the scales for group 1 and for group 2. That is, for any item in set A, b^A_{g1} and b^A_{g2} are values for the same parameter but are expressed on the scales for group 1 and 2, respectively. Therefore b^A_{g1} and b^A_{g2} must be related by

$$b^A_{g1} = kb^A_{g2} + m$$

Thus if we plot b^A_{g1} versus b^A_{g2}, the plot will be a straight line. The slope of this line is k and the intercept is m.

  Why would it be useful to have a bank of calibrated items? The utility of a calibrated item bank can be illustrated by considering a state where a teacher certification test is administered several times a year. Clearly it is undesirable to use the same test over and over again. If several forms of a test are assembled from a calibrated item bank it will be possible to locate examinees on the same latent trait scale even though different forms are taken at different times during the year. Comparing applicants who have taken different forms is possible because the item parameters have been estimated on the same scale during the calibration process, and this information can be used in scoring the test.

  In addition, a calibrated item bank permits parameters of new items to be estimated on the same scale as the original items. This is accomplished by administering a form of trial items along with the regular form during an administration of the test. A process analogous to the one used to transform the parameter estimates for item set C can be used to transform the parameter estimates for the new items to the scale used in the original item calibration.

  It seems natural to wonder why item parameters estimated with latent trait models should be invariant over different groups of examinees. There are at least two explanations of invariance to selection found in the literature. One, given by Hambleton and Cook (1977) and Lord (1980), treats the ICC as a regression curve. As Lord points out in many statistical contexts the regression function is unchanged when the distribution of the regressor variable (here, the latent ability) is changed. Although this is true, it does not imply that the ICC is automatically invariant to selection of examinees.

Lord (1980) and Lord and Novick (1968) related invariance to the concept of unidimensionality. They argued that if the ICC varies over subgroups of examinees, for example, males and females, there are systematic differences on item g between males and females who have the same latent trait score. Therefore the test cannot reasonably be considered to be unidimensional. Notice, however, that from this perspective, invariance to selection is not a property of latent trait models but rather is a logical requirement for unidimensionality. Therefore from this perspective, invariance to selection is an assumption that inadvertently may be violated in practice. As a result, in making applications that depend on the invariance assumption, provisions should be made to check the validity of assumption.

Tailored Testing

A problem that arises in using typical standardized tests is that they are not very useful measuring instruments for some examinees. For example on a standardized achievement test, many of the items will be too hard for the low-ability examinee. Since such examinees may guess at many of these items, the items contribute measurement error rather than useful information about the examinees. Also, consider a selective university that accepts only 10% of its applicant pool. The easier items on an admissions test will not help to discriminate among the examinees near the selection cut score since most of these examinees will tend to get these items correct. What these examples suggest is that rather than having every examinee respond to every item it may be better to match items to the examinee's ability. This is the goal of tailored (or adaptive testing). Technically these testing strategies depend on a concept known as *information*. The remainder of this section is devoted to developing this concept. To promote a better understanding of this important characteristic, consider the following simple example.

A test developer wants to construct a five-item test to locate a population of examinees on the latent trait scale, which in theory goes from negative infinity to positive infinity. However the developer knows that the latent trait scores of the examinees in this population run from -3.0 to 3.0 and are symmetrically distributed around 0. Suppose that it is possible to construct items with step function ICCs and vary the point at which the step occurs for each ICC. In the first attempt the test developer constructs five items, each of which has an ICC with the step at $\theta = 0$. When the test is administered 50% of students do not answer any items correctly and 50% answer five items correctly. Since all ICCs have a step at $\theta = 0$, the test developer concludes that the first 50% have latent trait scores less than 0 and 50% have latent trait scores greater than or equal to 0. Clearly this test only provides

TABLE 15.9.   Results on a Test Composed of Five Guttman Scalable Items

Score	Response Pattern	Ability Score Location
0	− − − − −	$-3.0 \leq \theta < -1.0$
1	+ − − − −	$-1.0 \leq \theta < -0.5$
2	+ + − − −	$-0.5 \leq \theta < 0.0$
3	+ + + − −	$0.0 \leq \theta < .05$
4	+ + + + −	$0.5 \leq \theta < 1.0$
5	+ + + + +	$1.0 \leq \theta < 3.0$

information about whether an examinee's latent ability is below 0 or not. Therefore all the information in the test concerns the scale point 0.

In the next attempt at test construction the steps in the ICC occur at -1.0, -0.5, 0, 0.5, and 1.0. Now the raw scores range from 0 to 5. The response patterns and locations of the examinees earning each score are given in Table 15.9. Notice that the test provides very little information for locating examinees below -1.0 or above 1.0. However it provides a good deal of information for locating examinees between -1.0 and 1.0.

In the third try five items are constructed with steps at $-2, -1, 0, 1$, and 2. Again all possible scores from 0 to 5 are observed. Table 15.10 gives the response patterns and locations corresponding to each score. Clearly this test provides more information than the second test did for locating examinees in the regions $-3 \leq \theta \leq 1.0$ and $1.0 \leq \theta \leq 3.0$. However it also provides less information for locating examinees in the region $-1.0 \leq \theta \leq 1.0$. Now the test developer realizes the dilemma. In order to construct a useful test, the first step must be to determine the regions of the latent trait scale for which fine discrimination among scale points is desirable. The next step is to construct a test that provides information for locating examinees in these regions.

From these examples it should be clear that a test provides differential information about different regions on the latent trait scale. Finer discriminations are made among examinees with latent trait scores in the regions where the test provides more information. Moreover the information in a test depends on the ICCs, and because of this we can speak of the information in an item.

Although this presentation conveys the general meaning of information, the con-

TABLE 15.10.   Results on a Test Composed of Five Guttman Scalable Items

Score	Response Pattern	Location
0	− − − − −	$-3.0 \leq \theta < -2.0$
1	+ − − − −	$-2.0 \leq \theta < -1.0$
2	+ + − − −	$-1.0 \leq \theta < 0.0$
3	+ + + − −	$0.0 \leq \theta < 1.0$
4	+ + + + −	$1.0 \leq \theta < 2.0$
5	+ + + + +	$2.0 < \theta \leq 3.0$

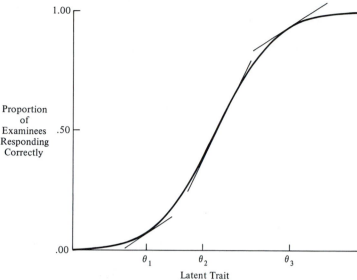

FIGURE 15.8   Illustration of Tangent Lines to an ICC

cept has a precise mathematical definition. Let $P'_g(\theta)$ denote the first derivative of the ICC. For readers unfamiliar with differential calculus, it should suffice to note that the value of the first derivative calculated at any value of θ is the slope of a line drawn tangent to the ICC at the point $P(\theta)$. Three such tangent lines are drawn in Figure 15.8. The tangent lines at θ_1 and θ_3 have relatively small slopes, and so the values of the first derivative at θ_1 and θ_3 are relatively small. The tangent line at θ_2 has a relatively large slope, and the value of the first derivative at θ_2 is relatively large. Let $Q_g(\theta) = 1 - P_g(\theta)$. The information provided by item g about any point on the latent trait scale is

$$I_g(\theta) = \frac{[P'_g(\theta)]^2}{[P_g(\theta)][Q_g(\theta)]} \tag{15.18}$$

The numerator of $I_g(\theta)$ is the first derivative of $P_g(\theta)$. Thus information tends to be larger when the first derivative is larger. As a result the item in Figure 15.8 provides more information at θ_2 than at θ_1 or θ_3 because the first derivative is larger at θ_2. Information can be evaluated at each and every point on the latent trait scale to yield the information provided by the item at each and every value of θ. Plotting $I_g(\theta)$ against θ yields the item information function. Figure 15.9 presents item information functions for three two-parameter logistic ICCs. Each of the three items have the same value for a_g. However the values of b_g vary over the three items. The smallest difficulty value is $b_1 = 0$. The information curve for this item is the furthest to the left. Note that it reaches its maximum over the score $\theta = 0$. This means that the first item provides the most information for examinees with a latent trait score of 0. Also note that the information curve for item 1 falls below .15 for latent trait

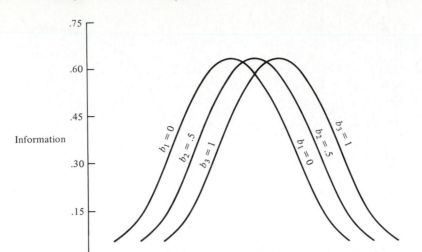

FIGURE 15.9 Illustration of Information Curves for Three Items, $b_1 = 0$, $b_2 = .5$, and $b_3 = 1$

scores less than -2.00 and greater than 2.00. This means that item 1 will provide very little information for examinees with latent abilities in these regions.

Having defined information, we can now describe tailored testing in somewhat more detail. One approach requires a large bank of calibrated items administered to examinees by a computer. The procedure begins by administering several items to each examinee. The responses are used to make a provisional estimate of each examinee's latent trait score. Then, for each examinee, the computer picks the item that provides maximum information at the latent trait score equal to the examinee's provisionally estimated latent ability. The examinee's response to the new item is used to update the estimate of his or her latent ability. Based on this updated latent trait score, a new item is picked and administered to the examinee. One possible stopping rule for the procedure is to set an accuracy criterion for the latent trait estimate. The testing procedure continues until a sufficiently precise latent trait estimate is obtained.

Information Provided by Different Scoring and Testing Procedures

The concept of information has proved useful in (1) comparing different formulas for scoring the same test, (2) comparing different tests that measure the same trait, and (3) comparing different testing procedures such as tailored and conventional testing. In making these comparisons the test information and score information functions are used, and so we begin this section by defining these functions.

The *test information function* is simply the sum of the item information functions for all items on the test. Symbolically,

$$I(\theta) = \sum_g I_g(\theta) \tag{15.19}$$

Since there are several possible ways to score most tests, it is appropriate to distinguish between the information provided by a scoring formula and the information provided by a test. For any scoring formula, denoted by X, the score information is denoted by $I(\theta,X)$. It can be shown that $I(\theta,X) \leq I(\theta)$. That is, the test information is an upper bound to the information obtainable from any particular scoring formula. The simplest possible scoring scheme is to award 1 point for each correct response and 0 for each incorrect response. This scoring formula can be expressed as

$$X = \Sigma U_g \tag{15.20}$$

where U_g is the score on item g and can be either 0 or 1. Birnbaum (1968) has shown that for the one-parameter model, this scoring formula yields the maximum obtainable score information function. This is also true for all tests in which all items have the same ICC, regardless of the form of the ICC. For the two-parameter logistic model, the scoring formula $X = \Sigma a_g U_g$ yields the maximum obtainable score information function. It can also be shown that for any other model, $I(\theta)$ cannot be obtained for all θ by any test scoring formula that (1) is a weighted sum of item scores and (2) uses the same weights for every examinee. For example, with the three-parameter logistic model, use of the weights

$$W_g = \frac{Da_g[P_g(\theta) - c_g]}{[1 - c_g]P_g(\theta)} \tag{15.21}$$

yields an information curve that equals the test information curve at all values of θ. These weights, however, depend on $P_g(\theta)$, and so the weights change for different examinees.

An important question is the loss of information when the optimal weighting system is not used as a scoring formula. For example, with the two-parameter model an important question is the loss of information when $X = \Sigma U_g$ is used as a scoring formula rather than $Y = \Sigma a_g U_g$. This question can be investigated through *relative efficiency,* which we define in the next paragraph.

Let X and Y denote two measures of the same latent trait. X and Y may be two different ways of scoring the same test or scores based on two different tests of the same latent trait. The *relative efficiency function* for these two measures is defined as

$$RE(\theta,X,Y) = \frac{I(\theta,X)}{I(\theta,Y)} \tag{15.22}$$

Like the information function, the relative efficiency function is evaluated at each point on the latent trait scale. That is, it indicates whether X or Y is a better measure of the latent trait at each point on the scale. For any latent trait score for which

$RE(\theta,X,Y) > 1$, X is a better measure. Similarly for any latent trait score for which $RE(\theta,X,Y) < 1$, Y is a better measure.

Relative efficiency has been used to investigate the loss of information when the optimal weighting system is not used as a scoring formula. For example, with the two-parameter model an important question is the loss of information when $X = \Sigma U_g$ is used as a scoring formula rather than $Y = \Sigma a_g U_g$. In this question relative efficiency is defined by $I(\theta,X)/I(\theta)$. Birnbaum (1968) referred to this special form of the relative efficiency function as the *efficiency function*. Since $I(\theta,X) \leq I(\theta)$, the value of the efficiency function is always less than or equal to 1. Hambleton and Traub (1971) found that for the two-parameter logistic model, the efficiency function of an unweighted score was generally above .85. This may be interpreted to mean that the length of a test scored with the unweighted scoring formula must be increased by a factor of $1/.85 = 1.18$ in order to reach the information obtainable with optimal scoring weights. Alternatively, use of the unweighted scoring formula is equivalent to reducing the test length by $100\ (1 - .85) = 15\%$ and using the optimal weights. Hambleton and Traub showed that using $X_g = \Sigma U_g$ with a three-parameter logistic model resulted in an efficiency function with values ranging upward from .60 to .70 at low ability levels.

Relative efficiency has also been used to compare conventional tests to adaptive tests. As noted, an adaptive testing procedure is one in which an attempt is made to match the difficulty of the items to the ability level of the student being measured. This is desirable since an item that is either too hard or too easy provides relatively little information about the level of the examinee's latent ability. Lord (1980) describes three different types of adaptive testing. One, the flexilevel test, consists of items that can be roughly ordered in terms of difficulty. An examinee begins by answering an item of moderate difficulty. If the examinee answers correctly, a more-difficult item is presented next; otherwise a less-difficult item is presented. Lord (1971) showed how to arrange the items in a test booklet so that the flexilevel test can be group-administered. A comparison of a hypothetical conventional test and a hypothetical flexilevel test can be accomplished by specifying parameters of the ICCs for each item of each test, specifying a scoring rule, and calculating relative efficiency. The results will show the regions of the latent trait scale for which the flexilevel test is more informative than the conventional test. This will help to indicate the assessment purposes for which a flexilevel test has advantages over a conventional test. By systematically varying the item parameters, one can determine rules-of-thumb for designing the most effective flexilevel test. These rules-of-thumb will consist of specifications of appropriate values for the item parameters. If we assume the availability of an item bank, it should then be possible to construct informative flexilevel tests. Of course it is important to have trial administrations of such tests in order to investigate the merits of using flexilevel tests with real examinees.

Procedures similar to those described for the flexilevel test can be used to develop design rules for two-staged and tailored tests. A two-staged test consists of a short routing test and several longer, second-stage tests. An examinee's score on the routing test is used to determine which second-stage tests the examinee should take. The results presented by Lord (1980) suggest that it is possible to construct two-stage and tailored tests that provide more information at all ability levels than conventional tests provide.

Finally, it is important to recognize that item response theory and its related concepts of information and relative efficiency may be applicable in comparing tests not originally developed with latent trait models. For example, Lord summarized a study comparing seven sixth-grade vocabulary tests using relative efficiency. The results show, for example, that when the Sequential Test of Educational Progress (STEP), Series II (1969), Level 4, Form A, Reading subtest is compared to the Metropolitan Achievement Test (MAT), Intermediate Level, Form F (1970), the former provided more information about the lower 20 percent of the students. For other students the MAT was more informative. Such studies indicate the potential of item response theory for making decisions about appropriate test use regardless of the original method of test development.

SUMMARY

This chapter presented an introduction to item response theory. Several basic concepts, item characteristic curves and latent traits, local independence and dimensionality, and test-free measurement were presented first. Next the normal ogive model and its parameters—item difficulty (b_g) and item discrimination (a_g)—were introduced. The relationship between the parameters of classical test theory and the parameters of the normal ogive model were presented and illustrated, as was the relationship between latent trait scores and true scores.

Three different logistic models were then presented. The one-parameter (or Rasch) model is the simplest model. Only an item difficulty parameter is estimated; it is assumed that all items are equally discriminating and that low-ability examinees do not answer correctly by guessing. The two-parameter model is qualitatively similar to the normal ogive model and includes a discrimination parameter. The three-parameter model includes a pseudoguessing parameter as well as discrimination and difficulty parameters, and so is the least-restrictive model. Parameter estimation was briefly discussed, followed by a fairly extensive presentation of the printout from BICAL, a program for estimation with the one-parameter model.

The chapter concluded with a description of several applications of item response theory: item banking, tailored testing, and the comparison of the accuracy of measuring devices at various points on the latent trait scale. The concepts of invariance to selection, information, and relative efficiency were introduced.

Exercises

1. Based on Figure 15.3 show that items 1 and 4 are locally independent for examinees with a latent trait score of θ_2. Show that items 2 and 3 are locally independent at any latent trait score in the range $\theta_2 < \theta < \theta_3$.

2. Suppose a two parameter logistic model is fit to data for a test. For the first two items $P_1(\theta) = .5$ and $P_2(\theta) = .7$ for a particular latent trait score. In addition, for these two items, $P(+,+|\theta) = .45$, $P(-,+|\theta) = .05$, $P(+,-|\theta) = .25$ and $P(-,-|\theta) = .25$. Do these results suggest the test is unidimensional? Why or why not?

3. Consider the following table of response patterns to a hypothetical five-item test:

Response Pattern	Item 1	2	3	4	5
a	+	+	−	−	−
b	−	−	−	−	−
c	+	+	+	+	+
d	+	−	−	−	−
e	+	+	+	+	−
f	+	+	+	−	−

Are these response patterns consistent with the claim that the items are unidimensional and the ICCs are step functions? If so draw the ICCs for the five items.

4. The following results are item-latent trait biserials (ρ_g) and item difficulties (p_g) for four items. Assuming θ is normally distributed with mean 0 and standard deviation 1, calculate a_g and b_g for each item. Based on these results does p_g suffer any deficits as a measure of item difficulty?

Item	ρ_g	p_g
1	.8	.7
2	.6	.7
3	.5	.7
4	.4	.7

5. The following tables contain information excerpted from a BICAL program printout providing data on 15 items for which responses of 474 examinees were used in calibration of item difficulty and subject ability parameters from the one-parameter logistic model.

   A. Identify three items for which examinee's response pattern shows the poorest fit to the model. What may account for this lack of fit?

   B. On a single continuum, using the data provided in the table for the six different ability levels, draw the item characteristic curve for items 1, 3, and 4 respectively. Then plot the six points for each item showing the actual proportions of examinees at those ability levels who responded correctly, using that same continuum. For each item, identify the ability region in which actual performance departed most markedly from expected performance.

   C. Rank order items 1, 3, and 4 in terms of their difficulties (based on your observations of their locations on the continuum drawn for B).

   D. Examinee A earned a raw score of 10 points on this test; Examinee B earned a raw score of 11 points. What is the estimated true score for each of these examinees?

Item Characteristic Curve

Seq. Num.	Item Name	1st Group	2nd Group	3rd Group	4th Group	5th Group	6th Group
1	0001	0.35	0.55	0.64	0.82	0.83	0.91
2	0002	0.84	0.86	0.94	0.99	1.00	0.98
3	0003	0.06	0.18	0.08	0.11	0.18	0.54
4	0004	0.49	0.54	0.47	0.56	0.61	0.71
5	0005	0.86	0.89	0.98	0.99	0.99	1.00
6	0006	0.51	0.71	0.89	0.86	0.92	0.99
7	0007	0.21	0.28	0.53	0.72	0.85	0.91
8	0008	0.56	0.86	0.88	0.97	1.00	0.99
9	0009	0.12	0.09	0.16	0.11	0.24	0.33
10	0010	0.26	0.35	0.28	0.35	0.51	0.69
11	0011	0.23	0.43	0.44	0.47	0.59	0.82
12	0012	0.40	0.68	0.78	0.88	0.94	0.96
13	0013	0.82	0.94	0.92	0.91	1.00	0.99
14	0014	0.25	0.17	0.36	0.49	0.48	0.68
15	0015	0.18	0.46	0.65	0.75	0.87	0.93
Score Range		1–7	8–8	9–9	10–10	11–11	12–14
Mean Ability		−0.50	0.19	0.55	0.92	1.33	2.05
Mean Z-Test		0.1	0.1	0.2	0.3	0.6	0.6
SD(Z-Test)		2.1	1.5	0.9	1.4	1.4	1.3
Group Count		77	65	85	80	71	96

Departure from Expected ICC

Seq. Num.	1st Group	2nd Group	3rd Group	4th Group	5th Group	6th Group
1	−0.05	−0.01	−0.01	0.10	0.03	0.02
2	0.02	−0.04	0.01	0.04	0.03	−0.00
3	0.01	0.08	−0.06	−0.09	−0.09	0.11
4	0.22	0.13	−0.03	−0.03	−0.08	−0.10
5	−0.00	−0.03	0.03	0.02	0.01	0.01
6	−0.08	−0.03	0.09	0.01	0.02	0.05
7	−0.09	−0.17	−0.01	0.10	0.13	0.07
8	−0.13	0.04	0.02	0.07	0.07	0.02
9	0.07	0.00	0.04	−0.06	−0.00	−0.06
10	0.10	0.09	−0.05	−0.08	−0.02	−0.00
11	0.01	0.08	−0.00	−0.06	−0.04	0.05
12	−0.11	0.00	0.03	0.06	0.08	0.03
13	0.02	0.05	−0.00	−0.03	0.04	0.01
14	0.09	−0.10	0.02	0.06	−0.05	−0.01
15	−0.17	−0.05	0.05	0.06	0.11	0.06

Plus = Too many right
Minus = Too many wrong

Item Fit Statistics

Seq. Num.	Err Impac.[a]	Fit Betwn.	T-Tests Total	Wtd. Mnsq.	Mnsq. SD	Disc. Indx.	Point Biser.
1	0.0	0.33	−1.88	0.92	0.04	1.17	0.42
2	0.0	0.65	−1.00	0.86	0.14	1.01	0.24
3	0.0	2.78	−1.07	0.93	0.07	1.14	0.33
4	0.09	4.47	5.10	1.18	0.03	0.28	0.15
5	0.0	0.35	−1.03	0.83	0.17	1.14	0.24
6	0.0	1.64	−2.18	0.85	0.07	1.28	0.42
7	0.0	3.40	−4.54	0.85	0.04	1.52	0.54
8	0.0	2.85	−2.39	0.79	0.10	1.46	0.45
9	0.02	1.76	0.63	1.04	0.07	0.67	0.20
10	0.03	1.82	1.55	1.06	0.04	0.76	0.29
11	0.00	0.17	0.17	1.01	0.03	1.00	0.37
12	0.0	1.69	−2.37	0.86	0.06	1.35	0.44
13	0.0	0.64	−0.84	0.89	0.13	0.94	0.21
14	0.02	1.34	1.03	1.04	0.04	0.86	0.31
15	0.0	3.09	−4.21	0.84	0.04	1.52	0.53

[a]ERROR IMPACT = Proportion error increase due to this misfit

6. The following table presents information $[I_g(\theta)]$ provided by nine items at each of nine points on the latent trait scale. For each of the nine items, $a_g = .5$. However, for the nine items, b_g ranges from −2.0 to 2.0. The information figures were calculated for the two-parameter logistic function, but very similar results would be obtained with the normal ogive model. Use the information figures to calculate
   A. the test information provided by a test which included these nine items. Calculate the test information values for the latent trait values used in the table.
   B. the test information provided by a test which includes nine items with $a_g = .5$ and $b_g = 00$.

θ	b_g −2.0	−1.5	−1.0	−0.5	0.0	0.5	1.0	1.5	2.0
−2.0	.18	.17	.15	.12	.09	.07	.05	.03	.02
−1.5	.17	.18	.17	.15	.12	.09	.07	.05	.03
−1.0	.15	.17	.18	.17	.15	.12	.09	.07	.05
−0.5	.12	.15	.17	.18	.17	.15	.12	.09	.07
0.0	.09	.12	.15	.17	.18	.17	.15	.12	.09
0.5	.07	.09	.12	.15	.17	.18	.17	.15	.12
1.0	.05	.07	.09	.12	.15	.17	.18	.17	.15
1.5	.03	.05	.07	.09	.12	.15	.17	.18	.17
2.0	.02	.03	.05	.07	.09	.12	.15	.17	.18

7. The following table presents test information for each of four tests at each of nine points on the latent trait scale. On the first two tests all items had $a_g = 1.0$; on the second two tests all items had $a_g = 1.5$. The first of each pair of tests contained nine items with the same b_g values as the nine items in A of question 6. The second included nine items each

with $b_g = 0.0$. Based on these results, your answers to question 6, and assuming you are not interested in accurate measurement for examinees with $\theta < -2.0$ or $\theta > 2.0$, what do you conclude about the utility of including items with a wide range of difficulty on a test? In answering this question you will want to consider that items with $a_g > 1.0$ are rare. An item with $a_g = 1.0$ has approximately a .80 biserial correlation with the latent trait. For items with $a_g = .5$ and $a_g = 1.5$, the corresponding biserials are .45 and .83.

θ	$a_g = 1.0$		$a_g = 1.5$	
	Mixed b_g	$b_g = 0$	Mixed b_g	$b_g = 0$
−2.0	2.06	.81	3.37	.36
−1.5	2.67	1.71	4.48	1.26
−1.0	3.04	3.42	4.92	3.96
− .5	3.21	5.49	5.06	9.99
0.0	3.26	6.48	5.09	14.67
.5	3.21	5.49	5.06	9.99
1.0	3.04	3.42	4.92	3.96
1.5	2.67	1.71	4.48	1.26
2.0	2.06	.81	3.37	.36

8. In testing programs, a short form composed of trial items is administered along with a regular form of the test. The items on the regular form have been chosen from a pool of calibrated items. A two-parameter latent trait model has been fit to the item data for the trial and regular forms. The scale has been chosen by setting the mean latent trait scale to 0 and the standard deviation to 1. How can the results be used to place the estimated item parameters for the trial items on the scale on which the parameters of the calibrated items are expressed?

Chapter 16

DETECTING ITEM BIAS

It is inevitable that test scores are affected by sources of variation other than the construct purportedly measured by the test. If this were not true, scores would be perfectly reliable and valid. Because irrelevant sources of variation are unavoidable, it is important that they should not give an unfair advantage to one subpopulation of examinees, such as males, over another subpopulation, such as females. Such an unfair advantage exists if within a group of examinees, all of whom have the same standing on the construct measured by the test, the irrelevant sources of variation are differentially distributed for the two subpopulations. To understand how this might occur consider the following situations:

1. An item on a well-known individual intelligence test asks, "What is the thing to do if you find someone's wallet in a store?" The correct answer is to report the discovery to someone in charge of the store; however, it is sometimes argued that such an item may be biased against children from low-income families since taking the money home to a parent might seem to be a more "sensible" response for these children than for children from more affluent homes.
2. An item from a self-concept scale asks students to respond in Likert format to the statement "My skin is nice looking." Again, it can be argued that such an item has different connotative meaning for white teenagers than for black teenagers, and thus similar responses might not indicate similar standings on the trait of interest.
3. An item on a math achievement test reads, "Ralph has 2 quarters. A pack of gum costs $.25. How many packs can he buy?" If this item were administered to a group of children, including some who cannot read English, it might be argued that the item measures different skills for different examinees.

Two notions are central to each of these arguments about item bias: first, the notion that examinees' performance on an item may be subject to sources of variation other than differences on the construct of interest, and second, the belief that these extraneous sources of variation influence performance in a way that differs systematically for some identifiable subgroups of examinees. It is also possible that test scores of different subpopulations may be affected by different sources of variation. Furthermore, the extent to which an item may be biased against specific subpopulations may not be apparent from inspection of its content. For example, on some occasions examinees from a given subpopulation actually have performed better on items that were judged by content reviewers to be "biased" against them, than on items which were judged to be "unbiased." Thus the test developer or test user who wishes to investigate whether items on a particular test are biased for certain groups must conduct an empirical study of how those groups perform on the items in question.

There are two purposes for item bias studies. One is to investigate whether test scores are affected by different sources of variance in the various subpopulations. If it is decided that test scores of all subpopulations are affected by the same sources of variance, a second purpose is to determine whether any of these irrelevant sources give an unfair advantage to some of the subpopulations. Based on these two purposes, we can formulate a definition of a set of unbiased items. A set of items is *unbiased* if (1) the items are affected by the same sources of variance in both subpopulations; and (2) among examinees who are at the same level on the construct purportedly measured by the test, the distributions of irrelevant sources of variation are the same for both subpopulations.

This chapter concerns methods of investigating item bias. Rather than trying to discuss all the available methods, we have chosen those that seem to be most prominent and promising in the current literature (Jensen, 1980, has offered a more exhaustive presentation). Three classes of methods are discussed: latent trait, chi-square, and item difficulty methods. No attempt is made to provide all the procedural details for all the methods presented. However, accessible references to these procedures are provided. In presenting each method two subpopulations are compared, but the methods can be used for comparisons of more than two groups.

METHODS BASED ON ITEM RESPONSE THEORY

In using item response theory to investigate item bias, a set of items is judged unbiased if the ICCs for every item are the same for both subpopulations. Then among examinees with the same latent trait score, the item is equally difficult for members of both subpopulations. Thus irrelevant sources of variance affect the subpopulations the same way. In addition, since the ICCs are the same for both groups, the items measure the same latent trait for each group. Thus if a set of items is unbiased according to the latent trait definition, it will also be unbiased according to the definition set forth earlier. (Actually, this conclusion is correct only if we are willing to assume that examinees who are homogeneous on the latent trait are also homogeneous on the construct of interest. If examinees, who are homogeneous on the latent trait, are substantially unhomogeneous on the construct of interest, then the test does not have substantial construct validity. Using a test with suspect valid-

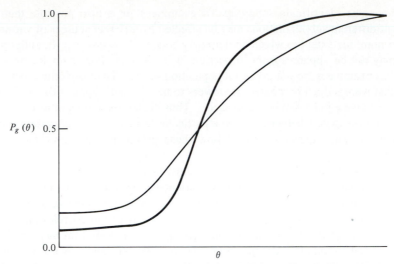

FIGURE 16.1   Illustration of an Item with Unequal ICCs in Two Subpopulations

ity to investigate item bias is analogous to conducting a reliability study for tests with suspect validity. Both activities seem rather pointless.) Items that are biased according to the latent trait definition may not be biased according to our definition. This point will be discussed in more detail at the end of this section. Figure 16.1 illustrates an item for which the ICCs are not the same for the two groups.

Because the ICCs for a set of unbiased items are invariant across subpopulations, most indices based on item response theory are measures of the extent to which the ICCs vary across these groups. Calculating these indices involves two steps. First the item parameters are estimated for each subpopulation and expressed on the same scale. Second an index of item bias is calculated for each item.

Scaling Item Parameters

Before the index of item bias is calculated the estimates of the item parameters must be expressed on the same scale for each subpopulation. One convenient way to do this is to constrain the estimates of the b_g's so that they have a mean of 0 and a standard deviation of 1 (Lord, 1980). This is known as "standardizing on the b_g's" and automatically places the parameter estimates on the same scale for each group. This procedure works for the three logistic models and for the normal ogive model. (For the one-parameter model it is only necessary to constrain the average item difficulty to 0.)

An alternate procedure involves standardizing on θ, the latent trait scores. In this procedure the scale for the estimates of the latent trait scores is set separately for each subgroup. In each subgroup the latent trait score estimates have a mean of 0 and a standard deviation of 1. Since the scales for the latent trait score estimates are different for the two subgroups, so are the scales for the estimates of difficulty and discrimination. However it is possible to transform the estimates of difficulty and discrimination for subgroup 1 to the scale for subgroup 2 by using the equations

$$\hat{b}_{1g} = k\hat{b}^*_{1g} + m \tag{16.1a}$$

and

$$\hat{a}_{1g} = \frac{\hat{a}^*_{1g}}{k} \tag{16.1b}$$

In these equations $\hat{a}^*_{1g}$ and $\hat{b}^*_{1g}$ represent the estimates for subpopulations 1 obtained by standardizing θ, and k and m are constants that are estimated as described subsequently. The values $\hat{a}_{1g}$ and $\hat{b}_{1g}$ are on the same scale as $\hat{a}_{2g}$ and $\hat{b}_{2g}$, the estimates obtained for subpopulation 2 by standardizing on θ. The quantity k can be estimated by the slope of the major axis of a scatterplot of $\hat{b}_{2g}$ versus $\hat{b}^*_{1g}$. The slope and intercept of this line are given by

$$\hat{k} = \frac{(\hat{\sigma}^2_2 - \hat{\sigma}^2_1) + \sqrt{(\hat{\sigma}^2_2 - \hat{\sigma}^2_1)^2 + 4\hat{\rho}^2_{12}\hat{\sigma}^2_1\hat{\sigma}^2_2}}{2\hat{\rho}_{12}\hat{\sigma}_1\hat{\sigma}_2} \tag{16.2a}$$

and

$$\hat{m} = \bar{b}_2 - \hat{k}\bar{b}_1 \tag{16.2b}$$

respectively. In Equation 16.2a, $\hat{\sigma}^2_1$ represents the variance over items of $\hat{b}^*_{1g}$, $\hat{\sigma}^2_2$ denotes the variance of $\hat{b}_{2g}$, and $\hat{\rho}_{12}$ represents the correlation over items of $\hat{b}^*_{1g}$ and $\hat{b}_{2g}$. In Equation 16.2b, $\bar{b}_2$ and $\bar{b}_1$ represent the average over items of $\hat{b}_{2g}$ and $\hat{b}^*_{1g}$, respectively. (Ironson, 1982, has pointed out that this procedure for estimating k and m is not entirely satisfactory and has discussed research directed to improving it.) The procedure will work for the one- and two- and three-parameter models. With the one-parameter model, k is set equal to 1. It should be noted that the pseudoguessing parameter, c_g, is not affected by a change of scale and there is no need to equate the $\hat{c}'_g$s for the two subpopulations.

Comparing ICCs

Once the parameter estimates are expressed on the same scale, the ICCs for the two subpopulations are compared. Several methods are available for making the comparison. Working with the three-parameter logistic model, Lord (1980) proposed a test of the null hypothesis that $a_{1g} = a_{2g}$ and $b_{1g} = b_{2g}$. It should be noted that this test is used in conjunction with the estimation procedure that standardizes on the b_g's for the groups. Because c_g is difficult to estimate accurately, it is not included in the test. The test is carried out for each item and leads to a chi-squared statistic which can be used to test the hypothesis in question. Each item for which the null hypothesis is rejected may be considered a biased item. Alternately the size of the chi-squared statistic may be considered to be a measure of the degree of bias in the item. Lord (1980) developed the test in the context of the three-parameter model. However a similar test is available for the two-parameter model. With the one-parameter model the null hypothesis $b_{1g} = b_{2g}$ may be tested with

$$z = \frac{\hat{b}_{1g} - \hat{b}_{2g}}{\sqrt{\hat{\sigma}_{b_{1g}}^2 + \hat{\sigma}_{b_{2g}}^2}}$$

where $\hat{\sigma}_{b_{ig}}$ denotes the standard error of the item difficulty for the gth item and ith group. The critical value is $\pm z_{\alpha/2}$, where $z_{\alpha/2}$ is $100(1 - \alpha/2)$ percentile of the standard normal distribution.

Rudner (1977) proposed calculating the area between the ICCs for two subgroups as a measure of the difference between two ICCs. This area can be approximated by using the formula

$$A_g = \sum_{\theta=-4.00}^{\theta=4.00} .005|P_{1g}(\theta) - P_{2g}(\theta)| \tag{16.3}$$

In Equation 16.3, $P_{1g}(\theta)$ and $P_{2g}(\theta)$ refer to the value of the ICC for each of the two groups. The value of $P_{ig}(\theta)$ is calculated for each value of θ from -4.00 to 4.00 in steps of $.005$. A variant of Equation 16.3 is

$$A_g(\text{signed}) = \sum_{\theta=-4}^{\theta=4} .005[P_{1g}(\theta) - P_{2g}(\theta)] \tag{16.4}$$

which yields a signed area measure. A numerical difference between the signed and unsigned measures occurs when the ICCs for the two subgroups cross, as illustrated in Figure 16.1. Because of the absolute value sign, use of Equation 16.3 converts negative values of $P_{1g}(\theta) - P_{2g}(\theta)$ to positive values. Thus all differences between the ICCs for the two subgroups are given a positive value by Equation 16.3. However, Equation 16.4 does not convert negative values of $P_{1g}(\theta) - P_{2g}(\theta)$ to positive values; thus the positive and negative differences balance out to some extent, and the unsigned area measure will be larger than the signed area measure. As a result, an item with the same ICCs and an item for which the signed differences exactly balance both yield $A_g(\text{signed}) = 0$. This seems undesirable since, even if the differences balance out, the item is biased.

Alternatives to Rudner's area measure have been suggested by Linn et al. (1981). These mean square item bias statistics are functions of $[P_{1g}(\theta) - P_{2g}(\theta)]^2$ calculated from $\theta = -3$ to $\theta = 3$. Both a weighted and unweighted version are available. The weighted mean square statistic weights more heavily those values $[P_{1g}(\theta) - P_{2g}(\theta)]^2$ that are accurately estimated more heavily. Computational details are given in Linn et al. More recent research on weighting has been conducted by Levine (1981) and Levine, Wardrop, and Linn (1982).

Which type of index of item bias is most appropriate? Is it better to report a statistic such as Lord developed for testing $b_{1g} = b_{2g}$ and $a_{1g} = a_{2g}$ or an area measure such as those developed by Rudner and Linn et al.? Although other criteria may eventually prove to be important in making this choice, it seems significant that ICCs can have quite different parameters and still be substantially the same (Linn et al., 1981). For example if $a_g = 1$, $b_g = 3.5$, and $c = .2$ in group 1, whereas $a_g = .5$, $b_g = 5.0$, $c_g = .2$ in group 2, the value of $P_{1g}(\theta) - P_{2g}(\theta)$ will not be greater than .05 for any value of θ between -3.0 and 3.0. In this case the large parameter difference may be a misleading indication of bias. This fact seems to favor the approach of Rudner or Linn et al. over that of Lord.

An Example Using Item Response Theory

To illustrate the use of item response theory in item bias investigations, responses of 150 males and 150 females to 10 items were analyzed. Table 16.1 reports estimates of item difficulty and item discrimination parameters of the normal ogive model for the male and female samples. (These estimates were obtained by using Equations 15.8 and 15.9, substituting the biserial correlation between total score and item score for ρ_g and the proportion correct measure of item difficulty. This estimation procedure is used for illustrative purposes only and probably should not be used in item bias research.) The values of $\hat{b}^*_{1g}$ and $\hat{a}^*_{1g}$ describe the male sample and were obtained by standardizing on θ for the males. The values of $\hat{b}_{2g}$ and $\hat{a}_{2g}$ describe the female sample and were obtained by standardizing on θ for the females. Since the parameter estimates for males and those for females are expressed on different scales, they are not directly comparable. To make these estimates comparable, $\hat{b}^*_{1g}$ and $\hat{a}^*_{1g}$ must be transformed with Equations 16.1a and 16.1b. This in turn requires calculation of $\hat{k}$ and $\hat{m}$. Table 16.1 reports $\bar{b}_1$, $\hat{\sigma}^2_1$, $\bar{b}_2$, $\hat{\sigma}^2_2$ and $\hat{\rho}_{12}$, which are necessary for calculating $\hat{k}$ and $\hat{m}$. Substitution in Equation 16.2a yields

$$\hat{k} = \frac{(1.055 - 1.343) + \sqrt{(1.055 - 1.343)^2 + 4(.769)^2(1.055)(1.343)}}{2(.769)(1.027)(1.158)}$$

$$= .798$$

TABLE 16.1.   Estimates of Item Difficulty and Discrimination for Male and Female Samples

	Sex			
	Male		Female	
Item	$\hat{b}^*_{1g}$	$\hat{a}^*_{1g}$	$\hat{b}_{2g}$	$\hat{a}_{2g}$
1	-3.726	.527	-1.467	1.198
2	$-.115$	1.000	.222	.723
3	-1.479	2.528	-1.602	.989
4	-2.966	.424	-1.734	.592
5	-2.614	.571	-3.202	.589
6	-1.375	1.730	-1.278	.909
7	$-.633$	.881	.139	.718
8	-1.196	.928	$-.428$	.963
9	$-.943$	1.920	$-.624$	.903
10	$-.083$	1.235	.115	.686

$$\bar{b}_1 = -1.513 \qquad \bar{b}_2 = -.985$$
$$\hat{\sigma}^2_1 = 1.343 \qquad \hat{\sigma}^2_2 = 1.055$$
$$\hat{\rho}_{12} = .769$$

Substitution in Equation 16.2b gives

$$\hat{m} = -.985 - (.798)(-1.513) = .222$$

Substituting for $\hat{k}$ and $\hat{m}$ in Equations 16.1a and 16.1b gives

$$\hat{b}_{1g} = .798\hat{b}^*_{tg} + .222$$

and

$$\hat{a}_{1g} = \frac{\hat{a}^*_{tg}}{.798}$$

as the equations for transforming from the scale for males to the scale for females.

Table 16.2 reports the values of $\hat{b}_{1g}$ and $\hat{a}_{1g}$ obtained from Equations 16.1a and 16.1b. It also reports $\hat{b}_{2g}$, $\hat{a}_{2g}$ and A_g, Rudner's area measure of item bias. Item 1 has the largest area measure of item bias, and item 7 has the smallest measure. Rules-of-thumb for deciding when an item is biased do not currently exist. The general practice seems to be to inspect items that have a relatively large measure of item bias and to try to rewrite these items to remove the source of bias. With this approach one might inspect items 1, 5, and possibly 3 since they have the largest item bias measures.

How well will the latent trait techniques meet the two purposes of item bias research we outlined earlier? We have already indicated that if all ICCs are equal for the subpopulations, the set of items are unbiased according to the latent trait definition and the definitions underlying our two purposes of item bias research. However items which are biased according to the latent trait definition are not necessarily biased according to the other definition. As Hunter (1975) has shown, if a set of items is multidimensional but a unidimensional latent trait model is fit to the data, the parameter estimates for this unidimensional model can vary across subgroups. Thus when ICCs for a unidimensional latent trait model vary across subgroups, it may indicate that the items are multidimensional. However from our point of view,

TABLE 16.2. Area Measure (A_g) of Item Bias

| Item | Sex | | | | |
| | Male | | Female | | |
	$\hat{b}_{1g}$	$\hat{a}_{1g}$	$\hat{b}_{2g}$	$\hat{a}_{2g}$	$\hat{A}_g$
1	−2.753	.672	−1.467	1.198	1.13
2	.130	1.252	.222	.723	.47
3	−.959	3.167	−1.602	.989	.77
4	−2.146	.531	−1.734	.592	.32
5	−1.865	.715	−3.202	.589	1.02
6	−.875	2.167	−1.278	.909	.60
7	−.283	1.103	.139	.718	.52
8	−.733	1.162	−.428	.963	.31
9	−.531	2.405	−.624	.903	.55
10	.155	1.546	.115	.686	.64

multidimensionality does not indicate bias unless (1) the other latent traits are irrelevant to the construct being measured, and (2) the distribution of these latent traits is different for the subpopulations. Thus varying ICCs do not necessarily indicate bias.

The second reason ICCs may vary is if different unidimensional latent traits are measured in the two subpopulations. From our point of view this situation does indicate item bias. How can the reason for the variant ICCs be ascertained? In principle the reason can be uncovered by establishing the dimensionality of the items in each subgroup. If the items are unidimensional in each group, the varying ICCs are due to measurement of different latent traits. If the items are multidimensional in each group, the variant ICCs are due to multidimensionality. The rub is that currently there are no entirely adequate procedures for establishing dimensionality. Therefore, when ICCs differ for two subpopulations the interpretation is always somewhat cloudy.

There is an important point to be made about the situation in which the items are unidimensional in each group but some of the ICCs vary across groups. The latter finding implies that the latent traits are different for each group. Therefore it is inappropriate to discard those items with different ICCs and claim that the remaining items are unbiased. Because the original item set was unidimensional for each group, these items that remain in the test still measure different latent traits for the two subpopulations and are therefore biased. Of course, in practice, we probably never have precisely unidimensional items. Therefore if only a few items vary across subpopulations, and these items have relatively low discrimination indices, it is reasonable to discard these items and claim that the remainder are unbiased.

CHI-SQUARE TECHNIQUES

Scheuneman (1979) and Camilli (1979) developed techniques that can be considered approximations to item response theory procedures. The advantage of these procedures is that they are simpler to apply than the procedures based on item response theory. These techniques essentially define an item as unbiased if, within a group of examinees with scores in the same test score interval, the proportion of examinees responding correctly to the item is the same for both subpopulations. These methods may be viewed as approximations to the latent trait methods since the observed test score is substituted for the latent trait in defining a biased item and the observed test score can be considered an errorful measure of the latent trait.

With the chi-square techniques the observed score scale is divided into several intervals. Within each interval the subpopulations are compared in terms of the proportions responding correctly to an item. If the proportions vary across groups, it is considered evidence of item bias. Table 16.3 presents some data for an example in which the score scale has been divided into four intervals. The symbols N_{1j} and N_{2j} refer to the number of examinees in the first and second subgroups, respectively, with scores in the jth interval. Thus 25 examinees from subgroup 1 had total scores in the first interval, and 315 examinees from subgroup 2 had scores in this interval. The symbols O_{1j} and O_{2j} refer to the number of examinees in subgroups 1 and 2 who had scores in the jth interval and answered the item correctly. The quantity P_{1j} is calculated by using

$$P_{1j} = \frac{O_{1j}}{N_{1j}} \qquad (16.5)$$

and is the proportion of examinees in the first group and jth interval who answered the item correctly. For subgroup 1 and interval 3 the proportion answering the item correctly is $P_{13} = 23/48 = .479$. The quantity P_{2j} is calculated and defined in a similar fashion for group 2. The quantity $P_{\cdot j}$ is calculated from

$$P_{\cdot j} = \frac{O_{1j} + O_{2j}}{N_{1j} + N_{2j}} \qquad (16.6)$$

and is the proportion of all examinees who scored in the jth interval and answered the item correctly. For examinees in interval 4, the proportion answering the item correctly is

$$P_{\cdot 4} = \frac{14 + 33}{65 + 92} = .299$$

Camilli's statistic is calculated by using the formula

$$\chi_c^2 = \sum_{j=1}^{J} \frac{N_{1j}N_{2j}(P_{1j} - P_{2j})^2}{(N_{1j} + N_{2j})P_{\cdot j}(1 - P_{\cdot j})} = \Sigma\chi_j^2 \qquad (16.7)$$

The χ_c^2 statistic can be tested for significance by comparing it to the $100(1 - \alpha)$ fractile of the chi-square distribution with J degrees of freedom. Here J denotes the total number of intervals. Alternately the magnitude of χ_c^2 can be considered an index of the amount of bias in the item. Table 16.4 illustrates the calculation of χ_c^2 using the data in Table 16.3. There is a signed version of Camilli's statistic which will be denoted by χ_c^2(signed). With this statistic each χ_j^2 is given a positive or negative sign according to whether P_{1j} is larger than or smaller than P_{2j}.

TABLE 16.3. Illustrative Data for Calculating χ_c^2 and χ_s^2

Interval	Score Level	N_{1j}	O_{1j}	P_{1j}	N_{2j}	O_{2j}	P_{2j}	$P_{\cdot j}$
1	13–14	25	22	.880	315	300	.952	.947
2	12	24	18	.750	110	99	.900	.873
3	10–11	48	23	.479	118	93	.788	.698
4	1–9	65	14	.215	92	33	.358	.299

From J. Scheuneman, A new method for assessing bias in test items, *Journal of Educational Measurement, 16*, 143–152. Copyright 1979 by the National Council on Measurement in Education, Washington, D.C. Adapted by permission.

TABLE 16.4.   Illustration of the Calculation of Camilli's χ_c^2

Interval	Substitution in χ_j^2	Result of Calculation
1	$\dfrac{25(315)(.880 - .952)^2}{(25 + 315).947(1 - .947)}$	2.392
2	$\dfrac{24(110)(.750 - .900)^2}{(24 + 110).873(1 - .873)}$	3.998
3	$\dfrac{48(118)(.479 - .788)^2}{(48 + 118).698(1 - .698)}$	15.455
4	$\dfrac{65(92)(.215 - .358)^2}{(65 + 92).299(1 - .299)}$	3.716

$$\chi_c^2 = 2.392 + 3.998 + 16.455 + 3.716 = 26.56$$

Scheuneman's statistic is calculated by using the formula

$$\chi_s^2 = \sum_{j=1}^{J} \frac{(O_{1j} - P_{.j}N_{1j})^2}{P_{.j}N_{1j}} + \sum_{j=1}^{J} \frac{(O_{2j} - P_{.j}N_{2j})^2}{P_{.j}N_{2j}} \tag{16.8}$$

Table 16.5 exhibits the steps in calculating χ_s^2. Scheuneman suggests that χ_s^2 is distributed as χ^2 with $J - 1$ degrees of freedom. Several authors (see, for example, Baker, 1981) have pointed out that this is not correct. However, the magnitude of χ_s^2 can be considered an indication of the amount of bias in the item. There is a signed version of χ_s^2 denoted by χ_s^2(signed), calculated by giving both $(O_{1j} - P_{.j}N_{1j})^2$ and $(O_{2j} - P_jN_{2j})^2$ a positive or negative sign according to whether O_{1j} is greater than or less than $P_{.j}N_{1j}$.

TABLE 16.5.   Illustration of the Calculation of Scheuneman's χ_s^2

Interval	Substitution for Group 1	Result of Calculation	Substitution for Group 2	Result of Calculation
1	$\dfrac{[22 - (.947)(25)]^2}{(.947)(25)}$	.118	$\dfrac{[300 - (.947)(315)]^2}{(.947)(315)}$	.009
2	$\dfrac{[18 - (.873)(24)]^2}{(.873)(24)}$	.415	$\dfrac{[99 - (.873)(110)]^2}{(.873)(110)}$	.091
3	$\dfrac{[23 - (.698)(48)]^2}{(.698)(48)}$	3.293	$\dfrac{[93 - (.698)(118)]^2}{(.698)(118)}$	1.373
4	$\dfrac{[14 - (.299)(65)]^2}{(.299)(65)}$	1.519	$\dfrac{[33 - (.299)(92)]^2}{(.299)(92)}$	1.096

$$\chi_s^2 = .118 + .415 + 3.293 + 1.519 + .009 + 1.373 + 1.096 = 7.89$$

A critical issue in use of the chi-square methods is the choice of cut scores for forming the intervals. This is an important decision since the choice of cut scores can affect the magnitude of both χ_c^2 and χ_s^2 (Ironson, 1982). The cut scores are chosen so that there are a sufficient number of examinees in each interval. Rules-of-thumb for the number of examinees in each interval are discussed subsequently. Scheuneman (1979) pointed out that unless some incorrect responses occur for each interval, the interval cannot possibly contribute to the detection of bias; however, she did not specify any particular number of incorrect responses. She also pointed out that her procedure may be especially dependent on the specific intervals chosen unless the total number of correct responses for each examinee group in each interval is at least between 10 and 20. Ironson implied that these criteria should be met for Camilli's technique also. In addition, Scheuneman suggested that to use χ_s^2, the expected number of correct responses in the ith group and jth interval, $N_{ij}P._j$, should be at least 5 for all i and j. In a similar fashion Ironson suggests that to use χ_c^2, the expected frequencies of $N_{ij}P._j$ and $N_{ij}(1 - P._j)$ should be at least 5.

One problem with the chi-square techniques is that evidence of item bias may be an artifact of measurement error. As we pointed out earlier, with the chi-square techniques the subpopulations are compared in terms of the proportion responding correctly to each item, but the comparison is made within each score interval. If the comparison were not made within each score interval, it would amount to comparing the proportion-correct measure of item difficulty. However a subpopulation difference in item difficulty is not necessarily an indication of item bias. It may reflect true differences between the subpopulations on the construct measured by the test. Making the comparisons within an interval is an attempt to control for such differences. The problem is that this device at best controls for observed score differences between the subgroups. However, it is desirable to control for true score differences (or equivalently, for latent trait score differences) rather than observed score differences. When observed scores are controlled, true score differences may exist between the groups even for examinees in the same observed score interval. In this situation, the subpopulation with the higher true scores will more frequently respond correctly to the item. This is true even if among examinees with the same true score, or the same latent trait score, the proportion responding correctly is the same for each group. Thus, the chi-square techniques may exhibit evidence of item bias that is an artifact of measurement error.

Comparison of Chi-square and Latent-Trait-Based Measures of Item Bias

Several authors have investigated the correlation between chi-square measures of item bias and measures of item bias based on item response theory. Ironson and Subkoviak (1979) analyzed five subtests used in the National Longitudinal Study (Hilton and Rhett, 1973) and reported correlations between χ_s^2 and A_g of .485 (total battery), .361 (vocabulary) .652 (picture-number), .742 (letter groups), .505

(math), and $-.047$ (mosaic comparisons). Ironson and Subkoviak also reported correlations between χ_s^2(signed) and A_g(signed). These were .575 (total battery), .561 (vocabulary), .754 (picture-number), .820 (letter groups), .543 (math), and .161 (mosaic comparisons). As Ironson and Subkoviak note, the range of these correlations is hard to interpret because it is unknown how well the three-parameter latent trait model fits the data in each subgroup. Shepard, Camilli, and Averill (1981) also investigated the correlation between chi-square and latent-trait-based measures of item bias. They analyzed data collected for black, chicano, and white samples on the Lorge-Thorndike Intelligence Test, Verbal and Nonverbal (Level 3, Form B, 1954). Correlations between the chi-square measures and latent trait measures of item bias are reported in Table 16.6.

Rudner, Getson and Knight (1980) simulated the responses of two groups of 1,200 examinees to 5,600 items with the three-parameter model. The situation simulated was that in which the items measure different latent traits for the two populations. This situation definitely involves item bias. Since the data were simulated, Rudner et al. could calculate the true values of A_g and correlate these with the estimated values of A_g and of χ_s^2. The former correlation was .80 and the latter was .73. These values suggest that when the items are unidimensional in both groups and when item bias exists, χ_s^2 will be almost as accurate an indicator of the amount of bias as A_g will be. Rudner et al. also reported a .73 correlation between the sample values of A_g and χ_s^2.

Taken as a group the correlations from the three studies are somewhat difficult to interpret. Rudner's study is the only one for which it is clear that item bias exists. The correlation between the estimated value of χ_s^2 and the true value of A_g was almost as large as that between the estimated and true values of A_g. This suggests that χ_s^2 can be substituted for A_g. The correlations in the Ironson and Subkoviak study and the Shepard et al. study suggest that the chi-square measures and area measures reflect something in common but that the chi-square measures are not adequate substitutes for the area measures. The problem with this latter conclusion

TABLE 16.6.   Correlations between Latent Trait and Chi-Square Item Bias Indices

Groups Compared	Chi-Square Measure	Subtest and Type of Index			
		Verbal		Nonverbal	
		Signed	Unsigned	Signed	Unsigned
Black-White	Scheuneman	.59[a]	.45	.63	.44
	Camilli	.68	.40[b]	.66	.41
Chicano-White	Scheuneman	.58	.40	.76	.28
	Camilli	.68	.37	.76	.03

[a] Correlation between χ_s^2(signed) and A_g(signed).
[b] Correlation between χ_c^2 and A_g.

From L. Shepard, G. Camilli, and M. Averill, Comparison of procedures for detecting test-item bias with both internal and external ability criterion, *Journal of Educational Statistics, 6*, 317–376. Copyright 1980 by the American Educational Research Association, Washington, D.C. Adapted by permission.

is that it is not clear that item bias actually exists for the tests studied by Ironson and Subkoviak and Shepard et al. As a result, it is not clear what A_g and A_g(signed) are measuring. Hence, the lack of substitutability of the chi-square measures for the area measures reported in these studies may or may not be important.

Techniques Based on Item Difficulty

A number of methods have been developed for using measures of item difficulty in item bias studies. These methods use either the proportion-correct measure of item difficulty (p) or some transformation of the item difficulty. All the methods are variations on a theme and are based on one of two definitions of a set of unbiased items.

The first definition is that a set of items is unbiased if the item difficulties for subpopulation 2 are perfectly correlated with the item difficulties for subpopulation 1. Think of constructing a scatterplot with item difficulties for subpopulation 2 plotted on the y axis and those for subpopulation 1 plotted on the x axis. The definition requires all points in the scatterplot to lie on a straight line. However, it should be noted that this requirement applies to item difficulties calculated for the subpopulations. With item difficulties calculated for samples from the subpopulations, some degree of scatter is to be expected even if the set of items is unbiased according to the first definition.

Perhaps the best-known method based on this definition was developed by Angoff and Ford (1973). This method uses the delta measure of item difficulty. For the gth item, delta is defined as $\hat{\Delta}_g = 4\hat{z}_g + 13$. Here, $\hat{z}_g$ is the z-score that cuts off the proportion, $\hat{p}_g$, in the standard normal distribution, and $\hat{p}_g$ is the proportion-correct measure of item difficulty. To apply the delta plot procedure, the $\hat{\Delta}_g$'s are calculated for each item and each subgroup and then the scatterplot, just described, is constructed. Table 16.7 presents hypothetical data describing the responses of samples from two subpopulations to 20 items. The statistics $\hat{p}_{g1}$, $\hat{z}_{g1}$ and $\hat{\Delta}_{g1}$ refer to the sample from the first subpopulation, and $\hat{p}_{g2}$, $\hat{z}_{g2}$ and $\hat{\Delta}_{g2}$ describe the sample from the second subpopulation. Figure 16.2 presents the scatterplot of $\hat{\Delta}_{g2}$ versus $\hat{\Delta}_{g1}$. The correlation for this scatterplot is .96, which may seem quite substantial. However, two of the points lie removed from the remaining points in the scatterplot, and these might be considered biased items.

A more formal method for detecting aberrant items involves fitting a straight line to the scatterplot and calculating d_g, the distance of the gth item from the line. The line fitted to the scatterplot is the major axis of the plot. Equation 16.2a can be used to calculate the slope of the line. However, here $\hat{\sigma}_i^2$ is the variance of the deltas for group i, and $\hat{\rho}_{12}$ is the correlation between the deltas for the two samples. In our example $\hat{\sigma}_1^2 = 20.068$, $\hat{\sigma}_2^2 = 17.926$, $\hat{\rho}_{12} = .961$, and $\hat{k}$ is calculated to be .936. The intercept is $\hat{m} = \overline{\Delta}_{g2} - \hat{k}\overline{\Delta}_{g1}$, where $\overline{\Delta}_{g2}$ and $\overline{\Delta}_{g1}$ represent the means of the $\hat{\Delta}_{g2}$'s and the $\hat{\Delta}_{g1}$'s. In our example, $\overline{\Delta}_{g2} = 11.851$, $\overline{\Delta}_{g1} = 12.063$, and $\hat{m}$ is calculated to be .558. The absolute value of the distance of the point, representing the gth item, from the major axis of the ellipse is

$$d_g = \frac{\hat{k}\hat{\Delta}_{g1} - \hat{\Delta}_{g2} + \hat{m}}{\sqrt{\hat{k}^2 + 1}}$$

(16.9)

Items with large d_g's deviate sufficiently from the line to be considered biased. Unfortunately there does not seem to be a rule-or-thumb for deciding when d_g is large enough to indicate bias. Table 16.7 reports the values of d_g for the twenty items. Inspection of the table shows that $d_{19} = -2.70$ and $d_{20} = 2.31$. These values are substantially larger than the values of d_g for the remaining items, which suggests that these items are biased. If several of the d_g's are not obviously larger than the others, interpreting d_g is more difficult.

One problem with the delta plot approach is that even though it is possible for the entire set of items to be unbiased according to the latent trait definition, the delta plot method may indicate bias. For example, considering the case in which the latent trait is normally distributed in each subgroup and all the ICCs are two-parameter normal ogives, Hunter (1975) showed that unless all item discrimination parameters (a_g) are equal, the delta plot will typically show some evidence of item bias. Moreover those items with large item discriminations will tend to appear the most biased. This problem arises when the latent trait distributions are not the same for each subpopulation. Even in this case the problem would be resolved if subgroups could be matched in terms of latent trait scores, or equivalently, in terms of

TABLE 16.7. Comparison of Item Difficulty Indices for Two Groups

Item	$\hat{p}_{g1}$	$\hat{z}_{g1}$	$\hat{\Delta}_{g1}$	$\hat{p}_{g2}$	$\hat{z}_{g2}$	$\hat{\Delta}_{g2}$	d_g
1	.407	−0.235	12.058	.447	−0.133	12.466	−0.45
2	.201	−0.837	9.648	.226	−0.752	9.988	−0.29
3	.788	0.802	16.209	.758	0.703	15.813	−0.06
4	.430	−0.176	12.293	.365	−0.344	11.620	0.33
5	.941	1.566	19.265	.918	1.394	18.578	0.01
6	.400	−0.251	11.993	.404	−0.241	12.036	−0.18
7	.062	−1.538	6.845	.065	−1.514	6.942	0.02
8	.002	−2.828	1.688	.001	−2.931	1.273	0.63
9	.390	−0.277	11.888	.369	−0.332	11.669	0.01
10	.003	−2.671	2.313	.005	−2.567	2.730	−0.00
11	.338	−0.417	11.331	.351	−0.382	11.470	−0.22
12	.674	0.452	14.807	.633	0.341	14.365	0.04
13	.235	−0.722	10.111	.183	−0.902	9.391	0.46
14	.781	0.777	16.108	.730	0.613	15.453	0.13
15	.516	0.041	13.166	.443	−0.143	12.427	0.33
16	.704	0.538	15.152	.663	0.423	14.692	0.04
17	.543	0.108	13.433	.543	0.109	13.436	−0.22
18	.488	−0.030	12.877	.486	−0.034	12.860	−0.18
19	.387	−0.287	11.850	.722	0.590	15.360	−2.71
20	.804	1.305	18.221	.641	0.362	14.449	−2.31

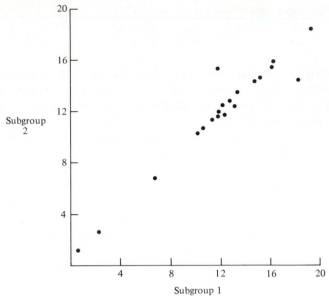

FIGURE 16.2   Delta Plot for Two Subgroups

true scores. As this is clearly impossible, several researchers have suggested some sort of matching that might approximate matching on latent trait scores.

Angoff (1982) suggested matching on variables that are external to the test and are correlated with the test scores. Jensen (1980) suggested using the total score on the test. Another possibility is to use estimated true scores. Work by Hunter and Cohen (1974) gives theoretical support to this alternative. However, two points about the use of matched groups should be borne in mind. First, examinees matched in terms of external variables, observed scores, or estimated true scores still differ in terms of latent trait scores, and as a result artifactual evidence of item bias may result. Second, the criterion for unbiased items should be different for matched groups than for unmatched groups since, for examinees matched on latent trait scores, unbiased items will be equally difficult. Thus, for matched groups a high correlation characterizing the delta plot is not necessarily evidence that the items are unbiased. Since with matched groups unbiased items will be equally difficult, bias can be investigated with McNemar's test (Marascuilo and McSweeney, 1977) for equality of proportions. Subject to the qualifications discussed, those items yielding significant test statistics might be considered biased. Alternately, the size of the test statistic can be considered to be a measure of the amount of bias in the item.

Another method for resolving the problem of different latent trait score distributions is the use of pseudogroups (Jensen, 1980). In a pseudogroup design the test score of each examinee in the smaller subgroup is matched to the score of an examinee in the larger subgroup. By this matching process the larger subgroup is divided into two pseudogroups. The distribution of test scores for one of the pseudogroups matches the distribution of the test scores from the smaller subgroup. The other pseudogroup consists of the remaining members of the larger subgroup. Angoff's analysis is then conducted twice, once for the two pseudogroups and once for the two subgroups. The delta plot correlations for the pseudogroups can be compared to that for the subpopulations. Item bias is indicated if the subgroup correlation is substantially smaller than the pseudogroup correlation. With this analysis there are again several cautions to be kept in mind. First, there is no hard and fast criterion for comparing the two correlations. Second, because the matching is not done by using true scores, the correlation for the pseudogroups can be expected to be somewhat larger than that for the subpopulations, even when the items are unbiased by the latent trait definition. Unfortunately there are no available guidelines to the amount of difference that might be expected.

Earlier we noted that item difficulty bias detection methods are based on one of two definitions, and that Angoff's method is based on the first. The second definition of a set of unbiased items requires the difficulty difference between the subgroups to be the same for all items. According to this definition, any item that exhibits a difficulty difference between subgroups which is larger than the difficulty difference typical for the set of items is a biased item. It should be noted that any set of items that meets the unbiasedness criterion of the second definition also meets the criterion of the first definition. The converse is not necessarily true. The analysis of variance approach employed by Cardall and Coffman (1964), Cleary and Hilton (1968), and Plake and Hoover (1977) uses this definition. See these articles for a description of the methodology. A graphical approach that uses the second definition was described by Echternacht (1974). Methods that are based on this second definition are subject to the same problem as those based on the first. Namely, evidence of bias may be an artifact of different levels of ability for the two groups. The designs for both matched groups and pseudogroups have some potential for ameliorating this problem, but their potential is limited by the factors just discussed.

Comparison of Latent-Trait-Based Indices with Delta Plot Indices

Several researchers have reported correlations between d_g and A_g as well as between the signed versions of these statistics. For Ironson and Subkoviak (1979) the correlation between the unsigned versions of d_g and A_g were .239 (total battery), .373 (vocabulary), .265 (picture-number), $-.161$ (lettergroups), .245 (math), and .088 (mosaic comparisons). The corresponding correlations for the signed versions were .491, .687, .675, .318, .419, and .364. Comparison of these correlations with the corresponding correlations for the chi-square methods shows that eight are smaller, two are about equal, and two are larger. The Rudner et al. study yielded a .61 correlation between the estimated values of d_g and the true values of A_g and a .60 correlation between the estimated values of d_g and the estimated values of A_g. These are smaller than their counterparts for χ_s^2. The study by Shepard, Camilli, and Averill (1981) yielded the following correlations between d_g(signed) and A_g(signed) for the black-white comparisons: .52 (verbal); .51 (nonverbal); and the corresponding correlations for the chicano-white comparison: .30 (verbal), .29 (nonverbal). Again these tend to be lower than the corresponding correlation for the chi-square methods. In summary there appears to be less justification for substituting d_g for A_g than for substituting χ_s^2 for A_g.

ADVANTAGES AND DISADVANTAGES OF DIFFERENT METHODS

The major advantage of using latent trait theory is that indications of item bias should not occur solely because of differences in the ability distribution. However, even when item bias does not exist, differences between the ICCs can occur if the items are not unidimensional. This is clearly a disadvantage of the methods based on item response theory. The disadvantage may eventually be negated through the development of multidimensional latent trait methods. Also, this disadvantage is shared by the chi-square and item difficulty methods. Another disadvantage is the sample size and number of items required for using latent trait methods. As noted in Chapter 15, Hulin, Lissak, and Drasgow (1982) found an acceptably low error in recovering three-parameter ICCs for 1,000 subjects and 30 items and for 500 subjects and 60 items. These size requirements would need to be met in each sample because accurate estimation is required in each sample. Fewer subjects and items may be required with the two-parameter and one-parameter models. For example Burril (1982) recommends a minimum of 500 examinees per group, and Wright and Stone (1979) suggest that 200 examinees are required in each group when the one-parameter model is used.

Major advantages shared by both the chi-square and item difficulty methods are the ease of computation and the relatively modest sample sizes required. Samples with between 100 and 200 examinees in each group are probably sufficient. A disadvantage of the item difficulty methods is that item bias can be an artifact of variation in the ability distributions of the subpopulations. In principle this problem can be circumvented by matching on latent trait scores. However this is clearly impossible, and matching examinees on other variables fails to resolve the problem entirely. The chi-square techniques may also be viewed as attempts to match on ability and share the problem of imperfect matching with the item difficulty methods.

SUMMARY

In this chapter a set of items was defined as unbiased if it meets two criteria:

1. In all subpopulations of interest the items scores are affected by the same sources of variance.
2. For examinees who are homogeneous on the construct purportedly measured by the test, the distributions of any source of item score variance, irrelevant to the intended construct, are the same across all subpopulations of interest.

Three classes of methods for investigating item bias were described, item response theory, chi-square, and item difficulty methods.

Item response theory methods involve a comparison of item characteristic curves for the several subpopulations using statistics for comparing item parameters or area measures. Chi-square methods involve the comparison across subpopulations of the proportion correct for examinees with observed scores in the same test score interval. Chi-square methods suggested by Scheuneman and by Camilli were discussed. Item difficulty methods involve comparisons of measures of item difficulty for the relevant subpopulations or for matched subgroups, one from each relevant subpopulation.

Each method can indicate item bias even when none exists according to the definition set forth earlier. With the latent trait methods multidimensionality can be mistaken for item bias. In addition to potentially confounding multidimensionality and item bias, the chi-square methods and item difficulty methods also potentially confound item bias and true differences on the construct being measured. In principle the latent trait methods appear to be the most promising. Development of trustworthy methods of detecting multidimensionality and/or the development of practical methods for estimating multidimensional latent trait models will resolve the problem of confounding multidimensionality and item bias. Practically speaking, the latent trait methods suffer because they require large data sets and complex computer programs, which can be expensive to run. Both the chi-square methods and item difficulty methods can be used with smaller data sets and are reasonably easy to implement. Of these two, the chi-square method appears to be more promising since there is more theoretical and empirical justification for substituting the chi-square methods for the latent trait methods.

Exercises

1. Following are item difficulties on each of 10 items for each of two groups. Using these indices, carry out Angoff's procedure and indicate those items that appear to be biased.

Item Difficulties for Two Groups
on the Same Test

Item	A	B
1	.540	.447
2	.132	.151
3	.629	.263
4	.308	.207
5	.085	.046
6	.020	.018
7	.273	.421
8	.978	.976
9	.833	.733
10	.040	.018

2. For each of four test score intervals, the following table presents the number of examinees (N_{1j} and N_{2j}) and the number of examinees answering the item correctly (O_{1j} and O_{2j}) in each of the two groups. Use these data to carry out Scheuneman's and Camilli's procedures. Use the appropriate critical value to determine whether there is statistically significant evidence of test bias.

Frequency Correct and Total Frequency
for Each of Two Groups Classified
into Four Test Score Intervals

Interval	O_{1j}	N_{1j}	O_{2j}	N_{2j}
1	16	56	36	100
2	31	47	48	72
3	41	53	44	62
4	40	43	33	35

3. A 25-item test was administered to 199 males and 269 females. Following is a frequency distribution for each gender group. Also reported for each score is the number of males and number of females who answered a particular item on the test correctly. Use these data to set up appropriate intervals and carry out Camilli's procedure. Use the appropriate critical value to determine whether there is statistically significant evidence of sex bias.

Total Frequency and Frequency Correct for Examinees Classified
by Total Test Score and Gender

	Sex			
	Male		Female	
Score[a]	Total Frequency	Frequency Correct	Total Frequency	Frequency Correct
5	1	1	0	0
7	0	0	1	1
8	2	1	2	1
9	2	0	2	2
10	4	2	7	4
11	4	2	5	2
12	4	4	7	2
13	4	3	7	6
14	5	2	18	9
15	11	7	28	14
16	19	7	23	15
17	25	15	35	15
18	22	12	37	19
19	27	12	34	18
20	26	14	38	19
21	24	15	19	12
22	13	8	15	13
23	6	6	1	1

[a] Missing scores had total frequencies of 0 for both males and females.

4. Rasch item difficulties and standard errors of the item difficulties were estimated separately for males and females. For each group the scale for the item parameters was set by constraining the average item difficulty to zero. The item difficulties and standard errors are reported in the following table. Use these results to determine which if any of the items are biased. (You may assume, for the purpose of this question, that there is sufficient evidence to conclude the items are unidimensional for males and females.)

Rasch Item Difficulties (b) and Standard Errors (SE)
for Males and Females

Item	Male		Female	
	b	SE	b	SE
1	−0.036	.169	−0.007	.138
2	−2.531	.369	−2.071	.252
3	2.367	.179	2.564	.170
4	0.758	.154	0.511	.130
5	−2.284	.335	−2.831	.341
6	−1.290	.235	−0.653	.158
7	0.341	.160	0.528	.130
8	−1.290	.235	−1.466	.202
9	2.832	.201	2.452	.165
10	1.469	.156	1.218	.131
11	0.829	.154	0.846	.129
12	−0.510	.188	−0.579	.155
13	−2.077	.310	−2.009	.246
14	1.102	.154	1.357	.133
15	0.238	.162	.142	.135

UNIT FIVE

Test Scoring and Interpretation

Chapter 17

CORRECTING FOR GUESSING AND OTHER SCORING METHODS

In conventional scoring of objective tests, each test score is the sum of the item scores for a given examinee, and the examinee is awarded one point for the correct item response and zero for any other response. This is sometimes called number-right scoring. The conventional scoring rule can be expressed as

$$X_a = \sum_{i=1}^{n} x_{ai} \tag{17.1}$$

where X_a is the total test score for examinee a and x_{ai} is the item score for examinee a to item i. When items are dichotomously scored, values of x_{ai} are 0 or 1, and no credit is given for blank or omitted items. With this scoring rule, all items are weighted equally. Although conventional scoring is simple and straightforward, it may pose problems when used with multiple-choice or true-false items.

It has long been recognized that examinees vary in their willingness to omit items for which they do not know the correct answers. This can contribute to variance in observed scores, which is unrelated to examinees' variation on the trait of interest. Suppose that Phyllis and George take an examination used to screen applicants for admission to a professional school. On this 100-item multiple-choice test, Phyllis knows the answer to 60 items but is unsure of the answer to the remaining 40 items and leaves them unanswered; George also knows the answer to 60 items but guesses at the answers to the remaining 40 items. Even if his guesses are entirely random, if there are four choices per item, George is likely to get 10 of these items correct by chance alone. If conventional scoring were applied, Phyllis would have a total score of 60 but George would be likely to have a total score of 70 points. Thus the observed score difference for these two candidates has nothing to do with their differences on the trait of interest but rather is a function of their propensities for guessing and random chance. This may present a serious concern to the examiner who must use scores from a single test to make decisions of import (e.g., selection of applicants for job or school admission or certification of members of a profession). It is in such situations that alternatives to conventional scoring typically have been considered.

FORMULA SCORING

The traditional approach to correction of test scores for differential guessing among examinees is through formula scoring. Rowley and Traub (1977) noted that formula scoring is based on a model which takes into account three possible situations: The examinee knows the correct option and chooses it, the examinee omits the item, or the examinee guesses blindly and selects one of the k item responses at random. Based on this *random-guessing* model, a basic formula for correcting raw scores for the effects of guessing can be written as

$$X_C = R + O/k \qquad (17.2)$$

where X_C is the corrected score; R, the number of correct answers; O, the number of items omitted; and k, the number of alternatives per item. (All items must have k alternatives.) Table 17.1 demonstrates the computation of corrected scores with this formula and presents results of its application to scores of three hypothetical examinees with differential guessing behaviors. Note that this correction increases an examinee's observed score by awarding additional points for omitted items on the assumption that if the examinee had attempted the omitted item, the probability of selecting the correct response is $1/k$. Thus it is assumed that all guesses at omitted items would be made at random.

A second formula, known as the *rights minus wrongs correction,* is

$$X_C' = R - W/(k - 1) \qquad (17.3)$$

TABLE 17.1. Illustrative Computation of Formula Scores for Three Examinees with Equal Raw Scores but Different Guessing Rates on a 20-Item Test with Four Responses per Item.

Examinee	No. Right	Omits	No. Incorr.	$X_C = R + O/k$	$X_C' = R - W/(k - 1)$
Ben R.	14	0	6	$14 + 0/4 = 14.00$	$14 - 6/3 = 12$
Louise M.	14	6	0	$14 + 6/4 = 15.50$	$14 - 0/3 = 14$
Tammy D.	14	3	3	$14 + 3/4 = 14.75$	$14 - 3/3 = 13$

where X_C' is the score corrected for guessing, W is the number of incorrect answers, and k is the number of alternatives per item. Table 17.1 also uses this formula to provide corrected scores for three examinees. At initial inspection, it may not be apparent why this formula should work as a correction. The underlying logic is to deprive the examinee of the number of points which are estimated to have been gained from random guessing. A basic assumption is that each incorrect response is the result of a random guess. To illustrate how this formula functions, suppose that we have a test composed of four-choice items, so $(k - 1) = 3$. With a random-guessing model, the quantity W represents only 3/4 of the items which the examinee did not know. Dividing W by $(k - 1)$, or 3, yields an estimate of the number of items which the examinee probably answered correctly by guessing. This latter quantity is subtracted from the examinee's score when making the correction for guessing.

Although Equations 17.2 and 17.3 yield numerically different values, the rank orders of the three examinees' scores in Table 17.1 are identical with these two corrections. In fact, Equation 17.3 can be shown to be a linear transformation of Equation 17.2, and thus if the two formulas are applied to the same set of item responses, the results will be perfectly correlated. Nevertheless, Traub and Hambleton (1972) have suggested that although the two correction formulas are mathematically equivalent, the instructions which accompany them may introduce different psychological factors into the examinees' test-taking behavior.

Rationale for Formula Scoring

Proponents of formula scoring have argued that this method should increase reliability and validity of scores because the corrected score should be a better estimate of the examinee's score on the underlying trait measured by the test than the uncorrected observed score. The theoretical rationale for this contention has been explained by numerous authors, with one succinct explication offered by Lord (1975). In this attempt to clarify the model underlying formula scoring, Lord identified two score values for an examinee, which we will here label X and X_C:

1. X is the score earned when an examinee is instructed to answer every item and number-correct scoring is employed.
2. X_C is the score earned when the same examinee is instructed to answer every item for which there is sufficient partial knowledge to eliminate one or more responses and to omit all other items, and scores are computed by Equation 17.2.

The use of formula scoring rests on the critical assumption that the difference between scores X and X_C for the same examinee on the same items is due only to random chance, which affects the X score because of lucky and unlucky guesses as the examinee is forced to respond to items which would be omitted under formula-scoring instructions. Lord further pointed out that for any given value of O (the number of items which should be omitted under the formula-scoring condition) the expected value of X and the expected value of X_C should be equal. However, for a given examinee on a given test, X and X_C may differ because on that particular occasion the examinee's lucky guesses may exceed or fall below O/k (the value by which the observed score will be adjusted under formula scoring). Because X values are affected by random guessing, its sampling variance should be greater than the sampling variance of X_C. Since the scores X and X_C are considered unbiased estimators of the same parameter (i.e., the examinee's true score), the estimator with the smaller sampling variance would be preferred. Thus in theory, X_C should be a better estimator of the examinee's ability than X. A review of empirical research, however, does not lend strong support to this contention.

Empirical Studies of Formula Scoring

In reviewing studies comparing results from conventional and formula scoring, Diamond and Evans (1973) found that reliability estimates were similar or in some cases slightly higher for the uncorrected scores; there was a trend, however, for validity coefficients to be slightly higher for corrected scores, but the magnitude of this effect was fairly small. Even Lord (1963) had concluded that the benefits of correction for guessing (in terms of validity) would be realized only where there is considerable variation among examinees in guessing behavior, there are fewer than five alternatives per item, and the test is fairly difficult. Lord (1975) suggested that perhaps examinees in previous studies had not been instructed when to guess and when to omit an item, in a manner consistent with the random-guessing assumption of the formula-scoring model. He called for empirical tests of the formula-scoring assumption by administering an examination with adequate formula-scoring instructions and then, on a second answer sheet, requiring examinees to respond to the items they had originally omitted. If the formula-scoring assumptions were correct, scores on the answer sheets obtained under formula-scoring directions should not differ from those on the second answer sheet when corrected for guessing. Empirical studies based on Lord's suggestions (Bliss, 1980; Cross and Frary, 1977), however, indicated that when students answer all items, they achieve higher raw scores than when they respond under formula-scoring instructions and scores are corrected as Lord suggested. This result suggests that examinees' behavior is not consistent with the assumptions of formula scoring. One possible explanation is that the formula-scoring model does not make adequate allowance for partial knowledge (or the way in which examinees make use of it during test taking), and hence the model is mathematically weak for explaining examinees' behavior in the real world (Gulliksen, 1950; Lord and Novick, 1968). Also although the greatest improvements in accurate score estimation from formula scoring should occur for low-ability examinees who omit many items (Lord, 1975), it may be that these are the examinees who are least likely to understand and correctly implement formula-scoring instructions. Still another possible explanation is that formula-scoring instructions introduce another factor into the test-taking situation which has nothing to do with the domain of tasks the test was designed to measure. Usually such influences are labeled as *risk-taking* or "willingness to gamble."

Studies of individual differences in risk taking have usually involved embedding nonsense items, which have no correct answer, within a set of legitimate test items. The number of nonsense items an examinee attempts to answer under formula-scoring conditions is taken as a measure of that person's propensity for risk taking. (See Slakter, 1968, 1969, for descriptions of this methodology.) Research summarized by Diamond and Evans (1973) indicates that students who are lower in risk taking are penalized more by formula-scoring instructions than those who are more prone to take risks on objective tests. Such findings raise questions about the interpretability of scores obtained under formula-scoring conditions. Consequently, in view of the somewhat questionable gains in reliability and validity that have been achieved, the time and effort required, and the potential for negative public relations which can result from use of the "penalty for guessing," routine use of formula scoring can hardly be justified.

Formula Scoring and Item Response Theory

More recently Lord (1980) described how the concept of formula scoring may be considered in estimation of true scores for tests developed with item response theory.[1] The reader should recall from Chapter 15 that $P_g(\theta)$ may be interpreted as the probability that an examinee with ability level θ will answer item g correctly. In Chapter 15, it was also noted that an examinee's true score may be estimated by summing these probabilities over all items. Lord, however, indicated that this practice may need to be modified if examinees have differentially omitted items. He suggested that a number-right true score for examinee a could be determined by the following process:

1. Identify all items which examinee a answers.
2. For each of these items, obtain $P_g(\theta)$, the probability that an examinee with a's estimated ability (θ) would answer this item correctly.
3. Sum these probabilities.

This process is denoted in the formula,

$$\xi_a = \Sigma^{(a)} P_g(\theta) \tag{17.4}$$

where ξ_a is the number-right true score for examinee a, and $\Sigma^{(a)}$ means to sum over only those items answered by examinee a. The number-right true score estimate for the examinee is then corrected for the effects of guessing by the formula

$$\eta_a = \Sigma^{(a)} P_g(\theta) - \frac{\Sigma^{(a)} Q_g(\theta)}{k - 1} \tag{17.5}$$

where $Q_g(\theta)$ is $[1 - P_g(\theta)]$, and k is the number of choices per item.

---

[1] This section may be omitted without loss of continuity with subsequent portions of this chapter.

The use of the formula true score in item response theory is based on two critical assumptions:

1. The examinees' responses to the items are due solely to their ability levels on the latent trait.
2. The examinees clearly understand and follow the formula-scoring instructions; that is, they omit an item if (and only if) they have no better than random chance ($1/k$) of choosing the correct response.

To illustrate the use of Equations 17.4 and 17.5 and the conditions under which they will give reasonable results, let us consider several cases in Table 17.2 which could arise in estimation of true scores in item response theory:

CASE I.   Here we have four examinees at the same ability level on the latent trait θ and four items, equivalent in difficulty. Each item has four options. At this particular value of θ_i, the probability of a correct response to each item is .25. Case I in Table 17.2 displays results that will be obtained for ξ_a if the examinees do not omit items at the same rate. Obviously the values of ξ_a vary, being greater for the examinee who omits fewest items. This is clearly undesirable because we know that all examinees have the same θ_i value; however, the formula true scores for these four examinees are identical, even though they have displayed very different response-omit patterns.

CASE II.   Here again we have four examinees at the same latent trait level. In this case, however, the items are not equal in difficulty. For examinees at the ability level, the probabilities of correct responses to items 1, 2, 3, and 4 are .25, .25, .50, and .50, respectively. Case II in Table 17.2 displays values of ξ_a and η_a for examinees with different response-omit patterns. Again we see that the ξ_a values will vary, favoring those who omit fewer items, but η_a values are equal for all four examinees.

CASE III.   In this case we have four examinees at the same latent trait level and four items which vary in difficulty. In Case III in Table 17.2 again, ξ_a values are higher for those omitting fewest items, but the values of η_a are not equal for all examinees. Examinee 1 and 4 have unique values of η_a. Why? For these two examinees, the basic assumptions of the model have been violated. Notice that examinee 1 responded to item 1 even though the probability of correct response was less than one-quarter, and examinee 4 did not respond to item 3, though the probability of a correct response exceeded one-fourth. Thus these examinees did not respond in a manner consistent with the formula-scoring instructions. Furthermore if examinees of the same ability level consistently demonstrate different degrees of willingness to respond, the items cannot be considered to measure a single trait.

In actuality, we can never know examinees' true scores and must rely on estimated values of $\hat{\theta}_a$, $\hat{\xi}_a$, and $\hat{\eta}_a$. Nor can we know when the assumptions required

TABLE 17.2.   Illustrative Probabilities of Correct Item Responses, Number-Right True Scores and Formula True Scores

	Item 1	2	3	4	ξ_a	η_a
Case I						
Examinee 1	.25	.25	.25	.25	1.00	0
2	.25	.25	.25	—	.75	0
3	.25	.25	—	—	.50	0
4	.25	—	—	—	.25	0
Case II						
Examinee 1	.25	.25	.50	.50	1.50	.67
2	.25	—	.50	.50	1.25	.67
3	—	.25	.50	.50	1.25	.67
4	—	—	.50	.50	1.00	.67
Case III						
Examinee 1	.10	.25	.50	.75	1.60	.80
2	—	.25	.50	.75	1.50	1.00
3	—	—	.50	.75	1.25	1.00
4	—	—	—	.75	.75	.67

for estimating the formula true score have been violated. As with formula scoring for conventional tests, the usefulness of this procedure will require empirical demonstration. Practical benefits derived from its application have yet to be demonstrated.

AWARDING CREDIT FOR PARTIAL KNOWLEDGE

Whereas the general intent of formula scoring is to prevent examinees from receiving "undeserved" points, another scoring problem that has received considerable attention is how to award credit for partial knowledge. The basic logic of these procedures is that among examinees who earn identical item scores on a conventionally scored multiple-choice item, there may be varying degrees of knowledge (partial knowledge) about that item. Scoring procedures designed to convey information about partial knowledge can be grouped into three general classes: confidence weighting, answer-until-correct, and option weighting. The general purpose of the following discussion is not to advocate use of any of the methods described but briefly to acquaint the reader with illustrative references from this substantial body of research and to point out difficulties that may arise when novel alternatives to conventional scoring practices are attempted.

With *confidence weighting,* the format and instructions are constructed so that the examinees must indicate how certain they are of the correctness of each response. A defining aspect of all confidence-weighting procedures is that two examinees choosing the same response may receive different scores for that item because of their indications of the degree of confidence in their responses. Echternacht (1972) reviewed confidence-weighting studies and concluded that although confidence-weighting schemes have substantial logical appeal, desired increases in reliability and validity coefficients generally have not materialized when these more complex test-taking and test-scoring techniques have been used. Perhaps the most disappointing aspect of confidence weighting has been the number of studies which have actually shown slight decreases in validity coefficients when it is employed. It is important to note that a scoring technique which requires some of the examinee's test-taking time must actually result in substantial increases in score reliability or validity to be comparable to that of a longer test which could be given in an equivalent amount of time. Consequently research and interest in this practice have waned in the last decade.

Another procedure suggested for giving credit for partial knowledge is the *answer-until-correct* (AUC) method. The examinee reads the multiple-choice test item, selects a response, and receives immediate feedback about the correctness of that selection. If the correct response has been chosen, the examinee is instructed to proceed to the next item; if an incorrect response has been chosen, the examinee is instructed to make another selection. This testing procedure must be used with special rub-out type or latent image answer sheets or with computerized testing so that a record is made of the number of responses attempted for each item. The traditional method for scoring AUC tests is to subtract the total number of responses made by an examinee from the total number of possible responses (Gilman and Ferry, 1972). Investigations of the reliability and validity of scores obtained from this procedure (Hanna, 1974 and 1975) have indicated that slightly higher estimates of internal consistency may be yielded than from conventional scoring, but mixed results have been found in attempts to improve criterion-related validity. Some interest in AUC methods has recently been revived by Wilcox (1981a, 1982) who developed a scoring procedure for the AUC method based on a strong true score model. Such models have been suggested for situations where the proportion-correct true score is defined as the proportion of items in the pool that the examinee can answer correctly. Use of such a model requires "strong" assumptions about the underlying true score distribution or the conditional distribution of observed scores. (Lord and Novick, 1968, Chapter 23, or Wilcox, 1981b, 1981c). One possible drawback to the use of AUC scoring is that some examinees' performance on the test may be differentially affected by factors such as test anxiety or ability to learn during the testing process. Hanna (1975) suggested the need for investigation of this issue.

The third broad class of scoring procedures involves differential *option weighting,* based on the assumption that item response options vary in degree of correctness and that examinees who select a "more correct" response have greater knowledge than those choosing "less correct" responses. These procedures usually require no special instructions or unusual test-taking behavior by examinees. Instead the options of a multiple-choice item are assigned different weighted values depending on the particular option chosen. One method for obtaining scoring weights for the options is through expert judgment. For example, Patnaik and Traub (1973) had judges rank order the alternatives to all test items on their relative correctness; they then used Thurstone's method of paired comparisons to determine the weight for each option. Davis and Fifer (1959) and Downey (1979) simply instructed judges to rate each option on a 1-to-7 scale, where 1 denoted a totally incorrect response and 7, a totally correct response. The judges' average rating was used as the weight for each option. These are called rational weighting methods. An empirical method for deriving option weights was described by Guttman (1941b) and Gulliksen (1950). Typically, a special scoring program is used, but the basic principle is that options chosen by examinees with higher total scores on the test (or some other designated criterion variable) receive greater weights than those chosen by examinees with lower total scores. In theory, scoring weights chosen in this manner should maximize coefficient alpha, but the results of empirical studies of option weighting generally have been disappointing. Although modest increments have sometimes been demonstrated in reliability estimates, gains in validity have been so small (or nonexistent) that the costs involved in the more complex scoring scheme hardly seem justified. Of particular concern have been findings by Hendrickson (1971) and Downey (1979) which showed that option weighting resulted in increases in coefficient alpha accompanied by the dubious side-effect of decreases in criterion-related validity coefficients. Thus, to date, the anticipated benefits of option weighting have not been realized. However, it is possible that future applications of item response theory to obtain scoring weights for wrong responses, as well as right responses, might prove fruitful. A promising study in this area has been described by Thissen (1976). In such studies, improvements in test-score information or in accuracy of item parameter and ability estimates could also be considered as criteria in evaluating the merits of new scoring systems.

SUMMARY

With conventional scoring of objective tests, the test score is defined as the sum of the item scores, and for dichotomously scored tests, item scores are 0 or 1. When the examiner is concerned that differential rates of guessing have affected scores, formula scoring may be used. Two formula-scoring procedures are based on the random-guessing model, which assumes that an examinee must guess among the k choices of an item at random. Despite a theoretical rationale for formula scoring, empirical studies have not supported the contention that substantial increments in test score reliability or validity result. Possible reasons are that the random-guessing model is too simplistic; that examinees do not understand or correctly implement formula-scoring instructions; or that test-taking behavior is influenced by other traits, such as risk-taking propensity, when formula scoring is introduced with conventional tests.

A method for estimating a formula true score based on item response theory and the assumptions necessary for its use were described. Lord (1980) suggested that this formula may be useful when examinees with similar levels of ability display different degrees of omission of test items; however, benefits can only be realized when examinees correctly follow formula-scoring instructions and item responses fulfill the requirements of unidimensionality and local independence common to all item response theory models.

Other procedures proposed for scoring tests are based on the assumption that examinees have varying degrees of partial knowledge about a test item. These procedures include confidence weighting, an answer-until-correct method and use of rational or empirically derived option weights, based on the assumption that various choices to a multiple-choice item may differ in their degrees of correctness, and that examinees who choose different options thus have differing amounts of partial knowledge about the content. To date, these methods have resulted in disappointingly small increases in test score reliability and sometimes even decreases in test score validity.

Exercises

1. The matrix contains item response scores of 5 examinees to 10 5-choice items.

Examinees	1	2	3	4	5	6	7	8	9	10
A	0	0	1	0	—	1	0	0	1	1
B	1	1	1	1	1	1	1	1	1	1
C	0	—	1	—	1	1	1	0	1	1
D	0	1	0	1	1	1	0	0	1	1
E	—	—	1	1	1	1	0	—	1	1

   A. Compute the total score for each examinee based on the number of items answered correctly.
   B. Do you consider examinees C, D, and E equally proficient in the material measured by this test? Explain your reasoning.
   C. What scores would be obtained if a correction for guessing were applied which would reduce scores of examinees who guessed?
   D. Verify that the rank order of the examinees would be the same if a correction had been applied which awards credit for omitted responses.
2. Suppose that a researcher were interested in comparing the reliability estimates for scores obtained by formula scoring, using only item data such as those shown in Exercise 1. Suggest a procedure that would be appropriate for estimating reliability of both the conventional scores and the formula scores without collection of additional data.
3. A physics professor is concerned about reducing effects of guessing on final examination scores and decides to apply formula scoring. In examining the students' answer sheets, the professor notes that all students answered all items. What will be the effect of the correction for guessing in this situation?
4. Using a new experimental test-taking procedure, which required examinees to indicate their confidence in their responses, a researcher found that the reliability estimate of the confidence weighted scores was .85, whereas the reliability estimate for the same items

administered in conventional format to a control group was .70. The experimental group required, on the average, 90 minutes to complete the test. The control group averaged 50 minutes to complete the test. What would you conclude about the effectiveness of the experimental scoring method?

5. Suppose that the response data presented in Exercise 1 were gathered on a test developed by item response theory (using the one-parameter logistic model) and that examinees C, D, and E all had the same estimated latent ability score (θ_i). From the item characteristic curve function, the following estimates for $P_g(\theta_i)$ are obtained for each item.

Item no.	1	2	3	4	5	6	7	8	9	10
$P_g(\theta_i)$	.20	.30	.60	.50	.80	.90	.20	.10	.95	1.00

A. What are the true score estimates for examinees C, D, and E?

B. What are the number-right true score estimates for these three examinees?

C. What are their formula true score estimates?

Chapter 18

SETTING STANDARDS

Many situations require the setting of cutoff scores before test performance is interpreted. For example, some instructional programs are divided into units. At the completion of a unit a student takes a test and is permitted to advance to the next unit only if the test score equals or exceeds a previously established cutoff score. In other cases, certification for practice of some professions and occupations requires completion of a test of professional knowledge. Certified status is granted only if the applicant's score equals or exceeds a specified cutoff score. The practice of setting cutoff scores is commonly called *standard setting*.

Broadly speaking there are three approaches to standard setting. The first involves an inspection of the content of a test by one or more expert judges who render a judgment based on a holistic impression of test content, and the second is based on judgments of individual item content. A traditional view of these approaches to standard setting is that they do not involve technical psychometric issues (Gallagher, 1979 and Linn, 1978). The third major approach to standard setting is based on the performance of examinees. This approach is somewhat more psychometric in orientation; however, it too involves an important element of informed judgment since all the methods classified under this approach require the standard setter to choose the examinee groups whose performance is examined. These three pragmatic approaches to standard setting are described in subsequent sections of this chapter.

Perhaps the most common way to *use* a cutoff score obtained by applying one of the standard-setting methods is to apply it directly to observed scores. That is, if the standard setters conclude that an appropriate cutoff score, for example, is .69, then an examinee must answer 69% or more of the test items correctly in order to pass the test. An alternate way to use the cutoff score is to apply it to the domain scores. In this approach the items on a specific test are treated as a sample from a larger domain of items. Each examinee is considered to have a domain (or true) score, which typically is defined as the proportion of the items in the domain that the examinee can answer correctly. The cutoff score set by the standard setters is used to divide the domain score scale into two regions and is called the *domain scale cutoff score*. In achievement measurement these regions are called *mastery states*. Examinees with scores at or above the domain scale cutoff score are called *true masters*. Other examinees are called *true nonmasters*. Once the domain scale cutoff score has been set, the problem is to identify the observed score cutoff that allows the test user to draw the most appropriate inferences about the examinees' true mastery states. The identification of the observed cutoff score can be accomplished by taking into account the relationship between observed and domain scores and the losses associated with misclassifying a true master as a nonmaster and a true non-master as a master. Methods for identifying the observed scale cutoff score and related issues are presented in the section of this chapter entitled Technical Considerations in Standard Setting.

Before turning to the main points of discussion, two minor points should be made. First, we have limited the discussion to setting a single cutoff score to divide the score scale into two regions, in part to keep the discussion relatively simple, and in part because use of a single passing score seems to be the most common case in practice. Nevertheless particular standard-setting situations may require the use of several cutoff scores to divide the score scale into several regions. In principle, all the methods discussed in the chapter can be generalized to handle problems involving several cutoff scores. Second, cutoff scores are also used in admissions and employment testing when tests are used to predict ultimate mastery states on an external criterion. These topics have already been addressed in Chapters 11 and 12 and are not directly addressed in this chapter.

APPROACHES TO STANDARD SETTING

Although more than 30 different methods of standard setting have been described in measurement literature in recent years (Behuniak, Archambault, and Gable, 1982), most of these techniques can be classified into one of three major categories. (Readers interested in additional categorization schemes should see Glass, 1978; Hambleton, 1980; Jaeger, 1979; Meskauskas, 1976; Millman, 1973.) The major approaches considered here involve

1. Judgments based on holistic impressions of the examination or item pool
2. Judgments based on the content of individual test items
3. Judgments based on examinee's test performance

Consensus Judgment Based on Holistic Impression

A panel of experts examines the test content, and based on an overall impression of the test and the content area, suggests what percentage of items should be correctly answered by an examinee who has attained the minimum level of competency to perform at the level of interest. Each judge normally sets a recommended standard, and these judgments are averaged for the final standard. Shepard (1976) suggested use of multiple groups of judges representing various constituencies who have an interest in the test results. For example, on a high school graduation certification test, groups of students, teachers, parents, and perhaps representatives of the community at large might be consulted.

At times, this judgment may be based on the allowance of tolerable error. Glass (1978) referred to this use as "counting backwards from 100%." That is, the standard setter assumes that the desired level of performance on the test should be 100% of the items correctly answered but makes allowance for some portion of incorrect answers because of misreading, mismarking, inattention, scoring errors, and so on. Some knowledge of the examinee population is probably implicitly employed by the judges. For example, Glass cited a report by Glaser that children in the primary grades can only be trained to about 70% accuracy in single-addition; thus it is not uncommon to find that classroom teachers will suggest that 60 to 70% is a reasonable standard on tests of this nature, perhaps because of their experience with examinees at this level.

Although holistic judgment is one of the most widely used methods of setting standards, it can be difficult to defend rationally or psychometrically. A common criticism is that the test developer can never know whether a different sample of experts might not have established the standard at a different point. One logical solution to this problem might seem to be to conduct replication studies; however, assuming that the overall number of judges available (or affordable) is fixed, if two replications are used, the number of judges for each individual study is reduced by half, and standards set by smaller numbers of judges will probably fluctuate more from sample to sample than standards set by a larger number of judges. Another problem is that there is no certainty that different judges will base their impressions on the same aspects of the test or hold similar perceptions of the content area. This may also result in undesirable fluctuation of the standard from one sample of judges to another. If this method is used, the test developer should at least provide careful documentation of the number of judges, their qualifications, the process for their selection, the instructions provided to them, and the distribution of their responses.

Judgments Based on Item Content

Perhaps the most widely studied methods of standard setting are those which require judgments at the individual item level. Three well-known procedures in this category will be considered here in order of their historic emergence. The first technique, proposed by Nedelsky (1954), is specifically designed for multiple-choice items. Nedelsky was particularly concerned with establishing standards of minimum competency for university-level examinations. Using this method, the standard is determined as follows:

1. Each judge (usually a qualified expert in the content area) is instructed to cross out for each item the number of responses that the "lowest D student" (or minimally competent examinee) should be able to eliminate.

2.   For each item, the judge records the reciprocal of the number of responses remaining. For example, on a five-choice item, if two responses were crossed out, the recorded reciprocal value would be one-third.
3.   The sum of the reciprocals over all items in the test is denoted as M and can be considered as the probable score of a minimally qualified examinee as determined from the ratings of that single judge.
4.   The M values are averaged over all judges (μ_M). Nedelsky originally suggested that the overall passing score for the test should be set at $\mu_M + k\sigma_M$, where the value of k would be arbitrarily chosen, probably between the range of .5 and 1.0. The logical assumptions involved in selection of k and adjustment of the value of μ_M have been criticized, and consequently some users of this technique prefer simply to set the minimum passing score at μ_M (Meskauskas, 1976).

The second method, proposed by Angoff (1971), was originally described in a footnote as the author offered illustrations of how various scale transformations could be created without normative data. Basically, the judges are instructed to think of a group of "minimally acceptable" persons, and for each item, to estimate the proportion of the minimally acceptable group who would answer the item correctly. (This can also be thought of as the probability that a minimally competent individual will answer the item correctly.) These probabilities are summed over all items to obtain the minimum passing score assigned by a single judge. The consensus of all judges' ratings is the minimum passing score.

Ebel (1972) proposed a similar system to Angoff's but recognized that both content relevance of the item and its difficulty level might influence judgments about how a minimally qualified examinee should be expected to perform on an item. This technique uses a two-dimensional grid for categorizing each item. One dimension (usually with four levels) is relevance; the second dimension (usually with three levels) is difficulty (see Table 18.1). First the test items are categorized

TABLE 18.1.   Illustrative Table and Percentages of Items Classified by a Single Judge Using Ebel's Standard-Setting Procedure for 200-Item Test

Levels of Relevance	Levels of Difficulty		
	Easy	Medium	Difficult
Essential	90%	50%	10%
	(20 items)	(25)	(5)
Important	60%	30%	20%
	(35)	(22)	(10)
Acceptable	40%	20%	10%
	(19)	(12)	(15)
Questionable	25%	—	—
	(7)	(20)	(10)

$X_C = \Sigma p(M) = .90(20) + .50(25) + .10(5) + .60(35) + .30(22) + .20(10) + .40(19) + .20(12) + .10(15) + .25(7) + 0(20) + 0(10) = 73.85$

into the cells of the grid, and then the judge assigns a percentage value to each cell, indicating the percentage of items in that cell that should be answered correctly by a minimally qualified examinee. Table 18.1 displays hypothetical percentages that might be obtained from a single judge. The numbers of items assigned to each cell are shown in parentheses. The minimal passing score recommended by a single judge is obtained by the calculation

$$X_C = \Sigma p(M) \tag{18.1}$$

where X_C is the cut score in terms of raw score points, p is the proportion of items in the cell that a minimally qualified examinee should answer correctly, and M is the number of items in that cell. The summation is over all 12 cells. Of course, when multiple judges are used, the final passing score could be obtained by computing the mean value for X_C over all judges. This value can also be converted to a proportion-correct passing score by simply dividing by the total number of items on the test.

Judgments Based on Performance of Examinees

Many advocates of criterion-referenced testing would decry the notion of setting a standard based on knowledge of performance during some trial administration of the test; yet there is no escaping the fact that the usual "expert" judges who would participate in standard setting would be chosen precisely because they have experience with how typical examinees might perform on such a test. For example, in setting performance standards for a test in high school plane geometry, we would be more likely to use as judges teachers of high school geometry rather than college professors of topology. Recognizing this, Shepard (1979) pointed out that since judges' standards are inevitably influenced by their perceptions of how examinees they know would perform on the test, it may be more appropriate to use actual data from a well-chosen sample of examinees than to rely on arbitrary judgments based on more limited (idiosyncratic) perceptions of examinees' abilities to perform on a given test.

A simple approach, using normative data, is to administer the test to a particular group of examinees who should be lower in the ability being tested than the ultimate target population and set a minimal competency standard based on the mean or median performance of this group. For example, Glass (1978) described setting a minimal standard for a high school diploma certification examination based on the median performance of ninth-graders. Another example of this approach is a standardized test used for screening children with language disabilities on which the cutoffs recommended for each grade level are the points 1 standard deviation below the mean for students at that grade level.

Another approach is to use data from examinee groups who should clearly differ in their proficiency levels on the material being tested and place the cut score to maximize discrimination between these two groups. Berk (1976) described a method using instructed and noninstructed groups of examinees. Nedelsky (1954) described a *contrasting groups method* for setting standards which consisted of six steps:

1. Select qualified judges who are familiar with the examinee population.
2. Allow the judges to discuss and, if possible, agree on what constitutes minimally competent performance.
3. Use the judges to identify examinees who are competent or incompetent performers (excluding any who appear to be borderline).
4. Test both groups of examinees.
5. Plot the score distribution for each group on the same continuum.
6. Set the performance standard at the intersection point of the two distribution curves (see Figure 18.1).

Additional procedures for setting the standard with data from the contrasting groups approach have been described by Koffler (1980) and Zieky and Livingston (1977).

Another procedure, also proposed by Nedelsky, is the *borderline group method.* Here the judges are selected and instructed as in steps 1 and 2, but they are then asked to identify examinees who appear to be borderline in competence. This group is then tested, and the median of their score distribution is used to define the point of minimal competence.

Critics of these approaches point out that setting standards based on examinees' performance is antithetical to the basic purpose of criterion-referenced testing because there is no regard for test content in designation of the performance standard. Glass (1978) further commented that the use of instructed versus noninstructed groups seemed a weak attempt to substitute "seat time" for demonstrated competence. A similar criticism applies if the criterion groups are composed of practicing members of a profession and aspiring students seeking the right to practice. If a standard is set to discriminate between such groups, there is an implicit assumption of the validity of the previous certification practice—which logically calls into question the need for the current test on which the standard is being set. Although such criticisms are worthy of serious consideration when a standard is established on the sole basis of examinees' performance, there is much more support for the use of performance data in the standard-setting process as a piece of supplemental information, which can be used in gauging the educational or societal consequences of imposing performance standards arrived at by other methods. Suppose, for exam-

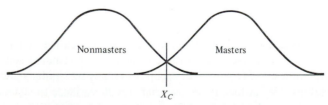

FIGURE 18.1   Cutoff Score Set at the Intersection of Frequency Distribution Curves for Two Contrasting Groups

ple, that a standard of 90% correct has been proposed for an entry-level certification in a health profession, but a preliminary field test indicates that fewer than 15% of the graduates from current baccalaureate programs in the profession can meet this standard. This information reveals that the licensure board now faces a serious dilemma: Either current academic programs are not doing an adequate job of preparing the vast majority of their students for professional practice, the process by which the test was constructed and the resultant content validity are in question, or the standard has been unreasonably set. All three possibilities would deserve serious consideration before instituting the testing program and the recommended standard for proficiency.

Jaeger (1982) proposed a process that combines features of holistic judgment, examinees' performance, and item judgment methods. This method is called an *iterative structured item judgment process,* and its application was demonstrated in establishing the standard for the North Carolina High School Competency Tests. Three groups of judges were used: high school teachers, school principals and counselors, and citizens of the state. Each judge was asked to complete the examination and rate each item on a yes-no scale in answer to the question, "Should every regular high school graduate in North Carolina be able to answer this item correctly?" Jaeger believed that this wording alleviated the need to define a construct such as minimal competence and allowed the judge to focus on the more observable act of conferring a diploma. The recommended passing score for each judge was determined by summing over the items (with a score of 1 point awarded for each "yes" response and 0 awarded for each "no" response). The distribution of recommended passing scores was determined for each group, and the yes-no response distribution of each group for each item was tallied. Then the judges were informed about how a sample of eleventh-grade examinees actually performed on the item (p-value) and how other judges in their group had rated the item. Judges were allowed to modify their original ratings in light of this information in two successive cycles. The median value of the distribution of passing scores recommended by each group was used as the standard for that group. (Although it was expected that greater convergence on the recommended standard would occur with successive rounds, this did not actually occur in Jaeger's study. Evidently different judges used the additional information in different ways as they reevaluated the items.)

EMPIRICAL RESEARCH ON STANDARD-SETTING METHODS

In view of the multiplicity of approaches, it is natural for measurement practitioners to raise questions such as these: Do different methods of standard setting lead to markedly different results? Do different groups of judges set similar standards using the same technique? What factors are associated with variance in standards set by different judges or samples of judges? To date, a number of empirical studies have been conducted to address these questions but definitive answers have not been forthcoming. A few illustrative findings will be discussed here to demonstrate.

First let us consider comparisons among item judgment methods. In one oft-cited study, Andrews and Hecht (1976) found that a group of eight judges, using Ebel's method, set the standard for minimal competency at 68% correct, but a standard of 49% correct was obtained with the same judges using Nedelsky's method. Glass (1978) further noted that a previously unreported finding from that study was that 95% of the examinee group would have achieved the Nedelsky criterion, but only 50% would have met the Ebel criterion. More recently, Behuniak, Archambault, and Gable (1982) reported a comparison of the Angoff and Nedelsky procedures for setting the standard on criterion-referenced achievement tests in reading and mathematics. For the reading test, a group of six judges established a mean proportion correct standard of 56.7% by the Angoff method and 43.2% by the Nedelsky method; however, on the mathematics test this finding was reversed (70.2% by Angoff's method and 77.1% by Nedelsky's). Although such comparison studies do not offer evidence of the superiority of one method over others, they clearly demonstrate that the various item judgment methods should not be considered ''Tweedle-Dum, Tweedle-Dee'' approaches to standard setting. A discomfitting finding of this latter study was that when groups of judges were split into two samples, there were substantial differences between standards recommended by different groups of judges using the same method.

Koffler (1980) and Mills (1983) compared results of standard setting from item judgment methods and methods using examinees' performance data. Specifically, Koffler investigated standard setting with Nedelsky's method and the contrasting groups approach, and Mills used the Angoff, contrasting groups, and borderline group techniques. Although again, results were somewhat mixed, Mills' study demonstrates that when three or more methods are used, it may be possible to obtain some convergence between at least two of the methods. For example, standards from Angoff's method and the contrasting groups method were more consistent with each other than with the standards from the borderline group method for most of the cases reported. To illustrate the variation in standards that may result from different methods, some results of the Mills study are reported for selected tests in Table 18.2a, where percentage-correct standards are listed, and in Table 18.2b, where the percentage of examinees achieving each standard are shown.

Other empirical studies of standard-setting processes have demonstrated that judges with different characteristics might arrive at quite different recommendations. For example, Jaeger (1982) reported considerable differences in standards obtained from groups comprised of teachers and of citizens when they reviewed items for the North Carolina High School Competency Tests. Furthermore Saunders, Ryan, and Huynh (1981) found a relationship between the judge's level of knowledge about the content and the passing score obtained from the judge using the Nedelsky procedure. In view of such findings, in any standard-setting study, it would be appropriate to estimate empirically the extent to which differences in judges and in methods may contribute to differences in the final standard recommendation. Brennan and Lockwood (1980) explored the potential applicability of generalizability theory in this context, and additional work in this area seems warranted.

TABLE 18.2a.   Minimal Passing Standard (in Terms of Proportion Correct) Obtained from Different Methods from a Study Reported by Mills (1983)

Test Form	Angoff Method	Contrasting Groups (Graph)	Borderline Group
G	.68	.68	.87
H	.68	.75	.88
I	.62	.65	.80
J	.78	.62	.90
K	.68	.70	.85
L	.68	.60	.83

TABLE 18.2b.   Proportions of Examinees Failing to Meet the Passing Standard Obtained from Different Methods

Test Form	Angoff Method	Contrasting Groups (Graph)	Borderline Group
G	7.06	6.30	29.75
H	6.03	8.19	22.09
I	7.60	9.42	26.66
J	9.10	4.07	23.71
K	7.82	9.32	25.40
L	7.95	5.38	23.11

From C. N. Mills, A comparison of three methods of establishing cutoff scores on criterion referenced tests, *Journal of Educational Measurement, 20*, 283–292. Copyright 1983 by the National Council on Measurement in Education, Washington, D.C. Adapted by permission.

Finally, in addition to the possibility that different samples of judges and different techniques may produce different results, van der Linden (1982) pointed out that intrajudge inconsistency may also be a problem. This occurs when a judge assigns a lower probability of a minimally competent examinee passing a relatively easy item and a higher probability of the same examinee passing a more difficult item. He proposed an index of discrepancy, based on item response theory, and demonstrated its application with judgments obtained from the Nedelsky and Angoff procedures. In considering the need for work in this area, Shepard (1980) suggested that additional practical research on the standard-setting process might be warranted for fairly large-scale certification-testing programs to learn more about the effects of different instructions to judges, the advantages or disadvantages of having judges work independently or in groups, and the most opportune time and desirable format for presenting normative data to judges.

PRACTICAL CONSIDERATIONS IN STANDARD SETTING

No matter what method is used, the need for well-considered judgment is inescapable in the establishment of test performance standards. It is imperative to recognize that although standard setting is an important psychometric problem, it is not solely a technical issue. The consequences of appropriate or inappropriate standards for individuals, for institutions, and perhaps for society as a whole must be considered. For some, such as Glass (1978), the theoretical foundation and empirical basis of knowledge that underlie current approaches to standard setting is so inadequate that the practice itself seems unjustifiable. For others (e.g., Hambleton, 1978, 1980; Popham, 1978; Scriven, 1978; Shepard, 1976, 1979), the need for standards as an aid to decision making in some educational and clinical contexts is a reality which cannot be avoided or ignored until all philosophical and methodological problems surrounding the practice are resolved.

Given this state of affairs, in approaching the problem of standard setting, a prudent first step is to *question whether there is a legitimate need for establishing a performance standard for interpretation of the test scores in question*. For example, in an area such as elementary school social studies it is probably unnecessary for students to completely "master" material in one unit before another instructional unit is introduced. Thus although assessment of student achievement is appropriate, the need for cutoff scores designating mastery levels on such a test would be questionable. Where there is a clear need for a performance standard for interpretation of test scores for decision making, it is probably advisable to review common approaches to standard setting and identify those that seem most rationally defensible for the given situation.

Next, it is important to *identify the likely threats to invalidity of the inferences that are to be made from the test scores*. Jaeger (1979) identified a number of threats to the validity of inferences drawn from test scores to domain scores and linked these various problems with particular standard-setting methods. Those which apply to all the judgment procedures based on item content were bias because of inadequate domain definition, random error affecting different judges' decisions, inappropriate or inadequate item sampling procedures to ensure representation of the domain, an inadequate number of items to represent the domain, and judgment bias in review of individual items. Note that the first, third, and fourth threats listed actually arise from faulty test construction procedures (or at least procedures inadequate to ensure the needed degree of content validity for the types of inferences desired from the test scores). It is probably only the second and fifth threats which can be controlled or reduced during the standard-setting process itself, assuming that the standard is established for scores on a previously developed test. Thus it would seem that using a large number of judges (preferably more than the six to eight that have been employed in some published studies), selecting them randomly from a carefully identified pool of qualified judges, providing them with clear instructions about the context in which test scores will be used, and training them in performance of the task would be valuable in reducing these potential problems. Zieky and Livingston (1977) and Hambleton (1978) provided additional guidelines and suggestions for implementing several of the methods of standard setting discussed here.

In addition, it is advisable to *use two or more different approaches to standard setting and multiple samples of judges,* chosen if necessary to represent different relevant constituencies. If these various methods fail to yield a single covergent standard (as is likely to occur), the questions of which should prevail or how to arbitrate a compromise solution will in the end require value judgment.

It is also advisable to *examine empirical evidence of how a typical sample of examinees perform on the test and to use this information in evaluating the consequences of setting a particular standard.* Consider, for example, a case where a performance has been established by one of the empirical item judgment methods at 87% for a mastery learning test in arithmetic for young children, but results of the field test show that only a small proportion of the children attain this criterion after instruction. The consequences of setting this standard must be considered from several perspectives. First, the consequences on subsequent learning must be considered; if children are advanced without having achieved this standard what will be the effects on their future learning? In addition, however, the effects on motivation from being forced to repeat instruction must also be considered. Opportunities lost (in terms of reduced instructional time for other subjects) may also be a factor. Similarly in areas such as professional certification, the consequences of certifying practitioners who may be less than minimally qualified must be weighed against the consequences of society's loss of services by truly qualified candidates who fail to meet an overly stringent standard. Obviously the establishment of useful performance standards requires a well-balanced blend of technical adequacy and a clear vision of the ultimate purposes and goals of the program which requires decisions about examinees based on their test performance. One approach that may allow the standard setter to consider these consequences systematically involves application of decision theory, which will be discussed in the following sections.

TECHNICAL CONSIDERATIONS IN STANDARD SETTING

The technical literature on standard setting has focused on one major issue, setting an observed scale cutoff score which permits the test user to make appropriate inferences about the examinees' true mastery states, which are defined on the domain score scale. As we shall see, the meaning of appropriate inferences depends on the procedure used to set the observed scale cutoff score. With some procedures, appropriateness is defined in terms of the probability of misclassification. With others it is defined in terms of losses due to misclassification. In this section several approaches to the problem at hand are described. Each procedure described in this section is an application of decision theory, which was introduced in Chapter 12. The technical literature has also addressed a somewhat more minor issue, the development of indices to quantify the quality of decision making based on an observed scale cutoff score. Research on this problem was reported by van der Linden and Mellenbergh (1977), Wilcox (1978), and Hunyh (1980c). The interested reader is referred to these papers.

Setting an Observed Scale Cutoff Score

MINIMIZING PROBABILITIES OF MISCLASSIFICATION. The domain scale cutoff score divides the domain score scale into two regions. Examinees with scores at or above the domain scale cutoff score are true masters, and examinees with scores below the cutoff score are true nonmasters. An examinee's domain score is interpreted as the proportion of the domain of items an examinee can answer correctly, and so the domain score scale ranges from zero to one. We will denote domain scores by τ and the domain scale cutoff score by τ_0. As we noted earlier, τ_0 may be based on one of the standard-setting methods described in preceding sections. However, since the domain score scale is a proportion-correct score scale, and the standard-setting methods yield scores on either a percentage or a number-correct scale, it is necessary to transform these cutoff scores before they can be interpreted as τ_0. If the cutoff score is expressed on a percentage-correct scale, it must be divided by 100 to yield τ_0. If it is expressed on a number-correct scale, it must be divided by the number of items used in the process of setting the cutoff score in order to obtain τ_0.

Once τ_0 is set, the problem is to determine the observed scale cutoff score that will permit the test user to make appropriate inferences about the examinees' mastery states. Typically this new cutoff score, denoted by X_0, will be expressed on the number-correct scale, denoted by X. Once a value is chosen for X_0, each examinee falls into one of four categories:

1. True positive—an examinee whose domain score is equal to or greater than τ_0 and whose observed test score is equal to or greater than X_0
2. True negative—an examinee whose domain score is less than τ_0 and whose observed test score is less than X_0
3. False positive—an examinee whose domain score is less than τ_0 and whose observed score is equal to or greater than X_0
4. False negative—an examinee whose domain score is equal to or greater than τ_0 and whose observed score is less than X_0

One way to approach the problem is to choose X_0 so the probability of misclassified examinees—false positives and false negatives—is minimized. Of course a problem in implementing this strategy is that we do not actually know the probabilities of false positive and false negative errors. This problem is overcome by using estimates of these probabilities. Estimation of these probabilities in turn requires us to make an assumption about the bivariate distribution of domain and observed scores.

The typical assumption is that the bivariate distribution of domain and observed scores is a beta-binomial distribution. Hunyh (1976b) used this assumption to derive results that permit the determination of X_0 (c_0 in his notation) that minimizes the probability of misclassification. The procedure derived by Hunyh for determining X_0 is somewhat complicated to apply. However, Hunyh showed that if the number of items is large and τ_0 is not too near .00 or 1.00, X_0 can be approximated by

$$\hat{X}_0 = \frac{n - KR(21)}{KR(21)} \tau_0 + \frac{KR(21) - 1}{KR(21)} \hat{\mu}_X + .5 \qquad (18.2)$$

where n is the number of items on the test. This approximation appears to be accurate if the test consists of 20 or more items and τ_0 is in the range .50 to .80 (Hunyh and Saunders, 1980).

Table 18.2 shows the approximate cutoff scores that result from applying Equation 18.3 for six different examinee groups. A similar pattern of results would have occurred if we had used Hunyh's exact procedure rather than his approximate procedure. Also a similar pattern of results would occur if we had population values for KR 20 and the observed score mean rather than sample estimates of these quantities. For each of the six groups $n = 28$ and $\tau_0 = .75$. However, they differ on KR 21 and/or $\hat{\mu}_X$. Inspecting the row for either KR 21 = .6 or KR 21 = .8, we see that $\hat{X}_0$ depends on the mean score for the group. As $\hat{\mu}_X$ increases, $\hat{X}_0$ decreases. To put these results in perspective, consider that with $\tau_0 = .75$ and $n = 28$, intuitively we might expect X_0 to be $n\tau_0 = 21$. That is, we might expect an observed scale cutoff score to require an examinee to answer 75 percent of the items correctly in order for the examinee to be declared a master. Inspecting either row we see that $\hat{X}_0$ is approximately 21 when $\hat{\mu}_X = 21$. However, $\hat{X}_0$ exceeds 21 when $\hat{\mu}_X$ is less than 21 and is less than 21 when $\hat{\mu}_X$ is greater than 21. Thus examinees from a group with a mean greater than $n\tau_0$ have a less stringent observed score scale cutoff than examinees from a group with a mean less than $n\tau_0$.

There are at least two intuitive explanations of the dependence of $\hat{X}_0$ on $\hat{\mu}_X$. One is that when members of an examinee group have scores that are predominantly above $n\tau_0$, most of these examinees are masters. The procedure for setting $\hat{X}_0$ reflects this belief by setting a lower observed scale cutoff score. The second explanation is related to regression estimates of true scores. Recall that the equation for an estimated true score is

$$\hat{T} = \hat{\mu}_X + \hat{\rho}_{XX'}(X - \hat{\mu}_X)$$

As this equation shows, examinees with observed scores below the mean are expected to have higher true scores than observed scores, and examinees with observed scores above the mean are expected to have lower true scores than observed scores. What would happen if we had two examinees with $X = 21$, but one came from the group with $\hat{\mu}_X = 17$ and the second came from the group with $\hat{\mu}_X = 25$? If KR21 = .6, the estimated true score of the first examinee would be 19.4, and that of the second examinee would be 22.6 (or 21). Thus if $n\tau_0$ were used as the ob-

TABLE 18.3.   Effect of Variation in KR 21 and $\hat{\mu}_X$ on $\hat{X}_0$

	$\hat{\mu}_X$		
KR 21	17	21	25
.6	23.43	20.76	18.10
.8	21.75	20.75	19.25

$n = 28$ and $\tau_0 = .75$ for each examinee group.

served scale cutoff score, the first examinee would be classified as a nonmaster and the second would be classified as a master. Rather than using estimated true scores, Hunyh's procedure adjusts $\hat{X}_0$ to reflect the relationship between observed scores and domain scores.

Table 18.3 also shows that as KR 21 increases, the variation in $\hat{X}_0$ as a function of $\hat{\mu}_X$ decreases. Indeed as KR 21 approaches 1.0, $\hat{X}_0$ approaches $n\tau_0 + .5$, regardless of the value of $\hat{\mu}_X$. Thus as the amount of measurement error decreases, the adjustment in $\hat{X}_0$ also decreases.

A practical problem can arise when methods like Hunyh's are used in ongoing testing programs. To illustrate, imagine a testing program in which the same secure test is to be used on three testing dates separated by a year. The test is 100 items long and τ_0 is .70. In the first year KR 21 $= .75$ and $\hat{\mu}_X = 71$, so the cutoff score X_0 is approximated by

$$\frac{100 - .75}{.75}.70 + \frac{.75 - 1}{.75}71 + .5 = 69.46$$

or 69 rounded to the nearest integer score. Suppose that in the second year KR 21 is again .75 but $\hat{\mu}_X = 74$. The new approximation to the cutoff score X_0 is 68 rounded to the integer score. The question that faces the test user in second year is which cutoff score to use, 69 from the first year or 68 from the second year. Notice that the mean scores for the two years are quite similar, which is evidence that the two samples of examinees are representative of the same population. Therefore the domain score-observed score bivariate distribution is the same for both years, and so 69 and 68 are estimates of the same cutoff score. The test user would be well advised to use 69 again to maintain consistency from year to year. Now suppose in the third year KR 21 is again .75 but $\hat{\mu}_X = 81$. The new estimate of the cutoff score is 66. Again the question is which estimated cutoff score to use. The mean score for the third year differs substantially from the mean scores for the previous years, which indicates that the sample in the third year and the samples in the first and second years are from different populations. Since the observed scale cutoff score depends on the population tested, the new cutoff score (66) and the old cutoff scores (68 and 69) probably estimate different cutoff scores. Thus to minimize the probability of misclassification for the examinees in the third year, it is appropriate to use $\hat{X}_0 = 66$. But using this estimated cutoff score could conceivably cause legal problems because examinees from the third year with $X = 66$ will pass the test but examinees from the first two years who earned $X = 66$ will have failed the test. Thus psychometric and legal principles may be in conflict.

There is an approach to setting an observed scale cutoff score that avoids this problem. Rather than setting τ_0 it is necessary to set

τ_1—the highest domain score that is definitely considered in the nonmastery region
τ_2—the lowest domain score that is definitely considered in the mastery region

The range between τ_1 and τ_2 is called an *indifference zone*. We are unsure whether an examinee with a domain score in this range should be considered a master or a nonmaster. As a result we do not care about the probability of misclassifying an examinee with a domain score in this range. We are concerned with the probability that an examinee with a domain score equal to τ_1 will be misclassified as a master and the probability that an examinee with a domain score at τ_2 will be misclassified as a nonmaster. As a result we determine X_0 so that the largest of these probabilities is as small as possible. This type of procedure is called a *minimax procedure* (Hunyh, 1980b) because it minimizes the maximum probability of misclassification. The X_0 set by the minimax procedure does not minimize the total probability of misclassification. On the other hand, the X_0 set by this particular minimax procedure does not change when the population being tested changes. (Other minimax procedures described by Hunyh result in an X_0 which can change as the population being tested changes.)

To implement the minimax procedure, the probability of misclassifying an examinee with domain score τ_1 and the probability of misclassifying an examinee with domain score τ_2 is calculated for every possible cutoff score. Table 18.4 shows these probabilities for $\tau_1 = .70$ and $\tau_2 = .85$ on a hypothetical seven-item test. Once these probabilities are calculated, the maximum probability at each cutoff score is determined. (These maxima are indicated by asterisks.) The score associated with the smallest of these maximum probabilities is then set as X_0. Inspection of the probabilities identified by asterisks indicate that $X_0 = 6$. With this cutoff score the larger probability of misclassification is for an examinee with domain score τ_1 and is equal to .3295. By virtue of the fact that X_0 is the minimax cutoff score, all other examinees have a misclassification probability smaller than .3295.

In order to calculate the probabilities of misclassification, it is necessary to make an assumption about the distribution of observed scores for examinees with a common domain score of τ_1 and for examinees with a common domain score of τ_2. One common assumption is that each of these distributions is a binomial distribution (previously introduced in Chapter 6). The binomial distribution can be used, for example, to calculate the probability that a coin will result in m heads in r coin flips. It can be used even if the probability of a head is not .5. A rationale for using the

TABLE 18.4. Probabilities of Misclassification for Domain Scores of .70 and .85 for All Possible Observed Scale Cutoff Scores

Cutoff Score	Domain Score	
	.70	.85
0	1.0000*	.0000
1	.9999*	.0000
2	.9963*	.0000
3	.9713*	.0011
4	.8741*	.0120
5	.6472*	.0737
6	.3295*	.2834
7	.0824	.6749*

*Indicates the maximum probability of misclassification for each cutoff score.

binomial distribution in standard setting is as follows. The domain score is the proportion of the domain of items that an examinee can answer correctly. Thus, the domain score can be interpreted as the probability that the examinee will answer a randomly chosen item correctly, and the binomial distribution is used to calculate the probability that an examinee with domain score τ will correctly answer X out of n randomly chosen items.

Table 18.5 shows the probability of each possible score on a seven-item test for examinees with domain scores of $\tau_1 = .70$ and $\tau_2 = .85$. These probabilities were calculated by using the binomial distribution. The probabilities in Table 18.4 are based on those in Table 18.5. To show how the results in Table 18.4 are obtained from those in Table 18.5, suppose that X_0 was set at 5. An examinee with a domain score of .7 (a nonmaster) will be misclassified if the examinee obtains a score of 5 or above on the test. According to Table 18.5 the probability that an examinee with domain score .7 will obtain a score of 5 or above is $.3177 + .2471 + .0824 = .6472$. This then is the probability of false-positive error for an examinee with domain score .7 when the cutoff score is 5. An examinee with domain score .85 (a master) will be misclassified if the examinee obtains a test score of 4 or less. Again, according to Table 18.5 this probability is $.0617 + .0109 + .0012 + .0001 + .000 = .0737$. The probabilities of misclassification can be determined in a similar fashion for the other cutoff scores.

Recall that for our hypothetical seven-item test, the maximum probability of misclassifying an examinee is .3295. Suppose a test user contemplating the use of this seven-item test finds this probability intolerably high. If it is practical to increase the test length, the probability can be reduced. This fact suggests a procedure for determining test length and X_0. First decide on the maximum tolerable probability of misclassification. Then construct a table like Table 18.4 for an initial test length, and choose a provisional X_0. If this X_0 does not give a maximum probability that is below the criterion probability set, increase the test length by one item and determine a new X_0 and the misclassification probabilities. Continue this procedure until an appropriate test length and X_0 are found. Fahner (1974) and Wilcox (1976) discuss this kind of procedure in more detail.

TABLE 18.5. Probability Distributions for a Seven-Item Test for Domain Scores of .70 and .85

Score	Domain Score	
	.70	.85
0	.0002	.0000
1	.0036	.0001
2	.0250	.0012
3	.0972	.0109
4	.2269	.0617
5	.3177	.2096
6	.2471	.3960
7	.0824	.3206

MINIMIZING THE EXPECTED COST OF MISCLASSIFICATION. The two approaches just described are concerned with minimizing the probability of misclassification. This approach is appropriate when false-positive and false-negative errors are equally serious. In many situations this is not true. For example, in an hierarchically organized curriculum the false-positive error may be more serious than the false-negative error. When a false-positive error is made, the student is moved to the next unit before the student is prepared to move. With false-negative error the student is retained in the same unit. Often this retention results in only a relatively short review of the material, and so it may not be a very serious error.

Procedures that take the misclassification losses into account use the concept of expected loss. We will illustrate this concept and this kind of procedure by applying a minimax procedure to the hypothetical seven-item test used in the preceding section. Rather than determining the cutoff score which minimizes the maximum probability of misclassification, the new minimax procedure will minimize the maximum expected loss due to misclassification.

Suppose that the loss for a false positive is 5 and the loss for a false negative is .5 (For the moment we will avoid the issue of how these values are obtained.) Let us consider the consequences of setting $X_0 = 4$. With this cutoff score an examinee with domain score $\tau_1 = .70$ has a .8741 probability of false-positive misclassification (see Table 18.4). The *expected loss* is the loss for misclassification multiplied by the probability of misclassification, or 5(.8741) = 4.3705. The expected loss for a false-negative misclassification of an examinee with domain score $\tau_2 = .85$ is .5(0120) = .006. Making these calculations for each possible cutoff score yields the results in Table 18.6. Asterisks indicate the maximum expected loss for each possible cutoff score. The cutoff score which results in the smallest of these maxima is $X_0 = 7$. Taking expected losses into account, then, results in a higher cutoff score than we obtained by minimizing the maximum probability of misclassification. This occurs because our losses imply that a false-positive error is 10 times as serious as a false negative. As a result we require a high score before we conclude that an examinee is a master.

TABLE 18.6. Expected Losses for Domain Scores of .70 and .85 for All Possible Observed Scale Cutoff Scores

Cutoff Score	Domain Score	
	.70	.85
0	5.0000*	.00000
1	4.9995*	.00000
2	4.9815*	.00000
3	4.8565*	.00055
4	4.3705*	.00600
5	3.2360*	.03685
6	1.6475*	.14170
7	.4120*	.33745

*Indicates the maximum expected loss for each possible cutoff score.

The minimax procedure minimizes the maximum expected loss. It is also possible to develop a procedure that minimizes the total expected loss. Hunyh (1976b) used the beta-binomial model to develop such a procedure. Again the results are somewhat complicated to apply, but an accurate approximation is available for use when $n \geq 20$ and τ_0 is between .50 and .80. This approximation is

$$\frac{n - KR(21)}{KR(21)} \tau_0 + z \sqrt{\frac{n - KR(21)}{KR(21)} \tau_0 (1 - \tau_0)} + \frac{KR(21) - 1}{KR(21)} \hat{\mu}_X + .5. \qquad (18.3)$$

In this expression z is the score in the standard normal distribution with an area of $Q/(Q + 1)$ to the left of it, and Q is the ratio of false-positive to false-negative losses. For example if this loss ratio is $Q = 4$, z is the score that cuts off an area of .8 to the left of it. Novick and Lewis (1974) used misclassification losses and the beta-binomial model to develop a procedure for setting testing lengths and observed scale cutoff scores.

In the preceding applications of decision theory, all false-negative misclassifications were treated as equally serious, as were all false-positive misclassifications. (Losses of this kind comprise a *threshold loss function*.) Yet it is logical to ask if it is not a more serious error to misclassify an examinee whose true level of ability is far away from the domain scale cutoff score than to misclassify one whose true level of ability is very near the domain scale cutoff score. To illustrate, suppose we are categorizing children in a reading instructional program and Ralph passes the test, even though his domain score is slightly below the master level. Susan also passes the test, but her domain score is far below the cut score. The loss associated with the false-positive decision made for Susan is greater than the loss associated with the false-positive decision made for Ralph. One loss function that expresses these kinds of losses is the *linear loss function*. Here the loss for a false-positive error is $a(\tau_0 - \tau)$ for $\tau \leq \tau_0$. The loss for a false negative is $b(\tau - \tau_0)$. Such linear loss functions are illustrated in Figure 18.2. This graph shows that the loss for a false-positive error only exists for domain scores less than τ_0 (i.e., for examinees who are true nonmasters). The loss for false-negative errors exists only for domain scores greater than or equal to τ_0 (i.e., for examinees who are true masters). For both types of errors, the degree of the loss increases as the distance between τ_0 and τ increases. Van der Linden and Mellenbergh (1977) have derived an observed scale cutoff score for the case with linear loss functions.

The threshold and linear loss functions are not the only possible loss functions that can be proposed. Any function of τ which is positive and does not increase from 0 (the smallest possible domain score) to τ_0 could serve as a loss function for false-positive decisions. Similarly, a positive function of τ which does not decrease from τ_0 to 1 (the largest possible domain score) can reasonably serve as a loss function for false-negative decisions. Hunyh (1980b) considered a minimax procedure that permitted the use of nonlinear loss functions.

It is important for practitioners to remember that the applications of decision theory presented here may be useful in setting a cutoff score that allows the test user to make appropriate inferences about examinees' true mastery states; however, such

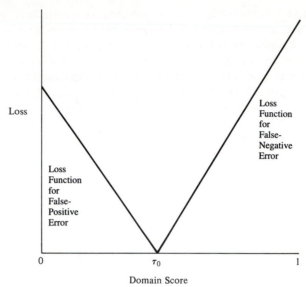

FIGURE 18.2   Illustration of a Linear Loss Function

procedures do not offer guidance in the initial issue of what level of performance constitutes "mastery" or what procedures should be used to define the standard.

So far we have not discussed the question of choosing the form of the loss function, for example, threshold or linear. Nor have we discussed choosing the particular loss function, for example, setting the values of the losses in a threshold loss problem. Basically, making these choices requires an assessment of the seriousness of the losses for each possible domain score. It is beyond the scope of the chapter to discuss in detail methods for making these choices. The interested reader is referred to Novick and Lindley (1978) and references therein.

SUMMARY

When items on a test are perceived as representing a performance domain, the examiner often desires to establish an observed score cutoff or standard which permits inference from the examinee's observed score to the true mastery state in the performance domain. This calculation is illustrated in situations where criterion-referenced test scores are used for making decisions about certification of minimal competency. In these situations the examiner must employ a rationally defensible procedure for location of the cutoff score. Three broad categories of standard setting are using panels of judges to review the test and make a holistic judgment about location of the standard, using examinees' performance data to set the standard, and using item judgment procedures. Two prominent methods of using examinees' performance data are the contrasting groups and borderline group methods. Three prominent methods based on judges' ratings of individual test items are Nedelsky's, Angoff's, and Ebel's procedures. In addition, there is a procedure proposed by Jaeger which combines several features of other methods in an iterative approach. Empirical studies comparing standards resulting from application of various methods were reviewed, and the general conclusion was that different approaches may result in different standards, and even different groups of judges using the same method may recommend different standards. In view of this variation, some practical recommendations for setting standards are (1) question whether a standard is really necessary for the testing situation; (2) identify the most likely threats to the validity of inferences that will be made by using the test; (3) select and instruct judges in a manner conducive to reducing bias in their judgments; (4) use multiple approaches to setting the standard and multiple panels of judges; (5) examine empirical evidence of how a typical group of examinees performs and use this to evaluate the consequences of the recommended standard.

There are two classes of methods for setting an observed scale cutoff score that permits the test user to make appropriate inferences about examinees' true mastery states. One is concerned with minimizing probabilities of misclassification. These procedures are appropriate when all false-positive and all false-negative errors are equally serious. A second class of methods is concerned with minimizing the expected losses due to misclassification. These methods use a threshold loss function which is appropriate when all false-positive errors are equally serious, all false-negative errors are equally serious, but false-positive and false-negative errors are differentially serious. Loss functions appropriate in other situations were introduced.

Exercises

1. A 30-item test is administered to 2,000 students. The mean score is 18 and KR 21 is .6. If τ_0 is .8, what is Hunyh's approximation to X_0?
2. Suppose that for the test situation in Exercise 1, the loss ratio for false positives to false negatives is 2. What will Hunyh's approximation to X_0 be?
3. Using the results for the hypothetical seven-item test, determine X_0 if the loss for a false positive is 1 and the loss for a false negative is 10. Determine X_0 if these losses are 2 and 20, respectively. Which is it necessary to set in implementing the procedure, the losses for false-positive and false-negative errors or their ratio?
4. Read Rowley's article, "Historical Antecedents of the Standard Setting Debate: An Inside Account of the Minimal Beardedness Controversy," published in the *Journal of Educational Measurement*, 1982, *19*, 87–96. Then answer the following questions:
   A. Should the variable of interest have been conceptualized as being measurable on a continuum or should it have been conceptualized as an all-or-none "state" variable?
   B. Match the methods of standard setting discussed in this chapter to those discussed by Rowley and identify at least two procedures presented here which Rowley failed to consider.
   C. Consider the "item" format suggested for assessment of beardedness. Would it be feasible to apply Nedelsky's item judgment process to these items? Why?

D. Rowley identified one or more major criticisms (or shortcomings) of each of the standard-setting methods: Angoff's method, contrasting groups method, and item response theory. For each method, describe Rowley's criticism and consider how serious it would be if applied to establishing a cutoff score on a minimum competency certification examination for beginning teachers.

E. In view of Rowley's findings (as reported in Table 1 of his article), consider whether it is logical that as the content validity of items (or their relevance to an important domain) increases, the recommended minimum passing score on that set of items should increase. How would you interpret the results of Rowley's study?

Chapter 19

NORMS AND STANDARD SCORES

In the preceding chapter we discussed criterion-referenced tests on which the raw scores are intended to have direct, interpretable meaning. In many cases, however, it may be difficult to make useful interpretations or inferences from examinees' raw scores alone. In this chapter we consider procedures for enhancing test score interpretability through the use of norms. Virtually all normative scores provide information about an examinee's performance in comparison to the score distribution of some norm sample or reference group. Consequently the meaningfulness of these scores depends on (1) the extent to which the test user is interested in comparing the examinee to the normative population and (2) the adequacy of the norming sample in representing that population.

At the outset, it is important to recognize that for some test uses, it is most appropriate to compare an examinee's performance to performance of a current peer norm group (i.e., all examinees taking this test at this time). Use of a current peer group may be appropriate for an employer who must fill a certain number of existing vacancies from the available applicant pool or for a classroom instructor who wishes to assign grades based on relative performance of students in the current class during the current term. In contrast, it seems less reasonable that a child's chance of placement in a special remedial program or a health professional's chance of state licensure should vary depending on the particular group of examinees who took the test on the same day. For these purposes it is helpful if the examinee's score can be compared to the test score distribution of an examinee sample representing a well-defined population. In such cases the normative sample should be described in sufficient detail with respect to demographic characteristics (e.g., gender, race or ethnic background, community or geographic region, socioeconomic status, and educational background) to permit a test user to assess whether it is meaningful to compare an examinee's performance to their norm group's. In some situations, test users prefer to develop norms, based on performance of a local norm group. In this case the test user must assume the responsibility for constructing an appropriate normative sample and making the score conversions. In this chapter we introduce some basic concepts relevant to developing test norms or to assessing the adequacy of norms which accompany a published instrument. Later we will review common score conversions used in comparing an individual examinee's raw test score to the distribution of a norm sample.

CONDUCTING A NORMING STUDY

In general, the recommended procedures for conducting a norming study are similar regardless of whether the norms are for local or broader use. The basic steps are as follows:

1. *Identify the population of interest* (e.g., all students in a particular school district or all applicants for admission to a particular program of study or type of employment).
2. *Identify the most critical statistics that will be computed* for the sample data (e.g., mean, standard deviation, percentile ranks).
3. *Decide on the tolerable amount of sampling error* (discrepancy between the sample estimate and the population parameter) for one or more of the statistics identified in step 2. (Frequently the sampling error of the mean is specified.)
4. *Devise a procedure for drawing a sample* from the population of interest. (Alternative sampling strategies will be briefly described in the following section.)
5. *Estimate the minimum sample size required* to hold the sampling error within the specified limits. Various formulas must be used depending on the sampling strategy employed.
6. *Draw the sample and collect the data.* Document the reasons for any attrition which may occur. If substantial attrition occurs (e.g., failure of an entire school to participate after it has been selected into the sample), it may be necessary to replace this unit with another chosen by the same sampling procedure.
7. *Compute the values of the group statistics of interest* and their standard errors. In practice the standard error of the mean is most often reported.
8. *Identify the types of normative scores that will be needed* and prepare the normative score conversion tables.
9. *Prepare written documentation of the norming procedure* and guidelines for interpretation of the normative scores.

PROBABILITY SAMPLING

Normative data for test scores are sometimes reported based on data from samples of convenience (i.e., intact groups of examinees who were available to the test developer). Norming a test on such a sample, however, increases the possibility that some systematic bias may influence examinees' performance. For example, examinees who volunteer to participate in the norming of a self-concept inventory may differ systematically in self-concept from nonvolunteers. Furthermore, because such samples are not chosen to represent any particular population, use of statistics, such as the standard error of the mean, to estimate the probable degree of error in the estimates is rather pointless. In contrast, when the test developer uses a probability sample for collection of normative data, the opportunity for systematic bias to influence test performance is reduced, and in addition it is possible to estimate the amount of sampling error likely to affect various statistics calculated from these scores. Simply defined, a *probability sample* is one in which every individual in a specified population has a known probability of selection. The simplest form of probability sampling (and the one to which other types are usually compared) is simple random sampling.

Simple random sampling may be likened to the process of assigning each member of the population a unique number, writing each number on a separate piece of paper, putting all the slips of paper in a hat, and drawing from the hat a given number of paper slips. Each examinee whose number is selected is chosen for the sample. In actuality, examinees are more often selected by choosing a random starting point in a random number table and selecting each examinee whose number appears sequentially in the list until the desired number of examinees for the sample has been reached.

When the value of the test score mean (or any other statistic) is computed for a norming sample, it is an estimate of that parameter for the population, and such an estimate is subject to sampling error. If many repeated random samples are drawn from a given population and the mean computed for each sample, it would be possible to describe a frequency distribution of these sample means around the single value of the population mean. According to sampling theory this distribution should approximate a normal curve. The standard deviation of this distribution of sample means is called the *standard error of the mean,* and we shall denote it as σ_M. This quantity is useful when we want to specify, with a certain degree of confidence, an interval around the sample mean which is expected to contain the population mean. Obviously the smaller this interval, the better, in terms of judging how adequately the normative sample represents the population.

The value of σ_M can be estimated from the data of a single sample by the formula[1]

$$\hat{\sigma}_M = \sqrt{\frac{\hat{\sigma}_X^2}{n}} \tag{19.1}$$

---

[1] This formula is used when the population size is so large that it is considered to approach infinity. When sampling from a finite population, the correct formula is

$$\hat{\sigma}_M = \sqrt{\frac{\hat{\sigma}_X^2}{n} \frac{(N-n)}{N}}$$

where N is the number of cases in the population. In most norming studies the correction for a finite population size is unnecessary.

TABLE 19.1.   Standard Errors of the Mean for
Samples of Differing Variability and Size

Sample Size (n)	Sample Variance ($\hat{\sigma}_X^2$)	$\hat{\sigma}_M = \sqrt{\dfrac{\hat{\sigma}_X^2}{n}}$
50	25	.71
100		.50
200		.35
50	100	1.42
100		1.00
200		.71
50	225	2.12
100		1.50
200		1.06

where $\hat{\sigma}_X^2$ is the variance of scores for the sample[2] and n is the sample size. Clearly the two determinants of the accuracy of the sample mean are the variance of the group and the size of the sample. Table 19.1 illustrates how $\hat{\sigma}_M$ decreases for a constant level of variability as sample size increases, and how it increases for a given sample size as group variability increases. Another way of putting this is that the greater the variability, the larger the sample size that will be necessary to achieve a given level of sampling error.

When the test developer can specify in advance the tolerable amount of error in the estimated mean for the norm sample, this information can be used in the formula for the standard error of the mean to estimate the minimal sample size that will be required. Thus on an 80-item achievement test, the test developer may want to be 95% confident that any estimate of the mean should lie within ± 1 point of the mean score that would be obtained if the entire population were tested. This means that the approximate point spread corresponding to $2\hat{\sigma}_M$ should be ≤ 1.00, and thus $\hat{\sigma}_M \leq .50$. To determine the minimum sample size needed to yield this degree of accuracy, it is necessary to have some idea of the size of the standard deviation of scores on the test. (This information may be obtained from some initial pilot-test data during earlier developmental efforts or by making an educated guess based on knowledge of how examinees typically perform on similar tests of this type.) Suppose now that the test developer has some reason to expect that the standard deviation on this 80-item achievement test will be 10 points. Substituting these values in Equation 19.1 and solving for n, we have $n = 100/.25 = 400$. Thus a minimum sample of 400 subjects will be needed to obtain the desired degree of accuracy for the sample estimate of the population mean.

In some norming studies it would be impossible to draw a simple random sample and test each examinee selected by this method. For example in norming a standard-

---

[2] It should be noted that when variance is estimated for sample data, the sum of the squared deviation scores is divided by $(n - 1)$ rather than by n.

ized achievement test, it would not be feasible to list all eighth-graders in the state and randomly select some for testing. Conceivably this sampling plan could cause the examiner to visit a much larger number of cities, schools, and classrooms than would be economically feasible. For other norming purposes, simple random sampling may not allow the investigator to control the composition of the norm sample in terms of some important relevant variables. Thus alternatives to simple random sampling are sometimes appropriate.

Systematic sampling is employed when subjects are listed in some order which is unrelated to the trait being measured (e.g. names in a telephone directory). The researcher identifies a random starting point in the list, and if the sampling ratio of $1/k$ subjects is to be chosen from the population, every kth subject on the list from that starting point is chosen. If the investigator reaches the end of the list before the entire sample quota has been filled, he or she simply goes to the front of the list and continues selection of every kth subject. Systematic sampling is especially useful where no advance list of subjects is available, as in a marketing survey where every kth customer is sampled as he or she enters the establishment or purchases a product. This method of sampling can be readily adapted to selecting a sample of entering patients or clients receiving services in diagnostic, remedial, or rehabilitative programs. If it can be assumed that the list of subjects was essentially in random order for the variable in question, standard errors of sample statistics can be estimated as for simple random sampling.

Stratified random sampling is similar to simple random sampling, but the researcher decides a priori that the sample must contain specific proportions of certain types of examinees. For example, the researcher may wish to insure that the sample selected will consist of 50% males and 50% females or of 70% whites and 30% blacks. If n represents the total sample size, separate random samples of males and females would be selected in this case by choosing a total number of .50(n) males and .50(n) females. If a sample of 70% whites and 30% blacks, with 50% males and 50% females in each racial group, is desired, and n is the total sample size, the researcher selects

One random sample of .30(.50)n, or .15n black males
One random sample of .30(.50)n, or .15n black females
One random sample of .70(.50)n, or .35n white males
One random sample of .70(.50)n, or .35n white females

Stratified random sampling may be preferable to simple random sampling for two reasons. The first reason for stratified sampling occurs when the stratification variable is related to test performance. Suppose, for example, that on a test of spatial relationships, there is a tendency for males to score higher than females and that males constitute 70% and females 30% of the population of interest. If a randomly drawn sample contained 80% males and 20% females, the sample mean would probably overestimate the population mean. If a simple random sample happened to contain 50% males and 50% females, the sample mean would probably underestimate the population mean. Thus drawing a stratified sample with 70% males and 30% females would increase the likelihood of obtaining a sample mean close to the population mean. With stratified sampling the test developer can produce norms with less sampling error for the same cost as a simple random sample of comparable size, or alternately the estimates from the two sampling strategies may have the same amount of error but a smaller, stratified sample could be used at reduced cost. As a general rule, it is advantageous to use a stratified sample whenever variance of examinees' scores within a stratum is less than total group variance. Also, a norm sample which is stratified to reflect the demographic composition of the population has greater credibility to test users. For example, even though there is no difference in performance of male and female students on an academic aptitude test for children, test users are likely to be more comfortable comparing their examinees' scores to a norm based on approximately 50% males and 50% females than in using a norm group based on 75% males and 25% females, which does not reflect the gender distribution in the general population.

When a stratified sample is used to norm a test, the sample mean is sometimes called a *weighted mean,* and the standard error of the weighted mean is calculated by

$$\hat{\sigma}_{M_w} = \sqrt{\Sigma W_h^2 \hat{\sigma}_{M_h}^2} \qquad (19.2)$$

where each stratum is assigned a decimal weight W_h denoting the proportion of cases it contains, and σ_{M_h} is the standard error of the mean for stratum h.[3]

When subjects are grouped together in natural aggregates or organizational units (e.g., classrooms, factories, hospitals, or perhaps city blocks of residences), it is possible to construct a sample by selection of a probability sample of these units. This is known as *cluster sampling.* In single stage cluster sampling, once a unit has been chosen, all individuals within that unit are in the sample. We shall limit consideration here to the case in which the investigator wants to sample clusters in such a way that each cluster has an equal chance of being selected. To draw the sample, the investigator would assign a number between 1 and K to each cluster in the population. Clusters would then be chosen using a random number table in the same way that simple random sampling is used for selection of individual subjects.

Typically cluster sizes vary, and Lord (1959a) suggested that an appropriate formula for estimating the standard error of the mean in this situation is

$$\hat{\sigma}_{M_C} = \frac{\hat{\sigma}_\mu}{\sqrt{k}} \sqrt{1 + (\hat{\sigma}_n / \hat{\mu}_n)^2} \qquad (19.3)$$

where k is the number of clusters in the sample, $\hat{\sigma}_\mu$ is the standard deviation of the cluster means, $\hat{\sigma}_n$ is the standard deviation of the cluster sizes, and $\hat{\mu}_n$ is the average

---

[3] When sampling from a finite population, this formula would be modified to

$$\hat{\sigma}_{M_w} = \sqrt{\Sigma W_h^2 \hat{\sigma}_{M_h}^2 (1 - f_h)}$$

where f_h is the sampling fraction, or proportion of examinees, sampled from strata h.

cluster size. In the case where all clusters are equal in size, $\hat{\sigma}_{M_C}$ can be estimated by

$$\hat{\sigma}_{M_C} = \frac{\hat{\sigma}_\mu}{\sqrt{k}} \qquad (19.4)$$

Examinees within a cluster (such as a classroom) typically are more homogeneous than the population as a whole. Thus the sample mean for examinees from a small number of clusters is likely to be farther from the population mean than a mean based on an equal number of examinees drawn by simple random sampling. If the test developer wants normative statistics for the cluster sample to have sampling errors similar to those obtained from a simple random sample of a given size, more individuals must be tested in the cluster sample. Lord (1959a) demonstrated that cluster sampling in a norming study for a standardized test might require testing as many as 12 to 30 times as many examinees to achieve norm estimates comparable in accuracy to those based on simple random samples. It should be noted that greater efficiency in cluster sampling may be achieved by sampling so that each cluster's chance of selection is proportional to its size. Jaeger (1984) has described sampling procedures and provided estimation formulas for this approach to cluster sampling.

Because standard errors of the normative statistics will generally be smaller as more clusters are used, the investigator should plan to collect data from as many sites (clusters) as possible. One way to contain the total cost of the study (and possibly to obtain better response rate from participating units) is through multiple stage sampling, which is most easily illustrated by two-stage sampling. Suppose that a test developer is interested in developing local district norms for an individually administered aptitude test for students at a particular grade level, but cannot afford to test all students in the district. A possible two-stage sample design is to (1) draw a random sample of schools and (2) within each school, sample a fixed proportion of examinees (e.g., 5%). This procedure essentially gives each school an equal chance of selection but ensures that larger schools are more heavily represented in the sample than smaller schools. For this two-stage sample, the standard error of the mean is affected by error variance due to sampling of schools and error variance due to sampling of individuals within schools. The error variance due to sampling of schools can estimated by $\hat{\sigma}_{M_C}^2$ (see Equation 19.3). Angoff (1971) and Lord (1959a) estimated error variance due to the sampling of individuals within clusters using formulas equivalent to

$$\hat{\sigma}_{M_w}^2 = \frac{(1-p)\overline{\hat{\sigma}_X^2}}{kp\hat{\mu}_n}$$

In the present example p is the proportion of students sampled in each school, k is the number of schools, $\hat{\mu}_n$ is the average school size, and $\overline{\hat{\sigma}_X^2}$ is an estimate of the average within-school variance for the population. Thus the standard error of the mean for this two-stage sample is

$$\hat{\sigma}_M = \sqrt{\hat{\sigma}_{M_C}^2 + \hat{\sigma}_{M_w}^2} \qquad (19.5)$$

Of course, the sampling design and estimation formulas presented here are not the only ways to select a two-stage sample of clusters and individuals. Another possible approach would be to select the cluster sample of schools in such a way that each school's chance of selection is proportional to its size with an equal number of students tested in each school. Angoff (1971) described a practical procedure for selecting such a two-stage sample and both Angoff and Lord (1959a) have provided formulas for estimation of the standard error of the mean for this type of sample. The main point that the reader should recognize is that for each successive stage in the sampling process an additional error variance term affects the standard error of the mean, and that when clusters or intact groups are used in constructing a norm sample, they should not be treated as a random sample of individuals drawn from the population. Furthermore different strategies for sampling clusters and individuals may require different error estimation formulas. A useful reference on construction of multiple stage samples is Kish (1965).

DESCRIBING THE NORMING STUDY IN THE TEST MANUAL

In describing the results of a norming study the test developer has several responsibilities. First, the general population of examinees for whom the test is intended should be described. Then the procedure by which the norming sample was selected must be documented. This should particularly include a detailed description of the sampling plan (e.g., type of sampling employed, identification of strata in stratified sampling, proportion sampled from each stratum, and number of clusters sampled). As a general suggestion, the description of the sampling plan should be sufficiently complete so that test users who may wish to estimate standard errors for statistics (other than those reported in the manual) would be able to do so.

In describing the sampling procedure it is also important to indicate the extent of refusal or nonresponse rate among the units originally sampled and to explain the possible impact which such refusals may have on generalizability of results from the sample to the population. For example, although the manual of the *Metropolitan Achievement Tests* (Prescott et al., 1978) indicates that over 550,000 students participated in some aspect of the standardization program, Baglin (1981) reported that a total of 88 school districts actually agreed to participate in the standardization and that these districts constituted only 32% of all districts invited to participate in the national norming study. (Similar or lower rates of participation were typically reported for other major achievement tests normed during this same period.) Furthermore, willingness to participate in a given publisher's norming study seemed to be influenced by what achievement test series was already in use in the district. Thus Baglin questioned whether it is reasonable to describe such norms as truly "nationally representative," suggesting that test publishers should be more thorough in describing how their norm samples are constructed.

Other critical information that should be reported includes the date of the norming study with a description of the composition of the norm sample in terms of gender, racial or ethnic background, socioeconomic status, geographic location, and types of communities represented (where appropriate). Any special conditions under which the test was administered should be noted. For example, if the norming sample for a professional certification examination consisted of applicants for certification who were required to take the test on an experimental basis only (so that their scores were not really considered in the certification decision), their motivational level and consequent test performance may have been lower than those of examinees who must later pass the test to be certified.

Group statistics reported to describe the performance of the norm sample on the test (e.g., mean and standard deviation), should be accompanied by information regarding the accuracy of these sample estimates. At the minimum, the standard error of the mean should be reported, accompanied by specific score intervals likely to contain the population mean for different levels of confidence. Angoff (1971) offered the rule-of-thumb for assessing whether the standard error of the mean is within reasonable limits by suggesting that the error at the mean due to the combination of sampling error and the standard error of measurement of the test should not exceed the standard error of measurement by more than 1%.

Finally, the test manual should contain clear explanations of the meanings and appropriate interpretations of each type of normative score conversion reported. Here it is also desirable to point out how much each type of score should be expected to vary because of measurement error. For conversions such as percentile ranks, this should be illustrated at various points of the score distribution.

TYPES OF NORMATIVE SCORES

Recall that in most cases a norming study is conducted for the purpose of constructing conversion tables so that a particular raw score value can be interpreted in terms of its relative location and frequency within the total score distribution. In the following sections some common types of normative scores will be described accompanied by considerations attendant in their interpretations.

Percentile Rank

Loosely speaking, the percentile rank corresponding to a particular raw score is interpreted as the percentage of examinees in the norm group who scored below the score of interest. Mathematically, the percentile rank is defined as

$$P = \frac{cf_l + .5(f_i)}{N} \times 100\% \tag{19.6}$$

where cf_l is the cumulative frequency for all scores lower than the score of interest, f_i is the frequency of scores in the interval of interest, and N is the number in the sample. Steps in computing percentile ranks for a raw score distribution are these:

1. Construct a frequency distribution for the raw scores as shown in Table 19.2.
2. For a given raw score, determine the cumulative frequency for all scores lower than the score of interest. (If we wanted the percentile rank corresponding to a score 17,

TABLE 19.2.   Raw Scores, Frequency Distribution, Percentile Ranks, and Linear z-Scores and Standard Normal z-Scores

Raw Score	f	cf	Percentile Rank[a]	Linear z	Normalized z
11	2	2	01	−2.53	−2.33
12	1	3	02	−2.17	−2.05
13	6	9	04	−1.80	−1.75
14	5	14	08	−1.44	−1.40
15	12	26	13	−1.07	−1.13
16	17	43	23	−.71	−0.74
17	21	64	36	−.34	−0.36
18	28	92	52	.02	0.05
19	19	111	67	.39	0.47
20	15	126	79	.75	0.81
21	10	136	87	1.12	1.13
22	5	141	92	1.48	1.40
23	3	144	95	1.85	1.64
24	4	148	97	2.21	1.88
25	2	150	99	2.58	2.33

[a]Rounded to nearest one-hundredth.
$\hat{\mu}_x = 17.94$, $\hat{\sigma}_x = 2.74$.

for the data in Table 19.2, we would determine the cumulative frequency for the score 16.)

3. Add half the frequency for the score of interest to the cumulative frequency value determined in step 2.
4. Divide the total by N, the number of examinees in the norm group and multiply by 100%.

For the percentile rank corresponding to a raw score of 17 in Table 19.2, the computation would be

$$PR_{17} = \frac{43 + (.5)(21)}{150} \times 100\% = 36$$

It may not be immediately obvious why only half the examinees who earned the raw score of interest are counted in computing the percentile rank. Although raw scores are discrete values, traditionally the underlying ability continuum is considered to be continuous. Thus each value on the raw score scale corresponds to a score interval on the ability continuum, and the point of interest is the midpoint of this interval. Theoretically half the examinees who earn any given raw score are considered to score below the midpoint of this interval, and half are considered to score above it. Thus in computing the percentile rank, we count only the number of examinees who score below the midpoint of the interval (half the total number of examinees who earned that raw score).

Percentile ranks are often recommended for communicating results of norm-referenced tests to students, parents, or clients. If we assume that the examinee were tested at the same time of year as the norm group, and test administration instructions and time limits were carefully observed, an appropriate interpretation would be illustrated by the statement, "Jane's score on this test was higher than the scores of 75% of the norm group." Nonetheless several cautions should be noted about percentile ranks. Most misinterpretations arise when test users fail to recognize that the percentile rank scale is a nonlinear transformation of the raw score scale. Simply put, this means that at different regions on the raw score scale, a gain of 1 point may correspond to gains of different magnitudes on the percentile rank scale.

To illustrate, let us consider Table 19.3, which contains examples of raw scores and corresponding percentile rank values from an elementary mathematics achievement test. The standard error of measurement for this test is approximately 3 points, and thus the fourth column of the table contains the raw score intervals corresponding to $(X \pm 1\sigma_E)$. Note that while these intervals are equal in width for all raw score values, their corresponding percentile bands in the last column vary considerably depending on location of the raw scores in the distribution. This occurs because of the greater relative frequency of scores in the middle of the distribution and the relative decrease in frequency toward the tails of the distribution. Thus test users should be aware that

1. Percentile rank scores are less stable (reliable) for scores in the central part of the distribution than for those in the extremes. For example, in Table 19.3, we see that the score of an examinee of medium ability may vary as much as 12 percentile rank points and still not exceed the standard error of measurement, whereas a similar increase in raw score for an examinee in the upper ability range would result in a change of only 5 percentile ranks. Consequently, a percentile band (an interval of percentile ranks corresponding to the points $X \pm 1\hat{\sigma}_E$) is often useful in score interpretation. Such percentile bands are shown in the rightmost column of Table 19.3.
2. Gains or losses of percentile ranks for individual examinees cannot be meaningfully compared for examinees at different points in the distribution. For example, suppose that all students in an experimental program gained 3 raw score points from pretest to post-test. Comparing gains in percentile ranks would lead to the inappropriate conclusion that the upper-ability examinees had gained least from the treatment and that the examinees in the middle had made the greatest gains.
3. Arithmetic and statistical computations of percentile rank scores cannot be mean-

TABLE 19.3.   Illustrative Raw Scores, Percentile Ranks, and Percentile Bands for an Elementary Mathematics Achievement Test

Distribution Region	Raw Score	Percentile Rank	$(X \pm 1\hat{\sigma}_E)$[a]	Percentile Band for $(X \pm 1\hat{\sigma}_E)$[a]
Upper	41	94	38–44	84–99
Middle	28	38	25–31	27–50
Lower	20	14	17–23	8–22

[a] $\hat{\sigma}_E$ is approximately 3 points.

ingfully interpreted in some situations. Suppose, for example, that a researcher wants to compare the means for two groups. The conclusion about the performance of the two groups might be different if the researcher averages the percentile ranks rather than the raw scores. This can be seen from a simple example with data from Table 19.2; suppose group A consists of two examinees with raw scores 12 and 20, and group B consists of two examinees with raw scores 15 and 17. Both group A and group B have a raw score mean of 16, yet the means of their corresponding percentile rank scores are considerably different (40.5 for group A and 24.5 for group B). Thus it is usually considered inappropriate to base group comparisons on the average of individual percentile rank scores.

Normalized z-Scores

Although most distributions of test scores are not absolutely normal (Lord, 1955), there are nevertheless some advantages in test score interpretation associated with creation of standard scores based on ''normalization'' of the original score distribution. The convenience of a normalized z-scale is that regardless of the test or examinee sample, for every point on the scale there are fixed percentages of cases falling above and below that point; the values of these percentages can be obtained from any standard normal z-table. Normalized z-scores are obtained by a nonlinear transformation of the original raw scores. Unlike linear z-scores (defined in Chapter 2), which retain the form of the raw score distribution, normalized z-scores have a distribution which approximates the normal curve. Thus the normalized z-score and linear z-score for a given raw score value will differ to the extent that the raw score distribution departs from normality.

A simple approach to converting raw scores to normal z-scores is to determine the percentile rank corresponding to each raw score value by the method previously described and then to look up the corresponding z-score for that percentile rank from a standard normal z-table, as we have done in Table 19.2. The z-scores thus determined for various raw score values would vary from sample to sample, depending on sampling variations in the frequencies for a given raw score. Thus in large-scale norming studies, test developers may employ a somewhat more sophisticated approach to determine percentile ranks and normalized z-scores. This involves a curve-fitting practice called *smoothing*. Smoothing processes vary considerably, so the reader should regard the description presented here as merely illustrative of the general concept.

Suppose that the raw score values of the distribution are plotted on the horizontal axis of a two-dimensional graph, and the percentile ranks associated with various raw scores are plotted on the vertical axis, as in Figure 19.1(a). The graph obtained is a plot of discrete points; however, it should be possible to fit an S-shaped curve to this set of points (see Figure 19.1(b). If the distribution of raw scores were perfectly normal, the curve obtained would be a normal ogive (discussed in Chapter 15). Two general approaches can be used to fit a smooth curve to a plot of points. One method is to draw the curve by hand, using a plot like that in Figure 19.1(a); however, Angoff (1971) suggests using normal probability paper (graph paper constructed so

Cumulative Frequency

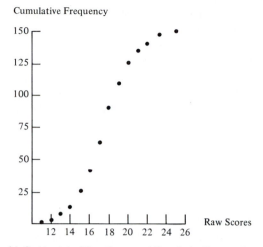

(a) Scatterplot of Raw Scores and Cumulative Frequencies

Cumulative Frequency

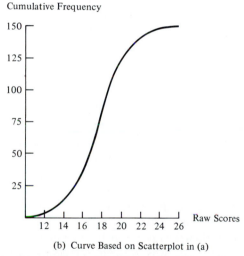

(b) Curve Based on Scatterplot in (a)

FIGURE 19.1   Scatterplot and Curve for Relationship between Raw Scores and Cumulative Frequencies for Data in Table 19.1

that a plot of points from a normal distribution will fall in a straight line). The second approach involves fitting a mathematical function to the frequency distribution and constructing the cumulative frequency distribution from the mathematical function. Keats and Lord (1962) and Lord and Novick (1968), illustrated the application of the negative hypergeometric function for this purpose.

Once a smooth curve has been drawn to depict the relationship between values on the raw score scale and values on the percentile rank scale, the percentile rank corresponding to any particular score is taken from the vertical coordinate of the point on the curve rather than from the original percentile rank calculated from the observed frequency data. The standard normal z-score is consequently also determined by finding the z-score in the normal curve table which corresponds to the "smoothed" percentile rank score. It should be noted that "smoothing," as a general process in scale construction, is not restricted to the graph showing the relationship between raw score values and percentile ranks. It can be applied to many different scale transformations.

The decision to normalize standard scores in development of norms is not always clear-cut. Historically the practice is well entrenched, especially for development of commercially published aptitude and achievement measures. For such tests, however, the point may be rather moot because in many instances item writing and item selection practices are employed to yield tests on which the examinee population should have a normal distribution and sample sizes are sufficiently large to represent the population distribution accurately. The issue of normalization becomes more critical, however, when the score distribution departs substantially from normal. This is not uncommon in small-scale research efforts or local norming studies where the size of the standardization samples may be fairly small. In such cases, the distribution of the normalized z-scores may differ markedly from that of the original raw scores. Then the question is whether the raw scores or the normalized scores most closely represent the distribution of scores that would have been obtained if the entire population had been tested. On the one hand, some measurement theorists would seem to maintain that normalization of scores is justified if the researcher believes that the psychological trait being measured is normally distributed in the population (Magnusson, 1967). Gulliksen (1950) submitted that normalization of scores is indicated when it is reasonable to believe that the ability measured by the test is normally distributed but that flaws in the test cause the observed scores to depart from normality. On the other hand, Angoff (1971) cautioned that transformation to a normal distribution is probably undesirable, especially if the nonnormal shape of the raw score distribution is suspected of being a function of the process for selection of examinees or of an atypical distribution of ability in the particular group that has been tested. It is thus somewhat ironic that normalization of scores is probably most justifiable when the raw score distribution does not depart too drastically from normal to begin with. It is difficult to imagine a situation in which the distribution of scores for a sample departs radically from normality and yet the examiner contends that the sample is an adequate representation of some population in which the trait is normally distributed.

Transformations of z-Scores

Whether linear or normalized, z-scores have the disadvantage of assuming decimal and negative values, which can be difficult to work with computationally and difficult to interpret to test users. (Consider, for a moment, the task of trying to explain to an examinee who has taken a 300-item test and answered 100 items correctly that he or she has earned a z-score of -1.5 points!) For this reason it is often more convenient to perform a linear transformation on z-scores to convert them to values that are easier to record or explain. It is important to recall, as noted in Chapter 2, that such linear transformations will not alter the shape of the z-score distribution. The general form of such a transformation is

$$Y = m + k(z) \tag{19.7}$$

where Y is the derived score, and m and k are constant values arbitrarily chosen to suit the convenience of the test developer. The value chosen for m will be the mean of the new distribution after transformation, and the value chosen as k will be its standard deviation.

Figure 19.2 displays several common transformed z-scales under the normal curve. One of well-known z-score transformations is the T score, developed by McCall (1939), who suggested this scale for reporting children's performance on a mental abilities test. The general formula for the T score is

$$T = 50 + 10(z) \tag{19.8}$$

On the T scale, the norm group will have a mean of 50 and a standard deviation of 10 points. Another transformed z-score, devised by the Educational Testing Service for reporting examinees' College Entrance Examination Board (CEEB) scores, takes the form

$$Y = 500 + 100(z) \tag{19.9}$$

so the mean of this transformed score distribution is 500 and the standard deviation is 100 points. Perhaps the most well-known of all the transformed z-scores is the deviation I.Q. score of the general form

$$DIQ = 100 + 15(z) \tag{19.10}$$

which was used by Wechsler (1939) for interpretation of scores on his adult intelligence scale. This derived score scale is designed to have a mean of 100 and a standard deviation of 15 points. Other intelligence tests (such as the Stanford-Binet scale) may use a standard deviation of 16 points. For historical accuracy it should be noted that the original concept of the intelligence quotient proposed by Wilhelm Stern for use with the Binet scale, was not a deviation I.Q. Kaplan and Saccuzzo (1982) give an account of this historical development in intelligence testing.

Finally some manuals for standardized achievement tests report tables for converting raw scores or percentile ranks to normal curve equivalents (NCEs). These standard scores have been particularly associated with the norm-referenced evaluation model for the ESEA Title I Evaluation and Reporting System (Tallmadge and Wood, 1976). The NCE scale has a mean of 50 and a standard deviation of 21.06. Values in normative tables for converting percentile ranks to NCEs are obtained by determining the normalized z-score associated with the percentile rank of interest and making a transformation of the form

$$NCE = 50 + 21.06(z) \tag{19.11}$$

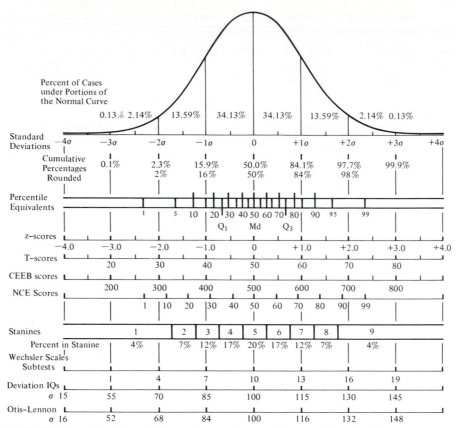

FIGURE 19.2   The Normal Curve, Percentiles, and Selected Standard Scores

Reprinted from Test Service Notebook 148 of the Psychological Corporation.

Stanines

Another standard score, particularly popular for use with standardized achievement tests, is the stanine, a scale consisting of single-digit numbers ranging from 1 to 9. This scale offers a method of describing examinees' performance in broad brush-strokes. Such scores are often used in school districts for communicating test results to parents since the nine-point scale has apparent simplicity and precludes the tendency for overinterpretation of small differences, which sometimes occurs when percentile ranks are reported alone. The mean on the stanine scale is 5 and the standard deviation is approximately 2. Typically, in a normal distribution, raw scores that correspond to the middle 20% of the distribution (i.e., from percentile ranks 40 to 59) are assigned to the middle stanine score of 5. Raw scores corresponding to the next 17 percentile rank points (i.e., from percentile ranks 60 to 76) are assigned a stanine of 6; raw scores corresponding to the next 12 percentile rank points are assigned a stanine of 7; raw scores corresponding to the next 7 percentile rank points are assigned a stanine of 8; and raw scores corresponding to the top 4 percentile rank points are assigned a stanine of 9. (See Figure 19.2.) The same procedure is used in the lower half of the distribution to assign stanines of 4, 3, 2, and 1 respectively.

Scaled Scores

Most standardized achievement test batteries are organized into levels, with the levels increasing in difficulty for higher grades. However a single level of the test is typically appropriate for two or more consecutive grades. For example, one level may be intended for students from the beginning of second grade to the end of third grade. Consider a second-grader who scores on a reading achievement test at the 50th percentile rank, compared to the second-grade norm group, and a third-grader who scores on the same test at the 50th percentile rank, compared to the third-grade norm group. Obviously these two examinees do not have the same absolute level of reading achievement, yet their grade-level normative scores do not convey this. On such tests, test users may be interested in a score-conversion table which permits normative comparisons of scores within each group but yet allows the distributions to be located on a single continuum, reflecting the higher educational or develop-mental level of the more advanced group (see Figure 19.3). Such normative scores, reflecting both peer group and longitudinal status, are commonly known as *scaled scores*.

The construction of a score scale on which scores from increasingly advanced groups may be expressed has evolved considerably over the last half century. One early procedure was Thurstone's method of absolute scaling. As applied to the current problem, Thurstone's absolute scaling is a method for transforming the raw scores of two groups who take the same test, and are known to differ on educational level or developmental status, to a scale on which the score distribution for each group is a normal distribution. Scores on the new score scale will appear as in Figure 19.3. Note that the main purpose is not simply to place the scores on the same scale. Since both groups took the same test, the raw scores were expressed on the same scale to begin with; however, the purpose is to normalize each of the two distributions, so that normative comparisons within a group can be made, while retaining the common scale for the scores for both groups. Gulliksen (1950) de-

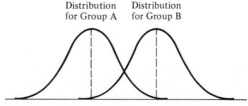

Distribution for Group A Distribution for Group B

FIGURE 19.3 Distributions of Normalized Scores for Groups A and B on a Common Scale

scribed the following process for determining the applicability of the procedure to scaled score development:

1. Administer a test to two groups (A and B) which overlap in their raw score distributions.
2. Select 10 to 20 raw score points (X_i) from the range of overlap.
3. For each of these X_i values, compute the two corresponding normalized z-scores $(z_{ai}$ and $z_{bi})$ in their respective distributions.
4. Plot the pairs of z_{ai} and z_{bi} values for all selected raw score values (X_i), with z_{ai} on the vertical axis and z_{bi} on the horizontal axis.
5. If this plot is linear, the two groups may be normalized on the same score scale.

Assuming that the plot meets the linearity requirement, we will now demonstrate how values on the common score scale can be established and related to the two score distributions. Let us denote the common scale as the Y scale. Note that since the Y scale and the z_a scale are simply linear transformations of one another, any value (z_{ai}) on the z_a scale can be related to the Y scale by the linear transformation

$$Y_i = \mu_{Ya} + \sigma_{Ya}(z_{ai}) \tag{19.12}$$

where μ_{Ya} and σ_{Ya} are the mean and standard deviation of the Y scores for group A. Now each value of Y_i can also be related to the z_b distribution by

$$Y_i = \mu_{Yb} + \sigma_{Yb}(z_{bi}) \tag{19.13}$$

Thus

$$\mu_{Ya} + \sigma_{Ya}(z_{ai}) = \mu_{Yb} + \sigma_{Yb}(z_{bi})$$

and we can solve the previous expression for z_{ai}:

$$z_{ai} = \left(\frac{\mu_{Yb} - \mu_{Ya}}{\sigma_{Ya}} \right) + z_{bi}\left(\frac{\sigma_{Yb}}{\sigma_{Ya}} \right) \tag{19.14}$$

The major axis of the scatterplot for the z_{ai}, z_{bi} paired scores can be described by the linear equation $z_{ai} = m + k(z_{bi})$. The values of k (the slope) and m (the intercept) can be estimated by procedures described in Chapter 16 (see Equations 16.2a and b). By setting $m = (\mu_{Yb} - \mu_{Ya})/\sigma_{Ya}$ and $k = (\sigma_{Yb}/\sigma_{Ya})$ and designating arbitrary values for μ_{Ya} and σ_{Ya}, we could then solve for values of μ_{Yb} and σ_{Yb} in the intercept and slope equations, respectively. Once we have values for μ_{Ya}, σ_{Ya}, μ_{Yb}, and σ_{Yb}, we can then convert any raw score value obtained in either the A or B distribution to the common Y scale. Although Thurstone's procedure allowed both the means and standard deviations of the distributions to differ, Gulliksen noted that it is still necessary to assume that otherwise the two distributions were similar in shape.

In the scaling problem just discussed two groups known to differ in educational level or developmental status took the same level of a test, and the object of the analysis was to normalize the two score distributions on the same score scale. A similar but more complicated problem is when two levels are intended for use with different groups, and we want to express the scores from the two levels on the same scale and normalize the scores for the two groups on the scale. Again the purpose is to use the normalized distributions to make within-level normative comparisons and to use the common score scale so that performances on the different levels can be compared. To solve the problem two steps are necessary. First, the scores from the two levels must be placed on the same scale. This is the problem of vertical equating and is discussed in the next chapter. Second, the scores on the scale resulting from the equating must be transformed so that the new score distributions for the two groups are normalized. This step can be accomplished by using the absolute scaling method previously outlined.

As an aid to interpreting scaled scores on standardized tests, users should know that typically the scaled score range lies between 1 and 100 or between 1 and 1000. For example, on the reading subtest of the Metropolitan Achievement Tests (Prescott et al., 1978), an examinee scoring at the 50th percentile rank in the fall of second grade has a scaled score of 571; a third-grader scoring in relatively the same place with respect to third-grade norms has a scaled score of 644; a fourth-grader with the same respective position to that grade norm has a scaled score of 674; and so on. Thus an examinee who makes normal educational progress will take a more difficult test each year and consequently earn a higher scaled score by simply remaining in the same relative position with respect to others at the same grade or age level. Also, two examinees may take tests at different levels and yet still earn the same scaled score if one examinee answers many items correctly on the lower-level test and the other answers fewer items correctly but takes a higher-level test.

Scaled scores are useful for two purposes:

1. When examinees have been administered a test above or below their actual grade level, their scaled scores can be used to relate their performance to percentile rank scores for the norm group at their actual grade levels.
2. In evaluation or research studies where average group performance must be determined for groups in which examinees may take different levels of a test, the mean scaled score can be computed, whereas the mean raw score or mean percentile rank would be misleading.

It is important to remember, however, that although scaled scores are useful in comparing examinees' performance at different levels within a single subject, they are not comparable across subtests for different subject areas within the same test battery. This fact also can be illustrated by the norms of the Metropolitan Achievement Tests, where a third-grader scoring at the 50th percentile in both reading and mathematics will have scaled scores of 644 and 532, respectively, in these subjects. These scores should not be interpreted to mean that the examinee's performance in math is weaker than in reading relative to that of his or her peers. The difference in scaled scores here reflects differences in the relative difficulty of the math and reading tests for the norm group at this grade level. Namely, the third-grade norm group as a whole performed somewhat better on the material covered by the reading test than on the material covered by the math tests relative to how norm groups at other grade levels performed.

Grade and Age Equivalents

When children are tested on aptitude or achievement measures, the test user often wants a normative score which will indicate how a given child's performance compares with that of others at a particular age or grade level. For this comparison, grade- or age-equivalent scores have sometimes been used. There are, however, severe limitations in these scores which should become apparent as the process of their development is described.

The general process by which test publishers construct grade-equivalent scores has been described by Echternacht (1977). This process can be characterized by the following steps:

1.   The raw score distribution for a test is converted to the scaled score distribution (discussed in the preceding section). This process is repeated for a test at several contiguous grade levels.
2.   The median scaled score for each grade level is determined and is plotted on a bivariate scatterplot. The horizontal axis of this scatterplot is marked into grade-placement years and months, and scaled score values are marked on the vertical axis. The median scaled score for a grade level is plotted above the year and month of the test-norming date.
3.   A smooth curve is drawn, connecting these points as shown in Figure 19.4. (Typically the relationship will be curvilinear rather than linear.)

Thus once an examinee's raw score is known, it can be converted to a scaled score and then converted to the grade-placement scale by means of this curve (or tabled values obtained from this curve). This procedure, however, permits extrapolation from raw scores on a particular test to grade levels at which the test has never been administered. It also permits a raw score to be converted to interpolated values within a grade-placement year representing times other than when the testing was conducted. As we shall see, this process gives rise to some telling criticisms of grade-equivalent scores.

The most frequently cited limitations of grade-equivalent scores are these:

1. Grade equivalents (GEs) are more subject to misinterpretation by laypersons and test users than other types of normative scores. Suppose, for example, a second-grader tested at the end of the year earns a GE of 5.3 in the areas of math, reading, and science. The appropriate interpretation is that on these tests, with second-grade content, this examinee scored similarly to how a typical fifth-year, third-month student would be expected to perform. It does *not* mean that the examinee could have performed in the same way on a test covering fifth-grade content, since obviously he or she would not have been exposed to instruction in that material; yet the

Raw Score Corresponding to Median Scaled Score at Each Grade

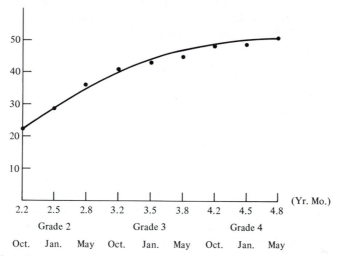

FIGURE 19.4   Plot of Selected Raw Score Values for Adjacent Grade Levels on Three Testing Occasions

name of the score may give the misleading impression that the student is capable of doing fifth-grade work.

2. Comparisons among GE scores across areas for the same individual also may be misleading. For example, a GE of 3.9 in reading and 3.9 in science would appear to imply equal proficiency in the two areas, but this is not necessarily true. Although an individual's GE scores for the two subjects may be equal, the percentile ranks in the on-grade norm group for those subjects could be, for example, 68 in reading and 82 in science.

3. The rate of growth on the GE scale within any particular grade or age level has been estimated from a small number of points, corresponding to the times at which testing occurred. The curve between these points is usually drawn by assuming that the rate of growth or progress between these points is even and continuous. In a subject such as reading, for example, this assumption of equal amounts of progress from month to month through the school year may be untenable. If two students have scores, respectively, of 3.8 and 3.9, it is not necessarily true that giving an additional month of instruction to the first student would place them at the same functional level.

4. For a single test, appropriate for examinees at a limited span of grade levels (e.g., third through fifth grade), raw scores in the tails of the distribution are converted to GE scores based on extrapolations of the curve to grade-level groups who did not actually take the examination. For example, it is possible for a fifth-grader to take a fifth-grade social studies test and earn a GE score of 1.0, although this fifth-grade test could not have been administered to entering level first-graders.

These extrapolated GE scores are obtained by the somewhat questionable assumption that the curve (or line) depicting the relationship between test score and grade level continues to be predictable for grades not tested. Thus the use of GE scores is probably most questionable for examinees in the upper and lower regions of the score distribution.

Age-equivalent scales are developed by the same general process used with grade-equivalent scales. With age-equivalent scales, however, some decision rule must be established for assigning examinees to respective age groups. For very young children (two years or less), age categories may be given in three-month or sixth-month intervals; for infants, age categories may be given in weekly or monthly intervals; for older examinees, yearly intervals are fairly standard. In assigning examinees to yearly intervals it is common to assign examinees who are within six months of their next birthdays to the age category above their current yearly age. It is also possible (although it results in loss of subjects from the norm group) to use only examinees who are within three to four months of their last birthday or those who are within three to four months of their next birthday, assigning the latter group to the next higher category.

SUMMARY

Normative scores are useful when test users want to compare an examinee's score to the distribution of scores for a sample from a well-defined population. The selection of a normative sample through probability sampling allows the test developer to estimate the degree of sampling error in sample statistics and reduces the opportunity for systematic bias in the normative data. Nine steps were suggested which can be followed in conducting a norming study. When the test developer can specify in advance the tolerable amount of error in the mean for the norming sample, the standard error of the mean can be used to solve for the minimum sample size needed.

Four types of probability sampling which may be used in norming studies are simple random sampling, systematic sampling, stratified random sampling, and cluster sampling. As a general rule, stratified random sampling results in more accurate sample estimates whenever the stratification variable is related to the performance on the variable of interest. Cluster sampling, which is often employed in norming of standardized tests for reasons of convenience, results in larger sampling errors and thus may require testing larger numbers of examinees to maintain the degree of sampling error that would result from testing a smaller simple random sample. Many norming studies for standardized tests actually involve multiple-stage sampling, which may involve various types of sampling at different stages. One common model is the selection of cluster samples of institutions followed by simple random or stratified sampling of individuals within each cluster.

In describing a norming study in a test manual, the investigator should document the sampling procedure used, the rate of refusal or nonresponse by those invited to participate, the date of the study, and demographic characteristics of the sample. Group statistics should be accompanied at the minimum by an estimate of the standard error of the mean.

To enhance the interpretive value of test scores, a number of normative score conversions have been developed which are useful for interindividual comparisons. In this chapter the following types of normative scores were described:

1. Percentile rank, reflecting the percentage of examinees in the norm group scoring at or below a given raw score value
2. Linear z-score, defined as the ratio of the individual's deviation score to the group standard deviation
3. Normalized z-score, which is the z-value from the standard normal z-table, associated with a given percentile rank
4. Derived scores, which are linear transformations of z-scores (including McCall's T score, derived IQ scores, and NCEs)
5. Stanines, which are created by dividing the raw score scale into nine sections so that a specified percentage of scores falls in each section
6. Scaled scores, which reflect both the examinee's score relative to the norm group and the location of that norm group's distribution in relation to that of other group distributions
7. Grade and age equivalents, indicating how a typical examinee for a given age or grade level might be expected to score on the test

Caution should be exercised in interpreting each type of normative score. It is highly desirable to present data showing how each type of normative score may be affected due to measurement error at various points of the score distribution.

Exercises

1. Following is an hypothetical distribution of a population of 50 examinees on a nonverbal problem-solving test. These examinees are from five separate classes within a single school. Assume that the test user wishes to develop local school norms for this test, but since it must be individually administered, the entire population cannot be tested.

   A. Construct a simple random sample of 20 persons from this population. Estimate the standard error of the mean.
   B. Using classes as cluster units, construct a cluster sample of 20 persons. Estimate the standard error of the mean.
   C. Using examinee membership in an exceptional student program as the stratification variable, construct a stratified random sample of 20 persons. The distribution of this variable in your sample should reflect its population distribution.
   D. Compare your sample means to the overall population mean. Does the accuracy of your sample means reflect what would be predicted according to sampling theory?
   E. Compare your results to those of others in the class. From the class results, construct the distribution of means obtained from each of the three sampling procedures. Which procedures appear to yield more-accurate estimates?

Class 1	Class 2	Class 3	Class 4	Class 5
101	96*	103	93*	104
102	97	100	91	96*
100*	96	101*	88*	100
99	95	104	90*	101
98*	91*	107*	92	101
100	97	102	89*	99*
97	93*	105	87	99
101	96	106*	88*	102
99	94	99	92	97*
97*	95*	103*	90*	101

*Exceptional student

2. For each of the following studies, a sampling procedure is described. Read each description and identify the type of probability sampling used:
   A. A psychology professor attaches a brief questionnaire about students' study habits to every fourth test and distributes the test to students as they walk into the room.
   B. In a survey of public offenders, the researcher randomly selects half the cell blocks in a state penitentiary and interviews all residents of each selected cell block.
   C. A university director of student services randomly chooses five dormitories on campus and from their residents selects a random sample of 60 percent freshmen and 40 percent upper classmen for a survey in alcohol use.
   D. Workers in a large company are chosen for a validation study if the last three digits of their social security numbers appear on a list of three-digit numbers in a random number table.

3. A health education specialist has designed a 30-item test to assess knowledge of basic hygiene facts. The specialist wants to norm the test on a sample of ninth-grade health science students and would like to be 95% certain that the population mean is within 1 point above or below the sample estimate. The specialist anticipates that the mean on the 30-item test will be about 25 points and the standard deviation about 5 points. What is the minimum sample size to insure the desired level of accuracy for the norm?

4. A. Complete the normative score-conversion table for the following data:

X	f	Raw Score PR[a]	Linear z	Normalized z	Normalized PR	Stanine
45	3					
44	7					
43	8					
42	15					
41	20					
40	15					
39	13					
38	9					
37	7					
36	3					

[a] PR: Percentile rank.

   B. Graph the points showing the relationship between the raw scores and the normalized percentile ranks (with raw scores on the horizontal axis and percentile ranks on the vertical axis). Draw a smooth curve which fits these points as well as possible.

C. Now on the same axis, plot the points showing the relationship between the raw scores and the original percentile ranks. Draw a smooth curve to fit these points. Explain the difference in the appearance of the two curves.

5. Read each situation description and answer the question at the end requiring your interpretation of various normative score scales.

A. Carl scores at the 89th percentile and Cathy at the 53rd percentile on a standardized achievement test. On a retest, each of their scores increases by 2 raw score points. Which examinee shows more gain in percentile rank? Why?

B. Joe scored in the second stanine last year and in the third stanine this year on a math computation test. Louise scored in the fourth stanine both times. Does this mean that Joe is making greater gains relative to the norm group than Louise? Why?

C. After retesting on the same test, Larry's score dropped from the 49th percentile rank to the 45th percentile rank. June's score dropped from the 89th to the 85th percentile rank. Were their losses of raw score points equivalent? Why?

D. At the end of grade 3, the grade-equivalent scores for Louise, Sandra, and Kim are 3.2, 3.5, and 3.8. Will these examinees have equal distances between their raw scores? Between their percentile ranks? Between their scaled scores?

6. Suppose that the normative tables of a standardized achievement test are based on administration of tests to students in the ninth month of each grade level. The following values are the median scaled scores obtained by students tested in each grade:

Grade Placement	Reading Scaled Score	Science Scaled Score
K.9	375	325
1.9	542	420
2.9	637	492
3.9	680	548
4.9	700	605
5.9	715	640

A. Use these data to draw a curve which represents the relationship between grade placement and scaled score for each test.

B. Offer some possible explanations for the difference in appearance of these two curves.

C. From your curve, identify grade-equivalent values corresponding approximately to scaled scores of 200, 350, 470, and 650 for each test. For which scaled scores are you more confident about the accuracy of your estimations?

D. If a group of examinees were tested in the third month of school at grades 1, 2, and 3, what would you predict to be their median scaled scores?

E. Suppose that a sixth-grader scores 1 year below grade placement in science and a second-grader scores one year below grade placement in this subject. Are these students probably similar in relative position with respect to their on-grade norm groups? Are the degrees of their deficiencies equally serious?

F. In terms of on-grade normative standing, is it as serious to be one grade-equivalent below grade in reading as in science? Why?

7. Using the normalized z-scores calculated in problem 4, set up a conversion table for converting the raw scores in that distribution to T scores; to deviation I.Q. scores; to the same score scale used by ETS in reporting subtest scores for the GRE or SAT.

Chapter 20

EQUATING SCORES FROM DIFFERENT TESTS

There are many situations in which different examinees are measured with different instruments that are supposed to measure the same trait. For example, in a professional certification program multiple forms of a test may be constructed so that the test can be administered several times during the year. However, if the score distributions for the forms are not the same, it may be necessary to determine equivalent scores on the forms. Establishing equivalent scores on different forms of a test is called *horizontal equating*. Also consider an achievement test battery composed of several levels. Each level is appropriate for testing students in a particular grade range. Suppose that one level of the battery is typically appropriate for students in the beginning of second grade, and a second level is typically appropriate for students in the end of second grade. However, for students who make slow progress in second grade, the second level may be too difficult to permit accurate measurement. A possible solution is to administer the first level to these students. To interpret the performance of these students, it may be necessary to determine equivalent scores on the two levels. This process is called *vertical equating*. Finally, suppose a researcher conducts a study in which variables derived from observations of teachers are to be correlated with scores on standardized achievement tests. If different districts use different test batteries, it may be necessary to try to equate scores on the various batteries. This may also be considered an example of horizontal equating.

The process of equating may be viewed as establishing the scores that are equivalent on different instruments. Thus, if two tests, X and Y, have been equated and an examinee takes test X, we can determine the equivalent score on the scale on which the Y scores are expressed. The function relating scores on X to equivalent scores on the Y score scale may be written as $Y^*=f(X)$. The score for an examinee who takes test X can be compared to examinees who take test Y by transforming the X scores to Y^* scores. The problem in equating is to determine the function $f(X)$. The function

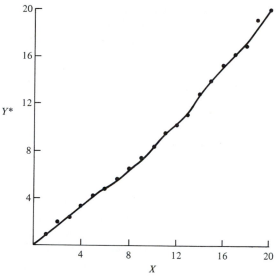

FIGURE 20.1   Plot of Equipercentile Equivalent Scores for Two Hypothetical 20-Item Instruments

may be represented as an equation such as $Y^* = a(X - c) + d$, or it may be represented as a graph, such as the one in Figure 20.1. The point on the Y axis corresponding to a score on the X axis is the Y^* score equivalent to that X score.

DEFINITION OF EQUATING

So far we have described equating as the process of establishing equivalent scores on two instruments. However we have not addressed the conditions that must be met in order for scores to be considered equivalent. A commonly accepted definition of equivalent scores is this: Two scores, one on instrument X and one on instrument Y, are considered equivalent if X and Y measure the same trait with equal reliability and the percentile ranks corresponding to the scores are equal. This definition of equivalent scores is the basis for the linear and equipercentile equating methods, which are presented in the next section.

DATA COLLECTION FOR EQUATING

There are three basic designs for collecting data to carry out an equating project. In the first design different instruments are administered to groups formed by random assignment. Thus if two forms of a test are to be equated, the total group of examinees is divided into two groups and each group takes one of the forms. In the sequel, this design will be called design A. In design B the same instruments are

TABLE 20.1. Schematic Presentation of Three Designs for Equating Studies

Design	Group	
	1	2
A	X	Y
B	$X:Y^a$	$Y:X$
C	X,Z^b	Y,Z

[a] Indicates that group 1 takes form X followed by form Y.
[b] Indicates that group 1 takes form X and anchor form Z.

administered to all examinees. To control for an order effect, the instruments are administered in all possible orders. The order that a particular examinee takes is determined by randomization. If two forms are to be equated, the total group is randomly divided into two groups. The first subgroup takes form X first, followed by form Y. The second subgroup takes the forms in the opposite order. In design C, different instruments are administered to different examinees. In addition a common instrument, or anchor test, is administered to all examinees. The anchor test is usually shorter than the forms to be equated. To equate two forms, each form is administered to one of two groups. These groups do not need to be created by random assignment. In addition the anchor test is administered to both groups. Table 20.1 presents a schematic diagram of these designs.

Linear Equating for Design A

Recall that design A requires randomly formed groups to take different instruments. In the following presentation it is assumed that there are two instruments to be equated. In this case two subgroups are formed by random assignment, and each subgroup takes one of the instruments. Linear equating is based on the assumption that, apart from differences in means and standard deviations, the distributions of the scores on form X and form Y are the same. If this is true, equivalent scores can be identified by determining the pair of scores, one on form X and one on form Y, that have the same z-score. Thus the two scores are equivalent if $(X - \hat{\mu}_X)/\hat{\sigma}_X = (Y - \hat{\mu}_Y)/\hat{\sigma}_Y$. These two scores will have the same percentile rank. The equation for transforming X to Y^* is

$$Y^* = a(X - c) + d \qquad (20.1)$$

(Angoff, 1971). In this expression

$$a = \frac{\hat{\sigma}_Y}{\hat{\sigma}_X} \qquad (20.2a)$$

$$c = \hat{\mu}_X \qquad (20.2b)$$

$$d = \hat{\mu}_Y \qquad (20.2c)$$

and X denotes a score on the first form. The symbol Y^* denotes the transformed score. A score of X on the first instrument is then equivalent to a score of Y^* on the second instrument. Suppose that group 1 takes form X and earns $\hat{\mu}_X = 50$ and $\hat{\sigma}_X = 10$, whereas group 2 takes form Y and earns $\hat{\mu}_Y = 52$ and $\hat{\sigma}_Y = 11$. Substituting in Equation 20.2, we obtain

$$a = 11/10 = 1.1$$
$$c = 50$$

and

$$d = 52$$

so Equation 20.1 becomes $Y^* = 1.1(X - 50) + 52$. Thus a score of 45 on form X is equivalent to a score of 46.5 on the scale for scores on form Y.

Linear equating is appropriate if the X and Y distributions differ *only* in the means and standard deviations. In other situations equipercentile equating may be more appropriate. As the name implies, equipercentile equating is determining which scores on the two instruments have the same percentile rank. Equipercentile equating will be discussed in more detail later in the section.

Linear Equating for Design B

In this design all examinees take all instruments. However different groups of examinees take the instruments in different orders, with the orders determined by random assignment. In equating two instruments there are two possible orders. The equation for carrying out the linear equating is again Equation 20.1. However for design B

$$a = \sqrt{\frac{\hat{\sigma}_{Y_1}^2 + \hat{\sigma}_{Y_2}^2}{\hat{\sigma}_{X_1}^2 + \hat{\sigma}_{X_2}^2}} \tag{20.3a}$$

$$c = \frac{(\hat{\mu}_{X_1} + \hat{\mu}_{X_2})}{2} \tag{20.3b}$$

and

$$d = \frac{(\hat{\mu}_{Y_1} + \hat{\mu}_{Y_2})}{2} \tag{20.3c}$$

(Angoff, 1971). In these expressions, the numerical subscripts indicate the subgroups formed to take the instruments in the two orders. Table 20.2 presents descriptive statistics for a hypothetical study conducted with design B. Substituting in Equation 20.3 we obtain

$$a = \sqrt{\frac{25.00 + 24.01}{28.09 + 31.36}} = .90$$

$$c = \frac{(25.2 + 24.8)}{2} = 25$$

and

$$d = \frac{(26.1 + 26.5)}{2} = 26.3$$

TABLE 20.2. Descriptive Statistics for a Hypothetical
Equating Study Using Design B

Group	Form	Statistic $\hat{\mu}$	$\hat{\sigma}$
1	X	25.2	5.3
	Y	26.1	5.0
2	X	24.8	5.6
	Y	26.5	4.9

Substituting in turn in Equation 20.1 we obtain

$$Y^* = .90(X - 25) + 26.3$$

as the equation for determining Y^*. Thus a score of 30 on form X is equivalent to a score of 30.8 on the scale of scores for form Y.

Linear Equating for Design C

With this design, each of the instrument, which are to be equated, is administered to a different group. These groups are not necessarily formed by random assignment. In addition a common anchor test is administered to all groups. Thus if two instruments are to be equated, each is administered to a different group of examinees, and a single anchor test is administered to both groups.

Let Z denote scores on the anchor test, and let the first group take instrument X and the second group take instrument Y. To describe the assumptions made in linear equating it is necessary to define subpopulation 1, the subpopulation from which group 1 is sampled, and subpopulation 2, the subpopulation from which group 2 is sampled. Subpopulations 1 and 2 comprise a total population. The assumptions made in linear equating are

1.   The slope, intercept, and standard error of estimate for the regression of X on Z in subpopulation 1 are equal to the slope, intercept, and standard error of estimate for the regression of X on Z in the total population.
2.   The slope, intercept, and standard error of estimate for the regression of Y on Z in subpopulation 2 are equal to the slope, intercept, and standard error of estimate for the regression of Y on Z in the total population.

These assumptions will certainly be reasonable if the two groups are formed by random assignment. However if the groups are not formed by random assignment, the assumptions may not be tenable. Angoff (1971) reports that the greater the difference between the groups on Z, the less likely it is that the assumptions hold.

As with design A, linear equating is carried out by using Equation 20.1, where

$$a = \sqrt{\frac{\hat{\sigma}_{Y_2}^2 + b_{YZ_2}^2(\hat{\sigma}_Z^2 - \hat{\sigma}_{Z_2}^2)}{\hat{\sigma}_{X_1}^2 + b_{XZ_1}^2(\hat{\sigma}_Z^2 - \hat{\sigma}_{Z_1}^2)}} \qquad (20.4a)$$

$$c = \hat{\mu}_{X_1} + b_{XZ_1}(\hat{\mu}_Z - \hat{\mu}_{Z_1}) \qquad (20.4b)$$

TABLE 20.3.   Descriptive Statistics For a Hypothetical Equating Study Using Design C

Group	Statistic	Variable X	Variable Y	Variable Z
1	$\hat{\mu}$	77.8		78.8
	$\hat{\sigma}$	12.7		11.2
	b_{XZ_1}	.9		
2	$\hat{\mu}$		83.5	83.4
	$\hat{\sigma}$		11.1	8.2
	b_{YZ_2}		1.2	
Total	$\hat{\mu}$			81.8
	$\hat{\sigma}$			9.3

and

$$d = \hat{\mu}_{Y_2} + b_{YZ_2}(\hat{\mu}_Z - \hat{\mu}_{Z_2}) \tag{20.4c}$$

In these expressions numerical subscripts indicate subgroup. Statistics without numerical subscripts are calculated for the total group. The symbols b_{XZ_1} and b_{YZ_2} denote the slopes for the regression of X on Z in group 1 and the regression of Y on Z in group 2, respectively. The reader should note that Equation 20.5b uses the relationship between X and Z to obtain an estimate of the mean X score for the entire group. Similarly Equation 20.4c yields an estimate of the mean Y score for the entire group. The numerator and denominator of Equation 20.4a are estimates of the variances of Y and X scores, respectively, for the entire group.

Table 20.3 presents descriptive statistics for a hypothetical equating study conducted with design C. Substituting in Equation 20.4, we obtain

$$a = \sqrt{\frac{11.1^2 + 1.2^2(9.3^2 - 8.2^2)}{12.7^2 + .9^2(9.3^2 - 11.2^2)}}$$

$$= \sqrt{\frac{150.93}{129.74}} = 1.07$$

$$c = 77.8 + .9(81.8 - 78.8) = 80.5$$

and

$$d = 83.5 + 1.2(81.8 - 83.4) = 81.58$$

Substituting for a, c, and d in Equation 20.1, we obtain

$$Y* = 1.1(X - 80.5) + 81.5$$

as the equation for determining the score on the scale for form Y that is equivalent to a score of X on form X.

Equipercentile Equating

Earlier we pointed out that equipercentile equating involves determining which scores on two instruments have the same percentile rank. The procedure for equipercentile equating is basically the same for designs A and B and will be described subsequently. The procedure for equipercentile equating with data collected in design C is somewhat complicated and will not be described. The interested reader is referred to Angoff (1971).

The first step in equipercentile equating is to determine the percentile ranks for the score distributions on each of the two instruments. (In design B two groups respond to each instrument. The score distribution for an instrument is obtained by combining the data for the two groups.) Table 20.4 presents mid-percentile ranks corresponding to scores on two hypothetical test forms. Percentile ranks are then plotted against the raw scores for each of the two instruments. A percentile rank-raw score curve is then drawn for each instrument. Such curves are illustrated in Figure 20.2 for two hypothetical 20-item instruments. In this figure, linear interpolation was used to connect the data points. Perhaps more typically, smooth curves are drawn by hand or the score distributions, on which the percentile ranks are calculated, are smoothed analytically. Once the percentile rank-raw score plots are constructed, equivalent scores can then be obtained from the graph. In Figure 20.2 this process is illustrated for a score of 12 on instrument X. The corresponding score on the Y^* scale is approximately 10.2. Table 20.5 presents percentile ranks, X scores, and corresponding Y^* scores determined by using Figure 20.2.

TABLE 20.4.   Midpercentile Ranks on
Two Instruments

| | Form | |
Score	Y	X
0	1	1
1	3	3
2	5	5
3	8	6
4	14	10
5	22	15
6	26	20
7	32	25
8	40	29
9	48	35
10	57	43
11	66	53
12	72	61
13	76	66
14	82	75
15	88	82
16	91	87
17	95	92
18	97	95
19	98	98
20	99	99

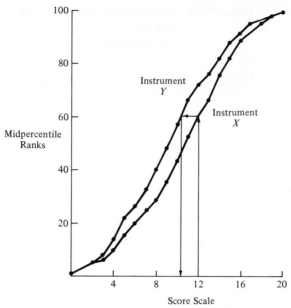

FIGURE 20.2   Plot of Percentile Ranks for Two Hypothetical 20-Item Instruments

TABLE 20.5.   Equipercentile Equivalent Scores on Two Instruments

Percentile Rank	X	Y*
1	0	0.0
3	1	1.0
5	2	2.0
6	3	2.3
10	4	3.3
15	5	4.2
20	6	4.7
25	7	5.6
29	8	6.4
35	9	7.3
43	10	8.3
53	11	9.4
61	12	10.1
66	13	11.0
75	14	12.8
82	15	14.0
87	16	15.2
92	17	16.2
95	18	16.9
98	19	19.0
99	20	20.0

TABLE 20.6.   Equipercentile Equivalent
Scores on Two
Hypothetical 20-Item
Instruments

Percentile Rank	X	Y[a]
1	0	0
3	1	1
5	2	2
6	3	2
10	4	3
15	5	4
20	6	5
25	7	6
29	8	6
35	9	7
43	10	8
53	11	9
61	12	10
66	13	11
75	14	13
82	15	14
87	16	15
92	17	16
95	18	17
98	19	19
99	20	20

[a] Scores obtained by rounding Y^* scores in Table 20.5.

After determining the X and Y^* scores, these scores are plotted against one another and a smooth curve is drawn through the points. This type of curve, which is illustrated in Figure 20.1, can be drawn by hand or determined analytically using a method presented by Kolen (1984). Equivalent scores are then read from the graph. For our example the new Y^* scores would be about the same as those reported in Table 20.5, and so we have not produced another table of equivalent scores.

To report the table of equivalent scores, the Y^* scores would be rounded and reported as Y scores, as illustrated in Table 20.6. An example of the interpretation of this table is as follows. A person who earns a score of 13 on the Y instrument is considered to have earned a score of 14 on the X instrument, and the percentile rank of either score is reported as 75.

Choosing among Equating Procedures

There are three main criteria for choosing an equating procedure: tenability of assumptions, practicality, and accuracy. These criteria apply both to the choice between linear and equipercentile equating for a particular design and to the choice among designs.

First consider the choice between linear and equipercentile equating. The following discussion applies to all three designs. Equipercentile equating makes fewer assumptions than linear equating, since the latter assumes the only differences between the distributions of X and Y are the mean and variance. Although making fewer assumptions is important, equipercentile equating also has several drawbacks. First, it is more complicated to carry out than linear equating and is therefore somewhat less practical. Second, in theory the equating error is much larger with equipercentile than with linear equating (Lord, 1982). For this reason linear equating may be preferable if the distributions of z-scores for X and Y are not too different.

In choosing among the three designs, practicality is frequently the prime criterion. Designs A and B require administration of two instruments with little or no time intervening between administrations. This may be impossible, and so design C may be preferable on practical grounds. Such a situation arises, for example, if different forms of a test must be used throughout the year and security issues preclude administering the forms in a separate equating study.

Although design C may be more practical in these situations, its equating procedures are based on assumptions in addition to those for designs A and B. Angoff (1971) warns that if the anchor score distributions for the two subpopulations are markedly different, the assumptions made in both linear and equipercentile equating are unlikely to be met. Angoff describes an alternative method for this situation. In addition, methods based on latent trait theory might be applied. However, both the method described by Angoff and the methods based on latent trait theory require assumptions in addition to those required by the methods used with designs A and B. The methods based on latent trait theory are introduced later in this chapter.

When it is possible to administer two instruments, with at most a short time intervening, all three designs may be used. In this situation the groups used in design C can probably be formed randomly, an assumption made in the ensuing discussion. In choosing among the three designs the issues of accuracy and practicality must be considered jointly in order to come to a reasonable choice. To illustrate, consider designs A and B. In design A each examinee takes one of the two instruments, whereas in design B each examinee takes both instruments. Design A, therefore, requires less testing time per examinee. However, this is only part of the story. The standard errors of linear equating for designs A and B are

$$SE_{Y*}^2 = \frac{2\sigma_Y^2}{N}(z_X^2 + 2) \qquad (20.5)$$

and

$$SE_{Y*}^2 = \frac{\sigma_Y^2(1 - \hat{\rho}_{XY})}{N}[z_X^2(1 + \hat{\rho}_{XY}) + 2] \qquad (20.6)$$

respectively. In these equations N refers to the total number of examinees in the equating and z_X refers to the z-score for the X score being transformed to $Y*$.

Comparison of Equations 20.5 and 20.6 shows that if N is the same for each design, the standard error of equating for design B is always smaller and is substantially smaller when $\hat{\rho}_{XY}$ is large. Therefore to achieve parity in accuracy, more examinees must be used with design A. The ratio of the number of examinees required to achieve equal accuracy is

$$\frac{N_A}{N_B} = \frac{2(z_X^2 + 2)}{(1 - \hat{\rho}_{XY})[z_X^2(1 + \hat{\rho}_{XY}) + 2]} \tag{20.7}$$

Suppose for example that $\hat{\rho}_{XY} = .8$. Then to achieve equal accuracy for an X score yielding $z_X = 0$, the required ratio is

$$\frac{N_A}{N_B} = \frac{2(0^2 + 2)}{(1 - .8)[0^2(1 + .8) + 2]} = 10 \tag{20.8}$$

That is 10 times as many examinees are required for design A. Thus design A is practical if a large number of examinees is available and the instruments are too long for each examinee to take both. Design B is practical if a smaller number of examinees is available and the instruments are short enough for each examinee to take both.

The other comparisons between designs follow along similar lines. To the degree that the anchor test is correlated with the two instruments, design C yields more accurate results than design A. However design C requires more testing time per examinee. A rule-of-thumb for the minimum length of the anchor test is the larger of 20 items or 20% of the number of items on either of the instruments (Angoff, 1971), so the anchor test may require substantial additional testing time. The formula for the standard error of equating for design C is essentially the same as that for design B, so the use of the anchor test can increase accuracy substantially. In a comparison of designs B and C, design B generally takes more testing time per examinee than design C. However, since the correlation between the instruments to be equated is generally larger than the correlations between the anchor form and the instruments, equating with design B also tends to be more accurate than equating with design C.

EQUATING WITH ITEM RESPONSE THEORY

As noted earlier, item response theory can be used to equate tests. In fact, it can be used with all three designs. However, it is probably most useful for design C when random assignment is not feasible; in this situation the assumptions made in using linear and equipercentile equating may not be met, and so an alternative procedure is required. In this section it will be assumed that the equating study is conducted with design C, with nonrandom assignment to forms. There is less need to use latent trait theory when design C is used with random assignment and when designs A and B are used. In these situations either linear or equipercentile equating will generally be adequate.

Currently there are several popular latent trait models. Perhaps the most widely used are the one-parameter logistic (Rasch) model and the three-parameter logistic model. Equating can be carried out with both models as well as with the two-parameter logistic and the normal ogive model. However, for ease of presentation, equating with the one-parameter logistic model will be treated here. Even with this limitation the discussion is not complete. A more-detailed presentation of equating with the one-parameter model is given in Wright and Stone (1979). Lord (1980) discussed equating with the three-parameter model.

A Brief Introduction to Latent Trait Theory

For the reader who has not read Chapter 15 a brief introduction to latent trait theory is provided here. Latent trait theory typically assumes that a single latent trait accounts for the relationships among responses to all pairs of items. A latent trait model is a statement of the relationship between scores on an item and scores on the latent trait. The one-parameter logistic model (or Rasch model, as it is also known) states that the proportion of examinees responding correctly to the gth item [$P_g(\theta)$] is related to scores on the latent trait (θ) by the equation

$$P_g(\theta) = \frac{e^{(\theta - b_g)}}{1 + e^{(\theta - b_g)}} \qquad (20.9)$$

Figure 20.3 presents graphs of the hypothesized item-latent trait relationship for three items with different values for b_g. These curves are called *item characteristic curves* (ICCs). The parameter b_g is a difficulty parameter, although it is not the same as the proportion-correct difficulty parameter used in classical test theory. Fifty percent of the examinees with a latent trait score equal to b_g will answer the gth

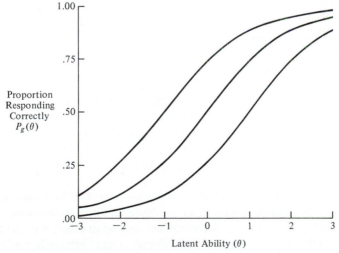

FIGURE 20.3   Item Characteristic Curves for Three Items

item correctly. Thus if $b_g = 1$, 50 percent of the examinees with a latent trait score of 1 will answer the gth item correctly. In Figure 20.3 the b_g for the first ICC is the smallest since the first curve reaches .5 before the other curves do. Notice that according to Equation 20.10, if two items have the same b_g the ICCs for the two items must be the same. This is true because the ICC depends only on θ and the latent trait score b_g. Thus under the one-parameter logistic model, items differ only in difficulty. All items are assumed to be equally discriminating. Loosely speaking this is equivalent to assuming the item-true score correlation is the same for every item.

Scaling Latent Trait Scores

With many physical measurements such as height or weight the zero point or origin of the scale of measurement represents absence of the property being measured. As a result, assignment of a score of zero to an object is not an arbitrary act. The score of zero can only be assigned to objects that do not have any of the property being measured. In latent trait theory a score of zero does not represent absence of the trait, and so a score of zero can be assigned to *any* group of examinees who are homogeneous on the latent trait. Of course once these examinees are given a score of zero, assignment of other scores is not arbitrary. Examinees with more of the latent trait than the "zero group" must be given a score that is larger than zero and so forth.

Another way to describe the arbitrary zero point is to say that given any scale θ for the latent trait scores, it is permissible to transform θ to $\theta^* = \theta + m$. Different values of m will assign the zero score to different groups of examinees. Notice that since the numeric value of b_g is a value on the latent trait scale, when θ is transformed to θ^*, b_g is transformed to $b_g^* = b_g + m$.

A common way to deal with the arbitrary zero point is to set the scale so that the average latent trait score in a particular sample or population is zero. To see the impact of this method of setting the zero point, suppose that a set of items is administered to two populations of examinees. Since the zero point is arbitrary, it is set separately for each population. This is accomplished by choosing a scale θ_1 for population 1, so that its mean latent trait score on this scale is zero, and by choosing a scale θ_2 for population 2, so that its mean latent trait score on this new scale is zero. Since the two scales are expressions of the same latent trait, the scales must be related by the equation $\theta_1 = \theta_2 + m$, where θ_1 is the scale for group 1 and θ_2 is the scale for group 2. This equation means that to transform a score on the scale for population 2 to a score on the scale for population 1, it is necessary to add m to the score on the scale for group 2.

Suppose it were possible to identify two examinees, one from each group, with the same amount of latent ability. Since the score on θ_1 for the examinee in population 1 and the score on θ_2 for the examinee on population 2 represent the same amount of ability but are expressed on different scales, subtracting θ_2 from θ_1 for these two examinees would give m. Unfortunately it is impossible to identify two such examinees. However, if item g is administered to each group, and its difficulty parameter is determined for each group, b_{g1} and b_{g2} also represent the same amount of ability but are expressed on different scales, and so $b_{g1} - b_{g2}$ will give us m. Given this value of m we can transform any score on the scale θ_2 to a score on the scale θ, using the equation $\theta_1 = \theta_2 + m$.

In using design C, only a subset of the items are taken by both groups. Nevertheless for any one of these items, $b_{g1} - b_{g2} = m$ and m can still be used to transform scores on the scale for population 2 to scores on the scale for population 1. Also, in practice, b_{g1} and b_{g2} must be estimated. As a result, $\hat{b}_{g1} - \hat{b}_{g2}$ is not the same for every anchor item, and so these differences are averaged to obtain an estimate of m. A more complete description of the equating procedure will be given after the nature of the anchor test is addressed.

Nature of the Anchor Test

Design C requires the administration of an anchor test along with each of the forms to be equated. To use latent trait theory with data collected under design C it is necessary for the items on both instruments and the items on the anchor test to measure the same latent trait. This requirement was not necessary for linear or equipercentile equating with data collected with design C.

Since all items administered to a group, including the anchor test items, are assumed to measure the same latent trait, it is possible to use all the item responses to obtain an examinee's test score, and this is the context we will use in our description of equating with latent trait theory. However, some testing companies use the anchor test for equating purposes only; an examinee's responses to the anchor items do not influence his or her score.

The Equating Procedure

Perhaps the easiest way to describe the equating procedure is to list the steps and illustrate them.

1.   Using the data for group 1, estimate the b_g's for all items taken by the group including the anchor items. This step is justified by the assumption that all items, including the anchor items, measure the same latent trait. In carrying out the estimation, the scale for these estimates is set by making the average latent trait score equal to zero. Table 20.7 presents estimates of the b_g's for 15 items taken by group 1. The last five items are the anchor items. (The BICAL program prepared by Wright, Mead, and Bell, 1979, was used to calculate these estimates. The data for the two groups were analyzed separately. Rather than setting the average latent trait score equal to zero, BICAL chooses the scale by setting the average of the latent trait scores assigned to each number-correct score equal to zero. This approach does not change in any important way the justification of using the group-to-group differences in the anchor item $\hat{b}_g$'s to estimate m.)

TABLE 20.7.   Difficulty Estimates for Items Taken by Group 1 and 2

| | Difficulty Estimates | | |
| | Group 1 (Form X) | Group 2 (Form Y) | Difference for Anchor Items $(\hat{b}_{g1} - \hat{b}_{g2})$ |
Item			
1	−1.867		
2	−0.727		
3	0.603		
4	0.061		
5	0.016		
6	−1.328		
7	−0.223		
8	0.321		
9	−0.223		
10	0.483		
11	−0.030	−0.185	.155
12	0.873	0.347	.526
13	0.797	0.159	.638
14	0.797	0.045	.752
15	0.444	−0.503	.947
16		−0.302	
17		−0.342	
18		0.159	
19		−0.714	
20		−0.069	
21		−0.185	
22		0.928	
23		0.159	
24		0.691	
25		−0.185	

2. Using the data for group 2, estimate the b_g's for all items including the anchor items, to which the group was exposed. Again the scale for these estimates is set by making the average latent trait score equal to zero. Table 20.7 presents estimates of the b_g's for 15 items taken by group 2. Here the first five items are the anchor items.

3. For each item on the anchor test calculate $\hat{b}_{g1} - \hat{b}_{g2}$. Then estimate m by calculating the average of these differences. In Table 20.7, the values of $\hat{b}_{g1} - \hat{b}_{g2}$ are reported in the third column. The average of these five numbers is $\hat{m} = .60$.

4. For each group, estimate the latent trait score corresponding to each number-right score. These estimates are reported in Table 20.8. The same runs of the BICAL program that calculated the item difficulties also produced the conversions of raw scores to latent trait scores for the two groups. The reader should recognize that the latent trait scores for the two groups are expressed on two different scales.

5. Add the estimate of m to the latent trait scores for group 2 to transform these scores to the scale used for group 1. For example, in Table 20.8, for group 2 the latent trait

TABLE 20.8.   Raw Score to Latent Trait Score Conversion Table [a,b]

Raw Score	Latent Trait Scores	
	Group 1 (Form X)	Group 2 (Form Y)
1	−2.91	−2.72
2	−2.07	−1.93
3	−1.53	−1.43
4	−1.12	−1.04
5	−.76	−.72
6	−.45	−.42
7	−.15	−.14
8	.15	.14
9	.45	.42
10	.76	.72
11	1.12	1.04
12	1.53	1.43
13	2.07	1.93
14	2.91	2.72

[a] With latent trait theory, latent trait scores, corresponding to perfect raw scores and zero raw scores, cannot be estimated.
[b] Latent trait scores are expressed on scales for the respective groups.

score corresponding to a raw score of 1 is −2.72. To transform this score to the scale used for group 1, add $\hat{m} = .60$ to −2.72 to obtain −2.12. All such transformed scores are displayed in Table 20.9, along with the original scores for group 1. Both sets of latent trait scores are expressed on the same scale, and therefore are equated.

TABLE 20.9.   Raw Score to Equated Latent Trait Score Conversion Table [a]

Raw Score	Latent Trait Scores	
	Form X	Form Y
1	−2.91	−2.12
2	−2.07	−1.33
3	−1.53	−.83
4	−1.12	−.43
5	−.76	−.12
6	−.45	.18
7	−.15	.46
8	.15	.74
9	.45	1.02
10	.76	1.32
11	1.12	1.64
12	1.53	2.03
13	2.07	2.53
14	2.91	3.32

[a] All scores are expressed on the scale for group 1.

TRUE SCORE EQUATING

Lord (1980) defined an equating method that uses latent trait theory and is known as *true score equating*. In this section we will explain and illustrate true score equating by using the example from the previous section. True score equating involves determining equivalent true scores on two test forms. The function relating equivalent true scores is then used to equate observed scores.

The relationship between latent trait scores and true scores is given by the equation

$$T = \sum_{g=1}^{G} P_g(\theta) \tag{20.10}$$

This equation says that for any value of θ, the corresponding true score can be determined by calculating $P_g(\theta)$ for each of the G items on a test and adding all the resulting terms. For example, with form X from the previous section, the true score T_X corresponding to $\theta = 1.5$ is

$$T_X = \sum_{g=1}^{15} P_g(1.5) \tag{20.11}$$

Recall that

$$P_g(1.5) = \frac{e^{(1.5-b_g)}}{1 + e^{(1.5-b_g)}} \tag{20.12}$$

Therefore substituting the estimates of b_g from Table 20.7, we obtain

$$T_X = \frac{e^{(1.5-b_1)}}{1 + e^{(1.5-b_1)}} + \cdots + \frac{e^{(1.5-b_{15})}}{1 + e^{(1.5-b_{15})}},$$

$$= \frac{e^{(1.5-1.867)}}{1 + e^{(1.5-1.867)}} + \cdots + \frac{e^{(1.5-.444)}}{1 + e^{(1.5-.444)}} = 11.9$$

Thus on form X a latent trait score of 1.5 corresponds to a true score of 11.9.

Figure 20.4 shows the curves relating T_X to θ and T_Y to θ. Each curve is called a *test characteristic curve*. Two true scores, one on form X and one on form Y are considered equivalent if they correspond to the same latent trait score. Equivalent true scores corresponding to $\theta = 1$ are indicated on Figure 20.4 by the dotted line. Figure 20.5 presents a plot of equivalent true scores on the two instruments.

If it were possible to measure an examinee on form X and obtain his or her true score on form X, we could use the equivalent true score plot to determine his or her true score on form Y even though we did not measure the examinee on Y. Thus the plot of equivalent true scores represents an equating of true scores. The problem with using the plot is that we cannot obtain an examinee's true score on X. Lord however has proposed using the plot of equivalent true scores by substituting raw scores for true scores. (An alternate proposal by Lord is to use latent trait theory to estimate true scores and then substitute these for actual true scores.) The plot of equivalent true scores is then used as the function $Y^* = f(x)$, which transforms an X score to the equivalent score on the scale for form Y.

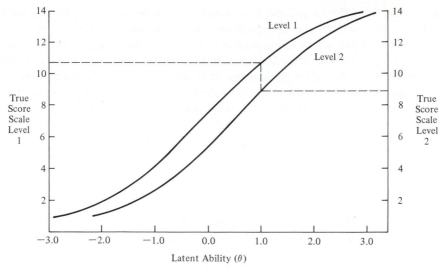

FIGURE 20.4   Relationship between Latent Trait Scores and True Scores on Two Levels of a Test

VERTICAL EQUATING

Vertical equating involves two or more tests that are supposed to measure the same trait and are designed to be different in difficulty. In the introduction to the chapter we pointed out that one reason for vertical equating arises in conjunction with out-of-level testing. There we pointed out that when a test battery has several levels

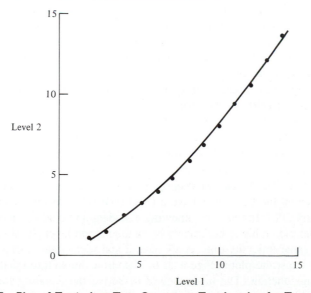

FIGURE 20.5   Plot of Equivalent True Scores on Two Levels of a Test

appropriate for different grades, it is sometimes considered advantageous for a student to be tested by a level appropriate for a grade other than his or her own grade. For example, a very bright student in the end of third grade might be tested with a level appropriate for the beginning of fifth grade. Similarly a student having difficulty at the end of third grade might be tested with a level appropriate for the end of second grade. In either case it is necessary to equate test scores from the two levels if the student taking the out-of-level test is to be compared to his or her contemporaries who took the on-level test.

A second reason for vertical equating derives from the need to chart growth of a child over his or her school years. What is desirable is to derive a common scale for reporting scores from all levels of an achievement battery, and this requires equating of the levels. If this scaling is accomplished, as a student moves through the grades and takes more advanced levels of a test, his or her score on an advanced level can be compared to his or her score on a less-advanced level. The scaled scores that are available for most standardized tests are created with vertical equating.

Vertical equating can be carried out with designs A, B, or C and linear, equipercentile, or latent trait methods. In the 1970s design A was used in conjunction with equipercentile equating to construct the scaled scores on many of the popular standardized achievement batteries. More recently test publishers have begun to use the latent trait methods described earlier to create the scaled score. For example, the scaled scores for the 1982 version of the Stanford Achievement Test were created with the one-parameter logistic model, and the scaled scores for the 1978 version of the Comprehensive Test of Basic Skills were created with the three-parameter logistic model.

An issue that must be considered in a vertical equating project is the possibility that tests that differ substantially in difficulty also differ in the traits they measure, despite having similar content. For example, in a popular standardized achievement test, one of the levels is intended for students from grade placement 1.5 to 2.4. A second level is intended for students from grade placement 2.5 to 3.4. The mathematics subtests of these two levels yield scores that have been placed on the same scale through a vertical equating program. Nevertheless, of the 57 objectives measured by one or the other of the levels, only 22 are measured by both levels. Although this is not definitive evidence that the levels measure different traits, it is certainly suggestive evidence.

What is the consequence if two levels measure different traits? We can only answer this question if we operationally define what we mean by two levels measuring the same trait. To this end we propose that two levels measure the same trait if the true scores on the two levels have a functional relationship such as that illustrated in Figure 20.5. In this case, knowing a student's true score on one level will allow us to determine his or her true score on the second level. If two levels do not measure the same trait, the true scores have a statistical relationship such as that illustrated by the scatterplot in Figure 20.6. The curve drawn through the scatterplot is an equating function. The method used to derive the equating function is not important for the purposes of the following discussion.

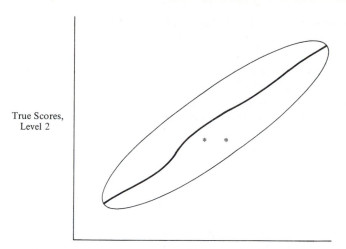

True Scores, Level 1

FIGURE 20.6   Scatterplot of True Scores on Two Levels of a Test

Consider two examinees with the same true score on level 2 but different true scores on level 1. The true score for two such examinees are indicated by asterisks on Figure 20.6. We refer to the examinee on the left as the first examinee. Since the first examinee has a lower true score on level 1 than the second examinee, the first examinee will tend to get a lower observed score on level 1. Thus if the level 1 scores for the two examinees are transformed to level 2 scores, using the equating function, the first examinee will probably have a lower score than the second examinee. This is true despite the fact that the two examinees have the same true score on level 2. Thus the first examinee is placed at a disadvantage. We can make the point in a somewhat different way if we consider an examinee who has true scores that place him or her below the equating function. If this examinee takes form 1 and has the score transformed to the scale for form 2, the score will tend to be higher then he or she would earn by taking form 2. The opposite is true for any examinee who has true scores that place him or her above the equating function.

The reader should recognize that horizontal equating will also be faulty if the instruments to be equated do not measure the same trait. However, in horizontal equating, the instruments are usually forms of the same test, are designed to match the same test specification, and are of equal difficulty. It seems reasonable to suppose that two such forms will measure the same trait. In some cases horizontal equating involves equating two different tests. Here, again, the question of whether the tests measure the same trait must be seriously considered.

In addition to the possibility that two levels of a test do not measure the same trait, additional problems can arise in using the latent trait methods of vertical equating. Here we focus the discussion on equating with the one-parameter logistic model, which is based on several key assumptions:

1.   The items on the test (or subtest) being analyzed measure a unidimensional latent trait.

2.   The items differ in difficulty but not in discrimination.
3.   Examinees do not attempt to guess the correct answers.

Because the model makes such strong assumptions, the question that arises is whether an equating function developed with the one-parameter model will be a good function if the assumptions are violated. Of course violation of these assumptions is a source of concern in horizontal equating, but it seems likely that violations will have a more serious impact in vertical equating. For example consider a project to equate two levels, one which is appropriate for grade 2 and one which is appropriate for grade 3. Students in grade 2 take level 1 plus the anchor test, and students in grade 3 take level 2 plus the anchor test. The anchor test is likely to be harder for second-grade students than for third-grade students. Thus guessing may differentially affect the second- and third-grade difficulty parameter estimates for the anchor test. Since the equating is based on the difference between second- and third-grade anchor test difficulty estimates, differential guessing may affect the equating.

There have been several studies that either directly (Holmes, 1982; Loyd and Hoover, 1980; Slinde and Linn, 1978, 1979) or indirectly (Forsyth, Saisangjan and Gilmer, 1981; Whitely and Dawis, 1974; Wright, 1968) investigated the utility of the one-parameter logistic model for vertical equating. As might be expected, the authors of these studies expressed different opinions about the usefulness of the one-parameter model for vertical equating. These differences in conclusions derive from at least four sources:

1.   The studies investigated different tests.
2.   The studies had somewhat different designs.
3.   The studies used different measures of the similarity of equated scores.
4.   The studies did not have clear criteria for judging the adequacy of equating.

To illustrate these differences let us review the studies reported by Holmes (1982) and Slinde and Linn (1979). The procedures used in these studies consisted of the following six steps:

1.   Create or locate two tests that differ in difficulty and a set of anchor items. The anchor items may actually be part of the two tests or they may constitute a separate test.
2.   Administer all items to the available sample.
3.   Identify a low- and high-ability group. These groups should ideally be based on a criterion other than the scores on the test created in step 1 (Slinde and Linn), but the criterion measure should be correlated with the trait measured by these tests.
4.   With the data for the low-ability group on level 1 and the high-ability group on level 2, carry out the equating procedure described in the section entitled Equating with Latent Trait Theory.
5.   Using a raw score to latent trait conversion table like that presented in Table 20.9, convert each examinee's raw scores, one from each level, to latent trait scores.
6.   Compare the two resulting latent trait scores.

Holmes concluded that the one-parameter model did not provide a satisfactory means of vertical equating across the entire ability range. Slinde and Linn were more optimistic about the use of the one-parameter model.

One difference between the two studies is that Holmes had available a sample of students who were not used to create her raw score to latent trait conversion table. Holmes repeated step 6 with this cross-validation sample. Slinde and Linn were unable to conduct this kind of cross validation. Holmes's results suggested that the equating was substantially less adequate for the cross-validation sample than for the original sample. A second difference was that the levels created by Holmes were shorter and exhibited larger difficulty differences than the tests used as levels by Slinde and Linn. In addition Holmes reported mean standardized differences between latent ability estimates at each of eight points on the ability scale for each of two grades. A standardized difference is calculated for each examinee by using

$$D = \frac{\hat{\theta}_1 - \hat{\theta}_2}{\sqrt{\hat{\sigma}_{\hat{\theta}_1}^2 + \hat{\sigma}_{\hat{\theta}_2}^2}} \tag{20.13}$$

$\hat{\theta}_1$ and $\hat{\theta}_2$ are estimates of latent ability based on level 1 and level 2 respectively, and $\hat{\sigma}_{\hat{\theta}_1}^2$ and $\hat{\sigma}_{\hat{\theta}_2}^2$ are estimated error variances for estimating θ_1 and θ_2. (If the equating works well, θ_1 should be equal to θ_2.) Slinde and Linn reported mean differences between latent ability estimates $(\hat{\theta}_1 - \hat{\theta}_2)$ for each of two grades but did not report mean differences at different points on the ability scale. Finally Holmes's conclusion seems to be based on the size and pattern of the differences she observed with no real attempt to show how differences of that magnitude would affect test-based decisions. Slinde and Linn attempted to judge their differences in terms of the magnitude of the standard error of measurement and the number of raw score points that the differences were equivalent to. However, they also did not attempt to relate the differences they reported to actual use of tests. An important point about this discussion is that even if these differences did not exist between the Holmes and Slinde and Linn studies, it is unlikely that such studies could ever unequivocally resolve the question of the adequacy of vertical equatings by using the one-parameter model or any of the other latent trait models. Each vertical equating project must include studies like those of Holmes and Slinde and Linn in order to examine the adequacy of equating in that particular project.

EQUITY IN EQUATING

As we noted earlier the problem in equating is to determine the equating function $Y^* = f(X)$, which will be used to transform an X score to the equivalent score on the Y score scale. (With some latent trait procedures both X and Y scores are transformed to the latent trait scale. With minor changes the following discussion also applies to this kind of equating.) The purpose of developing the equating function is to transform the scores of examinees who take instrument X to Y^* scores so that these scores can be compared to the scores of examinees who took instrument Y.

The question that arises is, ''What are sensible criteria for Y and Y^* to be comparable?''

Lord (1980) addressed the issue of criteria for comparability, although he referred to his criteria as criteria for equity in equating. Two of these criteria are of most concern here. First, an examinee's true score on Y must be equal to his or her true score on Y^*. Second, an examinee's distribution of error scores must be the same on Y and Y^*. If either of these criteria are not met, an examinee's chance of scoring well depends on the instrument administered. Thus Y and Y^* cannot be comparable, and X and Y are not equated. If Y and Y^* meet the criteria mentioned, Y and Y^* are parallel measures of the same trait and have the same distribution.

Two questions arise in reference to these criteria:

1. Is it possible for test score data to meet these criteria?
2. Is it possible to test whether these criteria are met?

Concerning question 1, Lord (1982) has shown that if the instruments to be equated measure a unidimensional latent trait, the scores on Y and Y^* cannot meet these criteria unless the X and Y have been constructed so that for each item on form X there is an item on form Y with the same ICC. Such tests will yield rigorously parallel test scores. However, if the tests are parallel in the first place, there is no need to equate them since the forms already yield equivalent scores.

Do Lord's results really mean that it is impossible for equated scores to be equivalent? First, latent traits are defined only in theory, and therefore the implications of latent trait theory may not be exactly true. Second, even if the implications are approximately correct, for long tests the form-to-form differences in true scores and personal standard errors of measurement may be inconsequential. Third, based on other theories, for example, classical test theory, it is possible for scores on nonparallel tests to be equivalent after equating.

Concerning question 2, it is possible to test whether Y and Y^* meet these criteria. For example if Y and Y^* meet the criteria, these scores should have equal correlations with all other variables. Therefore to check whether Y and Y^* meet the criteria, one can test whether Y and Y^* are equally correlated with several variables. Also if three or more instruments are equated, confirmatory factor analysis can be used to test the tenability of the assumptions.

SUMMARY

The purpose of equating is to establish the scores that are equivalent on different instruments that measure the same trait. If two instruments have been equated, the scores for two examinees can be compared even though the examinees have been administered different instruments.

There are three basic designs for equating. In design A each examinee is administered one of the instruments which are to be equated. The particular instrument administered is determined at random. In design B each examinee is administered all the instruments that are to be equated. The order in which the instruments are administered is determined at random. With design C each examinee is administered only one of the instruments which are to be equated. In addition, all examinees are administered a common or anchor instrument. The instrument administered can be determined at random but does not need to be. Perhaps most typically, the choice among designs hinges on questions of practicality.

Three methods of equating, linear equating, equipercentile equating, and latent trait equating, were described in the chapter. In principle each of these three methods can be used with each of the three designs. However, in practice the methods based on latent trait theory are perhaps most frequently used in conjunction with design C when random assignment of examinees to instruments is not feasible. In this situation the assumptions required to use linear or equipercentile equating are considered to be unreasonable assumptions, and therefore equating with these two methods may be inaccurate. The use of latent trait theory for equating was described in the context of using design C without random assignment. Linear and equipercentile equating are probably most frequently used with designs A and B. The choice between these two methods (or among the three methods if latent trait equating is considered) should be made on the basis of the accuracy of equating. There seems to be a general belief that if the test score distributions for the instruments are approximately the same, except for the means and standard deviations, linear equating is more accurate than equipercentile equating. However if the distributions differ in characteristics other than the means and standard deviations, equipercentile equating is more accurate.

Exercises

1. A researcher in special education created two forms of a scale to measure teachers' attitudes toward mainstreamed children. The researcher randomly assigned 10 teachers to take one form and 10 to take the second form. The data follow:

Scores on Two
Forms of a Teacher
Attitude Scale

Form A	Form B
50	31
41	38
42	42
51	39
37	41
53	46
50	34
54	42
48	37
53	52

Use these data to equate form B to form A.

2. A testing company, that wanted to equate two forms of a 10-item test, administered both forms to the same groups. Following is a frequency table for each form.

Score Frequency for Two Forms
of a Test

Score	Form A	Form B
0	0	13
1	2	19
2	17	54
3	28	36
4	39	39
5	50	40
6	65	49
7	56	27
8	27	17
9	11	12
10	4	5

Use these frequency distributions to equate form A to form B.

3. In the first table, Rasch item difficulties are presented for two forms of a 10-item test that includes 5-anchor items. For each form, the first 5 items are unique and the second 5 are the anchor items. In the second table, raw score to latent trait score transformations are presented for each form.

Rasch Item Difficulties
for Two Forms of a
Ten-Item Test

Form A	Form B
−.739	−.705
−.739	1.756
−.366	.051
−1.799	.073
−1.049	−.705
−1.372	−1.851
.118	−1.197
2.251	1.378
.767	−.147
2.929	2.379

Raw to Latent Trait Score
Conversion Table for Two Forms
of a Test

Raw Score	Latent Trait Score	
	Form A	Form B
1	−2.98	−2.89
2	−1.88	−1.82
3	−1.15	−1.12
4	−.55	−.53
5	0.00	0.00
6	.55	.53
7	1.15	1.12
8	1.88	1.82
9	2.98	2.89

Use these data to equate form B to form A.

4. An instructor with two sections of a course created two 50-item forms of a final examination. Each exam consisted of 10 items that were common to the two exams and 40 items that were unique to one exam. Scores on the unique and common items for 10 students from each section follow.

Scores on Unique and Common Items
on Two Forms of a Final Examination

Section			
I		II	
Unique Items	Common Items	Unique Items	Common Items
3	14	4	24
6	23	5	25
4	21	3	15
0	7	3	9
3	17	4	14
4	14	5	20
6	10	3	16
4	19	4	13
5	14	4	7
8	27	7	27

Use these data to derive a score for each examinee that reflects both the unique and common items and does not give an unfair advantage to either section.

5. A testing company plans to equate two forms of a test and to use design B and linear equating to equate the forms. Scores on form I are to be transformed to the scale for form II. From past research it is reasonable to expect the interform correlation to be .7 and the variance of either form to be 100. The company feels that the standard error of equating at the mean of form I should be no larger than one-tenth of a standard error of measurement. What sample size should be used to achieve this goal? How many students would be required if design A were used.

References

American Educational Research Association (AERA), American Psychological Association (APA), and the National Council on Measurement in Education (NCME). (1985). *Standards for educational and psychological testing*. Washington, D.C.: American Psychological Association.

American Psychological Association (APA), American Educational Research Association (AERA), and the National Council on Measurement in Education (NCME). (1974). *Standards for educational and psychological tests and manuals*. Washington, D.C.: American Psychological Association.

Anastasi, A. (1968). *Psychological testing* (3rd Ed.). New York: Macmillan.

Anderson, E. B. (1973). A goodness of fit test for the Rasch model. *Psychometrika, 38,* 123–140.

Anderson, L. W. (1981). *Assessing affective characteristics in the schools*. Boston: Allyn and Bacon.

Andrews, B. J., and Hecht, J. T. (1976). A preliminary investigation of two procedures for setting examination standards. *Educational and Psychological Measurement, 36,* 45–50.

Angoff, W. H. (1971). Norms, scales, and equivalent scores. In R. L. Thorndike (Ed.). *Educational measurement* (2nd Ed.). Washington, D.C.: American Council on Education.

Angoff, W. H. (1982). Uses of difficulty and discrimination indices for detecting item bias. In R. A. Berk (Ed.). *Handbook of methods for detecting item bias*. Baltimore: Johns Hopkins University Press.

Angoff, W. H., and Ford, S. F. (1973). Item race interaction on a test of scholastic aptitude. *Journal of Educational Measurement, 10,* 95–105.

Baglin, R. F. (1981). Does "nationally" normed really mean nationally? *Journal of Educational Measurement, 18,* 97–108.

Baker, F. B. (1981). A criticism of Scheuneman's item bias technique. *Journal of Educational Measurement, 18,* 59–62.

Behuniak, P., Jr. Archambault, F. X., and Gable, R. K. (1982). Angoff and Nedelsky standard setting procedures: Implications for the validity of proficiency test score interpretation. *Educational and Psychological Measurement, 42,* 247–252.

Berk, R. A. (1976). Determination of optimal cutting scores in criterion referenced measurement. *Journal of Experimental Education, 45,* 4–9.

Berk, R. A. (1978). The application of structural facet theory to achievement test construction. *Educational Research Quarterly, 3,* 62–72.

Berk, R. A. (1980a). A consumers' guide to criterion-referenced test reliability. *Journal of Educational Measurement, 17,* 323–350.

Berk, R. A. (1980b). Item analysis. In R. A. Berk (Ed.). *Criterion-referenced measurement: The state of the art*. Baltimore: Johns Hopkins University Press.

Beuchert, A. K., and Mendoza, J. L. (1979). A Monte Carlo comparison of ten item discrimination indices. *Journal of Educational Measurement, 16,* 109–118.

Binet, A., and Simon, T. (1905–1908). The development of the Binet-Simon scale. In W. Dennis (Ed.). *Readings in the history of psychology*. New York: Appleton-Century-Crofts, 1948.

Birnbaum, A. (1968). Some latent trait models and their use in inferring an examinee's ability. In F. M. Lord and M. R. Novick, *Statistical theories of mental test scores*. Reading, Mass.: Addison Wesley.

Bliss, L. B. (1980). A test of Lord's assumption regarding examinee guessing behavior on multiple choice tests using elementary school children. *Journal of Educational Measurement, 17,* 147–153.

Bloom, Benjamin S. (Ed.). (1956). *Taxonomy of educational objectives, handbook 1: The cognitive domain.* New York: McKay.

Bloom, B. S., Hastings, J. T., and Madaus, G. F. (1971). *Handbook on formative and summative evaluation of student learning.* New York: McGraw-Hill.

Bock, R. D., and Aitkin, M. (1981). Marginal maximum likelihood estimation of item parameters: Application of an EM algorithm. *Psychometrika, 46,* 443–460.

Bormuth, J. R. (1970). *On the theory of achievement test items.* Chicago: University of Chicago Press.

Boynton, P. L. (1933). *Intelligence, its manifestations and measurement.* New York: D. Appleton & Co.

Bray, J. H., and Maxwell, S. E. (1982). Analyzing and interpreting significant MANOVAS. *Review of Educational Research, 52,* 340–367.

Brennan, R. L. (1972). A generalized upper-lower item discrimination index. *Educational and Psychological Measurement, 32,* 289–303.

Brennan, R. L. (1980). Applications of generalizability theory. In R. A. Berk (Ed.). *Criterion-referenced measurement: The state of the art.* Baltimore: Johns Hopkins University Press.

Brennan, R. L. (1983). Elements of generalizability theory. Iowa City: The American College Testing Program.

Brennan, R. L., and Kane, M. T. (1977). An index of dependability for mastery tests. *Journal of Educational Measurement, 14,* 277–289.

Brennan, R. L., and Lockwood, R. E. (1980). A comparison of the Nedelsky and Angoff cutting score procedures using generalizability theory. *Applied Psychological Measurement, 4,* 219–240.

Brown, F. G. (1983). *Principles of educational and psychological testing.* New York: Holt, Rinehart, and Winston.

Brown, J. M., and Chang, G. (1982). The predictive validity of the Minnesota Reading Assessment in postsecondary vocational educational programs. *Educational and Psychological Measurement, 42,* 345–352.

Browne, M. W. (1975). Predictive validity of a linear regression equation. *British Journal of Mathematical and Statistical Psychology, 28,* 79–87.

Brownell, W. A. (1933). On the accuracy with which reliability may be measured by correlating test halves. *Journal of Experimental Education, 1,* 204–215.

Burke, C. J. (1963). Measurement scale and statistical models. In M. H. Marx (Ed.). *Theories in contempory psychology.* New York: Macmillan.

Burril, L. E. (1982). Comparative studies of item bias methods. In R. A. Berk (Ed.). *Handbook of methods for detecting item bias.* Baltimore: Johns Hopkins University Press.

Camilli, G. (1979). A critique of the chi-square method for assessing item bias. Unpublished paper, Laboratory of Educational Research, University of Colorado.

Campbell, D. T., and Fiske, D. W. (1959). Convergent and discriminant validation by the multitrait-multimethod matrix. *Psychological Bulletin, 56,* 81–105.

Campbell, D. T., and Stanley, J. C. (1963). *Experimental and quasi-experimental designs for research on teaching.* Chicago: Rand McNally & Company.

Cardall, C., and Coffman, W. E. (1984). A method for comparing the performance of different groups on the items in a test. (ETS Research Bulletin 64-61). Princeton, N.J.: Educational Testing Service.

Chissom, B. S., and Hoenes, R. L. (1976). A comparison of the ability of the D-48 test and the IPAT Culture Fair Intelligence Test to predict SRA achievement test scores for 8th and 9th grade students. *Educational and Psychological Measurement, 36,* 561–564.

Cleary, T. A. (1968). Test bias: Prediction of grades of Negro and white students in integrated colleges. *Journal of Educational Measurement, 5,* 115–124.

Cleary, T. A., and Hilton, T. L. (1968). An investigation of item bias. *Educational and Psychological Measurement, 28,* 61–75.

Cole, N. S. (1973). Bias in selection. *Journal of Educational Measurement, 10,* 237–255.

Coombs, C. H. (1950a). The concepts of reliability and homogeneity. *Educational and Psychological Measurement, 10,* 43–56.

Coombs, C. H. (1950b). Psychological scaling without a unit of measurement. *Psychological Review, 57,* 145–158.

Cox, R. C. (1965). Item selection techniques and evaluation of instructional objectives. *Journal of Educational Measurement, 2,* 181–185.

Cox, R. C., and Vargas, J. S. (1966). A comparison of item selection techniques for norm-referenced and criterion-referenced tests. Paper presented at the annual meeting of the National Council on Measurement in Education.

Cronbach, L. J. (1951). Coefficient alpha and the internal structure of tests. *Psychometrika, 16,* 297–334.

Cronbach, L. J. (1970). Review of *On the theory of achievement test items. Psychometrika, 35,* 509–511.

Cronbach, L. J. (1971). Test validation. In R. L. Thorndike (Ed.). *Educational Measurement* (2nd Ed.). Washington, D.C.: American Council on Education.

Cronbach, L. J. (1973). Disciplined inquiry. In H. S. Broudy (Ed.). *Philosophy of educational research.* New York: John Wiley.

Cronbach, L. J. (1975). Five decades of public controversy over mental testing. *American Psychologist, 30,* 1–14.

Cronbach, L. J. (1976). Equity in selection: When psychometrics and political philosophy meet. *Journal of Educational Measurement, 13,* 31–41.

Cronbach, L. J., Gleser, G. C., Nanda, H., and Rajaratnam, N. (1972). *The dependability of behavioral measurements.* New York: John Wiley.

Cronbach, L. J., Gleser, G. C. and Rajaratnam, N. (1963). Theory of generalizability. A liberalization of reliability theory. *British Journal of Mathematical and Statistical Psychology, 16,* 137–173.

Cronbach, L. J., and Meehl, P. E. (1955). Construct validity in psychological tests. *Psychological Bulletin, 52,* 281–302.

Cronbach, L. J., and Warrington, W. G. (1952). Efficacy of multiple choice tests as a function of spread of item difficulties. *Psychometrika, 17,* 127–147.

Cross, L., and Frary, R. (1977). An empirical test of Lord's theoretical results regarding formula scoring of multiple choice tests. *Journal of Educational Measurement, 14,* 313–322.

Cureton, E. E. (1950). Validity, reliability, and baloney. *Educational and Psychological Measurement, 10,* 94–96.

Cureton, E. E. (1958). The definition and estimation of test reliability. *Educational Psychological Measurement, 18,* 715–738.

Darlington, R. B. (1970). Some techniques for maximizing a test's validity when the criterion variable is unobserved. *Journal of Educational Measurement, 7,* 1–14.

Darlington, R. B. (1971). Another look at culture fairness. *Journal of Educational Measurement, 8,* 71–82.

Davis, C. E., Hickman, J., and Novick, M. R. (1973). A primer on decision analysis for individually prescribed instruction. (ACT Technical Bulletin No. 17). Iowa City: American College Testing Program.

Davis, F. B. and Fifer, G. (1959). The effect on test reliability and validity on scoring aptitude and achievement tests with weights for every choice. *Educational and Psychological Measurement, 14,* 159–170.

Dawes, R. M. (1972). *Fundamentals of attitude measurement.* New York: John Wiley.

Dennis, W. (Ed). (1948). *Readings in the history of psychology.* New York: Appleton-Century-Crofts.

Diamond, J., and Evans, W. (1973). The correction for guessing. *Review of Educational Research, 43,* 181–191.

Dixon, W. J., Brown, M. B., Engelman, L., Frane, J. W., Hill, M. A., Jennrich, R. I., and Toporek, J. D. (1981). *BMDP statistical software.* Berkeley: University of California Press.

Downey, R. G. (1979). Item-option weighting of achievement tests: Comparative study of methods. *Applied Psychological Measurement, 3,* 453–462.

DuBois, P. (1970). *A history of psychological testing.* Boston: Allyn and Bacon.

Ebel, R. L. (1951). Estimation of the reliability of ratings. *Psychometrika, 16,* 407–424.

Ebel, R. L. (1956). Obtaining and reporting evidence on content validity. *Educational and Psychological Measurement, 16,* 269–281.

Ebel, R. L. (1962). Content standard test scores. *Educational and Psychological Measurement, 22,* 15–25.

Ebel, R. L. (1965). *Measuring educational achievement.* Englewood Cliffs, N.J.: Prentice-Hall.

Ebel, R. L. (1968). The value of internal consistency in classroom examinations. *Journal of Educational Measurement, 5,* 71–74.

Ebel, R. L. (1972). *Essentials of educational measurement* (2nd Ed.). Englewood Cliffs, N.J.: Prentice-Hall.

Ebel, R. L. (1982). Proposed solutions to two problems of test construction. *Journal of Educational Measurement, 19,* 267–278.

Echternacht, G. J. (1972). The use of confidence testing in objective tests. *Review of Educational Research, 42,* 217–236.

Echternacht, G. J. (1974). A quick method for determining item bias. *Educational and Psychological Measurement, 34,* 271–280.

Echternacht, G. (1977). Grade-equivalent scores. *Measurement in Education, 8*(2), 1–4.

Englehart, M. D. (1965). A comparison of several item discrimination indices. *Journal of Educational Measurement, 2,* 69–76.

Fahner, S. (1974). Item sampling and decision making in achievement testing. *British Journal of Mathematical and Statistical Psychology, 27,* 172–175.

Fechner, G. T. (1860). Elements of psychophysics. In W. Dennis (Ed.). *Readings in the history of psychology.* New York: Appleton-Century-Crofts, 1948.

Findley, W. G. (1956). A rationale for evaluation of item discrimination statistics. *Educational and Psychological Measurement, 16,* 175–180.

Fishbein, M. (Ed.). (1967). *Readings in attitude theory and measurement*. New York: John Wiley.

Flanagan, J. C. (1954). The critical incident technique. *Psychological Bulletin, 51*, 327–358.

Forsyth, R., Saisangjan, V., and Gilmer, J. (1981). Some empirical results related to the robustness of the Rasch model. *Applied Psychological Measurement, 5*, 175–186.

Frederiksen, N. (1981). The real test bias. (Research Report No. 81–40). Princeton, N.J.: Educational Testing Service.

Frick, T., and Semmel, M. I. (1978). Observer agreement and reliabilities of classroom observational measures. *Review of Educational Research, 48*, 157–184.

Frisbie, D. A., and Brandenburg, D. C. (1979). Equivalence of questionnaire items with varying response formats. *Journal of Educational Measurement, 16*, 43–48.

Galton, F. (1883). Inquiries into human faculty and its development. In W. Dennis (Ed). *Readings in the history of psychology*. New York: Appleton-Century-Crofts, 1948.

Ganapole, S. J. (1980). The fundamental reading competencies test. *Journal of Educational Measurement, 7*, 71–73.

Gardner, P. L. (1975). Scales and statistics. *Review of Educational Research, 45*, (1), 43–58.

Gavin, A. T. (1977). Guide to the development of written tests for selection and promotion: The content validity model. (Technical memorandum 77-6). Washington D.C.: U.S. Civil Service Commission.

Gilman, D. A., and Ferry, P. (1972). Increasing test reliability through self-scoring procedures. *Journal of Educational Measurement, 9*, 205–207.

Glaser, R. (1963). Instructional technology and the measurement of learning outcomes. *American Psychologist, 18*, 519–521.

Glass, G. V. (1978). Standards and criteria. *Journal of Educational Measurement, 15*, 237–262.

Gleser, G. C., Cronbach, L. J., and Rajaratnam, N. (1965). Generalizability of scores influenced by multiple sources of variance. *Psychometrika, 30*, 395–418.

Gordon, I. J. (1967). *A test manual for the How I See Myself Scale*. Florida Educational Research and Development Council.

Gross, A. L., and Su, W. (1975). Defining a "fair" or "unbiased" selection model: A question of utilities. *Journal of Applied Psychology, 60*, 345–351.

Guertin, W. H., and Bailey, J. D., Jr. (1970). *Introduction to modern factor analysis*. Ann Arbor, Mich.: Edwards Brothers.

Guilford, J. P. (1954). *Psychometric methods* (2nd Ed.). New York: McGraw-Hill.

Guion, R. M. (1979). Content validity—the source of my discontent. *Applied Psychological Measurement, 1*, 1–10.

Guion, R. M. (1978). "Content validity"—in moderation. *Personnel Psychology, 31*, 205–213.

Guion, R. M. (1980). On trinitarian doctrines of validity. *Professional Psychology, 11*, 385–398.

Gulliksen, H. (1945). The relation of item difficulty and inter-item correlation to test variance and reliability. *Psychometrika, 10*, 79–91.

Gulliksen, H. (1950). *Theory of mental tests*. New York: John Wiley.

Gupta, S. S. (1963). Probability integrals of multivariate normal and multivariate t. *Annals of Mathematical Statistics, 34*, 792–828.

Gustafsson, J. E. (1980). A solution of the conditional estimation problem for long tests in the Rasch model for dichotomous items. *Educational and Psychological Measurement,* *40,* 377–385.

Guttman, L. (1941a). An outline of the statistical theory of prediction. In P. Horst et al. (Eds.). *The prediction of personal adjustment.* New York: Social Science Research Council.

Guttman, L. (1941b). The quantification of class attributes: A theory and method of scale construction. In P. Horst et al. (Eds.). *The prediction of personal adjustment.* New York: Social Science Research Council.

Guttman, L. (1945). A basis for analyzing test-retest reliability. *Psychometrika, 10,* 255–282.

Guttman, L. (1950). The basis for scalogram analysis. In S. A. Stouffer et al., *Measurement and prediction.* Princeton, N.J.: Princeton University Press.

Guttman, L. (1969). Integration of test design and analysis. *Proceedings of the 1969 invitational conference on testing problems.* Princeton, N.J.: Educational Testing Service.

Hambleton, R. K. (1978). On the use of cutoff scores with criterion-referenced tests in instructional settings. *Journal of Educational Measurement, 15,* 277–290.

Hambleton, R. K. (1980). Test score validity and standard setting methods. In R. A. Berk (Ed.). *Criterion-referenced measurement: The state of the art.* Baltimore: Johns Hopkins University Press.

Hambleton, R. K. (Ed.). (1983). *Applications of item response theory.* Vancouver: Educational Research Institute of British Columbia.

Hambleton, R. K., and Cook, L. L. (1977). Latent trait models and their use in the analysis of educational test data. *Journal of Educational Measurement, 14,* 75–96.

Hambleton, R. K., and Murray, L. (1983). Some goodness of fit investigations for item response models. In R. K. Hambleton (Ed.). *Applications of item response theory.* Vancouver: Educational Research Institute of British Columbia.

Hambleton, R. K., and Novick, M. R. (1973). Toward an integration of theory and method for criterion-referenced tests. *Journal of Educational Measurement, 10,* 159–170.

Hambleton, R. K., Swaminathan, J., Algina, J., and Coulson, D. B. (1978a). Criterion-referenced testing and measurement: A review of technical issues and developments. *Review of Educational Research, 48,* 1–47.

Hambleton, R. K., Swaminathan, H., Cook. L. L., Eignor, D. R., and Gifford, J. A. (1978b). Developments in latent trait theory: Models, technical issues, and applications. *Review of Educational Research, 48,* 467–510.

Hambleton, R. K., and Traub, R. E. (1971). Information curves and efficiency of three logistic test models. *British Journal of Mathematical and Statistical Psychology, 24,* 273–281.

Hanna, G. S. (1975). Incremental reliability and validity of multiple choice tests with an answer-until-correct procedure. *Journal of Educational Measurement, 12,* 175–178.

Harman, H. H. (1967). *Modern factor analysis* (2nd Ed.). Chicago: University of Chicago Press.

Harris, C. W. (1974). Problems of objectives-based measurement. In C. W. Harris, M. C. Alkin, and W. J. Popham (Eds.). *Problems in criterion referenced measurement.* (CSE monograph series in evaluation No. 3). Los Angeles: Center for the Study of Evaluation, University of California.

Harris, C. W., Alkin, M. C., and Popham, W. J. (1974). *Problems in criterion referenced measurement.* (CSE monograph series in evaluation, No. 3). Los Angeles: Center for the Study of Evaluation, University of California.

Harris, C. W., and Pearlman, A. P. (1977). Conventional significance tests and indices of agreement or association. In C. W. Harris, A. P. Pearlman, and R. R. Wilcox (Eds.). *Achievement test items—Methods of study*. (CSE monograph series in evaluation, No. 6) Los Angeles: Center for the Study of Evaluation, University of California.

Harris, C. W., Pearlman, A. P., and Wilcox, R. R. (1977). *Achievement test items— Methods of study*. (CSE monograph series in evaluation, No. 6). Los Angeles: Center for the Study of Evaluation, University of California.

Hartley, A. A., and Hartley, J. T. (1976). Predicting performance in the basic research methods course in psychology. *Educational and Psychological Measurement, 36*, 449–452.

Hays, W. L. (1981). *Statistics for psychologists*. New York: Holt, Rinehart and Winston.

Hendrickson, G. F. (1971). The effect of differential option weighting on multiple choice objective tests. *Journal of Educational Measurement, 8*, 291–296.

Henryssen, S. (1971). Gathering, analyzing and using data on test items. In R. L. Thorndike (Ed.). *Educational measurement* (2nd Ed.). Washington, D.C.: American Council on Education.

Hilton, T. L., and Rhett, H. (1973). The base year study of the national longitudinal study of the high school class of 1972. (Final Report Contract No. OEC-0-72-0903). Office of Education, National Center for Educational Statistics, U.S. Department of Health, Education, and Welfare. Princeton, N.J.: Educational Testing Service.

Hocking, R. R. (1976). The analysis and selection of variables in linear regression. *Biometrics, 32*, 1–49.

Holland, W. F., and Keller, R. T. (1978). A cross validation study of the Kirton Adaptation-Innovation Inventory in three research and development organizations. *Applied Psychological Measurement, 2*, 510–563.

Holmes, S. E. (1982). Unidimensionality and vertical equating with the Rasch model. *Journal of Educational Measurement, 19*, 139–147.

Hoyt, C. J. (1941). Test reliability estimated by analysis of variance. *Psychometrika, 6*, 153–160.

Hulin, C. L., Drasgow, F., and Parsons, C. K. (1983). *Item response theory*. Homewood Ill.: Dow Jones-Irwin.

Hulin, C. L., Lissak, R. I., and Drasgow, F. (1982). Recovery of two and three parameter logistic item characteristic curves: A Monte Carlo study. *Applied Psychological Measurement, 6*, 249–260.

Hunter, J. E. (1975). A critical analysis of the use of item means and item test correlations to determine the presence or absence of content bias in achievement test items. Paper presented at the National Institute of Education Conference on Test Bias, Annapolis, Md.

Hunter, J. E., and Cohen, S. H. (1974). Correcting for unreliability in nonlinear models of attitude change. *Psychometrika, 34*, 445–468.

Hunter, J. E., and Schmidt, F. L. (1976). A critical analysis of the statistical and ethical implications of various definitions of "test bias." *Psychological Bulletin, 83*, 1,053–1,071.

Hunyh, H. (1976a). On the reliability of decisions in domain-referenced testing. *Journal of Educational Measurement, 13*, 253–264.

Hunyh, H. (1976b). Statistical considerations of mastery scores. *Psychometrika, 41*, 65–78.

Hunyh, H. (1980a). Computation and inference for two reliability indices in mastery testing based on the beta-binomial model. In H. Hunyh and J. C. Saunders. Solutions for some technical problems in domain-referenced mastery testing. (Final Report, Project No. NIE-

G-78-0087). National Institute of Education, Department of Health, Education, and Welfare.

Hunyh, H. (1980b). A nonrandomized minimax solution for passing scores in the binomial error model. *Psychometrika, 45,* 167–182.

Hunyh, H. (1980c). A note on decision theoretic coefficients for tests. In H. Hunyh and J. C. Saunders. Solutions for some technical problems in domain-referenced mastery testing. (Final Report, Project No. NIE-G-78-0087). National Institute of Education, Department of Health, Education, and Welfare.

Hunyh, H. (1980d). Statistical inference for false positive and false negative error rates in mastery testing (computer program and tables added). In H. Hunyh and J. C. Saunders. Solutions for technical problems in domain-referenced mastery testing. (Final Report, Project No. NIE-G-78-0087). National Institute of Education, Department of Health, Education, and Welfare.

Hunyh, H., and Saunders, J. C. (1980). Accuracy of two procedures for estimating reliability of mastery tests. *Journal of Educational Measurement, 17,* 351–358.

Jennrich, R. I., and Sampson, P. F. (1966). Rotation for simple loadings. *Psychometrika, 31,* 313–323.

Ironson, G. H. (1982). Use of chi-square and latent trait approaches for detecting item bias. In R. A. Berk (Ed.). *Handbook of methods for detecting item bias.* Baltimore: Johns Hopkins University Press.

Ironson, G., Homan, S., Willis, R., and Signer, B. (In press). The validity of item bias techniques with math word problems. *Applied Psychological Measurement.*

Ironson, G. H., and Subkoviak, M. (1979). A comparison of several methods for assessing item bias. *Journal of Educational Measurement, 16,* 209–225.

Irvin, L. K., Halpern, A. S., and Landman, J. T. (1980). Assessment of retarded student achievement with standardized true/false and multiple-choice tests. *Journal of Educational Measurement, 17,* 51–58.

Jaeger, R. M. (1979). Measurement consequences of selected standard-setting models. In M. A. Bunda, and J. R. Sanders (Eds.). *Practices & problems in competency based measurement.* National Council on Measurement in Education.

Jaeger, R. M. (1982). An iterative structured judgment process for establishing standards on competency tests: Theory and application. *Educational Evaluation and Policy Analysis, 4,* 461–475.

Jaeger, R. M. (1984). *Sampling in education and the social sciences.* New York: Longman.

Jensen, A. R. (1980). *Bias in mental testing.* New York: The Free Press.

Jersild, A. J. (1952). *In search of self.* New York: Teachers College Bureau of Publications.

Joncich, G. M. (1968). *The sane positivist: A biography of Edward L. Thorndike.* Middletown, Conn.: Wesleyan University Press.

Jöreskog, K. G. (1969). A general approach to confirmatory maximum likelihood factor analysis. *Psychometrika, 34,* 183–202.

Jöreskog, K. G., and Sorbom, D. (1984). LISREL VI, Analysis of linear structural relationships by maximum likelihood, instrumental variables, and least squares methods. Mooresville, Ind.: Scientific Software, Inc.

Kaiser, H. G. (1958). The varimax criterion for analytic rotation in factor analysis. *Psychometrika, 23,* 187–200.

Kane, M. T. (1982). A sampling model for validity. *Applied Psychological Measurement, 6,* 125–160.

Kane, M. T., and Brennan, R. L. (1980). Agreement coefficients as indices of dependability for domain-referenced tests. *Applied Psychological Measurement, 4,* 105–126.

Kane, M. T., Gillmore, G. M., and Crooks, T. J. (1976). Student evaluations of teaching: The generalizability of class means. *Journal of Educational Measurement, 13,* 171–184.

Kaplan, R. M., and Saccuzzo, D. P. (1982). *Psychological testing principles, applications, and issues.* Monterey, Calif.: Brooks/Cole.

Katz, M. (1958). Selecting an achievement test: Principles and procedures. In V. H. Noll, D. P. Scannell, and R. P. Noll (Eds.). *Introductory readings in educational measurement.* Boston: Houghton Mifflin, 1972.

Keats, J. A., and Lord, F. M. (1962). A theoretical distribution for mental test scores. *Psychometrika, 27,* 215–231.

Kelley, T. L. (1927). *Interpretation of educational measurements,* New York: World Book.

Kelley, T. L. (1939). Selection of upper and lower groups for the validation of test items. *Journal of Educational Psychology, 30,* 17–24.

Kelley, T. L. (1942). The reliability coefficient. *Psychometrika, 7,* 75–83.

Kiefer, J., and Wolfowitz, J. (1956). Consistency of maximum likelihood estimates in the presence of infinitely many incidental parameters. *Annals of Mathematical Statistics, 27,* 887–890.

Kish, L. (1965). *Survey sampling.* New York: John Wiley.

Klein, S. P., and Kosecoff, J. P. (1975). Determining how well a test measures your objectives. (CSE Report No. 94). Los Angeles: Center for the Study of Evaluation, University of California.

Kleinbaum, D. G., and Kupper, L. L. (1978). *Applied regression analysis and other multivariable methods.* North Scituate, Mass.: Duxbury Press.

Koffler, S. L. (1980). A comparison of approaches for setting standards. *Journal of Educational Measurement, 17,* 167–178.

Kolen, M. J. (1984). Effectiveness of analytical smoothing in equipercentile equating. *Journal of Educational Statistics, 9,* 25–44.

Krathwohl, D. R., Bloom, B. S., and Masia, B. (1964). *Taxonomy of educational objectives, handbook II: The affective domain.* New York: McKay.

Kuder, G. F., and Richardson, M. W. (1937). The theory of the estimation of test reliability. *Psychometrika, 2,* 151–160.

Kurtz, A. K., and Mayo, S. T. (1979). *Statistical methods in education and psychology.* New York: Springer-Verlag.

Lam, T. C. M., and Klockars, A. J. (1982). Anchor point effects on the equivalence of questionnaire items. *Journal of Educational Measurement, 19,* 317–322.

Lange, A., Mehrens, W. A., and Lehmann, I. J. (1967). Using item analysis to improve tests. *Journal of Educational Measurement, 4,* 65–68.

Lawley, D. N. (1943). On problems connected with item selection and test construction. *Proceedings of the Royal Society of Edinborough, 6,* 73–287.

Lawley, D. N., and Maxwell, A. E. (1971). *Factor analysis as a statistical method* (2nd Ed.). New York: American Elsevier Publishing Company.

Lawshe, C. H. (1975). A quantitative approach to content validity. *Personnel Psychology, 28,* 563–575.

Levine, M. V. (1981). Weighted item bias statistics. (Report 81-5). Urbana-Champaign: Department of Educational Psychology, University of Illinois.

Levine, M. V., Wardrop, J. L., and Linn, R. L. (1982). Weighted mean square item bias statistics. Paper presented at the annual meeting of the American Educational Research Association, New York.

Likert, R. (1932). A technique for the measurement of attitudes. *Archives of Psychology,* (140), 44–53.

Lindquist, E. F. (1936). The theory of test construction. In H. E. Hawkes, E. F. Lindquist, and C. Mann (Eds.). *The construction and use of achievement examinations.* Boston: Houghton Mifflin.

Lindquist, E. F. (1953). *Design and analysis of experiments in education and psychology.* Boston: Houghton Mifflin.

Linn, R. L. (1973). Fair test use in selection. *Review of Educational Research, 43,* 343–357.

Linn, R. L., Levine, M. V., Hastings, C. N., and Wardrop, J. L. (1981). Item bias in a test of reading comprehension. *Applied Psychological Measurement, 5,* 159–173.

Livingston, S. A. (1972). Criterion-referenced applications of classical test theory. *Journal of Educational Measurement, 9,* 13–26.

Loevinger, J. (1947). A systematic approach to the construction and evaluation of tests of ability. *Psychological Monograph, 61,* No. 4.

Loevinger, J. (1954). The attenuation paradox in test theory. *Psychological Bulletin, 51,* 493–504.

Lomax, R. G. and Algina, J. (1979). Comparison of two procedures for analyzing multitrait multimethod matrices. *Journal of Educational Measurement, 16,* 177–186.

Lord, F. M. (1952a). The relationship of the reliability of multiple choice items to the distribution of item difficulties. *Psychometrika, 18,* 181–194.

Lord, F. M. (1952b). A theory of test scores. *Psychometric Monograph,* No. 7.

Lord, F. M. (1953). The relationship of test score to trait underlying the test. *Educational and Psychological Measurement, 13,* 517–548.

Lord, F. M. (1955). Sampling fluctuations resulting from the sampling of test items. *Psychometrika, 20,* 1–22.

Lord, F. M. (1957). Do tests of the same length have the same standard error of measurement? *Educational and Psychological Measurement, 17,* 510–521.

Lord, F. M. (1959a). Test norms and sampling theory. *Journal of Experimental Education, 27,* 247–263.

Lord, F. M. (1959b). Tests of the same length do have the same standard error of measurement. *Educational and Psychological Measurement, 19,* 233–239.

Lord, F. M. (1963). Formula scoring and validity. *Educational and Psychological Measurement, 23,* 663–672.

Lord, F. M. (1965). A strong true-score theory with application. *Psychometrika, 30,* 239–270.

Lord, F. M. (1968). An analysis of the Verbal Scholastic Aptitude Test using Birnbaum's three-parameter logistic model. *Educational and Psychological Measurement, 28,* 989–1020.

Lord, F. M. (1971). The self scoring flexilevel test. *Journal of Educational Measurement, 8,* 147–151.

Lord, F. M. (1975). Formula scoring and number-right scoring. *Journal of Educational Measurement, 12,* 7–12.

Lord, F. M. (1980). *Applications of item response theory to practical testing problems.* Hillsdale, N.J.: Lawrence Erlbaum.

Lord, F. M. (1982). The standard error of equipercentile equating. *Journal of Educational Statistics, 1,* 165–192.

Lord, F. M., and Novick, M. R. (1968). *Statistical theories of mental test scores.* Reading, Mass.: Addison-Wesley, 1968.

Loyd, B. H., and Hoover, H. D. (1980). Vertical equating using the Rasch model. *Journal of Educational Measurement, 17,* 179–193.

McCall, W. A. (1939). *Measurement.* New York: Macmillan.

McClung, M. S. (1978). Developing proficiency programs in California public schools: Some legal implications and a suggested implementations schedule. Sacramento: California State Department of Education.

McDonald, R. P. (1981). The dimensionality of tests and items. *British Journal of Mathematical and Statistical Psychology, 34,* 100–117.

McNemar, Q. (1962). *Psychological statistics.* New York: John Wiley.

McNemar, Q. (1975). On so-called test bias. *American Psychologist, 30,* 848–851.

Magnusson, D. (1967). *Test theory.* Boston: Addison-Wesley.

Marascuilo, L. A., and McSweeney, M. (1977). *Nonparametric and distribution free methods for the social sciences.* Monterey, Calif.: Brooks/Cole.

Marco, G. (1977). Item characteristic curve solutions to three intractable testing problems. *Journal of Educational Measurement, 14,* 139–160.

Marsh, H. W., and Hocevar, D. (1983). Confirmatory factor analysis of multitrait-multimethod matrices. *Journal of Educational Measurement, 20,* 231–248.

Marx, R. W., and Winne, P. H. (1978). Construct interpretations of three self-concept inventories. *American Educational Research Journal, 15,* 99–109.

Masters, J. R. (1974). The relationship between number of response categories and reliability of Likert-type questionnaires. *Journal of Educational Measurement, 11,* 49–53.

Matarazzo, J. D., Allen, B. V., Soslow, G., and Weins, A. N. (1964). Characteristics of successful policemen and firemen applicants. *Journal of Applied Psychology, 48,* 123–133.

Medley, D. M., and Meitzel, H. E. (1963). Measuring classroom behavior by systematic observation. In N. L. Gage, *Handbook of research on teaching.* Chicago: Rand McNally.

Mehrens, W. A., and Lehmann, I. J. (1984). *Measurement and evaluation in education and psychology* (3rd ed.). New York: Holt, Rinehart, and Winston.

Meskauskas, J. A. (1976). Evaluation models for criterion-referenced testing: Views regarding mastery and standard setting. *Review of Educational Research, 46,* 133–158.

Messick, S. (1975). The standard problem: Meaning and values in measurement and evaluation. *American Psychologist, 30,* 955–966.

Messick, S. (1981). Evidence and ethics in the evaluation of tests. *Educational Researcher, 10*(9), 9–20.

Millman, J. (1973). Passing scores and test lengths for criterion-referenced tests. *Review of Educational Research, 43,* 205–216.

Millman, J. (1974). Criterion referenced measurement. In W. J. Popham (Ed.). *Evaluation in education: Current applications.* Berkeley, Calif.: McCutcheon.

Millman, J., and Glass, G. V. (1967). Rules of thumb for writing the ANOVA table. *Journal of Educational Measurement, 4,* 41–51.

Millman, J., and Popham, W. J. (1974). The issue of item and test variance for criterion-referenced tests: A reply. *Journal of Educational Measurement, 11,* 137–138.

Mills, C. N. (1983). A comparison of three methods of establishing cutoff scores on criterion referenced tests. *Journal of Educational Measurement, 20,* 283–292.

Morrison, D. F. (1976). *Multivariate statistical methods* (2nd Ed). New York: McGraw-Hill.

Mosher, D. L. (1968). Measurement of guilt in females by self-report inventories. *Journal of Consulting and Clinical Psychology, 32,* 690–695.

Mosier, C. I. (1947). A critical examination of the concepts of face validity. *Educational and Psychological Measurement, 7,* 191–206.

Mulaik, S. A. (1972). *The foundations of factor analysis.* New York: McGraw-Hill.

Myers, J. L. (1979). *Fundamentals of experimental design* (3rd Ed.). Boston: Allyn and Bacon.

Nedelsky, L. (1954). Absolute grading standards for objective tests. *Educational and Psychological Measurement, 14,* 3–19.

Novick, M. R., and Lewis, C. (1974). Prescribing test length for criterion referenced measurement. In C. W. Harris, M. C. Alkin, and W. J. Popham (Eds.). *Problems in criterion-referenced measurement.* Los Angeles: Center for the Study of Evaluation, University of California.

Novick, M. R., and Lindley, D. V. (1978). The use of more realistic utility functions in educational applications. *Journal of Educational Measurement, 15,* 181–191.

Nunnally, J. C. (1967). *Psychometric theory.* New York: McGraw-Hill.

Osgood, C., Suci, G., and Tannenbaum, P. (1957). *The measurement of meaning.* Urbana: University of Illinois Press.

Oosterhof, A. C. (1976). Similarity of various item discrimination indices. *Journal of Educational Measurement, 13,* 145–150.

Overall, J. E., and Klett, C. J. (1972). *Applied multivariate analysis.* New York: McGraw-Hill.

Patnaik, D., and Traub, R. E. (1973). Differential weighting by judged degree of correctness. *Journal of Educational Measurement, 10,* 281–286.

Pearson, K. (1909). On a new method of determining a correlation between a measured character of A and a character of B, of which only the percentage of cases wherein B exceeds (or falls short of) intensity is recorded for each grade of A. *Biometrika, 7,* 96–105.

Pedhazur, E. J. (1982). *Multiple regression in behavioral research* (2nd Ed.). York: Holt, Rinehart, and Winston.

Peng, C. J., and Subkoviak, M. J. (1980). A note on Hunyh's normal approximation procedure for estimating criterion-referenced reliability. *Journal of Educational Measurement, 17,* 359–368.

Petersen, N. S. (1976). An expected utility model for "optional" selection. *Journal of Educational Statistics, 1,* 333–358.

Petersen, N. S. (1979). Review of *Achievement test items: Methods of study* by Chester W. Harris, Andrea Pastorak Pearlman, and Rand R. Wilcox. *Journal of Educational Measurement, 16,* 137–138.

Petersen, N. S., and Novick, M. R. (1976). An evaluation of some models for culture-fair selection. *Journal of Educational Measurement, 13,* 3–29.

Piers, E. V., and Harris, D. B. (1964). Age and other correlates of self-concept. *Journal of Educational Psychology, 55,* 91–96.

Plake, B. S., and Hoover, H. D. (1977). An analytic method of identifying biased test items. Paper presented at the annual meeting of the American Educational Research Association, New York.

Popham, W. J. (1974). Selecting objectives and generalizing test items. In C. W. Harris, M. C. Alkin, and W. J. Popham (Eds.). *Problems in criterion-referenced measurement.* (pp. 13–25). Los Angeles: Center for the Study of Evaluation, University of California.

Popham, W. J. (1978). As always, provocative. *Journal of Educational Measurement, 15,* 297–300.

Popham, W. J. (1981). *Modern educational measurement*. Englewood Cliffs, N.J.: Prentice-Hall.

Popham, W. J., and Husek, T. R. (1969). Implications of criterion-referenced measurement. *Journal of Educational Measurement, 6*, 1–9.

Pough, F. H. (1960). *A field guide to rocks and minerals*. Boston: Houghton Mifflin.

Powers, D. E. (1982). Long term predictive and construct validity of two traditional predictors of law school performance. *Journal of Educational Psychology, 74*, 568–576.

Powers, S., Slaughter, H., and Helmick, C. (1983). A test of the equipercentile hypothesis of the TIERS norm-referenced model. *Journal of Educational Measurement, 20*, 299–302.

Prescott, G. A., Balow, I. H., Hogan, T. P., and Farr, R. C. (1978). *Metropolitan Achievement Tests*. New York: The Psychological Corporation.

Prien, E. P. (1977). The function of job analysis in content validation. *Personnel Psychology, 30*, 1977, 167–173.

Rajaratnam, N. (1960). Reliability formulas for independent decision data when reliability data are matched. *Psychometrika, 25*, 261–271.

Rajaratnam, N., Cronbach, L. J., and Gleser, G. C. (1963). Generalizability of stratified parallel tests. *Psychometrika, 30*, 39–56.

Ree, M. J., and Jensen, H. E. (1980). Effects of sample size on linear equating of item characteristic curve parameters. In D. J. Weiss (Ed.). *Proceedings of the 1979 computerized adaptive testing conference*. Minneapolis: University of Minnesota, Department of Psychology, Psychometric Methods Program, Computerized Adaptive Testing Laboratory.

Rentz, R. R., and Bashaw, W. L. (1977). The national reference scale for reading: An application of the Rasch model. *Journal of Educational Measurement, 14*, 161–180.

Roid, G., and Haladyna, T. (1980). The emergence of an item writing technology. *Review of Educational Research, 50*, 293–314.

Roth, A. V., and Lubin, B. (1981). Factors underlying the depression adjective check lists. *Educational and Psychological Measurement, 41*, 382–385.

Rovinelli, R. J., and Hambleton, R. K. (1977). On the use of content specialists in the assessment of criterion-referenced test item validity. *Dutch Journal of Educational Research, 2*, 49–60.

Rowley, G. L., and Traub, R. E. (1977). Formula scoring, number-right scoring, and test-taking strategy. *Journal of Educational Measurement, 14*, 15–22.

Rozeboom, W. W. (1981). The cross validational accuracy of sample regressions. *Journal of Educational Statistics, 6*, 179–198.

Rudner, L. M. (1977). An approach to biased item identification using latent trait measurement theory. Paper presented at the annual meeting of the American Educational Research Association, New York.

Rudner, L. M., Getson, P. R., and Knight, D. L. (1980). A Monte Carlo comparison of seven biased item detection techniques. *Journal of Educational Measurement, 17*, 1–10.

Rulon, P. J. (1939). A simplified procedure for determining the reliability of a test by split-halves. *Harvard Educational Review, 9*, 99–103.

Saunders, J. C., Ryan, J. P., and Hunyh, H. (1981). A comparison of two approaches to standard setting based on the Nedelsky procedure. *Applied Psychological Measurement, 5*, 209–218.

Saupe, J. L. (1966). Selecting items to measure change. *Journal of Educational Measurement, 3*, 223–226.

Sawyer, R. L., Cole, N. S., and Cole, J. W. L. (1976). Utilities and the issue of fairness in a decision theoretic model for selection. *Journal of Educational Measurement, 13*, 59–76.

Sax, G. (1980). *Principles of educational and psychological measurement and evaluation* (2nd Ed.). Belmont, Calif.: Wadsworth.

Scheuneman, J. (1979). A new method for assessing bias in test items. *Journal of Educational Measurement, 16,* 143–152.

Schmidt, F. L., and Hunter, J. E. (1981). Employment testing: Old theories and new research findings. *American Psychologist, 36,* 1,128–1,137.

Schmidt, F. L., Hunter, J. E., and Urry, V. W. (1976). Statistical power in criterion-related validity studies. *Journal of Applied Psychology, 61,* 473–485.

Schmitt, N. (1978). Path analysis of multitrait-multimethod matrices. *Applied Psychological Measurement, 2,* 157–174.

Scriven, M. (1978). How to anchor standards. *Journal of Educational Measurement, 15,* 273–275.

Shavelson, R. J. (1981). *Statistical reasoning for the behavioral sciences.* Boston: Allyn and Bacon.

Shavelson, R. J., and Bolus, R. (1982). Self-concept: The interplay of theory and methods. *Journal of Educational Psychology, 74,* 3–17.

Shepard, L. A. (1976). Setting standards and living with them. *Florida Journal of Educational Research, 18,* 23–32.

Shepard, L. A. (1979). Setting standards. In M. A. Bunda and J. R. Sanders (Eds.). *Practices and problems in competency-based measurement.* National Council of Measurement in Education.

Shepard L. (1980). Standard setting issues and methods. *Applied Psychological Measurement, 4,* 447–465.

Shepard, L., Camilli, G., and Averill, M. (1981). Comparison of procedures for detecting test-item bias with both internal and external ability criterion. *Journal of Educational Statistics, 6,* 317–376.

Shoemaker, D. M. (1975). Toward a framework for achievement testing. *Review of Educational Research, 45,* 127–148.

Sirotnik, K. (1972). Estimates of coefficient alpha for finite populations of items. *Educational and Psychological Measurement, 32,* 129–136.

Slakter, M. J. (1968). The penalty for not guessing. *Journal of Educational Measurement, 5,* 141–144.

Slakter, M. J. (1969). Generality of risk taking on objective examinations. *Educational and Psychological Measurement, 29,* 125–128.

Slinde, J. A., and Linn, R. L. (1978). An exploration of the adequacy of the Rasch model for vertical equating. *Journal of Educational Measurement, 15,* 23–35.

Slinde, J. A., and Linn, R. L. (1979). The Rasch model, objective measurement, equating, and robustness. *Applied Psychological Measurement, 3,* 437–456.

Spearman, C. (1904). The proof and measurement of association between two things. *American Journal of Psychology, 15,* 72–101.

Spearman, C. (1907). Demonstration of formulae for true measurement of correlation. *American Journal of Psychology, 18,* 161–169.

Spearman, C. (1913). Correlations of sums and differences. *British Journal of Psychology, 5,* 417–426.

Stanley, J. C. (1971). Reliability. In R. L. Thorndike (Ed.). *Educational measurement* (2nd Ed.). (pp. 359–442). Washington, D.C.: American Council on Education.

Stevens, S. S. (1946). On the theory of scales of measurement. *Science, 103,* 677–680.

Subkoviak, M. J. (1976). Estimating reliability from a single administration of a criterion-referenced test. *Journal of Educational Measurement, 13,* 265–275.

Subkoviak, M. J. (1978). Empirical investigation of procedures for estimating reliability for mastery tests. *Journal of Educational Measurement, 15,* 111–116.

Subkoviak, M. J. (1980). Decision consistency approaches. In R. A. Berk (Ed.). *Criterion-referenced measurement: The state of the art.* Baltimore: Johns Hopkins University Press.

Swaminathan, H. (1983). Parameter estimation in item response models. In R. K. Hambleton (Ed.). *Applications of item response theory.* Vancouver: Educational Research Institute of British Columbia.

Swaminathan, H., and Gifford, J. (1979). Estimation of parameters in latent trait models. In D. Weiss (Ed.). *Proceedings of the 1979 computerized adaptive testing conference.* Minneapolis: University of Minnesota.

Swaminathan, H., Hambleton, R. K., and Algina, J. (1974). Reliability of criterion referenced tests: A decision theoretic formulation. *Journal of Educational Measurement, 11,* 263–268.

Tallmadge, G. K., and Wood, C. T. (1976). User's guide: ESEA Title I evaluation and reporting system. Mountain View, Calif.: RMC Research Corp.

Taylor, H. C., and Russell, J. T. (1939). The relationship of validity coefficients to the practical effectiveness of tests in selection: Discussion and tables. *Journal of Applied Psychology, 23,* 565–578.

Tenopyr, M. L. (1977). Content-construct confusion. *Personnel Psychology, 30,* 47–54.

Thissen, D. M. (1976). Information in wrong responses to the Raven Progressive Matrices. *Journal of Educational Measurement, 13* (3), 201–214.

Thorndike, E. L. (1904). *An introduction to the theory of mental and social measurements.* New York: Science Press.

Thorndike, R. L. (1949). *Personnel selection.* New York: John Wiley.

Thorndike, R. L. (1971). Concepts of culture fairness. *Journal of Educational Measurement, 8,* 63–70.

Thorndike, R. L. (1975). Mr. Binet's test 70 years later. *Educational Researcher, 4*(5), 3–7.

Thorndike, R. L. (1982). *Applied psychometrics.* Boston: Houghton Mifflin.

Thorndike, R. L., and Hagen, E. (1977). *Measurement and evaluation in psychology and education.* New York: John Wiley.

Thurstone, L. L. (1927). A law of comparative judgment. *Psychological Review, 34,* 273–286.

Thurstone, L. L. (1928). Attitudes can be measured. *American Journal of Sociology, 33,* 529–554.

Thurstone, L. L. (1942). *Multiple factor analysis.* Chicago: University of Chicago Press.

Thurstone, L. L., and Chave, E. J. (1929). *The measurement of attitude.* Chicago: University of Chicago Press.

Torgerson, W. S. (1958). *Theory and methods of scaling.* New York: John Wiley.

Traub, R. E., and Hambleton, R. K. (1972). The effect of scoring instructions and degree of speededness on the validity and reliability of multiple-choice tests. *Educational and Psychological Measurement, 32,* 737–758.

Traub, R. E., and Rowley, G. L. (1980). Reliability of test scores and decisions. *Applied Psychological Measurement, 4,* 517–546.

Traub, R. E., and Wolfe, R. G. (1981). Latent trait theories and assessment of educational achievement. In D. C. Berliner (Ed.). *Review of research in education 9.* Washington, D.C.: American Educational Research Association.

Travers, R. M. (1951). Rational hypotheses in the construction of tests. *Educational and Psychological Measurement, 11,* 128–137.

Tucker, L. R. (1946). Maximum validity of a test with equivalent items. *Psychometrika, 11,* 1–13.

Udinsky, B. F., Osterlind, S. J., and Lynch, S. W. (1981). *Evaluation resource handbook: Gathering, analyzing, reporting data.* San Diego, Calif.: EDITS.

van der Linden, Wim J. (1982). A latent trait method for determining intrajudge inconsistency in the Angoff and Nedelsky techniques of standard-setting. *Journal of Educational Measurement, 19,* 295–380.

van der Linden, W. J., and Mellenbergh, G. J. (1977). Optimal cutting scores using a linear loss function. *Applied Psychological Measurement, 1,* 593–599.

van der Linden, W. J., and Mellenbergh, G. J. (1978). Coefficients for tests from a decision theoretic point of view. *Applied Psychological Measurement, 2,* 119–134.

van der Ven, A. H. G. S. (1980). *Introduction to scaling.* New York: John Wiley.

Velicer, W. F., and Stevenson, J. F. (1978). The relation between item format and the structure of the Eysenck Personality Inventory. *Applied Psychological Measurement, 2,* 293–304.

Wainer, H., Morgan, A., and Gustafsson, J. E. (1980). A review of estimation procedures for the Rasch model with an eye toward longish tests. *Journal of Educational Statistics, 5,* 35–64.

Ward, W. C., Carlson, S. B., and Woisetschlager, E. (1983). Ill-structured problems as multiple-choice items. (GRE Board Professional Report No. 81–18P). Princeton, N.J.: Educational Testing Service.

Ward, W. C., Frederiksen, N., and Carlson, S. B. (1980). Construct validity of free-response and machine-scorable forms of a test. *Journal of Educational Measurement, 17,* 11–29.

Ware, W. B., and Benson, J. (1975). Appropriate statistics and measurement scales. *Science Education, 59* (4), 575–582.

Weber, E. H. (1846). The sense of touch and common feeling. In W. Dennis (Ed). *Readings in the history of psychology.* New York: Appleton-Century-Crofts, 1948.

Wechsler, D. (1939). *The measurement of adult intelligence.* Baltimore: Williams and Wilkins.

Wechsler, S. W. (1958). *The measurement and appraisal of adult intelligence* (4th Ed.). Baltimore: Williams and Wilkins.

Weitzenhoffer, A. M. (1951). Mathematical structures and psychological measurement. *Psychometrika, 16,* 387–406.

Whitely, S. E., and Dawis, R. V. (1974). The nature of objectivity with the Rasch model. *Journal of Educational Measurement, 11,* 163–178.

Wilcox, R. R. (1976). A note on the length and passing score of a mastery test. *Journal of Educational Statistics, 1,* 359–364.

Wilcox, R. R. (1977a). Estimating the likelihood of false positive and false negative decisions in mastery decisions: An empirical Bayes approach. *Journal of Educational Statistics, 2,* 289–307.

Wilcox, R. R. (1977b). New methods for studying equivalence. In C. W. Harris, A. P. Pearlman, and R. R. Wilcox (Eds.). *Achievement test items—New methods of study.* Los Angeles: Center for the Study of Evaluation, University of California.

Wilcox, R. R. (1978). A note on decision theoretic coefficients for tests. *Applied Psychological Measurement, 2,* 609–613.

Wilcox, R. R. (1981a). A closed sequential procedure for answer-until-correct tests. *Journal of Experimental Education, 5,* 219–222.

Wilcox, R. R. (1981b). A cautionary note on estimating the reliability of a mastery test with the beta-binomial model. *Applied Psychological Measurement, 5,* 531–537.

Wilcox, R. R. (1981c). Solving measurement problems with an answer-until-correct procedure. *Applied Psychological Measurement, 5,* 399–414.

Wilcox, R. R. (1982). Some new results on an answer-until-correct procedure. *Journal of Educational Measurement, 19,* 67–74.

Wood, R. L., Wingersky, M. S., and Lord, F. M. (1976). LOGIST-A computer program for estimating examinee ability and item characteristic curve parameters. (Research Memorandum 76-6). Princeton, N.J.: Educational Testing Service.

Wright, B. D. (1968). Sample free test calibration and person measurement. In *Proceedings of the 1967 Invitational Conference on Testing Problems.* Princeton, N.J.: Educational Testing Service.

Wright, B. D., and Douglas, G. A. (1977). Conditional versus unconditional procedures for sample-free item analysis. *Educational and Psychological Measurement, 37,* 47–60.

Wright, B. D., Mead, R., and Bell, S. (1979). *BICAL: Calibrating items with the Rasch model.* (Statistical Laboratory Department of Education RM 23b). Chicago: University of Chicago.

Wright, B. D., and Panchapakesan, N. (1969). A procedure for sample free item analysis. *Educational and Psychological Measurement, 29,* 23–48.

Wright, B. D., and Stone, M. (1979). *Best test design.* Chicago: MESA Press.

Wundt, W. (1873). Principles of physiological psychology. In W. Dennis (Ed.). *Readings in the history of psychology.* New York: Appleton-Century-Crofts, 1948.

Yalow, E. S., and Popham, W. J. (1983). Content validity at the crossroads. *Educational Researcher, 12*(8), 10–14.

Yerkes, R. M. (1921). Psychological examining in the United States Army. In W. Dennis (Ed.). *Readings in the history of psychology.* New York: Appleton-Century-Crofts, 1948.

Zieky, M. J., and Livingston, S. A. (1977). Manual for setting standards on the Basic Skills Assessment Tests. Princeton, N.J.: Educational Testing Service.

Zimmerman, D. W., and Williams, R. H. (1982). Gain scores in research can be highly reliable. *Journal of Educational Measurement, 19,* 149–154.

Appendix A

Probabilities and Y Ordinates Associated with given z-Score under the Standard Normal Curve

Absolute Value of z-Score	$Pr \leq -z$	$Pr \leq +z$	Y ordinate
.00	.500	.500	.3989
.05	.480	.520	.3984
.10	.460	.540	.3970
.15	.440	.560	.3945
.20	.421	.579	.3910
.25	.401	.599	.3867
.30	.382	.618	.3814
.35	.363	.637	.3752
.40	.344	.656	.3683
.45	.326	.674	.3605
.50	.309	.691	.3521
.55	.291	.709	.3429
.60	.274	.726	.3332
.65	.258	.742	.3230
.70	.242	.758	.3123
.75	.227	.773	.3011
.80	.212	.788	.2897
.85	.198	.802	.2780
.90	.184	.816	.2661
.95	.171	.829	.2541
1.00	.159	.841	.2420
1.05	.147	.853	.2299
1.10	.136	.864	.2179
1.15	.125	.875	.2059
1.20	.115	.885	.1942
1.25	.106	.894	.1827
1.30	.097	.903	.1714
1.35	.089	.911	.1604
1.40	.081	.919	.1497
1.45	.074	.926	.1394
1.50	.067	.933	.1295
1.55	.061	.939	.1200
1.60	.055	.945	.1109
1.65	.049	.951	.1023
1.70	.045	.955	.0941
1.75	.040	.960	.0863
1.80	.036	.964	.0790
1.85	.032	.968	.0721
1.90	.029	.971	.0656
1.95	.026	.974	.0596
2.00	.023	.977	.0540
2.05	.020	.980	.0488

Absolute Value of z-Score	$Pr \le -z$	$Pr \le +z$	Y ordinate
2.10	.018	.982	.0440
2.15	.016	.984	.0396
2.20	.014	.986	.0355
2.25	.012	.988	.0317
2.30	.011	.989	.0283
2.35	.009	.991	.0252
2.40	.008	.992	.0224
2.45	.007	.993	.0198
2.50	.006	.994	.0175
2.55	.005	.995	.0155
2.60	.005	.995	.0136
2.65	.004	.996	.0120
2.70	.003	.997	.0104
2.75	.003	.997	.0091
2.80	.003	.997	.0079
2.85	.002	.998	.0069
2.90	.002	.998	.0060
2.95	.002	.998	.0051
3.00	.001	.999	.0044

Appendix B
KEYS TO EXERCISES

Chapter 1

1. A. Testing
   B. Measurement
   C. Neither (no standard procedure for data collection)
   D. Testing and measurement
   E. Testing
   F. Measurement
2. A. Optimal performance measure
   B. Observational performance measure
   C. Typical performance measure
   D. Optimal performance measure
3. A. Defining the construct of fluency and determining a procedure for measuring it is a major problem. Different researchers might operationalize this construct differently from the ways chosen by this researcher.
   B. Sampling errors will be a major problem in generalizing from performance on this particular sample of passages to a greater domain of tasks. If different passages were used, students might score differently.
   C. In addition, students may make errors on a particular occasion which would not occur on retesting. This might be especially true on the listening test.
   D. Deciding on the number of points to be assigned to each correct response is another problem.
   E. Demonstrating that final scores obtained on the test have some direct relationship to other behaviors which represent ''fluency'' should be important.
4. A. Binet
   B. Wundt, Weber, and other German psychologists are often credited as among the first to use procedures for collection of observations in a standard way for all subjects.
   C. Galton
5. A. Research design
   B. Instrument development
   C. Inferential statistical analyses
   D. Sampling
6. B. Developing the 50-item test

Chapter 2

1. A. Group 2
   B. Group 1, group 2
   C. Group I
   D. For group 2, which has a slightly skewed distribution
2. $\mu_1 = 25$; $\sigma_1 = 1.378$, or 1.38; $\sigma_1^2 = 1.90$ (with standard deviations and variances calculated using N in the denominator)
   $\mu_2 = 26$; $\sigma_2 = 1.703$, or 1.70; $\sigma_1^2 = 2.89$ (with standard deviations and variances calculated using N in the denominator)
   $\mu_3 = 25$; $\sigma_3 = 1.673$, or 1.67; $\sigma_3^2 = 2.79$

3.

	Raw	*Dev.*	*z*
Joan	22	−3	−2.17
Peter	28	3	2.17
Edward	27	2	1.45
Cathy	24	−1	−.72

4. **A.** For $z = .00$, the raw score is the mean for each group.
   B. For $z = -1.00$:

   For group 1, $X = 23.62$ (approx. 24). Solve from equation: $-1.00 = \dfrac{X - 25}{1.38}$

   For group 2, $X = 24.3$ (approx. 24).
   For group 3, $X = 23.33$ (approx. 23).

5. No. The variability of group 3 is greater. For z-scores above .00, corresponding raw scores would be greater for group 3 than for group 1.

6. **A.** 1.6% scored lower than Rebecca.
   B. 1.6% scored higher than Sharon.
   C. 5.1% scored between Ronald and Sharon.
   D. Sheldon's score, which is closer to the mean, will be the most frequently earned among these four scores.

7. No. The scores are not normally distributed.

8. **A.** $z_u = \dfrac{55 - 50}{10} = .50$; $z_l = \dfrac{45 - 50}{10} = -.50$

   The area under the normal curve between z_l and z_u is $(.691 - .309)$, or .382.
   B. An equivalent question would be, "What proportion of the examinee group scored between 45 and 55 points?"

9. Aptitude and reading comprehension. Positive.

10. $\rho_{12} = .97$; $\rho_{13} = .07$; $\rho_{14} = .42$; $\rho_{12}^2 = .94$; $\rho_{14}^2 = .18$

11. No. Correlation between two variables does not imply that either variable can *cause* the other.

12. $z_Y' = (\rho_{XY})(z_X) = (.97)(-.75) = -.73$
    $z_Y' = (.42)(-.75) = -.32$
    $-.32 = \dfrac{Y' - \mu_Y}{\sigma_Y} = \dfrac{Y' - 20}{7.62}$
    $Y' = (-.32)(7.62) + 20 = 17.56$

13. Different sample sizes can account for these different conclusions. The standard error of the correlation can be estimated from

$$\sigma_\rho = \frac{1}{\sqrt{N - 1}}$$

14. Yes. No.
    $\sigma_{Y \cdot X} = \sigma_Y \sqrt{1 - \rho_{XY}^2} = 3\sqrt{1 - .63^2} = 2.33$
    95% confident that posttest scores (for $X = 15$) would fall in the range

$$34.1 - 1.96\,(2.33) \text{ and } 34.1 + 1.96\,(2.33)$$

   or 29.5 and 38.7.

15. $b_{Y \cdot X} = (.63)(3/5) = .38$ (for examinees 1 point apart on X).
    $(5)(.38) = 1.9$ points apart (for examinees 5 points apart on X).

16. slope: $b_{Y \cdot X} = \rho_{XY} \sigma_Y / \sigma_X = (.63)(3/5) = .38$
    intercept: $c = \mu_Y - b_{Y \cdot X}(\mu_X)$
    $c = 36 - (.38)(20) = 28.4$

17. **A.** The mean will be 5(10) = 50.
   B. Each examinee's deviation score will be 5 times larger.
   C. The variance will be $5^2(9)$, or 225 points.
   D. The correlation will be unchanged.

18. $\sigma_{X'}^{2} = \dfrac{\Sigma(X' - \mu_{X'})^2}{N}$

$= \dfrac{\Sigma(KX - K\mu_X)^2}{N} = \dfrac{K^2\Sigma(X - \mu_X)^2}{N} = K^2\sigma_X^2$

Chapter 3

1. **A.** Linear transformation: $y = 2x + 1$ (interval).
   B. Isomorphic (nominal)
   C. Monotonic (ordinal)
2. **A.** A (7), B (5), C (4), D (2)
   B. Subjects 2, 7, 8, 10
   C. 1; 3 and 5; 4 and 9; 6
   D. For S2, response to B
      For S7, response to B or response to C
      For S8, response to A
      For S10, response to B or A
      Because for most unscalable response patterns, B seems to be the problem, the test developer should question whether B is actually on the same dimension as the other items.
   E. $C = 1 - \dfrac{\text{Total errors}}{\text{Total responses}} = 1 - \dfrac{4}{40} = 1 - .10 = .90$
      (This scale barely meets Guttman's suggested criterion.)
   F. It is difficult and impractical to develop such a large number of items which can be scaled in this way.
4. A B C D—Region 1
   B C A D—Region 3
   C B D A—Region 5
   C D B A—Region 6
   B A C D—Region 2
   D C B A—Region 7
   B C D A—Region 4
5. **A.** stimulus-centered
   B. subject-centered
   C. response-centered

Chapter 4

1.

	Distribution Parameters	Normal Distributions	Correlation/ Regression	
Knowledge	C	C	C	10%
Comprehension	A	E	G, I	30%
Application	B, D	F	H, J, K, L	60%
	35%	15%	50%	

2. **A.** 10%, 30%, 60%
   B. 35% and 50%
   C. 30%
4. **A.** The temperature and pressure of gases could be varied.
   B. Students have told each other how to solve the problem so it no longer measures application.
5. **A.** Use of the "because" clause
   B. Use of an "If . . . then" clause.
   C. This is basically a factual statement; it is more like a true-false item than an attitude item.
   D. Use of the "not"
   E. Too long; vocabulary is too complex; use of a nonspecific determiner ("sometimes").
6. Possible procedures include using student self-descriptions in a content analysis; literature review; critical incidents reports by teachers or other professional child-care workers. (Expert opinions and observations are also possible but are probably less applicable than the three procedures already named.)

Chapter 5

1. **A.** $\mu_1 = 7$, $\sigma_1 = 1.41$ (Standard deviation calculated with N in the denominator.)
   $\mu_2 = 6$, $\sigma_2 = 1.90$
   $\mu_3 = 6.6$, $\sigma_3 = 1.36$
   B. 4
   C. 6.6
   D. $\sigma_1^2 = 2.0$
   E. .97
2. **A.** Item 1; $p = .90$; it is the easiest.
   B. Item 3; $pq = .25$
   C. .50
   D. .36
   E. .22
   F. .05
3. **A.** $\begin{bmatrix} 9.00 & 12.15 & 7.68 \\ & 25.00 & 18.00 \\ & & 16.00 \end{bmatrix}$

   B. 125.66
4. The approach is not very reasonable because although substantial variance may be achieved, the usefulness (or meaningfulness) of the scores will be reduced because of severe restriction of the behavioral domain represented by the test.

Chapter 6

1. **A.** Systematic
   B. Random
   C. Systematic
   D. Random
   E. Random

2. A. 2.5

   B. 1.5

   C. .5

   D. .25

   E. 1.25

   F. .50

   H. No. The actual true scores and error scores are not known, and consequently their variances cannot be directly computed.

3. No, although $\epsilon(E) = 0$ for each examinee over a large (infinite) number of repeated measurements, it is unlikely to equal 0 for only 3 repeated measurements.

4. John does not have a single true score, but in theory he has a different true score for each of two tests.

6. B. Although $\sigma_{T_i}^2$ can never be directly computed from empirical observations, σ_{ij} can be computed from a set of measurements i and j on the same persons.

7. $\rho_{YY'} = \dfrac{\rho_{11'}\sigma_1^2 + \rho_{22'}\sigma_2^2 + 2\rho_{12}\sigma_1\sigma_2}{\sigma_1^2 + \sigma_2^2 + 2\rho_{12}\sigma_1\sigma_2}$

8. A. .55

   B. 20.93

   C. 275.97 ($\sigma_Y^2 = \sigma_1^2 + \sigma_2^2 + 2\rho_{12}\sigma_1\sigma_2$)

   D. .97 (Use formula from Exercise 7.)

   E. .84 (Hint: Denote $Y_1 = X_2 + X_3$; $Y_2 = X_1 + X_4 + X_7$

$$\rho_{Y_1Y_2} = \frac{\sigma_{12} + \sigma_{24} + \sigma_{27} + \sigma_{13} + \sigma_{34} + \sigma_{37}}{\sigma_{Y_1}\sigma_{Y_2}}$$

   F. 19.9 to 24.1.

   G. Circular (no relationships)

Chapter 7

1. A. Internal consistency, probably using KR 21

   B. Alternate form or equivalence

   C. Coefficient alpha

   D. Internal consistency, with KR 20

   E. Test-retest with alternate forms (stability and equivalence)

2. A. Odd: 3,2,1,2,4,3,2,4,1,4.   Even: 3,2,2,1,4,2,3,3,1,3

   B. .74 (Variances computed with N in denominator.)

   C. .85

   D. Lower

   E. The odd-even split would be preferable. The first-half/last-half split seems to provide the most dissimilar sets of scores that could be obtained from all possible splits; thus an estimate based on this split would not be very close to coefficient alpha (the lower bound of the coefficient of precision.

   F. .63, .55

   G. The items are not equal in difficulty.

3. A. Form A: 3.3; form B: 3.1 No, the size of the standard error of measurement in relationship to the standard deviation of the test should be considered.

   B. 16.7–23.3; 13.4–26.6

C. 12.4; 27.6

D. .83

E. It made it an overestimate from the value that would have been obtained if all students had completed the test.

F. .40; .58

4. A. Coefficient for retest after 1 day (.95, .87, .91, .89)

B. .85, .89

C. .86, .80, .83, .78

D. .70, .68

E. Compare coefficients for retest after one week to form equivalence coefficients.

Chapter 8

1. A. $\hat{\rho}_I^2 = .926$

B. $15 \pm \dfrac{(\hat{\sigma}_i^2 + \hat{\sigma}_e^2)}{n_i'}$

$15 \pm .09$

C. $\hat{\rho}_{I*}^2 = .862$

2. $\hat{\rho}_i^2 = .355$

If examinees have a consistent option preference, the score on any one item should generalize to the universe score. Furthermore, generalization should occur even when different items are administered to different examinees.

3. A. i. Items

ii. The items facet is probably random. Typically examiners want to generalize to a set of items that is more extensive than the items on the test.

iii. Universe score variance, σ_p^2; expected observed score variance, $\sigma_p^2 + \sigma_e^2/n_i'$.

iv. $\hat{\sigma}_p^2 = \dfrac{(MS_p - MS_r)}{n_i}$

$\hat{\sigma}_e^2 = MS_r$

B. i. Cards (I) and psychologists (J)

ii. Most likely neither cards nor psychologists are fixed.

iii. Universe score variance, σ_p^2; expected observed score variance,

$\sigma_p^2 + \sigma_{pi}^2/n_i' + \sigma_{pj}^2/n_j' + \sigma_e^2/n_i'n_j'$

iv. $\hat{\sigma}_p^2 = \dfrac{(MS_p - MS_{pi} - M_{pj} + MS_r)}{n_i n_j}$

$\hat{\sigma}_{pi}^2 = \dfrac{(MS_{pi} - MS_r)}{n_j}$

$\hat{\sigma}_{pj}^2 = \dfrac{(MS_{pj} - MS_r)}{n_i}$

$\hat{\sigma}_e^2 = MS_r$

C. i. Modes (I) and topics (J)

ii. Modes are fixed since these exhaust the modes mentioned in most writing research.

iii. Universe score variance, $\sigma_p^2 + \sigma_{pi}^2/n_i'$; expected observed score variance,

$\sigma_p^2 + \sigma_{pi}^2/n_i' + (\sigma_{pj}^2 + \sigma_e^2)/n_i'n_j'$

iv. $\hat{\sigma}_p^2 = \dfrac{(MS_p - MS_{pi})}{n_i n_j}$

$$\hat{\sigma}^2_{pi} = \frac{(MS_{pi} - MS_r)}{n_j}$$

$$(\hat{\sigma}^2_{pj} + \hat{\sigma}^2_e) = MS_r$$

D.   i. Items (I) and students (J)

ii. Both are probably random.

iii. Universe score variance, σ^2_p; expected observed score variance,

$$\sigma^2_p + \sigma^2_{pi}/n'_i + (\sigma^2_{pj} + \sigma^2_j)/n'_j + (\sigma^2_{ij} + \sigma^2_e)/n'_i n'_j$$

iv. $\hat{\sigma}^2_p = \dfrac{(MS_p - MS_{pi} - MS_{j:p} + MS_r)}{n_i n_j}$

$$\hat{\sigma}^2_{pi} = \frac{(MS_{pi} - MS_r)}{n_j}$$

$$(\hat{\sigma}^2_{pj} + \hat{\sigma}^2_j) = \frac{(MS_{j:p} - MS_r)}{n_i}$$

$$(\hat{\sigma}^2_{ij} + \hat{\sigma}^2_e) = MS_r$$

4. A. $\hat{\rho}^2 = \dfrac{\hat{\sigma}^2_p}{\hat{\sigma}^2_p + \hat{\sigma}^2_{pi} + \hat{\sigma}^2_{pj} + \hat{\sigma}^2_e}$

$$= \frac{27.729}{27.729 + .015 + 41.732 + 1.261}$$

$$= .392$$

B. Increase the number of exhibits because $\hat{\sigma}^2_{pj}$ is the largest component of the error variance portion of the observed score variance.

C. Design 1 with 3 observers and 2 exhibits, design 2 with 2 exhibits nested in each observed, and design 3 with 3 exhibits and 3 observers are practical. The largest generalizability coefficient will result from the use of design 2.

D. $\hat{\rho}^2 = \dfrac{\hat{\sigma}^2_p + \hat{\sigma}^2_{pj}/n'_j}{\hat{\sigma}^2_p + \hat{\sigma}^2_{pi}/n'_i + \hat{\sigma}^2_{pj}/n'_j + \hat{\sigma}^2_e/n'_i n'_j}$

$$= \frac{27.729 + 41.732/3}{27.729 + .015/2 + 41.732/3 + 1.261/6}$$

$$= .99$$

E. It is most relevant to the study described in D.

Chapter 9

1. A. .029

B. .169

C. .036

2. A. .39

B. No, the relationship is low to moderate.

C. .63, .75, .88

D. $(MS_p - MS_r)/MS_p$

E. .40

F. KR 20

3. A. For cut score of .60, .80

For .70, .53

For .80, .67

For .90, .87

    B. .29, .08, .21, .42
    C. .60, .07, .33, .73
    E. .58
4. A. .51 (for a cut score of .50)
    B. In theory, M (C) should be smaller.
    C. .51 (for a cut score of .50)
    D. It is more an index of decision consistency. (See pp. 204–205.)
    E. The magnitude of the index depends on the amount of variation in individuals' domain scores.
5. A. .21
6. A. Variation in scores was relatively small.
    B. It should improve.
    C. It would be reduced because ρ_f^2 would be reduced.
    D. P^* and κ values would be lower than P values.
    E. The lowest cut score

Chapter 10

1. Identification of "important" objectives and percentages of items measuring these; correlation between "importance" ratings and number of items assessing those objectives; percentage of objectives not covered by items on this test.
2. A.

Item	Obj. 1	Obj. 2	Obj. 3
1	.67	−.08	−.59
2	.83	−.67	−.17
3	.50	−1.00	.50
4	−.50	1.00	−.50
5	.00	.00	.00

    B. Item measures the objective denoted by underlining.
    C. The index is lowered because item was judged to measure two objectives equally well.
4. As each test becomes more homogeneous, it is less likely to contain material on the other test form; thus error variances for G and H will be reduced and differences scores between G and H will increase, resulting in a smaller ratio.
5. A. Curtailment of variance (by explicit selection)
    B. Employees who have been on the job may not be representative of applicants for the job.
    C. Criterion contamination
    D. Test scores were not directly validated against the criterion of interest.
6. A. Construct validation
    B. Predictive criterion-related validation
    C. Content validation
    D. Concurrent criterion-related validation
    E. Predictive criterion-related validation and possibly construct validation
7. A. .70, .64, .73, .66 for Gordon's; .80, .79, .73, .80 for Piers-Harris
    B. .78, .59, .55, .80

  C. Physical appearance and academic/school studies
  D. The correlation between interpersonal adequacy and physical appearance as measured by method A and between school studies and physical appearance by method B
  E. The correlation between school studies (B) and social (A)

 8. .58; .42; .40; .58
 9. A hint to solving this derivation is to recognize that ρ_{XY} will be maximized when $\rho_{t_X t_Y} = 1.00$.
10. Strictly speaking the validity coefficient should not exceed the square root of the product of the reliability coefficients. The square root of a reliability coefficient is larger than the coefficient whenever the coefficient is less than 1.00.

11. $\dfrac{\rho_{XY}^2 (1 - \hat{\rho}_{XX'})}{\hat{\rho}_{XX'}(1 - \rho_{XY}^2)} \le K$ (assuming that criterion reliability is 1.00)

   where ρ_{XY} is the minimum desired validity coefficient and $\hat{\rho}_{XX'}$ is the reliability estimate for the initial set of items in the pilot study. There is no guarantee that lengthening the test will increase the validity to the desired level.

Chapter 11

 1. .14. It is the correlation between GPA and MRA for students who are homogeneous on TASK.
 2. For $R^2 = .50$, $R_{cv}^2 = .02$.
    For $R_2 = .70$, $R_{cv}^2 = .30$.
    Estimated cross validity is quite poor when the estimated squared multiple correlation is .5 or .7. The cross-validity coefficient is much more substantial when the estimated squared multiple correlation is .86. This suggests that ratios on the order of 3:1 can be tolerated if the population squared multiple correlation is quite substantial, perhaps .85 or above. Otherwise larger examinee-to-predictor ratios are required in order to have adequate cross validity.
 3. A. $Y' = 84.6 + 3.4$ [CFIT] $+ 2.2$ [D-48]
    B. $Y' = 218.6$
    C. $\hat{\sigma}_{Y \cdot X_1 X_2} = 42.7$
    D. (175.9, 261.3)
    E. No, the sample size is quite large.
 4. A. The means on Y for the two groups are 6.59 and 8.33, respectively. The average mean is 7.46. Classify any patient with a Y score of 7.46 or above as an uncontrolled drinker.
    C. Under the rule identified in A, all patients are correctly classified.
    D. Since the rule is applied to the patients on which the rule was developed, the method probably overstates the accuracy of classification.

Chapter 12

 1. A. Equal probability: $A/(A + B) = .75$ for males and .75 for females
                       (The selection procedure is fair.)
    Constant ratio: $(A + B)/(A + D) = 1.14$ for males and .57 for females
                       (The selection procedure is unfair.)

Conditional probability: $A/(A + D) = .86$ for males and $.43$ for females
(The selection procedure is unfair.)
Regression: $c = -1.873$, $b = .055$ for males
$c = -2.058$, $b = .061$ for females
(The selection procedure is unfair.)
  B. $X_C = 92$, males; $A/(A + D) = .43$
$X_C = 82$, females; $A/(A + D) = .43$
  C. $X_C = 70$, males; $X_C = 66$, females
  D. No. There is no single cut score on the test which would be exceeded by 70% of the males and 70% of the females.
2. 11.55 (majority); 11.65 (minority)
3. $\epsilon(U)_s$, maj. $= .80$ and $\epsilon(U)_r$, maj. $= .70$; therefore select.
  $\epsilon(U)_s$, min. $= 1.125$ and $\epsilon(U)_r$, min. $= .625$; therefore select.

Chapter 13

1. **A.** 2
   B. .291
   C. Sampling error
   D. .378
   E. .435
   F. .357
   G.

$$s_i^2 = \hat{\rho}_{xx} - \hat{h}_i^2$$

Gaelic	.263
English	.342
History	.393

No. Each variable has a substantial amount of true score variance not associated with common factors.
   H. Is $\hat{\rho}_{ij}$ approximately equal to $\hat{a}_{i1}\hat{a}_{j1} + \hat{a}_{i2}\hat{a}_{j2}$ for all $\hat{\rho}_{ij}$?
3. **A.** No. More than one factor was found.
   B. Because there were at least five factors with eigen-values greater than 1.00, it would be helpful to know the factor loadings from the 3-, 4-, and 5-factor solutions to see if they are reasonably "interpretable." Furthermore, use of a rotation to oblique solution (rather than the orthogonal varimax rotation) could also have been considered. Items 28 through 31 have sizable loadings on two factors, making it questionable whether simple structure criteria have been met by the solution reported.
   C. No. It seems inappropriate to say that these items do not load in factor 1 and yet to claim that item 13 (with a loading of .41) does. Similarly note loadings for items 14, 14, 19, and 22 on factor II.

Chapter 14

1. **A.** Item 1, $D = .00$ (for upper and lower 50%)
   Item 2, $D = .40$
   Item 1, $D = -.33$ (for upper and lower 30%)
   Item 2, $D = .67$
   B. Item 1, $-.23$ (total score variance computed using N in denominator)
   Item 2, .66

C. Item 1, −.18
   Item 2, .52

D. The biserial correlation requires the assumption that the variable underlying item performance is normally distributed. With the point-biserial correlation a truly dichotomous distribution is assumed to underlie item performances.

2. **A.** Item 23

B. Among those who chose the correct answer to item 25, there was a greater proportion of high-scoring students; for item 21, the situation was reversed (i.e., among those who chose the correct answer, there was a greater proportion of low-scoring students).

C. Rewrite response 2 to make it more plausible and attractive to those who are uncertain of the correct answer.

D. The item may be miskeyed (4 should be the correct response rather than 3); or there may be an ambiguity in the wording of the question stem or option 3, causing misunderstanding.

E. For 24, .66
   For 25, .52

F. +.15

G. .625

3. **A.** Chi-square test independence; 33.93. There is a significant relationship.

B. Large sample chi square; 12.25. There is a significant difference in item difficulties.

4. **A.** 3

B. 1

C. 2

D. 5

E. 4

5. 3.37; .13

Chapter 15

1. $P_{1,4}(\theta_2) = .00$
   $P_1(\theta_2) = 1.00$, $P_4(\theta_2) = .00$
   $P_{1,4}(\theta_2) = P_1(\theta_2)P_4(\theta_2)$
   $P_{2,3}(\theta_2 < \theta < \theta_3) = .00$
   $P_2(\theta_2 < \theta < \theta_3) = 1.00$
   $P_3(\theta_2 < \theta < \theta_3) = .00$
   $P_{2,3}(\theta) = P_2(\theta)P_3(\theta)$ for $\theta_2 < \theta < \theta_3$

2. $P(+,+|\theta) = .45$
   but $P_1(\theta)P_2(\theta) = (.5)(.7) = .35$
   $P(+,+|\theta) \neq P_1(\theta)P_2(\theta)$
   These items are not locally independent; thus the test is not unidimensional.

3. The response patterns indicate unidimensionality, and the ICCs would be step functions.

4. a_g: 1.33, .75, .58, .44
   b_g: −.66, −.87, −1.05, −1.31
   The index p_g reflects both difficulty b_g and discrimination (a_g) and therefore can be misleading as an index of difficulty.

5. **A.** Items 4, 7, and 15. These items may not be similar in discrimination to most items on the test. (Note their extreme point-biserial correlations with total score.)

B. Item 1, departure most severe for group 4.
Item 3, departure most severe for groups 4–6.
Item 4, departure most severe for group 1.
C. From easiest to hardest: 1, 4, 3
D. 9.81, 10.77

6.

$\theta =$	−2.0	−1.5	−1.0	−.5	0.0	.5	1.0	1.5	2.0
A.	.88	1.03	1.15	1.22	1.24	1.22	1.15	1.03	.88
B.	.81	1.08	1.35	1.53	1.62	1.53	1.35	1.08	.81

7. A wide range of difficulty can be justified only if the discrimination parameters are high. Even then it entails a severe loss of information for examinees with latent trait scores in the middle of the difficulty distribution.

Chapter 16

1. The d_g's for the items are .064, −.832, 2.121, .308, .310, −.446, −1.738, −.537, .364, .385. Items 3 and 7 have d_g's substantially different from the others and so appear to be biased.

2. $\chi^2_c = 1.40$, which is not significant.
$\chi^2_s = .76$, which is not significant.

3. Using the intervals 5–12, 13–15, 16, 17, 18, 19, 20, 21–23 gives expected frequencies meeting the criteria outlined in the chapter. The χ^2_j statistics for these intervals are .311, .164, 3.358, 1.714, .056, .434, .091, .887. These sum to 7.019. The .05 critical value is $\chi^2(8) = 15.507$, so there is insufficient evidence to conclude the item is biased.

4. The z-statistics for the 15 items are −.15, −1.04, −.65, 1.20, 1.13, −2.26, −.93, .55, 1.44, 1.20, −.10, .26, −1.27, and .43. Of these, only the t statistic for item 6 is significant at the .05 level. However, it is important to remember that if 15 items are tested for bias using a .05 level, and if all the items are in fact unbiased, the expected number of significant tests is .05 (15) = .75. Since only one test was significant, it probably is appropriate to view all 15 items as being unbiased.

Chapter 17

1. A. 4, 10, 6, 6, 6
B. Examinee D omitted no items but answered 4 items incorrectly; C omitted 2 and answered 2 incorrectly; E omitted 3 but answered 1 incorrectly. This leads us to believe that D guessed at more answers than C or E, and C guessed at more than E.
C. 2.75, 10, 5.5, 5, 5.75
D. 4.2, 10, 6.4, 6.0, 6.6

2. Correlation between split halves of the test, corrected by the Spearman-Brown formula

3. The rank ordering of examinees will not be changed if all students answered all items.

4. Increasing testing time from 50 to 90 minutes is equivalent to increasing test length by a factor of 1.8. The reliability estimate of the lengthened test would be .80, less than the reliability attained by the experimental procedure.

5. A. 5.55 for each
   B. C, 4.75; D, 5.55; E, 4.95
   C. C, 3.94; D, 4.44; E, 4.44

Chapter 18

1. 27.7
2. 28.9
3. Using the minimax procedure (to maximize the minimum expected loss), $X_0 = 5$; the ratio.

Chapter 19

1. A. Use formula $\hat{\sigma}_M = \sqrt{\dfrac{\hat{\sigma}^2}{N}}$

   When $N = 20$, $\hat{\sigma}^2$ is calculated by using $(N - 1)$ in denominator. Answers vary depending on the 20 scores selected for your sample.
   B. Randomly select any 2 of the 5 classes.
   The standard error formula is

   $$\hat{\sigma}_{M_c} = \frac{\hat{\sigma}_\mu}{\sqrt{k}}$$

   If classes 1 and 2 are chosen, $\hat{\sigma}_{M_c} = 1.55$.
   C. Your sample should contain 8 ESE students and 12 non-ESE students.
2. A. Systematic
   B. Cluster
   C. Two-stage: cluster sampling of dormitories and stratified sampling of individuals (stratified by class)
   D. Simple random sampling
3. 100
4.

A.

Raw Score	Raw Score P.R.	Linear z	Normalized z	Stanine	Normalized P.R.
45	99	2.04	2.17	9	98
44	94	1.59	1.51	8	94
43	86	1.14	1.08	7	87
42	75	.68	.66	6	75
41	57	.23	.18	5	59
40	40	−.23	−.27	5	41
39	26	−.68	−.66	4	24
38	15	−1.14	−1.06	3	13
37	7	−1.59	−1.51	2	6
36	2	−2.04	−2.17	1	2

5. A. Cathy gains more in percentile rank points.
   B. No. The 4th stanine contains a broader range of percentile rank points than the 2nd stanine.

    C. June probably had a greater loss in raw score points.

    D. No, there is not a linear relationship between these different types of score transformations.

7.

Raw Score	T-Score	DIQ	ETS
45	71.7	133	717
44	65.1	123	651
43	60.8	116	608
42	56.6	110	566

Chapter 20

1. $Y^* = 1.02 (X - 47.9) + 40.2$

3. The following is the table for transforming raw scores on form B to latent trait scores expressed on scale based on the examinees who took form A.

Raw Score	Latent Trait Score
1	−2.06
2	−.99
3	−.29
4	.30
5	.83
6	1.37
7	1.95
8	2.65
9	3.72

4. The scores based on the unique items for section II can be transformed to the scale for section I by using Equation 20.1, with a, c, and d calculated by using Equations 20.4a to 20.4c. The scores on the unique items can be added to the scores expressed on the section I scale to complete the solution to the problem. Substitutions in Equations 20.4a to 20.4c yield

$$a = \sqrt{\frac{46.222 + (1.412)^2(2.934 - 1.511)}{36.711 + (1.881)^2(2.934 - 4.677)}} = \sqrt{1.606} = 1.27$$

$$c = 16.600 + 1.881(4.250 - 4.300) = 16.51$$

$$d = 17.000 + 1.412(4.250 - 4.200) = 17.07$$

5. The standard error of measurement is

$$\hat{\sigma}_e = \hat{\sigma}_X \sqrt{1 - \hat{\rho}_{XX'}}$$
$$= 10\sqrt{1 - .7}$$
$$= 10\sqrt{3}$$

The standard error of equating is to be no larger than one-tenth the standard error of measurement. The target standard error of equating is therefore

$$SE_{Y^*} = .1(10\sqrt{3}) = \sqrt{3}$$

For design B the required N can be calculated by using Equation 20.6, which leads to

$$3 = \frac{2(100)(1 - .7)}{N}[0(1 + .7) + 2]$$

solving for N we obtain

$$N = 40$$

For design A use Equation 20.5 to obtain

$$3 = \frac{2(100)}{N}(0 + 2)$$

and

$$N = 134$$

Author Index

Aitkin, M., 355
Algina, J., 200, 234
Alkin, M. C., 329
Anastasi, A., 302
Anderson, E. B., 362
Anderson, L. W., 80
Andrews, B. J., 417
Angoff, W. H., 388, 390, 391, 413, 417, 418,
    429, 437, 438, 439, 442, 444, 458, 459,
    460, 462, 465, 466
Archambault, F. X., 411, 417
Averill, M., 387, 391

Baglin, R. F., 438
Bailey, J. D., Jr., 296, 297
Baker, F. B., 385
Bashaw, W. L., 346
Behuniak, P., Jr., 411, 417
Bell, S., 355, 356, 469
Benson, J., 62
Berk, R. A., 71, 193, 329, 330, 414
Beuchert, A. K., 314, 319
Binet, A., 9–10
Birnbaum, A., 369, 370
Bliss, L. B., 402
Bloom, B. S., 73, 75, 84
Bock, R. D., 355
Boles, R., 246
Bormuth, J. R., 71
Boynton, P. L., 10
Brandenburg, D. C., 81
Bray, J. H., 259, 260, 261
Brennan, R. L., 158, 193, 203, 204, 212, 330,
    331, 417
Brown, F. G., 68, 76
Browne, M. W., 251, 252, 259
Brownell, W. A., 138
Burke, C. J., 62
Burril, L. E., 392

Camilli, G., 383, 384, 386, 387, 391, 393
Campbell, D. T., 148, 232, 233
Cardall, C., 391
Carlson, S. B., 77
Cattell, J. M., 10
Chave, E. J., 11, 51
Cleary, T. A., 271, 272, 284, 391
Coffman, W. E., 391
Cohen, S. H., 148, 390
Cole, J. W. L., 278
Cole, N. S., 274, 277, 278
Cook, L. L., 363, 365

Coombs, C. H., 49, 56, 60, 64, 117, 142
Cox, R. C., 327, 330, 331
Cronbach, L. J., 5, 11, 67, 117, 119, 138,
    142, 152, 153, 158, 166, 179, 180, 194,
    217, 218, 222, 223, 267, 324
Crooks, T. J., 181
Cross, L., 402
Cureton, E. E., 142, 327

Darlington, R. B., 231, 271, 273–274, 275–
    276, 278, 284
Darwin, C., 8
Davis, F. B., 407
Dawes, R. M., 60, 80
Dawis, R. V., 476
Dennis, W., 9
Diamond, J., 402, 403
Dixon, W. J., 319
Douglas, G. A., 355
Downey, R. G., 407
Drasgow, F., 340, 355, 392
Dubois, P., 10*n*.

Ebel, R. L., 69, 73, 77, 219, 228, 315, 323,
    326, 413, 429
Echternacht, G. J., 391, 406, 450
Englehart, M. D., 314, 319
Evans, W., 402, 403

Fahner, S., 425
Fechner, G. T., 8, 50, 51
Ferry, P., 406
Fifer, G., 407
Findley, W. G., 319
Fishbein, M., 60
Fiske, D. W., 232, 233
Flanagan, J. C., 68, 137
Ford, S. F., 388
Forsyth, R., 476
Frary, R., 402
Frederiksen, N., 77
Frick, T., 143
Frisbie, D. A., 81

Gable, R. K., 411, 417
Gallagher, 410
Galton, F., 8–9, 24, 32
Gardner, P. L., 62
Gauss, C., 24
Gavin, A. T., 218*n*.
Getson, P. R., 387
Gifford, J., 355
Gillmore, G. M., 181
Gilman, D. A., 406
Gilmer, J., 476
Glaser, R., 69, 192

Subject Index